Bounded Rationality

Bounded Rationality
Heuristics, Judgment, and Public Policy

Sanjit Dhami and Cass R. Sunstein

The MIT Press
Cambridge, Massachusetts
London, England

© 2022 Sanjit Dhami and Cass R. Sunstein

All rights reserved. No part of this book may be reproduced in any form by any electronic or mechanical means (including photocopying, recording, or information storage and retrieval) without permission in writing from the publisher.

The MIT Press would like to thank the anonymous peer reviewers who provided comments on drafts of this book. The generous work of academic experts is essential for establishing the authority and quality of our publications. We acknowledge with gratitude the contributions of these otherwise uncredited readers.

This book was set in Sabon by Westchester Publishing Services. Printed and bound in the United States of America.

Library of Congress Cataloging-in-Publication Data

Names: Dhami, Sanjit S., author. | Sunstein, Cass R., author.
Title: Bounded rationality : heuristics, judgment, and public policy / Sanjit Dhami, Cass R. Sunstein.
Description: [Cambridge, Massachusetts] : The MIT Press, [2022] | Includes bibliographical references and index.
Identifiers: LCCN 2021037261 | ISBN 9780262543705 (paperback)
Subjects: LCSH: Rational choice theory. | Rational choice theory—Mathematical models. | Mathematical optimization. | Social sciences—Methodology.
Classification: LCC HM495 .D44 2022 | DDC 300.1—dc23/eng/20211108
LC record available at https://lccn.loc.gov/2021037261

10 9 8 7 6 5 4 3 2 1

Contents

Acknowledgments   xi

1   Introduction   1
2   What Is Rationality and What Is the Evidence for It?   23
   2.1   Introduction   23
   2.2   A Simple Taxonomy of Situations   29
   2.3   The Bayesian Rationality Approach   37
   2.4   Rationality under Certainty   38
   2.5   Rationality under Risk and Uncertainty   43
   2.6   Rationality in Choices Made over Time   47
   2.7   Rationality in Strategic Interaction   52
   2.8   What Rationality Is Not   54
      2.8.1   Rationality Does Not Imply Self-Regarding Preferences   54
      2.8.2   Rationality Does Not Imply Absence of Emotions in Decision-Making   55
      2.8.3   Rationality Does Require Perfect Attention and Unlimited Computing Power   56
   2.9   Evidence on Consistent Preferences   56
   2.10   Evidence on Limited Attention   59
   2.11   Evidence on Overconfidence   61
   2.12   Evidence on Rationality in Risk and Uncertainty   64
      2.12.1   Nonlinear Probability Weighting   64
      2.12.2   Reference Dependence   68
      2.12.3   More Violations   69
   2.13   Evidence on Rationality in Time Discounting   69
   2.14   Evidence on Rationality in Strategic Interaction   76

- 2.15 Do Humans Follow the Rules of Mathematical Statistics?   79
  - 2.15.1 Biases in Producing a Full Sampling Distribution   80
  - 2.15.2 Do People Use Bayes' Law?   84
  - 2.15.3 Conservatism   88
  - 2.15.4 A Modification of Bayes' Law   89
- 2.16 Appendix: A Primer on Decision Theory   92
  - 2.16.1 Expected Utility Theory   93
  - 2.16.2 Probability Weighting Function   96
  - 2.16.3 Rank Dependent Utility   99
  - 2.16.4 Prospect Theory   101

3 The Case for Bounded Rationality   109
- 3.1 Introduction   109
- 3.2 How Reasonable Is the Assumption of Mathematical Optimization?   114
  - 3.2.1 A Basic Problem in Dynamic Optimization   115
  - 3.2.2 Emotions and Optimization in Microfinance Contracts   119
  - 3.2.3 Bubbles in Financial Markets   126
  - 3.2.4 Will Non-Optimizing Individuals Simply Perish?   127
  - 3.2.5 Optimization or Heuristics? An Application from Microfinance Contracts   131
  - 3.2.6 Optimization or Heuristics? An Application to Tax Evasion   134
  - 3.2.7 Assessing a Three-Way Leaders Debate   138
- 3.3 Strategic Interaction   143
- 3.4 The Role of Social Norms   149
- 3.5 On Methodology in Economics   156
- 3.6 Preferences and Beliefs: The Role of History, Culture, and Institutions   161
  - 3.6.1 Effect of Preferences on Institutions   162
  - 3.6.2 Effect of Institutions on Preferences   163
- 3.7 The Macroeconomy as a Complex, Adaptive System   165

4 Behavioral Models of Heuristics-Based Choice   169
- 4.1 Risk as Feelings   177
- 4.2 Attribute-Based Models in Time Discounting   180
  - 4.2.1 Vague Time Preferences Model   181

- 4.2.2 The Similarity Relation and Time Preference 183
- 4.2.3 Trade-off Attribute Model of Intertemporal Choice 184
- 4.3 Heuristics and Optimization I: Heuristics for Temporal Choices and Delay-Discounting Models 185
- 4.4 Heuristics and Optimization II: Mental Accounting and Prospect Theory 188
- 4.5 Aspiration Adaptation Theory 190
  - 4.5.1 A Cooperation Problem 192
  - 4.5.2 A Coordination Problem 195
- 4.6 Evidential Reasoning 198
- 4.7 Kantian Rationality 203
- 4.8 Winner's Curse in Financial Markets 207
- 4.9 Complexity and Bounded Rationality: Thinking about Macroeconomics 211
  - 4.9.1 Inductive Reasoning, Adaptive Rules, and Emergent Phenomena 215
  - 4.9.2 Neighborhood Segregation as an Emergent Phenomenon 216
  - 4.9.3 Chaos: Extreme Dependence on Initial Conditions 219
  - 4.9.4 Agent-Based Models 221
- 4.10 Evolutionary Game Theory and Stochastic Social Dynamics 226
  - 4.10.1 Evolutionary Game Theory 226
  - 4.10.2 Stochastic Social Dynamics 231
- 4.11 Narratives and Contagion 234
- 4.12 Mental Models 242
- 4.13 Choice Bracketing 245
  - 4.13.1 Equity-Premium Puzzle 247
  - 4.13.2 Risk Aggregation 249
  - 4.13.3 Why Do People Engage in Narrow Choice Bracketing? 251
- 4.14 Attitudes toward Very Low Probability Events 251
  - 4.14.1 Original Prospect Theory 253
  - 4.14.2 The Evidence on Behavior under Low Probability Events 255
  - 4.14.3 So What Is the Way Forward? 258
- 4.15 Do People Take Account of Sunk Costs and Opportunity Costs? 259

5 Kahneman and Tversky's Research Program on Heuristics and Biases 265

- 5.1 Introduction 265
- 5.2 The Representative Heuristic 270
  - 5.2.1 The Gambler's Fallacy 273
  - 5.2.2 The Hot Hand Fallacy 274
- 5.3 Anchoring 275
- 5.4 Hindsight Bias 278
- 5.5 The Availability Heuristic 281
- 5.6 The Conjunction Fallacy 282
- 5.7 Regression to the Mean 284
- 5.8 Necessary and Sufficient Conditions 286
- 5.9 Confirmation Bias 286
- 5.10 The Affect Heuristic 288
- 5.11 Objections to the HBP 289
  - 5.11.1 Some Preliminaries 289
  - 5.11.2 Ecological Rationality 291
  - 5.11.3 One-Event Probabilities, Context, and Errors 292
  - 5.11.4 "We Cannot Be That Dumb" Critique 293
  - 5.11.5 Frequency versus Probability Format and the HBP 294
  - 5.11.6 Empirical Counterparts to the Heuristics 297
  - 5.11.7 How Can Heuristics Explain Events A and Not A? 298
  - 5.11.8 The Criticism of Appropriate Statistical Norms 300
  - 5.11.9 Systems 1 and 2 302
- 5.12 Experts and the HBP Heuristics 303

6 The Fast and Frugal Heuristics Research Program 305

- 6.1 Introduction 305
- 6.2 The FFP 309
- 6.3 A Critique of the FFP 316
  - 6.3.1 What Is the Benchmark for Comparison? 316
  - 6.3.2 Empirical Testing of Heuristics in the FFP 317
  - 6.3.3 Training People in Using Statistics 321
  - 6.3.4 Does the FFP Tell Us Which Heuristic to Use? 323
- 6.4 On Mathematical Optimization and As-If Theories 325
- 6.5 On Distinct Domains of Choices in the HBP and FFP 327

6.6 The Less Is More Effect   333
    6.6.1 A Critique of the Bias-Variance Trade-off   337
    6.6.2 Implications of the Less Is More Effect for the HBP   339

7 **Philosophical Foundations**   341
    7.1 Introduction   341
    7.2 Choices and Welfare   343
    7.3 Direct and Indirect Judgments   346
    7.4 Practice and Theory   351
    7.5 The Pervasiveness of Indirect Judgments   353
    7.6 Defining Direct Judgments   354
    7.7 Welfare   356
    7.8 Paths Forward   358

8 **Optimal Taxation and Regulation in Behavioral Economics**   361
    8.1 Introduction   361
    8.2 An Introduction to Multiple Selves   363
    8.3 Multiple Selves, Internalities, and Public Policy   366
    8.4 Limited Attention and Deadweight Loss from Taxation   374
    8.5 Tax Incidence under Limited Attention   380
    8.6 Internalities and Tax Efficiency: An Application to Sugar Taxes   382
    8.7 Present Biased Preferences and Procrastination: More Applications   385
        8.7.1 Procrastination: Fixing Ideas   386
        8.7.2 Job Search and Hard Paternalism   389
        8.7.3 Deadlines; Buying Single Cigarette Packs   390
        8.7.4 Inducing Farmers to Buy Fertilizers   391
    8.8 Behavioral Industrial Organization, Bounded Rationality, and Policy   392

9 **Libertarian Paternalism in Theory**   403
    9.1 Introduction   403
    9.2 Mistakes and Welfare   405
    9.3 Libertarian Paternalism   407
    9.4 Government Error   415
    9.5 Remedies   419

10 **Libertarian Paternalism in Practice**   423
    10.1 Behavioral Public Policy around the World   423

- 10.2 FEAST 426
- 10.3 Institutionalizing Behavioral Insights: Two Approaches 428
- 10.4 Examples of Behavioral Public Policies 429
  - 10.4.1 Default Rules 429
  - 10.4.2 Policies on Savings 431
  - 10.4.3 School Meals 432
  - 10.4.4 Finance 432
  - 10.4.5 Health Care 433
  - 10.4.6 Payroll Statements 434
- 10.5 Disclosure 434
  - 10.5.1 Nutrition 435
  - 10.5.2 Finance 436
  - 10.5.3 Health Care 437
  - 10.5.4 Fuel Economy 437
  - 10.5.5 Disclosure and Competition 438
- 10.6 Structuring Choices 440
- 10.7 Salience 440

11 Epilogue 443

Notes 445
References 455
Index 503

Acknowledgments

We are grateful to many people for help with this book. Thanks go first to Ali al-Nowaihi, coauthor on the essay out of which this book grew, for many indispensable contributions.

We are grateful to many people who were generous with their time and offered comments, suggestions, and advice on the manuscript that enabled us to effect many improvements. In particular, we would like to thank Junaid Arshad, Gary Charness, Vincent Crawford, Xavier Gabaix, Gerd Gigerenzer, Aditya Goenka, and Teimuraz Gogsadze. Three anonymous reviewers, chosen by MIT Press, provided numerous valuable comments and constructive criticisms, for which we are very grateful. Ali Mehdizadeh and Lia Cattaneo did a thorough job of checking the references for us. We would also like to thank Emily Taber, our editor, for her support and suggestions of many kinds.

Cass is grateful to many collaborators on other projects, who have also taught him much, even if they have not read this book (and have no responsibility for our errors). These are Daniel Kahneman, Sendhil Mullainathan, Lucia Reisch, Tali Sharot, and Richard Thaler. The Program on Behavioral Economics and Public Policy at Harvard Law School provided valuable support. Sanjit would like to acknowledge, without implicating for any errors, Ali al-Nowaihi, Vincent Crawford, Ernst Fehr, Herbert Gintis, and Peter Wakker, who have been generous with their time, support, and wisdom on behavioral economics over many years.

In some places, we have drawn on previous work, and we are grateful for permission to do that. The kernel of the book can be found in Sanjit Dhami, Ali al-Nowaihi, and Cass R. Sunstein, *Heuristics and Public Policy: Decision-making under Bounded Rationality*, Studies in Microeconomics 7 (Sage Journals,[1] 2019). Parts of chapters 7, 9, 10, and 11 draw from Cass R. Sunstein, *Behavioral Science and Public Policy* (Cambridge University Press, 2020).

A project of this size always requires enormous support and sacrifice from the family. Sanjit would like to express his gratitude to his parents, Manohar and Baljeet, his wife Shammi, his son Sahaj, and his niece Mehar. Cass would like to thank his wife, Samantha Power, his children Ellyn, Declan, and Rian, and his Labrador retrievers (and constant companions) Snow and Finley.

1
Introduction

In this book we have two main goals. The first is to offer a fresh understanding of *bounded rationality*—of how human beings depart from perfect rationality. This understanding will draw on, and attempt to clarify and formalize, decades of pathbreaking research about judgment and decision-making. The second is to explore the concrete implications of that understanding for public policy and law, with reference to foundational questions about choice, welfare, and freedom.

We aim to promote those goals both for specialists, who might benefit from a discussion of how the existing boundaries might be pushed forward, and for newcomers, who might be interested in the idea of bounded rationality and curious to learn what all the shouting is about. To promote our two goals, we offer a wide range of empirical findings about human behavior and also explore and assess theoretical work that attempts to explain those findings by reference to general models and to offer testable hypotheses. We show that the empirical evidence and the general models have important implications for public policy and law, for how to think about paternalism, and for how to improve human welfare, in part by lengthening lives. At the same time, we emphasize how much remains to be learned.

Rationality

A long-dominant framework in economics often called *neoclassical economics* has a rich intellectual history. Also known as the *Bayesian rationality approach* (BRA), it has a remarkable ability to deal with diverse human behaviors and to make precise and testable predictions. The BRA has been widely used in many social and behavioral sciences—for instance, in political science under the rubric of the rational actor model; in courses in law, management, and finance; and even in parts of neuroscience to model the behavior of individual neurons. The BRA has greatly, and formally, enriched our understanding of economic and social phenomena.

The BRA is a benchmark for what constitutes rational behavior and is a set of auxiliary assumptions, but (to put it mildly) it is not motivated by empirical evidence about how people actually behave. At its core are the assumptions that humans have unlimited computational and cognitive abilities; that they make considered choices that respect several axioms of rationality, such as completeness and transitivity; that they make cold, calculated decisions in the absence of emotions; that they effortlessly use all the available knowledge in mathematics and statistics (even including that which is just being published); and that they possess perfect and unlimited memory and attention. Importantly, some of those who employ the BRA relax these assumptions in various ways, but they are the starting points.

The vision of economics laid out in the BRA, and as described above, is much narrower than what the founding fathers of neoclassical economics themselves in the first half of the twentieth century, or classical economists such as Adam Smith, set out to construct. Indeed, there is a good argument that the classical economists and the founding fathers of neoclassical economists would have greater affinity for modern behavioral economics than for modern neoclassical economics. In order to avoid terms such as *modern neoclassical economics* and *classical neoclassical economics*, we shall throughout use the term BRA to refer to the practice in the teaching and research in the economics profession based on modern neoclassical economics. It is important to emphasize that in the last decades, the BRA has been under considerable pressure as a result of behavioral findings, and in economics departments and elsewhere, behavioral economics has made substantial inroads. Younger generations of economists are decreasingly committed to the BRA.

One of our main goals is to document and to specify the inroads. A great advantage of the BRA, and a continuing source of its appeal, is that it often makes extremely precise and testable predictions that can be used to test the underlying assumptions and the predictions of models based on these assumptions. This is an advantage that the BRA possesses relative to the other social and behavioral sciences. However, the BRA is ultimately a set of hypotheses about how people behave. The formal, technical, and mathematical language underlying the BRA does not make the predictions from these models self-evidently correct or in conformity with the evidence. These predictions must be stringently tested against the evidence, and they have been tested and often found wanting.

Several decades of testing the predictions of the BRA have shown, beyond doubt, that the data are not consistent with many of the central predictions and assumptions of the BRA. The data do not support the underlying assumptions of the BRA nor the individual theories within the BRA such as expected utility theory, exponential discounting, and various equilibrium concepts in game theory. Indeed, it has to be said that on any standards of acceptance of theories in the natural sciences, many of the key components of the BRA are rejected by the evidence. Adherents to the BRA hope that these rejections are in fact anomalies that successively more complicated BRA models will, in due course, be able to explain or that contrary evidence will itself be refuted. As we shall see, this is unlikely.

It is staggering that the features of the BRA have been widely accepted within the economics profession, although as noted, this is definitely changing (in some places too slowly). The empirical rejections of many of the key components of the BRA should not surprise us. The BRA made a bold and decisive move by creating an insular economics and, from around the second half of the twentieth century, undertook a process of purging insights from psychology, sociology, anthropology, and sociobiology. In addition, it has successively ratcheted up the rationality requirements on individual behavior.

Consider two highly influential examples in the BRA that are illustrative of how economics has progressed in recent decades.

1. The BRA used *rational expectations* to replace the cognitively simpler *adaptive expectations* process. The idea of rational expectations means that the subjective expectations of people are essentially the same as the mathematical expectations taken for the correct, possibly stochastic, underlying model that describes the economic phenomenon under study. The cognitive requirements behind such expectations are unlikely to be met in practice. Adaptive expectations, by contrast, require people to adjust their previous forecast by a fixed fraction of the previous forecast error; for that reason, they capture a simple adjustment process that is reminiscent of reinforcement learning. The 1976 Nobel Prize winner in economics, Milton Friedman, used adaptive expectations in his famous presidential address to the American Economic Association (Friedman, 1968) to make one of the most insightful predictions in modern macroeconomics.[1]

The switch to rational expectations from adaptive expectations did not occur by a process of stringent testing or as a result of the presence of compelling empirical evidence. Rather, the leaders in the field asserted, in an axiomatic fashion, that adaptive expectations is not rational enough and hence that people in economic models must follow rational expectations. This injunction was soon followed by others, and rational expectations quickly became an essential component of the BRA. This influenced not only macroeconomics, at least since the early 1970s, but also game theory. The latter imposed consistency between actions and beliefs as an equilibrium requirement, which is in the spirit of rational expectations. No empirical evidence was invoked in either case.

In accepting rational expectations, macroeconomics did not give serious consideration to insights from psychology on the expectations formation process. In accepting consistency between beliefs and actions, game theory also ignored insights from psychology and from sociology, where *social rationality*, not private rationality, plays the key role. We shall examine issues of social rationality in chapter 4. In laying the foundations of the BRA, theorists used axiomatic assertions rather than seeking guidance from the painful process of gathering empirical data. This is an interesting, but unfortunate, methodological feature of the BRA that is unparalleled in the natural sciences.

2. The BRA quickly adopted the newly discovered methods in mathematics, such as *dynamic programming*, developed in the 1950s for engineering control theory, and endowed humans with the ability to use these new tools seamlessly. The reasonableness of this assumption was asserted axiomatically without any empirical evidence and without invoking evidence from the related social and behavioral sciences on the plausibility of this method for human judgment and decision-making. We discuss a finite horizon dynamic programming model (see section 3.2.1) and outline the solution method. Even in fairly simple dynamic programming problems, which typically lack analytical solutions, we show that people have to be capable of making trillions of calculations in their heads in an instant. Or, and this is a point we deal with separately below, it is assumed that people act *as if* they can successfully perform these calculations.

Spurred and motivated by the evidence that rejected many of the assumptions and predictions of the BRA, behavioral economics has gained increasing acceptance within and outside the economics profession. It has a strong interdisciplinary focus, drawing liberally from the other social and behavioral sciences, and it explains far better the evidence arising from human behavior, not just within purely economic domains but also from law, politics, finance, and management. It must be stressed that to an increasing degree, behavioral economics is a fully rigorous and axiomatically founded framework. It certainly does not lag behind the BRA in making rigorous, falsifiable, and precise predictions, although it differs in its responsiveness to the empirical evidence and accepts refutation of existing theories.

Behavioral economics has been enormously successful in a relatively short period of time. It has produced a remarkable body of empirical evidence using the newer methods of lab studies and neuroeconomic studies and also using the existing methods of field studies and randomized control trials (RCTs). This has opened up the black box of human behavior, judgment, and decision-making as never before in economics. It has also produced new theoretical models that explain not only the empirical rejections of the BRA but also the emerging behavioral evidence.

Within behavioral economics, one might distinguish between two kinds of research programs, which for want of better terms we might call the *incremental program* and the *big-push program*. The incremental program seeks to replace selected components of the BRA with behavioral insights, hoping that gradual and incremental changes will produce a new set of better behaviorally founded theories within economics. For instance, it is typical to use mathematical optimization and relatively high-level rationality within these models while allowing people to be slightly inattentive, or boundedly rational, in other respects. The incremental program might, for example, emphasize that human beings are not attentive to *shrouded attributes* of products or activities but otherwise subscribe to the BRA.

The big-push program aims to undertake a more fundamental departure from the BRA and gives greater attention to *procedural rationality*, an important term popularized by Herbert Simon. The seminal work of Daniel Kahneman and Amos Tversky on heuristics and biases in the 1970s provides a foundation for this approach, and the work by Gerd Gigerenzer and his coauthors explicitly aims to model procedural rationality that underpins human choices.

Both these research programs are examples of boundedly rational models. They differ in how boundedly rational they wish to be. We focus on both approaches in this book, but due to the lesser attention given to the big-push program, we also highlight its essential features. In the process, we will also show, through several concrete examples, that there are bridges and connections between these two approaches. These connections show that in many cases the two approaches lead to either identical implied preferences or predictions.

In studying the rationale and the features of these programs, we must ask some fundamental questions. What precisely does rationality mean in the BRA? What is the evidence for the BRA? Is there merit in the position taken by the incremental program? Are optimization-based models tenable? How do we evaluate the *as-if* position within the BRA? Can we distinguish between the predictions made by the incremental and the big-push programs?

In the BRA, individuals have *well-behaved* and *consistent* underlying preferences (see chapter 2 for definitions) that give rise to choices. It is assumed in welfare analyses conducted in the BRA that individuals are the best judges of their own welfare and that observed choices reflect considered welfare judgments. For this reason, regulation is disfavored, though it still plays a role in policy analysis inspired by the BRA when, say, individuals ignore the externalities they impose on others. Long ago, John Stuart Mill argued for protection of liberty insofar as the decisions by individuals affected only themselves—but not insofar as their decisions affected others.

Followers of the BRA tend to embrace Mill's *harm principle*. For instance, they have no problem at all with pollution taxes. When individuals decide to buy a more polluting car, they are often required to pay higher taxes to help offset the social harm that they impose on others. But some forms of regulation are harder to defend by reference to externalities, such as those that ban menthol-flavored cigarettes or mandate wearing seat belts in cars and helmets on motorcycles, buying third party car insurance, or obtaining certification of the road worthiness of vehicles. Many followers of the BRA tend to be skeptical about such bans and mandates. Why force people to do something they do not want to do when they are the best judges of what will promote their own welfare? Insofar as the behavioral evidence rejects some of the key features of the BRA, it also calls into question the proposition that people can always be trusted to act in ways that promote their own welfare. Human beings can be inattentive, myopic, and lacking in self-control, and they might use convenient and generally reasonable heuristics that lead to systematic errors.

These findings have led to mounting interest in behavioral welfare economics, essentially welfare economics that takes account of the empirical evidence that is contrary to the predictions of the BRA. Some practitioners of behavioral welfare economics defend mandates and bans by reference to that evidence. A more cautious idea here is *libertarian paternalism*, which proposes minimally intrusive policies, such as warnings, reminders, and default options, that can be ignored by those who act as if they followed the BRA but can lead to welfare improvements for others. We shall explore the foundations of libertarian paternalism and its limits and evaluate some of the critiques. We shall also devote considerable attention to mandates and bans.

Aims

It is not possible to appreciate modern theorizing about bounded rationality and heuristics without an understanding of the central ideas of rationality and the BRA in economics. The work of Herbert Simon, Daniel Kahneman, Amos Tversky, Richard Thaler, and many others who made early and seminal contributions to bounded rationality was motivated by unease with the BRA framework. A large number of interdisciplinary researchers work, directly or indirectly, on bounded rationality but have diverse backgrounds in psychology, sociology, political science, anthropology, sociobiology, neuroscience, computer science, law, management, and finance. We suspect that for many interdisciplinary researchers, the BRA is nontrivial to follow. The formal approach in the graduate economics textbooks, and certainly in the leading journals in economics, can be fairly technical and opaque. One of our aims here is to give an accessible, and self-contained, treatment of the modern formal machinery in economics that is relevant for understanding some of the key features of the BRA. We hope that a common understanding of, and familiarity with, the tools of the BRA will facilitate more productive debate.

We also provide a gentle introduction to the frontiers and fairly technical material without compromising on the required understanding of the relevant theory. In almost all cases, we work through concrete examples, which should help the central points of the theory to stick. The mathematics requirements to read this book should not exceed what is needed for a well-taught high school mathematics course; any extra training in mathematics will be a bonus. Whenever we encounter more advanced material, we spend plenty of time on intuitive examples, on the basics, and on the intermediate steps. (We will also not be ashamed to repeat ourselves!) Any reader who is committed to understanding bounded rationality, and has a bit of patience, need not be familiar with advanced mathematics or statistics to understand the book. At the same time, we seek to provide enough information and material to keep the advanced reader interested.

Thus, for instance, we do not shy away from explaining concepts in evolutionary game theory, stochastic social dynamics, formal dynamic epidemiological models of the spreads of epidemics, dynamic programming, axiomatic foundations of utility functions, behavioral decision theory, complexity and chaos, and the bias-variance dilemma in machine learning.

We cover an extremely wide terrain, perhaps equivalent to what would be covered in a year long course on bounded rationality when augmented with other readings. We have tried to keep the references to a minimum, often pointing the reader in the direction of surveys that contain the relevant references, yet the number of references has exceeded our expectations. (We will encounter the planning fallacy, a form of bounded rationality to which we have fallen victim.) Although this is a long book, we do not provide a thorough survey of bounded rationality, of heuristics, or of policy ideas that are based on them. Our omission of some of the literature does not mean that we are unfavorably disposed toward it. We do not survey the earlier literature on bounded rationality, as this is covered elsewhere, and some of its insights are assimilated in the more modern literature (Simon, 1955; Cyert & March, 1963; Newell & Simon, 1972; Nelson & Winter, 1982; Radner, 1996). The reader interested in surveys of bounded rationality in firms can consult Harstad and Selten (2013) and Spiegler (2011).[2] However, we hope to provide enough in the way of formal models, and their variety, to give the reader a reasonably good picture of the literature and, we hope, the tools to form an assessment of where the field is headed.

In some places, it might seem that we pose more questions than answers. To that we plead guilty. The last decades have seen extraordinary progress, but thus far we have only scratched the tip of the iceberg of bounded rationality. This book is in some sense a manifesto for change in the social and behavioral sciences to incorporate even more bounded rationality. It highlights the problems with the BRA and points to empirical evidence that suggests promising future directions and also many dead ends. But we do not offer a coherent, well-defined, heuristics-based alternative to the BRA that can answer all the questions that the BRA has dealt with in the past, simply because such an alternative does not yet exist. Nonetheless, there has been much progress in the literature on heuristics and bounded rationality, and we are optimistic that there will be much more in the near future. One of our goals is to spur more researchers in more fields to think about these issues. Unless there is a minimum critical threshold of researchers working in this area, the speed of progress will not be satisfactory. And we are not even close to this threshold.

We should emphasize that applied economists reading this book—say, those who conduct RCTs in the field or others who use econometric methods to produce data-based inference—are hardly the main objects of criticism here. Applied economists have provided valuable empirical evidence to support research on bounded rationality. At the same time, we do have two concerns. First, many applied economists do actually subscribe to the BRA, and much of the applied research that they do is within the confines of BRA, not outside. Even now, findings that are supportive of the BRA stand a better chance of getting published in mainstream journals, particularly when they try to dispute behavioral models, often without a sufficiently strong basis. Tenure and career considerations can play a role in the sort of applied research in which economists choose to engage. Second, when teaching courses in economic theory most applied economists teach the standard BRA in economics, often omitting experimental findings that support behavioral theories and that are highly relevant to their courses. Fortunately, this is changing.

The intended audience of the book is quite diverse. We hope that our book will be useful not just for professional academics but also for policymakers and for members of the lay public who have an interest in the subject. The book is intended to be a research monograph on the subject, and as such we hope that it might be of interest to PhD students and career researchers in thinking about their research. We also hope that the audience for this book will be interdisciplinary and that, in addition to economists, it might be of interest generally to social and behavioral scientists. The book is also meant to work as a teaching resource in courses on behavioral economics and experimental economics and for courses in economic theory that are serious about explaining the evidence.

The Plan

Scope and Organization

The book comes in eleven chapters.

In many of the social and the behavioral sciences, and certainly in common discourse, the term *rationality* lacks a precise definition. By contrast, in the BRA, this term is clear, precise, and testable. In chapter 2 we first establish a common language by defining situations of risk, uncertainty, ambiguity, and true uncertainty. We then consider rationality in the various situations in which it is used in the BRA. In particular, we state and explain the *axioms of rationality under certainty*; the *axioms of rationality under risk*; and the *axioms of rationality under time discounting*. In each case, we show how preferences that respect these axioms can be represented by appropriate utility functions. Under risk, the relevant utility function is an *expected utility function*, and under time discounting it is the *exponential discounted utility function*. There are no specific axioms of rationality under strategic interaction, the subject matter of game theory. But the analysis of strategic interaction does need all the rationality requirements under the BRA and further restrictions such as methodological individualism, private rationality, *common priors* (which is sometimes relaxed), and *common knowledge of rationality*. The last two are extremely strong conditions for which there is little or no empirical evidence, except in cases where there is a public signal of some event or perhaps for behavior that is guided by social norms.

Next, we highlight typical auxiliary assumptions in the BRA that either are regarded as part of a broader concept of rationality or are sometimes mistakenly believed to be consequences of rationality. We show that self-regarding preferences are sometimes erroneously thought to be an implication of rationality in economics. The evidence supports other-regarding preferences, and these can actually be incorporated within the BRA, although this is seldom done. Similarly, emotionless deliberation is also sometimes mistakenly thought of as an essential component of rationality in the BRA. The BRA is flexible enough to incorporate emotions, although it does not often do so. By contrast, other-regarding preferences and emotions play a central role in behavioral economics.

Finally, in chapter 2, we also consider the evidence for the rationality axioms in the BRA. The weight of the evidence does not support the axioms of rationality in any of the following domains: certainty, risk, and time discounting. Furthermore, the predictions of neoclassical game theory do not find adequate support in the evidence. Some of the aspects on which we present evidence include *preference reversals*; *violation of completeness of preferences*; *nonlinear probability weighting*; *reference dependence*; *hyperbolic discounting*; *magnitude effect*; *gain-loss asymmetry*; *overconfidence*; *limited attention*; *violations of the predictions of equilibrium concepts in game theory*; *subjective probability distributions that have fat tails and do not respect sample size*; *base rate neglect*; and *conservatism*.

In the appendix to chapter 2, we give a relatively nontechnical primer on behavioral decision theory, which is important in understanding some parts of the book. Essentially, this is a set of tools about how people make decisions when they face risk and uncertainty. As promised earlier, nothing more than high school mathematics is required to understand this material. We outline three main decision theories, *expected utility*, *rank dependent utility*, and *prospect theory*. Of these theories, prospect theory is the only one that can cope with risk, uncertainty, and ambiguity. However, none of these theories is able to offer predictions under true uncertainty.

Chapter 3 offers an account of the role of bounded rationality in economics. Since it forms the core of our analysis, we give a detailed description of this chapter, which is also meant to serve as an introduction to the book as a whole. We use a wide variety of topics within the social and behavioral sciences to construct our arguments. These topics are not directly related to each other, but the common theme that runs through them is the role of bounded rationality and the implications for human behavior. We have said that in order to see why we need bounded rationality, it is essential first to consider the BRA, in which individuals use mathematical optimization to solve economic problems, using the existing repository of mathematical and statistical techniques. We show that simple bread and butter problems in economics require the assumption that people on the street can do trillions of calculations in their heads in an instant, or act as if they can. We also consider situations where it might be difficult to distinguish between the predictions of heuristics-based and optimization-based models. Introductory courses in the BRA generally teach, without evidence, that economic agents who do not optimize will perish, and any errors at the level of individuals will cancel out in the aggregate because positive and negative errors are equally likely to occur. We show that evidence does not support this axiomatic assertion, and neither do theoretical models in, say, finance; a prime example is that of noise trader risk.

In response to the empirical rejection of the BRA, we consider the relative merits of two possible ways forward. One possibility is to go for an all-out heuristics-based approach, the big-push approach. The BRA is based on *substantive rationality*, in which one judges whether the final choices made by individuals are rational. By contrast, the heuristics-based approach suggests using the concept of *procedural rationality*, which explicitly accounts for the procedure undertaken to arrive at the final choice (Simon, 1978, 1982, 1986). Procedural rationality would reject solution methods such as dynamic programming, which require trillions of calculations to be made in order to solve fairly simple dynamic problems, as being psychologically unrealistic. Procedural rationality also requires us to take account of the frame and context dependence of preferences and the circumstances in which events have greater or lower salience. These considerations are important for the procedure required to solve a problem.

A second possibility, currently favored in behavioral economic theory, is to make incremental changes in the BRA that replace individual features with more behaviorally informed features, one at time, but that keep faith with the other features of the BRA, including mathematical optimization. The choice between these two positions is not an easy one, even if the incremental approach appears to allow for faster progress, at least in the short run.

In considering strategic interaction within the BRA, we take as our main example the static prisoner's dilemma game, arguably the most recognized game in the social and the behavioral sciences, which also serves as a metaphor for human cooperation and conflict. Strategic interaction within the BRA assumes (1) *methodological individualism* (namely, individual motivation, cognition, and decision-making entirely explain all actions and social phenomena[3]), (2) *rationality*, and (3) *self-interested motivations*, (individual actions are motivated by self-interest only).

The BRA predicts that players who play the prisoner's dilemma game will never cooperate, yet we observe that about 60 percent of the players who play the static version of the game do cooperate. This relatively high degree of cooperation cannot be explained by lab subjects who are mistakenly importing repeated game experiences from outside the lab. We also reconsider this game in the subsequent chapters to illustrate how cooperation may be explained by newer heuristics-based solutions concepts. In particular, we show that social rationality as embodied, say, in a Kantian equilibrium, predicts cooperation in the static prisoner's dilemma game.

We offer the tantalizing possibility that under true uncertainty, *social norms*, possibly arising out of cultural adaptation, may offer us ready-made heuristics to make decisions. In the same situation, the BRA and optimization-based behavioral models may not be able to make predictions. Making decisions under true uncertainty is cognitively challenging, and social norms may offer us significant cognitive simplifications, requiring only that we have a proclivity to follow social norms, which has most likely arisen out of biological evolution and cultural adaptation.

In light of the evidence against the BRA, which has assumed mountainous proportions, what accounts for the continued adherence to it and the reluctance to accept the alternative frameworks such as behavioral economics? We believe that the reasons lie in a mistaken homespun approach to the methodology and the philosophy of science that has no precedent in any of the natural sciences. The most influential paper in economic methodology, by Milton Friedman, argues that we should look out only for the predictions of economic models, even if all assumptions are patently false and unrealistic. Should the model make successful predictions, he argues, we can conclude that people behave as if they follow the model, even if all the assumptions are false.

This has been used as license to build ad hoc models in economics without stringent empirical testing, which was unlikely to have been Friedman's position or motivation. The work by Daniel Kahneman and Amos Tversky in the 1970s showed that the predictions of economic models were rejected by the evidence and could not be accepted even in an as if sense (Kahneman & Tversky, 1972a, 1972b; Tversky & Kahneman, 1971, 1973, 1974). Since then, defenders of the BRA have argued that all theories/models are wrong anyway; that the purpose of economic models is to build intuition about the real world and to tell useful stories and fables but not to explain reality; that economics deserves special status because testing theories in it is nothing like testing theories in the natural sciences. These retrogressive and self-handicapping views on methodology, which have a fair bit of support within academia in economics, have not helped the field to make progress.

In the BRA, preferences are held fixed, while beliefs are allowed to be updated as new information arrives, typically by using Bayes' law. Many (not all) economists believe that departing from the idea that preferences are self-regarding and introducing other-regarding preferences will allow ad hoc explanations to flourish. Many are broadly skeptical of the idea that preferences shift with experiences and context (and are in that sense endogenous). But as we will show, preferences are indeed malleable and endogenous rather than fixed and exogenous, and there is feedback among preferences, history, culture, and institutions. With the proliferation of lab experiments, and in conjunction with field data, it is easier to produce data on these questions. For instance, the standards for theoretical models within behavioral economics to explain the data on other-regarding preferences are more stringent than any yardstick set within the BRA. Fehr and Schmidt (2006) argue that any candidate model of other-regarding preferences must explain the evidence on the relevant experimental games (dictator game, ultimatum game, gift exchange game, trust game, and public goods game with and without punishment).

Macroeconomic theory builds on the foundations provided by the BRA to construct models that contain several additional features. Very limited heterogeneity in preferences and technology is assumed in the most realistic of macroeconomic models. The vast majority of the macroeconomic models continue to embrace the *representative agent framework*, in which a single representative individual (a sort of Robinson Crusoe) represents all the consumers and firms in a $20 trillion economy. Despite much technical sophistication, the ability of such models, often lying within the rubric of dynamic stochastic general equilibrium (DSGE) models, to explain the data is questionable (Romer, 2016; Stiglitz, 2018). In the opening lines of his abstract, the 2018 Nobel Prize winner in economics, Paul Romer (2016), says: "In the last three decades, the methods and conclusions of macroeconomics have deteriorated to the point that much of the work in this area no longer qualifies as scientific research." Despite pushback against these dissenting views in the profession, it might not be possible to salvage the macroeconomic framework within the BRA.

Alternatively, in thinking about macroeconomic phenomena, it is worth focusing on insights from a *complex, adaptive, systems perspective*. Economic agents follow simple rules of thumb in a world where there is true uncertainty; they use simple adaptive learning rules that create feedback between macroeconomic aggregates and their own rules of thumb; fluctuations are caused endogenously without any stochastic terms; the dynamic system is characterized by *emergent phenomena* and *chaos*, or a high degree of sensitivity to initial conditions.

Chapter 4 outlines and discusses a set of models of heuristics-based choice that deal with a wide range of questions in the social and behavioral sciences. We use the *risk as feelings theory* to show that emotions and economic calculus, working in combination or alone, determine choices under risk. This offers a different set of predictions from the ones that we obtain in the standard decision theory models outlined in the appendix to chapter 2.

In chapter 3, we consider optimization-based models of choices made over time; by contrast, in chapter 4, we consider *attribute-based models of intertemporal choice* that act on outcome-time pairs as the relevant attributes. Among the models that we consider are the *similarity relation in time preferences* and the *trade-off model of attribute choice*. We show how preferences that are represented by attribute-based models can be given an equivalent representation under optimizing delay-discounting models. This opens up an important link between the models in the two classes, and we show how this framework can be used to improve delay-discounting models.

We formally consider Herbert Simon's work on *aspiration adaptation* that relies on procedural rationality and on the *satisficing heuristic* in providing an alternative to optimization-based models in the BRA. We also show how this work can give rise to cooperation in a prisoner's dilemma game. As noted earlier, neoclassical game theory is based on methodological individualism and private rationality. Several notions of social rationality have been proposed as alternative solution concepts. Examples include *team reasoning, joint intentionality*, and *Kantian rationality*. Of these, we show how Kantian rationality, based on the Kantian protocol, can be used to find social equilibria in games.

A *winner's curse* in public value auctions arises when bidders bid too optimistically and face potential losses, possibly bankruptcy. We examine the relevant empirical evidence. We then illustrate the heuristics on conditional probabilities that give rise to the problem of the winner's curse in a lab version of an auction experiment.

Next, we show how complexity theory and agent-based models can be used to provide an alternative account of macroeconomic phenomena. In these models, people follow simple adaptive rules of thumb and face true uncertainty, and there are simple feedback mechanisms between individual decisions and aggregate outcomes. The aggregate system exhibits emergent phenomena and chaos, and fluctuations are endogenous to the system. Continuing this theme, we present two topics in the next section: *evolutionary dynamics* and *stochastic social dynamics*. We provide the basic definitions of *evolutionary stable strategies, evolutionary dynamics*, and the *notion of asymptotically steady states*. We then discuss the basics of stochastic social dynamics and show how the resulting stability concept, *stochastically stable states*, can refine the set of asymptotically steady states. In these models, individuals follow simple rules of thumb and make mistakes, yet this low-level rationality can explain the emergence of institutions. We then move on to the intriguing new developments in *narrative economics* and explore how these could be key drivers in explaining social and economic phenomena. We use the classic Kermack-McKendrick model in epidemiology to show how *contagion* leads to the spread of epidemics, rumors, and narratives.

Since people often need to make choices under true uncertainty and cognitive constraints, they need simplified representations of reality to guide their decisions. In this regard, we consider *mental models* and how they can help, as well as harm, individual and collective interests. We show how cognitive simplifications are often obtained by *narrow bracketing* of options, in contrast to the recommendation of the BRA for *broad bracketing*. We apply the distinction between broad and narrow bracketing to financial market decisions and to the *equity-premium puzzle*.

Many people follow the heuristic of choosing to ignore *low probability events*. This poses tremendous difficulty for models within the BRA, as well as for models in behavioral decision theory, to explain the evidence on human decision-making for such events. Examples including the low take-up of insurance for low probability natural hazards, running red traffic lights, capital punishment, and wearing seat belts. We show how these behaviors can be accommodated within an extension of prospect theory, called *composite prospect theory*, that takes account of behavior toward low probability events. In the final section of chapter 4, we consider how *sunk costs* may influence human decisions. We also consider some evidence on the ability, or the lack thereof, to calculate opportunity costs.

In chapter 5, we consider the *heuristics and biases research program* (HBP) that started with the seminal research papers by Daniel Kahneman and Amos Tversky in the 1970s. The HBP took as its starting point the rationality assumptions embedded within the BRA and proceeded directly to test the individual assumptions and axioms that underlie it. The main message that emerged from the HBP was that the BRA was not tenable, not even in an as-if sense. Thus, even for those within economics who subscribe to an extreme version of Milton Friedman's approach to methodology, it ought to have led to a large-scale reconsideration of the BRA and their own research programs. To date, it has not had that effect, despite the growing influence of behavioral economics.

We do not provide a full survey of the HBP here. There are excellent sets of collected readings (Kahneman et al., 1982; Gilovich et al., 2002) and more recent surveys of the empirics and the theory within the HBP from a behavioral economics perspective (Dhami, 2020a). We begin by providing reasonably precise definitions of some of the important heuristics and biases outlined within the HBP. These include the *representativeness heuristic and its two exemplars, the hot hand fallacy and the gambler's fallacy*; *anchoring*; *availability*; *hindsight bias*; *confirmation bias*; and *affect heuristic*. We also discuss *regression to the mean* and the confusion between *necessary* and *sufficient conditions*.

The HBP has come under sustained attack from several quarters. While the HBP is sometimes dismissed outright within economics, often by those who do not understand it well, a public stand against the HBP has long been taken in another strand of research in bounded rationality. This work is most closely associated with Gerd Gigerenzer and his coauthors. Since this work is often associated with "fast and frugal heuristics," we abbreviate it as FFP, short for the *fast and frugal heuristics research program*. This is not the most suitable acronym because the HBP would enthusiastically agree that heuristics are fast and frugal. Chapter 6 offers an introduction to the FFP.

There is a great deal of confusion about the relative contributions of the two research programs, HBP and FFP, among their followers and their critics. The debate between the HBP and the FFP has come to be known as the *great rationality debate* in psychology. We believe that several aspects of this debate rely on confusion and misunderstanding about the relevant subject matter. We try to clarify several aspects of this debate in chapters 5 and 6.

In chapter 5, we consider a range of objections to the HBP that have been raised by the FFP. These objections are about *ecological validity* in the HBP; *one-event probabilities*; *"we cannot be that dumb" critique*; *frequency versus probability format*; *empirical counterparts to heuristics*; *how HBP can explain an event and its negation*; and the *criticism of appropriate statistical norms*. We agree that heuristics are fast and frugal, and we emphasize that with respect to bounded rationality, much can be gained by an understanding of the findings of the FFP. At the same time, we address the various criticisms and argue that, in general, they do not amount to convincing objections to the HBP. In some cases, they reflect a misunderstanding of the HBP position, and in other cases, they are based on a misunderstanding of statistics or of the methodology and philosophy of science.

Chapter 6 explores the FFP. The typical method of solving problems within the FFP is as follows. In order to make choices among competing options, people have a set of *cues* chosen from within a *reference class of cues*. The cues can either *discriminate* among the options, or they cannot. The *ecological validity* of a cue is the percentage of cases, within the reference class, in which it can discriminate among a pairwise comparison of the options. Several heuristics are then introduced in the FFP, each taking as given the data on reference classes, cues, and the ecological validities of the cues. For instance, in the case of two options, the *take-the-best heuristic* ranks the cues by their ecological validities, goes down the list of cues, picking the first cue that is able to discriminate between the options, and then picks the option recommended by the cue. Suppose that the problem is to determine which of two given German cities, A and B, is more populous. Suppose also that the first cue based on ecological validities that is able to discriminate between the populations of the two cities is whether the city has a football team. If this cue tells us that city A has a football team but city B does not, then the decision-maker is predicted to pick city A as the answer; this is known as the take-the-best heuristic. The particular example that we have chosen is also known as the *recognition heuristic*.

We highlight several concerns with the FFP. First, it is the typical practice in the FFP that the experimenter provides the reference class, the cues, and the ecological validities of the cues as data to the subjects before asking them to make a choice. Changing the reference class, for instance, will change the cues and their ecological validities. Insofar as this research program aims to discover how people make choices under true uncertainty, it is of the greatest importance to figure out how people search for the reference class of cues and how they discover the relevant information on their ecological validities. We suspect that most people would not know how to get this information under true uncertainty, or even if they should be looking for this information, if it were not provided to them by the experimenter. By providing this information, the FFP does not test its heuristics stringently enough.

By contrast, under prospect theory, the context of the problem often clarifies what an appropriate reference point is—for example, the status quo or an entitlement based on fairness, social norms, or conventions. In any case, tests of prospect theory do not provide subjects with a reference point. Such tests typically ask subjects to make choices between lotteries, and the relevant theory makes predictions based on the most sensible reference point. The model then stands or falls based on these predictions. Second, from choices made in the FFP, we cannot conclude what mental or cognitive process was used, nor is a direct test proposed within the FFP. The given choices could, in principle, be generated by several possible models. Thus, notwithstanding claims to the contrary and the FFP's criticism of the HBP on these grounds, the FFP is firmly an as-if approach, no less than prospect theory. The FFP provides no direct evidence that people actually use the heuristics that it proposes (even if it might be plausible to think that they do). We argue in this book that prospect theory is a good as-if theory, but is the FFP a good as-if approach?

A great difficulty in evaluating the FFP is that there is no benchmark against which one might compare the performance of the suggested heuristics. The situation is quite different for the HBP, where the BRA provided the relevant benchmark to test. However, under true uncertainty, which is the main situation of interest in the FFP, the BRA does not provide any benchmark because it really has no predictions to offer. The performance of some of the leading heuristics in the FFP, such as the take-the-best heuristic, is not satisfactory when the information on reference cues and ecological validities is directly, or indirectly (e.g., recall of cues from the given information), provided by the experimenter. Which heuristic in the FFP toolbox of heuristics is used in a given situation or context? This is one of the central questions in the FFP, but it is, as yet, unanswered.

We also argue that heuristics-based approaches may dominate optimization-based models in predictive ability only under true uncertainty, but not otherwise. Further, we contest the view that behavioral economics is a repair project for the BRA.

We also give a formal derivation of the *less is more effect*, sometimes known as the *bias-variance dilemma* in models of machine learning. The basic problem is one of fitting a function to a sample of noisy observations on the relation between two (or more) variables. Suppose that one undertook a standard statistical exercise of minimizing the sum of squares of the prediction errors. Then, it can be shown that an attempt to fit a function too close to the in-sample data overfits the function to the noise in sample. This increases the variance in the prediction errors, based on this function, in out-of-sample data. The optimal fitted function balances this trade-off. The FFP has alleged that the HBP has focused on the bias term alone and ignored the variance term. By contrast, the bias-variance trade-off is irrelevant to a large number of heuristics in the HBP—for example, the anchoring heuristic, conjunction fallacy, availability heuristic, confirmation bias, hindsight bias, and regression to the mean. In other cases, such as the representativeness heuristic, which includes the gambler's fallacy and the hot hand fallacy, the statistical inference problem is not of the nature of a bias-variance trade-off. Finally, it has not been demonstrated that human cognition and judgment necessarily work in a manner so as to resolve this trade-off; indeed, the evidence from behavioral economics suggests otherwise.

In chapter 7, we begin our discussion of *behavioral welfare economics*. In the BRA, it is assumed that people make fully rational and informed choices and that these choices must therefore be respected. Versions of these ideas go back to Mill, who argued that choosers know better than outsiders and hence in favor of respect for individual liberty unless choosers harm others; this is encapsulated in Mill's harm principle. By contrast, the evidence from behavioral economics shows that many people make choices that do not promote their own welfare. This empirical evidence has led to developments in the field of behavioral welfare economics.

In chapter 7, we explore the philosophical foundations of that field. We examine fundamental questions about how a third party—for example, a regulator or a government—should react to individual choices. Should these choices be respected under all circumstances? Contrary to Mill, our answer is no, even if the welfare of third parties is not at risk. We also ask about subjective well-being and about whether hedonic criteria, which are often used in welfare economics, provide the only or the best yardstick on which to evaluate human welfare. Our answer is again no. For instance, people might choose to have a more meaningful life, even if it does not make them happier in some simple sense. We also examine arguments for *means paternalism*, a relatively modest form of paternalism that respects people's judgments about their ends without necessarily respecting their judgments about the best means to their ends.

In chapter 8, we consider the use of traditional public policy instruments, such as taxation and regulatory mandates and bans, that arise from a consideration of behavioral findings. The emphasis in this chapter is on *hard paternalism*, which imposes material constraints on the choices of all individuals, whether they depart from the BRA or not. There are two main themes in this chapter that fall under the rubric of, respectively, *behavioral public economics* and *behavioral industrial organization*. Within behavioral public economics, we outline the model of multiple selves and consider the imposition of Pigouvian taxes to internalize *internalities*. These are costs and benefits that the self of an individual at time t creates for the future selves (of the same individual). We also consider the effects of limited attention and lack of self-control (e.g., the consumption of so-called sin goods such as sugary drinks and cigarettes) on the optimal design of public policy. Next, we consider the insights from the literature on behavioral industrial organization in the presence of boundedly rational consumers. We consider the interaction among bounded rationality, competition, and regulation when some consumers are inattentive while others are fully attentive.

In chapter 9, we focus on *libertarian paternalism* (LP), which strives to enable human beings to avoid errors, *as judged by themselves*, while also preserving freedom of choice. LP strategies are often described as *nudges*. A GPS device is an example; so are warnings, reminders, information disclosures (such as calorie labels), and automatic enrollment (in, say, pension plans). LP allows people to go their own way but helps them to arrive at their preferred destination. Most broadly, LP is an effort to increase navigability. It can be useful when people use heuristics that produce errors. Policies that are consistent with LP do not distort the choices of those who follow the BRA (or do so minimally) but are intended to improve the welfare of those who do not. Consider warnings and reminders, which may overcome the problem of limited attention.

Use of default options, an example of an LP policy, has been extremely effective in a large number of domains and can be more cost-effective than traditional tax/subsidy and direct regulation methods advocated in neoclassical welfare economics (Thaler & Sunstein, 2021; Thaler, 2016; Sunstein, 2016, 2017; Dhami, 2020c).

We show that endorsement of LP does not depend on a commitment to psychological claims that may be controversial. Most puzzlingly, the perceived adversarial position between the HBP and FFP approaches, described above, has nonetheless given rise to a critique of the LP approach (Gigerenzer, 2015). We consider the main elements of this critique. As we show, the rationale for many successful nudges lies in a lack of information, in limited attention, and in self-control problems (and imperfect awareness of such problems).

The *lack of a benevolent policymaker* criticism applies to any economic policy, not just nudges. This problem is well recognized in political economy, a well-established field in economics. For instance, there is an extensive literature on regulatory capture and how the problem of corruption may lead to inefficient outcomes; see the classic text by Laffont and Tirole (1993). If policymakers are not benevolent, the strongest objections should be to mandates and bans, not to nudges, which maintain freedom of choice (in part because of an insistence that policymakers may err). A primary reason for nudging, as opposed to mandates and bans, is precisely the possibility that policymakers are not benevolent (or adequately informed).

Objections to LP, based on psychological claims, do not sufficiently grapple with what LP means in practice (Sunstein, 2013; Halpern, 2015)—that is, with the particular policies that advocates or practitioners of LP have embraced in actual policymaking roles. At the same time, we emphasize that LP does not exhaust the category of interventions based on behavioral findings. For example, cigarette taxes and soda taxes might be understood as an effort to respond to present bias and unrealistic optimism (see chapter 8). Some mandates and bans can be defended in similar terms, at least if the goal is to improve human welfare. We would be cautious about coercive approaches of this kind, at least if people's choices are not harming others. But caution is not a rule, and in some cases, the argument for mandates and bans, on welfare grounds, is sufficiently strong. (A ban on menthol-flavored cigarettes is an example; so is a ban on trans fats.)

In chapter 10, we consider the practice of libertarian paternalism, with special reference to the United States. We begin by suggesting a simple organizing framework for behavioral public policy that is based on the acronym FEAST (fun, easy, attractive, social, and timely). We discuss possible institutional structures to implement behavioral public policy and several examples of behaviorally informed public policies and their impact. We consider the effects of mandatory disclosure requirements with respect to nutrition, finance, health care, and fuel economy and also the effect of disclosure on competition. Other topics in this chapter include the effects of structuring choices, both in terms of the number and the complexity of choices and the effect of salience on choices.

2

What Is Rationality and What Is the Evidence for It?

2.1 Introduction

Much debate, and confusion, in the social sciences arises from alternative meanings of the word *rationality*. The Cambridge dictionary defines *rationality* in a manner that is not unrepresentative of how rationality is viewed outside economics: "the quality of being based on clear thought and reason, or of making decisions based on clear thought and reason." The Oxford dictionary offers a similar definition: "(of behavior, ideas, etc.) based on reason rather than emotions." Neither of these definitions is precise. Arguing about rationality based on the content of these definitions is fishing in very muddy waters indeed.

A great strength of the BRA is that it defines rationality in a precise way that allows for sharp and testable predictions. In actual practice, many economists typically justify their rationality assumptions (and indeed the entire apparatus of the BRA) on the grounds of plausibility and tractability rather than on conformity with the empirical evidence. If challenged, they are likely to argue, without supporting evidence, that people act *as if* they were rational.

In section 2.2, we define situations of *risk, uncertainty, ambiguity*, and *true uncertainty*, as used in a formal sense in economics. Much confusion has arisen in the literature from debates between the different social and behavioral sciences in which researchers with different backgrounds use these terms to mean entirely different objects of interest. This section is intended to clarify the meaning of these foundational terms. Of these terms, *true uncertainty*, in which decision-makers cannot even imagine all possible outcomes (let alone the associated probabilities), sometimes referred to as a situation of *unknown unknowns*, is the least studied and arguably the most pervasive. For instance, can one specify/imagine all possible future outcomes from investing in a portfolio of assets, from choosing a partner to marry, or from having one more child? Can a firm specify/imagine all possible consequences from introducing a new product or from its merger, acquisition, and capital restructuring decisions? Alarmingly, the social and behavioral sciences, including economics, do not have definitive predictions to offer under true uncertainty. Yet, humans and firms do make decisions in such situations. A natural question then arises: How do people/firms/governments make decisions under true uncertainty? We shall explore potential answers to this question later in the book.

Section 2.3 sets out the main components of the *Bayesian rationality approach* (BRA). It provides the foundations of modern economics and constitutes the actual practice of neoclassical economics, the currently dominant paradigm in economics. Essentially, the BRA implies that humans have unbounded cognition, computational ability, and attention; perfect and everlasting memory; the ability to make cold, calculated decisions, without being swayed by emotions; and deep knowledge and understanding of all the mathematics and statistics that have ever been invented, including what has just been published in the research journals. Further auxiliary assumptions are added, such as equilibrium analysis, optimization, rational expectations, and rationality assumptions, which are equivalent to individuals following subjective expected utility under uncertainty; exponential discounting when making decisions over time; Nash equilibrium in static games; and perfect Bayesian Nash equilibrium in dynamic games of imperfect information.

Section 2.4 considers the meaning of *rationality under certainty*. We have defined *certainty* in section 2.2 as a situation where individual actions lead to certain outcomes that occur with probability 1. The main requirement for rationality under certainty is that for any pair of choices that are certain, the individual can express a preference or indifference for one over the other (completeness), and their choices are transitive—that is, if they prefer A to B and B to C, then they must prefer A to C. This is the requirement of *consistent preferences*, a fundamental concept in the BRA that forms the backbone for all formal analysis in modern economics. An important theorem in economics shows that individuals who have consistent preferences act *as if* they possessed a utility function, and vice versa. Although individuals may never even be aware that they have a utility function and only ever use their preferences, given this theorem, it is often pedagogically simpler to assume that they possess a utility function. But social scientists who argue that economics assumes that people carry around a utility function in their heads at all times are just wrong.

In section 2.5, we define *rationality under risk*. The objects of interest here are lotteries (see section 2.2). The decision-maker is now assumed to have preferences defined over the set of possible lotteries. Rationality under risk requires imposing certain restrictions on these preferences, the *axioms of rationality under risk*. The most important of these restrictions is given by the *independence axiom*: for example, if you prefer to eat apples to oranges, you will also prefer a 50-50 chance to eat either apples or grapes over a 50-50 chance to eat oranges or grapes. Thus, probabilistically adding a common third element to both choices leaves preferences intact. Any decision-maker who satisfies these restrictions also uses the *expected utility functional*. Conversely, anyone who uses this expected utility functional satisfies these preferences restrictions.

Section 2.6 considers the concept of rationality when decisions are made over time. The main object of interest here is outcome-time pairs—for example, the outcome time pair (z, t) that guarantees an outcome z with certainty at some future time t. The primitives are individual preferences over such outcome-time pairs. We outline the *axioms of rationality in time discounting* that impose suitable restrictions on these preferences. A key axiom is the *stationarity axiom*, along with other requirements such as consistency of preferences. The stationarity axiom requires that preferences between pairs of outcome-time pairs stay unchanged as the outcomes in both pairs are moved forward or backward in time by an identical number of time periods. For instance, the following statement satisfies the stationarity axiom: "At some initial time, say, $t = 1$, I prefer one apple today to two apples tomorrow; and, also at time $t = 1$, I prefer one apple in 50 days' time to two apples in 51 days' time" We then show that the preferences of decision-makers who satisfy the axioms of rationality in time discounting can be represented by a special utility function known as *exponential discounted utility* (EDU) function. Essentially, EDU discounts the sum of utilities from all outcomes today and in the future, but the discounting is done in an exponential manner (just as we would do discounting in the case of compound interest rates). Testing the axioms of rationality in time discounting can be undertaken either by empirically testing the individual axioms or by testing to see if decision-makers follow the EDU model. It is the former method that has been largely used, and it is the stationarity axiom that has been mainly tested. Any violation of the stationarity axiom is known as the *common difference effect*.

Section 2.7 considers the meaning of rationality when we have strategic interaction. Unlike the other cases considered above, there is no such thing as axioms of rationality under strategic interaction but rather a set of requirements that underpin the equilibrium concepts used in classical game theory (note that *classical game theory* is our term for the current practice of game theory within the BRA). For a start, all the features of the BRA are required. In other words, the rationality requirements in sections 2.4–2.6 are also essential requirements in classical game theory.

However, newer rationality restrictions are added. Of these, the main ones are *common priors* and *common knowledge*, although the common priors assumption is sometimes relaxed. Common priors requires that in thinking about the realization of some random variable (or any set of random variables), all players in a game have identical beliefs about the underlying distribution functions of the random variables. It is also typically assumed that players have common knowledge of these common priors. Common knowledge of an event, say, event A (e.g., that a player is never altruistic), requires that players know A; know that all other players know A; know that all other players know that all other players know A; and so on, ad infinitum. This *infinite regress problem* is quite difficult to write down beyond a few finite steps, but classical game theory requires that all humans can effortlessly engage in infinite regress. It is not clear what extraordinary magic, almost Harry Potteresque in nature, would lead to the satisfaction of these conditions. One could imagine the satisfaction of such conditions in a world governed by social norms (see section 3.4), but that would require a different sort of machinery based on empirical expectations, normative expectations, and sanctions. By contrast, classical game theory is not built on such foundations.

Section 2.8 considers auxiliary assumptions that are sometimes considered a part of the definition of rationality in economics. The main misconception is that *self-regarding preferences* (i.e., individuals care only about their own consumption bundles but not those of others) are an essential requirement. It is not. The BRA is amenable to an inclusion of other-regarding preferences, but it rarely, if ever, does so. Hence, for all practical purposes, the BRA only studies models in which individuals have self-regarding preferences. The same comment also applies to a consideration of emotions. In principle, we can incorporate emotional states in the BRA, but it is almost never done. It is not unusual for academic economists to express the opinion (although this trend has decreased over the last decade) that relaxing the assumption of self-regarding preferences will be disastrous for economics because it will compromise on a hard-won discipline in the field. This would be amusing if it were not so tragic for progress in economics. We have now unassailable evidence for other-regarding preferences, although it is the case that many people do act as if they had self-regarding preferences (Fehr and Schmidt, 2006; Dhami, 2019b). Good science is based on respect for the evidence, not on a hard-won discipline arising out of empirically rejected assumptions.

Our view of rationality is broadly based on the internal consistency of choices in various economic situations. This is the dominant view in economics. A critique and an alternative view, defended in Sen (2002), argues that internal consistency cannot be considered in isolation from external consistency of choices—that is, without considering an agent's values and the larger domain, external to the individual, within which choices are made. Suppose, for example, that an agent chooses A over B but also B over A, depending on the context. That would seem to be a violation of internal consistency. But perhaps the agent chooses B over A when there is an unchosen alternative C, on the theory that (say) one should always choose the second-largest piece of cake. Sen urges that to know whether a violation of internal consistency is irrational, we need to know what agents care about, and we need to know something about the domain in which choices are made.

As he puts it (Sen, 2002, p. 4), "Rationality is interpreted here, broadly, as the discipline of subjecting one's choices—of actions as well as objectives, values and priorities—to reasoned scrutiny.... Rationality is seen here ... as the need to subject one's choices to the demands of reason." The two key terms here are "reasoned scrutiny" and "demands of reason." Sen's interpretation certainly fits with conventional understandings of rationality. Still, it is more useful for normative purposes than for purposes of prediction. The criterion of internal consistency has the advantage of being eminently testable, and empirical evidence is the main, if not the only, yardstick on which we propose to evaluate alternative theories in this book. Furthermore, it would appear to us, in principle, that the binary preference relation we use in sections 2.4–2.6 can be indexed with the appropriate frame, context, and emotion. Such context-dependent preferences are commonplace in behavioral economics.

Importantly, objectives, values, and priorities, as described in Sen, have been incorporated in various forms within behavioral economics, including through precommitment strategies (often emphasized by Sen), planner/doer models, reference points, incorporation of human values and virtues in social preferences, explorations of altruism, and various formulations of the theory of goals. There is also work within behavioral economics, some of which we review in this book, on how preferences themselves may be influenced by external factors (including compromise effects, which occur when the introduction of some third option, C, switches people's preferences between A and B). Sen also argues against equating rationality with self-regarding preferences and with optimizing behavior. We agree, and we too make these arguments in this chapter.

In sections 2.9–2.15, we consider the empirical evidence for the rationality assumptions in the BRA. Section 2.9 considers the evidence on consistent preferences. In particular, we focus on the evidence from *preference reversals*. Section 2.10 considers a range of evidence on *limited attention* from the effectiveness of messages and reminders; tax salience; and left-digit bias in the odometer readings of used cars. Section 2.11 complements our discussion of the evidence in section 3.2.4 on *overconfidence*. We distinguish between the various senses in which we may classify an individual as overconfident (*overestimation, overplacement,* and *overprecision*) and cite evidence for individual overconfidence as well as overconfidence in the decision-making of firms and organizations. Section 2.12 considers the evidence on the axioms of rationality under risk and the expected utility representation of preferences given in section 2.5. We focus mainly on the *Allais paradox* to illustrate nonlinear probability weighting and some examples to demonstrate the importance of reference points.

Section 2.13 considers the evidence on the axioms of rationality under time discounting and the utility representation of these preferences, given by the exponential discounted utility (EDU) model. We outline three main refutations (sometimes called anomalies) of the EDU: *magnitude effect*; *gain-loss asymmetry*; and the *common difference effect*, which is a violation of the stationarity axiom in the axioms of rationality under time discounting. Of these three refutations, we focus mainly on the common difference effect and its resolution through *hyperbolic discounting*. Section 2.14 considers the evidence on strategic interaction that directly contradicts classical game theory. Our introduction to strategic interaction in section 3.3 is too brief to explain all the necessary aspects of classical game theory to an interdisciplinary audience. A fuller discussion would require greater familiarity with the tool kit of classical game theory. Hence, our discussion of the evidence is brief. Fortunately, there are comprehensive book-length treatments available for the interested reader to pursue this topic further (Camerer, 2003; Dhami, 2019d).

In section 2.15, we evaluate whether people do indeed follow the rules of mathematical statistics. We show evidence that people fail to produce statistically accurate probability distributions, and their elicited distributions have fat tails that neglect information on sample size; the majority of people fail to follow Bayes' law and, in particular, neglect base rates; sometimes people exhibit conservative behavior in estimating the likelihood of a sample (the opposite of overconfidence). We also consider simple modifications of Bayes' law and empirical estimates of the misperception parameters based on actual human choices.

Finally, in section 2.16, we give a primer on behavioral decision theory. The simplest economic (or noneconomic) problem arises when a decision-maker plays a game against nature and takes actions that probabilistically determine outcomes. We provide the reader with a working knowledge, using a minimum of the technical machinery and the jargon, of *expected utility theory*, *rank dependent utility*, and *prospect theory*. The reader will do well to get acquainted with the basics of these models, as they help to make sense of many different phenomena under bounded rationality.

2.2 A Simple Taxonomy of Situations

This section introduces a basic taxonomy of situations or environments that are important to understanding not just alternative concepts of rationality in the BRA but also the elements of bounded rationality. In particular, we define situations of *risk, uncertainty, ambiguity*, and *true uncertainty*. The main purpose is to ensure a common understanding and establish a common vocabulary because different social and behavioral scientists often speak at cross-purposes while discussing these situations.

Let $X = \{x_1, x_2, \ldots, x_n\}$ be a fixed, finite, set of real numbers such that $x_1 < x_2 < \ldots < x_n$. The outcomes can be positive, zero, or negative, but we find it convenient to order them such that their numerical value is increasing from left to right. The reader may think of these as possible outcomes, or wealth levels, or the level of returns arising from some choices exercised by a decision-maker. We can allow the outcomes to be nonmonetary, so long as you can put some monetary value on them, even if it is your subjective monetary value.

A *lottery*, or a *gamble*, is a technical term in economics (not to be confused with lotteries or gambles in common usage) that provides a simple way of listing all possible outcomes and their probabilities faced by a decision-maker. It is written as

$$L = (x_1, p_1; x_2, p_2; \ldots; x_n, p_n), \tag{2.1}$$

where $p_1, \ldots, p_n$, are the respective probabilities corresponding to the respective outcomes $x_1, \ldots, x_n$, such that probabilities are nonnegative and sum up to 1: $p_i \in [0, 1]$ and $\sum_{i=1}^{n} p_i = 1$. In words: In the lottery L, the decision-maker receives an outcome x_1 with probability p_1; x_2 with probability p_2; $\ldots$; x_n with probability p_n. It is also possible that we have a single outcome lottery, $n = 1$, which takes the form $(x, 1)$, where an outcome x is received with certainty. Since many decisions lead to uncertain outcomes, recourse has to be made to considering situations where different outcomes arise in a probabilistic manner. The purpose of behavioral decision theory is to study how people make choices among objects of the form given in (2.1).

For instance, you could invest in a stock or an equity that has a purchase price of \$40, and it gives you a 50-50 chance of winning \$30 and losing \$20. Thus, in effect, net of the purchase price, you face the two-outcome lottery $L_1 = (20, 0.5; 70, 0.5)$; this corresponds to the case $n = 2$ in (2.1). If you did not invest, then you get to keep the \$40 in your pocket, so, in effect, you face the lottery $L_0 = (40, 1)$, which gives \$40 with certainty. Will you make the investment? The answer depends on how you compare the two lotteries L_0 and L_1.

More generally, a decision-maker could typically take m different actions, say, $a_1, a_2, \ldots, a_m$, (e.g., invest in m different stocks). Each of the m actions results in a different lottery, say, $L_1, L_2, \ldots, L_m$. The decision-maker's choice between different actions can now be framed simply as a choice between different lotteries. The central question in behavioral decision theory is this: What is the most preferred action of the decision-maker, or equivalently the most preferred lottery? It is convenient to drop altogether the set of actions and simply focus on the most preferred lottery of the decision-maker. It is as if the decision-maker is playing a *game against nature*, in which an action leads to a set of probabilistic outcomes.

Behavioral decision theory is typically interested in the following four kinds of situations: certainty, risk, subjective uncertainty, ambiguity. There is a fifth type of situation, true uncertainty or Knightian uncertainty, that is typically not on the agenda, but arguably it is not less important than the other types of situations. These terms have a precise meaning in behavioral decision theory and in the judgment and decision theory literature; a lack of understanding of these terms may lead to much confusion. The key to understanding them lies in the nature of the outcomes and the probabilities and how much information one has about them.

1. *Certainty*: These are choices among outcomes received with certainty. Such lotteries are single-outcome lotteries ($n=1$) in which an outcome is received with certainty—for example, $L_1 = (x_1, 1)$, where outcome x_1 is received with certainty. A second lottery under certainty can be written as $L_2 = (x_2, 1)$ where the decision-maker receives x_2 with certainty. Thus, the choice between two different certain situations is simply a choice between two lotteries of the form $L_1 = (x_1, 1)$ and $L_2 = (x_2, 1)$. For instance, you could be choosing between two different kinds of sandwiches at a McDonald's restaurant that you frequent and have full information on the quality of the items ordered. In the remaining situations that we consider below, we are interested in the case $n > 1$.

2. *Risk*: These are choices among lotteries of the form given in (2.1) when the outcomes and probabilities are *objectively known*. We use the term *objectively known* in the sense that it is used in standard microeconomics books such as Mas-Colell et al. (1995, p. 168). This implies that there is common agreement among different people on the magnitude of these probabilities—for instance, a probability of 0.5 that heads will come up in an unbiased coin toss or a probability of 1/6 that the number five comes up in a single throw of a fair, six-sided die. If you invest in the stock market and you have a choice between two assets whose returns are probabilistic and the associated probabilities are objectively known, then in choosing one over the other, you face a situation of risk.

Consider another example of a risky situation. Suppose that you are in an economics experiment and the experimenter offers you the following choice. Would you rather have a fixed sum of money $10, as captured by the lottery $L_1 = (10, 1)$, or be willing to play the lottery $L_2 = (4, 0.4; 16, 0.6)$? The lottery L_2 gives a 40 percent chance of receiving 4 and a 60 percent chance of receiving 16. An experimenter may implement the lottery L_2 as follows. He puts four green balls and six red balls, that are otherwise identical in all respects, in an opaque urn and shakes the urn to thoroughly mix the balls. A ball is then randomly drawn. If a green ball comes up, you get $4, and if a red ball comes up, you get $16. You objectively know all the relevant probabilities and the outcomes, and so does the experimenter; hence, this is a situation of risk.

3. *Subjective uncertainty*: These are choices among lotteries of the form given in (2.1) when the outcomes are either *objectively* or *subjectively* known. However, the probabilities in (2.1) are *subjective probabilities* that are nonnegative and add up to one; indeed, no objective probabilities might be available. In this case, we have a situation of *subjective uncertainty*, sometimes just referred to as *uncertainty*.[1] For instance, in

November 2020, you might have assigned subjective odds that the Moderna vaccine for Covid-19 is the most likely to succeed and decided to invest in the shares of the company. However, no objective probabilities of the relative success of the different vaccines that are being simultaneously developed might be available. As a second example, let us alter the economics experiment under risk, discussed above, as follows. The lottery L_2 takes the form of a *Savage act*, $f = (4, \text{green ball}; 6, \text{red ball})$. To understand this, suppose that an opaque urn has six red and four green balls. A single ball is drawn randomly from the urn. You receive $4 if a red ball comes up and $6 if a green ball comes up. However, the catch is that the green balls used by the experimenter are larger than the red balls, and you know this. You also know the number of red and green balls. In this case, you are unaware of the objective probabilities of the events, green ball and red ball, when a single ball is randomly drawn from the urn. However, suppose that when you ponder over the probabilities, you are (subjectively) confident that, given their different sizes and numbers, a green ball and a red ball are equiprobable. So, you believe that you are actually facing a lottery of the form $L_2 = (4, 0.5; 6, 0.5)$. This is a situation of subjective uncertainty because no objective probabilities are known by the decision-maker. Other individuals, if they were asked to make choices in an identical situation, might assign very different subjective probabilities. This difference in subjective probabilities is often the reason that so much trade takes place in stock markets. Some traders might be subjectively bearish and others might be subjectively bullish. In contrast to risk, which applies to mechanistic stochastic processes such as the throw of a die, the toss of a coin or the outcome of playing a casino machine, in most situations of interest we are subjectively uncertain about the probability of future outcomes. For instance, even if you could somehow uncover all possible outcomes that could occur in the future if you married your current partner, you are unlikely to uncover objective probabilities of those outcomes.

4. *Ambiguity*: These are choices among lotteries when neither objective nor subjective probabilities exist that can explain choices. The leading example is the *Ellsberg paradox*, which can be set up in many ways (Dhami, 2019a, chapter 4), but here we choose the simplest setup, the so called *two-colors example*. Suppose you have two urns, an unknown urn U and a known urn K. In urn K are 50 red and 50 green balls. In urn U are 100 balls that are either red or green but the proportions are unknown. You are promised a prize of $10 if a red ball comes up. You assign an objective probability of 0.5 of a red ball being drawn from urn K. Also,

using the *principle of insufficient reason*, you may assign a probability 0.5 of a red ball being drawn from urn U; you have no reason to believe that a red ball is more likely to come up as compared to a green ball from urn U. Yet, when you are asked which urn you would prefer to bet on, U or K, you immediately prefer to bet on urn K rather than on urn U. However, you have assigned equal probabilities of drawing a red ball from each urn, so what explains your preference for urn K? This is the Ellsberg paradox.[2] In this case, individuals may assign *source-dependent probabilities* that depend on the underlying source of uncertainty. The basic idea is that the decision-maker views the uncertainty emanating from the two urns to be different. Source-dependent probability is an idea that goes back to Amos Tversky, and recent empirical research suggests that this may explain the Ellsberg paradox. A discussion of source-dependent probabilities will take as afield, so the interested reader can consult Dhami (2019a, chapter 4). The essential idea, in the context of the Ellsberg paradox, is that decision-makers distort objective probabilities in different ways depending on whether the urn is a known urn or an unknown urn. Hence, perceived probabilities are source dependent. However, surprisingly, ambiguity has not played a direct role in the literature on heuristics. In principle, individuals do make choices under ambiguity, and it might well be the case that they employ heuristics to do so. If you get an economist talking to a non-economist on issues of ambiguity, there is likely to be much talk at cross-purposes unless both understand the precise sense in which this term is used in decision theory. The emerging literature in economics offers several predictions in the presence of ambiguity. These predictions are based on correlating measures of ambiguity aversion arising from Ellsberg sorts of experiments with a range of human choices that include the following: stock market participation; the fraction of financial assets held in stocks; foreign stock ownership; ownership of stocks in one's own company; selling of stocks in the financial crises. See, for instance, Dimmock, Kouwenberg, et al. (2016) for a study on US households; Dimmock, Kouwenberg, & Wakker (2016) for a study on Dutch households.

There is fifth class of extremely important situations, arguably the most important, on which economic theory, and much of the social and behavioral sciences, have very little guidance to offer. Yet, in debates on risk and uncertainty, this situation is often mixed up with the other situations and is the source of much confusion.

5. *True uncertainty*: A situation of true uncertainty, or Knightian uncertainty (named after the Chicago economist Frank Knight), arises when

the outcomes and probabilities are unimaginable, as are their objective or subjective probabilities. The Ellsberg paradox, explained above, can be extended to balls of any number of colors and balls. Suppose that we carried out this extension. True uncertainty would arise if you could not imagine how many balls or what color balls are in urn U. The human eye can distinguish between 10 million colors, which are likely to be unimaginable to most people, and the number of balls could be very large. So, if you believe that this situation can be accommodated within classical subjective uncertainty (as in 3 above), then try to imagine the possible colors and the Cartesian product of colors and the number of balls over which you must form a subjective distribution. It is far-fetched to imagine that humans could do this sort of thing, even if in principle we could allow for this possibility and the use of subjective uncertainty. As a practical matter, it is better to classify such a situation as one of *true uncertainty*. Economists were aware of true uncertainty and debated its importance 100 years ago (Knight, 1921; Keynes, 1921). However, the main focus in economics has been on subjective uncertainty (what we refer to as *uncertainty* and *ambiguity* above). While this has allowed for rapid developments in formal decision theory, it has also compromised the ability of economics to make predictions in some of the most interesting and relevant situations. True uncertainty is different from ambiguity in that the main issue is not of source-dependent probability but the inability to imagine all possible outcomes and their probabilities. A common confusion is that true uncertainty can be subsumed within ambiguity, and many recent papers on ambiguity give such an impression. It is simply incorrect.

In example 2.1 below, we present a series of examples that are potentially consistent with the presence of true uncertainty. These examples may also be formally consistent with subjective uncertainty if people can foresee the entire time path of all possible events in the future and can assign subjective probabilities to them—which is unlikely. For a book-length treatment that offers many fascinating examples of true uncertainty, see Kay & King (2020).

Example 2.1. *True uncertainty seems to be reflected in the judgments of even experienced market participants. Thomas Watson, president of IBM, is said to have made the following statement in 1943, "I think there is a world market for maybe five computers." Indeed it would have been impossible to predict all possible eventualities (outcomes, technological* breakthroughs, tastes) relevant to this question in 1943. Consider some other examples that can plausibly be seen to reflect true uncertainty.[3]

> "Fooling around with alternating current (AC) is just a waste of time. Nobody will use it, ever." (Thomas Edison, 1889)

> "Television won't be able to hold on to any market it captures after the first six months. People will soon get tired of staring at a plywood box every night." (Darryl Zanuck, 1946, 20th Century Fox)

> "Nuclear powered vacuum cleaners will probably be a reality within 10 years." (Alex Lewyt, 1955, president of the Lewyt Vacuum Cleaner Company)

> "There is practically no chance communications space satellites will be used to provide better telephone, telegraph, television or radio service inside the United States." (T.A.M. Craven, 1961, Federal Communications Commission [FCC] commissioner)

> "Remote shopping, while entirely feasible, will flop." (Time Magazine, 1966)

> "There's just not that many videos I want to watch." (Steve Chen, 2005 CTO and cofounder of YouTube, expressing concerns about his company's long-term viability)

In example 2.1, Thomas Watson might have, in 1943, foreseen every possible event related to the computer industry (e.g., all possible innovations, supplies, demands, tastes, and prices) for all future time periods and assigned subjective probabilities to all these events. He might have then used expected utility (see the appendix to this chapter) to make a considered prediction. This would be consistent with the BRA and the standard way in which many economists would tackle this problem, but we are very doubtful of this possibility. It is more likely that Watson faced true uncertainty and employed suitable judgment heuristics or gut feelings to state his best guess.

Arguably, some of the most important problems that decision-makers face belong to the domain of true uncertainty. Even investing in the stock market for most investors, except perhaps the most professional, is arguably a problem in true uncertainty. Investment firms use complicated algorithms to make financial decisions, but the assumptions behind these algorithms often take the form of heuristics, educated guesses, homegrown thresholds, and margins of error that are chosen using rules of thumb. These appear to be sensible responses to true uncertainty.

Consider some other examples from individual decision-making: choosing a partner to marry; choosing a university course at age 19; investing in a pension fund at age 25 that matures when one is 60; and deciding on the number of children to have. It would be far-fetched to argue that in each of these cases, individuals could imagine all possible outcomes from their decisions, associate subjective probabilities to these outcomes, and then use expected utility to make decisions. If it is accepted that this is unlikely, as we believe, then economics does not have clear predictions to offer in these cases. Yet, these are often some of the most fundamental decisions that are made by humans. Equally important is the fact that people often do make decisions in such cases. People do invest in the stock market; people do choose marriage partners and divorce; students do choose universities to study; and young people do invest in pension funds (albeit sometimes with the aid of appropriate nudges) and decide on the number of children to have.

How do people make these decisions? It is surprising that this limitation of the scope of economic theory, and of much of social and behavioral theory, is inadequately recognized and almost never mentioned in economics courses. One of the authors did his bachelor's, master's, MPhil, and PhD degrees in economics and cannot recall a single instance when this problem was mentioned. Yet, given how basic and important problems in true uncertainty are, the relevant analogies with the natural sciences would be if physics was unable to explain why apples fell from trees; if chemistry was unable to explain why water turns into ice at zero degrees Celsius; and if biology was unable to explain how cells get their energy.

So how do individuals decide which lottery to choose under risk, uncertainty, and ambiguity? The appendix to this chapter offers a brief primer on the main decision theories. These are expected utility theory, rank dependent utility, and prospect theory. Of these, expected utility and rank dependent utility apply to risk and uncertainty, while prospect theory applies to the case of ambiguity. None of these theories applies to true uncertainty. These are, of course, not the only accounts of how people choose among lotteries. They might, for instance, make choices based on emotions; we consider Loewenstein's "risk as feelings" account of decision-making in chapter 4. Or individuals might use attribute-based models to make such choices, which we also consider in chapter 4. But this does not exhaust the scope of decision theories. For an account of other theories, such as those based on regret aversion; disappointment aversion; the query theory of value in explaining the endowment effect; case-based decision theory; or salience, see Dhami (2019a).

2.3 The Bayesian Rationality Approach

When economists deal with risk, uncertainty, and ambiguity, the dominant paradigm in economics, neoclassical economics in its actual practice, employs the *Bayesian rationality approach* (BRA). It typically delivers sharp, testable predictions, often in conjunction with other auxiliary assumptions. Understanding the elements of the BRA is the key to understanding modern economics, to understanding the rationale and the importance of bounded rationality, and to being able to judge economics theories. We shall consider some of the central features of the BRA later in the chapter where we specifically address the question of what economists mean by rationality.

In the BRA, the basic unit of analysis is *decision-makers*, or *economic actors*, or *agents*, or *players* (these terms are interchangeable in economics, and we use them as such), which could be either individuals, firms, or governments. The focus on individuals, and on individual firms, comes about due to the assumption of *methodological individualism* that has a long tradition in economics. Under the BRA, economic actors have complete, transitive, and continuous preferences (see section 2.4); possess unlimited attention, computation power, and memory; are not influenced by frame-dependence of problems if the frames are informationally equivalent; make cold, calculated decisions in which emotions play no role; effortlessly follow all the laws of statistics and mathematics including awareness of all the latest research; engage in instantaneous mathematical optimization in static and dynamic problems; and update their prior beliefs using Bayes' law.

Furthermore, and as we explain below, under the BRA, decision-makers conform to the axioms of expected utility theory under risk; subjective expected utility under uncertainty; exponential discounting when making decisions over time; and play a Nash equilibrium in static games and use appropriate modifications of this equilibrium concept in more complex games. In economics, it is assumed that economic actors either literally/axiomatically take these actions or act as if they do. This approach has gradually filtered into political science, under the rubric of the rational actor model, management, finance, law, and neuroscience.

The BRA is simply a set of conjectures and hypotheses about human behavior. Like all conjectures, these must be subject to stringent empirical tests, and they have been. Below we show that many of the assumptions and the theories in the BRA are violated by the empirical evidence. This will, we suspect, not surprise noneconomists. However, consistency of human behavior with the BRA is taught and accepted as an article of faith in most economics programs around the world. The most reasonable among the current practitioners of neoclassical economics will concede that humans do not literally follow the BRA. Yet, they will insist, often without any evidence, that humans act as if their behavior is consistent with the BRA. The as-if position is motivated by Milton Friedman's suggestion to evaluate economic theories by the accuracy of their predictions rather than by the realism of their assumptions. We shall consider issues of methodology in section 3.5.

Tversky and Kahneman (1971, 1974) prominently tested several of the assumptions that underlie BRA, although they were not the first to do so (see, e.g., the work of Maurice Allais in section 2.12 and Herbert Simon in chapter 4). Their program, the *heuristics and biases* research program (or HBP), which we consider in chapter 5, is one of the most significant achievements in all of social science. A most important finding from their research is that humans do not act as if they followed the BRA. This should, in principle, have been a massive setback for the existing theory and an exciting opportunity to move the subject forward by taking account of the newly discovered evidence. Of course, none of that ever happened. The work of Daniel Kahneman, Amos Tversky, and Herbert Simon is rarely mentioned in economics courses, and the experiments of Maurice Allais are often presented, at best, as a curious anomaly of the BRA.

2.4 Rationality under Certainty

In this section, we define rationality under situations of complete certainty. We proceed at a gentle pace in this section so that the reader becomes comfortable with the notation and the method. Recall from section 2.2 that under certainty, the individual takes an action that results in a guaranteed and perfectly foreseen outcome; nature is fully predictable in this case. In particular, there is no risk/uncertainty or temporal or strategic dimension to the problem.

For instance, one may choose between two brands of bread in a supermarket. More generally, one may choose bundles of goods (as in a grocery list). Suppose that one chooses different quantities of n such items. Then one's choices belong to the set of n positive real numbers (e.g., quantities of the n different grocery items). We denote by $\mathbb{R}^n$ the set of all such possible real valued choices. Within this very big set, the individual might be interested in a smaller subset X (we write this as $X \subset \mathbb{R}^n$, where the notation $\subset$ means *a subset of*). For instance, items in X may never be negative or are bounded above by some positive number (as in a grocery list).

Suppose that an individual has a set, $X \subset \mathbb{R}^n$, of choices, where $\mathbf{x} \in X$ may be interpreted as any bundle of n goods or services, and n is a finite positive integer number. The set X can be very large dimensional, so n is as large as we wish it to be. Let $\succeq$ be a *binary preference relation* defined over the set X. By this is meant that if we pick any two objects from the set X (say, apples and oranges), then the binary preference relation tells us which of the two objects the individual prefers. The individual's pairwise preferences over objects in the set X are given, and they do not change; this is the sense in which preferences are the *primitives* in economic models. For any two objects $\mathbf{x}, \mathbf{y} \in X$, $\mathbf{x} \succeq \mathbf{y}$ means that $\mathbf{x}$ is considered *at least as good as* $\mathbf{y}$ (in our groceries analogy, $\mathbf{x}$ and $\mathbf{y}$ are two different bundles of n grocery items).

The items in the bundles can be anything that you can imagine, so long as you can measure them in some way and impute a number to them.

Note: When we say that $\mathbf{x}$ is considered at least as good as $\mathbf{y}$, we follow the convention of writing it in two equivalent forms, either $\mathbf{x} \succeq \mathbf{y}$ or $\mathbf{y} \preceq \mathbf{x}$.

Example 2.2. *Let $n = 2$ so that the set X contains tuples or pairs of items; let these items be pairs of apples and oranges. Then, two possible elements of X are $\mathbf{x}_1 = (3, 7)$ (there are 3 apples and 7 oranges in $\mathbf{x}_1$) and $\mathbf{x}_2 = (4, 5)$ (there are 4 apples and 5 oranges in $\mathbf{x}_2$). Then, for a decision-maker, who has the binary preference relation $\succeq$, several of the following possibilities arise:*

1. *Either $\mathbf{x}_1 \succeq \mathbf{x}_2$ (i.e., $\mathbf{x}_1$ is at least as good as $\mathbf{x}_2$) or $\mathbf{x}_2 \succeq \mathbf{x}_1$ (i.e., $\mathbf{x}_2$ is at least as good as $\mathbf{x}_1$), or both $\mathbf{x}_1 \succeq \mathbf{x}_2$ and $\mathbf{x}_2 \succeq \mathbf{x}_2$ are true.*
2. *The decision-maker might say, "I don't have a clue how to compare $\mathbf{x}_1$ and $\mathbf{x}_2$."*
3. *The decision-maker might be able to make binary comparisons between objects when n is relatively low but not when n is relatively high (i.e., when there are lots more objects in the bundles). Indeed, in the latter case, say, for $n = 50$, the decision-maker might be completely overwhelmed by the pairwise comparisons needed to be made (1,225 such comparisons in this case) and find that they are unable to make the necessary calculations. Even if such calculations can be made, the decision-maker may feel that it is difficult to meaningfully process this amount of information.*

4. *The decision-maker sometimes expresses the preference $x_1 \succeq x_2$ but at other times expresses the preference $x_2 \succeq x_1$ in a manner that is difficult for the individual or an outside observer to understand or predict. Say, sometimes when choosing between the two options, the decision-maker simply tosses a coin to make the decision $x_2 \succeq x_1$.*

In the different social and behavioral sciences, even if (1)–(4) are true, the individual might not be termed as irrational. However, if any of (2)–(4) occur, then it falls outside the ambit of the economist's definition of rationality, as we show below. These sorts of situations are simply ruled out by the BRA.

Definition 2.1. *If $x \succeq y$, then we say that x is at least as good as y. If $x \succeq y$ and $y \succeq x$, then we say that x is indifferent to y, and we write this as $x \sim y$. On the other hand, if $x \succeq y$ but it is not the case that $y \succeq x$, then we say that x is strictly preferred to y, and we write $x \succ y$.*

We now formally define what rationality under certainty means for economists.

Definition 2.2. *The individual is rational; or equivalently, the preference relation $\succeq$ is rational; or equivalently, the individual has consistent preferences if the following conditions hold:*

1. *Completeness: For all $x, y \in X$, we have either $x \succeq y$ or $y \succeq x$.*
2. *Transitivity: Let $x, y, z \in X$, $x \succeq y$, and $y \succeq z$. Then $x \succeq z$.*

Thus, an individual satisfies the *assumption of rationality under certainty* if the individual has a preference relation, $\succeq$, on the set of choices, X, such that pairwise comparisons between any two alternatives can be made (completeness) and preferences are transitive. Such an individual is said to have *consistent preferences*.

What would violate rationality? Essentially, all of the cases in (2)–(4) in example 2.2 violate consistency of preferences. This is all that economists mean by rationality under certainty, although we require successively stronger assumptions as we expand the domain of choices to risky and temporal choices, which we do in the subsequent sections. A proper understanding of what is required in definition 2.2 should prevent endless confusion in debates on rationality between noneconomists and economists.

Definition 2.2, in itself, does not entail a violation of any laws of logic. There is a widespread consensus among economists that the assumption of rationality is plausible, and this lies at the heart of the BRA. Most academic economists would probably struggle to recall a single instance in their careers when they were challenged by a student in a lecture on the plausibility of definition 2.2, or indeed when they might have alerted students to potential problems with it or perhaps even questioned it themselves. Rationality, in this sense, is one of the most basic articles of faith within the economics profession.

Yet, an individual who violates definition 2.2 is not irrational in the literal sense of the word, nor is such an individual mad. Definition 2.2 is a hypothesis about human behavior, and like any hypothesis it ought to be stringently tested. Therefore, the crucial question is whether it is consistent with human behavior. We examine the evidence later in this chapter.

Gintis (2009) argues that the minimum requirements for rationality in definition 2.2 are always met if we take account of the context and frame dependence of preferences and that giving up on definition 2.2 would be disastrous for economics. The contrast between economics and the social sciences in terms of having a formal theory that makes very precise the relevant causal effects and makes very precise, concrete, and falsifiable predictions is quite noticeable. The worry is that giving up the minimum requirements for rationality, in the sense of definition 2.2, will compromise the ability of economic theory to make formal and precise predictions, which is one of its greatest strengths.

Being rational in the sense of economic theory is sometimes associated in the social and behavioral sciences with carrying a utility function around in one's head at all times. This is then criticized as being unrealistic. Only a little more work is required to debunk this erroneous claim. A utility function simply requires assigning each choice in the set of choices, X, a real number, such that more preferred choices are given higher numbers—nothing more, nothing less. Formally, this can be written as follows.

Definition 2.3. *(Utility function) A utility function* $u : X \to \mathbb{R}$ *represents the preference relation* $\succeq$, *if for* $\mathbf{x}, \mathbf{y} \in X$, $\mathbf{x} \succeq \mathbf{y}$ *if, and only if,* $u(\mathbf{x}) \geq u(\mathbf{y})$.

Thus, a utility function represents the preference relation $\succeq$ if it assigns a higher real number to the more preferred bundle. Under what conditions might a utility function exist? The next proposition answers this question.

Proposition 2.1. *Suppose that an individual has consistent preferences (or is rational) in the sense of definition 2.2. Then, there exists a utility function u that represents $\succeq$.*

Essentially, if individuals have consistent preferences, then they act *as if* they possess a utility function that represents their underlying preferences. The converse of proposition 2.1 also exists—that is, the existence of a utility function implies that individuals have consistent preferences; we state this in proposition 2.2.

Proposition 2.2. *If a utility function u represents the preference relation $\succeq$ on X, then $\succeq$ must be complete and transitive—that is, the individual must have consistent preferences.*

The proofs of propositions 2.1 and 2.2 are standard in economics and can be found in any microeconomics book, so we omit them. Together, the importance of propositions 2.1 and 2.2 is that we can treat preferences and utility functions interchangeably, depending on which is more convenient to use for any particular problem. The individual only needs to have preferences over objects, not utility functions. But these results allow us to use utility functions and completely omit any reference to preferences *as if* individuals do possesses utility functions in their heads, even if they do not. The utility function is one of the most basic constructs in the BRA.

The remaining material in this section might not interest all our readers, but it is necessary to include because our discussion above may have raised some questions.

Nothing so far rules out that the utility function may have jumps or discontinuities. As a practical matter, economists like to draw the utility function as a smooth continuous curve without lifting pen from paper; see, for instance, the utility function in figure 2.4. This requires imposing the assumption of *continuity* on the preference relation, $\succeq$.

To understand continuity, suppose that we have two different brands of soups—Chillidelight and Hotfresh. Suppose that within each brand, we have available a sequence of soup choices that differ only in having ever-decreasing salt content until the limiting member of the sequence has zero salt content. Suppose that this sequence of soups for Chillidelight is denoted by $\{x_n\}_{n=1}^{\infty}$ so that x_1 is the most salty version of Chillidelight, x_2 the next less salty, and so on, until the limiting member $x_\infty \equiv x$ is salt-free. The similar sequence for Hotfresh soups is given by

$\{y_n\}_{n=1}^{\infty}$, which has a limiting salt-free soup, $y_\infty \equiv y$. Suppose it is the case that $x_n \succeq y_n$ for all n (the individual finds Chillidelight at least as good as Hotfresh for all salt levels), then continuity requires that $x \succeq y$—that is, the individual also prefers the limiting version of salt-free Chillidelight to the limiting version of salt-free Hotfresh. We can now state this formally, and this definition can be extended to bundles of consumption goods.

Definition 2.4. *(Continuity) Suppose that we have a sequence of consumption bundles $\{\mathbf{x}_n\}_{n=1}^{\infty}$ and $\{\mathbf{y}_n\}_{n=1}^{\infty}$, $\mathbf{x}_n, \mathbf{y}_n \in X$, that converge to the respective bundles $\mathbf{x}$ and $\mathbf{y}$. If for all n, $\mathbf{x}_n \succeq \mathbf{y}_n$, then the preference relation $\succeq$ is continuous if $\mathbf{x} \succeq \mathbf{y}$.*

We can now state the analogues of proposition 2.1 and 2.2 by adding the continuity property. Essentially, if preferences are *consistent and continuous*, then a *continuous utility function* exists (the analogue of proposition 2.1). Conversely, if a continuous utility function exists, then the preferences that it represents must be consistent and continuous (the analogue of proposition 2.2).

The basic machinery in this section forms the basis for understanding utility functions in other situations also, such as when risk, or time, preferences are involved, as we shall see.

2.5 Rationality under Risk and Uncertainty

Having set the stage with the basics in section 2.4, we can now gather some speed and discuss the remaining forms of rationality. In this section, we outline the meaning of rationality under risk and uncertainty.

Let $X = \{x_1, x_2, \ldots, x_n\}$ be a fixed finite set of real-valued outcomes such that $x_1 < x_2 < \cdots < x_n$. Extensions to vector-valued outcomes are possible, as in section 2.4, where $X \subset \mathbb{R}^n$. A *simple lottery*, L, is written as

$$L = (x_1, p_1; x_2, p_2; \ldots; x_n, p_n), \tag{2.2}$$

where $p_1, \ldots, p_n$ are the respective probabilities corresponding to the outcomes $x_1, \ldots, x_n$ and $p_i \in [0, 1]$ and $\sum_{i=1}^{n} p_i = 1$. Suppose that the outcomes and the probabilities are objectively known, so that we have a situation of risk. The lottery $(x_i, 1)$ denotes an outcome x_i received with certainty; this was the situation considered in section 2.4. Thus, certainty is just a special case of risk when one of the outcomes is received with certainty, or with probability 1.

Let L be the set of all possible lotteries over the set of outcomes X. Which lottery will the decision-maker choose?

The most widely used theory under risk in economics is *expected utility theory* (EU) (see the appendix to this chapter). Its counterpart under uncertainty is known as *subjective expected utility* (SEU), but it requires a slightly different machinery in which individuals have preferences over Savage acts (defined in section 2.2). Yet, the utility representations under EU and SEU are remarkably similar with unique subjective probabilities under SEU replacing objective probabilities under EU. For the moment, we consider risk.

Under certainty, we required the individual to express preferences over a set, $X \subset \mathbb{R}^n$. Under risk, we require the decision-maker to express preferences over the set L of all possible lotteries over X. These preferences are the primitives under risk. Suppose that the decision-maker is endowed with a binary preference relation over L denoted by $\succeq$. To avoid introducing new notation, we use the same notation for a binary preference relation, $\succeq$, for different situations (e.g., under certainty, risk, and time preferences). So, for any two lotteries $L_1, L_2 \in L$, $L_2 \succeq L_1$ means that the lottery L_2 is *at least as good as* the lottery L_1.

Suppose that an individual faces a choice between two lotteries: $L_1 = (-75, 0.5; 100, 0.5)$, which is a 50-50 chance of gaining 100 and losing 75, and the lottery $L_2 = (-25, 0.5; 50, 0.5)$, which is a 50-50 chance of gaining 50 and losing 25. Thus, $(-75, 0.5; 100, 0.5) \succeq (-25, 0.5; 50, 0.5)$ means that the decision-maker finds the lottery L_1 at least as good as the lottery L_2, $L_1 \succeq L_2$. Of course, the decision-maker might also be indifferent to the two lotteries or might strictly prefer one to the other.

The EU functional (2.37) follows from certain axioms, the *axioms of rationality under risk*. We state these next, followed by an explanation and discussion.

Axiom 2.1. *(Order) Order requires the following two conditions.*

1. *Completeness: For all lotteries $L_1, L_2 \in L$, either $L_2 \succeq L_1$, or $L_1 \succeq L_2$, or both.*
2. *Transitivity: For all lotteries $L_1, L_2, L_3 \in L$: $L_1 \succeq L_2$ and $L_2 \succeq L_3$ $\Rightarrow L_1 \succeq L_3$.*

Two further binary relations between lotteries can be defined in terms of $\succeq$:

$$\begin{cases} \text{Indifference:} & L_1 \sim L_2 \Leftrightarrow L_2 \succeq L_1 \text{ and } L_1 \succeq L_2. \\ \text{Strict preference:} & L_2 \succ L_1 \Leftrightarrow \text{it is not the case that } L_1 \succeq L_2. \end{cases}$$

Axiom 2.2. *(Best and worst)* $x_n \succ x_1$ *(i.e., $(x_n, 1) \succ (x_1, 1)$).*

Axiom 2.3. *(Continuity) For each lottery, L, there is a probability $p \in [0, 1]$ such that $L \sim (x_1, 1 - p; x_n, p)$.*

Axiom 2.4. *(Independence) For all lotteries L_1, L_2, L, and all $p \in [0, 1]$, $L_2 \succeq L_1 \Leftrightarrow (L_2, p; L, 1 - p) \succeq (L_1, p; L, 1 - p)$.*

The axioms of completeness and transitivity together form the definition of consistent preferences under risk. These are analogous to the requirement for consistent preferences introduced in definition 2.2. The only difference is that these are introduced not on the set X but on the set of all possible lotteries over X given by L. Thus, consistent preferences here require that, for any two lotteries in the set L, we should be able to express them in order of preference and that these preferences should be transitive.

From axiom 2.2, under certainty a decision-maker strictly prefers receiving the highest outcome, $(x_n, 1)$, to receiving the lowest outcome, $(x_1, 1)$. The continuity property in axiom 2.3 asserts that every lottery, no matter how complex, is equivalent to a simple lottery obtained by probabilistically mixing the highest outcome, x_n, and the lowest outcome, x_1.

The independence axiom, axiom 2.4, is the main and the most critical axiom that gives rise to an expected utility representation of preferences. The requirement is that if a lottery L_2 is preferred to a lottery L_1, then mixing each of these lotteries with a third lottery, L (with the same mixing probability, p), does not alter the preference.

Example 2.3. *Suppose that you strictly prefer apples to oranges. Then, if you satisfy the independence axiom, axiom 2.4, you must also strictly prefer (1) an equal chance of receiving apples and bananas to (2) an equal chance of receiving oranges and bananas. Indeed, this preference stays the same for any probability in which you choose to mix the relevant choices.*

An implicit axiom that is often not directly stated but is required in the derivation of expected utility is the *reduction axiom*. In our notation, the lottery $((x, p), q)$, the simplest example of a *compound lottery* (i.e., a lottery of a lottery) means the following. A decision-maker gets to play the lottery (x, p) with probability $q \in [0, 1]$ and receives an outcome of 0 with the complementary probability $1 - q$. We now state the reduction axiom for the simplest compound lottery $((x, p), q)$, but it holds for any number of outcomes and probabilities; see Dhami (2019a) for the general case.

Axiom 2.5. *(Reduction axiom) For all $p, q \in [0, 1]$ and for all $x \in X$, the lottery $((x, p), q)$ is equivalent to the lottery (x, pq) in the sense that $((x, p), q) \sim (x, pq)$.*

The next definition gives *rationality* a precise meaning under risk.

Definition 2.5. *(Axioms of rationality under risk) The axioms order, best and worst, continuity, independence, and reduction, collectively, are termed the axioms of rationality under risk.*

Definition 2.5 specifies what economists mean by an individual being rational when facing situations of risk. In particular, this has nothing to do with the cleverness or the intelligence of the decision-maker, which is the sense in which the common discourse characterizes rationality. It simply requires that a decision-maker follow the given axioms that appear reasonable and persuasive.

It is important to stress that a violation of these axioms is not irrational in the sense in which the word is used in common discourse, nor does it imply a form of madness. The axioms themselves are hypotheses about human behavior and may or may not be confirmed when we examine human behavior, even if they might appear, ex ante, to be reasonable. Conformity with the evidence, and not perceived reasonableness of the theory by a researcher, is the appropriate scientific criterion in all the natural sciences.

Recall that when we defined the axioms of rationality under certainty in section 2.4, we asked next if the corresponding binary preference relation could be represented by a utility function (propositions 2.1 and 2.2), which often provides a more tractable way of solving many problems. We now ask an identical question: If a decision-maker satisfies the axioms of rationality under risk, then can one find a utility function that represents the corresponding risk preferences? In other words, suppose $L_2 \succeq L_1$. Can we find some utility function, denoted by EU, such that $EU(L_2) \geq EU(L_1)$? In their seminal work, Von Neumann and Morgenstern (1944) answered in the affirmative; we state their result next, followed by a discussion.

Proposition 2.3. *(Von Neumann-Morgenstern, 1944: Expected utility representation) Suppose that the binary relation, $\succeq$, on the set of lotteries L, satisfies the axioms of rationality under risk (definition 2.5). Then, there is an expected utility function, $EU : L \to \mathbb{R}$, that represents $\succeq$: $L_2 \succeq L_1$ if, and only if, $EU(L_2) \geq EU(L_1)$. For the lottery L in (2.2), this function takes the form*

$$EU(L) = \sum_{i=1}^{n} p_i u(x_i), \qquad (2.3)$$

where $u(x_i)$ is a real number assigned to the outcome x_i, also called the utility of x_i.

The converse of proposition 2.3 also holds. Namely, if a decision-maker makes choices between lotteries based on the expected utility function in (2.3), then the decision-maker must also satisfy the axioms of rationality under risk. The proofs can be found in Wakker (2010) or Mas-Colell et al. (1995).

Thus, the axioms of rationality are *equivalent* to an expected utility representation of preferences. If we wished to test this theory, we could either (1) test the axioms of rationality (a rejection of any one axiom is sufficient to reject the theory) or (2) test whether the decision-maker acts in conformity with the expected utility formula in (2.3). When constructing models, economists prefer to use, almost exclusively, the expected utility formula in (2.3). However, in testing the theory, it is much easier to test the individual axioms in definition 2.5. The main focus has been on testing the independence axiom. We report the results of some of these empirical tests later in this chapter.

This framework can be extended to uncertainty, where probabilities are subjective rather than objective (Savage, 1954; Dhami, 2019a, section 1.3). In this case, one gets a utility representation that is identical to (2.3), except that the probabilities $p_1, \ldots, p_n$ are now subjective probabilities, held inside the mind of the decision-maker, and may have no objective counterparts.

2.6 Rationality in Choices Made over Time

Many important decisions have a temporal dimension. For instance, consider saving money for retirement or saving money toward a college education fund for children. Many other important decisions such as marriage, having children, buying a house, buying consumer durables, and planning a vacation have a temporal dimension. What does it mean to say that someone is rational when they are making decisions over time? We address this question now.

In order to introduce a temporal dimension, we shall be interested in pairs of numbers of the form (z, t), where z is some monetary outcome that is to be received at a future time, t. If the outcomes are not monetary, but a monetary value can be assigned to them, that is fine too.

More formally, let $Z \subset \mathbb{R}$ be the set of possible outcomes that a decision-maker may receive now and in the future. Elements of the set Z are denoted by z_j, $j = 1, 2, \ldots$. Let $\Gamma \subset \mathbb{R}_+$ be the set of corresponding times at which these outcomes are realized and denote the elements of the set Γ by t_j, $j = 1, 2, \ldots$. Denote by (z_j, t_j) an *outcome-time pair*, which *guarantees* that the decision-maker will receive the outcome z_j at time t_j. For instance, if outcomes are dollar amounts and time is measured in months, then $(100, 8)$ means that the decision-maker will receive $100 in 8 months' time.

All possible outcome-time pairs are given by the Cartesian product of the two sets, $Y = Z \times \Gamma$. We now assume that the decision-maker has preferences that are defined on the set Y. Let $\succeq$ denote the binary preference relation *at least as good as* on the set Y (not to be confused with the binary preference relations in sections 2.4 and 2.5, which are defined on different sets). Also, let $\succ$, $\sim$ denote, respectively, the binary relations *strictly preferred to* and *indifferent to* on the set Y. These are the primitives of decision-making over time.

The following five axioms, B1–B5, in Fishburn and Rubinstein (1982) are typically called the *axioms of rationality for time discounting*. We state these first, followed by an explanation and a discussion.

Definition 2.6. *(Axioms of rationality for time discounting)* Let $z_m, z_n \in Z$, and $t_p, t_q \in \Gamma$.

B1. *Ordering*: $\succeq$ is complete and transitive.

B2. *Monotonicity*: If $z_m > z_n$, then $(z_m, t) \succ (z_n, t)$ for any $t \in \Gamma$ *(larger rewards are preferred, keeping time fixed)*.

B3. *Impatience*: Let $t_q < t_p$, and $z > 0$, $z \in Z$. Then, $(z, t_q) \succ (z, t_p)$ *(positive outcomes are preferred at an earlier date)*. Also $(0, t_q) \sim (0, t_p)$ *(no time preference for zero rewards)*.

B4. *Continuity*: Suppose that we have a sequence of outcome-time pairs $\{z_n, t_n\}_{n=1}^{\infty}$ and $\{z'_n, t'_n\}_{n=1}^{\infty}$ in the set Y that converges to the respective outcome-time pairs (z, t) and (z', t'). If for all n, $(z_n, t_n) \succeq (z'_n, t'_n)$, then the preference relation $\succeq$ is continuous if $(z, t) \succeq (z', t')$.

B5. Stationarity: *If $(z_m, t_q) \sim (z_n, t_p)$, then $(z_m, t_q + t) \sim (z_n, t_p + t)$ for any $t \in \Gamma$ (indifference between two outcomes depends only on the length of the time difference between the two).*

We have already encountered the analogues of axioms B1 and B4 in sections 2.4 and 2.5. axiom B1, which is a requirement for consistent preferences in section 2.4, requires that the decision-maker always be able to rank any two outcome-time pairs, say, (z_m, t_q) and (z_n, t_p), in some order—that is, one is preferred to the other or one is indifferent to the other. It is not permissible to say, "I am indecisive about which option I prefer" or "I am undecided yet." Furthermore, preferences are transitive, which is self-explanatory. Axiom B4 on continuity is identical to the definition of continuity in definition 2.4, extended to outcome-time pairs.

Axioms B2 and B3 are eminently reasonable. If two rewards are to be received at an identical future time, then the decision-maker prefers the outcome-time pair that contains the larger outcome (axiom B2). If the positive outcomes in two outcome-time pairs are identical, then the decision-maker prefers the outcome-time pair that is received earlier (this reflects impatience).

Axiom B5 is perhaps the most crucial axiom and the one that has been tested the most. Fishburn and Rubinstein (1982, p. 681) write: "However, we know of no persuasive argument for stationarity as a psychologically viable assumption."

When a decision-maker follows all the *axioms of rationality for time discounting* in definition 2.6, then the decision-maker is said to be rational while making temporal decisions. Obviously, violating these axioms is not a form of irrationality or madness, in the sense in which these terms are commonly used.

As in the previous two sections, we might now ask the following: Does there exist a utility function that represents preferences that satisfy the axioms of rationality for time discounting? This requires that if the decision-maker expresses the preference $(z_m, t_q) \succeq (z_n, t_p)$ for two outcome-time pairs, then we can find a utility function, U, such that $U(z_m, t_q) \geq U(z_n, t_p)$. The next result provides the answer, followed by an explanation and discussion.

Proposition 2.4. *(Fishburn & Rubinstein, 1982, p. 682) If axioms B1–B5 in definition 2.6 hold, then for any $\delta \in (0, 1)$, there exists a continuous increasing real-valued function, u, defined on the domain Z such that*

1. *for all* (z_m, t_q), (z_n, t_p) *in* $Z \times \Gamma$, $(z_m, t_q) \succeq (z_n, t_p)$ *if, and only if,*

   $U(z_m, t_q) = \delta^{t_q} u(z_m)$, $U(z_n, t_p) = \delta^{t_p} u(z_n)$; $\delta^{t_q} u(z_m) \geq \delta^{t_p} u(z_n)$;

2. *the outcome-time pair* $(0, t)$ *is treated as* $\delta^t u(0) = 0$; *and*
3. *given* δ, u *is unique up to multiplication by a positive constant.*

In proposition 2.4, the utility function that represents preferences consistent with the axioms of rationality for time discounting is given by

$$U(z, t) = \delta^t u(z); \delta \in (0, 1), \tag{2.4}$$

where u is sometimes known as the instantaneous utility function (or felicity) and δ^t is the value of the discount function at time $t \in \Gamma$ as viewed from the present. Since $\delta \in (0, 1)$, the successive terms $\delta, \delta^2, \delta^3, \ldots$ get smaller and smaller. Thus, the utility from future outcomes is shrunk more, the further out in the future they are. This reflects impatience (axiom B3). The converse of proposition 2.4 also holds—namely, if the decision-maker has the utility function U, then the axioms of rationality for time discounting also hold. Thus, to test the theory, we could either test any of the individual axioms in definition 2.6 or test that the decision-maker's behavior is consistent with the utility function U in (2.4). While models in economics prefer to use U to make predictions, tests of rationality under time discounting have relied on testing the individual axioms in definition 2.6.

The utility function U in (2.4) is called the *exponential discounted utility* (EDU) function. To see how it gets this name, we need a slightly different exposition that uses time dated streams of consumption rather than the outcome-time pairs that we have considered above. Both result in an identical utility representation of preferences.

Suppose that a decision-maker has available a stream of time dated consumption $c_0, c_1, \ldots, c_T$, so that c_t is some real-valued consumption at date $t = 0, 1, \ldots, T$. Let $\mathbf{c}_0 = (c_0, c_1, \ldots, c_T)$ be a shorthand way of writing this consumption stream. The *discounted utility* (DU) model, due to P. A. Samuelson (1937), can be written as

$$U(\mathbf{c}_0) = \sum_{t=0}^{T} D(t) u(c_t), \tag{2.5}$$

where $D(t)$ is a *discount function*. It is a decreasing function of time starting from $D(0) = 1$; thus, the weight placed on future utilities is lower, the further out into the future they are. The idea in the DU model is to have additive separability of the terms on the RHS of (2.5) (which can be written as $u(c_0) + D(1) u(c_1) + D(2) u(c_2) + \ldots$). Furthermore, the instantaneous utility at time t, given by u, depends only on the consumption at that time, c_t, but not explicitly on time itself.

The *discount rate*, $\theta(t)$, at time t is the rate of change of the *discount function* and, if the discount function is differentiable, it can be found from the relation

$$\theta(t) = -\frac{D'(t)}{D(t)}, \tag{2.6}$$

where $D'(t)$ is the first derivative of the discount function. The negative sign takes account of the fact that the discount function, D, is decreasing in time. This ensures that higher values of θ correspond to higher discount rates.

The EDU functional is a special case of the DU model in (2.5), where $D(t) = \delta^t$, $\delta \in (0,1)$. Thus, the EDU form can be written as $u(c_0) + \delta u(c_1) + \delta^2 u(c_2) + \ldots$, or more compactly as

$$U(c_0) = \sum_{t=0}^{T} \delta^t u(c_t), \text{ where } \delta = \frac{1}{1+\theta}. \tag{2.7}$$

If we were to shrink the gap between any two time periods and make this gap infinitesimally small, then we can write the continuous time analogue of (2.7) as

$$U(c_0) = \int_{t=0}^{T} e^{-\theta t} u(c_t) \, dt, \tag{2.8}$$

where $e^{-\theta t} u(c_t) \Delta t$ is the present discounted value of the utility from consumption at some future time t, evaluated over an interval of time Δt. The presence of the exponential term $e^{-\theta t}$ gives this utility function its name, exponential discounted utility (EDU). The necessary steps required in going from (2.7) to (2.8) require the same method that we need in going from simple interest rate calculations to compound interest rates used in high school maths. In (2.7) and (2.8), $\theta > 0$ is known as the *discount rate*, and it captures the impatience of the decision-maker (axiom B3). Under continuous discounting, and under the EDU model, we often compute the present discounted value, at time $t = 0$, of an outcome-time pair (z,t) by

$$e^{-\theta t} u(z). \tag{2.9}$$

We can now calculate the discount rate for the EDU model. The discount function in the continuous version of EDU in (2.8) is $D(t) = e^{-\theta t}$. Using 2.6, we get that the discount rate at time t is

$$\theta(t)=\theta, \tag{2.10}$$

which is independent of time. This is a direct consequence of the assumption of stationarity.

2.7 Rationality in Strategic Interaction

In this section, we consider the rationality assumptions that are implicit or explicit within classical game theory. Game theory deals with strategic situations in which individuals mutually influence each other's payoffs through their actions and beliefs. One of the simplest settings is captured by the prisoner's dilemma game, which we introduce in section 3.3. Rationality plays a key role in the development of the central concepts in game theory which uses the rationality requirements implicit in sections 2.4, 2.5, and 2.6. In game theory, players maximize their utility functions (section 2.4); they potentially employ mixed strategies in choosing their pure strategies probabilistically, using expected utility theory (section 2.5); and the players' analysis in repeated games assumes that they discount future payoffs using exponential discounted utility (section 2.6).

The refutation of any of the rationality axioms in sections 2.4, 2.5, and 2.6 creates potentially serious problems for game theory. For instance, in a fundamental result in game theory, Nash (1950), the 1994 Nobel laureate in economics, showed that every finite strategic-form game has at least one mixed strategy Nash equilibrium. This result assumes that players follow expected utility theory. The refutations of expected utility are well documented (Luce and Raiffa, 1957; Starmer, 2000; Wakker, 2010; Dhami, 2019a), and we shall outline a few of these below. Thus, there is no guarantee that a Nash equilibrium exists in mixed strategies. Furthermore, there is much evidence to suggest that although players try to randomize between their strategies, they do not randomize them in the proportions that are consistent with a mixed strategy Nash equilibrium (Camerer, 2003; Dhami, 2019d).

The entire set of assumptions in the BRA apply to any game theoretical analysis. For instance, people have unlimited cognitive and computational ability, unlimited and perfect memory, and perfect attention; are completely self-regarding (although this can be relaxed); make flawless use of Bayes' law; and typically employ no emotions in decision-making. Every one of these assumptions is called into question by the evidence.

In the simplest setting of a *static game of complete information*, such as the prisoner's dilemma game, a Nash equilibrium places no restrictions on the beliefs of players. In equilibrium, each player simply plays a best response to the equilibrium actions of the other player. However, belief restrictions that underpin a Nash equilibrium are studied in the *epistemic foundations of game theory*. These turn out to be extremely demanding and are unlikely to be met in practice. An important concept is *common knowledge*. There is common knowledge about an event, say, event A (or a set of events), if the players in a game know A, know that other players know A, know that others know that they know that others know A, and so on ad infinitum. This infinite regress problem is cognitively demanding and difficult to write down beyond a few steps, yet humans are assumed to be able to reason ad infinitum along these lines. In some cases, this is a plausible concept. For instance, consider a set of players in an experiment, and the experimenter publicly announces event A to all players. The public announcement makes it plausible that players have common knowledge of event A.

Suppose that the following conditions hold for each player: mutual knowledge of the payoffs, mutual knowledge of the rationality of players, common knowledge of the beliefs (or conjectures) each player has about the others, and common priors. Then, Aumann and Brandenburger (1995) showed that the common conjectures about what other players will do are in agreement and constitute a Nash equilibrium of the game. Polak (1999) showed that if mutual knowledge of the payoffs is strengthened to common knowledge of payoffs, then the Aumann-Brandenburger conditions imply common knowledge of rationality. It has never been empirically demonstrated that these assumptions hold in the real world, and recent research offers an unsettled view of the epistemic foundations (Gintis, 2009). But game theory courses almost never mention a shred of empirical evidence, relying instead on the underlying assumptions as a matter of faith. If the predictions of a Nash equilibrium and its refinements are empirically violated (as they are), then so are the epistemic conditions. We briefly summarize the empirical evidence below.

A central feature of game theory is that it relies on an equilibrium analysis. This is reflected in various equilibrium concepts for games of different types, such as Nash equilibrium, subgame perfect equilibrium, perfect Bayesian Nash equilibrium, and sequential equilibrium. For instance, in a perfect Bayesian Nash equilibrium, equilibrium analysis requires that the actions of players maximize their payoffs given their beliefs and the equilibrium actions and beliefs of the other players. Furthermore, the beliefs of the players in equilibrium are always correct, given the equilibrium actions; this is the analogue of the rational expectations assumption in macroeconomics. In games where players may make sequential decisions over time, or over various stages of the game, beliefs at any stage are correct given the subsequent equilibrium actions of other players (just as in dynamic programming; see section 3.2.1) and their own equilibrium actions.

Equilibrium analysis is sometimes justified using the following two arguments, but both are flawed.

1. Any game theoretic equilibrium is the outcome of a learning process where players in the game have had a chance to repeatedly try out their strategies and learn from their past strategies and outcomes. However, such processes do not guarantee convergence of play to a Nash equilibrium and, when convergence does take place, there is no guarantee that the underlying learning process is plausible (Fudenberg & Tirole, 1991, pp. 25–29; Dhami, 2020b). Even when convergence does take place under a plausible learning process, there is no guarantee that it does so in a reasonable amount of time that is representative of actual, real-world interactions.

2. Equilibrium game theoretic outcomes are to be interpreted as social norms. Consider, for instance, the static prisoner's dilemma game (see section 3.3). The strategy in which each player chooses to defect is the unique Nash equilibrium of the game. However, the joint payoff for each player is the lowest in this case. It is hard to believe that social norms would always pick such an inefficient outcome. Indeed, social norms of cooperation are likely to pick out the cooperative outcome. Not all social norms are a Nash equilibrium, although some might be, and not all Nash equilibria are social norms, although some might be.

2.8 What Rationality Is Not

Economists make several auxiliary assumptions in constructing models. It is sometimes mistakenly believed that these auxiliary assumptions are consequences of the rationality assumptions. At other times, they are regarded as part of a broader concept of rationality. We consider some mistaken notions in this section.

2.8.1 Rationality Does Not Imply Self-Regarding Preferences

The most common of these mistaken auxiliary requirements for rationality is that individuals have *self-regarding preferences*. Consider an individual i who has consumption x_i and let x_{-i} denote the consumption of all others. By *self-regarding preferences* is meant that the utility of individual i depends solely on own-consumption—that is, we have $u_i(x_i)$. On the other hand, individual i is said to have *other-regarding preferences* (or *social preferences*) if the individual cares about own-consumption, x_i, and the consumption of others, x_{-i}—that is, the individual's utility function is $u_i(x_i, x_{-i})$. In richer models, other-regarding preferences may also incorporate the inclusion of beliefs in the utility function, as in psychological game theory. In sections 2.4–2.7, the decision-maker always had self-regarding preferences because that has been the default assumption in the BRA. However, the results in sections 2.4–2.7 can be extended to other-regarding preferences. This is because the BRA is quite flexible in the definition of the initial set of choices, X. For instance, for individual i, elements in X may be appropriately defined as pairs of the form (x_i, x_{-i}). One can then proceed, as in sections 2.4–2.7, to derive a utility function with other-regarding preferences. However, in actual practice, the BRA has not taken account of other-regarding preferences. There are some models, in an older tradition of neoclassical economics, of *keeping up with the Joneses* and *snob consumption* (Duesenberry, 1949; Liebenstein, 1950), but these play, at best, a fringe role in modern economics.

By contrast, other-regarding preferences play a key role in behavioral economics. There is now extensive lab, field, and neuroeconomic evidence for such preferences. Behavioral models of other-regarding preferences have made several important predictions that have been confirmed by the data. Experiments, in turn, have played a key role in the precise identification of other-regarding preferences. For surveys, the interested reader may consult Fehr and Schmidt (2006) and Dhami (2019b).

2.8.2 Rationality Does Not Imply Absence of Emotions in Decision-Making

Rationality in economics is sometimes taken to imply cold, emotionless deliberation. While emotionless deliberation is standard in modern economics, the rationality requirements in the BRA can, in principle, be extended to allow for emotions. One could take account of a set of emotional states M (e.g., anger, guilt, frustration, shame, anxiety) and, for any $m \in M$, index the preference relation $\succsim$ in sections 2.4–2.7 by m to write $\succsim_m$ instead; this applies to situations of certainty and uncertainty and to the time dimension. This allows an individual's preferences to be dependent on the emotional state; for each m, the binary preference relation $\succsim_m$ represents different preferences.

By contrast, there has been growing interest in modeling emotions in behavioral economics (Dhami, 2020c). For instance, *anxiety* is an important emotion that has been used to explain the equity-premium puzzle in finance (Caplin & Leahy, 2001). We use the emotions of guilt and shame to explain contractual choices in microfinance contracts in section 3.2.2. We also show in section 3.4 that guilt and shame underpin moral and social norms, respectively. *Projection bias*, the tendency to project one's current emotional states to future states of the world, explains why those awaiting kidney transplants have reported relatively lower well-being as compared to a healthy control group, yet after the transplant, both groups report similar well-being (Loewenstein et al., 2003). There are also extremely important applications of emotions to strategic interaction that use the machinery of *psychological game theory*; see Dhami (2019d, section 2.5) and Battigalli and Dufwenberg (2020) for surveys.

2.8.3 Rationality Does Require Perfect Attention and Unlimited Computing Power

The choice set X, whether it be the space of outcomes, lotteries, or time-outcome pairs (sections 2.4–2.7), can be infinite. The most basic rationality requirement in section 2.4 requires individuals to engage in a potentially infinite number of pairwise preference comparisons in order to choose the most preferred, or maximal, element in the set X. In addition, transitivity must not be violated. This may require enormous computation power, memory, and attention. By contrast, the evidence shows that people are subject to inattention, misperception, and limited computation powers (Dhami, 2016). This could arise from many factors such as limited time, information/cognitive overload, deadlines, personal problems such as marital discord, and emotional lows that impair judgement. In turn, these rationality assumptions feed into optimization-based solutions to economic problems. We show in section 3.2 that the dimensionality issues that arise in such maximization exercises are nontrivial and appear beyond any reasonable human capabilities.

2.9 Evidence on Consistent Preferences

The most basic definition of rationality under certainty (definition 2.2) requires that preferences be complete and transitive—that is, that decision-makers exhibit consistent preferences. Both are violated in experiments. Iyengar and Lepper (2000) exposed subjects to either a limited choice condition (6 varieties of jams) or an intensive choice condition (24 varieties of jams). There was no difference in the percentage of jams sampled in both conditions. However, nearly 30 percent of the consumers in the limited choice condition purchased a jam jar. The corresponding number in the intensive condition was only 3 percent. This suggests that individuals may find it more difficult to make choices when there are too many options; this may violate completeness.

The most famous of the violations of transitivity occurs in the experiments on *preference reversals*, which were conducted in the domain of risk, where we also require transitivity (see axiom 2.1). Consider two probabilities $0 \leq p < P$, two outcomes $0 \leq z < Z$, and the following pair of lotteries:

$$P\text{-bet} = (0, 1-P; z, P), \quad \$\text{-bet} = (0, 1-p; Z, p). \tag{2.11}$$

In the P-bet, one can win the lower prize z with a higher probability, P (and win nothing with probability $1 - P$), and in the $-bet one can win the higher prize, Z, with a lower probability, p (and win nothing with probability $1 - p$). The decision-maker is given the following two tasks.

1. Which of the two lotteries, P-bet and $-bet, do you prefer?
2. The certainty equivalent is an outcome received for sure, which makes the decision-maker indifferent to the outcome and the given lottery (see definition 2.8). So, the second task for the decision-maker is this: Assign *certainty equivalents* to the P-bet and the $-bet; denote these, respectively, by C_P and $C_\$$. By the very definition of a certainty equivalent, we have that $-bet $\sim C_\$$ and $C_P \sim P$-bet, where $\sim$ denotes indifference.

The typical empirical finding, much replicated, is that the P-bet is chosen over the $-bet in the first task, but $C_P < C_\$$ in the second task (Lichtenstein & Slovic, 1971). Using the fact that (1) $-bet $\sim C_\$$, and $C_P \sim P$-bet, by definition, and (2) the empirically observed relation $C_P < C_\$$, we can show that transitivity fails because we have $-bet $\sim C_\$ \succ C_P \sim P$-bet $\succ $-bet (where $\succ$ denotes strict preference); clearly the $-bet cannot be strictly preferred to itself. The failure of transitivity means that we are no longer guaranteed that a utility function representing preferences exists.

These initial results are replicated in psychology. It was gradually realized that the implications for economics are profound. Grether and Plott (1979) examined the literature on preference reversals in psychology and pointed out serious shortcomings with it. For instance, subjects were often given hypothetical situations/rewards; sometimes the elicited information was of the nature of surveys; and the typical experimental study did not offer any incentives for choices made (a cardinal sin in experimental economics)—a charge that was also levied on the Lichtenstein and Slovic (1971) paper. However, when Grether and Plott reran the same experiments after eliminating the experimental confounds, much to their surprise, they found that the preference reversal effect was even stronger. For a review of some of the later literature, see Lichtenstein and Slovic (2006). Some decision theory models (e.g., regret theory) can account for intransitivity of preferences (Loomes & Sugden, 1982; Loomes et al., 1991).

We digress here, but this is an interesting methodological point. Most of the early work of Kahneman and Tversky, particularly their work on judgment heuristics and decision theory in the 1970s and even in the 1980s (which included work on fairness considerations with Richard Thaler) would be unpublishable in any economics journal today. The reason is that their subjects were not incentivized, and some of the experimental instructions may now be considered borderline subject deception, which is unacceptable in economics experiments but common in psychology experiments. Yet, when the original Kahneman-Tversky experiments were replicated with proper incentives, particularly in their work on prospect theory, the results stayed intact (Dhami, 2019a). Experimenters in psychology and economics ascribe different human motivations to lab subjects. The psychologists believe that most lab subjects would use their *intrinsic motivation* in making choices—hence, incentives do not have first order importance—while the economists place their faith in *extrinsic motivation* and reject non-incentivized lab studies. The actual empirical evidence on incentives is mixed, and we omit a discussion. Readers interested in these issues may consult Bardsley et al. (2010) and the introductory chapter in Dhami (2016).

It is also interesting that discussions of the BRA in economics courses rarely refer to the evidence on the consistency of preferences, a concept that is about as fundamental to the BRA as atoms are to physics and chemistry. The common consensus in economics, and in much of behavioral economics, is to maintain a minimum degree of rationality, as dictated by definition 2.2. Others are not persuaded by the evidence on preference reversals. For instance, Gintis (2017) dismisses the evidence on the grounds that the expected values of the two lotteries are very similar. In other contexts, the view in Gintis (2009, 2017) is that observed violations of the consistency of preferences are almost always due to a failure to take account of the context and frame dependence of preferences. A compromise could be to retain consistency of preferences, but only within a suitably narrow frame or context. However, it is an open empirical question whether all evidence that contradicts complete and transitive preferences could be explained by invoking different contexts and frames.

2.10 Evidence on Limited Attention

In this section, we consider the empirical evidence on *limited attention*. The evidence comes from many, and diverse, sources. We provide a selected review of the evidence here.[4]

Improving the information content of messages can be welfare improving. For instance, providing financial information on monthly repayments significantly reduces expensive payday loan borrowing (Bertrand & Morse, 2011). Insofar as borrowers may pay limited attention to the costs of borrowing, this result shows that mandatory borrower information may have huge welfare consequences. Reminders on the size of penalties for overdrawn accounts reduces overdraft fees for up to two years, and the effect is greater for individuals who have lower education and financial literacy (Stango & Zinman, 2014). Reducing the number of loan options presumably works to focus potentially inattentive minds, increasing loan take-ups; reducing the number of options from four to one increases borrowing by the same amount as a 2.3 percent reduction in the interest rate (Bertrand et al., 2010).

Giné et al. (2014) asked low-income individuals to spot the lowest-cost credit product in bank brochures in Mexico City; only 39 percent were successful. However, when the same information was provided in a user-friendly summary sheet, 68 percent were successful. Drexler et al. (2014) found that reducing the degree of sophistication of financial programs in the Dominican Republic by emphasizing simple heuristics improves financial literacy of firms and micro-entrepreneurs. The World Bank Development Report (2015) provides a wealth of information on diverse empirical studies of this form in developing countries.

There are well-documented institutional and cultural reasons that cause, and perpetuate, poverty. However, one consequence of poverty is that limited attention may take up scarce willpower. The poor in developing countries may have particularly depleted willpower due to pressing livelihood concerns (finding the next meal, finding clean drinking water, dealing with debt). Hence, problems of limited attention may be particularly severe for them, a form of *cognitive tax* (Shah et al., 2012; Mullainathan & Shafir, 2013). Thus, the poor may engage in insufficient deliberation or pay insufficient attention to many important issues (Banerjee & Mullainathan, 2008). This is sometimes referred to as the problem of *low bandwidth*. Hence, poor individuals may make suboptimal decisions, which perpetuate the poverty that is the cause of the initial problem.

Indeed, the actions of the poor may not fully reflect their intentions; this is known as the *intention-action divide*. Farmers score much lower on cognitive ability tests (up to 10 points lower on an IQ scale) before a harvest when they have high levels of financial stress (Mani et al., 2013). Goal-based text messages sent out to individuals in Peru, Bolivia, and the Philippines, reminding them of their savings goals, improved savings by 16 percent (Karlan et al., 2012). Poverty policy that takes account of limited attention can have low-cost welfare benefits—for instance, by targeting financial decisions when the bandwidth of poor is higher; Datta and Mullainathan (2014) term this as *low hanging policy fruit*.

Chetty et al. (2009) surveyed consumers at a grocery store where the sales tax was displayed for some consumer goods but not for others. Although consumers demonstrated awareness of the sales tax when asked, their purchase decisions suggested that taxes that are not displayed on price stickers reduce tax salience. The poor pay greater attention to sales taxes that are levied at the sales register but not displayed on the price sticker (Goldin & Homonoff, 2013). Attention, salience, and the marginal incentive effects of the earned income tax credit (EITC) are examined in Hotz and Scholz (2003). Political economy considerations may induce governments to use taxes that are less salient, in attentional terms, to fund growing public expenditures. This might explain the reluctance to alter income taxes (Buchanan, 1967; Brennan & Buchanan, 1980). We formalize some of these ideas in chapter 8. In a related application, customers who pay by manual tolls in car plazas have much greater awareness of the toll charged relative to customers who pay by electronic toll collections (Finkelstein, 2009).

People appear to give more attention to the leftmost digit of a multi-digit number, and less to the digits on the right (Korvost & Damian, 2008). This might explain the prevalence of prices ending in the digit 9—for instance, a price of $39.99 rather than $40. Lacetera et al. (2012) document left-digit bias in the wholesale used car market, and Busse et al. (2013) confirm these findings for the retail used car market. There are discontinuous drops in the retail prices of cars at 10,000-mile thresholds. For instance, cars with odometer readings 79,900–79,999 miles sell for $210 more than those with odometer readings in the range 80,000–80,100, yet they sell for only $10 less than those with odometer readings 79,800–79,899. There are also small discontinuities in the used car prices at the 1,000-mile thresholds. Sellers appear to be aware of the left-digit bias of buyers, and there are spikes in the number of cars offered for sale just before they hit these odometer thresholds.

2.11 Evidence on Overconfidence

In the BRA, individuals are neither underconfident nor overconfident. They use the statistically correct inference, which has no notion of underconfidence or overconfidence. Thus, observed departures from the correct statistical inference may indicate either underconfidence or overconfidence. Of these, overconfidence has been the more studied human trait and is the one that we focus on in this section (but see our discussion on underweighting of the sample likelihood in section 2.15.3).[5]

It is convenient to classify overconfidence into one of the following three types (Moore and Healy, 2008).

1. *Overestimation* occurs when individuals overestimate their own performance in a task, (e.g., an IQ test).
2. *Overplacement*, or the *better than average* or *better than median* effect (Larrick et al., 2007) arises when subjects rank themselves too favorably against some statistic of the rank order of others.
3. *Overprecision* occurs when subjects estimate confidence intervals of their predictions that are too narrow, relative to the correct statistical benchmark.

Empirically, we find that in domains where overestimation is high, underplacement is the highest. One explanation is a form of the *hard-easy effect*. People are imperfectly informed about their abilities and the abilities of others. In relatively easier tasks (e.g., driving a car), they underestimate their performance, but they underestimate the performance of others even more, leading to overplacement. For hard tasks, they overestimate their performance, but overestimate the performance of others even more so, leading to underplacement (Windschitl et al., 2003).

The *Dunning-Kruger effect* (Kruger & Dunning, 1999) arises when individuals of low ability hold the most inaccurate assessment of their skills/performance, relative to their peers. For instance, in tests of grammar and logical reasoning, students who perform in the bottom 25 percent believe that their performance is in the top 40 percentile. Similarly, those who performed in the top 25 percent underrated their performance (Dunning et al., 2003). Kruger and Dunning argue that low ability subjects score low because their ability is low, and in turn their low ability hampers recognition of their relative rank among their peers. Those who have high ability find the task easy and mistakenly infer that others will find it even easier, so they underestimate their ranks. However, there have been other explanations of the Dunning-Kruger effect, which include the *regression to the mean phenomena* (Krueger & Mueller, 2002) and the perceived difficulty of the task (Burson et al., 2006). The meta study by Ehrlinger et al. (2008) supports the original interpretation in Kruger and Dunning against both these alternatives.

The following question is often asked: Given the behavioral departures from the BRA for individuals, do these biases carry over to the behavior of firms, experts, and organizations? The work of Tetlock (2006) shows that experts also exhibit the relevant biases. In the context of the efficient markets hypothesis in finance, it has been shown that professional arbitrage does not achieve market efficiency either, and it is subject to its own biases (Dhami, 2020a).

In the specific context of overconfidence, Meikle et al. (2016) survey the evidence from firms and organizations. Greater feedback and consultative decision-making processes in organizational teams might mitigate against overconfidence. A countervailing factor is that the larger the team, the lower the responsibility and accountability for bad decisions that team members might feel. Just like individuals, organizations can make overconfident decisions—for example, overestimation of their future production/profitability—and team decision-making does not seem to mitigate such decisions (Buehler et al., 2005; Staats et al., 2012). Insofar that the mitigation channel is through feedback from team members, such feedback might be weak or might not have the desired effect because there are other benefits from staying optimistic. Another reason why negative feedback within firms might not have the desired salutary effect is the presence of *attribution bias* (Chen et al., 2015). The final outcomes of interest to firms, such as market shares and profits, are jointly determined by the quality of organizational decisions, which are endogenous, and the environmental factors, which are exogenous. Attribution bias arises when bad outcomes are ascribed to exogenous factors rather than bad decisions.

In a large study where experts from diverse fields were asked to construct confidence intervals, expertise did not necessarily shield against overprecision (Lin & Bier, 2008). More confident traders, as measured by their self-assessed overplacement, trade more (Glaser & Weber, 2007). Overconfidence may be correlated with other desirable traits in organizations (e.g., charm, passion, decisiveness). When coupled with attribution bias and/or the ability to persuasively deflect bad performance on exogenous factors, many individuals who rise to senior ranks in organizations may be the more risk-taking, overconfident types, yet they may cost the firm in terms of lower profits (Mabe & West, 1982; Anderson et al., 2012; Bonner & Bolinger, 2013; Tenney et al., 2015).

In section 3.2.4 we outline the evidence on overconfident CEOs and suboptimal decisions such as mergers. Since overconfident CEOs might be more willing to take risks, one may observe several effects. These CEOs can help increase a company's patent count, increase innovation, and lead to greater volatility in the company's stock market prices (Galasso & Simcoe, 2011; Hirshleifer et al., 2012). In other contexts, overconfident CEOs might engage in accounting fraud by engaging in riskier accounting practices (Ahmed & Duellman, 2013; Hribar & Yang, 2015). Overconfident leaders are also more likely to go to war (D. D. P. Johnson et al., 2006). There is also some evidence that overconfident CEOs make less aggressive choices following government intervention. This, for instance, was the case when the US Congress passed the Sarbanes-Oxley Act in 2002 (S. Banerjee et al., 2015).

Entrepreneurs are typically overconfident of the success probability of their start-ups; an early set of experiments that support this conclusion were conducted by Camerer and Lovallo (1999). Only 5 percent of startup entrepreneurs believe that their odds are any worse than comparable enterprises, and a third believe that their success is assured (Cooper et al., 1988). Based on French data, 56 percent expect "development," and only 6 percent of startup entrepreneurs expect "difficulty"; three years on, the respective figures are 38 percent and 17 percent (Landier & Thesmar, 2009). Empirically, only half of all start-ups survive beyond three years (Scarpetta et al., 2002), and the high failure rate among start-ups is widely reported in the popular press.

Unlike the correlation of some other behavioral phenomena with age (e.g., risk aversion), there is no clear relation between overconfidence and age. A positive relation is found in Hansson et al. (2008), while a negative relation is found in Touron and Hertzog (2004). For an overview of the literature, see Glaser et al. (2004). Menkhoff et al. (2013) find that different measures of overconfidence need not be highly correlated. They also find that, in their sample, investment advisors are most overconfident, while institutional investors are least overconfident.

Why are people overoptimistic or overconfident? The literature on *motivated cognition* offers some insights. The basic idea is that our beliefs may help us to preserve/enhance certain factors that are hedonically attractive. Humans often hold certain beliefs so as to preserve their ego, confidence, and optimism, which has several potential benefits. These include a positive self-image; heightened self-esteem; reduced disappointment and regret; improved motivation; reduction in self-control problems; and signaling desirable traits to oneself and others (Akerlof & Dickens, 1982; Bénabou & Tirole, 2002, 2016; Brunnermeier & Parker,

2005; Bénabou, 2015). The evidence suggests that motivated cognition is not necessarily related to one's IQ (Kahan, 2013; Kahan et al., 2017).

On the one hand, the benefits of holding motivated beliefs could be that they impart utility, but the cost may be a reduction in the quality of decisions. *Optimal belief management*, which individuals might actively pursue, trades off these benefits and the costs. On net, more optimistic people might achieve better life outcomes in terms of savings, income, retirement, and marriage (Puri & Robinson, 2007; Huck et al., 2018). Maintaining various forms of positive beliefs can come about from strategic self-manipulation (e.g., information avoidance, leading to confirmation bias; see chapter 5). Such beliefs can also come about from following a specific religion or set of cultural values that might provide comfort/reassurance and self-discipline (Bénabou & Tirole, 2016, p. 143).

2.12 Evidence on Rationality in Risk and Uncertainty

In this section, we provide selective and brief evidence for the axioms of rationality under risk (definition 2.5) and the expected utility representation of preferences (proposition 2.3). For book-length treatments, see Wakker (2010) and Dhami (2019a).

2.12.1 Nonlinear Probability Weighting

Probabilities enter linearly into the calculation of expected utility (EU); see (2.3). However, the evidence indicates that decision-makers weight probabilities nonlinearly in the manner shown in section 2.16.2. A nice example of nonlinear probability weighting comes from the play of Russian roulette (Kahneman & Tversky, 1979, p. 283). Some readers may remember the game of Russian roulette from the 1978 film *The Deer Hunter*. In a famous scene involving Robert De Niro, fewer than six rounds in a revolver are loaded, the cylinder is spun randomly, and he places the muzzle against his head and pulls the trigger.

In playing Russian roulette, most people would be willing to pay a higher amount of money to reduce the number of bullets from one to zero (to achieve complete certainty) than from four to three (reduction of risk). However, the reduction of a single bullet in the revolver results in an identical reduction in the probability of death, which is 1/6, irrespective of how many bullets one starts with. Hence, a decision-maker who follows expected utility should pay the same amount in both cases (the reader can try to construct the simple, but formal, proof). The payment of a higher amount to achieve complete certainty suggests that close to the end points of the probability interval ($p = 0$ and $p = 1$), there is a greater sensitivity to changes in probability, relative to the middle ranges, where such changes are more muted; this is exactly what we observe in the probability weighting function. See the continuous inverse S-shaped probability weighting function in figure 2.3.

The classic demonstration of the violation of linear probabilities is the *Allais paradox*, originally due to Allais (1953), which we now describe. Readers will need to be familiar with the material in the appendix to this chapter to understand the calculations. This example shows that a decision-maker who follows expected utility will violate the given pattern of choices. We then go back to the axioms of rationality and identify which axiom is violated.

Example 2.4. *(Allais paradox as a "common ratio violation"; Kahneman & Tversky, 1979) Consider a decision-maker who has zero initial wealth. The utility function for outcomes is given by u. Outcomes are in units of Israeli pounds (I£). Subjects choose between the following two lotteries,*

$$L_1 = (3000, 1) \text{ and } L_2 = (0, 0.2; 4000, 0.8), \tag{2.12}$$

where L_1 gives I£3,000 with certainty and L_2 gives an 80 percent chance of winning I£4,000 and a 20 percent chance of nothing extra. Of the 95 subjects who participated in the study, 80 percent chose L_1, and 20 percent chose L_2. In other words, if $\succ$ is the "strictly preferred to" binary preference relation under EU (see axiom 2.1), then we get that for the vast majority of subjects, the lottery L_1 is strictly preferred to the lottery L_1: $L_1 \succ L_2$. Using the expected utility calculations in (2.3) and the given lotteries in (2.12), we get

$$L_1 \succ L_2 \Leftrightarrow u(3000) > 0.8u(4000), \tag{2.13}$$

where the symbol $\Leftrightarrow$ means "equivalent to" (i.e., the LHS implies the RHS, and vice-versa).

In a second set of choices, 95 subjects were asked to choose between the following two lotteries,

$$L_3 = (0, 0.75; 3000, 0.25) \text{ and } L_4 = (0, 0.8; 4000, 0.2).$$

Of the 95 subjects, 35 percent chose L_3, and 65 percent chose L_4. Thus, we find that for the majority of the subjects,

$$L_4 \succ L_3 \Leftrightarrow 0.2u(4000) > 0.25u(3000). \tag{2.14}$$

The majority of the decision-makers would satisfy EU (and by implication, the axioms of rationality) if both (2.13) and (2.14) simultaneously hold. We can divide both sides of the inequality in (2.13) by 4 to get

$$L_1 \succ L_2 \Leftrightarrow 0.25u\,(3000) > 0.2u\,(4000). \tag{2.15}$$

There is no difference between (2.13) and (2.15) because dividing both sides by a positive number leaves the inequality unchanged. Yet, (2.14) and (2.15) cannot both be true at the same time. Hence, it must be that the majority of decision-makers do not follow EU.

In 1952 in Paris, Maurice Allais, who won the 1988 Nobel Prize in the economic sciences, presented the problem in example 2.4 to the then leading decision theorists, Leonard Savage, Paul Samuelson, and others.[6] He chose the following specific numbers (in units of millions of 1952 francs) for the lotteries given in example 2.4: $L_1 = (100, 1)$, $L_2 = (500, 0.98)$, $L_3 = (100; 0.01)$ and $L_4 = (4000; 0.0098)$; this leaves the conclusions of example 2.4 unchanged. To quote from Allais (1953): "The author of this memoir, who is perfectly familiar with Samuelson's arguments, unhesitatingly prefers lottery [L_1] to lottery [L_2] and lottery [L_4] to lottery [L_3] and he thinks that most of his readers will share his preference; yet to the best of his knowledge, he believes that he is not irrational." Savage (like Allais) initially chose L_1 over L_2 and L_4 over L_3. But after making an EU calculation, Savage concluded that he had made a mistake. Savage's response was that EU should be used for correct decision-making, and he might be right. However, Allais was also right to conclude that, in fact, most decision-makers do not follow EU.

The Allais paradox can be readily seen as one where nonlinear probabilities play a central role.

1. In the choice between lotteries L_4 and L_3, the decision-maker codes the two probabilities of nonzero outcomes, respectively, 0.2 and 0.25, to be nearly identical (the inverse S-shaped probability weighting function in figure 2.3 is quite flat in the middle); hence, he picks L_4 because it gives him a relatively higher outcome (4,000 instead of 3,000).
2. By contrast, in the choice between lotteries L_1 and L_2, the decision-maker does not code the two probabilities of nonzero outcomes, respectively, 1 and 0.8, as close to each other (the inverse S-shaped probability weighting function in figure 2.3 is quite steep as we approach a probability of 1) and prefers the complete certainty of receiving I£3,000 lottery L_1 (the *certainty effect*). In other words, he *underweights* the probability 0.8 in lottery L_2.

Hence, *nonlinear weighting of probabilities* is a potential explanation of the Allais paradox, but expected utility does not allow it.

It was realized later that the Allais paradox was part of a family of paradoxes that took two forms the *common ratio violation* form and the *common consequence violation* form. Both forms violate the independence axiom of EU (axiom 2.4) and have been widely replicated; see Starmer (2000) and Dhami (2019a). To see this violation, let us state the Allais paradox in example 2.4 a bit more generally.

Definition 2.7. *(Common ratio violation of expected utility)* Consider two probabilities $p, P \in (0, 1]$ and two prizes z, Z such that $p < P$ and $0 < z < Z$. Let $\mu \in (0, 1)$, and use the convention that (x, p) denotes the lottery $(0, 1-p; x, p)$. Consider a choice between the following pairs of lotteries.

$$L_1 = (z, P) \text{ and } L_2 = (Z, p) \tag{2.16}$$

$$L_3 = (z, \mu P) \text{ and } L_4 = (Z, \mu p) \tag{2.17}$$

The common ratio violation occurs if a decision-maker prefers (1) L_1 over L_2 and L_4 over L_3 or (2) L_2 over L_1 and L_3 over L_4. The name common ratio *derives from the fact that the ratio of probabilities for the outcomes in each of the two choices is the same: P/p.*

Example 2.4 is a special case of this violation if we set $p = 0.8$, $P = 1$, $z = 3000$, $Z = 4000$, and $\mu = 1/4$.[7] It is readily shown that the Allais paradox is a violation of the independence axiom. Below we give the proof for the interested reader; others who take our word for it may skip it.

Assume that $L_1 \succ L_2$, so $(z, P) \succ (Z, p)$. Hence, $(z, P) \succeq (Z, p)$. From the independence axiom (axiom 2.4), we get that $((z, P), \mu; 0, 1 - \mu) \succeq ((Z, p), \mu; 0, 1 - \mu)$, which, given our notation, can be written as $((z, P), \mu) \succeq ((Z, p), \mu)$. From the reduction axiom (axiom 2.5), it follows that $((z, P), \mu)$ and $((Z, p), \mu)$ are equivalent to $(z, \mu P)$ and $(Z, \mu p)$, respectively. Hence, $(z, \mu P) \succeq (Z, \mu p)$—that is, $L_3 \succeq L_4$. Thus, the observation of a common ratio violation—namely, $L_1 \succ L_2$ and $L_4 \succ L_3$—is a rejection of the independence axiom, given the other axioms of expected utility. Alternatively, we may view the observation of a common ratio violation as a rejection of the reduction axiom, given the other axioms of expected utility—an observation that is missed by many texts in microeconomics.

Another form taken by the Allais paradox is that of a common consequence violation; for the details and the empirical evidence, as well as more detailed evidence on nonlinear probability weighting, see Dhami (2019a).

2.12.2 Reference Dependence

As we note in the appendix to this chapter, *reference dependence* is a key feature of prospect theory. It is important to emphasize that reference dependence is not inconsistent with the axioms of rationality. The set of outcomes, X, that is used in the axioms of rationality under risk (see section 2.5) can simply be redefined by subtracting a reference point, r, from each outcome, and the analysis in section 2.5 still goes through—that is, we still obtain the expected utility representation of preferences in (2.3). Thus, while the evidence on nonlinear probability is fatal for the axioms of rationality under risk, the evidence on reference dependence is not; indeed, loss aversion is also not inconsistent with EU.

Whilst we may incorporate reference dependence under expected utility (EU) and split the set of outcomes into gains and losses, this is a largely vacuous exercise. The reason is that EU makes no meaningful distinction in human behavior in the domains of gains and losses. By contrast, prospect theory does make a critical distinction between the two domains that goes beyond the presence of loss aversion to different attitudes to risk in the two domains; see the *fourfold classification of risk* under prospect theory in section 2.16.4. We illustrate a related point through an example below.

Under EU, alternative ways of presenting the same information should be inconsequential for decision-making, provided that the information content is not changed; this is known as the *description invariance assumption*. Our next example shows that this assumption does not hold; that human behavior in the domains of gain and loss is different; and that attitudes to risk under prospect theory are richer than under EU.

In their experiments, Tversky and Kahneman (1981) gave the following problem to their subjects.

Imagine that the US is preparing for the outbreak of an unusual Asian disease, which is expected to kill 600 people. Two alternative programs to combat the disease have been proposed. Assume that the exact scientific estimates of the consequences of the programs are as follows.

Positive framing: If program A is adopted, 200 people will be saved. If program B is adopted, there is a one-third probability that 600 people will be saved and a two-thirds probability that no people will be saved. Which of the two programs would you favor?

Negative framing: If program C is adopted, 400 people will die. If program D is adopted, there is a one-third probability that nobody will die and a two-thirds probability that 600 people will die. Which of the two programs would you favor?

Under positive framing, the choices are framed in terms of their impact on *lives saved* (domain of gains); 72 percent of the subjects chose A, the safe program, and 28 percent chose the risky program B. Under negative framing, the choices are framed in terms of *lives lost* (domain of losses); 22 percent chose the safe program C, and 78 percent chose D, the risky program. Notice that the corresponding options in each frame are identical (A and C are identical; B and D are identical), yet description invariance is violated. Another important finding from this experiment is that decision-makers appear risk averse for gains and risk loving for losses, which is consistent with the predictions in prospect theory. Table 2.2 sharpens this result further by differentiating between small and large probabilities.

2.12.3 More Violations

In this section, we have merely scratched the tip of the iceberg on the refutations of expected utility. The interested reader can pursue Kahneman and Tversky (2000), Starmer (2000), and Dhami (2019a) for more details. Further refutations and applications, all covered in Dhami, include but are not restricted to unreasonable attitudes toward risk; the endowment effect; anomalies of tax evasion; the efficacy of goal-setting behavior; backward bending labor supply curve of taxi drivers; the equity-premium puzzle; contract choice and renegotiation; and the pricing of assets and the skewness of asset returns. Furthermore, close genetic relatives (e.g., primates such as capuchin monkeys) exhibit similar violations of expected utility, and their behavior is also consistent with prospect theory. The implication of this evidence is that preferences consistent with prospect theory are likely to have been hardwired into the common ancestors of humans and capuchin monkeys.

2.13 Evidence on Rationality in Time Discounting

As noted, the utility representation of rational time preferences takes the form of the exponential discounted utility (EDU) model; see proposition 2.4 for the rationality axioms and equations (2.7) and (2.8) for the EDU representation of the preferences. Under EDU, the discount factor, δ, is constant. From (2.7) and (2.8), this is equivalent to saying that the discount rate θ is constant. Thus, the instantaneous utility from an outcome of 15, denoted by $u(15)$, discounted back one period is $\delta u(15)$, no matter at what time the outcome 15 is received. This is violated by the evidence from *hyperbolic discounting*, which we consider below, where it does matter when the outcome of 15 is received.

Under EDU, the same discount factor, δ, applies (1) independent of the magnitude of an outcome (absence of *magnitude effect*) and (2) independent of the sign, positive or negative, of an outcome (*gain-loss asymmetry*). Furthermore, preferences are independent of the shapes of consumption profiles. For instance, most cultures typically prefer a dessert at the end of the meal but not at the beginning. By contrast, the evidence shows the presence of the magnitude effect, gain-loss asymmetry, and that the shapes of consumption profiles matter. Furthermore, behavioral models of time discounting have been proposed that are able to account for all of these violations (Frederick et al., 2002; Loewenstein, 2008; Dhami, 2019c).

The discounted utility (DU) model in (2.5) is often too general for making precise predictions. For instance, choices under the DU model could be *time inconsistent*—that is, decision-makers may wish to reschedule previously made plans to a later date even when there is no risk or uncertainty. The EDU model is the only one, within the much bigger class of DU models, that always results in *time consistent choices* (Strotz, 1955). Thus, choices made now for a future date continue to remain optimal when the future date arrives. This has been a major factor in the adoption of the EDU model in the BRA, but the empirical evidence (see, e.g., the discussion on the common difference effect) shows that people do make time inconsistent choices.

EDU is the dominant, perhaps the only, model of time discounting in the BRA. However, its psychological foundations are encapsulated in a single parameter, the *discount rate*, θ. P. A. Samuelson (1937, p. 156), who first proposed the EDU model, realized that it is completely arbitrary to assume that individuals behave in accordance with the EDU model, and he expressed reservations about its use for welfare comparisons. He wrote (p. 161): "In conclusion, any connection between utility as discussed here and any welfare concept is disavowed." Despite Samuelson's own reservations, the EDU model is still the dominant model used in economics, particularly in welfare economics.

We now consider some of the violations of the axioms of rationality under time discounting. Consider the violations reported in Thaler (1981). These findings have been confirmed by several subsequent studies; for surveys and potential confounds, see Frederick et al. (2002), Loewenstein (2008), and Dhami (2019c).

1. *Magnitude effect*: Subjects reported being indifferent to $15 received now and $60 in a year's time; $250 received now and $350 received in a year's time; and $3,000 received now and $4,000 in a year's time. EDU would require that in each case, the discount rate must be identical. However, the evidence indicates that larger amounts are more salient, so they are discounted less (i.e., the discount rate is lower for larger outcomes). To calculate the discount rates, we use (2.8): an outcome z received at time t (measured in, say, years) is currently worth $U(z,t) = e^{-\theta t} u(z)$. Let us assume that utility from outcomes is approximately linear, so $u(z) = z$. Then, we can write

$$U(z,t) = e^{-\theta t} z. \tag{2.18}$$

Consider the indifference between $15 received now and $60 in a year's time—that is, $U(15, 0) = U(60, 1)$. Using (2.18), we solve out for θ from $15 = 60 e^{-\theta}$, so $\theta = \ln 4 = 1.386$. The remaining two discount rates can be readily solved to give, respectively, $\theta = 0.336$ and $\theta = 0.29$.[8] Far from being constant, the discount rate declines as magnitudes grow—that is, larger magnitudes are discounted at a lower rate, so they are more salient (magnitude effect). But this is inconsistent with the axioms of rationality, where the discount rate is independent of the magnitudes.

2. *Gain-loss asymmetry*: In one set of choices, subjects had to say what amounts in 1 month, 1 year, and 10 years would make them indifferent to receiving $15, $250, and $3,000 today. In another set of choices, subjects had to reveal what fines in 3 months, 1 year, and 3 years would make them indifferent to being fined $15, $100, and $250 today. These calculations allowed Thaler (1981) to calculate the discount rates for gains and losses. The discount factors for gains turned to be 3–10 times larger than those for losses, so losses were discounted less than gains—that is, losses were more salient. This finding is reminiscent of losses being more salient than gains in static choices (loss aversion). By contrast, in the EDU model, the discount rate must be identical for gains and losses.

3. *Common difference effect*: A violation of the stationarity axiom of rationality under time discounting (axiom B5 in definition 2.6) is known as the common difference effect. This is by far the most studied refutation of the EDU model. When asked how much money in 1 month, 1 year, and 10 years would make them indifferent to receiving $15 now, the median response of subjects was $20, $50, and $100, respectively. We can now use (2.18) to calculate the respective implied annual discount rates to be 3.452, 1.204, and 0.190.[9] Hence, the shorter the horizon, the higher the implied annual discount rate (greater impatience); in contrast,

under EDU, the annual discount rate stays constant, provided we keep fixed the time interval between choices.

Recall the discounted utility model in (2.5), which evaluates the consumption stream $\mathbf{c}_0$ at time $t = 0$: $U(\mathbf{c}_0) = \sum_{t=0}^{T} D(t)u(c_t)$. In order to explain the magnitude effect and gain-loss asymmetry, there are two choices. We either explore further restrictions on the discount function D or restrictions on the instantaneous utility function u, or restrictions on both. The gain-loss asymmetry can be explained by using a utility function u that is more elastic for gains as compared to losses and the magnitude effect, in which we assume that the elasticity of the utility function must increase as the absolute magnitude of outcomes increases (Loewenstein & Prelec, 1992; al-Nowaihi & Dhami, 2008). Al-Nowaihi and Dhami (2009) provide a method for generating utility functions that satisfy these restrictions, which they call the *simple increasing elasticity*, or SIE, class of utility functions. Al-Nowaihi and Dhami (2008) demonstrate that the gain-loss asymmetry can also be explained by assuming that the discount function is different from gains and losses. We know far less about the empirical counterparts of these predictions, which remain an open question: as far as we know, the alternative explanations have not yet been tested.

The common difference effect suggests a taste for immediate gratification. A major thrust of the behavioral time discounting literature is to explain this phenomenon. Lest there be any confusion at this point, we point out that the EDU model also has built-in impatience (see, e.g., axiom B3 in definition 2.6) and, hence, a taste for immediate gratification. However, the empirical evidence on the violation of the common difference effect goes beyond this. It shows that impatience is so serious that it can lead to preference reversals between choices, as in example 2.5.

Example 2.5. *(Thaler's (1981) apples example) It is reasonable to assume that a person will prefer one apple today to two apples tomorrow. The same person will, however, in all likelihood, prefer two apples in 51 days to one apple in 50 days.*

One potential explanation for preference reversals is that individuals might be very impatient at short horizons (high discount rate) and much more patient at longer horizons (low discount rate)—that is, the discount rate itself changes even when a fixed interval of time is moved backward and forward, relative to the current date. By contrast, under the EDU model, the discount rate over a fixed interval is the same, no matter when the interval occurs.

It is straightforward to show that we cannot reconcile example 2.5 with EDU. Let $u(z)$ be the utility from outcome z, and consider the EDU utility function U in (2.4), so that the outcome time pair (z, t) is evaluated under EDU at date $t = 0$ as $U = \delta^t u(z)$. The preference for one apple today to two apples tomorrow implies that

$$u(1) > \delta u(2), \tag{2.19}$$

and the preference for two apples in 51 days to one apple in 50 days implies that $\delta^{50} u(1) < \delta^{51} u(2)$, or

$$u(1) < \delta u(2). \tag{2.20}$$

Obviously, the preference in (2.20) contradicts the preference in (2.19); hence, EDU cannot explain the stated preferences. This preference reversal is a violation of the stationarity axiom (axiom B5 in definition 2.6) because the two outcomes (one apple and two apples) are identical in each case, and the time difference (one day) is also identical in each case. Hence, stationarity would predict identical preferences in the two cases; by contrast, we observe preference reversals.

The evidence for preference reversals comes from several sources. Some of the earliest work to popularize *hyperbolic discounting* and its relation to preference reversals arose in the mid-1970s with articles by George Ainslie and several others; see Ainslie (1992, 2015) for a summary and Dhami (2019c) for a formal treatment. Recall that in (2.5), where we gave the DU model, $D(\tau)$ was the discount function for an outcome received at time $\tau \geq 0$ but evaluated at time $t = 0$. Human and nonhuman subjects (studies were conducted on pigeons in the 1960s) were given the choice between varying rewards with time varying delays. It was found by several researchers that their choices were well described by the *hyperbolic discount function*

$$D(\tau) = \frac{1}{1 + k\tau}; k > 0, \tau > 0, \tag{2.21}$$

where τ is the time delay between the current period, $t = 0$, some future period $\tau > 0$, and $k > 0$ is the single parameter. Using (2.6), we can calculate the implied discount rate at time τ as

$$\theta(\tau) = \frac{k}{1 + k\tau}, \tag{2.22}$$

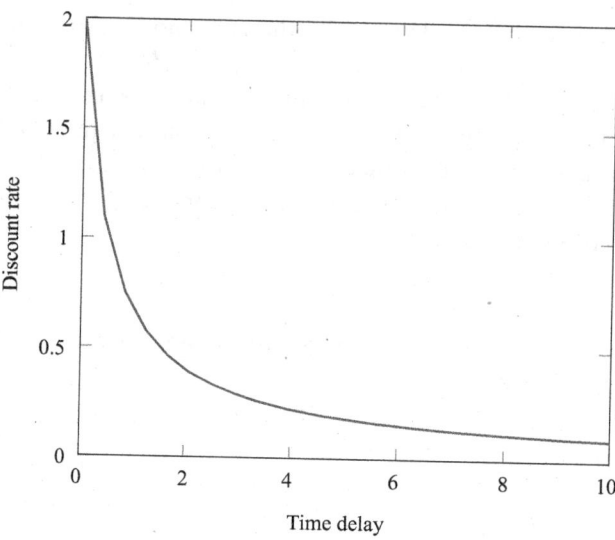

Figure 2.1
The discount rate in (2.21).

which depends on the time τ (through the presence of the term τ on the RHS). Comparing (2.10) and (2.22), we can see that the discount rate under the EDU model is independent of time, but the discount rate under hyperbolic discounting depends on time. Figure 2.1 plots the per period discount rate in (2.22) for the case $k=2$ for a fixed reward, but with varying time delays at which the reward is received.

Under EDU, a per period discount rate is constant for any time delay, while the plot in figure 2.1 shows hyperbolically decreasing per period discount rates. For this reason, the discount function in (2.21) is known as a hyperbolic discount function, and it violates the stationarity axiom under the EDU model. Thus, the shorter the time horizon at which a reward is received, the higher the per period discount rate, so the more impatient the individual. The hyperbolic discount function has also been used extensively, and successfully, in behavioral and experimental psychology to fit animal and human behavior (Logue, 1988). Another natural candidate is the simplest hyperbolic function $D(t) = \frac{1}{t}$, used by Chung and Herrnstein (1967) and Ainslie (1975), but (2.21) gives a better fit to the data.

When decision-makers are given a choice between a *smaller-sooner* (SS) reward and a *larger-later* (LL) reward, they may take actions to remove the SS choice from the menu. This indicates potential awareness of the preference for immediate gratification, hence, removing a tempting option from the menu. Indeed, sometimes individuals may pay others to undertake such a commitment. Such phenomena, while lying outside the scope of this book, are surveyed in Dhami (2019c, 2020c). The important implication for us is that the removal of the SS option cannot be explained by EDU; hence, one or more of the rationality assumptions under time discounting must fail.

Hyperbolic discounting is not the only method of explaining the common difference effect; there are other explanations such as *subadditivity* of the discount function (Dhami, 2019c). Subadditivity implies that the way we split a given interval of time into subintervals influences the extent of discounting.[10]

General and quite flexible forms of the hyperbolic discount function have been proposed (Loewenstein & Prelec, 1992; al-Nowaihi & Dhami, 2006a). However, a popular and tractable representation of hyperbolic discounting is via the *quasi-hyperbolic discounting* function (Phelps and Pollak, 1968; Laibson, 1997), in which time preferences for a consumption stream, $c_0, \ldots, c_T$, are represented by

$$U(c_0, \ldots, c_T) = u(c_0) + \beta \sum_{t=1}^{T} \delta^t u(c_t), \; 0 < \beta < 1. \tag{2.23}$$

In (2.23), other than the presence of the extra parameter, $\beta \in (0, 1)$, the utility function is identical to the EDU model (compare (2.7) and (2.23)). The parameter β shrinks the value of future lifetime discounted utility relative to current utility (given by $u(c_0)$), thereby creating an additional *present bias for current consumption*, or a taste for immediate gratification. This can potentially explain the pattern of choices in example 2.5, as we now show.

Example 2.6. *(explanation of Thaler's example) Let us use quasi-hyperbolic discounting to explain Thaler's (1981) apples example (example 2.5). Let $u(z)$ be the utility from outcome z. Under quasi-hyperbolic discounting, the preference for one apple today to two apples tomorrow implies that*

$$u(1) > \beta \delta u(2). \tag{2.24}$$

The preference for two apples in 51 days to one apple in 50 days implies that

$$u(1) < \delta u(2). \tag{2.25}$$

Notice that in (2.25) the parameter β cancels out on both sides. Together, (2.24) and (2.25) imply that

$$\beta\delta u(2) < u(1) < \delta u(2). \tag{2.26}$$

The inequalities in (2.26) can be consistent with hyperbolic discounting. For instance, for the values of the parameters used in Laibson (1997), $\beta = 0.5, \delta = 0.975$, and an identity utility function, $u(z) = z$, it can be checked that (2.26) is satisfied.

A taste for immediate gratification creates *self-control problems*. Furthermore, if people have imperfect awareness about their future self-control problems, as indicated by the evidence, they may take inadequate preventive measures. This may lead to the *time inconsistency problems* (i.e., choices made now about a future date t need not be optimal when the individual re-optimizes at time t). Time inconsistent choices are considered to be irrational in the BRA, and can never arise under EDU, but evidence suggests that they often occur (Loewenstein, 2008; Dhami, 2019c).

The quasi-hyperbolic framework resolves several problems that are unexplained by the axioms of rationality for time discounting (definition 2.6). Some of these are as follows (for details, see Frederick et al., 2002; Loewenstein, 2008; Dhami, 2019c): Why does consumption track income so closely? Why do individuals undersave for retirement? Why is there a sharp drop in consumption at retirement? Why do individuals hold illiquid assets and credit card debt simultaneously? What causes addictions? Why do some smokers pay more to buy smaller packs of cigarettes or support sales taxes on cigarettes? Why do some people buy annual gym memberships when they could save money by paying on a pay-as-you-go basis?

2.14 Evidence on Rationality in Strategic Interaction

Classical game theory, like other models in the BRA, makes precise and testable predictions. The empirical evidence shows that behavior in the early rounds of games, and in games unfamiliar to the players, is often inconsistent with the predictions. Learning—say, in repeated rounds of an experiment—and experience may or may not produce data consistent with the predictions either (Camerer et al., 2003; Dhami, 2019d, 2020a). Humans make many important decisions only a few times in their lives and experience limited learning opportunities (e.g., choosing a university degree or marriage partner, purchasing a house/consumer durables, or enlisting in a pension plan). Firms also make many important decisions that do not offer many learning opportunities (e.g., capital restructuring, mergers, sunk costs in major machinery and equipment, and the choice to make a new product).

Even in decisions that might be made frequently, the economic environment is ever-changing and uncertain, hence novel. Thus, arguably, the choices made in the early rounds of an experiment are vital to understanding strategic human behavior, yet these choices often do not conform to the predictions of classical game theory. On the other hand, these data are, in many cases, much better explained by *behavioral models of game theory* such as *level-k models, quantal response equilibrium, analogy-based equilibrium, cursed equilibrium, team reasoning,* and *evidential reasoning* (for details see Camerer et al., 2003; Dhami, 2019d).

Understanding the empirical evidence on strategic interaction does require a more sophisticated understanding of classical game theory than the one we provide in section 3.3. By contrast, we have provided enough background material on the relevant economic theory under certainty, risk/uncertainty, and time discounting to be able to lay out the basic evidence in sections 2.9–2.12. Given the interdisciplinary nature of our readership, we feel that it is better to simply summarize some of the evidence on strategic interaction for those readers who have some understanding of classical game theory. Fortunately, comprehensive book-length treatments survey the relevant evidence and the foundational issues that the interested reader can consult (Camerer et al., 2003; Gintis, 2009; Dhami, 2019d). This evidence calls into serious question the rationality assumptions under classical game theory (CGT).

1. In games requiring more than two steps of iterated deletion of dominated strategies, a majority of the players violate the predictions of CGT.
2. Extensive form games and their equivalent normal form representations often elicit different behavioral responses, even when CGT predicts identical responses.
3. The backward induction prediction of CGT in dynamic games of full information is refuted by the evidence, even when subjects highly trained in backward induction play centipede games.
4. Even when the simplest mechanisms are tested in experiments (e.g., the Abreu-Matsushima and the Glazer-Perry mechanisms, which are dominance solvable), the results are not supportive of CGT. This casts doubt on the implementability of more complex mechanisms.

5. Subjects play mixed strategies in experiments, but not in the proportions predicted by a *mixed strategy Nash equilibrium* in CGT. There is some positive evidence from some sports contexts, but there are many confounding factors in such experiments, and it is not clear if motor skills from a sports context have external validity in other economic contexts (e.g., choice of pension plans, choice of savings).

6. In games with multiple equilibria, none of the selection principles in CGT such as *payoff dominance* or *risk dominance* account fully for the data. The equilibria are strongly *history dependent*, and *preplay communication* in the form of promises / verbal pledges enhances coordination in a manner not predicted by CGT.

7. The CGT predictions of alternating-offers bargaining games are not supported by the evidence. When players reject an offer, they often make counteroffers that give them an even lower share (disadvantageous counteroffers). The predictions of bargaining under one-sided asymmetric information in CGT are not supported. But there is surprising and unexplained support for the predictions of two-sided asymmetric information under CGT, which bears further stringent testing before we can be sure. Under unstructured bargaining, which is more realistic, factors unimportant in CGT, such as *self-serving bias*, explain *bargaining impasse* under full information.

8. The pattern of searches and lookups in Rubinstein's alternative-offer bargaining game using the Mouselab software does not support the predictions of CGT.

9. In signaling games, there is no support for the predictions of CGT beyond the Cho-Kreps *intuitive criterion*.

10. In many experiments on games that have at least one Nash equilibrium, the choices made by the subjects are sensitive to the out-of-equilibrium payoffs. Increasing the out-of-equilibrium payoffs makes the corresponding non-Nash strategies less likely to be chosen. Yet, CGT predicts no such effects because these changes have no bearing on the Nash equilibria of the game. Behavioral game theory models can potentially explain these phenomena through two different kinds of models.

(a) The quantal response equilibrium explains this data by noisy best replies, so all strategies by a player have some probability of being played, and the probability of play depends on how high the payoffs are from that strategy.

(b) In level-k and cognitive hierarchy models, although players play a best response to beliefs, the level-0 players might play nonequilibrium actions, and others best respond to them. The rationality requirements in these models are more reasonable as compared to models of quantal response equilibrium.

11. There is evidence that several emotions such as guilt-aversion, surprise-seeking, and anger directly enter into the utility functions of players and influence equilibrium play. Players often try to infer the intentions behind the actions of others. These findings run counter to the framework of CGT, which does not allow beliefs to directly enter into the utility functions and forms the subject matter of the promising approach of *psychological game theory* within the ambit of behavioral economics.

Solution concepts in CGT rely on the twin concepts of (1) *methodological individualism* (all social and economic phenomena are the results of individual choices and actions) and (2) *instrumental rationality* (individuals use all possible means at their disposal to achieve their ends, e.g., utility maximization). An alternative framework, motivated by the inability of CGT to account for the data on strategic interaction, pursues radically different solution concepts that are based on *social rationality* (Gintis, 2017, p. 51; Dhami, 2019d, section 3.1). This overarching concept includes *team reasoning* but also Tomasello's concept of *joint intentionality* (Tomasello, 2014).

Joint intentionality implies that players have a shared common goal and common knowledge of trust in each other to implement the shared goal. In other words, players are able to collaborate, not just coordinate, independently of instrumental reciprocity. A related concept whose implications are being increasingly discussed in behavioral economics is *Kantian rationality* (Roemer, 2015, 2018). In the Kantian protocol, *players wish to take actions that they would like the other players to take*. Social rationality is then invoked to argue that players believe that other players will also take the same action. This obviously requires players to trust the social rationality of other players. Furthermore, players do not take such actions because they fear reprisals from other players but rather *because it is the moral thing to do*. This opens a completely new perspective in game theory, including why players cooperate in the prisoner's dilemma game (see section 4.7).

2.15 Do Humans Follow the Rules of Mathematical Statistics?

Central to the BRA is the supposition that humans effortlessly follow all the rules of classical statistics, including the recent advances in statistical theory, or act as if they did. We stress again that this is a central, not an auxiliary, assumption in economics. It is somewhat ironic that it takes great effort to teach the relevant statistical theory to economics students, yet not all receive a perfect grade.

The BRA makes a similar assumption about the ability of humans to effortlessly use modern mathematics. For instance, dynamic programming was developed by Richard Bellman in the 1950s. This is now the central method that is used in the BRA to solve problems involving choices over time. Some economists will, of course, protest and argue that they are not literally assuming that humans knowingly use mathematics and statistics. Rather, humans act as if they could effortlessly use modern mathematics and statistical theory. Our discussion in section 3.5 in chapter 3 will show that this view draws its inspiration from the work of Milton Friedman on methodology. We also offer an evaluation of this view.

This as-if argument is a testable hypothesis, and all the evidence indicates that humans are not intuitively good mathematicians and statisticians; not everyone in school, for instance, discovers that they are naturals at these subjects. There should be no presumption that the evolutionary development of humans would have produced in us the capacity to reason like mathematicians and statisticians. Indeed, the work of Daniel Kahneman and Amos Tversky in the 1970s refuted the notion that most humans act as if they could use modern mathematics and statistical theory. But this has had little effect in economics, certainly in courses in economic theory, that continue to maintain that the as-if assumption is true by definition wherever it is applied, but no evidence is cited to justify it. No natural science takes such a position.

In this section, we focus on two main themes. First, how do people view/construct probability distributions? Second, how do people update their prior beliefs in the face of new information? In the BRA, the maintained assumption is that humans use Bayes' rule, or simple variants of it. But the evidence does not support this assumption. However, these two topics comprise only a small subset of mathematical statistics. We continue our discussion of this theme in chapters 5 and 6.

2.15.1 Biases in Producing a Full Sampling Distribution

One test of the statistical sophistication of individuals is to see how well they understand basic properties of sampling distributions. For instance, one might ask individuals to produce a sampling distribution based on different sample sizes.[11] Consider the following basic result in statistics (we give a formal statement of this result in chapter 5). Suppose that we have a random sample of size N and that each set of observations $x_1, \ldots, x_N$ is drawn from independent and identically distributed random variables, $X_1, \ldots, X_N$, each of which has mean μ and finite variance σ^2. Then, before we draw the actual sample, the sample mean $\bar{x}(N) = \sum_{i=1}^{n} x_i/N$ is a random variable and has a sampling distribution. As the sample size increases, the sample mean $\bar{x}(N)$ gets closer and closer to the population mean μ, and the sampling distribution of $\bar{x}(N)$ has variance σ^2/N, which keeps shrinking as the sample size N increases.

The evidence indicates that individuals do not adequately take account of the properties of $\bar{x}(N)$ as the sample size N increases, provided the sample size is not too small—say, roughly not less than 10. Most people produce sampling distributions that are nearly identical for small and for large values of the sample size. In particular, individuals demonstrate limited awareness that the variance of the sampling distribution of the sample mean is σ^2/N and should shrink with an increase in sample size. As Kahneman and Tversky (1972b, p. 437) put it in the context of the representativeness heuristic (see chapter 5): "Thus, the event of finding more than 600 boys in a sample of 1,000 babies, for example, is as representative as the event of finding more than 60 boys in a sample of 100 babies. The two events, therefore, would be judged equally probable, although the latter, in fact, is vastly more likely."

Consider the following modern reproduction of the problem originally outlined in Kahneman and Tversky (1972b). Suppose that we toss a fair coin and consider the random variable that takes binary outcomes, heads or tails. For different values of $N = 10, 100, 1000$, subjects are asked to state the percentage of heads in the sample for 11 bin sizes (0%–5%, 5%–10%, ..., 95%–100%). For instance, for $N = 100$, the subjects are asked: How likely is it that there are 0%–5% heads in 100 tosses of the coin; 5%–10% heads in 100 tosses; and so on up to the 11th bin size of 95%–100% heads in 100 tosses? Once done, they are asked to repeat this exercise for other sample sizes.

Figure 2.2 shows the relevant data. The statistically correct distribution for each sample size $N = 10, 100, 1000$ is shown by the dotted curves. The variance of these distributions shrinks with an increase in the sample size. The median beliefs for each of the bins and for different sample sizes, $N = 10, 100, 1000$, are shown as different-colored histograms. In contrast to the statistically correct distribution, the variance of the estimated distributions stays the same; subjects do not appear to take account of the fact that the sampling variance of the distributions shrinks with an increase in N. For any bin size, there is not much to differentiate the beliefs for any sample size. One implication is that the tails of the estimated distribution

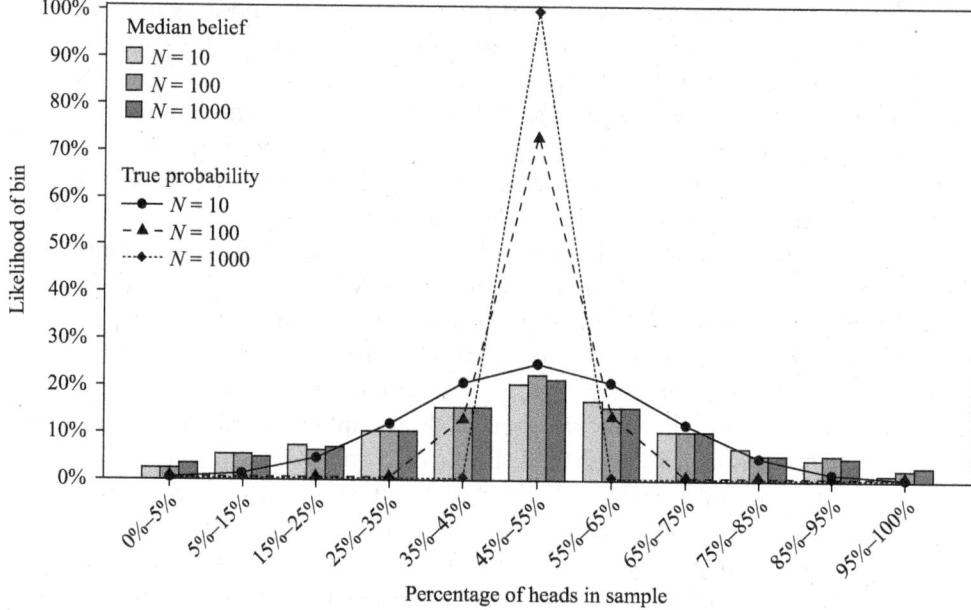

Figure 2.2
Sample size neglect for samples of 10, 100, 1000.
Source: Benjamin (2018).

are too fat relative to the true distribution, even for $N = 1000$. In applications in finance, fat tails imply that subjects might give too much attention to extreme returns. Indeed, the pricing of assets might reflect such beliefs (Barberis & Huang, 2008).

Subadditivity is an important issue in time discounting and in choices under risk. The basic idea is that time discounting over an interval depends on how that interval is split up; see Dhami (2019c) for a formalization. In particular, a time interval is discounted less when it is not broken up into its constituent parts (subadditivity). Under exponential discounted utility, breaking an interval into its constituent parts does not alter discounting. Under risk, Tversky and Koehler (1994) discuss the following issue of subadditivity in probabilities. Suppose that individuals need to assign a probability to an event. Then, the basic idea is that the assigned probability depends on how the event is unpacked. For instance, suppose that the event is homicide in an area over a time period. Subadditivity in probabilities arises when people assign a lower overall probability of homicide relative to the sum of the individual probabilities of its two constituent parts, (1) homicide caused by strangers and

(2) homicide caused by acquaintances. Statistically, and under the BRA, the two probabilities should be identical.

If we accept the evidence on subadditivity in probabilities, then different splits of the domain of a random variable (e.g., assigning different bins for the data in figure 2.2) may alter the elicited probability distribution leading to a violation of statistical theory. In their experiments with MBA students at Duke University, Clemen and Ulu (2008) asked subjects to assess the probability of temperatures in degrees Celsius, denoted by x, in Durham, NC, for different splits of the domain of temperatures. In the low partition condition, the set of possible temperatures was $x \leq 18$, $18 < x \leq 20$, $20 < x \leq 22$, $x > 22$. In the high partition condition, it was $x \leq 22$, $22 < x \leq 24$, $24 < x \leq 26$, $x > 26$. If the subjects used statistical theory correctly, then they would need to satisfy the following two axioms of probability.

1. The sum of probabilities across all bins in each partition condition must equal one; this turned out to be true for 115/145 subjects.
2. For each of the splits, six straightforward additivity conditions like the following must hold:

$$P(x \leq 22) = P(x \leq 18) + P(18 < x \leq 22). \tag{2.27}$$

It was found that 54.5 percent subjects satisfied all six, 23.4 percent satisfied 0–1 conditions; and 20 percent satisfied 2–5 conditions. Thus, about 45 percent of the subjects failed on at least one of the additivity conditions. In the low partition condition, the median estimate of $P(x \leq 22)$ was 42 percent and in the high partition condition it was 10 percent. Thus, different partitions of the domain of the random variable led to different estimates of probabilities for what was essentially the same split of the random variable; this violated correct statistical inference.

Subadditivity in probabilities challenges the notion that people may have well-defined probability judgments over events. It is similar to the problem of preference reversals that challenge the notion that individuals have a well-defined utility function. If different empirical studies use different partitions of the domain of the relevant random variable, then, under subadditivity, it is difficult to compare results across the studies. Finally, given that experimental researchers often stress the external validity of their results, this raises the question of what sort of typical partitions of the domain of random variables do people normally encounter or use in real life.[12]

2.15.2 Do People Use Bayes' Law?

Suppose that we have n mutually exclusive random variables $X_1, X_2, \ldots, X_n$ such that the sample space $X = X_1 \cup X_2 \cup \ldots \cup X_n$. For any event $A \subseteq X$ such that $P(A) > 0$, we would like to find the probability of X_i conditional on the event A having occurred: $P(X_i \mid A)$. Bayes' rule provides us with the following calculation, which uses the simple laws of conditional probabilities,

$$P(X_i \mid A) = \frac{P(A \mid X_i) P(X_i)}{P(A)} = \frac{P(A \mid X_i) P(X_i)}{\sum_{j=1}^{n} P(A \mid X_j) P(X_j)}. \tag{2.28}$$

In (2.28), $P(X_i)$ and $P(A)$ are referred to as the *base rates*.

An important empirical finding is that in calculating $P(X_i \mid A)$, individuals neglect to take full account of base rates.[13] Consider the following well-known *cab problem* introduced by Kahneman and Tversky (1972b); modified versions of this problem were subsequently studied by Bar-Hillel (1980) and Tversky and Kahneman (1980).

Example 2.7. *(The cab problem) There are only two cab companies in the city, Green and Blue; 85 percent of the cabs are Green. There was an accident last night. A witness comes forward to testify that the cab involved in the accident was Blue. In similar conditions, the reliability of the witness is 80 percent—that is, the probability that the witness incorrectly identifies the cab is 20 percent. What is the probability that the actual cab involved in the accident was Blue? The median and modal response was a probability of 80 percent, which is also the probability with which the witness correctly identifies a Blue cab as the one involved in the accident.*

In contrast to the subjects' responses, the statistically correct answer is 41.4 percent. To see this, define the events $X_1 =$ Blue cab and $X_2 =$ Green cab, and let the event "identification by the witness that the cab is Blue" be A. Then, using (2.28),

$$P(X_1 \mid A) = \frac{P(A \mid X_1) P(X_1)}{P(A \mid X_1) P(X_1) + P(A \mid X_2) P(X_2)}. \tag{2.29}$$

Using $P(A \mid X_1) = 0.8$ (probability of a correct identification), $P(A \mid X_2) = 0.2$ (probability of an incorrect identification), $P(X_1) = 0.15$ (base rate), and $P(X_2) = 0.85$ (base rate) we get the statistically correct answer, $P(X_1 \mid A) = 0.414$.

What accounts for the enormous difference between the median of the subject responses and the statistically correct answer? Individuals appear to underweight base rates—that is, the fact that only 15 percent of the taxis are actually Blue. The neglect of base rates reduces when greater salience is given to base rates in the design of experiments, but it does not disappear (Ajzen, 1977; Bar-Hillel, 1980).[14]

The reader might wonder if subjects with potentially greater cognitive ability conform to Bayes' law. The next example shows that this is not the case.

Example 2.8. *(Casscells et al., 1978) Consider the following problem, a variant of which was given to students at Harvard Medical School. Suppose that a police Breathalyzer test discovers false drunkenness in 5 percent of the cases when the driver is sober. However, the Breathalyzers are always able to detect a truly drunk person with complete certainty. In the general population, 1/1000 of drivers engage in driving while drunk. Suppose that a driver is checked at random and takes a Breathalyzer test, which shows that the driver is drunk. How high is the probability the driver really is drunk? The modal response was 95 percent, the mean response was 56 percent, and a sixth of the students gave the correct answer, which is approximately 2 percent. Thus, subjects with high cognitive and analytical abilities also underweight the base rate in relatively simple problems.*

Ajzen (1977) distinguishes between *causal* and *incidental* base rates. A causal base rate conveys information on some causal factors relevant to the problem, while incidental base rates do not. There is greater conformity with Bayes' law when base rates are causal, as shown in the following variant of the cab problem.

Example 2.9. *(Modified cab problem; Kahneman, 2011) There are only two cab companies in the city, Green and Blue, who own an equal number of cabs. Eighty-five percent of the cabs involved in accidents are Green. The rest of this problem is identical to the earlier cab problem following the instruction: "There was an accident last night...." This and the earlier cab problem are mathematically equivalent. Yet, one finds that subjects give more attention to the base rate in the second problem. The median response that the cab involved in the accident was Blue is 0.60, closer to the statistically correct answer of 0.41.*

The difference in answers in the original cab problem and the modified cab problem arises because base rates are incidental in the former and causal in the latter. Under causal base rates, the information given in the description of the problem suggests that drivers of Green cabs are particularly reckless. Hence, the individual assigns a lower probability to Blue cabs being involved in the accident, which reduces their tendency to underweight the base rate of Blue cabs.

Subsequent research has highlighted other factors that play an important role in increasing conformity with Bayes' law. These include combining information on base rates with other noncausal information (Bar-Hillel, 1980); instructing subjects to think like statisticians rather than like clinical psychologists (Schwarz et al. 1991); using individuals with higher measured intelligence (Stanovich & West, 2000); drawing attention to the different computations required in a Bayes' rule calculation (Girotto & Gonzalez, 2001); presenting the information in a diagram that highlights the set inclusion principle (Sloman et al., 2003). However, in the real world, these artificial cues that draw attention to the correct calculation using Bayes' law are unlikely to be available.

It has been claimed that presenting the information in a *frequency format* rather than a *probability format* (e.g., 10 in 100 rather than 10%) reduces base rate neglect. An evolutionary account has also been suggested (Brase, 2002b; Cosmides & Tooby, 1996; Gigerenzer & Hoffrage, 1995; Pinker, 1997).[15] In the *mind as a Swiss army knife view*, the brain consists of several modules. Each module is responsible for a specific set of functions and is not under the voluntary control of the individual. In this view, there is a specific module, with evolutionary origins, designed to process natural frequencies but not probabilities (Cosmides & Tooby, 1996; Gigerenzer & Selten, 2001a). A related view, which does not assume a modular structure for the brain but which is similar for all practical purposes, is that the brain has a *natural frequency algorithm* (Gigerenzer & Hoffrage, 1995). A natural advantage of the frequency format is that it makes transparent the sample size and the subset relation between two sets (e.g., 1 out of every 100 women have breast cancer). Barbey and Sloman (2007) take a system 1 and system 2 view of the brain and propose that a frequency format is more consistent with the natural inputs required by system 2 to process information.

Presenting the information in a frequency format appears to improve compliance with Bayes' law, but even in the most favorable results, the majority of people do not conform to Bayes' law; see table 2.1. The second column in table 2.1 shows that conformity with Bayes' law is poor when

Table 2.1
Percentage of responses consistent with Bayes' rule. Sample sizes in parentheses.

Study	Probability format	Frequency format
Casscells et al. (1978)	18(60)	—
Cosmides & Tooby (1996, Exp. 2)	12(25)	72(25)
Eddy (1982)	5(100)	—
Evans et al. (2000, Exp. 1)	24(42)	35(43)
Gigerenzer (1996b)	10(48)	46(48)
Gigerenzer & Hoffrage (1995)	16(30)	46(30)
Macchi (2000)	6(30)	40(30)
Sloman et al. (2003, Exp. 1)	20(25)	51(45)
Sloman et al. (2003, Exp. 1b)	—	31(48)

Source: Barbey and Sloman (2007).

the problem is presented in a probability format. Conformity improves in the third column, where the information is presented in a frequency format. The Cosmides and Tooby (1996) result could not be replicated by Sloman et al. (2003) or Evans et al. (2000).

On a closer examination, there are confounding factors that overplay the success of the frequency format; see discussion in section 5.11.5. The frequency format is also often used in conjunction with monetary incentives and the high ability level of subjects (e.g., students at top universities). In the presence of these confounding factors, we may obtain statistically significant differences in the facilitation role of natural frequencies (Brase et al., 2006). But this casts doubt on the evolutionary explanation, which lies at the heart of the facilitating role of the frequency format. Rather, these results are suggestive of the relation between cognitive effort and cognitive ability with the facilitation role of natural frequencies.

Along with the frequency format, the experimental instructions sometimes make the set inclusion relation too obvious relative to the probability format. When the set inclusion principle is not made too obvious, the facilitation role of natural frequencies drops significantly (Girotto & Gonzalez, 2001). Brase (2002a) finds that the probability and the frequency format are both perceived by subjects to be equally clear except when the probabilities are very low (see chapter 4). This result—that the probability format is perceived as equally clear—is difficult to reconcile with the claimed facilitating role of the frequency format.

Based on the evidence, the case for the frequency format reversing or eliminating base rate neglect is weak, although it might reduce base rate neglect.

2.15.3 Conservatism

Another departure of human behavior from the prescription of statistical theory is *conservatism*, or the *underweighting of the likelihood of a sample* (contrast this with underweighting of base rates).

Consider the following problem in Camerer (1995), originally due to Edwards (1968). Suppose that there are two urns A and B, each of which contains only red and blue balls. Urn A has 7 red and 3 blue balls and urn B has 3 red and 7 blue balls. A sample of 12 balls is drawn *with replacement* from one of the urns. Subjects do not know which urn was chosen to draw the balls from. But they do know that each urn was equally likely to be chosen—that is, $P(A) = 0.5$ and $P(B) = 0.5$.

Denote the number of red balls in a sample of size 12 by $x \in \{0, 1, \ldots, 12\}$. Consider the sample 8 red and 4 blue balls, which does not equal the exact proportions in any of the two urns. Hence, individuals cannot directly invoke the representativeness heuristic (we define this in chapter 5). Let p_A and p_B be the respective probabilities of drawing a red ball from urns A and B. The statistically correct prediction that the sample of 8 red and 4 blue balls came from urn A is $P(A \mid x = 8) = 0.967$. Here is how it is calculated.

Using the binomial distribution, the conditional probability of drawing x red balls in a sample of 12 balls from urn $i = A, B$ is

$$P(x \mid i) = \binom{12}{x} p_i^x (1 - p_i)^{12-x}; i = A, B \text{ and } x \in \{0, 1, \ldots, 12\}. \quad (2.30)$$

The Bayesian posterior belief that the sample came from urn A is given by

$$P(A \mid x = 8) = \frac{P(x = 8 \mid A) P(A)}{P(x = 8 \mid A) P(A) + P(x = 8 \mid B) P(B)}. \quad (2.31)$$

We already know that $P(A) = 0.5$, $P(B) = 0.5$. Since the respective probabilities of drawing a red ball from urns A and B are respectively, $p_A = 0.7$, $p_B = 0.3$, we get from (2.30) that $P(x = 8 \mid A) = 0.231$, $P(x = 8 \mid B) = 0.008$. Substituting these numbers in (2.31), we get that $P(A \mid x = 8) = 0.967$.

However, the typical response in experiments is that $P(A\,|\,x=8) \approx$ 0.7–0.8. Hence, subjects in experiments appear too conservative about sample likelihoods. The seemingly contradictory phenomena of base rate neglect and conservatism of sample was reconciled in a seminal paper by Griffin and Tversky (1992); the interested reader can read the details in Benjamin (2018) and Dhami (2020a).

2.15.4 A Modification of Bayes' Law

There have been several attempts to modify Bayes' law in order to provide a better explanation of the evidence. We outline some of these attempts here.

Suppose that there are two urns, $i = A, B$, and one is chosen randomly by nature. Each of the urns has a mixture of red balls and black balls, but in different proportions. In a single random draw of a ball from each urn, which we call a signal, S, suppose that we classify the event "success" as the draw of a red ball and the event "failure" as the draw of a black ball. Let the objective probability of success for urns A and B be, respectively, θ_A and θ_B. In N multiple draws of a ball from each urn, the balls are drawn *with replacement*; thus, N is the sample size. Subjects in experiments do not know which urn the balls are drawn from. However, it is common knowledge that nature chooses urns A and B with respective probabilities $p(A)$ and $p(B)$.

Throughout this section, we denote objective probabilities by p and subjective probabilities by q. From Bayes' law, we know that in a single random draw of the ball, giving rise to the signal, S, the conditional probability of urn $i = A, B$ is given by

$$p(i\,|\,S) = \frac{p(S\,|\,i)p(i)}{p(S\,|\,A)p(A) + p(S\,|\,B)p(B)}, \, i = A, B, \qquad (2.32)$$

where the denominator is $p(S)$. The signal S can arise in two different ways. Either nature chooses urn A with probability $p(A)$ (first term in the denominator) or urn B with probability $p(B)$ (second term in the denominator). Using (2.32) to divide $p(A\,|\,S)$ by $p(B\,|\,S)$, we get

$$\frac{p(A\,|\,S)}{p(B\,|\,S)} = \left[\frac{p(S\,|\,A)}{p(S\,|\,B)}\right]\left[\frac{p(A)}{p(B)}\right]. \qquad (2.33)$$

A decision-maker who follows the rules of classical statistics must satisfy (2.33).

From section 2.15.2, we know that the empirical evidence shows that the majority of subjects violate Bayes' law. In order to model departures from Bayes' law, we follow Grether (1980) in rewriting (2.33) in the modified form

$$\frac{q(A\mid S)}{q(B\mid S)} = \left[\frac{p(S\mid A)}{p(S\mid B)}\right]^a \left[\frac{p(A)}{p(B)}\right]^b, \tag{2.34}$$

where q denotes the decision-maker's subjective probabilistic beliefs, as compared to p, which denotes objective probabilistic beliefs. The parameters a, b are misperception parameters that are possibly heterogenous across individuals. An individual who uses statistical theory correctly (i.e., in this case, satisfies Bayes' law) will satisfy $a = b = 1$; for such an individual, we have $\frac{q(A\mid S)}{q(B\mid S)} = \frac{p(A\mid S)}{p(B\mid S)}$. Suppose that we could somehow use data on the choices made by individuals and form estimates of the parameters a, b. Denote the respective estimates by $\hat{a}, \hat{b}$. The case $\hat{a} < 1$ is termed as *underinference* (and $\hat{a} > 1$ as overinference), while the case $\hat{b} < 1$ is termed as *base rate neglect* (and its opposite, $\hat{b} > 1$, as base rate overuse).

We give below a summary of the estimates $\hat{a}, \hat{b}$ in empirical studies. However, it is important to give a caveat first in the following remark, which is missed in most of the literature.

Remark 2.1. *(Dhami, 2020a) In (2.34), we have a very specific functional form for the departure from Bayes' law that allows us to recover Bayes' law as a special case ($a = b = 1$). In actual practice, some individuals might follow yet another form of Bayes' law that does not collapse to the correct form of Bayes' law in (2.33) for any parameter values. Suppose, for instance, that an individual uses the subjective rule*

$$\frac{q(A\mid S)}{q(B\mid S)} = \left[\frac{p(S\mid A) - \varepsilon_1}{p(S\mid B) - \eta_1}\right]\left[\frac{p(A) - \varepsilon_2}{p(B) - \eta_2}\right],$$

where $\varepsilon_1, \varepsilon_2, \eta_1,$ and η_2 are individual-specific real numbers, such that the individual follows Bayes' law if $\varepsilon_1 = \varepsilon_2 = \eta_1 = \eta_2 = 0$. Still other individuals might be using any of the fast and frugal heuristics that we consider later in the book, or a combination of these heuristics. Or some individuals might simply ignore very small probabilities, or use attribute-based models (see chapter 4). The estimates $\hat{a}, \hat{b}$ derived in the literature have the maintained assumption that everyone, without exception, follows (2.34) and no other decision rule is used. Yet, if there is the sort of heterogeneity in decision rules that we refer to in this remark, then the estimated parameters for a and b could be telling us very little.

If the observations above are accepted, then the most favorable interpretation of the estimates $\hat{a}, \hat{b}$ is as follows. If $\hat{a} = \hat{b} = 1$, then we tentatively accept that the behavior of individuals conforms to Bayes' law (yet this might be rejected by future observations). If $\hat{a} \neq 1$ or $\hat{b} \neq 1$, then we cannot infer anything so that inferences of overinference and base rate neglect from these studies are, strictly speaking, not warranted and require further tests.

With the important caveat in remark 2.1, the results of the meta study of 16 studies by Benjamin (2018) are as follows. Consider symmetric updating problems, where $\theta_A = 1 - \theta_B = \theta$ (i.e., the probability of a red ball from urn A is identical to the probability of a black ball from urn B); θ is termed as the diagnosticity parameter. Taking logs on both sides of (2.34),

$$\ln\left[\frac{q(A\mid S)}{q(B\mid S)}\right] = a\ln\left[\frac{p(S\mid A)}{p(S\mid B)}\right] + b\ln\left[\frac{p(A)}{p(B)}\right]. \tag{2.35}$$

In order to estimate this equation, we can conduct the following two kinds of experiments.

1. A single draw of a ball ($n = 1$) from an unknown urn, and the data are collected from many individuals. In this case, the signal S is a single number (success or failure to draw a red ball).
2. Multiple draws of the ball ($N > 1$) with replacement from an unknown urn, and the data are collected from many individuals, in which case the signal S is a sequence of N numbers and each number is a success or failure to draw a red ball in a single draw.

The meta study contains both sorts of studies. If we restrict attention to the case of equal priors, $p(A) = p(B)$, then (2.33) implies that $\frac{p(S|A)}{p(S|B)} = \frac{p(A|S)}{p(B|S)}$, so using (2.35), and noting that $\ln 1 = 0$, we are required to estimate

$$\ln\left[\frac{q(A\mid S)}{q(B\mid S)}\right] = a\ln\left[\frac{p(A\mid S)}{p(B\mid S)}\right].$$

In the meta study, we find that $\hat{a} = 0.20 < 1$. If we further restrict the sample of studies to contain only incentivized studies, then the estimate is $\hat{a} = 0.38 < 1$. Hence, the data indicate underinference. The finding of underinference contrasts with casual empirical evidence that people often appear to jump to conclusions in real life. An increase in the sample size, N, reduces $\hat{a}$ (underinference is greater in larger samples). A value of $\theta > 0.5$ reduces $\hat{a}$ (underinference is greater when the diagnosticity parameter is high). We also find underinference when $N = 1$. If, on the other hand, we relax the restriction $p(A) = p(B)$ and estimate (2.35) but restrict $a = 1$, then the meta study gives $\hat{b} < 1$; this is the finding of base rate neglect in section 2.15.2.

For a formal model of sample size neglect, see Benjamin et al. (2018). Alternatives to the use of Bayes' law have been studied in economics. These include incorrect models of the world (Barberis et al., 1998; Rabin & Schrag, 1999); categorical thinking (Mullainathan, 2002; Mullainathan et al., 2008); and limited memory/recall (Gennaioli & Shleifer, 2010; Bordalo et al., 2016). However, these models do not explain departures from Bayesian updating when experiments clearly specify the prior probabilities and these are easy to refer to and recall during the experiment. Motivated by this problem, C. Zhao (2018) postulates, following Tversky and Kahneman (1974), that when decision-makers are asked to compute conditional probabilities $p(A \mid B)$, they substitute it by the potentially easier question: How similar or representative is A to B? For a simple model along these lines, see Dhami (2020a, chapter 4).

2.16 Appendix: A Primer on Decision Theory

In this appendix, we provide a brief and relatively gentle introduction to basic decision theory. We give a relatively nontechnical discussion at a basic level. However, we also provide sufficient exposure to the basic framework so that even the uninitiated can, hopefully, understand parts of this book that deal with risk and uncertainty. For an advanced treatment and applications, the more technically equipped reader can consult Kahneman and Tversky (2000), Wakker (2010), and Dhami (2019a).

The basic unit of analysis in decision theory is a *lottery*, which is a simple way of summarizing a risky or an uncertain situation. Consider, for instance, the lottery L,

$$L = (x_1, p_1; x_2, p_2; \ldots; x_n, p_n), \tag{2.36}$$

where $x_1 < x_2 < \ldots < x_n$ are n outcomes and $p_1, p_2, \ldots, p_n$ are the respective probabilities corresponding to these outcomes such that probabilities are nonnegative and sum up to one—that is, $p_i \in [0, 1]$, $i = 1, \ldots, n$, and $\sum_{i=1}^{n} p_i = 1$. Assume that the probabilities are either objectively known (risk) or subjectively known (uncertainty). How do decision-makers evaluate such lotteries?

It could be that decision-makers use a range of heuristics to evaluate such lotteries. For instance, *attribute-based models* (see chapter 4) view the lottery L as consisting of the outcome attributes $(x_1, x_2, \ldots, x_n)$ and the probability attributes $(p_1, p_2, \ldots, p_n)$. In comparing two lotteries, the decision-maker then compares the two attributes in each lottery using some rule that specifies the order in which the attributes are considered. For instance, a decision-maker may compare just the highest and the lowest outcome levels in each lottery and the associated probabilities. Then, the decision-maker may use simple threshold rules (e.g., that the outcome differences and the probability differences exceed a given threshold) to make the decision. Or, in other theories, the decision-makers could be particularly influenced by their emotional states and the salience of the attributes in making decisions (as in Loewenstein's *risk as feelings* hypothesis in section 4.1). We postpone a discussion of these theories to chapter 4.

In this appendix, we are interested in optimization-based approaches such as expected utility, rank dependent utility, and prospect theory. Since these theories require the decision-maker to engage in nontrivial calculations, we may think of these theories as as-if theories (see section 3.5). This, however, does not disqualify such theories for consideration (see discussion in section 3.2). There are good as-if theories that are broadly consistent with the evidence (prospect theory is the most prominent example) and some as if theories that are rejected by the weight of the evidence (expected utility theory is an example). We consider these theories next.

2.16.1 Expected Utility Theory

Expected utility theory (EU) is the main theory of decision-making under risk in the BRA. We discuss its axiomatic foundations and the evidence for it in sections 2.5 and 2.12. Here, we summarize its main features. A decision-maker who follows EU evaluates the lottery L in (2.36) as follows,

$$EU(L) = \sum_{i=1}^{n} p_i u(x_i), \qquad (2.37)$$

where $u(x_i)$ is the utility of outcome x_i. A special case of EU arises when $u(x_i) = x_i$, in which case (2.37) gives the calculation for expected value, $\sum_{i=1}^{n} p_i x_i$. However, the expected value criterion leads to the well-known *St. Petersburg paradox*, which led to the development of EU. A discussion

Example 2.10. *Consider the two-outcome lottery $L_1 = (4, 0.4; 16, 0.6)$ that offers a payoff of 4 with a 40 percent chance and a payoff of 16 with a 60 percent chance. Suppose that the utility function for outcomes is $u(x) = \sqrt{x}$. Then, $EU(L_1) = 0.4\sqrt{4} + 0.6\sqrt{16} = 3.2$. If the decision-maker were to be given another lottery, say, $L_2 = (0, 0.4; 25, 0.6)$, then it is worth $EU(L_2) = 0.4\sqrt{0} + 0.6\sqrt{25} = 3.0$. Since $EU(L_2) < EU(L_1)$, the decision-maker prefers L_1 over L_2.*

We take this opportunity to introduce another concept, that of a *certainty equivalent*. Suppose that a decision-maker faces the lottery L, which obviously imposes a risk due to the probabilistic nature of outcomes. Suppose that the decision-maker is asked, "What monetary outcome C_L, received for sure (i.e., a lottery of form $(C_L, 1)$), would you accept so that you are indifferent to facing the lottery L and accepting the sure amount $(C_L, 1)$? This sure amount, C_L, is the certainty equivalent of the lottery L. We record this in a formal definition for future use.

Definition 2.8. *(Certainty equivalent) Given any lottery L, an outcome C_L, received for sure, such that the decision-maker is indifferent to the two lotteries $(C_L, 1)$ and L, is known as the certainty equivalent of the lottery L.*

If we evaluate the lottery L using expected utility theory, as in (2.37), then the certainty equivalent, denoted by C_L, is found by solving the one equation in one unknown—that is, $EU(L) = u(C_L)$, or equivalently

$$\sum_{i=1}^{n} p_i u(x_i) = u(C_L). \tag{2.38}$$

In other decision theories, such as rank dependent utility and prospect theory, we use a different formula to evaluate the lottery L. This changes the calculation on the LHS of (2.38); hence, the certainty equivalent is also different. For instance, if we denote the prospect theory evaluation of lottery L by $PT(L)$, and if the utility function under prospect theory is given by v (instead of u; see reasons in section 2.16.4), then the certainty equivalent under prospect theory, C_L, is the solution to the equation

$$PT(L) = v(C_L). \tag{2.39}$$

There is no presumption that the solutions to the certainty equivalents in (2.38) and (2.39) are identical because their left-hand sides are different. Denote the expected value of the lottery L by E_L (by definition, $E_L = \sum_{i=1}^{n} p_i x_i$). Armed with the two numbers C_L and E_L, we can now determine the *attitudes to risk* of a decision-maker (e.g., whether the decision-maker is risk averse, risk loving, or risk neutral) under any decision theory.

Definition 2.9. *A decision-maker is risk neutral if $C_L = E_L$; risk averse if $C_L < E_L$; and risk loving if $C_L > E_L$.*

Attitudes to risk play a major role in answering a range of questions in economics, such as why individuals buy, or avoid, many different kinds of insurance; why individuals might insure and gamble at the same time; how extended families share or pool risks; how networks of individuals mitigate risks; how a firm should design its optimal incentive scheme if its workers are risk averse; and how the government provides insurance through social welfare schemes. As such, finding the numbers C_L and E_L often provides the basis on which the answers to these questions are formulated.

Example 2.11. *Let us consider the basic setup in example 2.10. A decision-maker faces the lottery $L = (4, 0.4; 16, 0.6)$ and has the utility function $u(x) = \sqrt{x}$, $x \geq 0$. We can then compute $E_L = 0.4(4) + 0.6(16) = 11.2$ and $EU(L) = 0.4\sqrt{4} + 0.6\sqrt{16} = 3.2$. The certainty equivalent is solved using (2.38); hence, it is the solution to the equation $EU(L) = \sqrt{C_L}$, or $3.2 = \sqrt{C_L}$, so $C_L = 10.24$. Since $C_L < E_L$, the decision-maker is risk averse.*

Remark 2.2. *In example 2.11, the utility function $u(x) = \sqrt{x}$, $x \geq 0$ is a strictly concave function; if you plot it and draw a tangent at any point, the entire curve lies below the tangent. It is no accident that the decision-maker was found to be risk averse in example 2.11. The reason is that under EU, attitudes to risk are determined entirely by the shape of the utility function. The decision-maker is risk averse if u is concave; risk loving if u is convex; and risk neutral if u is a linear function (this can be shown formally).*

To most psychologists, it often appears strange to characterize attitudes to risk entirely by the shape of the utility function, because psychologists instinctively feel that risk has something to do with probabilities, not the shape of the utility function. This misgiving has merit. In all the other decision theories in this appendix, in which probabilities are weighted nonlinearly, risk attitudes depend jointly on the shape of the utility function and the precise manner in which the decision-maker weights probabilities nonlinearly (section 2.16.2 shows how humans weight probabilities nonlinearly).

The predictions of EU are inconsistent with much human behavior (see section 2.12). There are two main features of EU that are contradicted by the empirical evidence.

1. Linear probabilities: Notice that the expected utility functional in (2.37) is linear in probabilities. Most evidence suggests that individuals weight probabilities in a nonlinear manner, which gives rise to a consideration of a *probability weighting function* (section 2.16.2).

2. Lack of a reference point: The utility function u for outcomes in (2.37) is defined over final outcomes, $x_1, \ldots, x_n$. By contrast, the evidence strongly suggests that people evaluate final outcomes relative to a *reference point*, or a *goal*, or a *target* (subsection 2.16.4).

While rank dependent utility (Quiggin, 1982) takes account of the first shortcoming—that is, nonlinear probability weighting (section 2.16.3)—prospect theory (Kahneman & Tversky, 1979; Tversky & Kahneman, 1992) takes account of both shortcomings—that is, nonlinear probabilities and reference points (section 2.16.4). But first, we define a probability weighting function, w, and give examples of it.

2.16.2 Probability Weighting Function

Under risk, while $p \in [0, 1]$ is the objective probability of an outcome, $w(p)$ captures how the individual mentally codes that probability. If an outcome is impossible, $p = 0$, then it is reasonable to assume that $w(0) = 0$—that is, the individual also subjectively regards it as impossible. If an outcome is certain, $p = 1$, then it is reasonable to assume that $w(1) = 1$—that is, the individual also subjectively regards it as certain. However, for probabilities in the interior $p \in (0, 1)$, there could be a mismatch between p and $w(p)$. At a minimum, it is reasonable to assume that as the probability of an outcome p increases, so does the subjective weight $w(p)$. A probability weighting function is a strictly increasing mapping from the set of probabilities $[0, 1]$ to the set of probability weights that also lie in the interval $[0, 1]$. All this is succinctly summarized in the next definition.

Definition 2.10. *(Probability weighting function) By a probability weighting function, we mean a strictly increasing function $w: [0,1] \to [0,1]$ such that $w(0) = 0$ and $w(1) = 1$.*

Definition 2.10 is quite general, so there are many different candidate probability weighting functions that satisfy it. After all, there is an infinite number of functions that begin at $w(0) = 0$, end at $w(1) = 1$, and are strictly increasing. Of these, the most satisfactory is the Prelec (1998) function, which is parsimonious, tractable, has axiomatic foundations, and empirical support. We define it next. For the axiomatic foundations, see either Prelec (1998) or al-Nowaihi and Dhami (2006a).

Definition 2.11. *(Prelec, 1998) By the Prelec function, we mean the strictly increasing probability weighting function $w(p): [0,1] \to [0,1]$ given by*

$$w(p) = e^{-\beta(-\ln p)^{\alpha}}, \, p \in [0,1], \, \alpha > 0, \, \beta > 0. \tag{2.40}$$

It is easy to check that the Prelec function in definition 2.11 also satisfies the conditions for a probability weighting function in definition 2.10. The Prelec function has two parameters $\alpha > 0$, $\beta > 0$ that can be used to fit the data on human choices under risk. Notice that under EU, $w(p) = p$—that is, the individual never distorts objective probabilities, mentally coding them exactly as they are. This turns out to be a special case of the Prelec function. The reader can readily check by substituting $\alpha = \beta = 1$ in (2.40) that $w(p) = p$. However, the restriction $\alpha > 0$, $\beta > 0$ in (2.40) allows for an infinite number of α, β values to capture human behavior. There is nothing particularly special about the case $\alpha = \beta = 1$ that gives rise to expected utility. Yet, it is this case that has dominated the BRA for the last seven decades or so, despite strong empirical rejections of it.

As the reader might have guessed, the parameters α, β control the shape of the Prelec function. The parameter α controls the convexity/concavity of the Prelec function. The parameter β controls the elevation, or height, of the Prelec function. In many empirical studies, the estimated parameter $\beta \approx 1$, so let us set $\beta = 1$ and focus on the other parameter, α, which leads to an important observation about heuristics-based choices later.

There is a critical value of α such that (1) if the estimated $\alpha < 1$ for a decision-maker, then the Prelec function is first concave, then convex, and (2) if the estimated $\alpha > 1$ for a decision-maker, then the Prelec function is

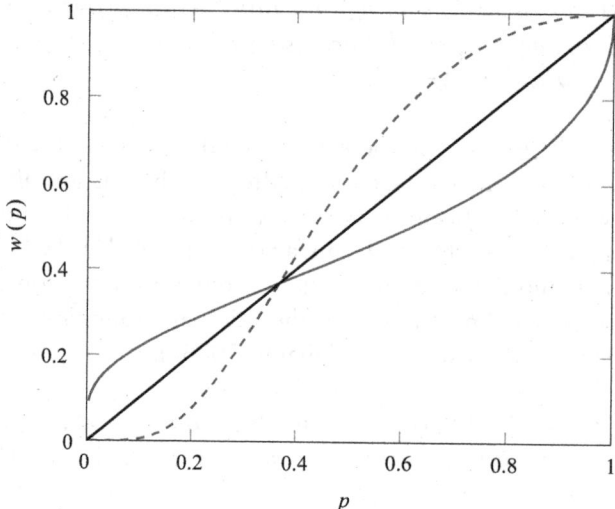

Figure 2.3

Plots of $w(p) = e^{-(-\ln p)^{0.5}}$ and $w(p) = e^{-(-\ln p)^2}$.

first convex, then concave. All this can be shown completely rigorously (Wakker, 2010; Dhami, 2019a). Figure 2.3 shows these two cases of $\alpha < 1$ and $\alpha > 1$. The diagonal 45° line is equidistant from both axes and represents the case $w(p) = p$, or the case of EU. Suppose that $\beta = 1$; then the Prelec function is given by $w(p) = e^{-(-\ln p)^\alpha}$. We now describe the two cases that we plot for this function.

1. We plot the case $\alpha < 1$ by choosing the illustrative example, $\alpha = 0.5$. This is shown as the continuous *inverse S-shaped curve* in figure 2.3, which is first concave, then convex. In this case, the decision-maker overweights low probabilities ($w(p) > p$) and underweights higher probabilities ($w(p) < p$). There is a point at which the Prelec curve cuts the 45° line. This is known as an interior fixed point, p^*, because $w(p^*) = p^*$ (note the other two fixed points are the two boundary fixed points, $p = 0$ and $p = 1$, because $w(0) = 0$ and $w(1) = 1$).
2. For the case $\alpha > 1$ we choose as an illustrative example, $\alpha = 2$. This is shown as the *dotted S-shaped curve* in figure 2.3, which is first convex, then concave. In this case, low probabilities are underweighted ($w(p) < p$) and high probabilities are overweighted ($w(p) > p$). There is an interior fixed point, p^*, and two boundary fixed points.

Suppose that we stay away from the end points of the probability interval $[0, 1]$—that is, ignore very low and very high probabilities at the moment. This is an important proviso in relation to our discussion about heuristics later on. Then, empirically, the median shape of the probability weighting function, as elicited from the actual choices, appears to be inverse S-shaped (Wakker, 2010; Dhami, 2019a), corresponding to the case $\alpha < 1$ in figure 2.3. However, there is heterogeneity in human choices and some individuals might well have a probability weighting function that is concave throughout (e.g., $w(p) = \sqrt{p}$ for all p) or convex throughout (e.g., $w(p) = p^2$ for all p).

Having discovered that people weight probabilities nonlinearly, as in figure 2.3, a sensible alternative to EU would appear to be the *decision weighted utility* of lottery L, denoted by *DWU* (L) (Edwards, 1954, 1962; Handa, 1977). This is given by

$$DWU(L) = \sum_{i=1}^{n} w(p_i)u(x_i), \qquad (2.41)$$

where $w(p_i)$ is the probability weight of outcome x_i given, say, by the Prelec function. Comparing (2.37) and (2.41), the only difference is that the weighting function w replaces objective probabilities. However, a decision-maker who uses (2.41) may also prefer lotteries that are *stochastically dominated* (Fishburn, 1978). When there are only two outcomes in each lottery, a stochastically dominated lottery offers a higher probability of a lower outcome and a lower probability of a higher outcome. Rational decision-makers are not supposed to choose stochastically dominated options (although it is an empirical question if they do, especially for more complex lotteries where dominance is hard to spot; see Kahneman & Tversky, 1979). Hence, the utility function in (2.41) was considered unattractive for decision theory.

2.16.3 Rank Dependent Utility

Quiggin (1982, 1993) proposed the first satisfactory solution to the problem of nonlinear probability weighting in the form of *rank dependent utility theory* (RDU). Decision-makers who use RDU do not choose stochastically dominated options. RDU could successfully resolve several paradoxes in EU, and in particular the *Allais paradox* (see section 2.12). The decision-maker's *rank dependent utility* from the lottery L is given by

$$RDU(L) = \sum_{i=1}^{n} \pi_i u(x_i), \qquad (2.42)$$

where the *decision weights* $\pi_1, \pi_2, \ldots, \pi_n$ replace the objective probabilities $p_1, p_2, \ldots, p_n$ in the expected utility representation in (2.37). The calculation of decision weights is given in the next definition. These are essentially cumulative transformations of the probability weighting function; we provide an example below to illustrate their usage.

Definition 2.12. *(Decision weights) Consider the lottery $L = (x_1, p_1; \ldots; x_n, p_n)$. Let w be the probability weighting function. For RDU, the decision weights, π_i, are defined as follows.*

$\pi_n = w(p_n)$

$\pi_{n-1} = w(p_{n-1} + p_n) - w(p_n)$

$\pi_i = w\left(\sum_{j=i}^{n} p_j\right) - w\left(\sum_{j=i+1}^{n} p_j\right)$

$\pi_1 = w\left(\sum_{j=1}^{n} p_j\right) - w\left(\sum_{j=2}^{n} p_j\right) = w(1) - w\left(\sum_{j=2}^{n} p_j\right) = 1 - w\left(\sum_{j=2}^{n} p_j\right)$

Since the probability weighting function is strictly increasing, it follows that $\pi_j \geq 0$, $j = 1, \ldots, n$. Adding up all the decision weights, it is straightforward to see that $\sum_{j=1}^{n} \pi_j = 1$.

Example 2.12. *Consider the lottery $L_1 = (4, 0.4; 16, 0.6)$ and the utility function $u(x) = \sqrt{x}$, as in example 2.10. The RDU of this lottery is given by $RDU(L_1) = \pi_1 \sqrt{4} + \pi_2 \sqrt{16}$. We have the case $n = 2$, so it follows directly from definition 2.12 that the two decision weights are given by $\pi_2 = w(0.6)$ and $\pi_2 = w(0.4 + 0.6) - w(0.6)$. Using the fact that $w(1) = 1$, we have $\pi_2 = 1 - w(0.6)$. Thus,*

$$RDU(L_1) = (1 - w(0.6))\sqrt{4} + w(0.6)\sqrt{16}. \tag{2.43}$$

If we specify a particular probability weighting function, say, the Prelec function, and insert the estimated values of its parameters α, β, then we can compute the RHS of (2.43).

The calculations in definition 2.12 may seem long-winded, but they provide a really simple way of capturing the *optimism* and the *pessimism* of the decision-maker based on the curvature of the weighting function; for the details, see Wakker (2010) and Dhami (2019a). We illustrate the flavor of this through the following example.

Example 2.13. *(Optimism and pessimism) Suppose that w is convex throughout (e.g., $w(p) = p^2$, which plots as a convex curve lying strictly below the diagonal 45° line in figure 2.3 except at $p = 0$ and $p = 1$). Consider the balanced risk lottery, L, that gives a 50-50 chance of receiving* two possible outcomes $x_1 < x_2$: $L = (x_1, 0.5; x_2, 0.5)$. Using (2.42), under RDU,

$$RDU(L) = u(x_1)[1 - w(0.5)] + u(x_2)w(0.5), \qquad (2.44)$$

where u is a strictly increasing utility function, so $u(x_1) < u(x_2)$. By contrast, under EU, and using (2.37), the worth of the lottery L is given by

$$EU(L) = 0.5u(x_1) + 0.5u(x_2). \qquad (2.45)$$

Since $w(0) = 0, w(1) = 1$ (see definition 2.10) and w is assumed to be convex throughout, we have that

1. $w(0.5) < 0.5$, and
2. $1 - w(0.5) > 0.5$.

Thus, comparing (2.44) and (2.45), a decision-maker who follows RDU, relative to an EU decision-maker, puts a smaller weight on the higher outcome and a higher weight on the smaller outcome. In other words, with EU as the benchmark, the decision-maker is relatively pessimistic.

The converse phenomenon (optimism) arises if w were concave throughout (e.g., $w(p) = \sqrt{p}$, which plots as a concave curve lying strictly above the diagonal 45° line in figure 2.3 except at $p = 0$ and $p = 1$). In this case, an RDU decision-maker puts a relatively higher weight on the higher outcome as compared to an EU decision-maker (and a relatively lower weight on the smaller outcome).

2.16.4 Prospect Theory

We consider here the version of *prospect theory* (PT) given in Tversky and Kahneman (1992); this is also sometimes known as *cumulative prospect theory* because it uses a modified form of definition 2.12 to compute decision weights. The original version of prospect theory in Kahneman and Tversky (1979), sometimes known as *original prospect theory* (OPT), proposed an evaluation of the lottery L that is similar to that in (2.41), except that the utility function took account of reference points. As noted above, this formulation allows for the choice of stochastically dominated options, which was criticized by decision theorists. OPT gave a psychologically rich account of human behavior. It made use of heuristics in an initial editing phase in which decision-makers simplified lotteries before applying any direct computations on them. This psychological richness and the use of heuristics were lost in the proposal for PT in 1992. We discuss OPT further in section 4.14.1.

PT relaxes both problematic features of EU described toward the end of section 2.16.1 (nonlinear probability weighting and reference points); hence, PT is a generalization of RDU, which in turn is a generalization of EU. The central idea in PT is that of a *reference point*. In particular, the utility function in PT is defined not over outcomes but on deviations of outcomes from a reference point (or a target level of outcomes, or a goal). Evidence indicates that when exposed to external stimuli, such as temperature, brightness, and pain, individuals are more sensitive to *changes* rather than *levels* (Helson, 1964). In a classic experiment in psychology, subjects first dip their right hand in cold water and the left hand in warm water until both hands have had time to adjust to the temperature. Then, simultaneously, both hands are taken out and dipped in lukewarm water. Although both hands experience the identical lukewarm temperature, the right hand feels warm and the left hand feels cold, suggesting that changes, rather than absolute levels, determine perception.

Kahneman and Tversky identified the *status quo* as a useful reference point, but other possibilities, depending on the context and the problem, could be an *expected outcome*, a *fair outcome*, or a *legal entitlement*. The reference point could also be state-dependent wealth, average wealth, or desired wealth. Or it could even be made endogenous by using the rational expectations of future wealth (Köszegi & Rabin, 2006), but this is cognitively very challenging and we do not have direct evidence to confirm or refute it yet. However, evidence is consistent with the view that reference points can be expected wealth (Dhami, 2019a).

The reference point splits the domain of outcomes into gains (outcome higher than reference point) or losses (outcome lower than reference point). The introduction of reference points is not just a renormalization of the space of outcomes. Lab and field evidence shows that human behavior is quite distinct in the domain of gains and losses.

1. Losses bite more than equivalent gains; this is known as *loss aversion* and is one of the most salient features of human behavior.
2. Attitudes to risk are different in both domains, and PT makes the prediction of a *four fold classification of attitudes to risk* (Kahneman & Tversky, 2000; Dhami, 2019a); we discuss this below.

To take account of reference dependence, we first define lotteries in *incremental form* by subtracting the reference point from each outcome in a lottery.

Definition 2.13. *(Lotteries in incremental form or prospects) Suppose that a decision-maker faces the lottery* $(x_1, p_1; x_2, p_2; \ldots; x_n, p_n)$ *and* the reference point is given by r. We say that a lottery is presented in *incremental form* if it is written as

$$L = (y_1, p_1; y_2, p_2; \ldots; y_n, p_n), \text{ where } y_i = x_i - r, \, i = 1, 2, \ldots, n. \tag{2.46}$$

If $y_i \geq 0$ the decision-maker is in the *domain of gains*, and if $y_i < 0$ the decision-maker is in the *domain of losses*.

It is pedagogically more convenient to refer to the y_i values as outcomes rather than using the more cumbersome but accurate expression *outcomes relative to the reference point*, so we shall follow this convention.

In PT, the *utility function* from an outcome, denoted by v (to differentiate it from the utility function u under EU and RDU), is defined over objects of the form y_i, and not x_i; that is, the reference point is explicitly taken into account. We first define such a utility function and then provide the discussion/intuition and a picture.

Definition 2.14. *(Utility function under PT) Let Y be the set of real-valued outcomes relative to a reference point. A utility function, v, is a continuous and strictly increasing function $v: Y \to \mathbb{R}$ that satisfies the following properties:*

1. $v(0) = 0$ *(reference dependence).*
2. v *is concave for $y \geq 0$ (declining sensitivity for gains).*
3. v *is convex for $y \leq 0$ (declining sensitivity for losses).*
4. $-v(-y) > v(y)$ *for $y > 0$ (loss aversion).*

Tversky and Kahneman (1992) propose the following power form of the utility function, which satisfies all the conditions required in definition 2.14:[16]

$$v(y) = \begin{cases} y^\gamma & \text{if } y \geq 0 \\ -\lambda(-y)^\gamma & \text{if } y < 0 \end{cases}, \tag{2.47}$$

where γ and λ are constants such that $0 < \gamma < 1$, and $\lambda > 1$ is known as the *coefficient of loss aversion*. One may also impose separate powers in the domain of gains and losses, respectively, γ^+ and γ^-. Tversky and Kahneman estimated that the median values are $\gamma^+ \simeq \gamma^- = \gamma = 0.88$ and $\lambda \simeq 2.25$.

We can now plot the function in (2.47), which should clarify all the features in definition 2.14. In order to plot it, we assign the following values to the parameters, $\lambda = 2.5$, $\gamma = 0.5$. The resulting plot of v is shown in figure 2.4 as the continuous, strictly increasing function. Along the

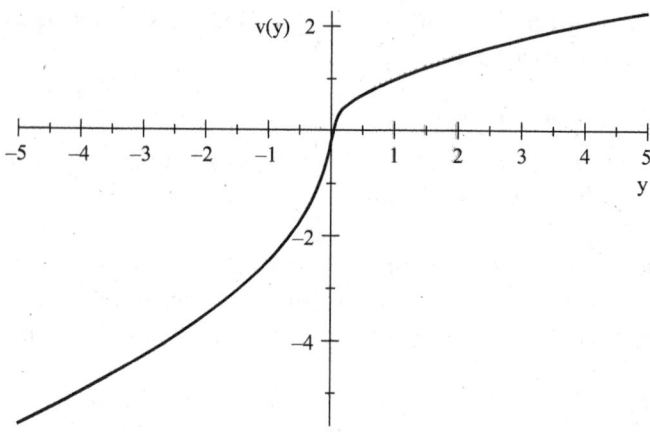

Figure 2.4
The utility function under prospect theory.

horizontal axis, we measure outcomes relative to the reference point, $y_i = x_i - r$. When an outcome equals the reference point, we have $y_i = 0$; this is the origin in figure 2.4. To the right of this point, $y_i > 0$, we are in gains, where the utility function is concave. To the left, $y_i < 0$, we are in losses, and the utility function is convex.

In order to describe the construction of decision weights under PT, it is more convenient to assume that we have a total of $m + 1 + n$ outcomes. Of these, there are m distinct outcomes in the domain of losses ($y_i < 0$), n distinct outcomes in the domain of gains ($y_i > 0$), and one reference outcome for which $y_i = 0$. We denote the reference outcome as y_0. So, the n outcomes in gains are $y_1 < y_2 < \cdots < y_n$ and the m outcomes in losses are $y_{-m} < y_{-m+1} < \cdots < y_{-1}$. Using definition 2.13, we can define the following lottery in incremental form,

$$L = (y_{-m}, p_{-m}; y_{-m+1}, p_{-m+1}; \ldots; y_{-1}, p_{-1}; y_0, p_0; y_1, p_1; y_2, p_2; \ldots; y_n, p_n). \tag{2.48}$$

The probabilities are, as usual, nonnegative, $p_i \geq 0$ for all i, and sum up to 1: $\sum_{i=-m}^{n} p_i = 1$.

We also denote by L_P the set of all lotteries of the form given in (2.48). The *prospect theory utility* of any lottery $L \in L_P$ to the decision-maker is given by

$$V(L) = \sum_{i=-m}^{n} \pi_i v(y_i), \tag{2.49}$$

where π_i, $i = -m, \ldots, n$ are the decision weights corresponding to each of the $m+1+n$ outcomes and are given in definition 2.15, while v is the prospect theory utility function of an outcome, given in definition 2.14. The decision weights under PT are very similar to those in RDU (see definition 2.12) except that, under PT, we need to take account of the separate domains of gains and losses (by contrast, under RDU there is only one domain because there is no reference point). In principle, one could have different probability weighting functions in gains and losses; denote these respectively by w^+ and w^-.[17]

Definition 2.15. *(Tversky and Kahneman, 1992) For PT, the decision weights, π_i, are defined as follows:*

$$\pi_n = w^+ (p_n)$$

$$\pi_{n-1} = w^+ (p_{n-1} + p_n) - w^+ (p_n) \ldots$$

$$\pi_i = w^+ \left(\Sigma_{j=i}^n p_j \right) - w^+ \left(\Sigma_{j=i+1}^n p_j \right) \ldots$$

$$\pi_1 = w^+ \left(\Sigma_{j=1}^n p_j \right) - w^+ \left(\Sigma_{j=2}^n p_j \right)$$

$$\pi_{-m} = w^- (p_{-m})$$

$$\pi_{-m+1} = w^- (p_{-m} + p_{-m+1}) - w^- (p_{-m}) \ldots$$

$$\pi_{-j} = w^- \left(\Sigma_{i=-m}^{-j} p_i \right) - w^- \left(\Sigma_{i=-m}^{-j-1} p_i \right) \ldots$$

$$\pi_{-1} = w^- \left(\Sigma_{i=-m}^{-1} p_i \right) - w^- \left(\Sigma_{i=-m}^{-2} p_i \right)$$

The decision weights $\pi_1, \ldots, \pi_n$ are defined exactly as they were for RDU in definition 2.12 except that we are using the probability weighting function for the domain of gains, w^+. The decision weights for the domain of losses, $\pi_{-1}, \ldots, \pi_{-m}$, are then defined in exactly the same way, starting from the lowest outcome in losses, y_{-m}, and moving up toward the highest outcome in losses, y_{-1}. To illustrate the use of these decision weights, now consider the same lottery as in example 2.12.

Example 2.14. *Suppose that a decision-maker faces the lottery $(4, 0.4; 16, 0.6)$ and has the reference point $r = 9$. The lottery in incremental form, obtained by subtracting the reference point $r = 9$ from each outcome, is given by $L = (-5, 0.4; 7, 0.6)$. Thus, we have one outcome each in the domain of gains and losses—that is, we have the case $m = n = 1$. Using the empirically supported power form of utility function*

Table 2.2
Fourfold classification of risk under prospect theory.

Probability	Domain of gains	Domain of losses
Low	$L=(100, 0.05; 0, 0.95)$ $C_L = 14, E_L = 5$	$L=(-100, 0.05; 0, 0.95)$ $C_L = -8, E_L = -5$
High	$L=(100, 0.95; 0, 0.05)$ $C_L = 78, E_L = 95$	$L=(-100, 0.95; 0, 0.05)$ $C_L = -84, E_L = -95$

of the decision-maker in (2.47), and using the parameter values $\gamma = 0.88$ and $\lambda = 2.25$, we get

$$v(y) = \begin{cases} y^{0.88} & \text{if } y \geq 0 \\ -2.25\,(-y)^{0.88} & \text{if } y < 0 \end{cases}.$$

The PT evaluation of the lottery L is given by

$$PT(L) = \pi_{-1}\left(-2.25\,(5)^{0.88}\right) + \pi_1\,(7)^{0.88}.$$

Directly, using definition 2.15, the two decision weights are given by $\pi_1 = w(0.6)$ and $\pi_{-1} = w(0.4)$. Thus,

$$PT(L) = w(0.4)\left(-2.25\,(5)^{0.88}\right) + w(0.6)\,(7)^{0.88}. \tag{2.50}$$

An explicit value for the RHS of (2.50) can be found by specifying a probability weighting function and its parameters.

Recall our discussion on attitudes to risk under expected utility (definition 2.9 and remark 2.2). Attitudes to risk are quite subtle under prospect theory and are determined jointly by the shapes of the probability weighting function and the utility function; for the formal details see Wakker (2010) and Dhami (2019a). Tversky and Kahneman (1992) provide evidence on the *fourfold pattern of attitudes to risk* under prospect theory.

Consider two-outcome lotteries in incremental form given by $L = (0, 1-p; y, p)$, where the outcome $y \gtreqless 0$ occurs with probability p. This is a gain, $y > 0$, or a loss, $y < 0$, relative to the reference point. The reference outcome 0 occurs with the complementary probability $1 - p$. We vary the outcomes and the probabilities. In particular, we consider either a low value of p of 5 percent ($p = 0.05$) or a high value of 95 percent

($p = 0.95$), and we consider both gains ($y > 0$) and losses ($y < 0$). Let C_L denote the certainty equivalent of the lottery and E_L the expected value of the lottery L.

Table 2.2 shows the empirically observed values of C_L, E_L for each of four different lotteries in each cell. Recall from definition 2.9 that attitudes to risk in any decision theory are determined by a comparison of the values of C_L and E_L. If $C_L < E_L$, then the decision-maker is risk averse, and if $C_L > E_L$, then the decision-maker is risk loving. Using this definition, we can directly read off the following information from table 2.2. For low probabilities ($p = 0.05$), there is risk seeking in the domain of gains but risk aversion in the domain of losses. For high probabilities ($p = 0.95$), we observe risk aversion in the domain of gains but risk seeking in the domain of losses. This pattern is hard to explain under EU or RDU but is easily explained by PT.

3
The Case for Bounded Rationality

3.1 Introduction

This chapter makes the case for bounded rationality in the social and behavioral sciences. We use a two-pronged approach. On the one hand, we highlight the requirements for unbounded rationality, as encapsulated in the BRA, focusing particularly on the required degree of cognitive sophistication and on some of the evidence. On the other hand, we demonstrate, using concrete examples, how bounded rationality provides an alternative, more compelling account of human behavior. Since our intention is to provide a systematic treatment of the subject with concrete examples and the evidence, we proceed as follows.

Mathematical optimization is the main solution method used by households and firms in the BRA. In section 3.2, we examine the reasonableness of this solution method from several different angles that we now explain.

In section 3.2.1, we consider *dynamic programming*, the main solution method in the optimization toolbox of the BRA, when the future is uncertain. Dynamic programming was introduced into mathematics in the early 1950s with the work of Richard E. Bellman. The maintained assumption in the BRA is that all economic agents use (or act as if they use) the sum total of existing knowledge in mathematics and statistics, including research that has just been published. Thus, it was only a matter of time before economic agents in economic models were endowed with the ability to use dynamic programming. We work through the basics of a simple intertemporal optimization problem under uncertainty, albeit in a gentle manner for interdisciplinary readers, to demonstrate the computational requirements and the method followed in this approach. For instance, in a simple 30 time period problem with just three possible realizations of a single random variable in each time period (e.g., uncertain income that takes three possible values every period), we show that an individual must make 68 trillion calculations to solve a dynamic programming problem. Economic problems, by contrast, typically have an infinite number of time periods and an infinite number of realizations of several random variables in every period. Economists rarely if ever ask whether, in this basic bread and butter problem in economics, the required number of calculations is within the realm of human cognitive and computational limits.

Emotions are notably absent in the BRA, which in its actual practice deals with cold economic calculus, although we argue in chapter 2 that emotions can be included within the BRA. In section 3.2.2, we set up a problem in microfinance contracts that enables us to illustrate several essential issues in this and other subsections. Consider *joint liability contracts* in which a group of borrowers jointly borrows money from a microfinance institution; each borrower has an independent project that is likely to be more successful if each borrower puts in more effort. Importantly, in a joint liability contract, each borrower in the group must successfully repay their loan; otherwise all group members forgo the privilege of all future borrowings. We use an optimization-based model using *psychological game theory*[1] to predict that *guilt averse* borrowers will feel guilty from letting down the expectations of other borrowers in their group in the joint liability contract. Thus, they put extra effort on their independent projects. The evidence is consistent with this prediction. Similarly, when borrowers have to repay their loans in front of their social group / peers, the model predicts that *shame averse* borrowers would feel shame if they publicly defaulted on their loans. Hence, they would work harder on their projects to ensure the project's success. The evidence is also consistent with this prediction.

Thus, on the face of it, optimization seems to do rather well, although emotions, which are not a part of the BRA, at least in its actual practice, provide the key explanation. However, when the microfinance model is repeated over two periods (so that the second period is the last period), in the second period, there are no future consequences of current actions (i.e., effort choices of the borrowers). But there are consequences of first period effort choices, as higher effort makes it more likely that the project will be successful and a second period loan can be obtained from the bank. Hence, first period effort gives more bang for the buck, relative to second period effort (technically, the marginal product of first period effort is higher). Yet, contrary to the predictions of any optimization-based model, we find that the second period effort is identical, or higher, relative to first period effort. We suggest simple heuristics that borrowers could be using in this case.

Section 3.2.3 considers the empirical finding of bubbles in financial markets, in which the price moves away from the fundamental value of an asset for an extended period of time. This is often considered inconsistent with optimization-based models in finance. However, any empirical test of the BRA is a joint test of the assumption of optimization and other auxiliary assumptions. In this case, it is difficult to reject optimization unless other potential confounds, such as common knowledge, and heterogeneity of investors are not simultaneously ruled out.

In introductory courses in economics, mathematical optimization and rationality is typically motivated as follows. Non-optimizing economic agents, particularly firms, will make lower profits as compared to optimizing firms; hence, market competition will ensure that they must perish. Furthermore, if there exist any irrational agents (relative to the BRA benchmark) who make errors in their choices, then positive and negative errors are likely to cancel out in the aggregate. Hence, at the aggregate, we should observe the error-free outcomes of only rational choices. This is symptomatic of a method of proof that is not unusual in economics. Economic theory, and assertions such as the ones above, are constructed in an axiomatic manner, without designing stringent empirical tests for them. Indeed, when tested stringently, many of these assertions fail on the evidence. We consider these issues, and the relevant evidence, in section 3.2.4. Non-optimizing individuals and firms can survive even in market competition, and errors, rather than canceling out in the aggregate, may accumulate in one direction, often leading to large movements in financial markets.

In sections 3.2.5 and 3.2.6, we consider two applications in which the data appear to be consistent with either an optimization-based approach or a heuristics-based approach. Section 3.2.5 continues with our example of microfinance contracts, and section 3.2.6 considers an example from tax evasion. In cases such as these, we need to generate other predictions that enable us to differentiate between optimization and heuristics-based models. Also of relevance are the kinds of questions that we are interested in and whether the answers that we wish to seek are qualitative or quantitative. For instance, optimization-based and heuristics-based models are both likely to predict that greater deterrence deters crime (e.g., more policing reduces street crime). However, if we are interested in the extent to which crime is deterred, which is a quantitative question, then the choice between optimization and heuristics-based models could be critical.

Section 3.2.7 evaluates a three-way debate between some of the leaders in the field. The question of interest is which of the following two approaches to follow: (1) Embrace heuristics in an all-out manner, which is the *big-bang approach*, or (2) engage in an *incremental approach*, where incremental changes to the BRA are made by incorporating successively more realistic behavioral assumptions, keeping intact the remaining apparatus of the BRA?

Section 3.3 offers an introduction to *strategic interaction*, the subject matter of game theory. Game theory offers a powerful framework, and potentially a common language, that can be used to address the two central questions in the social and behavioral sciences—that of *cooperation* and *coordination* among humans. We take the archetypal game in the social sciences, the static prisoner's dilemma game, that is used to study cooperation and conflict. In this case, the prediction of *classical game theory* (a term that we reserve for game theory, as used in the BRA) is that there should be no cooperation. Yet, we find that the cooperation rate is about 60 percent. This is problematic not just for classical game theory but also for those behavioral game theory models that require players to play a best response to beliefs. We outline some of the possible explanations (explored further in chapter 4) that are based on heuristics-based choices (e.g., evidential reasoning) and on notions of *social rationality* rather than the private rationality that characterizes classical game theory.

As noted in chapter 2, under true uncertainty, the BRA is unable to make predictions. Evolution, both biological and cultural, has produced humans that have a proclivity to follow social norms. Section 3.4 considers the intriguing possibility that social norms provide us with guidance on making decisions under true uncertainty. A simple heuristic of following the social norm may provide a cognitive shortcut to making decisions in situations that have the characteristics of true uncertainty.

Section 3.5 asks why many economists are not willing to accept refutations to various elements of the BRA in the face of overwhelming evidence that began to emerge about seven decades ago and has snowballed since then. It locates the answer in homegrown methodological positions within economics that are widely subscribed to yet bear little relation to the positions taken in any of the successful natural sciences. The basic position, due to work by the 1976 Nobel laureate in economics, Milton Friedman, suggests that even if a model is based on patently incorrect assumptions, if the predictions are correct, then it is a good model. Furthermore, in this case, the decision-makers may be considered to behave *as if* they followed the model. However, the work of Kahneman and Tversky in the 1970s on judgment heuristics showed that the predictions of the BRA did not hold true, even in an as-if sense; this is the subject matter of chapter 5.

The methodological position in economics has since gradually evolved to shield the BRA from empirical refutation. A flavor of some of the arguments made by the leading economists, in print we might add, may be summarized as follows. All models are wrong anyway, so there is nothing particularly concerning about economic models whose predictions are not correct; the purpose of economic models is to tell useful stories, fables, and to build our intuition, not to explain the complex reality out there; and the purpose of economic models is to convey a message, not to describe reality. These positions, coupled with the view that economics is not a natural science and hence is deserving of special status that protects it from refutation, have had a cumulatively disastrous effect on research in economics. It has not only led to a massive production line of empirically rejected model, but also ensured that the evidence on refutations of the BRA has not been given as much attention as it deserves.

The BRA uses preferences and beliefs as the primitives, allowing beliefs to be updated as new information arrives. However, it draws the line at changing preferences. The view in economics has been that changing preferences can allow one to explain anything. This argument is only partially correct. It would be correct if one tweaked preferences arbitrarily and in an ad hoc manner to provide explanations for outstanding puzzles and problems. However, this is not how behavioral economics has developed and not how it is practiced. It has taken a fairly disciplined approach as far as preferences have been concerned. Lab experiments are relatively cheap to run, so any new proposed preferences in behavioral economics are quickly tested to either confirm or reject the new proposal. However, the issue of malleability of preferences is an empirical one, and not one to be decided on a priori grounds. Section 3.6 outlines the empirical evidence on the feedback between preferences, history, culture, and institutions.

The BRA also forms the basis on which modern macroeconomic theories are constructed. It is the chassis on which additional elements are bolted to produce macroeconomic models. These additional elements include a representative individual framework (a single representative individual represents all consumers and firms in a $20 trillion economy); market clearing equilibrium analysis (all markets clear at equilibrium prices); and rational expectation (on average, people make no forecasting errors, certainly not systematic ones). The quality and accuracy of the predictions of macroeconomic models is debatable. Section 3.7 presents an alternative way of viewing the macroeconomy as a *complex adaptive system*. Such systems are in a constant state of flux, never settling down;

heterogenous consumers and firms use simple rules of thumb and try to find their way under true uncertainty; fluctuations are caused by endogenous rather than exogenous factors; small changes in the parameters lead to large changes, or *chaos*; and the dynamic system exhibits *emergent properties*. In macroeconomics, *agent-based models* (ABMs) are typically used to implement the elements of the complexity approach. We give a critical assessment, followed by a more detailed discussion, of some of these issues in chapter 4.

3.2 How Reasonable Is the Assumption of Mathematical Optimization?

Optimization, as in *mathematical optimization*, is part of the requirement for a BRA. After all, why would rational economic actors not wish to utilize the limitless cognitive, informational, computational, and attentional resources at their disposal and their knowledge of all existing mathematics and statistics to compute a mathematical optimum (or optima) of whatever it is they wish to optimize? Or, even if they did not literally optimize in this way, perhaps they act in a manner as if they could do so. Surely, it would be irrational otherwise. As with other components of the BRA, we require the relevant empirical evidence to make such a determination rather than assert it axiomatically as an article of faith.

Profit maximization by firms requires that they maximize the difference between total revenues and total costs. Optimizing firms should produce output up to the point where producing an extra unit of output generates the same extra revenue (marginal revenue) as it adds to the costs (marginal cost). In other words, profit maximizing by firms is synonymous with equating marginal revenues and marginal costs. Producing either beyond, or below, this point will reduce profits. The entire corpus of the modern economic theory of the firm is based on this equilibrium condition.

In his Nobel Prize acceptance speech, Herbert Simon (1978) noted: "But there are no direct observations that individuals or firms do actually equate marginal costs and revenues." This is almost as serious and astonishing as a physicist saying in a Nobel Prize acceptance speech, "But there is no evidence that electrons exist." One would imagine that, in an ideal world, Simon's observation would have prompted immediate soul-searching about the basic tenets of the BRA. Nothing of this sort ever happened. The relevant debate, in our view, is not whether economics is a science but rather whether economists respect and abide by the scientific method.

The 1994 Nobel laureate in economics, Reinhard Selten, has argued on many occasions that economic problems are *NP complete,* a term that is borrowed from the computer science literature. The solution to such problems is hard/impossible to obtain. While no analytical solution may obtain, numerical solutions may be possible with high-powered computers and sophisticated algorithms. Yet, in the BRA, the people on the street are assumed to solve such problems in their heads, in an instant. Selten's work on subgame perfection plays a central role in game theory courses in economics. However, Selten was aware that its empirical performance was poor, and for that reason, he was skeptical of it. Yet, the area that he gravitated toward and contributed significantly to, bounded rationality, is hardly taught in courses on economic theory. To say that this work poses problems for the BRA is an understatement.

3.2.1 A Basic Problem in Dynamic Optimization

It is perhaps useful to explore the hidden assumptions behind optimization-based methods in economics, using an example that forms the basis of any dynamic model in economics, and certainly all of macroeconomics. Indeed, no dynamic economics (that is to say, there is some time element to the decisions being made) is possible without assuming that individuals can effortlessly solve problems of this kind, or act as if they could. Although the underlying material is technical, we go through it in a relatively gentle manner. The main purpose is to demonstrate the calculations that individuals using the BRA are supposed to effortlessly make. The reader who has a particular aversion to anything even mildly technical may just read the last two paragraphs of this subsection.

Suppose that we index time by $t = 1, \ldots, T$, so there is a total of T time periods, and suppose also that there is no population growth. An individual economic agent in competitive markets starts life with an initial stock of savings s_0 that earns a market interest rate of r_t at time t. The individual also supplies one unit of labor, every period, that earns a market wage of θw_t at time t, where θ is a random variable that captures labor market shocks at time t. We assume that θ is independently and identically distributed in every period and takes only positive realized values. Since θ is a random variable, its future value is not known. However, once the future does arrive, the random variable does take a particular value that is observed by the individual. Denote the time t realization of θ by θ_t (we conserve on notation by using θ for the random variable and its realization).

In every time period, t, the individual chooses to either consume or to save that period's income for the next period. The budget constraint of the individual, once the realization of the random variable is known, is given by

$$c_t + s_t = \theta_t w_t + r_t s_{t-1}; \quad t = 1, \ldots, T. \tag{3.1}$$

In (3.1), the RHS is the total income of the individual at time t. It is the sum of labor income, $\theta_t w_t$, from the currently supplied 1 unit of labor, and capital income, $r_t s_{t-1}$, on account of the savings made in period $t-1$. The LHS of (3.1) is the total expenditure, the sum of consumption expenditure, c_t, and savings s_t.

In the background, competitive firms use labor supplied by individuals and capital (which is the savings of the individuals in the previous period) to produce output under constant returns to scale.[2] Factor prices at any time t—that is, the wage $\theta_t w_t$ and the rental rate r_t—are determined in competitive factor markets that equate demand and supply in each market.

The individual derives utility from the sequence of temporal consumption $c_1, c_2, \ldots, c_T$. At time $t = 1$, the individual maximizes the expected present discounted value of utility, also known as the exponential discounted utility model (see section 2.6). This is given by

$$U = E_1 \left[u(c_1, \theta) + \delta u(c_2, \theta) + \delta^2 u(c_3, \theta) \ldots + \delta^{T-1} u(c_T, \theta) \right],$$

where E_1 is an expectation operator that is conditional on all available information to the individual at time $t = 1$, and u is a utility function for outcomes, so that $u(c_t)$ gives the utility at time t from consumption c_t. The individual knows that at each date, $t = 1, 2, 3, \ldots$, there will be an opportunity to maximize the date t objective function. Such maximization at time t is subject to the initial stock of savings s_{t-1}, carried over from the savings made at time $t-1$; the budget constraints in (3.1); and a terminal condition on savings, $s_T \geq 0$, which requires the individual does not die in debt.

We have a simple T period *dynamic optimization problem* that underlies any dynamic model in economics. A method of finding a solution to these problems is described in Bellman (1952), who suggested a recursive method, based on the Bellman equation, to solve such problems; for the definitive treatment of this method in economics, see Stokey et al. (1989). Economists quickly adopted the idea that humans use the Bellman equation in solving problems too. Indeed, entire courses in macroeconomics are based on this as the main, or even the exclusive, method of solution. Our interest here is not in applying the Bellman equation to the problem above but to give a flavor for how we might solve this problem using dynamic programming, assuming that a solution exists. It is typical that no analytical solution exists to such problems and a numerical solution has to be found.

The idea is to start with the last time period, $t = T$, and work our way backward toward time $t = 1$, one time period at a time.

- Time period T: Once the realization of the random variable θ, denoted by θ_T, is known, then the income of the individual, $\theta_T w_T + r_t s_{T-1}$ is also known. The individual pays off all debts, if any, in order to satisfy the terminal requirement $s_T \geq 0$ and consumes the rest. Denote the optimal period T consumption by $c_T(s_{T-1}, \theta_T)$. It depends on the savings made at time $T-1$ and the realization of the random variable θ_T.
- Time period $T-1$: The individual knows the time $T-1$ realization of θ, given by θ_{T-1}, but not the time T realization of θ, which is θ_T. Assuming that the choice made at time T will be optimal—that is, given by $c_T(s_{T-1}, \theta_T)$—the individual, at time $T-1$, wishes to choose the optimal value of c_{T-1}, taking into account all possible future realizations θ_T of the random variable. This is the solution to the following problem. Choose c_{T-1} to maximize

$$u(c_{T-1}) + \delta E_{T-1} u(c_T(s_{T-1}, \theta_T)),$$

subject to the budget constraint at time $T-1$, given by $c_{T-1} + s_{T-1} = \theta_{T-1} w_{T-1} + r_{T-1} s_{T-2}$. E_{T-1} is the time $T-1$ expectation operator based on what the individual knows at this time. For instance, if θ takes only two values, θ_H with probability p and θ_L with probability $1-p$, then

$$E_{T-1} u(c_T(s_{T-1}, \theta_T)) = p u(c_T(s_{T-1}, \theta_H)) + (1-p) u(c_T(s_{T-1}, \theta_L)).$$

Solving the time $T-1$ problem will give the solution to consumption at time $T-1$, denoted by $c_{T-1}(s_{T-2}, \theta_{T-1})$.

This sets the pattern of recursion and we solve next for the optimal consumption at time $T-2$, given by $c_{T-2}(s_{T-3}, \theta_{T-2})$. We continue moving backward toward time $t = 1$, one period at a time, and choose optimally in each period, assuming that we shall choose optimally in all future periods. This gives us the sequence of optimal consumption choices: $c_T(s_{T-1}, \theta_T), c_{T-1}(s_{T-2}, \theta_{T-1}), \ldots, c_2(s_1, \theta_2), c_1(s_0, \theta_1)$. Using the initial value of savings, s_0, we can start by solving $c_1^* = c_1(s_0, \theta_1)$, which gives optimal first period savings, s_1^*, by using the budget constraint in (3.1): $s_1^* = \theta_1 w_1 + r_1 s_0 - c_1^*$.

We then plug s_1^* into the solution for second period consumption, $c_2(s_1, \theta_2)$, to get optimal second period consumption $c_2^* = c_2(s_1^*, \theta_2)$, which gives optimal second period savings, $s_2^* = \theta_2 w_2 + r_2 s_1 - c_2^*$. In turn, this can be used to solve for $c_3^* = c_3(s_2^*, \theta_3)$ and s_3^*. Proceeding in this manner toward time T, we can generate the entire sequence of optimal choices of consumption, $c_1^*, c_2^*, \ldots, c_T^*$. This completes the dynamic programming solution.

People on the street are supposed to do these calculations in their heads, in an instant, without breaking a sweat (or behave as if they can). This is the standard assumption in the BRA about how humans make decisions over time.

To see the cognitive burden that solving such problems requires of humans, return to time $T-1$. Suppose that there are only three possible realizations of θ, say, $\theta_L, \theta_M, \theta_H$, with associated nonnegative probabilities $p, q, 1-p-q$ that sum up to unity. Then, at time $T-1$, the individual needs to take account of three possible contingent consumption levels for time T, each corresponding to an unknown future realization of θ: $c_T(s_{T-1}, \theta_L), c_T(s_{T-1}, \theta_M), c_T(s_{T-1}, \theta_H)$. The problem is a little bit more difficult for the individual at time $T-2$, where they need to take account of three possible contingencies at $T-1$, followed in each of these three cases by a further three possible contingencies at time T. This gives rise to $3^2 = 9$ contingencies, and, hence, at least nine simultaneous calculations. If we keep going backward to time $T-(T-1) = 1$, or to the first time period, the individual will have to make 3^{T-1} calculations in their head in order to generate the optimal time path of consumption.

But how large is 3^{T-1}? The answer obviously depends on the chosen value of T. In courses in economic theory, and in any of the professional journals in economics, it is routine to assume that $T \to \infty$. Let us do some calculations for relatively small values of T. Pick a reasonably small value of $T = 30$, in which case $3^{T-1} = 3^{29} = 68$ trillion. If, on the other hand, θ took only two values, θ^L, θ^M, then for $T = 30$ we have $2^{T-1} = 2^{29} = 0.53687 \times 10^9$, which is more than half a billion calculations and contingencies. While noneconomists might be somewhat staggered at this point, the basic article of faith among economists is that these calculations are effortlessly done by people on the street in the blink of an eye!

Similar problems of unreasonable assumptions on computational ability apply to the behavior of firms within the BRA. If anything, the computational problems appear even more complicated for the firm, particularly when we try to open the black box of decision-making within firms and consider it as a formal and informal network of dynamic contracts (Simon, 1955; Cyert & March, 1963; Nelson & Winter, 1982; Radner, 1992, 1996).

One of us has taught advanced economic theory courses at four universities for more than 20 years. He has never heard any student object to the notion that humans can engage in dynamic programming (or act as if they can), nor did he ever hear any of his teachers or fellow students express any reservations about these issues while working on his PhD at a leading Western university, nor has he ever heard any reservations about this expressed in any of the mainstream economic theory articles (sans the behavioral economics articles) that he has read in his 20-plus years in academia.

All the evidence contradicts the assertion that humans behave in this manner or act as if they behaved in this manner (Dhami, 2016; Dhami, 2019c). This is symptomatic of how unbelievable and unquestioning so many of the core economics models have become. Successive generations of bright students in economics are successfully brainwashed into not questioning the basics and are not typically exposed to the reasonably well developed alternatives that exist in behavioral economics. Younger academics often toe the line, worried about their tenures and wary of the gatekeepers in some of the leading journals in economics or, worse, being brainswashed into believing that the evidence supports their theories.

3.2.2 Emotions and Optimization in Microfinance Contracts

Some readers, schooled in the BRA, might at this stage say, "Hang on, but perhaps people are myopic and maximize their objectives over very short time periods, say, today and tomorrow, ignoring the rest. Perhaps in these models, optimization is a good approximation." We should point out that while myopia is probably an excellent description of how many people behave, it is not consistent with the BRA; after all, why should fully rational individuals ignore the full future consequences of their current actions? Other readers, who are mainly trained in microeconomic theory, say, in game theory, might look upon the problems arising in the previous subsection as specific to the domain of macroeconomics. It is not uncommon to hear microeconomic theorists in the wake of the 2007–2008 financial crises speak of macroeconomic theorists with apparent disdain. Such readers might find this subsection, and several subsequent sections, sobering. This subsection also illustrates a variety of problems with the BRA that tie in with our discussion of methodological issues and issues of social norms below.

The paper by Dhami et al. (2020) on the economics of microfinance contracts illustrates several issues that are pertinent to the debate. Microfinance borrowers are individually small and lack any security to offer as collateral, so the formal banking sector refuses to lend to them. However, the Grameen Bank, founded by Muhammad Yunus, successfully solved the supply side problem of microfinance contracts and won the 2006 Nobel Peace Prize. In 2017, estimates suggest that 130 million microfinance borrowers took $114 billion in loans.

To see how this model works, suppose that we have just two time periods, $t = 1, 2$ and the following two main kinds of microfinance contracts.

1. *Individual liability (IL) contracts:* Individual borrowers borrow money from a microfinance institution (MFI) in the first period, and each such borrower is given a second period loan *only* if the first period loan is repaid.
2. *Joint liability (JL) contracts:* Groups of borrowers, say, groups of two, jointly borrow money in the first period, typically for different and unrelated projects. Both borrowers are given a second period loan *only* if *both borrowers* repay the first period loan; otherwise, if the project of any single borrower fails, then *both* borrowers are refused a second period loan. Each borrower in a JL contract creates a positive externality for the partner because by working harder one ensures that one's own project is more likely to be successful, which also increases the chances that the partner in the joint liability contract will also get a second period loan.

The basic BRA, in the absence of moral hazard or asymmetric information, predicts that JL contracts should not exist. This is because in a JL contract, groups of borrowers will ignore the positive externalities that they create for each other, so they both will not work hard enough.[3] Yet, the initial business model of the Grameen Bank was based on JL contracts, and the repayment rate was extremely high: in 2017 it was 99.6 percent. It is well-known that the Grameen Bank started by offering JL contracts (also known as *Grameen I*), but many commercial microfinance banks have, in recent years, moved toward IL contracts (now known as *Grameen II*). We offer potential explanations for why this might have happened. By contrast, models in the BRA that rely on explanations based on asymmetric information or moral hazard typically struggle to explain this switch.

Another important institutional factor in microfinance contracts is the *public repayment of loans*. Essentially, the loan officer visits a village, say, once a month and gathers around all borrowers to declare their loan repayments. So, defaults or repayment delays become public information in front of one's peers and the relevant social group. Consider a 2 × 2 design in which we vary the liability structure (IL or JL) and also the mode of repayment, which is either public repayment in front of peers (P) or individual repayment to the bank without peer observation (I). This gives rise to four possible contracts: ILI (individual liability with individual repayment), ILP (individual liability with public repayment), JLI (joint liability with individual repayment), and JLP (joint liability with public repayment).

In its actual practice, the BRA advocates emotionless deliberation that is based solely on monetary costs and monetary benefits. However, in their formal theoretical model, Dhami et al. (2020) propose emotional factors such as *guilt* and *shame* as being decisive in the choice between contracts and also for the choice of effort by borrowers. Formally, they use the machinery of *psychological game theory*, in which beliefs directly enter into the utility function, which allows for an explicit and formal modeling of emotions.[4]

1. *Guilt:* In JL contracts (i.e., in contracts JLI and JLP), borrowers might feel guilty about not meeting the expectations of their partners about how hard they will work to repay their loans. Hence, they may work harder, potentially explaining why borrowers put in higher effort in JL contracts. In order to create variation in guilt, the authors conveyed a private signal of the effort expectations of each player in a JL contract to their partner (e.g., if Jim and Jane are the two partners, then Jim received a private signal about how hard Jane expected him to work on the project, and vice-versa). The prediction of a model based on guilt aversion is that a higher private signal induces higher effort. In the standard model in the BRA, such signals should have no effect on effort.

2. *Shame:* In contracts with public repayment (i.e., in contracts ILP and JLP), borrowers may work harder to avoid defaults because the default information is revealed publicly, in front of one's social group or peers. Thus, defaulters experience the emotion of shame from the act of defaulting on loans. This is particularly the case when borrowers (a) receive a *social signal* from their relevant social group (perhaps as part of a social norm) about how hard they are expected to work and (b) are likely to receive social disapproval from their social group by putting in effort that is below the expectations of the social group.

In particular, the contrasts between the two pairs of treatments, ILI versus ILP and JLI versus JLP, tease out the effect of shame by keeping fixed the liability structure but varying the mode of payment, private or public. The prediction of a model based on shame aversion is that there should be greater effort in the public repayment treatments as compared to the private repayment treatments. In the basic model in the BRA, there should be no difference in effort levels between private and public repayments.

Incidentally, the public repayment feature is common in Grameen I and Grameen II and was unaffected by the switch from IL to JL contracts. This is not formally explained by any of the existing models. However, a model that formally includes the possibility of shame has the potential to explain why, as we shall see below.

Dhami et al. (2020) made formal predictions based on a model that included both guilt and shame and then put the model to the test using an artifactual, between-subjects field experiment with 400 microfinance borrowers in Pakistan. In each contract between borrowers and an MFI, subjects first borrowed money from the MFI, under limited liability, and then chose their first period effort. Effort probabilistically determined the outcomes of their projects such that a higher effort increased the success probability of the project. However, due to moral hazard, effort levels were unobserved by the lender and could not be written down in a formal contract. Once the outcome (success or failure) for the first period project was known, the MFI made the decision to give or withhold second period loans.

Under ILI and ILP contracts, borrowers with successful first period projects were automatically given second period loans, and they chose again their effort in the second period. Under JLI and JLP contracts, if both borrowers in the group had successful first period projects, then they both received a second period loan and chose their effort level in the second period. Otherwise, both borrowers were denied a second period loan and could not proceed to the second period.

The results on the first period effort choices by the subjects in the four different contracts are summarized in the *box and whiskers plot* in figure 3.1. The distribution of effort choices by the subjects in each of the four contracts are to be read vertically upward. Under the parameterization chosen by the authors, the BRA, in the absence of the emotions of guilt and shame, predicts an effort level of approximately 3. This is comfortably rejected and there is a great deal of heterogeneity in choices. In the two public repayment treatments (ILP, JLP), players are told before choosing their effort levels that their social group expects them to put in an effort level of 6; this was the relevant social signal. The expectation was that effort levels below the social signal, when observed under public

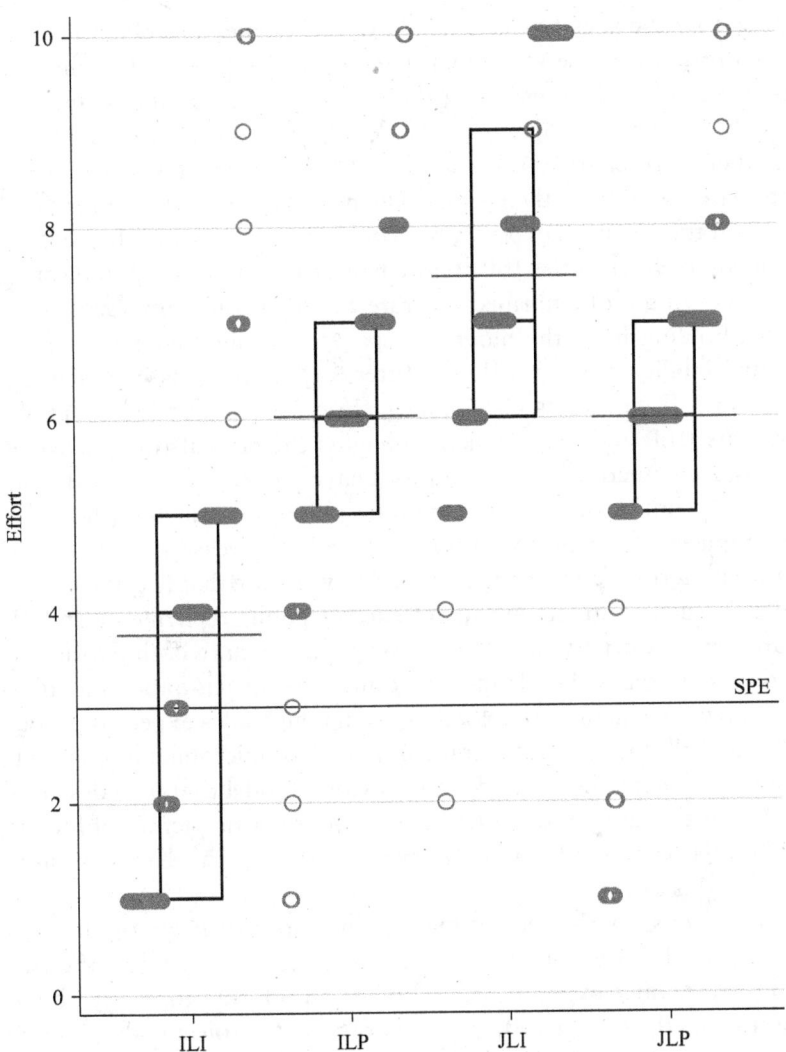

Figure 3.1
First period effort levels in different contracts / treatments.

repayment by the social group, would create shame. The effort level of 6 turned out also to be the actual mean/median effort level in the two public treatments, demonstrating the critical role of shame (confirmed separately by regression analysis). On average, borrowers in JLI contracts expect their partners to choose an effort level of 6.67; this was the relevant private signal from the partner. The prediction is that an effort level lower than the partner's expectation would give rise to guilt. Indeed, the mean/median effort in the JLP contracts is also close to 6.67, indicating the presence of guilt (confirmed separately by regression analysis).

Thus, holding fixed the mode of repayment, guilt aversion explains why joint liability contracts, JL, do better than individuals contracts, IL. Both IL and JL contracts elicit higher effort in the presence of public repayments (ILP and JLP), which highlights the critical role played by shame. Indeed, microfinance institutions have moved away from JL contracts to IL contracts, while maintaining public repayments (the move from Grameen I to Grameen II noted above). The reasons that IL contracts are preferred to JL contracts in recent years are that (1) effort levels are high in such contracts in the presence of public repayments and (2) they are not as restrictive as JL contracts, which require both partners in a JL contract to repay their loans before any of them gets another loan, so fewer individuals qualify for a loan, reducing the bank's expected profits.

In a nutshell, the relevant empirical facts from microfinance contracts have a natural explanation under a behavioral model that includes emotions, because such a model offers a far more realistic picture of human behavior relative to the BRA. This is the first main point that we wish to make with this example.

We now consider the second main point: Do borrowers optimize in a mathematical sense? The second period is the last period of the two period microfinance experiment, and there is no future to worry about. By contrast, in the first period, greater effort on the project makes it more likely that an individual (in an individual liability contract) or a group of individuals (in a joint liability contract) will be able to repay their loan and so successfully obtain a second period loan. In other words, the marginal benefit of first period effort is always greater than second period effort. So, we should expect first period effort to exceed second period effort. It is problematic for any optimization model to explain why second period effort should be equal to or greater than first period effort. Figure 3.2 shows the distribution of effort levels in the four contracts in the second period. Comparing figures 3.1 and 3.2, we see that second period effort is equal to or greater than first period effort.

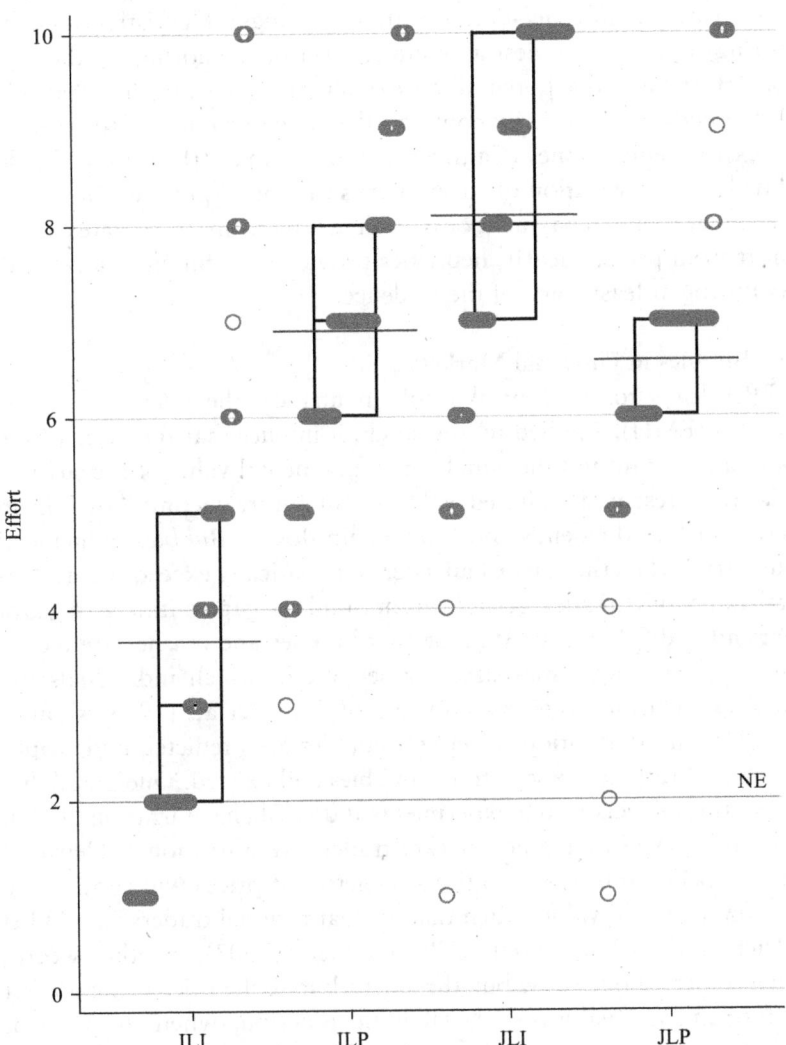

Figure 3.2
Second period effort levels in different contracts / treatments.

What can possibly account for these findings? Heuristics such as anchoring on a socially desirable effort level or anchoring on the first period effort have the potential to explain these results that defy the predicted endgame effect. By contrast, the endgame effects produced in many experimental games (Camerer, 2003; Dhami, 2019d) typically do not involve the invocation of social norms that underpin the emotion of shame under public repayment or of guilt arising from the private signals of effort from peers. Clearly, heuristics provide a useful alternative way of organizing at least some of the evidence.

3.2.3 Bubbles in Financial Markets

The BRA leads to the central result in finance, the *efficient markets hypothesis* (EMH). Applied to any stock, it implies that the price of the stock at any instant in time equals the fundamental value of the stock—that is, the present discounted value of all future income flows from the stock such as dividends and capital gains/losses. *Bubbles* in financial markets arise when the price of an asset systematically exceeds the fundamental value for extended periods of time and the gap continues to grow.

Harstad and Selten (2013) argue that bubbles and crashes are inconsistent with an optimizing-based framework in which individuals use rational expectations. The experiments of Smith et al. (1988) showed that under full information, where no bubbles are predicted under optimization and rational expectations, bubbles still existed. One possibility was that the subjects in the experiments did not behave irrationally but may have believed that other market traders were irrational. Hence, if others are believed to have irrational beliefs that prices will continue to exceed fundamental values, then that is what rational traders should bet on (Allen et al., 1993; Abreu & Brunnermeier, 2003). In other words, rational traders should now buy the asset (despite the price being greater than fundamental values) and sell it next period, when the price is expected to increase even further on account of the presence of irrational beliefs. Indeed, such expectations cause the price of the asset to actually increase—a sort of *self-fulfilling prophesy*.

Using field data, it is quite difficult to test this explanation because one has to determine who is rational and then devise a method to elicit their beliefs about the irrationality of others. However, the great advantage of experiments is that they allow one to test models in a way that field data rarely allows. Lei et al. (2001) reran the original experiments in Smith et al. (1988) but forbade buyers of assets to resell them. Clearly, this shuts down the channel through which rational traders may be influenced by other irrational traders. However, the bubbles reemerged in the data.

From this evidence, Harstad and Selten (2013, p. 501) conclude that "no model based on optimization can explain the bubbles that arise in the Lei, Noussair, and Plott experiments." Although it might indeed be the case that the data arise from non-optimization, it is also possible that the data arise from other assumptions made within the model. Crawford (2013) makes the point that the results in the experiments on bubbles are a joint test of optimization, rational expectations, and *common knowledge of beliefs*. Hence, the experimental results do not necessarily invalidate optimization—perhaps they invalidate common knowledge. Thus, this is an example of a situation where unambiguous conclusions about optimization are difficult to draw. Much modern game theory, certainly most applied game theory, is based on the notion of common knowledge of beliefs. Roughly speaking, common knowledge about an event, say, event A, arises if the relevant population knows A, knows that others know A, knows that others know that they know that others know A, and so on ad infinitum.

The precise mechanism through which common knowledge might arise in these models is almost never spelled out. The issue of how common knowledge might arise in economic models is also almost never addressed in courses in economic theory, which tends to be taught in an axiomatic fashion, without recourse to the evidence. Coming back to financial markets, if market participants were following different belief formation heuristics, which they probably are, then it is very unlikely that we would have something like common knowledge in asset markets. Indeed, Hong and Stein (1999, 2007) show that heterogeneity in the beliefs of market traders and lack of common knowledge is necessary for there to be momentum in stock market prices and for high trading volumes, even when prices equal fundamental values.

For this reason, some have argued for dropping the common knowledge assumption altogether (Gintis, 2009). But this would imply a radical rewriting of existing economic theory, including altering the focus from Nash equilibrium and its extension to different classes of games to other sorts of equilibria, such as a correlated equilibrium and a Kantian equilibrium Gintis (2009, 2017) or to an evidential equilibrium (al-Nowaihi & Dhami, 2015). We consider some of the alternative notions of social rationality, such as Kantian equilibrium, below.

3.2.4 Will Non-Optimizing Individuals Simply Perish?

A common preamble to most economics and finance courses, in order to justify the methods used, runs as follows.

> Individuals who fail to optimize will receive inferior payoffs. Thus, in a competition with other individuals who do optimize, and hence receive higher payoffs, the non-optimizing types will perish under market competition. It follows that any individual who has to survive in competitive conditions must optimize. Henceforth, we shall only consider optimizing individuals in this course. QED

This preamble is typically followed by a corollary:

> We do not deny that there could be individuals who make errors, or are irrational. However, the positive and negative errors cancel out in the aggregate and what remains is purely rational behavior. Hence, there is no merit in considering any form of irrationality in this course. QED

The preamble and the corollary are, of course, simply hypotheses about human behavior and the likely outcomes. These hypotheses also play a central role in the justification of the efficient markets hypothesis (EMH). However, the evidence does not support these hypotheses. Various implications of the EMH fail when confronted with the evidence (Shiller, 1981, 2015; Shleifer, 2000; Akerlof & Shiller, 2009; Dhami, 2020a).

Financial market participants have been shown to use a range of judgment heuristics in making financial decisions that collectively give rise to *investor sentiment*. These heuristics, surveyed in chapter 5, include, but are not restricted to, using representativeness to infer from small samples the properties of the population distribution (the gambler's fallacy and the hot hand fallacy are special cases); anchoring on irrelevant anchors; using the hindsight bias to misperceive one's own previous predictions, hence, underestimating stock market volatility; not following the prescriptions of Bayes' law; using trends and trying to infer patterns in inherently noisy data (Shleifer, 2000; Dhami, 2020a). The following quotation from Shleifer (2000, p. 10) illustrates a set of other judgment heuristics and biases that run contrary to the assumption of EMH, further undermining the case for EMH.

> It is difficult to sustain the case that people in general, and investors in particular, are fully rational. At the superficial level, many investors react to irrelevant information.... Investors follow the advice of financial gurus, fail to diversify, actively trade stocks and churn their portfolios, sell winning stocks and hold on to losing stocks thereby increasing their tax liabilities, buy and sell actively and expensively managed mutual funds, follow stock price patterns and other popular models. In short, investors hardly pursue the passive strategies expected of uninformed market participants by the efficient market theory.

Thus, many investors make important financial decisions based on their investor sentiment (or *animal spirits*, as in Akerlof & Shiller, 2009) rather than employing the prescriptions of the BRA. Such investors are sometimes also known as *unsophisticated investors* (Kyle, 1985) or *noise traders* (Black, 1986). Noise traders is not just a theoretical construct. For instance, the closed-end puzzles can be explained by the existence of noise traders (Lee et al., 1991). Indeed, if rational financial market traders, known as *arbitrageurs*, take into account the behavior of noise traders, then they might bet on mispricing getting worse, giving rise to bubbles. Laypersons and experts make *persistent errors* and exhibit *systematic biases* (Dhami, 2020a). Hence, the probability that positive and negative errors simply cancel out in the aggregate is low, perhaps vanishingly low, with serious implications for financial stability. Noise traders may take a long time to lose money and to exit the market; however, arbitrageurs may have to liquidate their positions before noise traders can exit the market (Figlewski, 1979). Thus, the non-optimizing traders might outlast the arbitrageurs. De Long et al. (1990) show that noise traders, who trade simply on investor sentiment, may earn higher profits as compared to arbitrageurs, provided that they are bullish.

In the BRA, and in finance, non-optimizing managers of companies are predicted to perish because they will make lower profits for their companies and hence be fired. Managers with behavioral biases that might not be conducive to maximizing company profits could be hard to get rid of in practice (Lazear, 2004). Here are some reasons for why this might be the case (Dhami, 2020, Vol. a).

1. Many corporate decisions are of an infrequent nature and do not allow sufficient learning opportunities to develop the requisite skills. Furthermore, outsiders such as shareholders, evaluating the decisions of managers, often do so in an environment of true uncertainty (unknown unknowns); hence, the optimal decisions may be unclear to them. These include infrequent decisions such as choosing specialized investments, making long-term technological choices, making merger and acquisition choices, and capital restructuring.
2. In some domains, models in the BRA and in behavioral finance often do not offer a clear yardstick to judge what really are the most efficient corporate decisions. For instance, what is the appropriate method to evaluate the long-run effects of a merger decision taken by a CEO? This makes it quite difficult to evaluate some CEO decisions on any objective yardstick.
3. Managers might be able to protect themselves, and successfully shade bad decisions, by influencing the board of directors, and the board might not always act in a manner that maximizes shareholder value (Bebchuk et al., 2002).

4. It might be hard to evaluate the performance of managers/CEOs because of *attribution bias*. The cash flow of companies depends both on managerial competence/skills and on purely random luck / external factors. However, the board of directors or shareholders might underestimate the effect of luck / external factors, particularly when faced with a charming and smooth-talking manager who articulates and rationalizes well the earlier decisions, even if they were inappropriate.

Self-serving bias on the part of managers ensures that when companies do badly, external factors beyond the managers' control are blamed in annual reports (attribution bias). By contrast, when the cash flow of companies increases, perhaps purely due to luck, managers may be mistakenly attributed as the cause, and their self-serving bias ensures that annual reports highlight the critical role they have played to ensure a good outcome (Bettman & Weitz, 1983). For instance, world oil prices are determined by events outside the control of managers of oil companies and are determined by the world demand and supply conditions of oil. Yet, as oil prices increase, the compensation of executives in oil companies increases (Bertrand & Mullainathan, 2001).

But if markets are efficient, how do biased managers make it to the top? Do not the firms' internal selection processes work well? Indeed, these processes do not always work well. Overconfidence is a well-documented human trait (Weinstein, 1980), although in the BRA, managers are never overconfident. The BRA would predict that overconfident managers are likely to make rash decisions and also perish in a competition with rational managers. However, in actual practice, more overconfident managers may take more risks, could be successful purely by chance, and leapfrog managers who are not overconfident. This is particularly the case in a tournament setting where relative performances are compared (Goel & Thakor, 2008). More confident managers might have masking traits (e.g., they may be inspiring or charming or have a positive outlook) that give rise to a misperception of their being in control of the ship. Managers are likely to be overconfident in domains where they think that they have control (*illusion of control*) and in domains where they have a *personal commitment*. Overconfidence in managers is well supported by the evidence (March & Shapira, 1987; Ben-David et al., 2013). Security analysts who are more optimistic, rather than more accurate, are more likely to move up to a high-status brokerage house, and brokerage houses offer relatively higher rewards to optimistic analysts who promote stocks as compared to more accurate analysts (Hong and Kubik, 2003).

CEO overconfidence is also reflected in the practice of CEOs holding on to their own company stock for too long, hence forgoing a profitable opportunity to sell company stock (Meulbroek, 2001; Hall & Murphy, 2000, 2002). Malmendier and Tate (2015) use this proxy to determine managerial overconfidence. They show that overconfident CEOs are one and a half times more likely to engage in merger activities with other firms relative to the fully rational benchmark. Malmendier and Tate (2008) confirm the relation between overconfident CEOs and mergers and find a smaller stock market reaction to mergers when investors perceive CEOs to be more overconfident. Malmendier et al. (2011) show that more overconfident managers are also more likely to believe that their stocks are undervalued by the market. Hence, they perceive that external finance is overpriced and may forgo profitable opportunities for their companies that rely on external borrowings. Aktas et al. (2016) measured narcissism in managers, a trait possibly linked to overconfidence, by the ratio of the number of times that CEOs used first person singular pronouns to the total number of first person pronouns in transcribed speeches. Managers who were more narcissistic were more active in the role of acquiring firms in mergers, negotiated faster, and were more likely to have initiated and completed mergers, potentially disadvantaging their companies because most mergers, in fact, fail.

In sum, managers who depart from the optimizing benchmark and exhibit a range of behavioral biases are not only likely to survive, but might never be found out despite making suboptimal decisions for their companies.

3.2.5 Optimization or Heuristics? An Application from Microfinance Contracts

In many cases, the predictions of optimization-based models and heuristics-based models may be identical or very similar. In this case, it becomes critical to derive further predictions that help us distinguish between the two sets of models. For instance, we would need to derive implications that are predicted under optimization-based but not under heuristics-based models or vice-versa. We offer the first of two examples in this subsection, immediately followed by the second example in the next subsection.

Consider the predictions for the microfinance game in section 3.2.2 that were based on an optimization framework. Consider the following two predictions of the optimization model:

1. In joint liability contracts, guilt averse borrowers should respond to higher expectations of effort from their partners by putting in more effort. The reason is that guilt averse borrowers suffer disutility from falling below the expectations of their partners. This channel was confirmed by the data; see figure 3.1.
2. Shame averse borrowers respond to higher effort expectations of their social group / peers (i.e., how much effort they *ought to* contribute, as deemed appropriate by the social group) by exerting higher effort. The reason is that shame averse borrowers suffer disutility from falling below the expectations of their social group. This was also confirmed by the data; see figure 3.1. Such borrowers might also anticipate being sanctioned by their social group if their effort falls below their group's expectations. Sanctions were allowed in the microfinance game, and borrowers who fell below these expectations were indeed found to be sanctioned. These results are consistent with effort being influenced by social norms (see the discussion on social norms in section 3.4).

It may be tempting to conclude from 1 and 2 that in choosing their effort level, borrowers indeed optimize in a precise mathematical sense. However, such a conclusion might be premature. Consider the following two examples from Dhami et al. (2020) that invoke a heuristics-based choice yet lead to conclusions that are observationally equivalent to an optimization-based approach.

Example 3.1. *Norma enters into an individual liability contract with public repayments (ILP) with a microfinance institution that requires her to make repayments that are publicly observed by her social group / peers. Norma does not engage in mathematical optimization when making decisions but relies on simple heuristics. The relevant social group forms expectations about the effort that its group members ought to exert. Bicchieri (2006) calls such expectations normative expectations (see section 3.4). These expectations are known to Norma because she observes a clear social signal of these expectations. The social group can also observe the repayments and defaults by the group members and impose costly social sanctions on those who fall below the normative expectations.*

Norma is shame averse because she experiences shame from falling below the social group's normative expectations. This could be because, like most humans, Norma is conditioned by evolution or culture to follow social norms (Bowles & Gintis, 2011; Henrich, 2017; Gintis, 2017). In order to avoid shame, Norma uses the following simple rule of thumb, or heuristic. She puts in an effort level that equals her social group's normative expectations. If instead Norma were asked to repay in private (i.e., if she had chosen the contract ILI), then she would not anticipate any shame from defaulting on the loan repayment; hence, she would be likely to put in lower effort. However, this set of predictions, based on a heuristics-based approach, is observationally identical to Norma using optimization within a psychological game theory framework.

Example 3.2. A microfinance institution enters into a two-person joint liability (JL) contract with Gill and a partner, who do not use mathematical optimization in making their decisions but use heuristics in making choices. Before choosing their own effort levels, Gill and her partner form expectations about each other's actual effort levels because their effort and the partner's effort will jointly determine whether they get second period loans or not. In contrast to the normative expectations in example 3.1, such expectations are known as positive expectations in the literature (see Bicchieri, 2006, and section 3.4). Gill and her partner are also aware of each other's positive expectations because they receive a clear private signal of these mutual expectations.[5]

If Gill is guilt averse, then she experiences disutility from guilt by exerting effort below her partner's positive expectations (Battigalli & Dufwenberg, 2007). Thus, Gill follows a simple heuristic of matching her partner's positive expectations in order to avoid guilt. If, on the other hand, Gill had taken up an individual liability (IL) contract with the microfinance institution, then she would not have a partner. Hence, she would not have to take account of a partner's positive expectations, so she puts in a lower effort. This is one reason why, under private repayments, joint liability may induce higher effort and loan repayments relative to individual liability contracts. In this case, too, the heuristics-based approach generates predictions that are observationally identical to an optimization-based approach.

Examples 3.1 and 3.2 show that individuals who follow simple heuristics may also enable us to explain the data in figure 3.1. Hence, we cannot necessarily conclude that the data establish that people optimize. In this case, we need to look for other implications of the optimization and the heuristics frameworks that may help us to distinguish between the two.

As discussed above, the second period effort choices in figure 3.2 are not consistent with an optimizing model because there are no endgame effects (i.e., sharp drop in effort in the last period, which is the second period). Any optimization-based model would predict that effort should be lower in the second period, as compared to the first period. The conclusion? First period effort is consistent with either a heuristics-based or an optimization-based model, but second period effort is not consistent with an optimization-based model. Is second period effort necessarily consistent with a heuristics-based model? Dhami et al. (2020) do not establish the precise heuristic that borrowers might be using, but they offer conjectures that include the possibility that borrowers simply anchor their second period effort choices on the first period effort choices in order to economize on scarce cognitive resources.

3.2.6 Optimization or Heuristics? An Application to Tax Evasion

The next example poses a slightly more complicated problem in which there is an issue of distinguishing the predictions of two competing optimizing models and a further issue of distinguishing their predictions from a heuristics-based approach. However, this example also demonstrates the critical insight that optimization-based models may also provide good as-if approximation. This allows us to develop the theme that there are good as-if optimization-based models and bad ones, so one cannot, on a priori grounds, always argue that optimization-based models are an unmitigated bad idea.

Consider the classic problem of tax evasion in public finance. In the UK, HMRC estimates that the tax gap (the difference between taxes owed and taxes paid) for 2018–2019 is £31 billion. Some rough, back of the envelope calculations show this money could be used to fund 40 new state of the art NHS hospitals in the UK. The corresponding tax gap for the US for 2019 is estimated by the IRS to be $441 billion.

In this section, we consider tax evasion by individuals only. A central question that we ask is this: Why do individuals, whose income is not deducted at source, pay any taxes?

The seminal application of expected utility theory to the tax evasion problem is by Allingham and Sandmo (1972) and Yitzhaki (1974). This model is sometimes known as the Allingham-Sandmo-Yitzhaki, or AYS, framework; it has been adopted by much of the subsequent literature. In the AYS framework, an individual taxpayer has some privately known, but exogenous, income W that is unobserved by the government. The individual makes a voluntary decision to declare an amount $D \in [0, W]$ of the income for tax purposes, which is taxed at the constant tax rate $t > 0$. The taxpayer is audited by the tax authorities with probability $p \in (0, 1)$. If audited, the tax authorities discover hard evidence of the taxpayer's evasion that is sufficient to gain a conviction in a court of law. If caught, a tax evader has to (1) repay the owed taxes and (2) pay a penalty proportional to the evaded taxes at a rate, $\theta > 0$.

How much should the taxpayer evade? How do changes in the deterrence parameters, p, θ, and the tax rate, t, influence the evasion decision?

An expected utility analysis predicts that deterrence is effective in the sense that an increase in the probability of detection, p, and in the audit penalty, θ, induces the taxpayer to declare more income. This was generally taken as a validation of the joint assumptions of optimization and of expected utility theory. Since the early 1970s, the AYS framework has spawned a huge literature that has extended the basic model in several directions that incorporate moral costs of tax evasion, norms of evasion, line reporting of items in evasion decisions, nonlinear taxes, dynamic considerations, nonmonetary penalties, simplification of the tax system.[6]

However, the predictions of an expected utility framework for the response of tax evasion to changes in the tax rate, t, are counterintuitive; this has been known since the mid-1970s as the *Yitzhaki puzzle* (Yitzhaki, 1974). The assumption of *decreasing absolute risk aversion* in the BRA is reasonable and it is empirically supported. It implies that, if given a choice between investing in a risky asset and a riskless asset, the richer are less risk averse in the sense that they will invest a higher absolute amount in the risky asset. Applying this assumption to tax evasion, we can trace out the effect of a change in the tax rate, t. An increase in the tax rate reduces the incomes of taxpayers, making them poorer and hence also more risk averse, so they evade less (Yitzhaki puzzle). In the limit, at a tax rate of 100 percent, evasion can be eliminated altogether under reasonable conditions. This is not just counterintuitive; it is rejected by most of the empirical evidence, which shows that at higher taxes people try to evade more income (Slemrod & Yitzhaki, 2002; Alm, 2019). Among researchers working in this area, this was considered to be an *anomaly* of an otherwise good theory, but not worthy enough to reject the theory, as evidenced by thousands of subsequent papers in this tradition.

However, there was an undercurrent of concern among an admittedly small number of researchers, who pointed out several other anomalies of an expected utility approach to the AYS framework.[7] One of the striking anomalies was the following. The audit probability, p, for an amateur tax evader is extremely low, with realistic magnitudes ranging from $p = 0.01$ to $p = 0.05$ (i.e., 1%–5%) (Skinner & Slemrod, 1985). The penalty rate θ ranges from 0.5 to 2.0 (i.e., if caught, one pays evaded taxes, plus a fine that equals half to two times the tax evaded). Suppose that we take the tax rate at 30 percent (i.e., $t=0.30$), which is representative of Western democracies.

Under expected utility, it can be shown that the taxpayer will choose to evade taxes if the *expected return per dollar of evaded tax*, $1-p-p\theta$, is positive. To see this, suppose that a tax evader evades \$1 in taxes. Then, the evader is caught with probability p and must pay the \$1 in evaded taxes plus $\$1 \times \theta$ in fines. If not caught, the evader can keep the \$1 in evaded taxes. For small amounts, the utility function is approximately linear. Hence, the expected return from evading \$1 in taxes is $(1-p) \times 1 + p(1-1-\theta) = 1-p-p\theta$. Let us use the midpoints of the representative range of values of the deterrence parameters, $p=0.03$ and $\theta=1$. Then, $1-p-p\theta=0.94$. In other words, tax evasion under expected utility has a 94 percent rate of return, which is unmatched relative to most assets that would be held in the portfolio of any ordinary Joe or Jane on the street. This begs the question of why people would pay any taxes at all.

Dhami and al-Nowaihi (2007, 2010a) applied all the components of prospect theory for the first time in an optimization-based analysis of the AYS framework (for a primer on prospect theory, see the appendix to chapter 2). In effect, they continued to use optimization but dropped expected utility in favor of prospect theory. Prospect theory, like expected utility, predicts that greater deterrence (higher probability of detection and higher fines) reduces evasion. But importantly, their analysis was able to solve the known anomalies/puzzles that arose under expected utility. Consider two of the anomalies/puzzles that they explained.

1. *Yitzhaki puzzle:* A rough and ready, but not entirely accurate, intuition is that an increase in the tax rate pushes the taxpayer into the domain of losses. Under prospect theory, the decision-maker is risk seeking in the domain of losses (see appendix in chapter 2), hence, choosing the riskier activity of tax evasion. Thus, an increase in the tax rate increases evasion, which is consistent with the empirical evidence. It follows that the Yitzhaki puzzle does not arise under prospect theory.

2. *Explanation of why people pay taxes:* Two features of prospect theory are critical in this regard. First, decision-makers overweight low probabilities; hence, the detection probability of, say, $p=0.03$, has a higher subjective weight in the mind of the taxpayer, giving rise to greater deterrence (see the appendix to chapter 2 for nonlinear probability weighting). Using the terminology in sections 2.16.2 and 2.16.4, we have $w(0.3) > 0.3$, where $w(0.3)$ is the subjective weight assigned to a probability of 0.3 by the taxpayer.

Second, loss aversion, a central feature of prospect theory, implies that when the taxpayer is caught evading taxes, giving up the $1 in evaded taxes and paying a penalty of θ causes total disutility not of $(1+\theta)$ but of $\lambda(1+\theta)$, where λ is the parameter of loss aversion. Empirical magnitudes of λ vary between taxpayers, but the median estimate reported in Tversky and Kahneman (1992) is $\lambda \approx 2.25$. It follows that the higher is loss aversion, the lower will be tax evasion.[8] However, Dhami and al-Nowaihi (2007, 2010) did not provide a taxpayer-specific measurement of λ. Subsequent empirical work found indirect measures of loss aversion and related it to tax evasion (Engström et al., 2015; Rees-Jones, 2018). However, direct individual-level estimates of loss aversion were first obtained by Dhami and Hajimoladarvish (2020), who showed that loss aversion significantly reduced evasion, exactly as predicted in Dhami and al-Nowaihi (2007).

It follows that a tax evasion analysis based on an underlying optimizing model where decision-makers follow prospect theory, which is an as-if theory, provides a highly satisfactory account of the data. In this sense, it might be premature to simply discard optimization and as-if theories. The reason prospect theory is a good as-if theory embedded within an optimization framework is because it contains psychologically salient and critically important features of human behavior. These include reference dependence, loss aversion, diminished sensitivity for gains and losses, and nonlinear probability weighting. By contrast, expected utility, the dominant approach in economics, is a poor as-if theory and fails to fully account for the empirical evidence. The numerical estimates in Dhami and al-Nowaihi (2007) show that expected utility makes predictions that are wrong by a factor of 100.

Yet, we cannot rule out the possibility that a heuristics-based approach may also explain well the evidence on tax evasion. Individuals may, for instance, have internal moral norms and, depending on the strength of these norms, choose to comply or not with the deterrence parameters.[9] Others might follow a simple heuristic of not breaking the law; the data does show that a significant number of people do not evade, even when there is an opportunity to do so. Dhami and Hajimoladarvish (2020) show that many people still do not evade taxes even when there is a 100 percent subsidy to tax evasion. Loss aversion might induce heuristics-following individuals to evade even lower taxes.

The way forward in deciding between a prospect theory analysis of tax evasion and a heuristics-based analysis is to seek further implications of both these frameworks in domains where they give different predictions.

Furthermore, for those interested in this area, the precise heuristics that taxpayers use to pay taxes ought to be identified and then stringently tested against optimization-based frameworks.

3.2.7 Assessing a Three-Way Leaders Debate

In this section, we consider a three-way debate between some of the leaders in the field on the relative merits of optimization and bounded rationality models, which appeared in the 2013 issue of the *Journal of Economic Literature* (51:2). The three papers, by Harstad and Selten (2013), Crawford (2013), and Rabin (2013a), present different points of view. Roughly speaking, Harstad and Selten recommend on all-out heuristics approach based on procedural rationality as the way forward; Rabin argues for an optimization-based approach with incremental replacements of the assumptions in the BRA by behavioral assumptions; and Crawford takes a middle ground. Our views do not fully endorse in all the details any of these three thoughtful and enlightening papers, but lie between the positions taken by Harstad and Selten on the one hand and Crawford on the other.

Crawford (2013) and Rabin (2013a), two of the leaders in the field of behavioral economics, recommend maintaining an optimization-based framework (in contrast to a heuristics-based framework) but relaxing the assumptions in the BRA in favor of behavioral economics assumptions. For instance, one might replace expected utility with prospect theory; self-regarding preferences with other-regarding preferences; exponential discounting with hyperbolic discounting; and equilibrium concepts in classical game theory with level-k models, quantal response equilibrium, and other models in behavioral game theory. In their view, this endeavor is likely to be more successful than an all-out heuristics-based approach.

Rabin (2013a) offers the view that the steepest trajectory is likely to arise from incremental changes to existing optimizing models in the BRA that incorporate successively realistic behavioral assumptions. In particular, he is in favor of models that have the feature that for certain parameter values, they reduce to the standard models in the BRA and for other parameter values, to behavioral models. An example is the model of Fehr and Schmidt (1999) of other-regarding preferences, which reduces to the model of self-regarding preferences when the parameters of advantageous and disadvantageous inequity are set equal to zero. Another example comes from our model of microfinance contracts above. By setting the parameters of guilt aversion and shame aversion equal to zero, a model that is otherwise grounded in psychological game theory reduces to the standard model in the BRA.

This model building suggestion allow us to derive empirically testable restrictions within the same model and, hence, choose between theories. For instance, for the Fehr-Schmidt model, we can test if the data satisfy the restriction that the parameters of advantageous and disadvantageous inequity are statistically zero. If yes, then the self-regarding model would be vindicated for now; otherwise, which is the case, the inequity aversion model is confirmed by the data. However, a downside to this model building suggestion is that it is likely that for no parameter values do optimization-based models reduce to models of simple heuristics. Or the optimization-based model that reduces to a heuristics-based model is too restrictive. In these cases, it is difficult to take account of *procedural rationality* embedded within the model, which appears to be the main concern of Harstad and Selten (2013).

On the other hand, Rabin makes a case for constructing enlightening models of heuristics that use an underlying optimization framework (Rabin & Schrag, 1999; Rabin, 2002; Rabin & Vayanos, 2010); for an introduction to these models, see Dhami (2020a). In Rabin's view, heuristics-based models may lack ecological validity, not alert us to the precise domains in which they apply, and, in particular, assume too little rationality relative to what humans possess. This leads (Rabin, 2013a, p. 536) to a view diametrically opposite to that of Harstad and Selten (2013): "My worry is that, short of extremely tight empirical attention, applications of the models as replacements for the neoclassical paradigm may worsen our predictions in general." However, an analogous argument can be given for optimization-based models, even when they include some behavioral components—namely, that they may lack ecological validity, not alert us to the precise domains in which they apply, and, in particular, assume too much rationality relative to what humans possess.

Crawford (2013, p. 524) offers the following conclusion:

> But to move forward, those who advocate bounded rationality modeling must find comparably convincing, evidence-based ways to choose among the equally enormous number of possible non-optimizing models. This, I think, will prove a more difficult task than finding empirical support for optimization-based deviations from neoclassical models, because the benchmark that optimization provides seems to aid the evidence-gathering process.

We suspect that many behavioral economists would agree with the spirit of this, if not the details. It might well be the correct worldview, even if many neoclassical economists are willing to entertain neither optimization-based behavioral models nor a heuristics-based framework. We also agree that the evidence for heuristics in many domains is patchy and that we do not have an overarching model of heuristics that tells us precisely which heuristics are used when. However, it is difficult to offer a definite conclusion that an optimization framework plus behavioral features will necessarily offer a steeper gradient to progress in the social and behavioral sciences, as compared to a heuristics-based framework plus behavioral features.

Many of the arguments above are for improving the quality and focus of research on heuristics. Harstad and Selten (2013), who make a case for replacing optimization with an all-out heuristics-based boundedly rational framework, also lament the lack of progress in developing boundedly rational alternatives. They write (p. 497):

> However, generations of scholars proposing boundedly rational approaches to economic analysis have not yet led us to a coherent body of behavior-based (as opposed to optimization-based) theory that can offer a legitimate challenge to the primacy of neoclassical theory in economics scholarship, teaching, and policy analysis.

Our own view is that the pace of progress in this area has quickened in recent years. Harstad and Selten advocate neither incremental change nor an optimizing framework but rather a decisive move toward bounded rationality models that rely on procedural rationality and incorporate heuristics as the core components.

Ultimately, and best practice in the natural sciences teaches us this, the only safety net for social and behavioral scientists is to religiously follow the evidence and the facts. After all, and if we were to play the devil's advocate, arguments given in favor of models in the BRA relative to behavioral economics also have a somewhat similar flavor to the arguments for sticking only to optimization-based incremental models relative to heuristics-based models. Indeed, the position of those who prefer to keep unchanged the status quo on the BRA may be characterized as follows (for details, see the introductory chapter in Dhami, 2016):

> We must not abandon neoclassical models, because they tell us useful stories and help us to gain intuition about the real world; provide a tractable framework to make predictions; and that there is inadequate evidence for the behavioral theories, which, furthermore, lack discipline, and are ad-hoc. Hence, we believe that the greatest empirical success is likely to arise from following neoclassical models, relative to models in behavioral economics.

We believe that there is no inherent contradiction between incorporating more behavioral features into our models and thinking about the decision-making process in the spirit of procedural rationality, even if it requires heuristics instead of optimization. If we do not invest adequately in a heuristics-based framework plus behavioral features, we will never know its potential. However, the evaluation of such an investment must be in terms of conformity with the empirical evidence. Empirical conformity is also central to the development of behavioral models of game theory that relax the equilibrium in beliefs assumption in classical game theory as, say, in the applications of level-k models to bilateral trading mechanisms (Crawford, 2021). In this regard, Crawford (2013, p. 525) writes: "The reciprocal challenge for strategic modeling is to find evidence-based boundedly rational models that have the precision, generalizability, and portability to be worthy competitors to Nash equilibrium."

As a final point in this subsection, we consider the commonly repeated assertion among economists that the BRA provides a coherent body of theory with clear predictions while nothing comparable is available among bounded rationality / behavioral economics models. In a similar spirit, Rabin (2013a, p. 531) writes: "I am struck by Harstad and Selten's thoughtful observation that generations of scholars have put effort into bounded rationality without delivering a serious rival to the neoclassical model." We believe that this issue deserves to be examined further, and we discuss it below.

What is meant by the standard BRA, or the currently practiced neoclassical framework to model construction? At its most basic level, in a world of certainty and in the absence of strategic concerns, it simply requires individuals to maximize their utility function subject to budget constraints that govern how scarce resources, such as income or time, are allocated. This already requires making assumptions that guarantee the existence of a utility function; thus, individuals are assumed to (1) pay enough attention to all the alternatives, no matter how many, (2) rank all alternatives in order of preference, and (3) satisfy preference assumptions such as transitivity. Almost all of these assumptions have faced serious challenges from the empirical evidence (see chapter 2). What predictions do we get from such a model? Very little, in fact, without making further auxiliary assumptions; see any graduate textbook in microeconomics, say, Mas-Colell et al. (1995). When applied to general equilibrium, there is again very little that we get out of this most basic model in terms of predictions; see, for instance section 17.E in Mas-Colell et al., titled "Anything goes."

The real predictive power of the BRA framework, and its presumed prowess, comes only from adding extra auxiliary assumptions and from considering successively richer situations that require further assumptions. These assumptions guarantee, for instance, that under risk and uncertainty, decision-makers follow *expected utility*; when making temporal choices, they follow *exponential discounted utility*; when engaged in strategic interaction, they follow equilibrium concepts such as a *perfect Bayesian Nash equilibrium*; and when updating information, they use *Bayes' law*. Thus, it is correct to say that the BRA does provide a coherent body of theory with clear predictions. Yet, there is now enough evidence that rejects all of the theories mentioned in this paragraph in italics and, by implication, the main and auxiliary assumptions behind these theories (see chapter 2). Indeed, as Thaler (2015) notes, the heuristics-based framework of Kahneman and Tversky has shown that the predictions of the BRA do not hold, even in an as-if sense.

Often the rejection of a model in the BRA tradition is a potential rejection of any combination of the elements of a BRA, including optimization. The case for the incremental changes argument, therefore, boils down to altering one component (or a few components) of the BRA and keeping faith with the rest. For instance, we may simply replace exponential discounted utility in the BRA with hyperbolic discounting (see chapter 2). What if the resulting model explains well the data under consideration in a statistical sense, despite the fact that most other components of the BRA in that model are rejected? This could be put down to pure luck. Or, it could be due to the fact that some component of hyperbolic discounting is particularly decisive in explaining the problem at hand, and we chose reasonably nonstringent tests to pass the model through. Or, it could be that in our empirical tests we do not take account of enough alternative explanations of the same phenomena. Or, it could be due to the fact that hyperbolic discounting in conjunction with a heuristics-based approach gives very similar predictions, but we have chosen not to explore this path. We have seen examples (e.g., examples 3.1 and 3.2) where simple heuristics and optimization-based models make observationally identical predictions.

It will be difficult to declare victories for any theory in such a process, and any claimed victories are likely to be very messy. This leads us to the question of judging what exactly is a good incremental change and how can we be sure. There are no simple answers. Almost certainly, claims that optimization-based models will provide a steeper trajectory to progress than heuristics-based models are likely to be gut feelings or just one's personal subjective opinions.

3.3 Strategic Interaction

Strategic interaction, which is the subject matter of game theory, lies at the very heart of modern economics and indeed of all social science. The explanation of *cooperation* and *coordination* is a central task in the social/behavioral sciences, and game theory is well suited to address this task. Indeed, in the absence of a common language and lacking adequate interdisciplinary research in the past, the different social and behavioral sciences have contrived to offer different and mutually inconsistent explanations for cooperation and coordination. Gintis (2009), who makes this point, advocates the unification of all social and behavioral sciences using game theory as the common language. A rigorous treatment of game theory is, therefore, an important part of the toolbox of all social scientists. Modern economics is written in the language of game theory.

Game theory, as practiced in economics (for which we use the term *classical game theory*), relies on (1) a variety of equilibrium concepts, (2) methodological individualism, and (3) auxiliary assumptions that are often unjustified by the evidence, such as the assumption of common knowledge and common priors that different players have about the same event. The equilibrium concepts in economics include Nash equilibrium in static games; subgame perfection in sequential games of perfect information; and perfect Bayesian Nash equilibria in dynamic games of imperfect equilibria. In addition, we have a range of refinements of the equilibrium concepts that require increasingly, and often incredibly, stringent cognitive requirements from the players. The typical requirement in these equilibrium concepts, roughly speaking, is that the equilibrium actions of players are a best response to their beliefs and the equilibrium actions of the other players. Furthermore, equilibrium actions and beliefs are consistent with each other.

As noted in the introduction, methodological individualism is the assumption that individual motivation, cognition, and decision-making entirely explains social phenomena. To explain the assumption of common priors, suppose that a new candidate in the US primary elections for president has potentially one of m different levels of competence, $c_1, c_2, \ldots, c_m$. The candidate knows his competence privately, but voters do not. However, any voter j, in the set of voters, has subjective beliefs about these levels of competence given by $p_{1j}, p_{2j}, \ldots, p_{mj}$, where p_{ij} is the probability assigned by voter j that the competence is given by c_i, $i = 1, \ldots, m$. Common priors requires that all voters in the US who consider voting must assign identical probabilities, $p_1, p_2, \ldots, p_m$, independent of the voter index j, to the different levels of competence. Furthermore, to make progress, we need common knowledge of the common priors: all know that others assign these probabilities; all know that others know that all others assign these probabilities; and so on. This is absurd and unlikely to ever be satisfied in practice but it facilitates a formal and tractable analysis. Almost no reservation is expressed to justify these heroic assumptions in standard theoretical models of political economy that are published in the top journals in economics. A similar situation holds when these models are taught in courses in game theory, which is typically an exercise in axiomatic model building.

But does classical game theory serve the purpose of addressing the critical questions of cooperation and coordination, and is it consistent with the evidence on human behavior? We examine some of these questions here; for a summary of the relevant evidence on strategic interaction, see section 2.14.

The most important game of strategic interaction in the social and behavioral sciences is the static *prisoner's dilemma game* invented by the Canadian mathematician Albert W. Tucker. Indeed, this is the canonical game theoretic model of cooperation and conflict that is taught to almost all social and behavioral science students. If classical game theory is not able to explain the empirical evidence from such a game, then its ability to explain the stylized facts of human cooperation and conflict may need to be questioned.

In the static prisoner's dilemma game, two players (or prisoners) who are caught for the same crime are being interrogated simultaneously in separate rooms. The payoffs and the strategy choices of the two players are represented by the *normal form game* in table 3.1.

The two players cannot observe the choices made by each other; hence, they simultaneously choose from among the available strategies. Each player has one of two strategies: either cooperate, C (the analogue of not snitching on the other accused prisoner), or defect, D (the analogue of snitching on the other accused prisoner). If both simultaneously choose

Table 3.1
The prisoner's dilemma game

	C	D
C	2, 2	0, 3
D	3, 0	1, 1

C, they are both let off by the legal system on account of insufficient evidence; in this case they both get a payoff of 2, measured in some monetary units. The worst possible joint payoffs arise if both choose D, providing enough evidence to convict them; in this case, they get a payoff of 1 each. If one player snitches (chooses D) and the other does not (chooses C), then the snitch gets away with a relatively high monetary payoff of 3 because there is no evidence against them, while the unfortunate player who did not snitch gets a payoff of 0.

The strategies of the row player/prisoner are C, D, and the strategies of the column player/prisoner are also C, D.[10] In any of the four cells corresponding to a pair of strategies chosen by the row and the column players, the first number is the row player's payoff and the second number is the column player's payoff.

Is there an obvious way to play this game? Irrespective of the choice of the other player, each player has a dominant strategy, D; this is to say that this strategy gives a higher payoff to a player for any strategy choice of the other player. On this criterion, the strategy C is a dominated strategy because it gives a lower payoff, relative to D, for any choice of the other player. The *best response* of a player, given the strategy of the other player, is a strategy that gives the highest payoff. The profile of strategies (D, D), in which each player plays a best response to the other player's equilibrium strategy, despite the fact that the strategies are chosen simultaneously and without observing the other player's chosen strategy, is said to be a *Nash equilibrium*. Indeed, in this case, the Nash equilibrium is unique and quite easy to find.

Remark 3.1. *We shall use the prisoner's dilemma game in several places in this book to illustrate the outcomes in a variety of cases (e.g., in aspirations-based models and in demonstrating a Kantian equilibrium; see sections 4.5 and 4.7). There is nothing particularly salient about the numbers used for the payoffs in the prisoner's dilemma game in table 3.1. We could have used any numbers for payoffs that respect the following restrictions: (1) (D, D) is the unique Nash equilibria of the game. (2) The outcome (C, C) is not a Nash equilibrium, but it ensures each player a higher payoff as compared to (D, D) and the highest joint payoff. (3) Conditional on the other player choosing the strategy C, each player gets a higher payoff from choosing the strategy D rather than the strategy C.*

There is no obvious problem of bounded rationality in this low-dimensional and simple problem. Irrespective of the beliefs about what the other player will choose, one must never play C, the strictly dominated strategy. However, when this game is played once (a *static game*), we observe that between 50 and 60 percent of the outcomes are (C, C), and there is a greater incidence of the cooperative outcome if this game is framed as a *cooperative game* rather than an *adversarial game*; see Dhami (2019d, section 2.7.4). Rapoport (1988) finds cooperation rates of 50 percent in the prisoner's dilemma game. In a study of the prisoner's dilemma game based on high-stakes outcomes from a British TV show called *Goldenballs*, Darai and Grätz (2010) find unilateral cooperation rates of 55 percent for stakes above £500 and cooperation rates of 74 percent for stakes below this level. Zhong et al. (2007) show that the cooperation rates in prisoner's dilemma studies go up to 60 percent when positive labels are used (such as a *cooperative game* rather than *prisoner's dilemma game*. When purely generic labels are used (such as C and D), then the cooperation rates are about 50 percent. In a novel study, Khadjavi and Lange (2013) find that actual prison inmates cooperate far more than the student population. In particular, they find that while the cooperation rates among students playing the static prisoner's dilemma game is 37 percent, the cooperation rate among prison inmates is 56 percent.

To see how shocking the empirical results are for any theory that predicts the unique play of (D, D), imagine you were asked if you would take an offer to travel in an airplane in a one-off flight with the probability of safely landing at the destination being 40 to 50 percent. Will you take the flight, even if it is free? Classical game theory predicts you will.

How could a classical game theory course hope to go beyond this point?

Perhaps, because not a shred of empirical evidence is ever presented in a typical game theory course. This is a staggeringly self-handicapping strategy, with tragic consequences for the students, consciously chosen by the instructors in such courses given that the evidence is readily available from so many sources. As to how we might explain the choices of instructors in such courses, see section 3.5 on methodology.

The outcome (C, C) is problematic for many popular behavioral game theories as well (e.g., *level-k models*, where players play a best response to beliefs, so they cannot play C for any beliefs because it is strictly dominated by D). This is not the place to outline models of behavioral game theory. For two fairly comprehensive book-length treatments, see Camerer (2003) and Dhami (2019d). The explanation of the outcome (C, C) is also problematic for evolutionary game theory (see section 4.10.1 for an introduction); the set of evolutionary stable equilibria is a subset of the set of Nash equilibria, so (D, D) is the only possible evolutionary equilibrium. *Quantal response equilibria*, in which players play noisy best replies, can explain the outcome (C, C), but it is not clear what the source of this noise might be in such a simple game. Furthermore, the cognitive requirements for quantal response equilibrium are very stringent.

On the other hand, if we move away from the assumptions of classical game theory, then group selection theories could result in a play of (C, C), as could other behavioral theories based on a notion of social rationality, such as Kantian rationality, joint intentionality, and team reasoning (see Gintis, 2017, who makes this point very well, and Dhami, 2019d, section 3.2). We pursue some of these approaches in section 4.7.

In the context of social preferences, it is considered as desirable that any reasonable theoretical model of other-regarding preferences must first satisfy the evidence from the main experimental games, such as the ultimatum game, trust game, and public goods game (Fehr & Schmidt, 2006). Perhaps one could also propose, in a similar vein, that any model of strategic interaction that wishes to be taken seriously must, as a minimum, explain the evidence from the static prisoner's dilemma game. It could be that people use simple heuristics in game theoretic situations. Al-Nowaihi and Dhami (2015) introduce *evidential reasoning* (which has a rich tradition in psychology; a special case is sometimes referred to as the *false consensus effect* in economics) and *evidential equilibrium* into game theory as useful heuristics with which people think about strategic situations. While we explore this in greater detail in section 4.6, the essence of the idea is this: When uncertain about what other like-minded individuals will do, there is strong evidence that people assign diagnostic significance to their own actions in forming beliefs about what others will do. Furthermore, the default frame for most *conditional reciprocators* is to begin with cooperation and then conditionally reciprocate. This provides a plausible explanation for why the majority of people choose (C, C) in the prisoner's dilemma game. Following Kahneman and Tversky's work on heuristics in judgment and decision-making, perhaps we need a heuristics and biases revolution in game theory too.

At this point, someone trained in classical game theory might protest that it also allows for the cooperative outcome (C, C). However, this requires either an infinitely repeated game, or a game that ends with some probability in each period, or a finitely repeated game in which players have some doubt about the rationality of other players. The explanation of cooperation in this case, elegant in the opinion of some (but elegance is not a scientific criterion), is entirely *instrumental*; people calculate the current benefits and costs of cooperation, and if the benefits are high enough, they cooperate. However, real world people often cooperate because they would like to do so *intrinsically*, not instrumentally, and they often cooperate even with strangers. In other words, conditionally cooperative behavior is a part of our preferences (Bowles and Gintis, 2011; Dhami, 2019b). Furthermore, the evidence presented for the outcome (C, C) arises in the static case, where none of the classical game theoretic explanations have any bite.

In explanations of cooperative play in the repeated prisoner's dilemma game, players often play mixed strategies (i.e., they choose their pure strategies probabilistically). However, Harsanyi's purification agenda, which is used to justify mixed strategies, does not have any bite for this class of games. The cooperative results for repeated games hold mainly for public signals received commonly by all the players, but little is known for the more realistic case of private signals. The available results obtain only for private signals that are "ε close to public signals"; we get no idea of how small ε must be. For the claims in this paragraph, see Gintis (2009). It is also noteworthy that the classical game theory solution for finite repeated games uses backward induction, a solution method that repeatedly fails in experiments (e.g., in experiments on the centipede game) (Dhami, 2019d, section 1.2.3).

Finally, consider the general criticism that the experimental evidence in static games, such as the static prisoner's dilemma game, is flawed because subjects cannot distinguish between repeated and static interactions. For instance, they could mistakenly apply repeated game heuristics and social norms that they use outside the lab to make their choices in a static lab game (Binmore, 1998). This criticism is flawed. It is true that there are cross-cultural differences in the behavior of subjects in games, possibly reflecting different social norms; indeed the evidence from the ultimatum game and other games reflects this (Henrich et al., 2001; Henrich, 2017). However, the prisoner's dilemma games are conducted with fairly uniform subject pools, such as Western university students, in which there is probably less diversity in norms. We know from many experiments that the extent of cooperation and punishment differs in static and repeated games, ruling out the possibility that subjects mistakenly apply repeated game heuristics to static choices (Andreoni & Miller, 1993; Fehr & Fischbacher, 2004; Gächter & Falk, 2002; Seinen & Schram, 2006; Engelmann & Fischbacher, 2009).

It is difficult to explain cooperation in the prisoner's dilemma game by using models of social preferences for plausible parameter values (al-Nowaihi and Dhami, 2015). Since the action C is a dominated strategy, it is not *rationalizable* and cannot be supported in a *correlated equilibrium* either.

Another potential problem arises in games where the strategy spaces are too large. This can arise if each player has too many strategies or there are too many players in the game. We have already seen a variant of this dimensionality problem in section 3.2.1. It has been suggested that players trim their strategies in some manner to simplify the choices that they have (Arad & Rubinstein, 2012; Harstad & Selten, 2013). For instance, players with multiple goals may pick just a few desirable goals in order to determine their choices. They then use the trimmed strategy spaces to use boundedly rational solution concepts such as level-k models or cognitive hierarchy models and choose an optimizing solution over the remaining choices. The trimming stage is reminiscent of the editing phase in Kahneman and Tversky (1979) in their original formulation of prospect theory, in which individual decision-makers trimmed large-dimensional lottery choices to achieve cognitive simplicity (see section 4.14).

3.4 The Role of Social Norms

We have reviewed some evidence on the computational and cognitive requirements that are implicit in the BRA. These requirements are unlikely to be satisfied in real life. For instance, it could be that the computational requirements in solving a problem are beyond any reasonable human limits (section 3.2.1); or humans might not pay adequate attention to all the possibilities (section 2.10); or they may use some form of heuristics rather than optimization (chapters 5, 6); or they might not follow Bayes' law to update probabilities (section 2.15.2). It is also possible that individuals face true uncertainty, in which case the BRA is not suitable to make predictions.

Yet, individuals do make decisions in these sorts of situations. How do they do it?

One tantalizing possibility is that social and/or possibly moral norms provide appropriate heuristics to individuals, enabling them to make choices. It cannot be ruled out that some social norms exist mainly to facilitate such choices. There has been a proliferation of research papers on social norms in economics in recent years; for a survey and the references, see Dhami (2019b, section 5.7). Our intention here is not to survey the literature but to offer some thoughts on a potentially novel role for social norms. Let us first consider a motivating example.

Example 3.3. One of the authors of this book spent his formative years in India and often came across anecdotal evidence of the ideas in this section. Consider, for instance, the choice of a marriage partner in a society where such marriages are often arranged. Arguably, this is a decision where by all possible future outcomes are likely to be unimaginable. By contrast, the prescription in economics, if one could miraculously imagine all the possible future outcomes and their probabilities, is to use dynamic programming (in conjunction with expected utility) as in section 3.2.1. But there are serious dimensionality problems associated with such a method. Yet, people do marry. So, how are marriage partners picked?

In traditional Punjabi villages, arranged marriages among farming families (and perhaps elsewhere) are traditionally initiated with the parents and other senior members of the family of a potential partner visiting the family of the other. In order to reach the momentous decision, custom has dictated a simple heuristic, and since there is a shared understanding of this heuristic with clear social expectations, it is a candidate social norm (Fehr & Schurtenberger, 2018a).

The heuristic was to go through a checklist, which included, but was not restricted to, observations on how well fed the animals in the host family were (indicating compassion, care, and responsibility); how well organized the winter haystacks were (indicating organizational skills, responsibility, and farsightedness); and how well the host family was greeted by other villagers as they escorted the visiting family to the village boundaries on their way home (indicating social capital and trust).

The short of the story is that an incredibly difficult decision problem under true uncertainty can be routinely solved by ordinary individuals using social norms. Since social norms govern the entire network of human relations and the decision-making processes within it, they are likely to be employed to solve similar problems under true uncertainty elsewhere too.

If social norms give us useful heuristics to follow in some domains, aiding us in making our decisions, almost as if we were on autopilot, then it is worth exploring the meaning and scope of social norms in more detail. Unfortunately, the sizable recent literature in economics lacks clarity and does not have a uniform definition, which creates difficulties in interpreting and comparing the results (Dhami, 2019b, section 5.7). We completely concur with Schram and Charness (2015), who write: "It has become fairly common practice to refer to 'social norms' or 'internalized social norms' when discussing experimental (or field) data that appear unexplainable by existing economic theories of behavior. Essentially, much of this literature has used 'social norms' as a black box meant to capture some of the influence of the social environment on individuals' decisions."

Following Bicchieri (2006) and Elster (2011), we propose the following framework. There is a social norm to choose action A in some social situation S, in a social group G, if three conditions, stated below, hold for all, or most, individuals in G. Note that not everyone in the social group, G, may follow a social norm, even if most people do.

1. *Empirical expectations*: Individuals observe that many other individuals in their social group are choosing the action A (or an action that is reasonably close to A).
2. *Normative expectations*: Individuals in G know that group members expect that other group members ought to choose action A.
3. *Punishments/sanctions*: Individuals in G know that if they do not choose the action A, then they are likely to be sanctioned by the group members. Such sanctions are typically costly and reduce the social capital of the punished individuals.

Empirical expectations are typically generated by direct observations of the behavior of others. However, when individuals are not fully informed by direct observation of behavior, then they might use social projection or evidential reasoning to infer what other like-minded people are likely to do in the given situation (Cialdini et al. 1990; al-Nowaihi & Dhami, 2015). Normative expectations—that is, how one is expected to behave in a group—can be transmitted through many different social signals (e.g., normative injunctions received from parents, family, elders, and other group members).

These expectations are different from *personal normative expectations*—that is, self-generated expectations of one's own behavior that underpin many *moral norms* (Elster, 1989). Normative expectations are critical in sustaining norms, while empirical expectations alone might not be enough (Bicchieri, 2006; Sugden, 1998, 2004). Sometimes, a distinction is drawn between *descriptive norms* (actions of players are based on empirical expectations alone) and *injunctive norms* (actions of players are based on normative expectations alone). However, most successful social norms are likely to have a combination of empirical expectations, normative expectations, and sanctions.

Finally, the role of sanctions is important in many kinds of social norms. For instance, Fehr and Schurtenberger (2018b) consider the formation of social norms of cooperation in a repeated public goods game using all three features of norms listed above. Without a punishment option, cooperation in the public goods game decays over successive rounds, despite the presence of normative expectations. The presence of normative expectations differentiates these experiments from earlier work such as Fehr and Gächter (2000, 2002). However, when punishments/sanctions are allowed, a successful norm of cooperation successfully develops. There is a sizable experimental and nonexperimental literature that supports this view.[11] Thus, empirical and normative expectations are necessary but not sufficient for norm compliance. Should a successful social norm exist, it creates a *shared understanding* among the group members in G that action A is appropriate in social situation S (Fehr & Schurtenberger, 2018a). Ostrom (2000), in a much-cited passage, writes (pp. 143–144): "Social norms are shared understandings about actions that are obligatory, permitted, or forbidden." We believe that the shared understanding part is the outcome of, and not necessarily the definition of, a social norm.

Why might humans wish to conform to norms? The typical explanation is that human evolutionary history has self-selected those individuals who have a desire to conform to social norms provided that the necessary conditions for norm compliance are met (Bowles & Gintis, 2011; E. O. Wilson, 2012; Gintis, 2017). The desire to comply with social norms is underpinned by *internal psychological mechanisms*, such as *guilt* or *shame*, that create disutility from violating social norms (Elster, 1989, 1999, 2011). Shame arises when one's norm violation is observed by the social group, G, which has the ability to sanction norm violation. This was important in explaining the results from microfinance contracts under public repayment in section 3.2.2.

Example 3.4. *Consider, for instance, the prisoner's dilemma game in table 3.1. The strategy cooperate, C, is strictly dominated by the strategy defect, D, for each player; hence, under the BRA we should never observe the play of C. The empirical evidence shows that many subjects do indeed cooperate even in the static game. We have noted above the limitations of explaining cooperation in repeated games.*

Indeed, we often observe cooperation between complete strangers, which is akin to a one-shot static game. Should such a cooperative norm exist, then individuals do not need to indulge their scarce cognitive resources in thinking through the game. They can simply invoke their social norm of cooperation and pick C, as if they were following a simple heuristic. If both players pick C, then the outcome (C, C) is Pareto optimal—that is, it is not possible to have another outcome in which the payoffs of both players are strictly higher or the payoff of one player is unchanged but that of the other player is strictly higher. If humans are hardwired to follow social norms of cooperation, even in one-shot games, then the outcome (C, C) follows from the simple heuristic of choosing the social norm. An intriguing possibility is that Pareto optimal outcomes may be particularly salient focal points for cooperative social norms, and one finds several oblique references to this in Henrich (2017).

We give a semiformal definition of Pareto optimality for any two-player game for later use, although the concept can be extended to any number of players.

Remark 3.2. *(Pareto optimality) Suppose that there are two players $i = 1, 2$ and their respective utilities/payoffs are given by u_1 and u_2, which are drawn from some feasible set of utilities of the two players $U \subset \Re^2$. Then, a combination of utilities of the two players (u_1^*, u_2^*) is Pareto optimal if it is not possible to increase the utility of one player without decreasing the utility of the other player. Pareto optimality is a relatively weak welfare criterion in the sense that it imposes minimum value judgments on comparing interpersonal welfare, and it is the one that economists prefer.*

The emotion of guilt is typically invoked in supporting *moral norms*. Moral norms are rules of behavior followed by an individual that do not require observation or sanctions by group members. Examples of moral norms include being punctual for appointments, waiting in a queue, being honest in one's public dealings, and keeping one's promises. Moral norms arise from ingrained or acquired human virtues; we do not explore their origin here. For instance, in the context of public goods games, Dhami et al. (2019) show that guilt aversion is a powerful determinant of public goods contributions (guilt arises here by subjects falling below the expected contributions of their partners), even when there are no normative expectations or sanctions.

Consider models of multiple selves, where different time dated selves of the same individual make decisions that affect all future selves; see chapter 8 for an exposition of these models. It could be the case that all future contingencies and outcomes are difficult to guess for any current self of the individual (true uncertainty). Or it could be the case that all possible outcomes and their subjective probabilities can be imagined and accounted for (uncertainty). Under uncertainty, the BRA recommends that we use dynamic programming and proceed as in section 3.2.1. Or, alternatively, it could be that moral norms provide the individual with simple rules of thumb to choose their actions. Should an individual waiting in a long queue, or deciding whether a promise should be kept, use dynamic programming to make this decision, taking account of the consequences for all future selves? Or should they use the moral norm of waiting in the queue, and keeping a promise, because their moral compass refuses to entertain any other possibility? We believe that many reasonable people will choose the latter option. Thus, moral norms too can provide ready-made heuristics that enable one to take decisions where computational and cognitive requirements are high. The real benefits of this approach, as in the case of social norms, is likely to arise in the case of true uncertainty, where none of the existing theories offers predictions.

It is sometimes useful to distinguish a social norm from a *convention*. A convention is an action C, such that it is in the material best interests of any individual to choose C if others choose it too (Sugden, 1989). Successful conventions do not require sanctions to support them. The British constitution is a good example of a set of unwritten conventions.

Consider another normal form game in which there is only bilateral interaction between group members in some group G. When two group members meet, they can simultaneously choose actions/strategies s_1, $s_2, \ldots, s_n$, where n is some large number. By *simultaneously* is meant that when choosing their own strategies, players cannot observe the strategy of their partners. The normal form game is shown in table 3.2.

Table 3.2
A two-player, large-dimensional coordination game

	s_1	s_2	.	.	.	s_n
s_1	1, 1	0, 0	.	.	.	0, 0
s_2	0, 0	2, 2	.	.	.	0, 0
.	.	.	.	.	.	.
.	.	.	.	.	.	.
.	.	.	.	.	.	.
s_n	0, 0	0, 0	.	.	.	n, n

All off-diagonal cells of the game in table 3.2 give each player a payoff of zero. Any diagonal cells corresponding to a strategy profile (s_k, s_k), $1 \leq k \leq n$, give each participant a monetary payoff of k (e.g., the payoffs from the strategy profile (s_2, s_2) are two each). This is a large-dimensional coordination game in which strictly positive payoffs for the players arise only if they coordinate and pick identical strategies; otherwise both receive a payoff of zero. Which strategy should each player choose? Classical game theory would proceed as follows. Any symmetric choice of strategies, (s_k, s_k), $1 \leq k \leq n$, is a Nash equilibrium—that is, if one player chooses s_k, the best response of the other player is also to choose s_k (but remember that when choosing their strategies, players do not know the strategy chosen by the other player—they pick strategies simultaneously, without communication).

Given there are multiple Nash equilibria (in fact, n such equilibria), which equilibrium is likely to be played? One may impose additional refinements of Nash equilibrium such as *payoff dominance* to try to pin down (s_n, s_n) as the unique Nash equilibrium, which is also a Pareto optimal outcome. But this requires common knowledge among the players that the other player finds payoff dominance to be a compelling principle. Why should there be common knowledge of such things? If players are not sure about the rationality of their partners, and if common knowledge of such rationality is missing, then there is very little that classical game theory could say about the eventual outcome of this game. Since there are no dominated strategies (unlike the prisoner's dilemma game), even rationalizability, which imposes relatively weak restrictions, does not narrow down the set of equilibria.

A more persuasive argument is that the social group would, over time, have evolved social norms to deal with these sorts of coordination problems among its group members. Indeed, Henrich (2017) offers a book-length treatment on this theme, where the cultural practices of groups give rise to such norms. Imagine a band of prehistoric hunters from a tribe, hunting in the ice ages. Lack of coordination could be catastrophic by opening them up to injuries or losing their lives, and putting their tribe at starvation risk. It is likely that there is a social norm to choose the highest action, s_n, in coordination games such as these. The existence of social norms gives the necessary shared understanding of the action to be taken, a form of common knowledge. Thus, faced with the real-life analogue of this situation, a group member follows a simple heuristic, almost on autopilot: follow the social norm of playing s_n. Social norms themselves may arise purely as accidents of history; a deductive/inductive problem-solving approach taken by the group may have been a catalyst. Yet, even this might not be necessary, as we discuss next.

There is another approach that is used to justify the play of s_n and achieve the Pareto optimal outcome. Suppose that we gave up the BRA and used relatively low-level rationality. It is possible that players make small errors or mistakes in playing their strategies and use fairly simple rules of thumb in making choices. In this case, one may invoke the machinery of *stochastic social dynamics* in order to pick an action in the coordination game above (P. H. Young, 1998). Under certain conditions, the chosen action can be a Pareto optimal choice. We examine this method in section 4.10.2. Another possibility is that players use a different notion of rationality while playing the coordination game above. They may use notions of social rationality, which involve looking for, say, the Kantian equilibrium or invoking concepts of joint intentionality; see section 4.7.

3.5 On Methodology in Economics

In the last few decades, behavioral economics has made a tremendous impact on research and teaching within economics. It has offered a far better empirically supported account of human behavior as compared to the BRA. Some researchers, and this includes many behavioral economists, are reluctant to pit behavioral economics and the BRA against each other. After all, the founding fathers of neoclassical economics, and even the classical economists, were aware of many of the current themes and arguments within behavioral economics. However, recall that we have restricted our usage of neoclassical economics to the *commonly practiced version in academia*, which allows us to draw a distinction between the two. Otherwise, we are in agreement with the sentiments often expressed by Richard Thaler that he would like to see a gradual assimilation of behavioral economics within the economics profession and the gradual dropping of the prefix *behavioral* in behavioral economics.

The main difference between behavioral economics and the BRA is methodological. A behavioral economics approach requires stringent empirical testing of the predictions of the proposed theory using lab, field, and neuroeconomic evidence and a willingness to abandon or modify theory that is not in conformity with the evidence.[12] In introducing the *theory of relativity* to readers of *The London Times* on November 28, 1919, Einstein made three specific predictions and noted that if his theory failed on any of the predictions, it was untenable. The appeal of behavioral economics to many lies in its methods, based on an underlying Popperian approach (and its extensions), which is consistent with best practice in the natural sciences (Popper, 1959/1934, 1963; Lakatos, 1970). The drive to falsify theories and design innovative and stringent tests required to falsify theories is central to physics and plays a major role in the emergence of new and better theories. This is captured in the words of the Nobel Prize–winning physicist Feynman (1965), who once said along the following lines: "We are trying to prove ourselves wrong as quickly as possible, because only in that way do we make the fastest progress." It is also the result of a better methodological approach, we believe, that behavioral economics has solved important and outstanding problems in economics in such a short span of time.

The dominant view in economic methodology is associated with the name of Milton Friedman, the 1976 Nobel laureate in economics. In this view, economic models need only be true in an *as-if sense*—that is, even if the assumptions are patently incorrect and unrealistic, good predictions make a good model (Friedman, 1953). If the predictions turn out to be correct, then, the argument goes, we may legitimately conclude that people act *as if* they conformed with the assumptions of the theory even if the assumptions are patently unrealistic. It is unfortunate that the only exposure to methodology that most economists have had is Friedman's views, coupled with the basics of Kuhn (1962). This work has often been used as a license to build models based on ad hoc assumptions that are justified by using bogus as-if arguments that are never subject to stringent empirical tests. For instance, from the observation that birds fly, we may conclude that they act as if they understand the laws of aerodynamics and the closely related laws of hydrodynamics. Yet, most birds left underwater try to fly their way under water, rather than swim, and drown even more quickly. One would not observe this if birds really understood hydrodynamics or acted as if they did.[13]

There are likely to be several reasons why bounded rationality and behavioral economics more generally have not received an even warmer response in the economics profession. After all, it is demonstratively true that behavioral models outperform existing models in the BRA in many different domains (Kahneman & Tversky, 2000; Camerer, 2003; Loewenstein, 2008; Dhami, 2016). It is important to understand the reasons, and we outline our views below. But first, let us dismiss some common arguments up front.

One common argument given for the continued use of the BRA is that it is tractable, simple, and parsimonious and makes precise predictions.

It is not clear to us why a bounded rationality model or a behavioral economics model should be intractable and complex and make imprecise predictions. As noted above, in order to derive interesting predictive content, one needs to substantially enhance the set of assumptions in models in the BRA with auxiliary assumptions. In particular, if a standard model in the BRA does not adequately capture the realism in human behavior yet wishes to explain the data well, then it needs to employ auxiliary assumptions that will take up the slack of unrealistic assumptions on human behavior. If anything, our contention is that behavioral models are simpler because they are based on a more realistic picture of human behavior; hence, they require fewer auxiliary assumptions to explain the data.

A second argument is that the BRA provides a disciplined approach and that bounded rationality / behavioral economics, because they often, allegedly, furnish ad hoc explanations, will fritter away that hard-won discipline. This is not supported by the actual practice of bounded rationality / behavioral economics models, and the BRA appears to preach what it does not often practice. First, it is hardly good discipline to add arbitrary and ad hoc auxiliary assumptions within the BRA to explain the data. Second, a founding principle of behavioral economics is stringent testing of the theoretical predictions of behavioral models using many diverse kinds of evidence from lab experiments, field studies, survey data, and neuroeconomic data. If anything, behavioral theories face more testing than models in the BRA.

Is the slower than expected take-up of bounded rationality / behavioral economics the result of natural inertia? After all, new ideas take time to percolate through any science. However, this does not explain the continued popularity of many of the components of the BRA, despite decades of refutation. For instance, Luce and Raiffa (1957) comment (p. 35) on "utility theory and rational choice" by writing that "reported preferences almost never satisfy the axioms." On page 37, they describe these refutations as "bolstered by a staggering amount of empirical data." Now we are at a stage where it appears pointless to test expected utility any further (Wakker, 2010; Dhami, 2019a). Similarly, the demonstrated failure of the as-if position held by the BRA, in Kahneman and Tversky's work on judgment heuristics in the 1970s, has had very little impact on the BRA either in research or in teaching.

Our preferred explanation for resistance to bounded rationality / behavioral economics is the particular brand of homespun methodological positions that are used in economics, largely relying on Friedman's as-if position as a starting point. In many instances, these homegrown methodological positions are retrogressive and bear no relation to the methodology of science, or to the philosophy of science. Many otherwise reasonable economists use the as-if argument to justify almost any assumptions, including completely false assumptions, without testing them or offering clear tests for them. The standard texts in microeconomics, game theory, and contract theory contain almost no empirical evidence whatsoever. This is in sharp contrast to the natural sciences. This situation is well summed up in the following quotation from Herbert Gintis (2009, p. xvi):

> Economic theory has been particularly compromised by its neglect of the facts concerning human behavior.... I happened to be reading a popular introductory graduate text on quantum mechanics, as well as a leading graduate text in microeconomics. The physics text began with the anomaly of blackbody radiation.... The text continued, page after page, with new anomalies ... and new, partially successful models explaining the anomalies. In about 1925, this culminated with Heisenberg's wave mechanics and Schrödinger's equation, which fully unified the field. By contrast, the microeconomics text, despite its beauty, did not contain a single fact in the whole thousand-page volume. Rather the authors built economic theory in axiomatic fashion, making assumptions on the basis of their intuitive plausibility, their incorporation of the "stylized facts" of everyday life, or their appeal to the principles of rational thought.... We will see that empirical evidence challenges some of the core assumptions in classical game theory and neoclassical economics.

A professional economist cannot fail to notice these problems. In Dhami and Beinhocker (2019), one of the authors, narrating his personal experiences, writes:

> Many years ago, a reasonably well known economic theorist was appalled that I should suggest testing his model—"But my model is a branch of mathematics—what has empirical testing got to do with it?" he protested. A prominent game theorist, when challenged on the evidence for his applied game theory model in a seminar in which I was present, responded that he was only interested in the "mathematical structure of game theory." An editor of a leading economics journal once told me that he immediately rejects experimental papers because they are too easy—"Theory is hard and more important," he insisted.

Beyond these subjective personal anecdotes, there are published accounts from some of the leading economists that give a similar impression and reflect homegrown and entrenched positions within economics. Here are some well-known published examples.

> Hence the choice of a model will depend on the purpose for which the model is used, the modeler's intuition, and the modeler's subjective judgment of plausibility.... One economist may reject another's intuition, and, ultimately, the marketplace of ideas will make some judgments. (Dekel & Lipman, 2010, p. 264)
>
> In particular, we agree that: economic models are often viewed differently than models in the other sciences; economic theory seems to value generality and simplicity at the cost of accuracy; models are expected to convey a message much more than to describe a well-defined reality; these models are often akin to observations, or to gedankenexperiments; and the economic theorist is typically not required to clearly specify where his model might be applicable and how. (Gilboa et al., 2014, p. F516)
>
> As in the case of fables, models in economic theory are derived from observations of the real world, but are not meant to be testable. As in the case of fables, models have limited scope. As in the case of a good fable, a good model can have an enormous influence on the real world, not by providing advice or by predicting the future, but rather by influencing culture. Yes, I do think we are simply the tellers of fables, but is that not wonderful? (Rubinstein, 2006, p. 882)

The introductory chapter in Dhami (2016) rejects each of these positions, but then it is not hard to do so. These positions should inform us what anyone who desires to see quick changes in the status quo in economics is up against. The field's core theories and models still typically rely on the BRA. However, behavioral economists should continue to point out the evidence and build better models of economic behavior that are based on a more realistic picture of human behavior. This is likely to involve a deeper examination of procedural rationality and heuristics than behavioral economics has done so far.

We should also continue to robustly challenge the core assumptions in the BRA that are decisively rejected by the bulk of the evidence arising from several decades of research. These include, among other things, expected utility theory, exponential time discounting, universal self-regarding preferences, Nash equilibrium, mixed strategy Nash equilibrium and refinements, unbounded rationality, unlimited attention, and emotionless deliberation (see chapter 2 for some details). Some argue that the profession will give up rejected models suddenly and unexpectedly like the fall of the Berlin Wall and the collapse of the Soviet Union as we tip into the basin of attraction of a good equilibrium as under stochastic social dynamics (see section 4.10.2). However, it is also possible that change occurs more gradually via the next generation of newly minted PhDs who are likely to be more open minded and better trained in the evidence and in the new behavioral models (this is the view that science progresses funeral by funeral, as the current adherents die out).

It is encouraging that several student movements in the West now explicitly demand a more empirically relevant economics to be taught in their curriculum. It is not clear if these movements have had far-reaching effects yet. Ultimately, the change must come from a change in the way economists practice their craft. But that would require deeper training in methodology; understanding the best practices in the natural sciences; dropping demands for a special status for economics that prevents refutation of theories; and dropping religious attachment to the BRA in favor of a religious attachment to stringent empirical testing of theories and accepting refutation of theories.

3.6 Preferences and Beliefs: The Role of History, Culture, and Institutions

In the BRA, preferences and beliefs are the primitives. Beliefs may change as new information becomes available, in which case, beliefs are updated using Bayes' law or, in more enlightened models, some variant of it that takes account of, say, the evidence on base rate neglect. However, preferences are held fixed. In behavioral economics, by contrast, preferences can be malleable, and the role of culture, history, institutions, and even recent, but salient, events may alter preferences significantly.

Preferences and beliefs may also serve as primitives under behavioral economics, except that they are not immutable and are likely to be influenced by a richer variety of factors on account of the explicit consideration of psychological and social factors. In heuristics-based models, changes in preferences and beliefs may induce individuals to switch heuristics or induce a period of reexamination of the existing heuristics. Furthermore, culture, history, and institutions might have important feedback effects on preferences, beliefs, and the boundedly rational rules that people use. Hence, at a bare minimum, we need to pause to briefly consider some of these factors, although they probably require a book-length treatment in their own right.

Institutions can be defined as formal constraints on human behavior, such as the legal system, rules, and written or unwritten constitutions (North, 1990). By contrast, *culture* may be defined as informal constraints on human behavior, such as norms and conventions in a society (North,

1990; Alesina & Giuliano, 2015). One may also define culture as the set of beliefs and preferences acquired by nongenetic transmission (Bowles & Gintis, 2011). Cultural values are typically transmitted in ethnic, religious, and social groups from one generation to another, sometimes in a relatively unchanged manner. For instance, Luttmer and Singhal (2011) find that the redistribution preferences of second generation immigrants are correlated with the extent of the welfare state in their parents' country of origin. Social learning is one channel of cultural transmission and takes the forms of vertical (parents to children), horizontal (peer to peer), and oblique (nonparental elder to younger) transfers of information.

One of the best-known works on the link between culture and institutions in behavioral economics is Henrich et al. (2001). They find that prosociality is positively correlated with (1) market integration in the community (predominance of buying/selling for a wage) and (2) cooperation in production. The opposite is taught in most introductory courses in economics—namely, that markets eliminate prosociality. Markets may reduce *ethicality*, but not *prosociality*, which is an important but subtle distinction; see Dhami (2017). There has also been an examination of the link between individualistic preferences that promote innovation but also reduce cooperation and collectivist preferences that reduce innovation but increase cooperation (Gorodnichenko & Roland, 2020).

3.6.1 Effect of Preferences on Institutions

Weber's account of the Calvinist doctrine of predestination and capitalist development in Northern Europe provides a link between culture and development. Al-Nowaihi and Dhami (2015) link this to evidential reasoning in games (see section 4.6). In this context, there is a question in the World Values Survey (WVS) that asks respondents if success is determined by hard work or luck. The percentage of people who believe in the relative importance of hard work is greater in the US relative to Europe. Another similar question in the WVS asks respondents if they believe that the poor could become rich if they tried hard enough. Alesina and Glaeser (2004) use differences in the responses to this question to explain why the welfare state is more generous in Europe relative to the US; clearly society is more willing to help the poor if their lower income is believed to be a result of bad luck rather than an unwillingness to work hard.

Trust is by far the most studied cultural trait in experiments. Education is associated with higher trust, and history matters. For instance, Africans whose ancestors were raided during the slave trade display lower trust, relative to those who were not raided (Nunn & Wantchekon, 2011). In general, communities that have been discriminated against in the past show lower levels of trust. When the *trust game*[14] is played, a robust finding is that in-group members are trusted more than out-group members. For instance, Fershtman and Gneezy's (2001) study demonstrated such in-group effects with descendants of Ashkenazi Jews, who have a European origin, and Eastern Jews, who have an African or Asian origin.

Empirical evidence also uncovers a relationship between the strength of family ties with the following two factors: (1) labor force participation / political participation (Alesina & Giuliano, 2014) and (2) extent of family-run business in society (Bertrand & Schoar, 2006). The relative presence of nuclear families and clans explains different patterns of urbanization in Europe and China (Greif & Tabellini, 2012).

Consider the following fascinating account of how preferences influence institutions and how accidents of history determine current institutions and values. Successive waves of immigrants into the US brought with them their own cultural values that were translated into different institutional arrangements (Fischer, 1989). Puritans from East Anglia believed in education and order, so they introduced laws promoting universal education. Virginia Cavaliers came from South West England, and their beliefs accepted income inequality, so they promoted low taxes and low government spending, including on education. Quakers came from the North West Midlands in England and valued personal freedom, so they promoted laws emphasizing equal rights.

Cultural beliefs can influence institutions and actual economic outcomes. For differences in cultural beliefs of Maghribi and Genoese traders leading to different institutions, the former based on informal legal and enforcement institutions and the latter on formal legal institutions codified in contract law, see Greif (1994). Trust, interpreted as a cultural variable, is positively correlated with several indicators of financial markets—for example, use of cash, participation in the stock market, and the use of bank loans versus loans from friends (Guiso et al., 2004, 2008a, 2008b).

3.6.2 Effect of Institutions on Preferences

Institutions can also change preferences. For instance, Carpenter and Seki (2011) find that fishermen who work under shared costs/benefits, called the poolers, are also more cooperative when playing the *public goods game*,[15] relative to the nonpoolers, who engage in fishing on an independent basis.

The unification of Germany and the collapse of the Soviet Union provide two interesting examples of the effects of a change in institutions. Did 50 years of the separation of East and West Germany lead to different cultural attitudes? Early studies find no difference, suggesting that institutions do not influence culture, but some of this work had a small sample size. However, with a larger sample size, Alesina and Fuchs-Schündeln (2007) find that there are differences between the two peoples in how pro-government they are (Eastern Europeans were more pro-government). However, any remaining differences are closing fast, and the authors predict they might be eliminated in two generations.

The experience of war can change some preferences but not others. Using a sample of 681 Muslims, Croats, and Serbs in postwar Bosnia and Herzegovina, Whitt and Wilson (2007) identify in-group favoritism in *dictator game experiments*[16] that suggests the effects of war on preferences. Yet, a norm of fairness prevails in the sense that dictators transfer to out-group members some socially acceptable fraction of their endowment; this component of preferences was not changed by war. In a field experiment, people in Burundi who have experienced war-related violence share more with neighbors (Voors et al., 2012).

Herrmann et al. (2008) find that antisocial punishments in public goods games (noncontributors punishing contributors) are higher in societies where the norm of civic cooperation and the rule of law are weak. Fishermen who practice more cooperative modes of fishing (bigger hole sizes in nets allow young fish to escape on a common property resource, a lake) also contribute more in public goods games experiments (Fehr & Leibbrandt, 2011). There is less antisocial punishment (a cultural value) in public goods games when the punishments are originally decided by a referendum among members (institutions) (Tyran & Feld, 2006; Ertan et al., 2010; Sutter et al., 2010).

Increases in female labor force participation (institutions) gave rise to family size reductions, feminism, and changes in sexual practices (culture) (Bowles, 1998). Repeal of the law of no shopping on Sundays (institutions) alters the opportunity cost of participating in Sunday church and reduces church attendance/donations (culture) (Gruber & Hungerman, 2008).

There are also models of the two-way interaction between culture and institutions. Tabellini (2008) considers the interaction between morality as a cultural value and legal institutions. Better legal institutions reduce the need for private punishments and may also increase the proportion of cooperators, an improvement in morality on some yardstick. On the other hand, when there are more cooperators, it reduces the load on the legal system through, say, reduced caseload.

Norms of cooperation may change quickly due to inspired leadership or other institutional changes (Acemoglu & Jackson, 2012). The tiny nation of Georgia eliminated police corruption within a few days in a dramatic move following the election of the new government in November 2003 on an explicit agenda of fighting corruption. The reforms targeted the ministry of internal affairs, and it was decided to outright dismiss a large fraction of the police force, particularly the traffic police, which was exceptionally corrupt. Steps were immediately taken to begin a new public servants / police recruitment drive. This changed the norm for police corruption in Georgia, and the police no longer harass people for bribes. However, in other cases, such norms are hard to change and survive changes in leadership and political parties (Bicchieri, 2006).

3.7 The Macroeconomy as a Complex, Adaptive System

It is natural to presume that the bounded rationality of humans would have profound influence on the way we think about macroeconomic aggregates such as employment, GDP, interest rates, and inflation. Yet, the BRA applied to microeconomic models is typically scaled up to macroeconomic questions, keeping intact the basic framework and the rationality assumptions. This is normally referred to as *microfounded macroeconomic models* and cited as a strength of modern macroeconomic theory. The key solution method in these models is dynamic programming, which we have encountered in section 3.2.1. Yet, these microfoundations inherit all the problems of the BRA and liberally add extra problems. Of these, the one that is particularly contentious is the *representative agent framework* (fairly conservative agent heterogeneity is added in recent models), in which a single representative individual represents all the consumers and all the firms in an economy; for a devastating and authoritative critique, see Kirman (1992).

Microfounded macroeconomics uses an equilibrium analysis that requires all markets to clear; this follows from the tradition of general equilibrium analysis in microeconomics. This is somewhat unfortunate because economists have substituted a hard but empirically more relevant question (how do we understand the dynamics of an economy?) for an easier, but not easy by any yardstick, yet less empirically relevant question (what happens in equilibrium?). Very little justification is given for an equilibrium analysis in university courses in economics except to say that economics is about equilibrium analysis and that economists have among their many gifts the ability to construct elegant and beautiful models. The admiration of such elegance and beauty is a common exercise in economics, but much like the emperor and his new clothes, commoners (read noneconomists) may struggle to spot it. For an entertaining and beautifully written parody of economists as a primitive tribe in which status is governed by the construction of modls (analogy for a primitive tool), see Leijonhufvud (1973).

In contrast to microfounded macroeconomics, the real world looks something like the following description of it. The macroeconomy is incredibly complex, and no individual agent has a decisive understanding of all the underlying mechanisms and features of the economy, not even the central bank. People follow simple adaptive rules of thumb and face conditions of true uncertainty. The future is simply unknowable to any single agent or group of agents, although they may have hunches and employ useful heuristics, some better than others. The standard macroeconomics model in the BRA cannot make predictions in this case, unless it focuses on quite narrow questions. The economy is always in a state of flux, constantly buffeted by random shocks whose origin and effects are often mysterious; it never settles down to a steady state.

Under these conditions (true uncertainty, nonequilibrium analysis, and agent heterogeneity), the economy may be viewed as a *complex adaptive system*. We outline this in more detail in section 4.9. *Agent-based models* (ABMs) have been employed in this case, and they are able to incorporate an unprecedented level of institutional detail within the confines of the model; all agents use simple, plausible, adaptive rules of thumb; and equilibrium is not imposed on the system (Beinhocker, 2006; Beinhocker et al., 2016; Colander & Kupers 2014; Farmer et al., 2019; Dhami, 2020b). By contrast, microfounded macroeconomic models are too parsimonious and based on rationality assumptions that are too fantastic to reasonably capture the empirics of many real-world economic phenomena. Indeed, their parsimony is designed to fit analytical solutions, or those that can be solved numerically in reasonable time, not necessarily to capture all relevant aspects of economic phenomena.

An attractive feature of ABMs that they share with other models of complex adaptive systems is that fluctuations (e.g., business cycles) typically arise not from external shocks but from the endogenous behavior of adaptive agents. This gels well with many observed phenomena that are puzzling for the BRA, such as stock market crashes without any accompanying news about changes in fundamental values. To be sure, there is an earlier and quite well-developed literature on self-fulfilling prophecies in macroeconomics that arose in the 1970s and 1980s, but it relied on rational expectations and full economic rationality (Blanchard & Fischer, 1989); these assumptions are less attractive for a behavioral economist.

However, there are several features in ABM models that have caused concern. These include too many degrees of freedom to fit the data; postulated behavior of economic agents in the model that is no better than guesses; inadequate incorporation of the insights from behavioral economics on human behavior and on behavioral learning frictions; and an arbitrary division of the economy into various sectors and arbitrary choice of the types of agents (Dhami, 2020b). In spite of these drawbacks, the ABM literature is still young and growing and needs to be encouraged. An immediate improvement in this literature can be made by incorporating more empirically realistic boundedly rational behavior. ABMs, like models of bounded rationality, are hampered by the relatively small base of researchers who actively work in these areas. By contrast, the BRA is hugely popular and occupies the minds and times of the very vast majority of the best researchers within the economics profession.

4
Behavioral Models of Heuristics-Based Choice

In this chapter, we cover a wide terrain as we consider some of the behavioral models of heuristics-based choices of individuals as well as the implications for aggregate outcomes.

The standard decision theory models in the BRA and in behavioral economics, such as expected utility, rank dependent utility, and prospect theory (see appendix to chapter 2) are *consequentialist*. They take as the relevant data the outcomes and probabilities in a lottery and then apply different formulae to summarize the worth of a lottery in a single number. In section 4.1, we consider the *risk as feelings theory*, which explicitly models the possibility that the choice procedure can be *nonconsequentialist*. In this richer framework, the final choice among risky outcomes may well be based on outcomes alone, probabilities alone, or a mix of both, or on anticipatory emotions and the vividness of risky choices. This can explain why, for instance, people buy extended warranties for consumer durables, which are not good value for money. Yet, the buyers and sellers of these warranties emphasize other features of warranties, such as peace of mind, which appears to guard against the anticipatory negative emotions associated with the breakdown of consumer durables.

In section 4.2, we consider *attribute-based models of time discounting*. In the models of time discounting considered in chapter 3, particularly the exponential discounted utility (EDU) and the hyperbolic discounted utility models, outcome-time pairs are translated into a number that is based on a formula (see, e.g., equations (2.18) and (2.23)). A different approach is pursued in attribute-based models. The idea is that an outcome-time pair (z, t), where the outcome z is received at some time t in the future, consists of two attributes: an outcome attribute z and a time attribute t. In comparing two such outcome-time pairs, say, (z_1, t) and (z_2, s), where z_1, z_2 are outcomes and t, s are the respective times at which they are received, attribute-based models directly compare the attributes and make choices based on this comparison.

We consider three such attribute-based models in section 4.2: the *vague time preferences model*; *the similarity relation* in time preferences; and the *trade-off model of attribute choice*. In the similarity relation, if two outcomes are deemed similar, then the decision-maker simply chooses the outcome-time pair that is available earlier. On the other hand, if the two time dates are deemed similar, then the outcome-time pair with the larger outcome is chosen. The vague time preferences model posits that future choices might not be clear enough relative to current choices—that is, they might be vague. Hence, the discounted utility from the preferred outcome-time pair must not only be higher but exceed a certain threshold to ensure that the decision-maker is confident in choosing it. Choices are made here using a primary criterion, a secondary criterion, and a tertiary criterion. Finally, in the trade-off model, the two outcome attributes are directly compared with the two time attributes in making choices; here outcomes and times can be directly compared. Two features stand out in these three models. First, they do not use optimization but focus on the procedural rationality of the solution. Second, they are able to explain several anomalies of the EDU model outlined in section 2.13.

Heuristics-based choices and optimization-based choices are often considered to be two distinct class of models of human decision-making. However, in section 4.3, we show that there is an equivalence between these two classes of models for some of the recent heuristics-based models of intertemporal choice. For a given heuristics-based model, we show that preferences implied in that model are also consistent with a general model of delay-discounting (see section 2.6). We show this to be the case for three recent heuristics-based models, the *trade-off model*, the *DRIFT (difference, ratio, interest, and finance) model*, and the *ITCH (intertemporal choice heuristic) model*. Establishing this equivalence is a powerful result because it shows a link between heuristics and optimization-based choices in some cases. However, this investigation also shows that in some cases we need to modify the existing delay-discounting optimization models to take account of the evidence from heuristics-based choices. This can be a potentially fruitful line of research in the future.

In section 4.4, we revisit the point made in chapter 2 that the choices arising from heuristics-based models can sometimes be explained by optimization-based models. This is the case when such models are based on psychologically rich assumptions, as is the case with prospect theory. In this section, we show that the heuristics that people follow to aggregate or segregate monetary amounts are also implied by a prospect theory model.

In section 4.5, we consider *aspiration adaptation theory*, a leading alternative to optimization in the bounded rationality approach. This was proposed by Herbert Simon, the 1978 Nobel laureate in economics, as an alternative to the optimization-based approach in the BRA by emphasizing the role of *procedural rationality* (Simon, 1982, 1986, 2000). The basic idea is that individuals have initial aspirations that evolve over time, depending on the payoffs (or utilities) from outcomes that they experience. If they experience good (resp. bad) payoffs, aspirations increase (resp. decrease). At any time, if the payoffs exceed aspirations, then the individual stays with the current choice. If, however, the payoffs fall below the aspiration level, then the individual experiments with alternative choices to see if payoffs can be increased. In the BRA, individuals are always looking for choices that will increase their payoffs, and they keep doing this until they arrive at a global maximum (in the sense of mathematical optimization). However, Simon argued, in a world where searching for the possible set of unknown actions/strategies is costly, one cannot formulate an optimal search strategy because of the infinite regress problem in search costs, which we explain in section 4.5. Hence, he postulated a stopping rule, whereby individuals stop the search for more actions and strategies once they achieve a payoff that is at least as great as their aspiration levels. We apply this framework to two situations that lie at the heart of the social and the behavioral sciences—cooperation and coordination. In particular, we show how this theory can support cooperation in a prisoner's dilemma game and also how it might lead to coordination on the Pareto optimal outcome in a simple coordination game.

In section 4.7, we consider an alternative solution concept in game theoretic situations that eschews *private rationality* in the BRA in favor of *social rationality*. Examples of solution concepts that rely on social rationality include *team reasoning*, *joint intentionality*, and *Kantian rationality*. Of these three, we explore *Kantian rationality* and the related concept of *Kantian equilibrium* in some detail. In the *Kantian protocol*, players prefer to make choices that they would like the other players to make. In making these choices, players do not act strategically (in the sense of classical game theory) nor out of fear but rather because it is the moral thing to do. We apply Kantian reasoning to the prisoner's dilemma game and show that it can explain the cooperative outcome.

In section 4.8, we consider bidding behavior in *common value auctions*. These are auctions, such as oil lease auctions, in which the value of the oil under the surface is the same for anyone who drills it. In order to decide on their optimal bids, potential bidders must form a cost estimate of drilling the oil. Bidders who form the most optimistic, rather than the most realistic, cost estimates are likely to bid high and win the auction. However, in due course, true costs are revealed, often leading to losses or bankruptcy for the winner. This is known as the *winner's curse*, and we present the relevant empirical evidence. In order to explore this phenomenon further, we consider the *acquire a company* game, which offers a stylized version of the problem that is suitable for testing in the lab. It turns out that the winner's curse arises in this game from using a simple heuristic to calculate conditional probabilities, but it is statistically incorrect, contrary to the assumptions made in the BRA.

Section 4.9 considers applications of bounded rationality to macroeconomics.[1] Modern macroeconomics relies on the rationality assumptions in the BRA that we outlined in chapter 2 but adds a further set of assumptions, many of which are contentious. Many macroeconomic models assume that the entire economy can be studied as a representative agent model in which a single representative individual represents all consumers and firms. In the recent literature, there has been increased recognition of some degree of heterogeneity in consumers and also a greater importance given to the financial sector, but such heterogeneity is minimal relative to the real world. Furthermore, agents in such models use rational expectations, which imposes extreme cognitive requirements, and there is no persuasive evidence for this; the analysis is equilibrium analysis; no predictions can be made under true uncertainty, which arguably is of the utmost importance for macroeconomic phenomena; and economic fluctuations arise from exogenous shocks to the system.

In contrast to this view of macroeconomics, section 4.9 presents the outline of an approach based on *complexity theory*, which is applied in economics under the rubric of *agent-based models* (ABMs). In this approach, all economic actors face true uncertainty, and they respond by following simple rules of thumb that are updated by using simple learning strategies based on the feedback between aggregate outcomes and individual choices. No use is made of rational expectations; there is no equilibrium, so the dynamic system is in a constant state of flux, or *persistent randomness*; and fluctuations arise not from exogenous factors but endogenously, from the simple rules of thumb followed by economic agents; *emergent phenomena* arise, in which individual decisions/outcomes cannot be simply aggregated to produce macroeconomic outcomes; and *chaotic dynamics* emerge as the system shows extreme sensitivity to initial conditions. The ABM framework is not without limitations, and we highlight many of them, but if we wish to develop a more empirically relevant macroeconomics, then perhaps we cannot avoid taking a complexity-based approach more seriously.

Section 4.10 continues our discussion of dynamics under bounded rationality and the implications for aggregate behavior. This section is divided into two subsections that illustrate the concepts by using an identical coordination example. In section 4.10.1, we consider the basics of *evolutionary dynamics*, which we might consider as the most boundedly rational situation in which genes, or individual players, are hardwired to follow a particular strategy without conscious deliberation, which may also describe the behavior of system 1 in a dual systems view of the brain. We take as our basic approach the Darwinian idea of survival of the fittest. *Fitness* itself is defined as the ability of the strategies to cope with the environment. Fitter strategies proliferate among the population, while less fit strategies decay over time. One of the central questions here is, What sort of strategies survive the long-run evolutionary processes?

We introduce the two main dynamic concepts in these models. The concept of an *evolutionary stable strategy* (ESS) formalizes the sense in which an existing strategy can survive against random mutations that produce alternative strategies. It turns out that the set of ESS is a subset of the set of Nash equilibria of the underlying game. The concept of an *asymptotically stable steady state* then summarizes a state of rest for the system after it has passed through its dynamic time path. In order to model the dynamics of the system and to incorporate Darwin's idea of survival of the fittest, we introduce *replicator dynamics*, which allow fitter strategies to proliferate in the population. There could be a unique asymptotic steady state in which all players, in the long run, get hardwired to play an identical strategy (*monomorphic equilibrium*). Or, there could be an asymptotic steady state in which we observe two or more distinct sets of hardwired behaviors (*polymorphic equilibrium*). When there is more than one asymptotic steady state, we cannot use evolutionary dynamics to predict which of the two will arise—it all depends on the initial starting point.

An alternative approach that we consider in section 4.10.2, known as *stochastic social dynamics* (SSD), can refine the set of equilibria when we have multiple asymptotic steady states. SSD apply to situations where there is persistent randomness (i.e., constant shocks in every period that never cease or settle down). In this case, asymptotic stability does not help us pin down the long-run state in which a system is more likely to end up. Persistent randomness can be created by players who mutate or make mistakes, by unpredictable technological shocks, or by the random entry and exit of players. Suppose that in every period, players pick their optimal action with some probability, but with the complementary probability they make mistakes / mutate and pick other strategies. Now, the system never really settles down into any asymptotic steady state. If it does arrive in such a steady state, then as random mistakes / mutations of the players accumulate, they tip the system out of the basin of attraction of the steady state and, over time, into the basin of attraction of another steady state. Thus, the system achieves different steady states over time and keeps tipping in and out of them, giving rise to *punctuated equilibria*. The SSD then ask the question: Which of these steady states does the system spend most of its time in, or in which of the steady states is the long-run frequency of play concentrated? These steady states are the stochastically stable steady states and provide the main equilibrium prediction of these models. We show how the multiple asymptotic steady states in a coordination game in section 4.10.1 can be refined to give a unique stochastically stable steady state.

In section 4.11, we consider the emerging work in *narrative economics*. Narratives are stories and easily understood explanations of otherwise potentially difficult-to-understand phenomena that typically rely on eliciting an affective response. As such, narratives need not fully reflect all the facts; indeed narratives can often, but not always, provide an inaccurate explanations of events. The spread of narratives through contagion can influence economic outcomes, and Robert Shiller, the 2013 Nobel laureate in economics, has highlighted its importance. We use the classic Kermack and McKendrick model from epidemiology to demonstrate how epidemics, rumors, and narratives might spread in the population. In the BRA, economic agents are not persuaded by narratives. They are only interested in the information content of messages. However, in recent decades, narratives have been increasingly used in the social sciences as explanations for important social phenomena. While economics has lagged behind the other social sciences in this respect, there is now increased interest in narratives in economics. From our perspective, another interesting aspect of narratives is their interface with heuristics, which Shiller exploits in his work. In particular, we show that the representativeness heuristic, the anchoring heuristic, the availability heuristic, and the affect heuristic play important roles in the dynamic evolution of narratives.

Individuals often face true uncertainty and have limited cognition to deeply understand their complex environment. Yet, the drive to make sense of their world is an intrinsic human trait and, indeed, a valuable tool in judgment and decision-making. In section 4.12, we consider the possibility that individuals use *mental models*, which are simple hypotheses about the causal relationships that humans observe or convenient explanations/simplifications of events or observations that are otherwise difficult to explain. The mental models used by an individual need not arise from self-introspection and self-inference. In fact, most mental models are socially and culturally inherited. Mental models share many similarities with narratives and with social norms, but unlike social norms there are no explicit sanctions from not following mental models. Yet, conforming to a group's mental models can enable individuals to gain acceptance and trust within the group. Mental models can be fairly accurate, but they can also be incorrect and sometimes harmful (e.g., the formation of racial prejudices, stereotypes, and discriminatory practices against ethnic or religious groups). Mental models can be fairly inertial and difficult to change, just like social norms. Public policy can offer significant welfare improvements in cases where mental models are harmful.

In the BRA, decision-makers take account of all information in making decisions. In actual practice, individuals may achieve cognitive simplification in solving problems by grouping information and choices into convenient subsets. Furthermore, they could focus on only a few of these subsets and not take account of differences in elements within each subset. Such behavior is known as *narrow bracketing*. By contrast, the approach in the BRA recommends *broad bracketing*, a consideration of all information. Section 4.13 considers these issues. For instance, a smoker who uses narrow bracketing and consumes a pack of cigarettes a day will consider the health consequences of smoking just the next cigarette. On the other hand, if the smoker were to consider the health consequences for a longer horizon, say, one year (broad bracketing), then they would need to take account of the health consequences of smoking 7,300 cigarettes during the year. Clearly, the choice of bracketing, narrow or broad, will have a massive effect on the decision to quit smoking.

Section 4.13 is divided into three subsections. In section 4.13.1, we apply these ideas to the equity-premium puzzle, the empirical finding of expected returns on stocks relative to bonds, which are too high to be explained by any reasonable degree of risk aversion in the BRA. This puzzle is resolved when we apply prospect theory, along with narrow bracketing of the time over which the return evaluations are carried out. In section 4.13.2, we consider a classic example of narrow bracketing in the economics folklore. Paul Samuelson, the 1970 Nobel laureate in economics, asked a colleague if he would accept a bet that offered a 50-50 chance of winning $200 and losing $100. The colleague replied that he would not but that he would accept 100 such bets. Using reasonable parameter values, prospect theory, and broad bracketing, we show that the colleague would have also found it profitable to accept even two such bets. Under narrow bracketing, any number of such bets should be unacceptable. In section 4.13.3, we explore some of the reasons, such as cognitive simplification and self-control problems, for why people might wish to engage in narrow bracketing.

Consider the inverse S-shaped probability weighting function in figure 2.3. It is very steep near the endpoints of the probability interval. One implication of the steepness near zero probabilities is that many decision theories such as rank dependent utility and prospect theory predict that humans ought to be very sensitive to low probability events. Thus, for instance, we should rush to buy insurance against very improbable events (e.g., being bitten by a dog on the street or being hit by a stray bullet), provided that such insurance is available. But what is the evidence on human behavior for low probability events that also have significant economic importance? Section 4.14, which has three subsections, considers these issues.

In section 4.14.1, we briefly outline *original prospect theory* (OPT), proposed in Kahneman and Tversky's (1979) seminal paper; by contrast, the version of prospect theory that we describe in the appendix to chapter 2 is the 1992 version of the theory, which is also known as *cumulative prospect theory*, or just prospect theory. Kahneman and Tversky were fully aware of the empirical evidence that showed that many people use the simple heuristic of ignoring very small probability events altogether, but others did not. In an editing phase in OPT, decision-makers prune their lotteries of very low probability events before evaluating them in an evaluation phase. This psychological richness of the OPT was lost in the 1992 version of prospect theory. In section 4.14.2, we consider the evidence on human behavior for low probability events that supports the insights already present in OPT. Many humans are reluctant to buy insurance against low probability natural hazards, even when it is on overfair terms; in the BRA, decision-makers are predicted to buy such insurance. We also highlight the evidence from red traffic light running, capital punishments, recommended breast cancer examinations, and seat belt usage, which shows that many people simply ignore very low probability events. Section 4.14.3 shows how we might accommodate the evidence on low probability events by modifying prospect theory in a proposal that has been called *composite prospect theory*.

In the BRA, two basic lessons are taught within the first few introductory lessons in any economics course, even those in high school. First, human decisions are guided by the marginal costs and the marginal benefits (or the incremental costs and benefits) of taking an action. In particular, the fixed costs or the *sunk costs* that precede the taking of the action are predicted to be irrelevant. Second, individuals fully understand and use the concept of *opportunity costs*—that is, what needs to be forgone to obtain a good/service. It is difficult to proceed with any economic model if any of these assumptions are violated. Yet, we show persuasive evidence in section 4.15 that people violate both these principles. It is likely that experienced individuals in the field might exhibit greater conformity with these principles, but the lab evidence with nonprofessionals is not encouraging. This suggests that the BRA needs to widen the scope of human motivation and make more realistic assumptions on the scope of human cognition.

4.1 Risk as Feelings

Existing decision theory in economics, as encapsulated in, say, the models outlined in the appendix to chapter 2, is almost entirely *consequentialist*. Individuals evaluate the consequences of their actions in terms of outcomes and probabilities, as summarized in a lottery, and then choose an appropriate decision theory (expected utility, rank dependent, or prospect theory) to evaluate the lottery. Loewenstein et al. (2001) present an alternative approach to decision-making under risk, which they term as *risk as feelings theory*. It a mixture of consequentialist and nonconsequentialist reasoning. The predictions of this theory in some domains can differ substantially from standard decision theory, particularly when anticipatory emotions are important.

The basic idea of *anticipatory utility*, which plays an important role in this theory, is *anticipal utility*—that is, anticipation about future outcomes gives rise to current utility. The idea, which goes back to Bentham (1789) and was later extended by Jevons (1905), postulates that the anticipation of future events is as important as the physical experience of an event. Anticipal utility may be the reason we sometimes postpone desirable consumption (e.g., a dessert at the end of a meal) as if we had a negative time discount rate.

Loewenstein (1987) provides a theoretical framework for anticipal utility under certainty and reports the following experiment. Students were asked how much they would pay now to (1) obtain a kiss from a movie star of their choice and (2) avoid receiving a nonlethal 110 v shock. These events occurred at various time delays: 0, 3 hours, 24 hours, 3 days, 1 year, and 10 years. In the presence of a positive discount rate, the exponential discounted utility (EDU) model (see chapter 2) predicts that the decision-maker will value the pleasant event (kiss) most highly if it occurs immediately; if it occurs in the future, its discounted utility is lower. However, subjects were willing to pay the most for the kiss to be delayed by three days; this is consistent with the prediction of anticipal utility but not the EDU model. Anticipal utility for a kiss exhibits a hump-shaped pattern, peaking at three days. The EDU model also predicts that the unpleasant event (shock) should be delayed because the discounted value of a negative event is lower. However, subjects found the unpleasant event more painful the longer the delay (e.g., the desire to get an aching tooth out earlier rather than later). Thus, subjects act as if they wish to avoid the anticipal pain of an unpleasant event in the future.

Figure 4.1 represents a schematic outline of the risk as feelings theory. On the left, we have the primitives of the theory, and on the right, we have the two objects of interest, behavior and outcomes. Among the primitives are anticipated outcomes with their associated emotions;

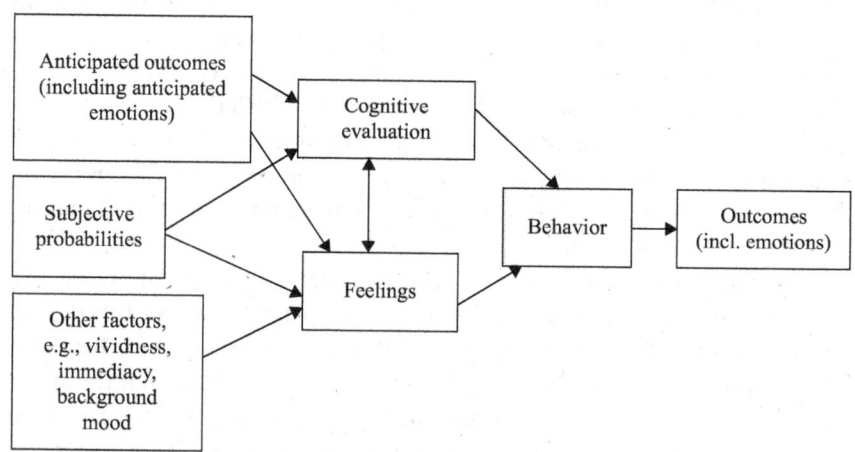

Figure 4.1
Schematic description of the risk as feelings thesis.
Source: Copyright © 2001 by the American Psychological Association. "Risk as feelings." Loewenstein et al., Ned. *Psychological Bulletin*, 127(2), March 2001, 267–286.

subjective probabilities; and a set of factors that capture the vividness of a risky situation, its immediacy, and one's background mood while making a risky choice. If we follow the lowermost arrows directed from left to right, then it is clear that the theory allows behavior under risk to manifest entirely independently of the associated probabilities and outcomes. In other words, lotteries that are the primitives in the theory in the appendix to chapter 2 may play no role at all. However, in other situations and contexts (follow the upper and middle arrows directed from left to right), both outcomes and probabilities, or either outcomes alone or probabilities alone, may be sufficient to explain behavior.

The vividness of risky outcomes, where vividness may be perceived in different ways by individuals, can affect risky choices. For instance, individuals could be reluctant to buy insurance for risks that cannot be vividly imagined. Personal experience may enhance or dim vividness, which could also depend on personally knowing someone who has suffered from the negative consequences of a risky situation. This invokes the anchoring and availability heuristics that we discuss in chapter 5. A common finding is that individuals are less affected by statistics associated with risk (e.g., 1 in 100,000 houses in my area can catch fire) and more affected by personal human stories of suffering that evoke greater emotion (e.g., my neighbor's house burned down and they lost all their possessions). In some cases, such as the risky effects of smoking / drinking / drug use, public information may create anxiety and lead individuals to avoid the relevant public information, resulting in suboptimal risk mitigation activities. Women are often more risk averse than men and also less overconfident, so for instance, they churn their assets relatively less in the stock market (Charness & Gneezy, 2012). Since women are also known to possess more vivid imagery, on average, as compared to men, perhaps they feel greater negative emotions associated with losses, resulting in relatively higher risk aversion.

Contrary to consequentialist models of risk, decision-makers typically do not react as much to changes in probability from, say, 1 in 100,000, to 1 in 1,000,000. In several experiments in psychology, the probability of receiving an impending shock had little effect on anticipatory anxiety. In particular, for vivid outcomes, say, a brief and painful electric shock, the sensitivity to probabilities is low. On the other hand, for nonvivid outcomes, sensitivity to probabilities is relatively higher (Loewenstein et al., 2001). Recall that the *probability weighting function* is relatively flat for probabilities in the middle ranges, say, between 30 and 70 percent; see the inverse S-shaped curve in figure 2.3. However, the predictions under the risk as feelings theory go further. Even for probabilities in this middle range, the theory relates behavior to whether an experience is vivid or not, which has no counterpart in the consequentialist models.

An interesting application of the theory is to the high take-up rates of expensive warranties, which are often shown not to be good value for money. When buying these warranties, people often ignore the probability of product breakdown but appear to think of the peace of mind associated with the warranty, which is an anticipatory emotion. Indeed, salespeople rarely highlight probabilities of breakdown but emphasize the convenience and peace of mind aspects of owning the warranty. Lottery sellers similarly appeal to anticipatory emotions when they use slogans such as "Buy a dream" rather than emphasize the odds of winning the lottery.

4.2 Attribute-Based Models in Time Discounting

In section 2.6, we outlined an optimization-based approach to making choices over outcome-time pairs of the form (z, t), where the outcome $z \in Z$ is received at some time $t \in \Gamma$ in the future. Z and Γ are, respectively, the sets of all possible outcomes and times. We then outlined the exponential discounted utility (EDU) model. In section 2.13, we considered models of hyperbolic discounting. In these optimization models, the decision-maker evaluates either outcome-time pairs or entire temporal profiles of consumption by using a utility functional that reduces these choices to real numbers. Comparing two temporal profiles of consumption then becomes a simple matter of comparing the corresponding real numbers as dictated by the relevant utility functional.

Consider the delay-discounting model in equation (2.5) so that the present discounted utility at time 0 of an outcome z received at time t, written as (z, t), is given by

$$D(t)u(z), \qquad (4.1)$$

where $D(0) = 1$ and D is a decreasing function of time, t.

In this section, we consider a very different approach, one that is based on heuristics and falls under the rubric of *attribute-based models*. The outcome-time pairs that are to be compared by decision-makers consist of two natural attributes: the time of delivery and the outcome. One can then consider the trade-off between the two attributes to determine which outcome-time pair will be chosen. We consider below a range of attribute-based models.[2]

4.2.1 Vague Time Preferences Model

Manzini and Mariotti (2006) use a delay discounting model so that the present discounted utility of an outcome-time pair (z, t) is given by (4.1). They propose a theory of *vague time preferences* and argue that the choice between, say, receiving \$1,000 now and \$1,100 next year is *clearer* than the choice between these two sums received 10 and 11 years from now, respectively. Since we shall be interested in several possible outcomes, it is convenient to use the symbols $z_1, z_2, \ldots$ for different outcomes and the symbols $s \geq 0, t \geq 0$ for different time periods. Suppose that the decision-maker makes choices at time 0.

They propose a heuristics-based decision process that consists of three criteria in order to make a choice between two future outcome-time pairs (z_1, t) and (z_2, s), so the outcome z_1 is received at time t and the outcome z_2 at time s. Let $\prec_V$ be a binary preference relation in the vague preferences model between two outcome-time pairs when the decision-maker makes a choice in the current time period, say, at time 0. Thus, the notation $(z_1, t) \prec_V (z_2, s)$ means that a decision-maker, who subscribes to the vague time preferences model, strictly prefers (z_2, s) to (z_1, t) at time 0.

The preference $(z_1, t) \prec_V (z_2, s)$ occurs at some initial time 0, if and only if, for some real number $\sigma > 0$, one of the following holds:

1. *Primary criterion:* $D(s) u(z_2) - D(t) u(z_1) > \sigma$,
2. *Secondary criterion:* $D(s) u(z_2) - D(t) u(z_1) \leq \sigma$, and $z_1 < z_2$, or
3. *Tertiary criterion:* $D(s) u(z_2) - D(t) u(z_1) \leq \sigma$, $z_1 = z_2$, and $s < t$.

The primary criterion states that the difference in present discounted values of the outcome time pairs (z_2, s) and (z_1, t) must exceed a threshold value, $\sigma > 0$. The justification is that the decision-maker is vague about the appropriate objective function, or discount function, to use. Hence, a preference is expressed for one of the options not only if the preferred option has a higher discounted utility but also if the difference in discounted utilities exceeds a positive threshold σ. If, on the other hand, we have that $D(s) u(z_2) - D(t) u(z_1) \leq \sigma$ (i.e., the threshold is not met), then the two outcome-time pairs are too similar to make a direct choice. In this case, the *secondary criterion* is invoked to choose the alternative that has the highest monetary value ($z_1 < z_2$). If even the two outcomes are identical (i.e., $z_1 = z_2$), then a *tertiary criterion* is invoked: "Choose the outcome that is delivered sooner." If all three criteria fail, then the subject is indifferent to the two alternatives.

This model achieves a complete, but intransitive, preference ordering. In particular, indifference here is not an equivalence relationship.[3] Recall from section 2.13 that the stationarity axiom in the EDU model is not supported by the evidence. Hence, the typical finding is of a common difference effect (of which the Thaler's apples example is particularly illustrative). We have argued in section 2.13 that one advantage of hyperbolic discounting is that it is capable of explaining the common difference effect. However, the vague preferences model too can explain the common difference effect, as we now show.

Example 4.1. *(al-Nowaihi & Dhami, 2008) Consider the choice between receiving $1,000 now and $1,100 next year and the choice between these two sums received 10 and 11 years from now, respectively. We use the identity utility function for outcomes, so $u(x) = x$; thus, $u(1000) = 1000$ and $u(1100) = 1100$. We use the exponential discount function $D(t) = e^{-\theta t}$ with the discount rate $\theta = 0.1$. Suppose that $\sigma = 3$.*

1. *Consider the first set of two choices, receiving $1,000 now or $1,100 next year; in other words, the choice between $(1000, 0)$ and $(1100, 1)$. Using the primary criterion, we have*

$$u(1000) - u(1100)e^{-0.1} = 1000 - 1100e^{-0.1} = 4.68 > 3.$$

Hence, the primary criterion is satisfied, so the decision-maker prefers $1,000 now to $1,100 next year: $(1100, 1) \prec_V (1000, 0)$.

2. *Let us now consider the choice between the two sums received 10 and 11 years from now: the choice between $(1000, 10)$ and $(1100, 11)$. Using the primary criterion, we have*

$$u(1000)e^{-0.1(10)} - u(1100)e^{-0.1(11)} = 1000e^{-0.1(10)} - 1100e^{-0.1(11)}$$
$$= 1.72 < 3.$$

Hence, the primary criterion fails, because the present discounted values of the two choices are closer than the threshold value of 3. Thus, recourse must be made to the secondary criterion. Since $1000 < 1100$, the secondary criterion requires that the decision-maker prefer $1,100 received 11 years from now to $1,000 received 10 years from now: $(1000, 10) \prec_V (1100, 11)$. We then have an illustration of the common difference effect using the model of vague time preferences.

If, however, in the secondary criterion we replace $z_1 = z_2$ by $s < t$ (i.e., sooner in time is better than larger in outcome), then, in example 4.1, we have $(1100, 11) \prec_V (1000, 10)$—that is, we would not get a common difference effect. The priority order, $z_1 < z_2$ or $s < t$, is an empirical question and requires further research.

4.2.2 The Similarity Relation and Time Preference

A. Rubinstein (2003) argues that hyperbolic discounting is a conservative extension of EDU, so he proposes a heuristics-based decision framework that relies on the *procedural aspects of decision-making*. The central idea is to use a *similarity relationship* in evaluating outcome-time pairs. Suppose that a decision-maker needs to compare two outcome-time pairs: (z_1, t_1) and (z_2, t_2). There are two *attributes*: *size* of the outcomes, z_1, z_2, and the *time delays*, t_1, t_2. The decision-maker is then assumed to apply the following three-stage procedure.

1. If $z_1 > z_2$ and $t_2 > t_1$, then the larger prize is available at an earlier date; hence, (z_1, t_1) is the preferred alternative.
2. If there is *similarity* in one attribute dimension, it ceases to be relevant for a comparison between the two choices. The decision-maker then compares the two alternatives in the remaining attribute dimension. For instance, if z_1 and z_2 are deemed to be similar, then the decision-maker chooses the alternative that is available earlier ($\min\{t_1, t_2\}$). Similarly, if t_1 and t_2 are deemed to be similar, then the alternative that offers the larger outcome is picked ($\max\{z_1, z_2\}$).
3. If there is no similarity in either dimension, then no decision criterion is provided by the theory. Hence, the preference relationship in this model is incomplete; that is, the decision-maker may not be able to express any preferences between some outcome-time pairs.

This model is a promising step, insofar as it attempts to open the black box of human decision-making. However, in order to make this procedure operational, one needs to specify the similarity relation in more detail. First, the similarity relationship does not specify how close two entities must be in order to qualify to be *similar*. Second, the procedure does not apply to choice situations when there is no similarity in either dimension and preferences may be incomplete. Third, the procedure becomes less suitable as the number of outcome-time pairs (z_i, t_i) increases. In this case, theory must specify the order in which the various outcome-time pairs are to be compared. The order might be critical to the final choices made (no order independence theorem is provided in the relevant theory). Fourth, even in the simple setup above, it is not clear which attribute, outcome or time, to choose first in order to use the similarity relation. Thus, although the similarity relationship is a promising choice heuristic, its current scope for applications appears to be limited.

4.2.3 Trade-off Attribute Model of Intertemporal Choice

So far, the models in this section have considered one attribute (outcome or time) at a time. However, Scholten and Read (2006, 2010) proposed the *trade-off model of intertemporal choice*, in which a decision-maker trades off the relative benefits in each dimension in arriving at a choice. A great strength of this model is that it can explain the magnitude effect, present bias, and gain-loss asymmetry (see section 2.13 for these rejections of the EDU model), which is no mean achievement.

Suppose that a decision-maker has a choice between a smaller-sooner (SS) reward, (z_S, t_S), and a larger-later (LL) reward, (z_L, t_L), such that the LL reward has the higher outcome ($0 < z_S < z_L$), but the SS reward is available at an earlier date ($t_S < t_L$). The outcomes, z_S and z_L, are measured relative to some reference point. If the reference point is current wealth, then the restriction $0 < z_S < z_L$ can be understood as the two outcomes being gains relative to current wealth. This framework can be extended to outcomes that are losses relative to the reference point, $z_L < z_S < 0$. We omit the treatment of losses here, but see Dhami (2019c) for the details.

The advantage of the SS reward, denoted by the function $a_S = a_S(t_S, t_L)$, is that it arrives earlier; notice that this term depends only on the time attributes in the two choices. The disadvantage of the SS reward, denoted by the function $d_S = d_S(z_S, z_L)$, is that one forgoes the larger outcome in the future; this term depends only on the outcome attributes in the two choices. In the simplest form, the functional forms for a_S, d_S are linear:

$$a_S = \kappa(t_L - t_S); d_S = z_L - z_S, \tag{4.2}$$

where $\kappa > 0$ ensures compatibility between the units in which time and outcomes are measured. For instance, moving from time units of weeks to months increases κ by a factor of four. The theory does not provide us with a method to guess κ; hence, this must somehow be inferred from individual choices.

Let $\sim_T$ denote the binary indifference relation and $\succ_T$ the strict binary preference relation between two outcome-time pairs in the trade-off model. Using (4.2), the decision-maker uses the following decision rule:

$$\begin{aligned} a_S = d_S &\Leftrightarrow \kappa(t_L - t_S) = z_L - z_S \quad \text{then} \quad SS \sim_T LL \\ a_S > d_S &\Leftrightarrow \kappa(t_L - t_S) > z_L - z_S \quad \text{then} \quad SS \succ_T LL \\ a_S < d_S &\Leftrightarrow \kappa(t_L - t_S) < z_L - z_S \quad \text{then} \quad LL \succ_T SS \end{aligned} \tag{4.3}$$

The decision rule in (4.3) is cognitively simple. Suppose that the advantage and the disadvantage of the SS reward are identical, $a_S = d_S$. Then, from the first row of (4.3), the trade-off model predicts $SS \sim_T LL$. The SS reward is strictly preferred when the advantage of the SS reward relative to the disadvantage is higher, $a_S > d_S$ (second row of (4.3)). Finally, the LL reward is preferred if $a_S < d_S$ (third row of (4.3)).

Starting with $a_S = d_S$, let us explain the magnitude effect (i.e., that larger magnitudes are discounted less).[4] Suppose that both outcomes z_S and z_L are multiplied by a factor, $\gamma > 1$. Then, we need to compare the two outcome-time pairs $(\gamma z_S, t_S), (\gamma z_L, t_L)$. Since $a_S(t_S, t_L) = d_S(z_S, z_L)$, from (4.3) we get that $\kappa(t_L - t_S) = z_L - z_S$, or $\kappa(t_L - t_S) < \gamma (z_L - z_S)$. This implies that $a_S(t_S, t_L) < d_S(\gamma z_S, \gamma z_L)$, so, using the second row in (4.3), we have $(\gamma z_S, t_S) \prec_T (\gamma z_L, t_L)$, or $SS \prec_T LL$, as predicted by the magnitude effect (larger magnitudes are more salient). The advantage and the disadvantage of the SS reward relative to the LL reward can also be nonlinear functions of the attributes. In this case, in principle, the trade-off model may also explain the common difference effect, which is a violation of the stationarity axiom (see sections 2.6 and 2.13). However, we have, as yet, no empirical evidence for the precise nonlinear forms that the relevant functions may take.

4.3 Heuristics and Optimization I: Heuristics for Temporal Choices and Delay-Discounting Models

In this section, we follow al-Nowaihi and Dhami (2008) to show that heuristics-based choices in time discounting can be shown to be equivalent to the optimizing choices in a delay-discounted utility model, as in (4.1). Consider first a utility function for outcomes, u, so that $u(x)$ is utility from outcome x. Now define a function, $v(x) = v(u(x))$, which is an increasing monotonic transformation of the utility function u (e.g., if $u(x) = \sqrt{x}$, then one possible example is $v(x) = 2\sqrt{x}$). If u is a utility function, then so is any increasing monotonic transformation of it; hence, $v(x)$ is also a utility function. We also assume, for simplicity, that outcomes are positive, $x \geq 0$, although al-Nowaihi and Dhami give this analysis for both positive and negative outcomes. Consider the following example of an exponential function.

$$v(x) = e^{u(x)}, x \geq 0 \qquad (4.4)$$

Consider first the trade-off model of choice in section 4.2.3. Let $(x, s) \preceq_T (y, t)$, where (x, s) is the SS option and (y, t) is the LL option. For the trade-off model, from (4.3), we get

$$(x, s) \preceq_T (y, t) \Leftrightarrow a_S \leq d_S \Leftrightarrow \kappa(t - s) \leq y - x.$$

Let $u(x) = x$ for all x. Thus,

$$(x,s) \preceq_T (y,t) \Leftrightarrow \kappa(t-s) \leq u(y) - u(x). \quad (4.5)$$

Since the exponential function is a strictly increasing function (e.g., $e^3 > e^2$), we can write (4.5) as

$$(x,s) \preceq_T (y,t) \Leftrightarrow e^{\kappa(t-s)} \leq e^{u(y)-u(x)} = \frac{e^{u(y)}}{e^{u(x)}}.$$

Simplifying this expression, we get

$$(x,s) \preceq_T (y,t) \Leftrightarrow e^{u(x)} e^{\kappa(t-s)} \leq e^{u(y)}. \quad (4.6)$$

From (4.4), (4.6), we get

$$(x,s) \preceq_T (y,t) \Leftrightarrow v(x) \leq e^{-\kappa(t-s)} v(y). \quad (4.7)$$

Recall that under the EDU model, an outcome time pair (z,t) is evaluated at time 0 as $e^{-\theta t} u(z)$ (see equation (2.8)), and if we wish to evaluate this choice at some time $s: 0 < s < t$, it is given by $e^{-\theta(t-s)} u(z)$. Thus, from (4.7), it follows that $v(x)$ is the EDU of the outcome-time pair (x,s) evaluated at time s and that $e^{-\kappa(t-s)} v(y)$ is the EDU of the outcome-time pair (y,t) when evaluated at time s. Thus it follows that the decision-maker behaves as if they followed the exponential discounted utility model with the discount rate given by κ and the utility function v given in (4.4).

This is a fairly powerful result. It shows that, in time discounting problems, there is sometimes a close relation between models of heuristics-based models and standard optimization-based models in the discounted utility class of models. Following al-Nowaihi and Dhami (2018), we can extend this result to some of the newer models of heuristics-based choice. Below we give a flavor of these results.

In order to give a general framework for considering some of the modern literature on heuristics-based temporal choice, suppose that we have a smaller-sooner (SS) choice (x,s) and a larger-later (LL) choice (y,t). Suppose that the decision-maker expresses a preference for (y,t) over (x,s). Then, we assume that

$$(x,s) \preceq (y,t) \Leftrightarrow f(s,t,\theta) \leq g(x,y,\theta), \quad (4.8)$$

where f is the advantage of the SS reward (it is available earlier); this depends on the time attributes and a vector of parameters θ only. $g(x,y,\theta)$ is the advantage of the LL reward (it contains a higher outcome), and this depends on the outcome attributes and θ only. For the trade-off model, using (4.2), we get the special case $f = \kappa(t_L - t_S)$ and $g = z_L - z_S$ (the disadvantage of the SS reward, d_S, is the same as the advantage of the LL reward).

We consider two different, but related, classes of attribute models in this section, the DRIFT (difference, ratio, interest, and finance) model of Read et al. (2013) and the ITCH (intertemporal choice heuristic) model of Ericson et al. (2015). These models formalize (4.8) in alternative ways by assuming that there is linear combination of different factors that define $f(s, t, \theta)$ and $g(x, y, \theta)$. The empirical evidence in both papers leads the authors to claim that the attribute-based models outperform the commonly known time-discounting models. We present our results with the DRIFT model below.

Denote the binary preference relation under the DRIFT model by $\preceq_D$. So, if the decision-maker considers that (y, t) is at least as good as (x, s), we write $(x, s) \preceq_D (y, t)$. In the DRIFT model, f and g are specified as

$$f(s, t, \theta) = \omega_T (t - s); \quad g(x, y, \theta) = \omega_D (y - x) + \omega_R \left(\frac{y - x}{x}\right) + \omega_I I + \omega_F F,$$

where $\omega_T, \omega_D, \omega_R, \omega_I, \omega_F$ are nonnegative weights; I is a dummy variable that captures an interest rate context (i.e., whether an experimental interest rate is highlighted in the experiment); F is a a dummy variable that captures framing in the experiment (e.g., whether the outcomes are presented as an opportunity to invest or to consume). Then, the relevant decision criterion in (4.8), under the DRIFT model, can be written as

$$(x, s) \preceq_D (y, t) \Leftrightarrow \omega_T (t - s) \leq \omega_D (y - x) + \omega_R \left(\frac{y - x}{x}\right) + \omega_I I + \omega_F F.$$

Simplifying, we get

$$(x, s) \preceq_D (y, t) \Leftrightarrow \omega_T (t - s) \leq \omega_D y - \omega_D x + \varphi,$$

where $\varphi = \omega_R \left(\frac{y}{x} - 1\right) + \omega_I I + \omega_F F > 0$. \hfill (4.9)

Let $u(x) = \omega_D x$ for all x. Then, using (4.4), (4.8), and (4.9), we get

$$(x, s) \preceq_D (y, t) \Leftrightarrow v(x) e^{-\omega_T s} \leq v(y) \left(e^{-\omega_T t + \varphi}\right). \hfill (4.10)$$

From (4.10), there is again an equivalence between the preferences in the DRIFT model and an appropriately defined discounted utility model. However, in this case, things are more complicated. The reason is that the outcomes x, y directly enter into the exponent on the RHS through the term $e^{-\omega T t+\varphi}$. This is a significant discovery because if the DRIFT model does indeed well explain human choices, then we cannot have the clean separation between time and outcomes that characterizes the discounted utility model, as stated in equation (4.1). We would then need a more complex class of models that goes well beyond the delay-discounting model. However, within this more complex class of models, there is a clear equivalence between heuristics-based and optimization-based choices.

4.4 Heuristics and Optimization II: Mental Accounting and Prospect Theory

Suppose that the data suggest that people are using heuristics in making choices. An interesting situation arises when optimization-based models that rely on psychologically realistic theories, such as prospect theory, also make predictions that are consistent with the data. In cases such as these, we do not always face a stark choice between heuristics and optimization. As noted in chapters 2 and 3, some optimization theories are good as-if theories. The prime example is prospect theory.

Thaler (1985) argues that when presented with multiple gains, multiple losses, or a combination of gains and losses, people appear to use the following simple heuristics.

1. People prefer to *segregate multiple gains*—that is, when faced with multiple gains, they wish to receive these gains separately, rather than aggregate the gains. The following analogies are helpful: If one receives a box of sweets, one typically does not finish it all at once but tries to savor the enjoyment over time. Also, we typically do not like to wrap all Christmas presents in one box.

2. People wish to *integrate multiple losses*—that is, when faced with multiple losses, they wish to incur these losses in one fell swoop, rather than incur them separately. As an example, sellers attempt to lump together items for sale—for instance, adding options to a car at the time of purchase. It is as if the additional options have an inelastic demand once they are combined with a larger purchase.

3. When there are both losses and gains, but the gains are large relative to the losses, people try to *integrate small losses with larger gains*—for instance, hiding a little bit of negative news within several bits of positive news in annual company reports.

4. When there are both losses and gains, but the losses are large relative to the gains, then it is difficult to discern preference patterns. However, one

suggestion is that people prefer to *segregate large losses from small gains*, which is known as the *silver lining principle*. For instance, rather than selling a car for $32,000, car dealers would prefer to sell it for $33,000 and then offer an upgrade, say, a better sound system, worth $1,000, for free (expensive car, but the silver lining is that it has a free sound system).

On the face of it, this is a potentially challenging set of observations to explain. Anticipal utility can explain some but perhaps not all of these phenomena. However, applying prospect theory calculations, within an optimizing framework, one can show that all these observations are easily explained. The results can be demonstrated with fairly general utility functions that satisfy the conditions of a utility function under prospect theory (definition 2.14). However, below we use only simple illustrative numerical examples; see Dhami (2019a) for a more general treatment.

Denote wealth by x and the reference point by r. Define $y = x - r$ as the increment in wealth relative to the reference point. Let us use the power form of the utility function, v, taken from (2.47), for empirically reasonable median values of the parameters.

$$v(y) = \begin{cases} y^{0.88} & \text{if } y \geq 0 \\ -2.25(-y)^{0.88} & \text{if } y < 0 \end{cases} \quad (4.11)$$

1. *Multiple gains are segregated*: Suppose that $y = 100$, and one has an option to split it up into two equal gains of 50 each. Using (4.11), the utility from receiving 100 is $(100)^{0.88}$ and the utility from splitting it into two equal parts is $(50)^{0.88} + (50)^{0.88}$. We have

$$(100)^{0.88} < (50)^{0.88} + (50)^{0.88} \Leftrightarrow 57.544 < 62.535.$$

Thus, the individual prefers to segregate multiple gains.

2. *Multiple losses are integrated*: Suppose that a decision-maker has a choice between receiving a loss of $y = -100$ (using (4.11), this gives a utility $-2.25(100)^{0.88}$) and splitting it into two equal losses of 50 (using (4.11), this gives utility $-2.25(50)^{0.88} - 2.25(50)^{0.88}$). We have

$$-2.25(100)^{0.88} > -2.25(50)^{0.88} - 2.25(50)^{0.88} \Leftrightarrow -129.47 > -140.7.$$

Thus, the decision-maker prefers to integrate the two losses into a single loss of 100.

3. *Mixed net gains are integrated*: Consider a loss of 5 and a gain of 15, so there is a mixed net gain of $15 - 5 = 10 > 0$. The decision-maker can

either receive the integrated amount, 10, or the two individual amounts, -5 and 15. We have

$$-2.25\,(5)^{0.88} + (15)^{0.88} < (10)^{0.88} \Leftrightarrow 1.56\,(10)^{0.88} < 7.59.$$

Thus, the decision-maker prefers to integrate the two amounts in the net gain.

4. *Mixed net losses and the silver lining principle*: We cannot say anything in general in this case. A special case arises when there is a very small gain and a very large loss. Consider, for instance, a gain of 10 and a loss of 5000, so that we have a large net loss of 4990. We have

$$(10)^{0.88} - \left(2.25\,(5000)^{0.88}\right) > -2.25\,(4990)^{0.88} \Leftrightarrow -4040.7 > -4041.2.$$

In this case, we get the silver lining principle: the decision-maker prefers to *segregate large losses from small gains*.

Thus, prospect theory explains all four segregation/integration heuristics, suggesting that for many questions of interest, it is a good as-if theory.

This is not the only example that illustrates the power of a prospect theory–based analysis. The impulse balance equilibrium is a heuristics-based learning procedure (Ockenfels & Selten 2005; Selten & Chmura 2008; Brunner et al., 2011; Selten et al., 2011; see also Dhami, 2020b for a detailed treatment). Crawford (2013) shows that the impulse weights in this theory play a role akin to loss aversion. On this interpretation, Crawford argues that "the impulse balance equilibrium is equivalent to Nash equilibrium in a game with payoffs transformed to reflect loss aversion." This shows a clear link between what is believed to be a heuristic-based model and an optimization-based model, in which loss aversion, a key insight from prospect theory, is critical.

4.5 Aspiration Adaptation Theory

Simon (1957) provides one of the most important alternatives to the BRA in his work on bounded rationality. In particular, he proposes replacing mathematical optimization with *satisficing*, which offers a simple heuristics-based solution relying on procedural rationality. The starting point of this theory is that individuals and firms might have an initial *aspiration level*, which is reminiscent of the concept of a reference point in prospect theory. Thus, an aspiration level could, for instance, be a goal or a self-determined target, some socially determined share in a common resource problem, or a legal, cultural, or social entitlement. A decision alternative is *satisfactory* if it meets or exceeds the aspiration level. Saurmann and Selten made an early attempt at a formal model of *aspiration adaptation* in 1962; an English version was published as Selten (1998).

In many games, there is potentially a large number of alternatives or strategies that an individual might be able to use, including those that the individual does not currently know or perhaps cannot imagine. Searching for these options leads to the well-known *infinite regress problem in search*. Namely, in order to search for the relevant alternatives, the decision-maker has to search for the unknown costs of searching for these alternatives, but in order to search for unknown costs requires knowing the unknown costs for the search of the unknown costs, and so on, ad infinitum. In order to avoid these problems, Simon proposed that decision-makers use a simple stopping rule. Stop searching for more options when the outcome from the current choice exceeds the aspiration level. Such an approach has also been called *satisficing* (a neologism that combines the words *satisfy* and *suffice*) in order to distinguish it from *optimization*.

The aspiration levels are themselves updated over time through a dynamic process that depends on past payoffs and past aspirations. For instance, aspiration levels may be adjusted downward if payoffs from a choice fall below the aspiration level, much as one would reduce the sale price of a house that has been on the market for too long. As Simon (1978) puts it: "In a benign environment that provides many good alternatives, aspirations rise; in a harsher environment, they fall."

The individual does optimize in a limited sense, given the rules described above, but not in the sense of discovering a global maximizer, as in the typical mathematical optimization exercise in the BRA. Yet, optimization is invoked in a limited sense because the individual does strive to find an alternative that meets or exceeds the aspiration level. The stopping rule and the updating of aspirations take the form of simple heuristics that enable choices to be made. Satisficing respects the limited cognitive abilities of individuals, as embodied in a stopping rule, and takes account of the structure of the environment, as embodied in the formation of aspirations.

Two of the central problems in the social and the behavioral sciences are the explanation of human cooperation and coordination. We give an example from each of these problems below and show how aspirations adaptation can make predictions in this case.

4.5.1 A Cooperation Problem

In order to illustrate how aspiration adaptation might explain cooperation, consider once again the prisoner's dilemma game that we introduced in chapter 3. We reproduce this game in table 4.1 for the benefit of the reader.

Suppose that the prisoner's dilemma game is played repeatedly over time. Each player has access to two alternatives or actions that we term respectively as *cooperation* (C) and *defection* (D). Time is discrete and denoted by $t = 0, 1, 2, \ldots$. Time $t = 0$ captures the history of the game, such as initial aspirations. The two players simultaneously choose either C or D starting from $t = 1$ onward in every period.

The two players are indexed by $i = 1, 2$, and the aspiration level of player i at time t is denoted by a_{it}. The initial time $t = 0$ aspirations of the players, a_{10} and a_{20}, are given exogenously, and the aspirations of the two players at time t are summarized by the vector $a_t = (a_{1t}, a_{2t})$. The action/strategy of player i at time t is denoted by $s_{it} \in \{C, D\}$. Note that we are not using strategies in the sense of complete contingent plans of action in dynamic games in classical game theory. Here the choice in each period (which we call *strategy*) is more mechanical and governed by simple rules of thumb, as we show below.

The action/strategy profile of both players at time t is denoted by $s_t = (s_{1t}, s_{2t})$, so if both choose C at time t, the action profile is (C, C). The initial strategies are exogenously given by $s_0 = (s_{10}, s_{20})$. We also assume that the payoffs in the payoff matrix in table 4.1 represent utilities. Thus, if both players play C at some time t, then the instantaneous utility of player i is given by $u_i(s_t) = u_i(C, C) = 2$.

Assume that the aspiration levels of the two players evolve in a dynamic manner as follows.

$$a_{it} = a_{it-1} + [u_i(s_{t-1}) - a_{it-1}]; t = 1, 2, \ldots \quad (4.12)$$

From (4.12), aspirations evolve according to a simple *adaptive expectations* rule. At the beginning of time t, current aspirations of player i,

Table 4.1
The prisoner's dilemma game

	C	D
C	2, 2	0, 3
D	3, 0	1, 1

denoted by a_{it}, equal the aspirations in the previous time period, a_{it-1}, adjusted for the difference between the previous period utility and the previous period aspiration level. If the past payoff, $u_i(s_{t-1})$, was high (resp. low), then current aspirations are also high (resp. low). A more general form of (4.12), and the one typically used, is given by $a_{it} = a_{it-1} + \omega [u_i(s_{t-1}) - a_{it-1}]$, where $0 < \omega < 1$, but we choose the simpler form in (4.12) (which effectively requires $a_{it} = u_i(s_{t-1})$) to illustrate the basic ideas.

Since player $i = 1, 2$ has only two strategies at any time, we denote the chosen strategy at time t by $s_{it}^c \in S_i$ and the unchosen strategy by $s_{it}^u \in S_i$. For example, if player i chooses strategy C at time t, then $s_{it}^c = C$ and $s_{it}^u = D$. The individual uses the following simple behavioral rule or heuristic to choose strategies:

$$s_{it+1} = \begin{cases} s_{it}^c & \text{if } u_i \geq a_{it} \\ ps_{it}^c + (1-p)s_{it}^u & \text{if } u_i < a_{it} \end{cases}, \quad (4.13)$$

where $0 < p < 1$ and $ps_{it}^c + (1-p)s_{it}^u$ is a *mixed strategy* in which the player picks s_{it}^c with probability p and s_{it}^u with probability $1-p$. The idea behind the heuristic is the following. If, at time t, the current utility of player i after choosing the action s_{it}^c is at least as great as the current aspiration level ($u_i \geq a_{it}$), then continue playing the current action, s_{it}^c, at time $t+1$. Otherwise, switch to the unchosen action, s_{it}^u, with some probability $1-p$. Thus, p represents a measure of *inertia*. If $p = 0$, then the individual always switches to the unchosen action (no inertia), and if $p = 1$, then the individual never switches (full inertia). Inertia may arise, for instance, from potential switching costs that we have not modeled.

For pedagogical simplicity, we only consider the special case of no inertia, $p = 0$, below, but the results can be extended to the more general case in (4.13).

Given the initial aspiration levels, a_0, and the initial strategies, s_0, of the two players, we can solve for the time path of aspirations and the strategies, $\{a_\tau, s_\tau\}_{\tau=1}^\infty$, by using the definition of aspirations in (4.12) and the heuristic for strategy choice in (4.13). We are agnostic about where the data for initial time $t = 0$, on a_0, s_0, come from. It is simply given by history, and we need an initial set of conditions to kickstart any dynamic system. Assume, for illustrative purposes, that the initial aspiration levels are given by

$$a_{10} = a_{20} = 1.5. \quad (4.14)$$

1. Suppose that the initial strategy profile is $s_0 = (C, C)$. Then, the utilities of the two players at time $t = 0$ are given by

$$u_1(C, C) = u_2(C, C) = 2.$$

Since $u_i(C, C) > a_{i0}$, (4.13) implies that the strategy profile at $t = 1$ continues to be unchanged: $s_1 = (C, C)$. From (4.12), the aspiration level for either player i in period $t = 1$ is given by $a_{i1} = a_{i0} + [u_i(C, C) - a_{i0}] = 2$. Now consider period $t = 2$. Since at $t = 1$, aspirations and utility are equal for both players ($u_i(C, C) = a_{i1}$), it follows from (4.13) that neither of the players switches their strategy from the chosen strategy, C. Thus, at time $t = 2$, the strategy profile is again (C, C). The aspiration level at $t = 2$ is $a_{i2} = 2 + [2 - 2] = 2$. Repeating the same steps, in every future time period, the aspiration level stays at 2, and the action profile also stays unchanged at (C, C).

Thus, the prediction of the aspirations model is that if both players start by cooperating, they cooperate forever. The reason is that the utility from (C, C) is always at least as good as the aspiration level; hence, the players never feel the need to experiment and choose a different strategy. This result stays unchanged even if we set a finite terminal date $t = T$ beyond which the game ends.

Notice that cooperation in a finite period game cannot arise under classical game theory (unless players believe that their opponents are irrational). This is because, in finite period games where players have mutual knowledge of rationality, players defect in the last period, T, by choosing D. The reasoning given in classical game theory is that if the other player had stayed honest and played C, then the defector gets a higher payoff, $3 > 2$ (and players only care about payoffs). In period $T - 1$, rational players are supposed to foresee this eventuality and also choose the action defect, D. Unraveling backward, defection, D, is the optimal choice in every period.

Under the aspirations model, by contrast, players do not use such reasoning. They play more mechanically by using simple rules of thumb that do not create the incentive for spectacularly ditching your partner in the last period. So why should we expect players to choose (C, C) in the very first time period, $t = 0$? The reason is that the evolutionary origins of humans have ensured that they are *conditional cooperators*. Perhaps the fitness of this phenotype was the highest among the available phenotypes; this is often suggested in models of multilevel selection (Bowles & Gintis, 2011; Gintis, 2017; Dhami, 2020b). Conditional cooperation requires that when most humans encounter a new social situation, their initial default frame is to cooperate (Gintis, 2009).

2. Suppose that the strategy profile $s_0 = (D, C)$ is played in the initial period. The game is symmetric, so the results with the strategy profile (C, D) in the initial period are identical. The initial aspirations are given by (4.14), $a_{10} = a_{20} = 1.5$. The utilities of the two players at time $t = 0$ are given by $u_1(s_0) = 3; u_2(s_0) = 0$. It can be shown that in this case, the course of play in successive time periods goes as follows with no discernible trend: $s_1 = (D, D)$, $s_2 = (C, D)$, $s_3 = (D, D)$, $s_4 = (D, C)$, $s_5 = (D, D)$, $s_6 = (C, D)$, $s_7 = (D, C) \ldots$ Dynamic play does not settle down. The calculations are not particularly enlightening, so we omit them. It is possible that for a different level of initial aspirations, we get different results.

3. Suppose that the initial strategy profile is (D, D). Using table 4.1, the first period utilities are then $(1, 1)$. Since $1 < a_{i0}$, both players' aspiration levels are violated, and at $t = 1$, they both switch to the strategy profile (C, C) (recall that we have assumed the case of no inertia $p = 0$). At $t = 1$, their aspiration levels are given by $a_{i1} = 1 < u_{i1} = 2$. So neither of the players alters their strategy for $t = 2$, which remains at (C, C), and $u_{i2} = 2$ for both players. Using (4.12), at $t = 2$, the aspiration levels of both players are given by $a_{i2} = 2$, and since $a_{i2} = u_{i2} = 2$, from (4.13), neither of the players alters their strategy for the next period, which remains at (C, C). This gives a steady state of the system, where the aspirations of both players and their respective utilities equal 2 in every period and the cooperative strategy profile (C, C) is played every period.

It should be quite intuitive that this framework can be used to support the cooperative outcome in a range of games (Colman et al., 2010). For various formalizations of these ideas, see Börgers and Sarin (2000), Karandikar et al. (1998), Cho and Matsui (2005), Ray (2006), Genicot and Ray (2017).

4.5.2 A Coordination Problem

Consider the two-player coordination game below.

	C	D
C	1, 1	−1, −1
D	−1, −1	0, 0

In this game, coordination refers to choosing the strategy profile (C, C), which is also the Pareto optimal outcome. If both players coordinate on (C, C), they get the highest payoff of 1 each. If players do not coordinate their actions (any of the two profiles (D, C) or (C, D)), then each receives the lowest possible payoff of -1. However, if they coordinate on (D, D), then both get a zero payoff.

In classical game theory, there are two Nash equilibria in this game (C, C) and (D, D). However, it is not clear without further refinements of equilibrium (e.g., imposing payoff dominance that would give rise to (C, C) in equilibrium) which of these two equilibria will be played. However, under aspiration adaptation, the predictions are different, as we show below.

Assume that the initial aspiration levels are given by

$$a_{10} = a_{20} = -0.1. \qquad (4.15)$$

The solution to this problem is obtained in the same way as for the case of the prisoner's dilemma game. Maintaining the same assumptions as in that case, we directly summarize the results, leaving the details for interested readers to work out themselves.

1. Suppose that the initial strategy profile is $s_0 = (C, C)$. The prediction of the model is that if both players start by coordinating on (C, C), they will continue coordinating at (C, C). The reason is that the payoff from (C, C) is always at least as good as the aspiration level; hence, the players never feel the need to experiment and choose a different action.
2. Suppose that the initial strategy profile is $s_0 = (C, D)$. Since the game is symmetric, the results with the profile (D, C) are identical. Assume that there is no inertia, $p = 0$. If $s_0 = (C, D)$, the strategy profile settles at (D, C) for all time periods, starting at $t = 1$. If on the other hand, $s_0 = (D, C)$, the strategy profile settles at (C, D) from $t = 1$ onward.
3. If the initial strategy profile is (D, D), then it is followed in every period. The aspiration level improves in every period and converges eventually to zero, from below.

An important finding from the empirical literature on coordination games is that the final outcome is history dependent and the initial state of play is quite important (Camerer, 2003; Dhami, 2019d). In both cases, the cooperative and the coordination games, the cooperative outcome (C, C) can be sustained in an equilibrium of the aspirations adaptation game, depending on the initial conditions, such as initial aspiration levels and initial strategy choices. The aspiration adaptation model might also lead to undesirable solutions. For instance, in the coordination game, and for the initial aspirations in the example above, if players begin by coordinating on (D, D), they stay at (D, D) forever and never coordinate at (C, C), which is a rather grim prediction.

The aspiration adaptation process in (4.12) and the strategy updating rule in (4.13) are plausible and intuitive. However, ultimately, empirical evidence must be the sole arbiter to determine the precise aspiration adaptation process. Humans might exhibit substantial heterogeneity that is interpersonal, cultural, and context dependent. However, the general principles behind aspiration adaptation are supported by the evidence. Using data on Ethiopian households, Bernard and Taffesse (2014) find that watching inspirational videos based on the actual life stories of successful people leads to higher savings and higher aspirations, particularly about the children's educational future. Poverty has been found in empirical studies to lower aspirations and create greater hopelessness (Ray, 2006; Haushofer & Fehr, 2014). In richer countries, poorer students have relatively lower aspirations toward education and employment (Guyon & Huillery, 2014). Lower aspirations may cause the poor to put in a lower effort and result in poor economic outcomes, perpetuating poverty (Dalton et al., 2016).

The setup in our formal model is relatively simple. In actual practice, the link between actions and outcomes might not be obvious due to the presence of noise or other confounding factors: there could be multiple goals, complex goals, or conflicting goals (e.g., short-term and long-term goals), and it might not be clear how to achieve them. These are interesting problems for future research. Selten et al. (2012) outline a formal model of the decisions taken by a monopolist, which has some of the abovementioned features, in an approach that they call *goal systems*.

We note the cognitive requirements for classical game theory in section 2.7. The evidence in section 2.14 does not support the predictions of classical game theory. One potential solution is to take social rationality more seriously; we consider this in section 4.7. Another potential solution is to explore cognitive simplifications that people might engage in when they are presented with strategic contexts. Aspiration adaptation is an obvious exemplar. In section 4.6, we consider another cognitive simplification based on evidential reasoning, which can also explain cooperation in the prisoner's dilemma game.

4.6 Evidential Reasoning

In static strategic interactions, such as the prisoner's dilemma game, each player is uncertain about the action that the other player will take. It could be that players do not know each other very well, or even if they did, they could be facing a novel social situation. In cases such as this, the evidence suggests that players assign *diagnostic significance* to their own actions in forming inferences about how others will behave. Such reasoning is known as *evidential reasoning* (ER), also sometimes known as *social projection* or the *false consensus effect*. The likelihood that players use ER is even higher when the other players are viewed as *like-minded*.

Robbins and Krueger (2005) describe ER as follows: "Using their own disposition or preferences as data, people can make quick predictions of what others are like or what they are likely to do." In a survey article, Krueger (2007) writes: "*The concept of social projection is once again generating vigorous theory development and empirical research . . . . Social projection is among the simplest, oldest, and arguably most central concepts of the field.*" By contrast, players in classical game theory use *causal reasoning*. Causal reasoners assign no diagnostic value to their own actions in inferring the actions of others.

Let us first consider some examples of evidential reasoning.

Example 4.2. *(False consensus effect) Ross et al. (1977) asked subjects if they would walk around a university campus wearing a sandwich board with the word "REPENT" written on it. Those who agreed to do so estimated that 63.5 percent of their peers would also agree to do so, while those who refused expected 76.7 percent of their peers to also refuse. Since these percentages add up to more than 100 percent, they cannot constitute consistent beliefs in the sense of classical game theory. This evidence is consistent with two-thirds to three-quarters of the subjects using evidential reasoning to impute diagnostic significance to their own preferred actions in forming beliefs about the likely actions of other like-minded people (the student population in the university, in this case). This is an example of the false consensus effect.*

Example 4.3. *(Contributions among like-minded people in public goods games) Voluntary public goods contribution games are those in which a group of players voluntarily, and simultaneously, contribute toward a public good that provides all players with an identical public benefit* *irrespective of the individual contributions—for instance, a lighthouse that is constructed by pooling together the voluntary contributions of fishermen in the vicinity. Public goods are, thus, nonrival in consumption (use by one person does not diminish use by another, at least not until there are too many users), and they are nonexcludable (e.g., it is difficult to exclude a fisherman who did not contribute from using the lighthouse). How much should each person contribute toward the public good? Under classical game theory, under reasonable conditions, it is a Nash equilibrium for each player to free-ride (i.e., make zero contributions) on the contributions made by others. The experimental evidence shows that in the absence of punishment of noncooperators, contributions decay over successive rounds, while punishments are conducive to high levels of contributions (Ledyard, 1995; Fehr & Gächter, 2000).*

Gächter and Thöni (2005) investigate whether cooperation in public goods games is higher among like-minded people in the absence of punishments. Based on the contribution choices of players in a single round of the public goods game experiment, subjects are grouped into categories. The top three contributors are grouped into a separate group (the top group) as having the greatest inclination to contribute. Other groups are constituted on the basis of lower contributions; the lowest three contributors constitute the bottom group. The public goods game is then played separately for each of these groups. Players know the contributions of other group members; hence, they know that they are grouped with like-minded people, which might particularly facilitate the use of evidential reasoning in guessing how much others will contribute. Over the next 10 rounds, contributions are much higher and free riding much lower in the top group, which achieves nearly the first best level of contributions in several rounds. Even the endgame effect—that is, the sharp drop in contributions in the last round of the experiment—is most pronounced among the bottom group.

Example 4.4. *(Evidential reasoning about states of other humans) Van Boven and Loewenstein (2005) asked subjects, who were made to experience the physiological states of either thirst or hunger, to imagine a hiker who is lost in the woods. They were then asked whether the hiker was more likely to be thirsty or hungry. Participants attributed their own physiological states to the hypothetical hiker despite their being no obvious correlation. Thus, participants seem to assign diagnostic significance to their own state in inferring the state of the lost hiker.*

Table 4.2
Expectations of voters from each political party

Year	Candidates	% Democrats expecting Democrat win	% Republicans expecting Republican win
1988	Dukakis vs. Bush	51.7	94.2
1984	Mondale vs. Reagan	28.8	99.8
1980	Carter vs. Reagan	87.0	80.4
1976	Carter vs. Ford	84.2	80.4
1972	McGovern vs. Nixon	24.7	99.6
1968	Humphrey vs. Nixon	62.5	95.4
1964	Johnson vs. Goldwater	98.6	30.5
1960	Kennedy vs. Nixon	78.4	84.2
1956	Stevenson vs. Eisenhower	54.6	97.6
1952	Stevenson vs. Eisenhower	81.5	85.9

Source: Forsythe et al. 1992.

Example 4.5. *Survey evidence from US presidential elections shows that voters who intend to vote Democrat assign higher probabilities to the Democrat candidate winning; see table 4.2. Voters who intend to vote Republican assign higher probabilities to a Republican win. The assigned probabilities often add up to 150 percent or above. Yet, most people get their information from potentially identical public sources (social media had little presence for the dates shown in table 4.2). This is consistent with voters taking their own actions as diagnostic of what other like-minded voters might do. Quattrone and Tversky (1984) use these insights to explain why voters vote in elections. Voters who have a predisposition to vote (say, due to a sense of civic responsibility) believe that other like-minded responsible voters will also vote. On the other hand, if they were to procrastinate and choose not to vote for their party, they believe that other like-minded people might also reason in a similar manner, and the other party could win the election. So they vote.*

It is important to highlight that people who use evidential reasoning do not believe that by altering their own actions they are able to alter the actions of the other players. They simply take their own predisposition to follow, or not, an action as diagnostic evidence for what other, like-minded players might do. Economists accustomed to traditional notions of rationality may find evidential reasoning to be less than fully rational. Evidential reasoning equips players with a simple heuristic that is *fast* in computation time and *frugal* in the use of information.

Other evidence supports our interpretation of ER as a heuristic. People who use evidential reasoning are not aware of using it, despite their behavior being obviously consistent with evidential reasoning. Evidential reasoning appears to manifest as an *automatic* response rather than as a *deliberate* response—that is, it does not require awareness, effort, or intention. Evidence supporting this view comes from experiments that show that evidential reasoning was not hampered by cognitive load or the time required to complete an action; see Krueger (2007). Furthermore, other evidence, also reported in Krueger, suggests that considerable cognitive effort is required to suspend evidential reasoning.

Al-Nowaihi and Dhami (2015) provide a theoretical framework that replaces causal reasoning in classical game theory with evidential reasoning in static games of complete information.[5] Such games may be called *evidential games*. Al-Nowaihi and Dhami propose an equilibrium for such games, known as *evidential equilibrium*, identify conditions for its existence, and show its relation to a Nash equilibrium. The cognitive requirements required for solving evidential games are very reasonable and turn what is essentially a strategic situation into a simpler decision theoretic situation.

Consider once again the prisoner's dilemma game in table 4.1. How might we explain the observed cooperative outcome (C, C) using evidential reasoning? A formal treatment, along the lines of al-Nowaihi and Dhami (2015), requires introducing additional technical machinery. So we make do here with the basic intuition for the solution that goes back to Lewis (1979), who invokes evidential reasoning to explain the unexpectedly high levels of cooperation in the one-shot prisoner's dilemma game. Mutual cooperation is better than mutual defection, and players know this. Furthermore, some players may be hardwired to cooperate and/or they may be inequity averse. If such players use evidential reasoning, they may take their own preference for mutual cooperation as diagnostic evidence that their rival also has a preference for mutual cooperation, so they are more likely to cooperate. This intuition is borne out by the evidence. Players who cooperate by playing C believe that 60 to 70 percent of others will also play C; those who play D also believe that 60 to 70 percent of others will also play D (Krueger, 2007). This is reminiscent of the message that emerges from the data on US presidential elections in table 4.2.

Adherents of classical game theory may object and argue that even in classical game theory, if players believe that others are irrational, then they might choose C. But this begs the question of why super-rational players in classical game theory should believe that others are irrational enough to play a strictly dominated action in a game with such a simple structure. What hope do we have for much more complex games, where common knowledge of rationality is essential for the results in classical game theory?

Evidential reasoning is likely to be facilitated if players believe that others are like-minded. Such confidence in the like-mindedness of others may increase if there is the possibility of preplay promises that players will cooperate with each other and shake hands on it. The empirical evidence in Darai and Grätz (2010) is consistent with this channel. By contrast, in classical game theory, such preplay promises should have no effect. The reason is that in classical game theory, players have no hesitation in breaking a promise if the current benefits exceed the future costs; their morality is instrumental, not intrinsic.

Like-mindedness is compatible with both outcomes, C and D, depending on one's own predisposition to play a particular strategy. Thus, evidential reasoning also predicts the play of (D, D). We observe both outcomes in the prisoner's dilemma game, however. Why then do we observe so much cooperation in the static prisoner's dilemma game, which also incidentally leads to a Pareto optimal outcome? The reason is that most humans intrinsically like to cooperate, particularly when they encounter a new social situation. This is an essential part of the definition of conditional reciprocity. As Gintis (2009, p. 145) eloquently puts it: "It is not reason but humanity that leads us to believe that the Pareto-superior equilibrium is obvious. We humans by virtue of our gene-culture coevoluationary history and our civilized culture, harbour a default frame that says 'in coordination games, unless you have some special information that suggests otherwise, conjecture that the other player also considers the frame to be a default frame and reasons as you do, and choose the action that assumes your partner is trying to do well by you.'" This also explains the label salience of outcomes in the prisoner's dilemma game: when framed as a cooperative game, the cooperation rate is higher.

For a range of other applications of evidential reasoning, such as those to oligopoly theory and Nash bargaining, see al-Nowaihi and Dhami (2015).

4.7 Kantian Rationality

Consider once again our discussion of the prisoner's dilemma game in table 4.1 and the difficulty of explaining the empirical evidence using classical game theory. Roemer (2018) views the explanation of cooperation in classical game theory thusly: "I will maintain that this is an unappealing solution, and too complex as well. It is a Ptolemaic attempt to use non-cooperative theory to explain something fundamentally different."

In response to the evidence, we have examined several alternative explanations of cooperation in this book, such as *aspiration-based models* and *evidential reasoning*. Yet another approach is to move away from notions of individual rationality to consider what Gintis (2017, p. 51) calls *social rationality*. This is an overarching concept that includes team reasoning (Bacharach 1999, 2006) and Tomasello's (2014) concept of *joint intentionality*.

Joint intentionality implies that players have a shared common goal and common knowledge of trust in each other to implement the shared goal. In other words, players are motivated not just by instrumental reciprocity, as in classical game theory, but also by the desire to collaborate and coordinate to achieve shared goals. These insights arose from Tomasello's work on comparing infant humans and chimps; the former are hardwired to collaborate, but chimps, our nearest genetic relatives, are not. Chimps can cooperate to, say, hunt monkeys, but their primary motivation is based on "me-thinking" rather than the "we-thinking" that is characteristic of human collaboration.

In this section, we explore a specific notion of social rationality, the *Kantian equilibrium* (Roemer, 2015, 2018). In the Kantian protocol, *a player wishes to take the action that they would like the other players to take*, not out of fear but *because it is the moral thing to do*. Social rationality is then invoked to argue that players believe that other players will also take the same action. This obviously requires players to trust the social rationality of other players.

We explain the idea behind a Kantian equilibrium using two-player static games of full information in which players make their choices simultaneously. Denote the two players by $i = 1, 2$; when referring to a player, we sometimes call the other player the opponent. Let $S = [n_1, n_2]$, $i = 1, 2$ be the identical common pure strategy set of both players, where $n_1 \leq n_2$ are real numbers. Thus, the strategy of player i, denoted by s_i, is to choose any number in the interval $[n_1, n_2]$. The number could be, say, the choice of an effort level or the contribution to a joint project. Since these are numbers in an interval, we can speak of an *increase* or *decrease* in the strategy of a player as an increase or decrease, respectively, of these numbers. The strategy of the opponent, denoted by s_{-i}, is to simultaneously choose a number in the same interval $[n_1, n_2]$.

The strategy profile of the two players is denoted by $\mathbf{s} = (s_i, s_{-i})$. The two players interact in a strategic manner in the sense that their choices affect their own payoffs and the payoffs of the opponent. The interaction lasts for only one time period. Denote by $u_i(s_i, s_{-i})$ the payoff, or utility function, of player i when player i chooses the strategy s_i and the opponent chooses the strategy s_{-i}. Denote by S^I the subset of $[n_1, n_2]$ when each player chooses an identical strategy. Thus S^I contains elements of the form $\mathbf{s} = (s, s)$, where $s \in [n_1, n_2]$. A normal form game is denoted by $G = \{1, 2, S, u_1, u_2\}$—that is, it lists the two players, their strategy sets (which are identical in this case), and their payoffs.

Definition 4.1. *(Kantian equilibrium) Consider a normal form game G. A strategy vector $\mathbf{s}^* = (s^*, s^*) \in S^I$ is a Kantian equilibrium if*

$$u_i(\mathbf{s}^*) \geq u_i(\mathbf{s}) \text{ for all } i \text{ and for all } \mathbf{s} \in S^I.$$

From definition 4.1, in a Kantian equilibrium, where each player chooses an identical strategy, s^*, each player gets a higher payoff than any other identical strategy $s \in S^I$.

To make progress, we need to specify how the payoffs of each player change as the strategy of the other player increases or decreases. There are two distinct possibilities.

1. *Monotone increasing game*: In public goods games (see example 4.3), the payoffs of players are strictly increasing in the contributions of the other players to the public good.
2. *Monotone decreasing game*: In a common-pool resource problem, the payoffs of players are strictly decreasing in the actions of the other players, which run down the common-pool resource.

The prisoner's dilemma game that we describe to illustrate the Kantian equilibrium is an example of a monotone increasing game. Hence, we focus only on this case, although the results, particularly proposition 4.1, hold also for the monotonically decreasing case.

Definition 4.2. *(Strictly monotone increasing games) A normal form game G is strictly monotone increasing if*

$$u_i(s_i, s_{-i}) > u_i(s_i, s'_{-i}) \text{ for all } i, s_i, s_{-i}, s'_{-i} \text{ such that } s_{-i} \geq s'_{-i}. \tag{4.16}$$

From definition 4.2, an increase in the strategy of the opponent from s'_{-i} to s_{-i}, but holding fixed the strategy of player i at s_i, increases the payoff of player i. This must hold for both players and for all possible strategies of the player and the opponent. The next result shows that the Kantian equilibrium has desirable welfare features because it achieves a Pareto optimal outcome (see remark 3.2). In this sense, Kantian equilibria might make a compelling case for social rationality to apply.

Proposition 4.1. *The Kantian equilibrium of a strictly monotone increasing game is Pareto optimal.*

Proof of Proposition 4.1. Let $\mathbf{s}^* = (s^*, s^*) \in S^I$ be a Kantian equilibrium (definition 4.1). We use the method of proof by contradiction. Suppose that $\mathbf{s}^*$ is *not* Pareto optimal. Then, there exists some other equilibrium, say, $\hat{\mathbf{s}} = (\hat{s}_i, \hat{s}_{-i}) \in S$ (notice we have not restricted this to the set S^I), where the payoffs of both players are higher (if not, then $\mathbf{s}^*$ would be Pareto optimal):

$$u_i(\hat{\mathbf{s}}) \geq u_i(\mathbf{s}^*) \text{ for all } i, \text{ with strict inequality for at least one } i. \tag{4.17}$$

Let $s_{\max} = \max\{\hat{s}_i, \hat{s}_{-i}\}$ be the higher of the two strategies $\hat{s}_i$ and $\hat{s}_{-i}$. Define a new strategy $\mathbf{s}_{\max} = (s_{\max}, s_{\max}) \in S^I$. From (4.16), we get

$$u_i(\mathbf{s}_{\max}) > u_i(\hat{\mathbf{s}}) \text{ for all } i. \tag{4.18}$$

From (4.17) and (4.18), we get

$$u_i(\mathbf{s}_{\max}) > u_i(\mathbf{s}^*) \text{ for all } i, \text{ and } \mathbf{s}_{\max}, \mathbf{s}^* \in S^I,$$

which contradicts the fact that $\mathbf{s}^*$ is a Kantian equilibrium. Hence, $\mathbf{s}^*$ must be Pareto optimal. □

Let us consider an application of this framework to the prisoner's dilemma game in table 4.3, where $0 < b < c < 1$. The game satisfies the requirements for a prisoner's dilemma game (recall remark 3.1). It is a symmetric game in which the row and the column players have two strategies, cooperate (C) and defect (D). The unique Nash equilibrium is (D, D) because $-b > -c$ by assumption ($0 < b < c < 1$). One reason that we use the prisoner's dilemma game in a slightly different format in this section, as compared to the game in table 4.1, is that we want to ensure that the strategy set is of the form $S = [n_1, n_2]$ so that the results derived above can be used.

Table 4.3
A prisoner's dilemma game

	C	D
C	0, 0	$-c, 1$
D	$1, -c$	$-b, -b$

Suppose that the row player (player 1) plays C with probability $p \in [0, 1]$ and D with probability $1 - p$. The column player (player 2) plays C with probability $q \in [0, 1]$ and D with probability $1 - q$. It follows that the outcome (C, C) arises with probability pq; the outcome (D, D) arises with probability $(1 - p)(1 - q)$; the other two outcomes (C, D) and (D, C) arise with respective probabilities $p(1 - q)$ and $q(1 - p)$. Let $n_1 = 0$ and $n_2 = 1$, so that the strategy sets of the players are given by $S = [0, 1]$. Thus, the strategy of the row player is to choose a probability $p \in [0, 1]$ and the strategy of the column player is to choose a probability $q \in [0, 1]$.

We assume that each of the payoffs in table 4.3 is the corresponding utility from a pair of strategies and that both players wish to maximize expected utility (this is not critical, as we could have presented the results with prospect theory). Thus, the respective expected utilities of the players from the strategy choices are

$$\begin{cases} EU_1(p, q) = -p(1-q)c + (1-p)q - (1-p)(1-q)b \\ EU_2(p, q) = -q(1-p)c + (1-q)p - (1-q)(1-p)b \end{cases} \quad (4.19)$$

Differentiating the expected utility of player 1, u_1, with respect to q (the strategy of the opponent, player 2), we get $\frac{\partial EU_1}{\partial q} = pc + (1-p)(1+b) > 0$. Similarly, differentiating EU_2 with respect to p, we get $\frac{\partial EU_2}{\partial p} = qc + (1-q)(1+b) > 0$. Thus, we have a strictly monotone increasing game (definition 4.2) because an increase in the strategy of the opponent increases the payoff of each player.

To find the Kantian equilibrium of the prisoner's dilemma game, we need to restrict attention to the symmetric strategy set $S^I \subset S$. Hence, elements of S^I take the form (p, p), where $p \in [0, 1]$ (or alternatively, we could have written this as (q, q), where $q \in [0, 1]$). Using (4.19), and restricting attention to the set S^I, the maximization problem of player 1 is

$$p^* \in \arg\max EU_1(p, p) = -p(1-p)c + (1-p)p - (1-p)^2 b.$$

It follows that

$$\frac{dEU_1(p,p)}{dp} = 2b(1-p) + (1-c)(1-2p).$$

The second order condition is $\frac{d^2 EU_1(p,p)}{dp^2} = -2b - 2(1-c) < 0$, where the sign follows from the condition $0 < b < c < 1$. Thus, the objective function of player 1, EU_1, is strictly concave in p, so the first order condition is sufficient to find the unique solution. Solving $\frac{\partial EU_1}{\partial p} = 0$ for p, we get the Kantian solution p^*,

$$p^* = \frac{1}{2} + \frac{b}{2(b+1-c)}. \qquad (4.20)$$

Since $\frac{b}{(b+1-c)} < 2$, $0 < p^* < 1$ is the identical probability chosen by each player to play C (and play D with probability $1 - p^*$).

In the Nash equilibrium solution under classical game theory, we have $(p, q) = (0, 0)$, because players never play the strictly dominated strategy C. However, since $0 < p^* < 1$, in the Kantian equilibrium, players play the strictly dominated strategy C with a strictly positive probability. Furthermore, using proposition 4.1, (p^*, p^*) must be a Pareto optimal equilibrium (see remark 3.2 for the definition of Pareto optimality). In particular, as c becomes arbitrarily close to 1, we can use (4.20) to see immediately that $\lim_{c \to 1} p^* = 1$. Hence, in this case, both players play the cooperative outcome with probability 1.

Thus, social rationality, of which the Kantian protocol is an example, provides a powerful and plausible justification for the cooperative outcome, relative to the instrumental view that is embodied in classical game theory.[6]

4.8 Winner's Curse in Financial Markets

In common value (CV) auctions, bidders for an object do not have access to any private signals about the value of the object. The value of the object depends only on a common public signal, S. Hence, the value of the object perceived by bidder $i = 1, \ldots, n$ is $v_i = v_i(S)$. Suppose that the object that is up for auction in a CV auction is indivisible, so that the winner takes all. How much should bidders bid? Several aspects of this question have been studied in economics. From a behavioral economics perspective, the most important result is the *winner's curse*, first discovered in oil lease auctions.

In oil lease auctions, bidders bid for drilling rights for oil on a tract of land. The value of the oil can be estimated, and it is the same for all companies; hence this is a common value auction. The estimation of the costs of drilling, c, however, lead to uncertainty and must be estimated. Suppose that the estimate of c for bidder i is given by $C_i = c + \varepsilon_i$, where c is the objectively correct cost of drilling, and the noise term ε_i is independently distributed across bidders and has zero mean. In actual practice, bidders may differ in the precision with which they estimate the true underlying costs, and they may also differ in their optimism in their estimates; these factors may lead to variation in the noise term, ε_i, but let us abstract from these for the moment. Since $E[C_i] = c$, the cost estimates of all bidders are unbiased, but in any particular draw of the estimate, there is random error, as captured by ε_i.

It follows that the winner of the CV auction is the most optimistic bidder who has the lowest realization of ε_i. Ex post, the actual costs are likely to turn out to be higher than the estimated costs for the most optimistic bidder. Hence, the winner might go bankrupt or the profits might turn out to be unexpectedly low. This is known as the *winner's curse*.

Capen et al. (1971) provide the first field evidence for the winner's curse using outcomes of the US government's outer continental shelf oil lease auctions, which are of the nature of CV auctions. Thaler (1988) summarizes the findings from this study and the follow-up study by Mead et al. (1983), as follows.

1. Restricting oneself to serious bids, the ratio of the highest to the lowest bids is commonly between 5 to 10 and as high as 100.
2. The sum of winning bids in the 1969 Alaska North Slope sale was $900 million, while the sum of the second highest bids was $370 million. The winning bid was at least four times higher than the next highest bid in 26 percent of the auctioned tracts and at least two times higher than the next highest bid in 77 percent of the cases.
3. Calculating the before-tax returns on 1,223 leases over the period 1954–1969 in the Gulf of Mexico, only 22 percent of the leases turned out to be profitable, but the after-tax earnings were not very high; 62 percent of the leases were dry and another 16 percent were unprofitable.

Bazerman and Samuelson (1983) used MBA students at Boston University to conduct 48 first price sealed-bid auctions (highest bidder wins the object) in 12 classes. The object up for auction was a jar full of coins or small and large paper clips with a value of $8. All bidders observed the same object, but they were not informed of the value of the items in the jar and had to guess the value. The bid that was closest to the actual value of the item won a $2 prize. The mean bid across all auctions was $5.13, but the average winning bid was $10.01, and it led to losses in half of the auctions. The authors then followed up this game with the *acquire a company* game in Samuelson and Bazerman (1985), which we explain in example 4.6. In this game, the rational bid is zero; however, 90 percent of the subjects bid between 50 and 75. These results are suggestive of a winner's curse.

There are many empirical findings of a winner's curse. Lind and Plott (1991) find the winner's curse for above-average-ability students; Dyer et al. (1989) find that only 17 percent of the winners in a CV auction earn any profits and 59 percent of all bids were greater than the expected value of the object, conditional on winning it. Empirical studies have also explored other implications of the predictions under classical game theory in CV auctions that fail the empirical test. These include (1) the prediction that as the number of bidders increases, the optimal bids should fall (Kagel et al., 1995) and (2) the predicted effects of information provision on the value of the object (Kagel & Levin, 1986). Experienced auction players in lab experiments also exhibit the winner's curse (Dyer et al., 1989). There is some evidence that very highly experienced subjects may not be subject to the winner's curse, but their profits fall below the predictions of classical game theory (Kagel & Richard, 2001). However, Kagel and Levin (2001, pp. 32, 33) caution us in interpreting these results by arguing that the winner's curse is avoided in experimental settings only with strong information feedback that is unlikely to be present in field settings. There are additional reasons, they point out, relating to the incentive and organizational structure, to suspect that other factors in field settings might work in favor of producing the winner's curse rather than removing it.

Harrison and List (2008) conducted two experiments with sports cards dealers and argue that experienced dealers do not suffer much from the winner's curse. For instance, under asymmetric information they suffer from the winner's curse in 24 to 30 percent of the cases, and this incidence is lower under symmetric information. Kagel (2015) argues persuasively that there are alternative, plausible explanations for the results from both experiments. In the first, dealers could simply be using their common heuristic of buying at a low price to sell at a higher price, which protects them from the winner's curse. In the second experiment, there is no scope for a winner's curse because the package of 10 sports cards has a publicly known retail value.

The source of the winner's curse appears to be that bidders do not use the statistically correct conditional expectations. Rather, they appear to use a simple heuristic in calculating conditional probabilities. Consider the following game introduced by Samuelson and Bazerman (1985) that clarifies the necessary calculations.

Example 4.6. *(Acquire a company (takeover) game; Samuelson & Bazerman, 1985) An acquiring firm (A) bids an amount $b \geq 0$ to acquire a target firm (T) whose value, $v \geq 0$, is private information to firm T. Firm T agrees to the bid by firm A if $b \geq v$; otherwise it rejects the bid. Firm A has beliefs that v is uniformly distributed in the interval $[0, 100]$. Firm A knows that if it acquires firm T, the value of firm T will increase to γv, $\gamma > 1$. For instance, firm A could add value due to its specialized expertise in this area. How much should firm A bid?*

When $\gamma = 1.5$, experimental results suggest that about 90 percent of the subjects in their role as firm A bid in the range 50–75.[7] These subjects typically reason as follows: "Since v is uniformly distributed in $[0, 100]$, the average value of T is 50. By acquiring it, the value increases by 50 percent, so that post-acquisition the expected value is 75."

This is a plausible heuristics-based way of thinking about conditional probabilities, but it is statistically incorrect. It ignores the adverse selection problem by making unconditional probability calculations. In particular, it ignores the expected value of the firm, conditional on the bid being accepted. After all, if a bid b is accepted, then the conditional value of the firm, v, can be no higher than b. In fact, since v is uniformly distributed, the average value of T is then simply $\frac{b}{2}$. But since A adds value to T, the post-takeover expected value of T is $\gamma \frac{b}{2}$, which exceeds the bid, b, only if $\gamma \frac{b}{2} > b$, or equivalently if $\gamma > 2$. However, if $1 < \gamma \leq 2$, then, on average, the value of the firm is lower than the bid, making a loss for A, which gives rise to the winner's curse. Thus, classical game theory predicts that the rational bid equals zero if $\gamma < 2$ and equals 100 if $\gamma \geq 2$.

For those who prefer a slightly more formal treatment of the same result, we can see how the optimal bid of A is calculated. The expected profit of firm A, for any bid b, is

$$\pi(b) = \Pr(v \leq b) \int_0^b [\gamma v - b] \, dv, \qquad (4.21)$$

where $\Pr(v \leq b)$ is the probability that A's bid is accepted by T. We can ignore the case $\Pr(v > b)$ on the RHS of (4.21) because in that case the bid is rejected and both firms get a zero profit. If a bid b is accepted, which occurs with probability $\Pr(v \le b)$, then firm A must infer that the value of T lies uniformly in the interval $[0, b]$, which accounts for the upper and lower limits on the integral. In this case, the profits for A equal $\gamma v - b$ for any true, but unknown, value of v in the relevant range. Since v is believed to be uniformly distributed in the interval $[0, 100]$, so $\Pr(v \le b) = \frac{b}{100}$, hence we can rewrite (4.21) as $\pi(b) = \frac{b}{100} \int_0^b [\gamma v - b] \, dv$. Evaluating this integral we get $\pi(b) = \frac{b^3}{100} \left[\frac{\gamma}{2} - 1\right]$, which gives the optimal rational bid as

$$b^r = \begin{cases} 0 & \text{if } 1 < \gamma \le 2, \\ 100 & \text{if } \gamma > 2. \end{cases} \quad (4.22)$$

The existence of the winner's curse in the takeover game identifies as the key explanation a failure to calculate conditional probabilities. It is unlikely that human evolution has prepared us to calculate conditional probabilities in classical statistics. Humans tend to use simple heuristics in making statistical inferences, and by not taking account of the evidence on these heuristics, the BRA struggles to account for the evidence.

The winner's curse can also be explained by several models in behavioral game theory that include *cursed equilibrium* and *level-k models*; for details see Dhami (2019d). However, these models do not well fit the data from the acquire a company game (Charness & Levin, 2009). One possible reason is that the main insights in a cursed equilibrium and level-k models do not directly arise from the failure to take the statistically correct conditional probabilities.

4.9 Complexity and Bounded Rationality: Thinking about Macroeconomics

In this section, we explore some of the macroeconomic implications of bounded rationality and heuristics-based choices. Modern macroeconomics, within the neoclassical tradition, assumes that individuals satisfy all the rationality requirements in the BRA (see chapter 2). It then proceeds to study market equilibrium, in which demands and supplies are in balance. In a competitive general equilibrium, under the assumption that all individuals are price takers, the task is to find a price vector such that individuals maximize their utility, firms maximize their profits, and all markets clear. The expectations of individuals and firms are met, in the sense of rational expectations.[8] Rational expectations is a scaling up of the assumption of sequential equilibrium in microeconomics, where, in equilibrium, the beliefs and actions of all players are in conformity with each other. Once the macroeconomic system is in equilibrium, it stays there unless there are exogenous shocks, such as technology shocks. Furthermore, there is minimal heterogeneity of consumers and firms, and the analysis is often conducted using a single representative individual. The state of modern macroeconomics has divided opinion within the profession and has led to serious doubts about its ability to explain the data.

This is not a debate we wish to get into here in any detail. Rather, we are interested in the more limited question of the insights that one might derive from a bounded rationality approach to macroeconomics in which the economic actors face true uncertainty; they follow simple heuristics and use simple learning strategies; there are feedback loops between these learning strategies and aggregate behavior; and neither market equilibrium nor rational expectations are required. Such an approach is provided by complexity theory, which is implemented in macroeconomics under the rubric of *agent-based models,* or ABMs. We do not intend to survey here the state of complexity theory or agent-based models in economics but rather sample some of the insights from this literature.[9]

In nature, there are several examples in which animals, neurons, and cells follow fairly simple rules of thumb and learn and adapt using simple learning strategies. In these cases, the aggregate behavior is not controlled or coordinated by a central planner/controller. However, miraculously, the aggregate behavior is *complex* and appears to an outside observer as if it were purposeful and guided by a central planner.

Example 4.7. *(Emergent behavior) Each bird in a flock of starlings follows simple heuristics; for example, it maintains a fixed flying distance from the immediate neighbors and follows the flight movements of a few immediate neighbors. To an outside observer, this produces stunning visual patterns, known as starling murmurations, that appear to be complex and highly choreographed. An outside observer would draw similar observations from the behavior of ants in ant colonies (say, forming an ant bridge to cross a swollen stream of water); individual neurons in a brain (say, coordinating to produce complex thought and consciousness); individual white blood cells in an immune system (apparently coordinating to attack a virus infection); and individual cells that form an eye (coordinating to produce visual signals and detecting very subtle difference in color). Such complex aggregate behaviors are known as* emergent behaviors *or* emergent properties *of the system. They do not arise from* *conscious actions by individual entities but are the surprising products of uncoordinated actions of dispersed and large numbers of individual entities who use simple adaptive rules of behavior.*

Emergent behavior, as described in example 4.7, arises in the absence of any central planner to design or choreograph such behavior. No individual unit (such as a starling, neuron, or white blood cell) whose heterogenous and boundedly rational behavior leads to this behavior exhibits any awareness of it. Further, there is no evidence that the goal of any individual unit is to produce the observed emergent behavior. Yet, the purposeful nature of the outcomes leads to the justifiable characterization of such systems as *self-organizing systems*.

It is interesting that there is no widely accepted definition of complex systems, and characterizations of such a system list its salient properties and features. For instance, Mitchell (2009, p. 13) proposes the following definition of a complex system: "a system in which large networks with no central control and simple rules of operation give rise to complex collective behavior, *sophisticated information processing, and adaptation by learning or evolution*." She also gives an alternative definition on the same page: "*a system that exhibits nontrivial emergent and self-organizing behaviors.*"

Under *complexity*, the system never settles down to an equilibrium; it is in a constant state of flux or *persistent randomness*. There is constant feedback between the actions of individuals, based on simple learning strategies and the complex aggregate outcomes. Equilibrium in these systems takes a very different nature from the one in economics—for instance, it could be a *statistical equilibrium*, say, the Boltzmann equilibrium for molecules in a gas; but even a statistical equilibrium may not exist.

Persistent randomness can also occur in neoclassical macroeconomics. For instance, this could arise from technology shocks or from consumer sentiment as described in Akerlof and Shiller (2009). Importantly, in modern macroeconomics, these shocks are external to the system. However, even in these cases, the source of these shocks (e.g., investor sentiment) can lie beyond the scope of economic models in the BRA (but not always: e.g., the oil shocks of the 1970s). By contrast, persistent randomness under complexity arises from two endogenous sources of uncertainty: (1) true uncertainty (see chapter 2 for the definition) and (2) uncertainty arising from technological innovation that creates ripple and cascading effects—for instance, those arising from the steam engine, air travel, computer chips, telephones, and gene splicing. This gives rise to the endogenous creation of new technologies (Arthur, 2015).

Modern economics does not provide guidance on making decisions under true uncertainty and technological uncertainty. Certainty, the sort of deductive reasoning that is characteristic of the BRA, is unlikely to lead to useful inferences under true uncertainty. Not only is it impossible to deduce what the future holds, but it is also impossible to deduce how others will react to an unknowable future. Given bounded rationality and the uncertain environment, individuals may then resort to simple adaptive heuristics and mental models. It is very likely that individuals use *inductive methods* in this case. These models involve groping around in their set of possible actions, perhaps picking first the subjectively most promising action, persisting with it for a while, then evaluating and possibly changing it on the basis of feedback from the aggregate patterns. The result is that future movements of the economy are also often unknown and unknowable. This continual feedback between individual actions and the complex patterns in the economy create emergent phenomena in a system that is in a constant state of flux.

As the reader will have guessed, under complexity it is highly unlikely to obtain neat analytical solutions that one can often obtain in modern macroeconomics. Hence, the main solution tools are computational; algorithms, not equations, lie at the heart of these models. As Bookstaber and Kirman (2018, p. 770) write: "And this in turn means that rather than seeking a theoretical result, we are in the world of pragmatism, of engineering, of case studies. And, it means we must delve into the real world."

Does the presence of algorithms, instead of equations, mean that there is no such thing as an economic theory to explain macroeconomic phenomena? In this context, Arthur (2015, p. 21), one of the leading advocates of complexity in macroeconomics, writes:

> *Consider a parallel with biology. Even now, 150 years after Darwin's Origin, no one has succeeded in reducing to an equation-based system the process by which novel species are created, form ecologies, and bring into being whole eras dominated by characteristic species.... Equations do well with changes in number or quantities within given categories, but poorly with the appearance of new categories themselves.... Biology then is theoretical but not mathematical; it is process-based, not quantity-based. In a word, it is procedural. By this token, a detailed economic theory of formation and change would also be procedural.*

The current practice in neoclassical economics is to linearize the Euler equations that arise from dynamic general stochastic equilibrium (DGSE) models. Furthermore, it is not an uncommon mistake to linearize the behavioral equations, which can radically alter the dynamics of the system. What should be linearized are the reaction functions. However, under complexity, we cannot analytically derive the Euler equations either, let alone guess their linearized version. Hence, the complexity framework for thinking about macroeconomics requires fundamentally new machinery. Modern macroeconomics, particularly the dominant school based on DGSE models, predicts that most macroeconomics variables should have a Gaussian distribution. Yet, empirical analysis shows that most such distributions are nonnormal and have fat tails, which is consistent with an analysis based on complex systems. However, fat tails might also be consistent with individuals using a variety of judgment heuristics and behavioral expectations, such as diagnostic expectations. On this, see section 2.15 and Dhami (2020a).

4.9.1 Inductive Reasoning, Adaptive Rules, and Emergent Phenomena

We now give an example of *inductive reasoning* and an emergent property of a simple system.

Consider the El-Farol problem due to Arthur (1994). El-Farol is the name of a bar in Sante Fe and the behavior of customers in this bar first gave Brian Arthur this idea. The bar has a maximum capacity of 60 places. A pool of 100 people simultaneously, and privately, decide, at each time, $t = 1, 2, 3 \ldots$, to either undertake a costly visit to the bar (say, time and taxi costs) or not. After the first 60 people are admitted in the bar, the rest are turned back. How should any particular individual form expectations about how many others will decide to turn up?

Suppose that, at time t, the attendance rate at the bar (number of people who chose to visit it) for the past n time periods is given by the set $A = \{a_{t-1}, a_{t-2}, \ldots a_{t-n}\}$; so a_{t-j} is the attendance rate j time periods ago. Individuals have m possible candidate predictors for the attendance rate at time t that are summarized in the set $P = \{p_1, p_2, \ldots p_m\}$. Each predictor, $p_i, i = 1, \ldots, m$, takes account of past attendance rates, summarized in the set A, and predicts the current attendance at time t, so technically, we can write $p_i : A \to [0, 100]$, $p_i \in P$. If the predictor being used at time t is $p_i(A)$, then individuals decide to go to the bar if the predicted attendance is less than 60 (or $p_i(A) \leq 60$); otherwise they decide to stay at home. Here are some examples of the different predictors used by Arthur (1994).

$$p_1 = a_{t-1}; \ p_2 = 100 - a_{t-1}; \ p_3 = \frac{1}{4} \sum_{i=1}^{i=4} a_{t-i}; \ p_4 = a_{t-2}; \ p_5 = a_{t-5}; \ldots$$

For instance, the predictor p_3 uses the average attendance in the past four periods to predict current attendance. Individuals are also given an initially active predictor to start off the problem. If a predictor does not predict well (e.g., a costly trip to the bar and no admittance), then individuals might choose a different predictor from the set of available predictors. Bar attendance is then simulated over time using computational methods with 100 agents. Over 100 repetitions of this game, the mean attendance converges to 60 over time. Interestingly, individuals use an inductive process of reasoning, there is no central planner, yet they are led to an efficient solution.

The convergence to 60 is an emergent property of the system. The intuition for this result is as follows. Toward the end of the simulation, we obtain a polymorphic mix of predictors for the 100 agents in the simulation: 60 percent of the predictors used predict an attendance below 60 (so 60 agents go to the bar), and 40 percent of the predictors used predict attendance above 60 (so 40 agents decide not to go). To see how individuals switch predictors, suppose that at some time t, 20 percent of the predictors predict attendance over 60 and 80 percent predict attendance below 60. Then, 20 out of the 80 people who make the decision to go to the bar will be dissatisfied with their predictors and may wish to switch to a new predictor. Such switching behavior continues until we get the required 60-40 ratio.

4.9.2 Neighborhood Segregation as an Emergent Phenomenon

An interesting application of the ideas sketched above is to the problem of neighborhood segregation. We follow here an adapted version of the simple and insightful approach of Schelling (1971). Suppose that there are two types of households: *immigrant households*, denoted by I, and *native households*, denoted by N. In all other relevant respects (say, income, number of children), these households are identical. They live within a population that resides in a city that, for pedagogical simplicity, is arranged in a single row of identical houses, sometimes known as a linear city in the urban economics literature. Each household, of type I or N, uses a simple rule of thumb to make a locational choice: they wish to stay in a neighborhood where the majority of the households are of their type.

For simplicity, we allow a free and costless relocation of households to what they perceive as a more desirable neighborhood. Despite identical households (except for their types, I or N) and identical houses, it can be shown that segregation (clusters of houses of each type of households) emerges in equilibrium. This is an emergent property of the model because it arises from a simple behavioral rule that each household follows: relocate so that the majority of neighbors are of the same type. There are obviously many other reasons for segregation and we do not wish to downplay their importance, but this is not our focus here.[10]

In our illustrative exercise, households are assumed to use a simple rule for deciding whether to relocate or not. A *neighborhood* for each household includes that household and both neighbors on either sides (one on the left and one on the right). When a household does not have any neighbors on one side (e.g., corner households), then the neighborhood of a household includes that household and the single neighbor on the other side. Of course, we could have defined the neighborhood to consist of any number of neighbors on each side, but it does not change the results. So, we consider here the simplest case that will drive home the central message of this model.

Households decide not to relocate if the majority of their neighbors are of the same type—that is, two out of three households, including their own; these are *contented households*. Otherwise, they relocate to the nearest point along the line (either to the left or to the right) where such a majority exists; these are *discontented households*.

Once the discontented households are identified, we need to specify the order and direction of relocation. We assume that the households move in order from the left to the right, beginning with the leftmost discontented household. The relocation by each discontented household will alter the neighborhoods for other households. Thus, relocations create two effects.

1. Some originally discontented households will become contended and will not move.
2. Some originally contended households will find that they have become discontented and so would like to relocate.

We assume that all newly discontented households will move in a separate round, once all the currently discontented households have completed their moves.

Table 4.4 shows an example with 10 households of two possible types, *I* and *N*. In the very first row, we show the initial list of households of both types that is given by history at time $t = 0$. We now apply the criterion for contended/discontented households and show the discontented

Table 4.4
A model of neighborhood segregation

$t=0$	N_1	I_1	I_2	N_2	I_3	N_3	N_4	I_4	N_5	I_5
$t=1$	I_1	I_2	N_1	N_2	I_3	N_3	N_4	I_4	N_5	I_5
$t=2$	I_1	I_2	I_3	N_1	N_2	N_3	N_4	I_4	N_5	I_5
$t=3$	I_1	I_2	I_3	N_1	N_2	N_3	N_4	N_5	I_4	I_5

households at any time, $t = 0, 1, \ldots$, in bold type. At the initial time, $t = 0$, five households are discontented (N_1, N_2, I_3, I_4, N_5). Based on the relocation order (left to right) specified above, the very first household who relocates at time $t = 1$ is the native household N_1. Household N_1 moves to the nearest point on the linear city that enables it to live in a majority-native neighborhood: just next to household N_2. The relocation is shown in the second row of table 4.4 (see the row corresponding to $t = 1$). On account of the relocation of N_1, the originally discontented native household N_2 is no longer discontented because it now lives in a majority-native neighborhood; hence, N_2 is not shown in bold at $t = 1$.

At $t = 2$, the next discontented household to move is I_3, and it moves left to the nearest point where it can live in a majority-immigrant neighborhood. It could equally have moved right, an equal distance, toward I_4. Since the household is indifferent either way, we have picked the leftward move. At $t = 3$, the leftmost discontented household, I_4, moves right and relocates next to the immigrant household I_5 to establish an immigrant-majority neighborhood.

At this point, there are no discontented households left, so this is the final equilibrium configuration of households along the linear city. There are two clusters of immigrant neighborhoods at each end of the city, and all the native households cluster in the middle. To an outside observer, it might appear that a central planner has purposefully arranged the households in segregated clusters. Yet, each discontended household followed a simple rule of thumb—simply relocate next to another household of the same type, and there is no central planner. Hence, segregation of this sort is an example of an emergent phenomena. It is also striking that it takes just two rounds of relocation to achieve this outcome. This simulation can be run with a larger number of households, with more complicated rules for what constitutes a majority neighborhood, and with different rules for relocation, yet similar results are relatively easy to obtain (Schelling, 1971), which highlights the robustness of the underlying insights.

4.9.3 Chaos: Extreme Dependence on Initial Conditions

An important feature of complexity, and one that has particular bite for the current practice in neoclassical macroeconomics, is the sensitivity of the model to initial conditions. In common discourse, one often hears the mind-bending analogy of a butterfly flapping its wings in Mexico and setting off a tornado in Brazil or of one flap of a seagull's wings changing weather forever. Such chaotic dynamics often arise in nonlinear systems, of which the economy is an excellent example.

Example 4.8. *Suppose that we change the temperature of pure water between 0 and 100 degrees Celsius. We do not observe extreme changes in the state of the water. However, under ideal conditions, dropping the temperature to 0 degrees Celsius suddenly changes its state to a solid and raising it to 100 degrees Celsius suddenly changes its state to a gas. Hence, initial conditions can create massive changes.*

There are several other ways of illustrating this point more formally. The simplest formal method is to consider the *logistic map*, which is a simple nonlinear first order difference equation.[11] First published by Pierre Verhulst in 1845, the logistic map describes the time evolution of a population. Suppose that some species of animal begins with an initial population y_0, and its population in future time periods $t = 1, 2, \ldots$ is denoted by y_t. Suppose that the birth rate and the death rates in the population are fixed for all time and are given, respectively, by b and d; denote the difference by $\lambda = b - d$. Let $m > 0$ be the maximum sustainable population of the species, conditional on the environment. Then, the logistic map is given by

$$y_{t+1} = \lambda \frac{y_t}{m}(m - y_t). \quad (4.23)$$

Let us transform variables so that $x_t = \frac{y_t}{m} \in [0, 1]$ is the current population of the species relative to the maximum sustainable population. The corresponding initial value in terms of the transformed variables is $x_0 = \frac{y_0}{m} \in [0, 1]$. Then (4.23) can be written as

$$x_{t+1} = f(x_t) = \lambda x_t (1 - x_t), \quad (4.24)$$

which is the final form of the logistic map that we are interested in. We are not interested in the complete dynamics and stability properties of the logistic map here (see Dhami, 2020b for details). We simply summarize the results in a footnote for interested readers.[12]

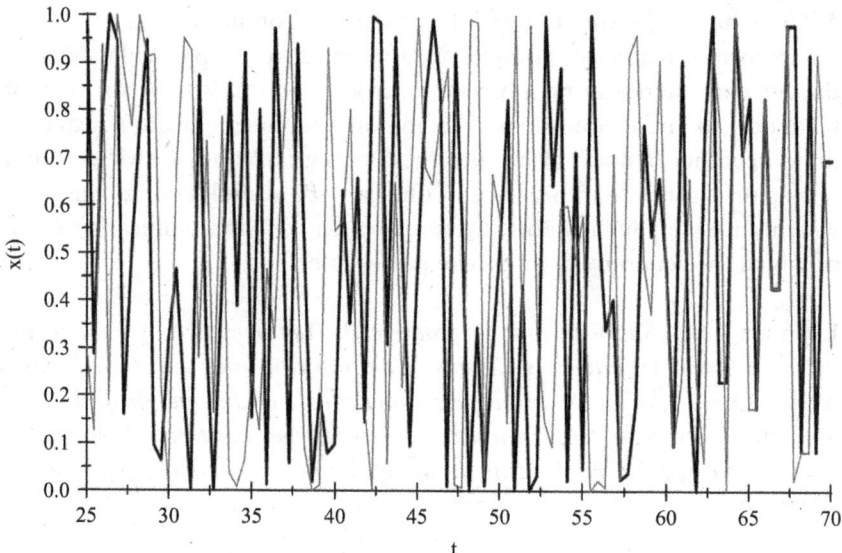

Figure 4.2
A plot of the logistic map for λ = 4 and for two initial conditions: (a) $x_0 = 0.2$ (thicker curve) and (b) $x_0 = 0.20001$ (dashed curve).

When $\lambda \geq 3.56995$, then starting from any initial value x_0, it is hard to say where the system will end up, and we get chaos. Consider the case shown in figure 4.2 for $\lambda = 4$. For the initial value $x_0 = 0.2$, the dynamic path of the population, shown as the thicker of the two paths, exhibits fluctuations when plotted for 70 time periods. If we now start from a nearby initial value $x_0 = 0.20001$ (which differs by only 0.00001), the dynamic path is shown as the thinner of the two paths. The two paths are virtually identical for approximately the first 30 periods. However, after $t = 35$, the time paths differ significantly and appear to arise from two different dynamic systems. Yet, they arise from an identical dynamical system where the initial conditions are extremely close. Thus, initial conditions matter greatly for the future time path of the dynamic system under complexity.

What is quite surprising is that the logistic map is a very low-dimensional nonstochastic difference equation. It produces highly complex behavior, even chaos, and the system is extremely sensitive to minute variations in historical conditions. These problems are likely to be even more serious for macroeconomic models with multiple heterogenous economic actors and complex interrelations.[13] As illustrated by the logistic map, nonlinearities provide the key feature through which chaotic behavior arises. Hence, the current practice of log-linearizing the Euler equations in macroeconomic models (e.g., in the DSGE model) effectively shuts down this channel. So, while in a complex system the economic shocks in 2007-2008 could have arisen from chaotic dynamics caused by small endogenous shocks and would, hence, be unpredictable, this account is not consistent with a log-linearized version of a Euler equation in a DSGE model.

4.9.4 Agent-Based Models

In economics, applications of complex systems lie under the rubric of *agent-based models* (ABMs). ABMs share most of the features of complex systems that we have already highlighted, which include the following: agent heterogeneity; true uncertainty; agents following simple behavioral strategies with learning, mutation, adaptation, and combination of existing strategies; there is a two-way and continuous feedback between aggregate variables in the economy and the behavioral strategies of individuals; a selection mechanism that chooses the more successful behavioral strategies and discards the less successful ones; disequilibrium, not equilibrium, as the persistent state of the system; final outcomes may be highly sensitive to the initial conditions (history dependence); complex nonlinear outcomes and emergent behavior; and the source of fluctuations being typically endogenous rather than exogenous.

In ABMs, as in complexity, emergent behavior is not uncommon. Thus, simply aggregating individual behavior does not adequately describe the aggregate behavior, but such aggregation is the current practice in general equilibrium in economics. It is also difficult to predict the future path of an economy under complexity, even when the underlying system is non-stochastic, because small changes in initial conditions may imply vastly different dynamic time paths (see, e.g., figure 4.2).

Unlike models in modern macroeconomics, it is not possible to give a neat analytical example of an ABM. The reason is that in an ABM economy, there is a very large number of heterogenous individuals, firms, and sectors, and a large variety of behavioral rules are ascribed to them. The model allows for complex interlinkages between them. Hence, one cannot fully describe these models through a select number of equations, and there are typically no analytical solutions. Powerful numerical methods are used to derive the time path of such economies within the neighborhood of a chosen set of parameters and initial conditions.

For a succinct introduction to an ABM of the UK housing sector based on Baptista et al. (2016), see Dhami (2020b). To obtain a flavor of the detail involved in an ABM of just a single sector in their paper, the housing market, consider the following brief description. This level of detail is unprecedented in modern macroeconomics, and there are no models in the BRA that can match the level of detail on the housing market that is embedded in this single ABM.

There are approximately 60 calibrated parameters / initial values (see appendix B in Baptista et al., 2016). The source of the house price cycles in ABMs is entirely endogenous. Economic actors employ simple behavioral rules that use data on past observations of various housing-relevant variables to create price dynamics. By contrast, in macroeconomic models of the housing markets, one needs to rely on forward-looking beliefs under rational expectations that generate bubbles, which is extremely cognitively challenging for economic agents. Agents in the ABM expect that house price growth, g_t, at time t depends only on the past observations of the house price data, $p_{t-1}, p_{t-2}, \ldots$, and in particular

$$g_t = \alpha \left(\frac{p_{t-1} + p_{t-2} + p_{t-3}}{p_{t-13} + p_{t-14} + p_{t-15}} - 1 \right), \tag{4.25}$$

where either $\alpha > 0$ is a parameter that is replaced by its real world proxy value or the researcher varies α to ensure that the distribution of outcomes matches the real world distribution. The three main actors in this model are households, commercial banks who give mortgages, and central banks. Among households, there are three further types. *Renters* rent a house, and when their rental contracts run out, they bid for either new rentals or owner-occupied houses. *Owner-occupiers* decide whether to keep their house or sell it. If they decide to sell, they must decide on the selling price (their ask price) and also how much to bid for a new house. The *buy to let investors* (BTL) must decide whether to sell their existing properties, buy new ones, or rent out their properties again and how much rent to ask for.

Banks give mortgages to those seeking to become owner-occupiers and to BTL investors who wish to buy new properties. The central bank is responsible for macroprudential policy and sets the loan to income (LTI) and loan to value (LTV) ratios.

Among households, there is heterogeneity with respect to age and incomes. Each period, some households die and new ones are born with new age, income, and house ownership profiles. Of the new households born, $x\% > 0$ have the BTL gene. This fraction can be varied in various simulations and plays an important role in the results. The housing stock relative to the households is kept fixed at 82 percent, so if there is a housing shortfall, new houses enter the market. BTL investors collect rent, receive income each period, pay taxes, and enjoy nonhousing consumption. The ownership market is cleared first (by using the bids and asks between buyers and sellers), followed by the rental market.

Several data sources are then used to calibrate the economy. For instance, the relation between income and wealth is lognormal in the data; this is directly imposed on the model. Behavioral rules are then specified for the decisions made by each of the agents. These decisions depend on house prices, capital gains from owning houses, the rent, cost of the mortgage, and the policy parameters. Particular functional forms are chosen for these behavioral rules (e.g., logistic).

A great strength of the ABM approach is that it takes account of bounded rationality and considers a far richer economic environment than modern macroeconomics. However, there are also several drawbacks of the ABM approach, and there are no easy fixes for a model that aspires to explain economic phenomena in such detail.

Many of the decision rules imposed on economic agents in such models appear to be, at best, guesses. Conformity with several features of the data is already built into the model (e.g., real world lognormal distributions for income and wealth are used in the model above). Consider another example. In order to decide whether households should pay for a house by cash or get a mortgage, the following rule is imposed. If the financial wealth of the household exceeds the price of the house by a factor of 2, they will pay cash, otherwise, they apply for a mortgage. The justification used for this rule is given in Baptista et al. (2016, n. 9): "This ensures a roughly correct proportion of cash buyers, calibrated against WhenFresh/Zoopla data." Another example is the choice of α to ensure that the distribution of outcomes matches the real world distribution in (4.25). This often gives rise to the criticism that such a model might have too many degrees of freedom to match real world data. It is also not clear whether real economic agents in the economy follow the precise behavioral rules ascribed to them by the ABM modeler. By contrast, it is easier to ascertain by experiments in behavioral economics whether economic agents follow these rules.

An ABM modeler would respond that ABMs cannot possibly explain everything. They would also argue that they wish to perform simulations on economic variables of interest in response to changes in a small number of parameters—for example, policy changes (this comprises comparative statics in these models)—by keeping the rest of the model as close as possible to the real world. However, critics of ABM would argue that selectively fixing individual parts of the model to match the empirical data and the freedom to choose parameters / initial values may give misleading comparative static results or perhaps even any results that the ABM modeler would like to achieve. The problem of extra degrees of freedom is, of course, not unique to ABMs. It also arises in economic theory when ad hoc assumptions are used to explain a phenomenon and less than stringent tests are used to evaluate the relevant theory. The problem also arises in many other areas in social science (e.g., models of climate change), so one has to be mindful of applying the appropriate statistical tests to guard against it.

The learning channels in ABMs do not adequately recognize *behavioral frictions to learning*. These include, but are not restricted to, representativeness, availability, anchoring, overconfidence, attribution bias, confirmation bias, hindsight bias. A closer interface between behavioral economics and complexity has the potential to enrich both.

The errors in the specification of the parameters/initial conditions can propagate exponentially through an ABM. There are two channels for this. First, there are a large number of equations and parameters in ABMs, giving rise to the complex error propagation paths that macroeconomists know very well from the large-scale macroeconomic models of the 1970s–1980s. This, the inability to explain the empirical evidence (stagflation), as well as being subject to the Lucas critique, ultimately led to their demise relative to much more parsimonious models. Second, due to chaotic nonlinear dynamics, even minute changes in the values of the parameters used for simulation may lead to very large changes in the dynamic paths (think, for instance, of the logistic map in figure 4.2). Yet, given the degrees of freedom in adjusting the parameter values and initial conditions in ABMs, such error propagation may go unnoticed.

Suppose that the empirical estimates of risk aversion used in an ABM come from an existing empirical study. The typical empirical estimates of risk aversion are based on an expected utility theory analysis. We now know that most of what we observe as risk aversion is possibly loss aversion (Novemsky & Kahneman, 2005). However, this would be hard to uncover from an ABM, which lacks tests of the validity of these individual components. Given the very large number of variables and transmission channels at work, it is difficult to establish cause and effect in ABMs. As such, the results from ABMs can be put on a stronger footing by incorporating insights from behavioral economics, which would have recommended using loss aversion in the first place. It is problematic, however, that by using estimates based on empirically refuted models (expected utility in the case of estimates of risk aversion), ABMs still claim to match well the real world data. This will only raise the suspicions of those who believe that ABMs have too many degrees of freedom to make choices.

Which calibration values to use, then, when there is no consensus on the underlying values? Suppose that one needs to use labor supply elasticities for calibration purposes in ABMs. James Heckman, one of the leaders in this field, and the 2000 Nobel laureate in economics, once reportedly said that several decades of research have shown that labor supply elasticities lie between $-\infty$ and $+\infty$. So which of the large number of available estimates should an ABM researcher use? Furthermore, a great deal of the data on labor supply elasticities comes from situations where the individual really does not have a choice to vary the hours worked (see Dhami, 2019a), while such choice might have been explicitly modeled in an ABM. Would an ABM researcher happen to be aware of all the nuances about the very large number of calibrated values in their model, which only specialists in the field might know about? This suggests the usefulness of teams of researchers with different expertise working on any ABM project.

The calibrated values for ABMs, such as behavioral parameters (risk aversion, marginal propensity to consume and invest, labor supply elasticities), are often taken from real world data. However, as one changes the initial conditions and policies, these behavioral parameters themselves will change. Hence, the well-known *Lucas critique*, which bedevils many economic models (changes in policies change the behavioral responses of economic agents), also applies to ABMs. Thus, ABMs need to develop satisfactory methods of addressing this problem.

One mitigating factor for ABMs is that there is a relatively small set of people working in this relatively young field. It is quite likely that, as the criticisms are taken into account, in due course, this field will continue to gain acceptance and grow within mainstream economics.

ABMs have also been applied to other areas in economics, including the explanation of fish prices in the Marseille fish market (Härdle & Kirman, 1995; Weisbuch et al., 2000; Kirman & Vriend, 2001); monetary and fiscal policies under complexity (Dosi et al., 2015); corporate bond trading (Braun-Munzinger et al., 2016); and learning to play correlated equilibrium (Arifovic et al., 2019). To see how fat tails and clustered volatility might arise in ABMs, see Thurner et al. (2012). For business fluctuations in the presence of highly leveraged firms (financial fragility) that are also accompanied by Zipf's law for the distribution of firms, see Delli Gatti et al. (2005).

4.10 Evolutionary Game Theory and Stochastic Social Dynamics

Another approach in which economic agents follow simple heuristics, do not formally optimize yet focus on macro-level outcomes, and find persistent randomness as under complexity theory can be found in the literature on *stochastic social dynamics*. In order to provide an introduction to stochastic social dynamics, it is first worthwhile to explore the basics of evolutionary dynamics. We shall then take a concrete coordination game and give its solution under evolutionary dynamics and then under stochastic social dynamics. There is an earlier approach to modeling evolutionary dynamics in economics that highlights problems of innovation and growth (Nelson & Winter, 1982); for a later summary of this approach, see Nelson and Winter (2002). However, this approach, which has not been followed up in economics, shares similarities not just with the material in this section but also with the material on complex adaptive systems in section 4.9.

4.10.1 Evolutionary Game Theory

In Darwin's account of evolutionary theory, a gene is the basic unit of analysis. So, rather than focusing on an animal, we focus on its *genotype*, or its exact genetic structure. We make the pedagogically simple assumption that each distinct genotype corresponds to a unique behavior for the animal, which constitutes its phenotype.[14] Thus, animals are *hardwired* to follow certain strategies, which for purposes of exposition, we take to be their phenotypes. This can be taken to represent an extreme form of bounded rationality. In theories in the social and behavioral sciences, by contrast, the strategies and the behavior of humans are also influenced by conscious deliberation.

How do we know which phenotype is the most suitable for an animal? In Darwinian models, different phenotypes have different levels of *fitness* that give rise to differences in the *reproductive success* of the animal. The fitness of a phenotype depends on how well adapted to the environment it is, relative to other phenotypes. *Natural selection*, then, as embodied in the principle of the survival of the fittest, works as follows. In any time period, phenotypes with higher current fitness *proliferate* relatively more in numbers in the next time period, while those with lower fitness

Table 4.5
A simple coordination game

	L	H
L	1, 1	0, 0
H	0, 0	2, 2

reduce in numbers. New phenotypes arise randomly through a process of *mutation* of the underlying genotype.

In *evolutionary game theory*, if the existing phenotypes (or *resident phenotypes*) can survive invasion by mutant phenotypes, then they are said to be *evolutionary stable*; these phenotypes are also called *evolutionary stable strategies* (ESSs). If there is only one phenotype that is an ESS, then the resulting population of animals is said to be *monomorphic*; if there is more than one, then it is said to be *polymorphic*.

Consider the simple two-player coordination game shown in table 4.5. The row and the column players have two identical strategies, L and H. The strategy pairs (L, L) and (H, H) are Nash equilibria (check that each player plays a best response to the other's equilibrium strategy). However, in an evolutionary account, players do not consciously pick these strategies. Evolution, through a process of natural selection, picks the strategy that has the highest fitness. The resulting equilibrium can either be monomorphic or polymorphic. We show how such equilibria are arrived at in the context of the coordination game. We need to introduce a few basic concepts first.

Consider a fixed population size. To simplify our exposition, assume that players are hardwired to play one pure strategy at a time (i.e., either L or H). Mixed strategies in which players are hardwired to play L with a probability $p \in (0, 1)$ and H with a probability $1 - p$ can be accommodated, but we abstract from these. We denote a pure strategy by $s \in \{L, H\}$. We assume that mutant strategies, denoted by $\hat{s}$, are also in pure strategies (i.e., either L or H), so $\hat{s} \in \{L, H\}$.

Suppose that a fraction $x \in [0, 1]$ of the population is hardwired to play L and the remaining fraction $1 - x$ is hardwired to play H. Define the average strategy in the population, $\bar{s}$, by

$$\bar{s} = xL + (1-x)H. \tag{4.26}$$

We assume that members of the population meet randomly in pairwise meetings. In any such random pairwise meeting, with probability x, each player meets an opponent who plays L, and with probability $1-x$, an opponent who plays H. In other words, in any pairwise meeting, it is as if a player meets an opponent who plays the average strategy $\bar{s}$. We would like to see how each of the strategies, L, H, fares against the average $\bar{s}$. Denote by $\pi(s, \bar{s})$ the payoff, or fitness, of a player who is hardwired to play the pure strategy $s \in \{L, H\}$ and expects to meet an opponent who plays the average strategy $\bar{s}$. Let $\pi(\bar{s}, \bar{s})$ be the payoff, or fitness, of the average strategy against itself.

We now define an *evolutionary stable strategy* for the case of the coordination game in table 4.5, when players are hardwired to play pure strategies only. For a more general treatment and the formal derivations, see Hammerstein and Selten (1994).

Definition 4.3. *(Evolutionary stable strategy [ESS]; Maynard Smith & Price, 1973):* Consider the coordination game in table 4.5. A pure strategy $s \in \{L, H\}$ is said to be an ESS, if for all mutant strategies, $\hat{s} \in \{L, H\}$, $\hat{s} \neq s$, the following two conditions are satisfied.

1. Equilibrium condition or primary criterion: $\pi(s, s) > \pi(\hat{s}, s)$.
2. Stability condition or secondary criterion: If $\pi(s, s) = \pi(\hat{s}, s)$, then $\pi(s, \hat{s}) > \pi(\hat{s}, \hat{s})$.

The primary criterion for s to be an ESS requires that the payoff, $\pi(s, s)$, of a player who plays s against an opponent who also plays s is higher as compared to the payoff, $\pi(\hat{s}, s)$, of a player who plays $\hat{s}$ against a player who plays s. Using the informal definition of a Nash equilibrium (see section 3.3), the primary criterion reveals that an ESS is also a Nash equilibrium. If, however, $\pi(s, s) = \pi(\hat{s}, s)$, then we cannot invoke the primary criterion. In this case, we use the secondary criterion, which proposes a strengthening of Nash equilibrium. Hence, the set of ESS is a subset of the set of Nash equilibrium. The secondary criterion requires that the strategy s against the mutant $\hat{s}$ gives a higher payoff than the mutant strategy $\hat{s}$ against itself.

Let us now use definition 4.3 to check for the evolutionary stability of the two pure strategies in our coordination game. Using table 4.5, we have $\pi(L, L) = 1, \pi(H, L) = 0$. Since $\pi(L, L) > \pi(H, L)$, the primary criterion in definition 4.3 implies that all players playing L is an ESS. Similarly, $\pi(H, H) = 2 > \pi(H, L) = 0$, so all players playing H is also an ESS. This is all that we can say in terms of ESS. It does not help us to predict which of the two strategies, L or H, we should observe in the long run.

ESS is an equilibrium concept, and as such it is static. Yet, we expect an ESS to be the outcome of a dynamic process in which competition between alternative strategies leads to an equilibrium. Hence, we expect ESS to arise as a steady state (or a state of rest, which leads to no further changes) of some dynamic process. Indeed, several dynamic processes are available that incorporate the Darwinian idea that fitter strategies proliferate in the future, while less fit strategies decay over time. A popular dynamic adjustment process, which we outline below, is the *replicator dynamics* introduced by Taylor and Jonker (1978).[15]

Suppose that time $t \in [0, T]$. At any instant in time, t, a fraction $x_t(s)$ of the population plays the pure strategy $s \in \{L, H\}$ such that $x_t(L) + x_t(H) = 1$. The state of the system at time t is summarized by the fractions that play each of the two pure strategies, $(x_t(L), x_t(H))$. While each individual plays a pure strategy, the state of the system represents frequencies of play of each pure strategy, by different players, that sum up to one. The replicator dynamics specify how the state of the system evolves over time and is influenced by the fitness of various pure strategies. It is given by the following differential equation.

$$\dot{x}_t(s) = [\pi(s, \bar{s}_t) - \pi(\bar{s}_t, \bar{s}_t)] x_t(s); \; s \in \{L, H\}, 0 \leq t \leq T, \quad (4.27)$$

where $\dot{x}_t(s) = \frac{dx_t(s)}{dt}$ shows how the fraction of the population that plays the pure strategy s changes at time t. Recall that $\bar{s}_t$ is the average strategy in the population at time t, given by $\bar{s}_t = x_t L + (1 - x_t)H$. Since there are two pure strategies, and (4.27) holds for each of these strategies, the *replicator dynamics* are given by a system of two equations. Since $x_t(L) + x_t(H) = 1$, it is sufficient to consider just one of the two equations. Obviously, in more complex problems, with a higher number of pure strategies, there will be a larger number of differential equations to consider. Replicator dynamics can be used to model the time path of different strategies. Suitably adapted to different contexts, these strategies can also represent norms, conventions, and cultural forms; for a formal model of gene-culture coevolution, see Dhami (2020b).

Starting from the monomorphic population in which all players play L, suppose that at time t there is an invasion by a small fraction $1 - x_t$ of mutants who play H. Then, the replicator dynamics in (4.27), which give the evolution of the strategy L, are given by

$$\dot{x}_t(L) = [\pi(L, \bar{s}_t) - \pi(\bar{s}_t, \bar{s}_t)] x_t(L). \quad (4.28)$$

Suppose that payoffs are as given in table 4.5. Then, we can compute the expected payoff, $\pi(L, \bar{s}_t)$, when a player plays L but there is a probability $x_t(L)$ of meeting an opponent who also plays L, which gives a payoff of 1, and a probability $(1 - x_t(L))$ of meeting an opponent who plays H, which

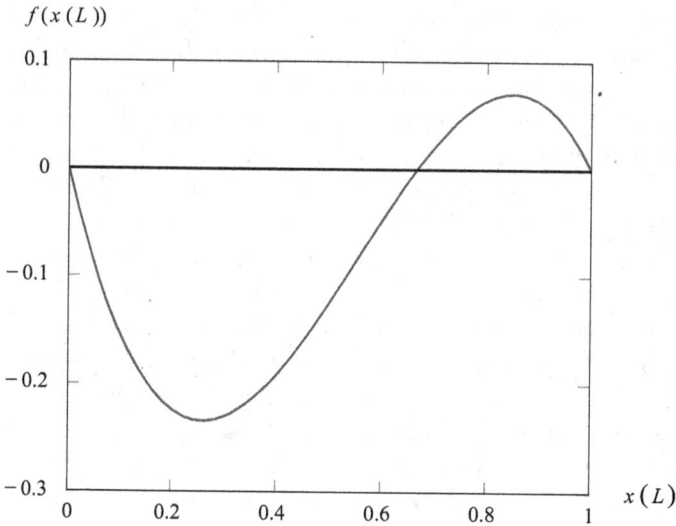

Figure 4.3
A plot of $f(x(L))$ in (4.29).

gives a payoff of 0; hence, $\pi(L, \bar{s}_t) = x_t(L) \times 1 + (1 - x_t(L)) \times 0 = x_t(L)$. We can also compute $\pi(\bar{s}_t, \bar{s}_t)$, the expected payoff to playing the average strategy $\bar{s}_t$ when the opponent is expected on average to also play $\bar{s}_t$. The required calculation is given by $\pi(\bar{s}_t, \bar{s}_t) = x_t[x_t \times 1 + (1 - x_t) \times 0] + (1 - x_t)[x_t \times 0 + (1 - x_t) \times 2]$, or $\pi(\bar{s}_t, \bar{s}_t) = x_t^2(L) + 2(1 - x_t(L))^2$. Substituting these calculations in (4.28), we get a nonlinear, first order, differential equation

$$\dot{x}_t(L) = f(x(L)) = \left[x_t(L) - x_t^2(L) - 2(1 - x_t(L))^2\right] x_t(L). \tag{4.29}$$

We show a plot of f against $x(L)$ in figure 4.3. In the interval $\left(0, \frac{2}{3}\right)$, we have $f < 0$; hence, from (4.29) we have $\dot{x}_t(L) < 0$, so the fraction of people playing L decays in every period. In the interval $\left(\frac{2}{3}, 1\right)$ we have $f > 0$; hence, from (4.29) we have $\dot{x}_t(L) > 0$, so the fraction of people playing L proliferates in every period. The relevant steady state in which a dynamic system settles down when we allow sufficient time to pass is known as the *asymptotically stable steady state*; this is a steady state in the sense that if the dynamic system finds itself close to this state, it reverts back to it. On this definition, the steady state $x^*(L) = \frac{2}{3}$ is asymptotically unstable because, as argued above, to the left of it, $x_t(L)$ decays, and to its right, $x_t(L)$ proliferates. The *basin of attraction* of a steady state is the set of states $x_t(L)$ such that once the system is in any state in this set, then it must eventually arrive at that steady state (by definition, $x_t(H) = 1 - x_t(L)$, so we could have equivalently expressed the basin of attraction in terms of $x_t(H)$).

In other words, if the initial fraction of the population playing the strategy L is exactly $\frac{2}{3}$, say, on account of an accident of history, then the dynamic system stays there forever. In this case, we have a polymorphic equilibrium where $\frac{2}{3}$ of the population plays L and $\frac{1}{3}$ of the population plays H for all times to come. However, even the slightest movement away from $x^*(L) = \frac{2}{3}$ tips the dynamic system toward the two extreme steady states. Any increase in the fraction of the population playing L beyond $\frac{2}{3}$ tips the system into the basin of attraction of the steady state $x^*(L) = 1$; thus, the basin of attraction of the steady state $x^*(L) = 1$ is the set of states $x_t(L) > \frac{2}{3}$. The dynamic system then begins an inexorable move toward a situation where the entire population eventually plays the strategy L. Similarly, the slightest decrease in the fraction playing L below $\frac{2}{3}$ ($x_t(L) < \frac{2}{3}$) tips the system into the basin of attraction of the steady state $x^*(L) = 0$, and the dynamic system eventually ends up in a state where all play H.

By contrast, the two extreme steady states $x^*(L) = 0$ (all play H) and $x^*(L) = 1$ (all play L) are both asymptotically stable. Any random shock that moves the fraction of the population playing these strategies, even if ever so slightly, will be self-correcting in the sense that the fractions revert back to where they started from. This is because, as noted above, to the right of $x^*(L) = 0$ we have $\dot{x}_t(L) < 0$ (fraction playing L is decreasing), and to the left of $x^*(L) = 1$ we have $\dot{x}_t(L) > 0$ (fraction playing L is increasing).

4.10.2 Stochastic Social Dynamics

In deterministic situations, as under the evolutionary dynamics in section 4.10.1, random shocks are one-off, isolated, and rare events. In a deterministic system, if we are in some asymptotically stable steady state (e.g., $x^*(L) = 0$ or $x^*(L) = 1$ in the coordination game in section 4.10.1), then a rare, small deviation pushes the system back to the asymptotically stable state. Thus, once the system arrives into the basin of attraction of an asymptotically stable state, it stays there forever.

In many cases of interest, there is reason to believe that *persistent randomness* is not an exception but the norm. For instance, random mutations might alter the types of players; payoffs might be random; there might be immigration and emigration of players within distinct populations; there could be unpredictable technological shocks; and players might play their strategies with errors. In any case, the economic environment is rarely stationary and is constantly buffeted by shocks.

The behavior of a system subjected to persistent random shocks is very different from the deterministic dynamics in section 4.10.1. The system is ever-changing, in a constant state of flux. These persistent shocks, even if they arise with a small probability, can accumulate gradually over time and force the system out of the basin of attraction of an asymptotically stable steady state. Asymptotically stable steady states do not provide a useful prediction of the long-run behavior of a stochastic dynamic system. The focus under persistent randomness is on the long-run frequency with which various strategies are played as the dynamic system keeps tipping in and tipping out of the basin of attraction of asymptotically stable steady states. This is formalized using *stochastic social dynamics*. A *stochastically stable steady state* is one where, informally speaking, the dynamic system spends most of its time, or it is the steady state where the long-run frequency of play is concentrated. For formal definitions, see Kandori et al. (1993), H. P. Young (1993), Ellison (1993), and P. H. Young (1998). For an introduction to this approach and for applications, see P. H. Young (1998) and Dhami (2020b).

Bounded rationality plays a key role in this approach. We can summarize the basic ingredients as follows. First, players have *limited information* and *limited cognitive ability*, and their memory goes back only a finite number of past periods. Second, although players learn from the limited history of play by the opponent, they play *myopic best replies* (as, say, under models of fictitious play in learning). By *myopic best replies* is meant that players choose an action that maximizes their payoff in the short run without taking account of the long-run consequences of their actions. Third, players *mutate* or make *mistakes* in the following sense. They play their myopic best replies with a probability $1 - \varepsilon$, where $\varepsilon > 0$ is small. With the complementary probability ε, they mutate / make mistakes by randomly choosing any pure strategy in their strategy set, say, set S. Relative to the BRA, the rationality requirements are reasonable and plausible.

When there are multiple asymptotically stable states (as in our coordination example in section 4.10.1), under stochastic social dynamics, history plays a powerful role in choosing the stochastically stable steady state. However, since there is persistent noise created by the small probability of mistakes / mutation, ε, howsoever small, the system keeps tipping in and tipping out of the basin of attraction of different asymptotically stable steady states. This gives rise to a *punctuated equilibrium* where a long period of stay in one asymptotically stable state is followed by tipping into the basin of attraction of another asymptotically stable state. The asymptotically stable state that has a greater likelihood of being observed in the long run, as the noise $\varepsilon \to 0$, is a *stochastically stable state*. If some stochastically stable states are reached with greater likelihood, *irrespective of the initial conditions*, these states are said to be *ergodic*.

This bounded rationality framework has been used to analyze the evolution of institutions. In one theory, institutions are driven by the individual or by pivotal actions of key individuals (e.g., Napoleon and the legal code; Bismarck and social security; and Gandhi and nonviolence). Stochastic social dynamics provide an alternative account in which small and dispersed individuals, who use adaptive learning, shape institutions through small mutations, as captured by the term ε. Each mutation is individually small, almost unnoticeable, yet, over time, successive mutations create punctuated equilibria, some or none of which might be ergodic.

Let us adapt the coordination example in section 4.10.1 to stochastic dynamics. Under stochastic dynamics, and following Wallace and Young (2015), we can write the replicator dynamics in (4.29) as a stochastic differential equation as follows.

$$\dot{x}_t(L) = \left[x_t(L) - x_t^2(L) - 2(1 - x_t(L))^2 \right] x_t(L) + \varepsilon dW_t, \quad (4.30)$$

where W is a Wiener process such that $W_t - W_0 \sim N(0, t)$. A Wiener process is a stochastic process such that the initial value of a Wiener process is W_0 and the time t value is W_t. In each time period, there are independent increments to the process, $W_{t+1} - W_t$, that are independent of the past values of the Wiener process, $W_{t-1}, W_{t-2}, \ldots$. Increments to the process, say, $W_t - W_0$, are distributed normally with mean 0 and variance that equals the length of the time difference between them, t.

The only difference between (4.29) and (4.30) is the presence of the last term in (4.30), which creates random shocks to the dynamic system and captures mistakes and mutations in the decisions made by the players.

The evolutionary dynamics in section 4.10.1 show that both L and H are asymptotically stable states with equal asymptotic status. Yet, under stochastic dynamics, and using the notion of a stochastically stable steady state, we can single out the state H where the system is likely to spend most of its time. This can be seen from figure 4.4, which shows the proportion

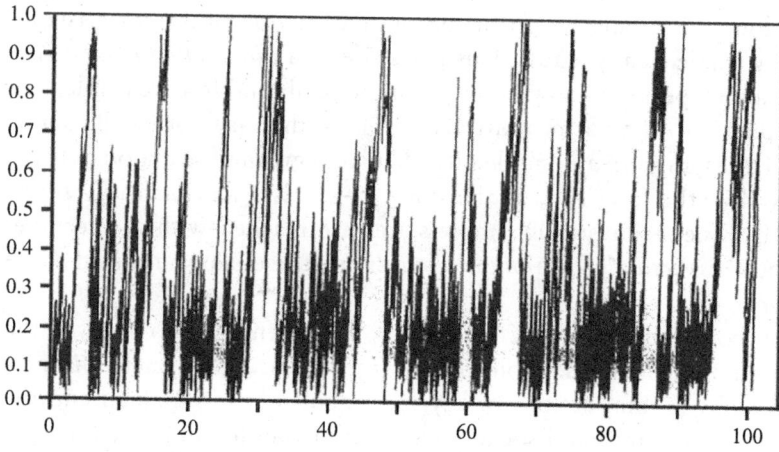

Figure 4.4
Simulated plot of the transitions between the two states. The vertical axis is the fraction of players who play L; the horizontal axis is the time (step size 0.05).
Source: Wallace, C., & Young, P. (2015). Stochastic evolutionary game dynamics. In P. Young & S. Zamir (Eds.), *Handbook of game theory with economic applications* (Vol. 4, pp. 327–380). Copyright © 2015 Elsevier.

of the population that plays the strategy L over time and how punctuated equilibria arise. Over time, we sometimes have all players playing L (i.e., $x_t(L) = 1$) and sometimes all players play H (i.e., $x_t(L) = 0$). Yet, the system spends most of its time in the monomorphic state $x_t(L) = 0$, where all play H. It is also the case that coordinating at H rather than at L is payoff improving for the players. The reader will have guessed that when we interpret strategies as institutions, such a framework can help weed out inefficient institutions. Thus, this framework provides a low rationality, heuristics-based, alternative explanation for the development of institutions. For further discussion and applications, see P. H. Young (1998) and Dhami (2020b, chapter 3).

4.11 Narratives and Contagion

In the BRA, the framing of information does not matter. So long as the information content of two signals or messages is identical, they produce identical outcomes. In recent decades, there has been a spurt in the use of *narratives* to explain diverse phenomena in the social and behavioral sciences. In this respect, economics has lagged behind psychology, anthropology, history, criminology, and sociology, yet important recent work in economics sheds light on disparate phenomena (Shiller, 2017, 2019;

Bénabou et al., 2018). Our treatment in this section follows Shiller; Bénabou et al. use the slightly more technically demanding framework of linear networks that not all readers might be familiar with. Another important difference in the two approaches is that narratives in Bénabou et al. are endogenous (e.g., arising from a desire to maintain a positive social image), while in Shiller they are largely exogenous. An important interface between narratives and judgment heuristics is highlighted in the work of Shiller; we discuss these heuristics in chapter 5. Economic agents who follow the BRA as in Bénabou et al. do not follow these heuristics.

Shiller (2017) defines *narrative* as "a simple story or easily expressed explanation of events that many people want to bring up in conversation or on news or social media because it can be used to stimulate the concerns or emotions of others, and/or because it appears to advance self-interest."

This definition reveals several interesting features of narratives. Since narratives are often simplified stories, they might not be factually accurate and might evolve with successive retelling. Consider, for instance, past narratives on gender and race that are not acceptable now because those narratives no longer hold sway. Narratives can take the form of a legend, a mythical tale, an urban legend, a joke, a poem, stories told within families or groups of people, or personal anecdotes. Yet, narratives contain a core feature that makes them particularly suitable for contagion and retelling. Once a narrative begins, it can be difficult to control the precise direction. Random mutations can make it difficult to predict its effects and possible steady states. Since reality can be quite difficult to comprehend fully, and cognitive resources are scarce, it is not uncommon for societies to create easily expressed explanations of events. Such narratives can also take the form of mental models; see section 4.12 for several examples.

Particularly intriguing is the idea of narratives as *scripts* (Schank & Abelson, 1977). Individuals might face true uncertainty and could find it difficult to compute their most desired action. In such cases, they might recall certain narratives, say, a mythical religious story, and adopt a role/injunction from the narrative (e.g., the injunction to not deviate from moral actions, even when tempted), as if they were acting in a play. How do individuals choose to recall certain narratives and then pick certain role models within those narratives? We suspect that the heuristics of representativeness, availability, and anchoring (which we consider in chapter 5) might play an important role in answering this question.

The last part of Shiller's definition considers the possibility that narratives may be used to advance self-interest. Thus, they could be designed to manipulate others. Consider the example of a competitive equilibrium in economics where competitive firms, in equilibrium, make long-run zero profits (or normal profits below which firms will have to quit). If some firms manipulate customers (e.g., by peddling misleading narratives about their product), and this increases their profits, then all competitors must do the same, so that the manipulation-inclusive long-run profits are zero. Firms that do not engage in manipulation must exit the competitive markets. This is the equilibrium notion considered in Akerlof and Shiller (2016), which they call a *phishing equilibrium*.

Narratives have a core that people find appealing enough to retell to others. What might be the constituent elements of this core? It is very difficult to predict ex ante whether a narrative will be successful, just like it might be difficult to predict whether a forthcoming film will be successful and click with the audience. In the context of folk stories, which is one of the most popular forms of narrative in human history, one can think of several core elements. Shiller (2017, p. 970) cites two different sources. Tobias (1999) says that, in all of fiction, there are only twenty master plots: "quest, adventure, pursuit, rescue, escape, revenge, the riddle, rivalry, underdog, temptation, metamorphosis, transformation, maturation, love, forbidden love, sacrifice, discovery, wretched excess, ascension and descension." Booker (2004) argues that there are only seven basic plots: "overcoming the monster, rags to riches, voyage and return, comedy, tragedy, and rebirth." These core elements probably form a part of the narratives in successful propaganda (e.g., military propaganda), and in the formation of social norms. The news media might also attempt to push self-serving narratives (e.g., traditionally, Fox News and CNN have presented different narratives on many important news stories). Narratives may also play an important role in maintaining and heightening social identity by disseminating favorable information about the in-group and unfavorable information about the out-group.

The *affect heuristic*, which we consider in chapter 5, highlights the affective response to events and outcomes, and it captures the positive or negative valence of an experience. Many narratives work on inducing an affective response in others. For instance, the risk assessment of a stock market crash by individuals might be particularly influenced by (1) news stories that invoke the emotion of fear and (2) natural hazards that create an affective response, such as an earthquake within close locational and temporal proximity (Goetzmann et al., 2016). In other cases, a positive affective response that is created from positive narratives can have a positive effect on perceptions of economic outcomes—for example, arising from the national football team's performance in the World Cup (Dohmen et al., 2006).

Given that narratives play an important role in human judgment and decision-making and also have an interface with heuristics, it is important to model the spread of narratives through contagion. The machinery used in modern economics for such purposes is network theory, but it has been largely silent on narratives; however, see Bénabou et al. (2020). An alternative method is to use models from epidemiology that take account of the spread of infectious diseases among the population. The hugely influential model by Kermack and McKendrick (1927) forms the basis of all modern epidemiological models; for a survey of the extensions to the basic model, see Lamberson (2016). Daley and Kendall (1964, 1965) conjecture that this model may also explain the spread of ideas and rumors. This idea is equally applicable to model the spread of narratives.

Consider a society with a fixed population of N members that faces an infectious disease. The Kermack and McKendrick model divides the society into three different groups, S, I, and R, so that $N = S + I + R$, where S is the number of people who are susceptible to the disease; I is the number of people who are infective and may spread the disease; and R is the number of people who have recovered from the disease. For this reason, the Kermack-McKendrick model is sometimes known as the *SIR* model.

It is convenient to solve the model in continuous time. Denote by $[0, \infty)$ the time interval over which we are interested in studying the changing composition of the three groups. Let $S(t)$, $I(t)$, and $R(t)$ be, respectively, the number of individuals at time t in the three groups, S, I, and R. The population is held fixed, so we have $N(t) = N$ for $t \in [0, \infty)$),

$$N = S(t) + I(t) + R(t), t \in [0, \infty). \tag{4.31}$$

All dynamic models require initial conditions to start off the dynamic process. Let the initial number of people in each group be given by

$$S(0) > 0, I(0) > 0, R(0) = 0. \tag{4.32}$$

Notice that $R(0) = 0$ so that in the initial period nobody in the population has recovered yet, although there is a strictly positive number of people who have been infected and others who are susceptible. We assume that members of the population mix freely with each other. Our interest is in the time path of the numbers in each group, $S(t)$, $I(t)$, and $R(t)$, $t \in [0, \infty)$.

The model is based on three first order differential equations, each representing a proposed transmission channel linking the time evolution of the populations in the three groups S, I, and R.

1. Change in the susceptible population: At any time t, the change in the number of susceptible people depends on how many infected people, $I(t)$, come into contact with the susceptible people, $S(t)$—that is, on the product $S(t)I(t)$. This intuition is represented by

$$\frac{dS(t)}{dt} = -cS(t)I(t), \, t \in [0, \infty), \tag{4.33}$$

where $c > 0$ is know as the *contagion rate*. Thus, in the existing pool of susceptible people at time t, $S(t)$, a total of $cS(t)I(t)$ people become infected and move out of the pool of susceptible people into the pool of infected people (hence the negative sign in (4.33)). Notice that since we have continuous time, the change described in (4.33) occurs instantaneously at time t. If, in contrast, we had written this model in discrete time, where time is given by $t = 0, 1, 2, \ldots$, then (4.33) would have been written as $S(t+1) - S(t) = -cS(t)I(t)$, where the LHS denotes the change in the number of susceptible people between time periods t and $t+1$ and the RHS gives the number of such people. However, the continuous time version is more amenable to analysis, and we persist with it below.

The rule in (4.33) is a reduced form way of capturing at least two different underlying, but unmodeled, channels: (a) the frequency with which people in the infected and susceptible groups meet each other and (b) the infectiousness of the disease. In the context of the current Covid-19 pandemic, it would also capture factors such as the fraction of the people wearing face masks, using hand sanitizers, and self-isolating. An obvious extension of this model would be to impose more realistic conditions on the contagion rate, c, and perhaps recognize its time varying nature; see Lamberson (2016) for a survey.

2. Change in the infected population: This depends on two different channels. (a) We already know from (1) that a total of $cS(t)I(t)$ new people are infected at time t. (b) A fraction of the people in the pool of infected people recover from the disease and move into the pool of recovered people, $R(t)$. We assume that there is a constant exponential recovery rate, $r > 0$, among the infected. Both these features are incorporated into the change in the pool of infected people at time t, $\frac{dI(t)}{dt}$, as follows:

$$\frac{dI(t)}{dt} = cS(t)I(t) - rI(t), \, t \in [0, \infty) \tag{4.34}$$

In extensions of this model, it is possible to consider a time varying recovery rate, r.

3. Change in the recovered population: This follows directly from (2). At each instant in time, people move from the pool of the infected into the pool of the recovered (captured in the second term on the RHS of (4.34)).

$$\frac{dR(t)}{dt} = rI(t), \ t \in [0, \infty) \tag{4.35}$$

A solution to the model, denoted by $S^*(t)$, $I^*(t)$, $R^*(t)$, $t \in [0, \infty)$, is a time path of the three groups of people starting from the initial condition in (4.32). This framework can describe the spread of contagious diseases, but equally well the spread of narratives, rumors, and ideas with appropriate change in interpretation. It does not require an explicit modeling of networks, as the model predates developments in this area. There should be no presumption that the predictions it offers are necessarily inferior to the current generation of network models. The network models are likely to provide additional information about the shape of the network of the relevant groups of people and its evolution over time. But this extra information comes at a cost in terms of additional assumptions that require high levels of rationality, such as requiring all players in the network to observe the network in real time and then make optimal decisions using the BRA.

It is difficult to obtain closed form solutions to the model, and we typically need to rely on simulated time paths. This requires us to specify the initial conditions in (4.32) and the parameters of the model, c, r. Consider, for instance, the simulations reported in figure 4.5 for the case $N = 100$, $I(0) = 1$, $c = 0.005$, $r = 0.05$. Out of 100 people in the population, initially there is only 1 infected person and the contagion and the recovery rates are, respectively, 0.005 and 0.05. The dark bell-shaped curve plots the infected people. The number of infected people increases rapidly, reaches a peak, and then, as recovery sets in, the infected numbers fall rapidly. The number of recovered people increases continuously, and after the first 100 time periods, most people have recovered and new infections are down to a very low level. Not everyone is infected in the population. At its peak, only 70 percent of the population is infected.

The bell-shaped pattern in the numbers infected is found repeatedly in many different contexts—for instance, internet memes (Bauckhage, 2011) and mentions of names of famous people (J. B. Michel et al., 2011). The reader can go to Google Ngrams (a free service available at https://books.google.com/ngrams) to generate plots for well-known names such as Adam Smith, Karl Marx, Marlon Brando, and Mahatma

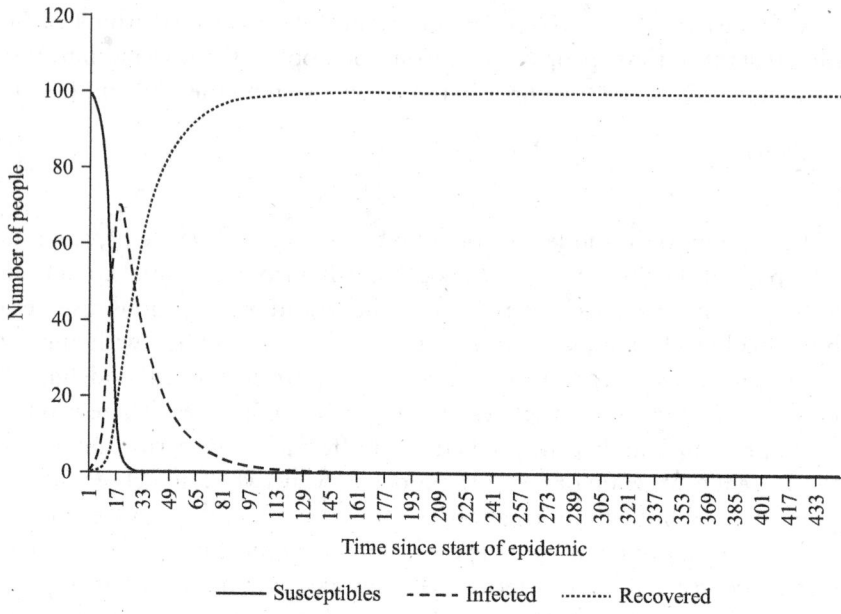

Figure 4.5
Simulated values for $S(t)$, $I(t)$, $R(t)$ for the case $N = 100$, $I(0) = 1$, $c = 0.005$, $r = 0.05$.
Source: Shiller (2017).

Gandhi (or ideas such as the Laffer curve) and check whether the frequency with which their names are mentioned plots as a bell-shaped curve over time. In some cases, when there is a renewed interest, due to potentially random events, there can be more than one bell-shaped curve. In order to accommodate these, a slightly more complicated stochastic version of the *SIR* model is needed. In the context of models of epidemics, this requires that some of the people who recovered once lose their immunity subsequently, perhaps leading to another wave of the epidemic that produces yet another bell-shaped curve for the infected. Or, perhaps the disease mutates slightly, leading to another round of infections in which the infected exhibit a bell-shaped pattern over time. We observe this for common colds every year.

The important questions are the following.

1. What is the size of the epidemic? In related contexts, one might ask, How widespread is a narrative or rumor?
2. What are the conditions for an epidemic or narrative going viral?

Both questions require us to compute $R(\infty)$—that is, what is the limiting number of people who have been infected and have recovered? $R(\infty)$

is taken to be synonymous with the size of the epidemic (or the extent of the spread of the narrative), and $R(\infty) > \frac{N}{2}$ is often taken to be the definition of a viral epidemic (or a viral narrative).

Dividing (4.33) by (4.35), we get $\frac{dS(t)}{dR(t)} = -\frac{c}{r} S(t)$, or $\frac{dS(t)/dR(t)}{S(t)} = -\frac{c}{r}$. Thus, the instantaneous percentage rate of growth of S with respect to R is a constant, $-\frac{c}{r}$. Hence, we can write the solution as $S(t) = S(0) e^{-\frac{c}{r} R(t)}$. Using (4.31) and (4.32), we get $S(0) = N - I(0)$. Hence, we have

$$S(t) = [N - I(0)] e^{-\frac{c}{r} R(t)}. \tag{4.36}$$

From (4.31) and (4.32), we have $N = S(\infty) + R(\infty)$ (we have used $I(\infty) = 0$) or $S(\infty) = N - R(\infty)$. Evaluating (4.36) at $t \to \infty$ and using $S(\infty) = N - R(\infty)$, we get $N - R(\infty) = [N - I(0)] e^{-\frac{c}{r} R(\infty)}$. Taking logs on both sides, we get that $R(\infty)$ is given implicitly by the solution to the following nonlinear equation:

$$\frac{1}{R(\infty)} \ln \left(\frac{N - I(0)}{N - R(\infty)} \right) - \frac{c}{r} = 0 \tag{4.37}$$

In other words, if we substitute the parameters c, r and the initial condition $I(0)$ in (4.37), then we can recover the value of $R(\infty)$. We can implicitly differentiate the equation in (4.37) to see that $\frac{dR(\infty)}{d(c/r)} > 0$. Thus, a higher value of $\frac{c}{r}$ increases the size of the epidemic and makes it more likely that it will go viral. Using the parameter values that we used above, $N = 100$, $I(0) = 1$, Shiller (2017) reports the calculation for the epidemic/narrative to go viral as $R(\infty) > \frac{N}{2} \Leftrightarrow \frac{c}{r} > 0.14$.

Many people now receive their information from social and news media. Thus, contagion, in the context of narratives, need not only arise from face-to-face interaction. However, the prediction of the *SIR* model is likely to still hold because (1) face-to-face communication may still be more effective and (2) the role of social and other news media can be accommodated within the *SIR* model as an increase in the contagion rate, c (L. Zhao et al., 2013). The roles of the representativeness, anchoring, availability, and affect heuristics mentioned above may also be usefully translated into changes in the contagion rate, c. For instance, if the 2007–2008 financial crises seemed to many people to be representative of the financial crash of the 1930s and if such a narrative were to spread, then greater representativeness is likely to translate to a greater contagion rate. Similarly, when people are in a heightened affective state and are fearful of future events, say, in times of crises, then narratives are more likely to go viral; this corresponds to an increase in the contagion rate.

Shiller (2017) gives a fascinating account of narratives that underlie major events and the heuristics that might be implicated in the spread of the narratives. We give two examples below.

1. The Laffer curve is a bell-shaped curve that plots tax revenues as a function of the tax rates. The implication is that once the Laffer curve reaches a peak, further increases in the tax rate will decrease tax revenues. Shiller argues that the narratives around the Laffer curve were possibly instrumental in reducing income tax rates and corporate tax rates in the UK during the Reagan years.

2. The 1920–1921 recession in the US, the sharpest since records began, was preceded by narratives around the end of World War I, the influenza epidemic, public fear of Communism, oil price shocks, and race riots that reduced optimism and possibly consumer confidence. Shiller advances the idea that narratives possibly underpinned the stock market crash of the 1930s (the Great Depression) and the Great Recession of 2007–2009. Incidentally, during the time of the Great Recession, there was a great spurt in narratives about the Great Depression (a Google Ngram for the term *Great Depression* plots as the usual bell-shaped curve). This indicates that people might have used the representativeness heuristic and believed that the Great Recession was representative of the Great Depression and using this to make inferences about the future in the face of true uncertainty. Many of these narratives were driven by an affective response to the bank runs starting with Northern Rock in the UK in 2007–2008, followed by Washington Mutual Bank and the Reserve Primary Fund in the US.

4.12 Mental Models

Many important decisions are made under true uncertainty, under cognitive constraints, and under limited attention. Hence, it is useful for individuals to form *mental models*, or useful and tractable models of the world and of the different phenomena around them. Narratives, which we have considered in section 4.11, may be one possible mechanism for forming mental models. A useful working definition of *mental models*, based on Denzau and North (1994), is given in World Bank's *World Development Report* (WDR; 2015, p. 11): "When people think, they generally do not draw on concepts that they have invented themselves. Instead, they use concepts, categories, identities, prototypes, stereotypes, causal narratives, and worldviews drawn from their communities." Chapter 3 in WDR gives an excellent introduction to mental models. WDR (p. 11) further says: "There are mental models for how much to talk to children, what risks to insure, what to save for, what the climate is like, and what causes disease. Many mental models are useful; others are not as useful and may even contribute to the intergenerational transmission of poverty."

A bit like social norms, mental models can be passed down from generation to generation and can be learned from other members of one's social group. Like social norms, the use of mental models is inertial, so they can persist even when they are harmful or no longer useful. They can sometimes lead to relatively efficient decisions but at other times lead to suboptimal decisions. Stereotyping of other individuals and racial discrimination based on social group identities are examples that fit both social norms and mental models. An essential difference between social norms and mental models is that while there may be sanctions from violating social norms, typically there are no explicit sanctions for not subscribing to existing mental models.

Datta and Mullainathan (2014) document several examples of incorrect mental models that are detrimental to self-interest. Let us consider some of these.

1. In many developing countries, there is a low take-up of the oral rehydration solution (ORS), a relatively cheap and effective mix of essential salts to treat diarrhea. However, 35 percent of poor women surveyed in India believed that the best response to diarrhea is to reduce, not increase, fluid intake. They possibly draw an incorrect analogy to a leaky bucket. Since ORS saves lives but does not alleviate the symptoms of diarrhea, it allows many people to hold on to an incorrect, and potentially fatal, mental model.
2. Farmers might overuse nitrogenous fertilizers because they believe that such fertilizers promote greener plants. This model works well for plants like spinach but not as well for grains, because it overencourages the production of green healthy leaves, which results in lower crop yields.
3. Parents in Morocco and Madagascar pull their children out of school too early. In their incorrect mental model, education only pays if children go all the way up to secondary school. However, evidence shows that every extra year of schooling is equally valuable. Thus, while parents could afford to send their children to school for longer, doing so is inconsistent with their mental models (Banerjee & Duflo, 2011).

There are several explanations for inertia in abandoning harmful mental models.

1. Under true uncertainty, the yardstick against which the quality of a mental model is to be judged might not be clear to individuals.
2. Mental models dovetail with several judgment heuristics that humans might be hardwired to follow; see chapter 5 for a discussion of these heuristics. For instance, since mental models provide a ready-made template that is culturally or socially learned, they may serve the purpose of *anchors* in making decisions, particularly when it is not clear what to do. The *availability heuristic* dictates that individuals are likely to draw on existing mental models when making decisions. Even when there is some yardstick on which mental models might be judged, individuals subject to the *confirmation bias* are likely to ignore information that contradicts their existing mental models.
3. Social identity may play an important role. By conforming to preexisting and shared mental models in a social group, individuals may wish to demonstrate that they belong to the group of insiders and gain greater acceptance and trust within the group.
4. Inadequate social exchange between traditional communities that mistrust each other can allow mutual stereotypes to persist. Female genital mutilation may persist in parts of the world because contact with the nonmutilated genitalia may be perceived to be harmful. Thus, individuals could be unwilling to experiment with alternative mental models because they perceive that it is too costly to do so (Mackie, 1996; Gollaher, 2000).

There is no presumption that all individuals hold identical mental models. Indeed, there could be heterogeneity in mental models. Yet, shared mental models are also essential to developing institutions, and there could be a two-directional feedback between mental models and institutions (Acemoglu et al., 2013). Not all mental models are cultural and social. Some mental models are hardwired in humans due to their evolutionary history (e.g., fear of snakes and spiders). Other mental models might be the result of historical accidents. For instance, the current low levels of trust in parts of Africa can be traced back to the slave trade (Nunn, 2008; Nunn & Wantchekon, 2011). Gender inequalities may have their roots in the historical technological breakthroughs, such as the plow, which favored males due to their physical strength. Hence, gender inequities are more pronounced in societies with an agricultural history rather than a nomadic history (Alesina et al., 2013).

Mental models could also arise because, on account of cognitive limitations, individuals organize different events into coarse categories (Mullainathan, 2002; Mullainathan et al., 2008). They then treat all events in the same category in an identical manner, so that there is across-category heterogeneity and within-category homogeneity; such thinkers may be termed as *coarse thinkers*.

While there is likely to be substantial inertia to change mental models, can public policy or outside agencies influence a change in mental models? Datta and Mullainathan (2014) argue that rather than simply alerting people that they hold the wrong mental models, it is more productive to provide evidence that falsifies the core beliefs in an incorrect mental model. For instance, rather than telling people they are wasteful in their energy consumption, they could be given information on a comparison of their electricity consumption relative to neighbors. This was found to reduce electricity consumption by as much as that caused by an 11 to 20 percent increase in the price of electricity (Allcott & Mullainathan 2010; Allcott & Rogers, 2014); a similar effect is documented for water consumption (Ferraro & Price 2013). Providing information to poor villagers on the availability of jobs for girls with high school degrees is more likely to induce them to educate their girls (Jensen, 2012). Soap operas in Brazil that emphasized small family size led to reduced fertility (La Ferrara et al., 2012). Exposure to cable TV in India appears to have altered existing mental models by leading to a reduction in fertility, an increase in women's status, a reduction in domestic violence, and an increase in children's school enrollment (Jensen & Oster, 2009). Legal or regulatory changes can also lead people to question existing mental models (Sunstein, 1996); indeed, this might well have been the case in changes in attitudes toward slavery, wearing motorcycle helmets, smoking, and racism.

4.13 Choice Bracketing

In the BRA, individuals consider all available information and all available choices in making their decisions. Ignoring information is typically never optimal in the BRA. But do individuals take account of all available information when making choices? The answer to this question cannot be asserted axiomatically; it is matter of the relevant empirical evidence.

When individuals are faced with information or choices, *choice bracketing* occurs when the individual decides to group the available information/choices into different sets. Often, the individual might treat these sets in isolation from one another. When making the actual choice, if individuals only consider a subset of these sets and ignore the others, then they are said to be engaged in *narrow choice bracketing*. This is broadly the idea behind some of the newer equilibrium concepts in behavioral economics—for instance, the idea of a cursed equilibrium (Eyster & Rabin, 2005) or an analogy-based equilibrium (Jehiel, 2005).

The maintained assumption under the BRA is that individuals take account of all relevant information—that is, they are engaged in *broad choice bracketing*. For instance, in making temporal choices under the BRA, individuals are expected to use the EDU model, in which they take account of all current and future time periods (broad bracketing). However, what we often observe is that individuals are myopic—that is, they do not consider the consequences of their choices for all possible future time periods (narrow bracketing). There is much empirical evidence to support this assertion, particularly the finding that people are loss averse and myopic, a phenomenon known as *myopic loss aversion* (Gneezy & Potters, 1997; Haigh & List, 2005; Sutter, 2007).

Consider some further examples that are based on Read et al. (1999).

Example 4.9. *(Smoking) Consider a smoker who is engaged in narrow choice bracketing. Thus, in choosing to smoke each cigarette, the individual only takes account of the current costs and benefits from smoking, while ignoring the effect on future health outcomes. In this case, myopic decisions, caused by narrow choice bracketing, are likely to hamper efforts to quit smoking and may have adverse long-term health consequences. On the other hand, an individual who consumes a pack of cigarettes each day and engages in broad bracketing will take into account that they will end up smoking 7,300 cigarettes a year. Such an individual might decide not to smoke the next cigarette. For addictive substances, the choice of narrow or broad bracketing might also involve issues of emotions and temptation, over which the individual could have limited self-control.*

Example 4.10. *(New York cab drivers) Under the BRA, one cannot a priori decide whether an increase in the wage rate will induce workers to work harder. The outcome, as any first-year undergraduate student in economics is taught, depends on opposing income and substitution effects. Suppose that an individual allocates total available time between labor, which sells in the market for a wage, and leisure, which provides direct utility. An increase in the wage makes a worker richer, so the worker consumes more leisure and supplies less labor (income effect). However, the wage increase also raises the opportunity cost of leisure, so the worker takes less leisure and supplies more labor (substitution effect). The net effect on labor supply is ambiguous.*

In New York, it is hard to find a taxi on a rainy day. Clearly some of the effect arises because the demand for taxis is higher on such days. Since taxi drivers have to wait less between consecutive taxi hires on rainy days, the effective wage is much higher than on normal days. However, the main effect appears to arise from too many taxi drivers quitting early on the day. This corresponds to reducing their labor supply, precisely when the wage is high.

One can, of course, invoke the BRA to explain this, but since the BRA can account for an increase as well as a decrease in labor supply following a wage increase, it is not very helpful. Camerer et. al. (1997) found that New York cab drivers employ a simple heuristic that is based on narrow bracketing. They have a particular earnings target for the day (much like a reference point in prospect theory), which is achieved much more quickly on a busy day; thus, they quit earlier on the day. Interestingly, more experienced drivers do not necessarily quit early. This suggests that they might be using a form of broad bracketing, say, in the form of maximizing earnings over a longer period. On the other hand, we argue below that in some contexts the gain from narrow bracketing might be an improvement in personal motivation.

We now give further applications of narrow bracketing for a few other economic problems.

4.13.1 Equity-Premium Puzzle

In the simplest portfolio analysis, suppose than an individual wishes to hold both stocks (such as equity that offers variable and unpredictable returns) and bonds (such as fixed rate bank deposits and fixed interest government treasury bills) in their portfolio of assets. The main distinction between stocks and bonds is that stocks exhibit variability in returns, imposing relatively greater risk on stockholders. Clearly, more risk averse individuals (in the sense of definition 2.9) will demand a higher expected return on stocks relative to bonds as a premium for holding a risky asset.

Benartzi and Thaler (1995, p. 73) make the following observation: "Since 1926 the annual real return on stocks has been about 7 percent, while the real return on treasury bills has been less than 1 percent." The quantitative difference in returns between the two assets is too large to be explained by differences in the standard deviations; the annual standard deviation of stock returns over the period 1926–1997 is about 20 percent. This is known as the *equity-premium puzzle*. In other words, the average returns on stocks relative to bonds are too high to be accounted for by the greater risk of holding stocks.

These results are difficult to explain if one uses expected utility theory, which is the main decision theory in the BRA. The *coefficient of relative risk aversion* captures, in a unit-free single number, the extent of risk aversion exhibited by a decision-maker.[16] A higher coefficient of relative risk aversion signifies greater risk aversion. Mehra and Prescott (1985) find that for expected utility theory to explain the equity premium puzzle, the coefficient of relative risk aversion should be about 30. The actual empirical estimates of the coefficient of risk aversion are close to 1 (Bombardini & Trebbi, 2012), and in extreme cases up to about 5. Mankiw and Zeldes (1991) illustrate the absurdity of such a high level of risk aversion. A decision-maker with a relative risk aversion coefficient of 30 evaluates the certainty equivalent (see definition 2.8) of the lottery $L = (100,000, 0.5; 50,000, 0.5)$ to be 51,209. Thus, the decision-maker is indifferent to receiving the sure amount of 51,209 or playing the lottery L, which is absurdly cautious behavior.

Benartzi and Thaler (1995) invoke narrow bracketing (i.e., stock returns are considered in isolation from all other returns and other sources of wealth) and prospect theory to explain the equity-premium puzzle. They first ask, What planning horizon must investors be choosing so that they are indifferent to stocks that give a 7 percent return and bonds that give a 1 percent return? Their empirical results give a best estimate of one year, which is again a form of narrow bracketing because decision-makers do not consider the consequences of current choices for all future outcomes. Yet, this is plausible, given that individuals prepare tax returns and receive annual company newsletters over the same horizon. Benartzi and Thaler term a one-year planning horizon as *myopic investor behavior*. Furthermore, most stock returns exhibit significant fluctuations over a one-year horizon; hence, the investor potentially experiences repeated gains and losses (relative to some reference point), even if these are not actually realized. Loss aversion (recall definition 2.14 and equation (2.47)) magnifies losses, hence also magnifying the downside risk from holding stocks. Loss averse decision-makers will demand a much higher rate of return on stocks to hold them in their portfolios. Under these assumptions, it turns out that a 7 percent return on stocks is indeed required to explain the observed composition of portfolios between stocks and bonds. Both narrow bracketing and loss aversion play a key role in this analysis.

There is an important corollary to these results. The more frequently someone checks the market performance of their portfolio of assets, the more likely it is that they will observe losses relative to their reference point, since stocks do fluctuate in value in real time with real time trading. Such individuals will demand even higher risk premia to hold stocks in their portfolios relative to others who check the market value of their stocks on a more irregular basis. Yet the frequency of checking the market performance of one's stocks may also be considered to be a form of choice bracketing. More frequent checking is akin to being engaged in narrow choice framing. Rather than being affected by the longer-run return on the equity, such an individual is too sensitive to frequent fluctuations. Engaging in broad bracketing, where one is interested in the market performance of one's portfolio over a longer horizon, should reduce the premium required to hold stocks. The actual market return reflects the composition of different types of individuals who wish to hold stocks.

4.13.2 Risk Aggregation

The decision to engage in narrow or broad bracketing can also determine which of two risky options one chooses. Since risk and uncertainty are pervasive, the implications are far reaching. Paul Samuelson, who in 1970 was the first American to win the Nobel Prize in economics, famously asked a colleague at MIT if he would accept the following gamble: win $200 or lose $100 with equal probability (Samuelson, 1963). In our terminology (see section 2.16.4), this lottery in incremental form is given by $L_1 = (-100, 0.5; 200, 0.5)$. The colleague replied that he would reject this bet but would accept 100 such bets. In this section, we require the reader to be familiar with the material in the appendix to chapter 2.

We can show that if the colleague is a prospect theory maximizer, he would prefer even two such bets to a single bet. Suppose that the utility function is given in (2.47). For simplicity, let us use the parameter values $\gamma = 1$ and $\lambda = 2.25$ for the utility function. Then, the utility function is given by

$$v(y) = \begin{cases} y & \text{if } y \geq 0 \\ -2.25(-y) & \text{if } y < 0 \end{cases}.$$

For pedagogical simplicity, assume that the decision-maker weights probability in a linear manner so that $w(p) = p$, where $w(p)$ is the probability weighting function (see appendix to chapter 2). Our insights are not altered if we use nonlinear probability weighting, but it adds algebraic complexity. Thus, the utility of lottery L_1 under prospect theory is given by

$$V(L_1) = \frac{1}{2}(200) - \frac{1}{2}2.25(100) = -12.5 < 0. \tag{4.38}$$

Samuelson's bet is costless, so not playing the bet results in a utility of $v(0) = 0$. A decision-maker who uses prospect theory derives negative utility from the bet in (4.38), so it is best to decline the single bet.

Now suppose that the bet L_1 is offered twice in succession, say, in two different time periods, $t = 1$ and $t = 2$. Consider the following two types of decision-makers.

1. A type 1 decision-maker uses narrow bracketing, hence treating the two bets as two separate single period bets. Since the bets are identical, using (4.38), we know that the combined utility of the bets is $V_1 + V_1 = -25.0 < 0$. Thus, such a decision-maker will not accept a sequence of two bets. It is straightforward to use induction and see that the decision-maker will not accept any number of bets offered in succession, where each bet is to play the lottery L_1.

2. A type 2 decision-maker uses broad bracketing and aggregates the risky income over both time periods. When the single period bet L_1 is played twice, the following four mutually exclusive outcomes are equally possible: $(200, 200), (200, -100), (-100, 200), (-100, -100)$. Since the decision-maker derives utility from the sum of the payoffs over the two periods, there are the following four possible equally likely outcomes $400, 100, 100, -200$; the individual is in the domain of gains in the first three cases and in the domain of losses in the last case. Thus, we can write the lottery faced by the decision-maker as $L_2 = \left(-200, \frac{1}{4}; 100, \frac{1}{4}; 100, \frac{1}{4}; 400, \frac{1}{4}\right)$. Since we are using linear probability weighting, we can add together the probabilities for the two identical outcomes of 100 to rewrite $L_2 = \left(-200, \frac{1}{4}; 100, \frac{1}{2}; 400, \frac{1}{4}\right)$. A type 2 decision-maker who faces the lottery L_2 and uses prospect theory derives the utility

$$V(L_2) = -\frac{1}{4}2.25(200) + \frac{1}{2}(100) + \frac{1}{4}(400) = 37.5 > 0.$$

Since not accepting the bet gives the decision-maker a utility of zero, and accepting the two successive bets gives the utility $V(L_2) > 0$, the decision-maker who uses broad bracketing accepts the bet.

Thus, the nature of choice bracketing, narrow or broad, is likely to play an important role in financial decisions.

4.13.3 Why Do People Engage in Narrow Choice Bracketing?

One possible explanation for narrow bracketing is that it conserves scarce cognitive resources that would be expended if the entire domain of choice was taken into account. However, there is some experimental evidence that the heuristic of narrow bracketing arises even in the absence of cognitive limitations (Read et al., 1999). Choice bracketing could also be acquired by social norms and conventions. For example, we often divide the week into two unequal lengths: the working week and the weekend, and we label food as meals or snacks.

A potentially important justification for narrow bracketing is that it enables one to deal with the problems associated with self-control. For instance, alcoholics under treatment are usually asked to be sober one day at a time (narrow bracketing) because the possibility of lifetime abstinence (broad bracketing) is too daunting. Narrow bracketing, in this case, improves motivation by setting attainable goals. Nonattainable goals can reduce motivation and the individual may simply give up; see the discussion in the special issue of The Journal of Economic Perspectives Vol. 30, No. 3, Summer 2016.

In the game of cricket, particularly in the Test match version that lasts for five days, surviving for long periods of time is essential. Successful batsmen in cricket, when asked about their batting strategy, often say that they take one session of play at a time (narrow bracketing) rather than planning the entire day. Successful tennis players might focus on winning one game at a time to keep motivation at a high level rather than think about all of the sets. Motivation might also explain the behavior of the New York cab drivers mentioned earlier; by setting an attainable target over a short period of time, they are less likely to be daunted by the prospect of achieving a more ambitious target, say, a yearly income amount.

Another factor that may work in favor of narrow bracketing is that individuals often make errors in computation and prediction; a simultaneous consideration of too large a set of factors could magnify these errors. There are other associated transaction costs of engaging in broad bracketing, such as more record keeping.

4.14 Attitudes toward Very Low Probability Events

Recall the inverse S-shaped continuous plot of the probability weighting function in figure 2.3. In figure 4.6, we plot the same curve, but we restrict attention to probabilities close to 0, in the interval $[0, 0.05]$ to be precise.

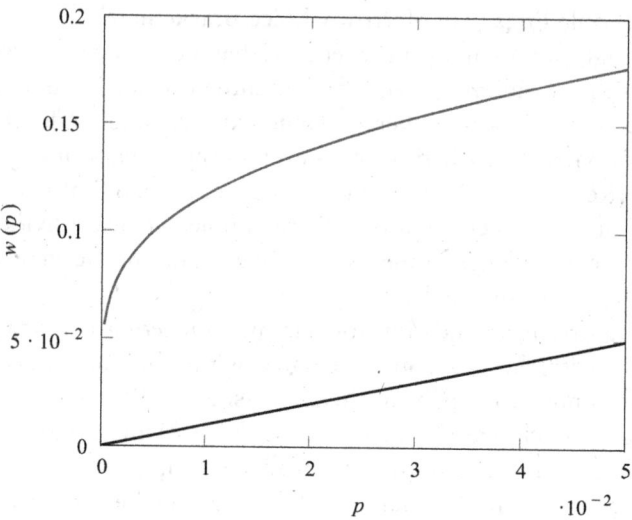

Figure 4.6
A plot of the Prelec function for low probabilities.

We also show the 45° line that represents the case of expected utility (i.e., $w(p) = p$). The range of probabilities, 0 to 5 percent, is where most of the interesting action occurs for many important economic problems. Consider, for instance, the purchase of private insurance. In home insurance, the probability that one's house burns down could be 1 in 100,000 or $p = 0.00001$. The probability that one is involved in a car accident could be 1 in 50,000 or $p = 0.00002$. Some people would still buy insurance against these extremely low probability events, even if it were not mandatory to do so, but others do not choose to insure themselves against such risks, effectively ignoring very low probability risks.

For probabilities close to 0, $p = 0$, the probability weighting function in figure 4.6 is incredibly steep. The mirror image of this is that the probability weighting function is also incredibly steep for probabilities around $p = 1$ (this is not shown in figure 4.6, but see figure 2.3).[17]

As noted earlier, expected utility is rejected by several decades of evidence. The main competitors in economics, rank dependent utility and prospect theory, both use the probability weighting function. The upshot of these remarks is that since the probability weighting function is so steep around $p = 0$ (and also around $p = 1$), decision-makers ought to be incredibly sensitive to changes in probability in this range. In particular, since small probabilities are so massively overweighted by the probability weighting function (relative to the 45° line where $w(p) = p$) individuals should be extremely eager to buy insurance against very low probability hazards—for instance, being run over by a car or being hit by an asteroid the next time they walk outside.

Do decision-makers exhibit such sensitivity? The evidence appears to indicate that there are two kinds of decision-makers (Dhami, 2019a, Section 2.11.2). A fraction $\mu \in [0, 1]$ of decision-makers follow the simple heuristic of (1) ignoring events of extremely low probability and (2) treating extremely high probability events as certain. In the context of the take-up of insurance for low probability natural hazards, the results from one set of experiments by Kunreuther et al. (1978) are consistent with $\mu = 0.8$ (see al-Nowaihi & Dhami, 2010). For all other, nonextreme probabilities, the median behavior of decision-makers is consistent with the standard inverse S-shaped probability weighting function shown in figure 2.3—that is, they overweight small probabilities and underweight large ones. It also appears that the fraction μ depends on the context and the type of problem, and it can be influenced by the media, family, friends, and public policy. The size of μ is also likely to be influenced by personal circumstances such as emotions, experience, time available to make a decision, bounded rationality, framing, and incentive effects (Kunreuther & Pauly, 2005, chapter 4). The remaining fraction of decision-makers, $1 - \mu$, behaves as described in figure 2.3 for all probabilities.

4.14.1 Original Prospect Theory

The only mainstream decision theory that incorporates realistic behavior toward low probability events is Kahneman and Tversky's (1979) *original prospect theory* (OPT). Recall that our presentation of prospect theory in the appendix to chapter 2 was based on *cumulative prospect theory* (Tversky & Kahneman, 1992), which is now simply referred to as *prospect theory*. Under OPT there is an *editing* phase, followed by an *evaluation/decision* phase. Critically, under OPT, the decision-maker decides *which improbable events to treat as impossible and which probable events to treat as certain*. Kahneman and Tversky (1979) knew that the behavior of decision-makers was complicated in the promixity of the endpoints of the probability interval—that is, around $p = 0$ and $p = 1$. Hence, in drawing their probability weighting function, they left gaps at the endpoints, as shown in figure 4.7.

Kahneman and Tversky (1979, pp. 282–283) beautifully summarize the evidence for human behavior close to the endpoints of the probability interval $[0, 1]$ as follows.

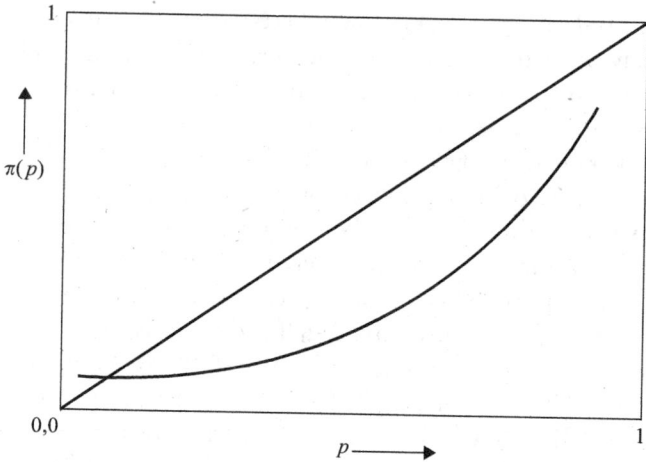

Figure 4.7
A hypothetical probability weighting function.
Source: Kahneman & Tversky (1979, p. 282).

The sharp drops or apparent discontinuities of $\pi(p)$ at the end-points are consistent with the notion that there is a limit to how small a decision weight can be attached to an event, if it is given any weight at all. A similar quantum of doubt could impose an upper limit on any decision weight that is less than unity.... The simplification of prospects can lead the decision-maker to discard events of extremely low probability and to treat events of extremely high probability as if they were certain. Because people are limited in their ability to comprehend and evaluate extreme probabilities, highly unlikely events are either ignored or overweighted, and the difference between high probability and certainty is either neglected or exaggerated. Consequently $\pi(p)$ is not well-behaved near the end-points.

One of the attractive features of OPT is the use of heuristics by decision-makers in the editing phase. Of these heuristics, ignoring probabilities close to $p=0$ is just one of many examples. Another heuristic employed by the decision-maker is *coalescing* or *combination*, which ensures that if an outcome appears more than once in a lottery, its probabilities can be added. For instance, the lottery $(-30, 0.2; -30, 0.3; 175, 0.5)$, also known as a *split lottery*, is equivalent to the lottery written in the coalesced form as $(-30, 0.5; 175, 0.5)$. The *cancellation heuristic* is used to eliminate common components among the lotteries being compared. The *dominance heuristic* is used to recognize and eliminate lotteries that are obviously stochastically dominated. Interestingly, this only rules out stochastically dominated lotteries when such dominance is obvious to the decision-maker but not when dominance is not obvious. By contrast, and as noted earlier, under the BRA, decision-makers can never choose stochastically dominated options. The *editing phase* is followed by the *evaluation phase*, in which the heuristically edited lotteries from the editing phase are evaluated using the prospect theory utility functional (this roughly corresponds to our treatment of prospect theory in the appendix to chapter 2, but setting decision weights the same as probability weights).

Recall from the appendix to chapter 2 that the 1992 version of prospect theory (Tversky & Kahneman, 1992) used cumulative transformations of probabilities following the insights developed by Quiggin (1982, 1993). Hence, the authors wrote down the objective function of the decision-maker as shown in (2.49). By contrast, the 1979 version (Kahneman & Tversky, 1979) simply used a probability weighting function in place of decision weights, so the objective function was given by the analogue of (2.49),

$$V(L) = \sum_{i=-m}^{n} w(p_i) v(y_i).$$

Since no distinction is made between decision weights π and the probability weighting function w in OPT, the vertical axis in figure 4.7 is labeled π rather than w. Recall also, in the discussion following equation (2.41), that such decision-makers can also choose stochastically dominated options. This led to much criticism of OPT in economics. Perhaps in response to this criticism and due to the insights of Quiggin (1982), Tversky and Kahneman (1992) gave up the psychologically important and heuristics-rich editing phase in OPT and replaced it with prospect theory. However, prospect theory is unable to explain the behavior for extreme probability events in the vicinity of $p = 0$.

4.14.2 The Evidence on Behavior under Low Probability Events

Compelling evidence that many people use the simple heuristic of ignoring events of low probability comes from many different sources. We provide several examples below.

Example 4.11. *(Reluctance to insure for low probability events)* Kunreuther et al. (1978) find that decision-makers are reluctant to buy nonmandatory insurance against low probability natural hazards (e.g., earthquakes, floods, and hurricane damage). Updated evidence can be found in Kunreuther and Pauly (2004, 2005). The study of insurance is one of the central questions in microeconomic theory. Under expected utility theory, a risk averse decision-maker facing an actuarially fair premium will, in the absence of transaction costs, buy full insurance for all probabilities, however small. By contrast, Kunreuther et al. (1978, chapter 7) find that decision-makers who face actuarially fair, and even overfair, insurance refuse to take up insurance as the probability of the loss decreases, and below a certain probability, the take-up of insurance drops dramatically. These results are unaltered despite government subsidies to overcome transaction costs and the reduction of premiums below their actuarially fair rates. A very large number of potential confounds were controlled for, yet the results did not change.

Kenneth Arrow, the 1972 Nobel Prize winner in economics, writes in his foreword (Kunreuther et al., 1978, p. viii): "Clearly, a good part of the obstacle [to buying insurance] was the lack of interest on the part of purchasers." Kunreuther et al. (1978, p. 238) write: "Based on these results, we hypothesize that most homeowners in hazard-prone areas have not even considered how they would recover should they suffer flood or earthquake damage. Rather they treat such events as having a probability of occurrence sufficiently low to permit them to ignore the consequences." Thus, the researchers seem to suggest that a proportion $\mu > 0$ of decision-makers (using our framework above) simply ignore the very low probability of a loss; hence, they are unwilling to buy insurance.

Example 4.12. *(Does capital punishment work?)* In a celebrated result in economics, known as the Becker proposition, the 1992 Nobel laureate in economics, Gary Becker (1968), proposed that the most efficient way to deter crime is to impose the "severest possible penalty with the lowest possible probability of detection and conviction." The idea was that by reducing the probability of detection, society can economize on the costs of enforcement, such as policing and trial costs. But by increasing fines, which are less costly, the deterrence effect of the punishment is maintained. So long as infinitely high fines/punishment is available (e.g., capital punishment), a risk neutral or risk averse offender will be deterred from crime, however small the probability of detection and conviction. This is shown formally in Dhami and al-Nowaihi (2013), who also showed that this result extends to rank dependent utility and to prospect theory. The main intuition is that since the probability weighting function is so steep around $p = 0$ (see figure 4.6), potential offenders infinitely overweight the small risk of facing infinite punishments. Kolm (1973) memorably phrases the Becker proposition as "It is efficient to hang offenders with probability zero."

Empirical evidence shows that the behavior of a significant number of people does not conform to the Becker proposition; this is known as the Becker paradox. For instance, Levitt (2004) shows that the estimated contribution of capital punishment to deterring crime in the US, over the period 1973–1991, was zero.[18] A natural explanation for the Becker paradox is that a fraction $\mu > 0$ of individuals use the simple heuristic of completely ignoring (or heavily underweighting) the very low probability of getting caught, so they commit a crime despite high levels of punishment.

Example 4.13. *(Why do people run red traffic lights?)* In running a red traffic light, there is at least a very small probability of an accident. Running red traffic lights is pervasive in real life. Bar-Ilan and Sacerdote (2001, 2004) estimate that there are 260,000 accidents per year in the US caused by red-light running, with implied costs of car repairs alone on the order of $520 million per year. It is implausible to assume that the act of running red traffic lights is simply a mistake. Using Israeli data, Bar-Ilan (2000) calculated that the expected gain from jumping one red traffic light is, at most, one minute (the length of a typical light cycle). Given the known probabilities, they find that if a slight injury causes a loss greater or equal to 0.9 days, a risk-neutral person who follows EU will be deterred by that risk alone. However, the corresponding numbers for the additional risks of serious and fatal injuries are 69.4 days and 13.9 days, respectively, which should ensure complete compliance with the law. However, evidence is to the contrary.

Expected utility combined with risk aversion will struggle to explain this evidence, as will rank dependent utility and prospect theory, due to the steep overweighting of small probabilities. The most plausible explanation for observed red traffic light running is that a fraction $\mu > 0$ of individuals run red traffic lights because they ignore or seriously underweight the very low probability of an accident.

Example 4.14. *(Other examples)* Many other examples can be given in which individuals use the simple heuristic of ignoring potentially large losses that arise with a relatively small probability. These include the use of handheld mobile phones in moving vehicles, which increases the risk of an accident by two- to sixfold. In the UK, up to 40 percent of individuals drive and talk on mobile phones while two-thirds of Finnish *drivers and 85 percent of American drivers use their phones while driving (Royal Society for the Prevention of Accidents, 2005; Pöystia et al., 2005). Hands-free equipment does not seem to offer essential safety advantages. Prior to 1985, in the US, only 10 to 20 percent of motorists wore seat belts voluntarily (Williams & Lund, 1986). For a typical driver, an accident with serious consequences may occur with a small probability. Empirical evidence shows that seat belts save lives; thus, not wearing seat belts is consistent with the inference that some people simply ignore the very low probability of an accident.*

Despite publicly announced risks, initially women only sparingly took up the offer of breast cancer examination (small probability of a large loss). In the US, this changed only after the greatly publicized mastectomies of Betty Ford and Happy Rockefeller; see Kunreuther et al. (1978, pp. xiii, 13–14). This indicates that salient events, and active public policy, may be able to influence the fraction of individuals who ignore events of very low probability.

4.14.3 So What Is the Way Forward?

The discussion above leaves us at an interesting juncture. On the one hand, there is sufficient evidence that for many activities of great economic importance, some individuals use the heuristic of ignoring very low probabilities. On the other hand, none of the existing optimization-based approaches—expected utility, rank dependent utility, and prospect theory—is able to take this into account. Hence, the predictions arising from these theories for low probability events are not consistent with the data. How should we proceed to take account of the relevant evidence?

One approach would be to develop new heuristics-based models of decision-making that take account of this evidence. The other possibility, pursued by al-Nowaihi and Dhami (2010), is to incorporate the relevant heuristic directly within an optimization-based approach, in this case, prospect theory. They propose an extension to prospect theory that takes account of human behavior toward low probability events. In their framework, a fraction $1 - \mu \geq 0$ of the decision-makers have the classical inverse S-shaped probability weighting function, so they are quite sensitive to low probability events. However, the remaining fraction μ of the decision-makers have the axiomatically derived probability weighting function shown in figure 4.8—the *composite Prelec probability weighting function* (CPF), which is generated by smooth pasting three Prelec probability weighting functions.

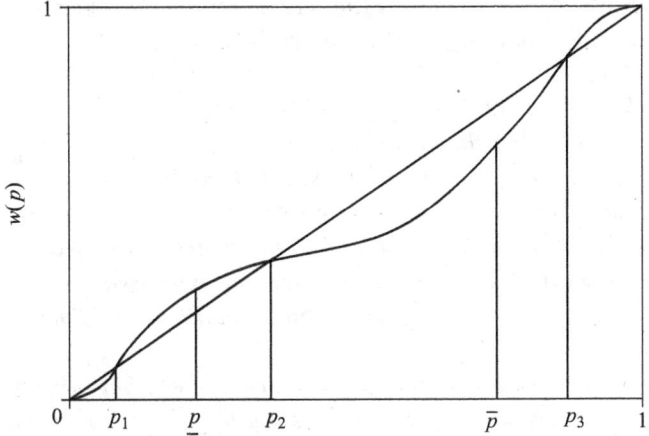

Figure 4.8
The composite Prelec weighting function (CPF) in al-Nowaihi and Dhami (2010).

In figure 4.8, decision-makers heavily underweight very low probabilities in the range $[0, p_1]$. Indeed, the probability weighting function infinitely underweights small probabilities; roughly speaking, it is very flat near $p = 0$.[19] Thus, in this range of probabilities, the fraction μ of the decision-makers ignore very low probability events. At the other extreme, in the range of probabilities $[p_3, 1]$, the decision-maker overweights probabilities; thus, these probabilities are particularly salient. However, in the middle segment, $p \in [p_1, p_3]$, the CPF is inverse S-shaped, which is consistent with the evidence. Al-Nowaihi and Dhami (2010) show formally that CPF can explain all the paradoxical examples in section 4.14.2. It remains to empirically test the CPF, but in principle, it shows how heuristics can be usefully incorporated within an optimizing theory such as prospect theory.

4.15 Do People Take Account of Sunk Costs and Opportunity Costs?

A basic lesson in any first-year undergraduate economics course is that sunk costs (fixed costs incurred prior to taking an action) should be ignored and should not determine the optimal action. The optimal action, in turn, is guided by the *marginal costs* and the *marginal benefits* of the action (these are the incremental costs and incremental benefits from an action that exclude the fixed costs). Yet, experimental evidence indicates that sunk costs do matter for the actual action taken. Alternatively, individuals follow a simple heuristic of taking account of sunk costs.

However, there are associated heuristics that create interactions between mental accounting and sunk costs, as we shall see below.

Example 4.15. *(Kahneman & Tversky, 1984) In an experiment, subjects in the first group are told that they purchased a theater ticket for $10 in advance (sunk cost) but have subsequently lost it before the event. A second group of subjects is told that they have lost $10 before the event. Which group would be more willing to buy another ticket? Forty-six percent in the first group and 88 percent in the second expressed a desire to buy another ticket. Yet, both groups of subjects had lost an identical monetary amount.*

The type of sunk costs matters in this case. It is very likely that subjects keep a system of mental accounts, and money is not fungible across these accounts. By contrast, in the BRA, money is perfectly fungible across all mental accounts. It is tempting to conclude that subjects have a mental account on theater outings and losing the ticket is seen as an outflow from this account, while losing an equivalent amount of money leaves this account unaffected. A second feature of mental accounts is that humans dislike mental accounts that are in the red, which occurs when debits in that account are greater than credits; this is a form of debt aversion for the mental account. Rather, they appear to prefer mental accounts that are in the black—that is, when the credits in an account are greater than the debits (Prelec & Loewenstein, 1998).

Example 4.16. *(Thaler, 1980) Suppose that you purchased a ticket for $100 to see a basketball game, but there is a blizzard on the day of the game. Will you go to the game? The cost of the ticket is a sunk cost and should not influence the decision to undertake potentially risky travel in a blizzard. Thus, the optimal action predicted by the BRA (to go or not) for ticket holders is identical to those who have not purchased the ticket. However, it is very likely that ticket holders would be more willing to travel in the blizzard. The explanation is similar to that for example 4.15. Individuals appear to have a mental account for the basketball game, which is debited for $100 when the ticket is purchased. If the game is missed, then this account must be closed in the red, which is aversive. However, non–ticket holders do not face this calculation, and they decide on the basis of how safe it is to travel in a blizzard to see the game.*

Example 4.17. *(Thaler, 1999) By having a real effect on decisions, sunk costs overturn one of the most basic lessons in economics—namely, that* optimal decisions equate marginal costs and marginal benefits, independent of sunk costs. However, the effects of sunk costs may not last forever. Sunk costs can depreciate over time. Suppose that you buy shoes that seem comfortable at the time of buying, but after wearing them for a day, they feel uncomfortable. You try wearing them for the next few days, but it gets worse. At this point, the shoes cannot be returned because of the wear and tear on them. If the shoes cannot be returned, then their purchase is a sunk cost. Thaler conjectures that the more expensive the shoes, (1) the longer one persists in wearing them despite the discomfort, and (2) the longer they stay in the closet before being thrown away. Yet, irrespective of their costs, the shoes are eventually thrown away (full payment depreciation in the long run).

The concepts of *acquisition utility* and *transaction utility* given in Thaler (1985/2008) [reprint info given in 1985 reference listing] can be used to illustrate the findings in example 4.17. Suppose that an individual has a valuation for an object, $v > 0$, and pays a price p to acquire it. Then, the net valuation of the object, or the *acquisition utility*, U_A, is $U_A = v - p$.

Acquisition utility corresponds to consumer surplus or the net satisfaction derived by the individual from consumption of the object (sometimes also referred to as *experienced net utility*). A related concept is *transaction utility*, $U_T = \bar{p} - p$, where $\bar{p}$ is the reference price or the regular price that the consumer expects to pay. Thaler (1985/2008) feels that the most important determinant of $\bar{p}$ is fairness, which depends on the costs of the seller.

At the time of the purchase, the consumer is guided by transaction utility alone. For instance, the behavior of the sales staff and the services they provide or the hype around a sales event, might directly influence $\bar{p}$ and the decision to buy the object. Transaction utility might not be a good predictor of acquisition utility. Transaction utility would dictate buying the good only if the actual price is below the reference price—that is, $\bar{p} \geq p$. On the other hand, if acquisition utility had been invoked at the time of purchase, then the consumer would buy only if $v \geq p$.

In example 4.17, suppose that the individual uses transaction utility U_T to purchase the shoes and acquisition utility U_A to evaluate the subsequent experience. Since the shoes turn out to be smaller than expected, they provide low utility, v. Suppose we take the extreme case that $v = 0$, so that the acquisition utility is $U_A = -p$ in every period. One way of thinking about the depreciation of sunk costs is that they fall continuously at the rate $\delta > 0$ each period, so that at time t in the future, sunk costs equal $-pe^{-\delta t}$. The individual can close the shoes' mental account (i.e., throw the shoes out or give them away) when the sunk costs have depreciated to some predetermined low level, $\underline{c}$, that is too low to care about the shoes any more. Thus, it is time to discard the shoes when $t=t^*$ solves $pe^{-\delta t^*}=\underline{c}$. The larger is p (i.e., the more expensive are the shoes), the larger is the value of t^* at which the shoes are thrown away. This explains the conjectures that Thaler (1999) makes in example 4.17.

Another well-known example of sunk costs comes from Shafir and Thaler (2006); it illustrates several heuristics that people use in judging *opportunity costs*. The concept of opportunity cost is perhaps the most fundamental in all of economics. The opportunity cost of a good/service is what needs to be forgone to obtain a unit of the good/service. For instance, if you pay $10 to get a CD, then the opportunity cost of the CD is $10. If you exchange your CD for another CD from a friend, then the opportunity cost of the CD given up is the CD that you received. Almost everything has an opportunity cost, which is sometimes summarized in the popular saying "There is no free lunch."

Shafir and Thaler (2006) asked the question in example 4.18 of subscribers to a wine newsletter, *Liquid Assets*, which used to be published by the economist Orley Ashenfelter. The subscribers are extremely knowledgeable wine consumers who have substantial home cellars. In many cases, these are economists or business executives, so they should, in principle, be able to fully comprehend the choices in the experiment.

Example 4.18. *(Shafir & Thaler, 2006) Suppose you bought a case of a good 1982 Bordeaux in the futures market for $20 a bottle. The wine now sells at auction for about $75 a bottle. You have decided to drink a bottle. Which of the following best captures your feeling of the cost to you of drinking this bottle? The respondents were given five answers to choose from: $0, $20, $20 plus interest, $75, and −$55. The percentage of respondents choosing each answer was 30, 18, 7, 20, and 25.*

An opportunity cost calculation immediately leads to the correct answer of $75; the sunk cost of $20 is irrelevant. Yet, more than half the respondents report that drinking the bottle either costs nothing or actually saves them money. There is a wide range of answers among these seasoned wine drinkers who should be well versed in economic and financial calculus. When the experiment was posed in terms of giving the bottle away (rather than drinking it), then 30 percent gave the correct answer,

$75. The authors conclude that wine drinkers think of their initial purchase as an investment. People who choose the $-\$55$ option, for instance, think that the value of the investment turned out to be $75, but they paid $20, so they saved $55. Thus, more than half the responders think that drinking the bottle either costs them nothing or actually constitutes a saving. It was also found that 55 percent of the individuals start thinking in terms of the opportunity cost ($75) if the question is posed in terms of the wine bottle having been broken accidentally. Breaking the bottle makes the replacement cost of the bottle more salient.

Sunk costs need not be just monetary. The sunk cost phenomenon has also been found when there are *sunk time costs*, although they have a smaller effect on actions relative to monetary sunk costs (Soman, 2001; Navarro & Fantino, 2009). Furthermore, time is also found to be non-fungible across mental accounts (Rajagopal & Rha, 2009). Sunk costs have also been documented for risky choices (Okada & Hoch, 2004).

5
Kahneman and Tversky's Research Program on Heuristics and Biases

5.1 Introduction

Daniel Kahneman and Amos Tversky published a set of seminal papers in the 1970s that tested various aspects of the BRA (Kahneman & Tversky, 1972a, 1972b; Tversky & Kahneman, 1971, 1973, 1974). A major finding from their work was that people followed simple *heuristics* in making decisions and that their behavior differed significantly from the predictions of the BRA. In other words, people's choices were *biased* relative to the BRA benchmark. Hence, this research program, which since then has blossomed in many directions, is known as the *heuristics and biases research program* (henceforth, HBP). The word *bias* in this research program is a bit unfortunate; it is not to be read as suggesting any incompetence or shortcoming on the part of individuals, other than to say that their behavior is *different* from the predictions of the BRA. The HBP was able to demonstrate that the BRA in economics is not tenable, not even in an as-if sense.

In the past, the HBP was influential outside economics, but not within economics; this has changed with the advent of behavioral economics. However, the HBP has also come under intense criticism from another school within bounded rationality that is most associated with the name of Gerd Gigerenzer, although there are a large number of other contributors to it as well. It identifies Herbert Simon's bounded rationality approach as its intellectual fountainhead and focuses on *procedural rationality* and the *ecological rationality of heuristics*, terms that we shall define below. This approach stresses that heuristics are *fast* in terms of the computational time required to make decisions and *frugal* in the use of information. Hence, we abbreviate this approach as the FFP (*fast and frugal heuristics research program*).

In this chapter, we mainly focus on the HBP; in the next chapter, we focus on the FFP. We offer very limited discussion on the relevant mental or neural processes that are to be implicated in the use of heuristics or the appropriate normative benchmark models of the brain to be employed. The interested reader can pick up these aspects of the debate in Stanovich and West (2000) and Stanovich (2012). Our acronyms, HBP and FFP, are based on convenience of use, for want of better standardized acronyms in this literature, but it is important to emphasize that they are not literally accurate. The HBP approach (1) does not deny that heuristics are fast and frugal and (2) has been influenced by the work of Simon. Indeed, Herbert Simon was appreciative of the work done by Kahneman and Tversky in the HBP (Gigerenzer, 2008, p. 86).

In sections 5.2 to 5.10, we outline the main heuristics in the HBP. A major criticism of the HBP by the FFP is that the relevant heuristics are not stated formally, so it is not clear what they mean, and that heuristics can be used arbitrarily to give any desired explanation of events (Gigerenzer, 1991, 1996a; Gigerenzer & Gaissmaier, 2011). For instance, talking of representativeness and availability, Gigerenzer (1991, p. 102) writes that these are "largely undefined concepts and can be post hoc used to explain almost everything." Kahneman and Tversky (1996, p. 585) respond that since representativeness can be elicited experimentally, there is no need to define it a priori. We give reasonably precise mathematical definitions of the heuristics in the HBP that directly address the criticism in the FFP that heuristics are not formally defined, and we also briefly describe the evidence consistent with the use of these heuristics. We keep references to a minimum. For a detailed treatment of the HBP, we refer the reader to two excellent edited collection of readings, Kahneman et al. (1982) and Gilovich et al. (2002). For a treatment from the standpoint of behavioral economics, see Dhami (2020a).

In section 5.2, we consider the *representativeness heuristic*. In judging the likelihood that a sample is drawn from a particular population, people use *superficial similarity* between the sample and the population that is not supported by statistical inference. For instance, many people believe that a sequence of five consecutive heads in successive coin tosses is likely to have come from a biased coin rather than a fair coin. Yet, there is no result in statistics that states that the 50-50 split between heads and tails in a coin toss should also arise in a small number of coin tosses. The 50-50 proportion between heads and tails is a limiting result that arises only in very large samples. By contrast, many individuals appear to follow the *law of small numbers* in the sense that they ascribe to small samples the properties of large samples.

We consider two of the leading applications/examples of representativeness—the *gambler's fallacy* and the *hot hand fallacy*. The gambler's fallacy arises when people assign too much *negative autocorrelation* to an inherently random process. For instance, many people are reluctant to bet on the winning numbers from the last draw of a lottery, believing that the probability of drawing these numbers is now lower, although statistically the probability does not change. Similarly, when people are asked to produce hypothetical sequences of random numbers (e.g., hypothetical repeated tosses of a coin), they alternate too much between heads and tails, even though in small samples, the proportions of heads and tails need not be 50-50. The hot hand fallacy is the opposite—perceiving too much *positive autocorrelation* in an inherently random process. For instance, stores that sell the winning lottery ticket see elevated sales for an extended time in the future. People appear to assign a higher probability to the store selling a winning ticket again in the future, even though the tickets are randomly allocated to stores.

In section 5.3, we consider the *anchoring heuristic*. Many people appear to anchor on irrelevant information that is provided to them prior to making a decision. In a well-known experiment, a wheel of fortune was spun in front of subjects and they observed a number come up. Their subsequent estimates of the percent of African nations in the UN were clustered close to the irrelevant number on the wheel of fortune. This extremely robust heuristic has been found in many domains for both experienced and inexperienced subjects.

In section 5.4, we consider *hindsight bias*. This arises when subjects are initially asked to make a *predictive judgment* for an uncertain event that is to occur in the future. Once the uncertain event is realized and it has been observed, they are asked to recall their prediction, which is also known as the *postdictive judgment*. In the BRA, predictive and postdictive judgments coincide. By contrast, many people recall their predictive judgment in a biased manner, so their remembered prediction is too close to the actual realization of the uncertain event. Hence, they appear to be saying "I knew it all along." We show how market investors subject to this bias may underestimate stock market volatility and, hence, pursue suboptimal investment strategies.

In section 5.5, we consider the *availability heuristic*. Unlike the assumption of perfect memory recall in the BRA, many people do not use the entire stock of possible memories that they have. They use a subset of these memories, and in choosing their memories they use various cues, such as the vividness and salience of past events and whether they or their acquaintances personally experienced these events.

Section 5.6 describes the *conjunction fallacy*, which arises when people assign a greater probability to the intersection of two sets as compared to either of the two sets. Consider, for instance, a famous problem, the Linda problem. On hearing the description of a person, many people assign a higher probability that they could be a librarian and a bank clerk relative to the probability that they are a librarian alone or a bank clerk alone. This is a misunderstanding of the set inclusion principle. We also consider the evidence on the extent of the fallacy when incentives are introduced.

Section 5.7 shows that people may not fully understand the statistical phenomenon of *regression to the mean*. Suppose that you ask someone to toss a fair coin and give them nothing if tails comes up and $10 if heads comes up. Clearly, the expected or mean payment in this task is $5. Some people, purely by luck, will get a heads and earn $10 and others, also purely by luck, will get a tails and earn $0. If we now asked all those with above-average earnings ($10 in the first toss) to toss a coin with identical rewards a second time, then their mean/expected earnings from the second toss are $5. Similarly, those with below-average earnings in the first toss ($0 in the first toss) also have a mean/expected earning of $5 in the second toss. This phenomenon is known as regression to the mean. Both groups, one above average and the other below average, regress toward the mean earnings of $5 in the second toss. This is an important heuristic in situations where outcomes are governed by luck, but if we are subject to this bias, then we may ascribe the better-than-average performance (in this case, earnings on the first toss of the coin) to other factors that may be spuriously correlated with good luck and assign causal significance to them.

Section 5.8 shows that many people may not be able to distinguish between *necessary and sufficient conditions*. For instance, it is necessary for an animal to have a tail to be a horse, but having a tail is not a sufficient condition to be a horse. In the BRA, people should have no such confusion. Hence, this is a bias relative to the predictions of the BRA. We show that, from the observation that it is difficult to make money on the stock market, it is erroneous to conclude that the stock market is efficient. This is essentially a confusion between necessary and sufficient conditions.

Section 5.9 considers *confirmation bias*, the tendency to hold on to our initial beliefs even in the face of contrary evidence. For instance, just after we buy a new car, the same model of the car appears more numerous on the road. Individuals subject to the confirmation bias seek the evidence that they are looking for and ignore or pay less attention to contrary evidence. Confirmation bias is likely to play a major role in entrenching one's initially held views, leading, for instance, to the formation of stereotypes and maintaining racial prejudices.

Finally, section 5.10 considers the *affect heuristic*. People often associate events and experiences with an emotional valence, positive or negative, and this influences their decisions. The evidence suggests that this heuristic applies both to laypeople and experts. Unlike the other heuristics, this is more difficult to define in precise mathematical terms. However, the emerging literature in psychological game theory, within behavioral economics, does achieve precision and formalism in the modeling of emotions such as guilt, shame, reciprocity, anger, and frustration. We have already seen an example of this in section 3.2.2.

Section 5.11 considers a range of objections to the HBP, mainly leveled by the FFP. We discuss several objections such as the lack of ecological validity in the HBP; one-event probabilities; "we cannot be that dumb" critique; frequency versus probability format; empirical counterparts to heuristics; how the HBP can sometimes explain an event and its negation; and the criticism of appropriate statistical norms. We believe that it is possible to address these objections.

Briefly, HBP respects ecological validity if the environment is understood as the context and the frame of a decision. Outcomes in the HBP are context and frame dependent. The issue of one-event probabilities pertains to the debate between frequentists and Bayesians, and it is not a specific issue for the HBP. Most of the work done in applied economics is in the tradition of frequentist statistics, where the researcher has a single sample and then proceeds to draw probabilistic inferences on its basis. The "we cannot be that dumb" critique questions why humans need to employ heuristics in the face of major scientific achievements such as landing a man on the moon and decoding the structure of DNA. This is a misunderstanding of how science progresses. Good science begins with intuition, intuitive guesses, and sometimes serendipity, and researchers use different heuristics in generating insights. In conjunction, the institutions in science (peer review, refutability, replication, respect for the evidence, willingness to ditch empirically refuted models) function in a manner that is conducive to making progress. Thus, there is no conflict between the use of heuristics by researchers (obviously backed by great expertise, skill, and competence) and progress in science.

Most of the heuristics in the HBP do not depend on a distinction between the frequency and the probability format (e.g., hot hand fallacy, gambler's fallacy, anchoring, availability, hindsight bias, confirmation bias, affect heuristic). This distinction applies only to a few heuristics such as the conjunction fallacy and base rate neglect. Even where it applies, the weight of the evidence suggests that a frequency format can at best reduce the associated biases but not eliminate them; the majority of the subjects still exhibit the relevant bias. Furthermore, there are potential confounds that arise from subtle framing effects when the frequency format is reported as being too successful in reducing base rate neglect. We show that a theory can still be a good theory even if it cannot always specify the exact empirical counterparts. Indeed, subsequent empirical work, by examining the channels suggested by the relevant theory, can offer more precise identification of the empirical counterparts. We illustrate this using the highly influential work of three Nobel Prize winners in economics.

We show how the representativeness heuristic can sometimes be used to explain an event and its negation by exploring the underlying inference problem that subjects are trying to solve. It is a mistake to argue that the HBP advocates or endorses normative standards such as expected utility theory, or the axioms of rationality, under the BRA. The HBP takes as given the normative standards in the BRA and then proceeds to test them. This is a perfectly acceptable practice in any science.

Finally, in section 5.12, we show that experts are subject to biases, just like laypeople, in several different domains. However, experts are more likely to be able to offer better ex post explanations for why their predictions failed. This addresses an important criticism of behavioral economics by some within the economics profession that the relevant biases do not apply to experienced subjects and to experts. In some areas, experience does mitigate some of the behavioral features highlighted in behavioral economics, but we know of no examples where the qualitative findings for experts are the reverse of those found for lay subjects (Dhami, 2016).[1]

5.2 The Representative Heuristic

The representativeness heuristic is one of the most widely applicable and useful heuristics (Kahneman & Tversky, 1984). Gigerenzer and Brighton

(2011, p. 18) write: "On the other hand, there is the label 'representativeness,' which was proposed in the early 1970s and means that judgements are made by similarity—but how similarity was defined is left open. A label can be a starting point, but four decades and many experiments later, representativeness has still not been instantiated as a model." We shall examine the validity of this claim.

The representativeness heuristic has been defined and formalized (Rabin, 2002; Dhami, 2020a, section 1.2). Consider first the weak law of large numbers. It essentially says that if we have a random sample of size n in which each observation comes from independently and identically distributed random variables, then as the sample size increases, we get closer and closer to the population mean. In the limit, as the sample size becomes infinitely large, then the sample mean is virtually identical to the population mean.

Theorem 5.1. *(Weak law of large numbers; Hogg et al., 2005) Let $\{X_n\}$ be a sequence of independently and identically distributed random variables, with a common mean μ and finite variance σ^2. Denote the sample mean based on n observations by $\bar{x}(n) = \sum_{i=1}^{n} x_i/n$, where x_i is the sample realization of the random variable X_i. Then, $\bar{x}(n)$ "converges in probability" to the population mean, μ—that is, $\lim_{n \to \infty} P[|\bar{x}(n) - \mu| \geq \varepsilon] = 0$, $\forall \varepsilon > 0$.*[2]

In the BRA, since people effortlessly subscribe to the laws of classical statistics, they subscribe to the law of large numbers in theorem 5.1. In particular, they do not ascribe to small samples the properties of large samples. For instance, they do not subscribe to the belief that the sample mean based on small samples is close to the population mean. However, the evidence suggests that many people act as if they believe that even small samples mimic the properties of large samples; we have already considered evidence for this in section 2.15. One of us recalls an admissions tutor in a university who rejected an applicant from a particular foreign university on the grounds that, a few years ago, a different student from the same university did not do well when granted admission. Clearly, the admissions tutor is basing the decision on a sample of size 1, which does not permit strong inferences.

Definition 5.1. *(Law of small numbers) An individual subscribes to the law of small numbers if the individual holds the belief that for a finite sample size the sample mean is either identical to the population mean or close to it.*

Example 5.1. *(An illustration of the law of small numbers)* Consider the following experimental instructions from Tversky and Kahneman (1974). "A town is served by two hospitals. In the larger hospital, about 45 babies are born each day, and in the smaller hospital, about 15 babies are born each day. As you know, about 50 percent of all babies are boys. However, the exact percentage varies from day to day. For a period of one year, each hospital recorded the days on which more than 60 percent of the babies born were boys. Which hospital do you think recorded more such days?"

In the sample, 53 students said that both hospitals are equally likely to have recorded such days, and an equal split of 21 students chose the larger and the smaller hospital, respectively. The statistically correct answer is the smaller hospital because as the sample size grows, the sample proportions become closer to the population proportions. Thus, the choices of 74 percent of the respondents violate the law of large numbers because many are likely to have subscribed to the law of small numbers.

We now provide a working definition of representativeness.

Definition 5.2. *(Representativeness) Suppose that there are m categories of objects, $C_1, \ldots, C_m$. An individual is asked to guess the likelihood of the category to which a given sample, S, of n objects belongs. This is the probability that the sample comes from category C_i, $i = 1, \ldots, m$—that is, $P(C_i \mid S)$, which can, for instance, be found by using Bayes' rule. Denote the statistically correct conditional probability of category C_i, as $n \to \infty$, by P_i^*. Individuals use the representativeness heuristic if, even for small values of n, they assign a subjective probability $\tilde{P}_i$ to the category C_i that has the following property. When the sample S has high superficial or outward similarity to the category C_i, decision-makers assign $\tilde{P}_i > P_i^*$.*

Definition 5.2 is not entirely rigorous. What does *superficial or outward similarity* mean? These terms are very hard to define given that there is potentially an infinite number of ways in which similarity can be defined. We have come across this problem before in the definition of a similarity relation in section 4.2.2. But this should not distract us from the importance of the concept of similarity and that humans and animals use it in some form. For instance, penguin mothers are able to locate their chicks in a colony of tens of thousands when they come back from their feeding grounds, despite all chicks looking almost identical to an outside observer. They use several similarity-based cues in homing in on their chicks, and it is difficult to give a precise mathematical definition of the relevant similarity. Fortunately, in specific circumstances, similarity is quite obvious, as in our next example (and as in the previous example of the admissions tutor).

Example 5.2. *Consider the experiments reported in Camerer (1987, 1990, 1995). Suppose that there are two urns, $i = A, B$, and one is chosen randomly by nature (the two urns are the two categories in terms of definition 5.2). Urn A has 1 red ball and 2 black balls. Urn B has 2 red balls and 1 black ball. Players know that nature chooses urn A with probability 0.6, so $P(A) = 0.6$ and $P(B) = 0.4$. A sequence of three balls ($n = 3$) is drawn with replacement from one of the urns. Suppose that the sample is 1 red and 2 black balls; denote this sample by RBB (the exact order of the colored balls is not important). Experimental subjects do not know which urn the balls are drawn from. What is the posterior probability that the sample came from urn A?*

Using Bayes' law, the statistically correct answer can be computed to be $P(A \mid RBB) = 0.75$. In contrast to the Bayesian estimate, an individual who uses the representativeness heuristic assigns a subjective probability estimate between 0.75 and 1.00 (compare this with definition 5.2). In the extreme case of representativeness, the individual assigns a subjective probability estimate equal to 1.00, based on the similarity of the sample to the composition of urn A.

The formal model of small numbers due to Rabin (2002) examines representativeness in a particular context; see Dhami (2020a, section 1.2.3).

5.2.1 The Gambler's Fallacy

One implication of the law of small numbers is that many people are unable to generate a truly random sequence of events. For instance, when asked to write down a random sequence of coin tosses, subjects alternate too much between heads (H) and tails (T). So, the sequences generated by humans to represent an underlying random process have too much negative autocorrelation. Most people believe that when a fair coin is tossed five consecutive times, the sequence H, H, H, H is very likely to be followed by T, although the a priori chance of H or T in the fifth toss is identical (Bar-Hillel & Wagenaar, 1991; Rapoport & Budescu, 1992, 1997).

Definition 5.3. *If subjects infer negative autocorrelation when asked to make an inference about a hypothetical random process, they are said to commit the gambler's fallacy.*

When subjects were shown a subset of 3 coin tosses from an underlying set of 150 coin tosses, they assigned the subjective conditional probability P that the fourth toss will be H as follows: (1) $P(H|HHH) = 0.30$; (2) $P(H|HTH) = 0.412\%$; (3) $P(H|THT) = 0.588$; (4) $P(H|TTT) = 0.70$ (Rapoport & Budescu, 1997; Rabin & Vayanos, 2010). In each case, the ex ante statistically correct probability of H in the fourth toss is 0.50, but the behavior of subjects is consistent with the gambler's fallacy in definition 5.3. Rabin and Vayanos (2010) propose a formal and more general model that can account for the gambler's fallacy when the outcomes are neither binary nor independently and identically distributed.

There is reduced betting on a winning number in subsequent lottery draws, which is consistent with the gambler's fallacy (Clotfelter & Cook, 1993). Many individuals assign a lower probability that the currently winning number will come up a winner the next time, just as they assign a probability lower than 0.5 of heads in a random coin toss if there have already been three successive heads (e.g., $P(H|HHH) = 0.30$ in the evidence reported above). Much evidence for the gambler's fallacy has come from the study of betting behavior—for example, horse races (Metzger, 1984), dog races (Terrell & Farmer, 1996; Terrell, 1998), and gambling in casinos (Croson & Sundali, 2005). There is now a large literature on applications of the gambler's fallacy to finance. For instance, there is a tendency to sell winning stocks and hold on to loss-making stocks for too long (*disposition effect*). The idea is that people think that a stock that has risen in the past is now due for a fall and vice-versa, which is consistent with the gambler's fallacy (Dhami, 2020a, section 1.2.2).

5.2.2 The Hot Hand Fallacy

The hot hand fallacy is the statistical opposite of the gambler's fallacy; it produces positive autocorrelation in random processes.

Definition 5.4. *If subjects infer positive autocorrelation when asked to make an inference about a hypothetical random process, they are said to engage in the hot hand fallacy.*

The *hot hand fallacy* has been documented in many contexts. In a basketball game, a player might be particularly successful in a sequence of successive attempts to shoot the ball in the basket. Such success might, however, arise purely from luck. Data from betting behavior indicate that bettors assign a high probability that such a player will be successful in making the next shot too (Camerer, 1989). In contrast, the underlying data, at least in the early studies, were found not to reveal a hot hand effect; thus, players shoot at a mean level of skill that depends on their ability, and there are random departures from the mean level caused by variation in luck. Several studies have shown that the observed sequence of successful basketball shots is statistically a random sequence (Gilovich et al., 1985; Tversky & Gilovich, 1989a, 1989b).

Recent research has raised the possibility of actual streaks, or the hot hand phenomenon, in basketball and baseball (Green & Zwiebel, 2013; Bocskocsky et al., 2014; Miller & Sanjurjo 2018). In other words, these are departures from the mean ability level of a player that are systematic and not based on random luck. However, a statistical demonstration of the hot hand phenomenon, a nontrivial task involving advanced statistics, does not imply that individuals, both players and bettors, are able to see through the pattern of shots and discover the hot hand effect. For instance, when testing for a mixed strategy Nash equilibrium, it has been discovered, statistically, that there is serial correlation in tennis serves and in penalty kicks in football. Yet, opponents do not discover such serial correlation in actions (Dhami, 2020d, section 1.3.4).

Some of the clearest and most persuasive evidence for the hot hand phenomenon comes from a novel field experiment by Guryan and Kearney (2008). They find that sales at lotto stores that have sold a winning ticket soar in the immediate weeks following the lotto win. Yet, the likelihood that this store sells a winning ticket now or in the future has not changed. Figure 5.1 shows a plot of the log sales at lotto stores for 81 weeks. This includes the date, t, at which the winning ticket from a lottery store was sold, and the 40 previous and the 40 subsequent weeks. There is an immediate upward jump in sales following the sale of the winning ticket, and this effect lasts for 40 weeks following the win. The authors checked for several confounding factors, such as that a lottery win in a zip code may give rise to greater salience to playing the lottery; there is some spillover effect of increased sales at other stores within the same zip code, but the increase in sales in the winning store is significantly higher. This store-specific effect indicates the hot hand fallacy. Furthermore, the higher is the size of the win, the higher is the store-specific effect on sales.

5.3 Anchoring

It is probably best to begin with the following classic example of anchoring.

Example 5.3. *Tversky and Kahneman (1974) rigged a wheel of fortune with the numbers 1–100 to come to a stop at either of the two*

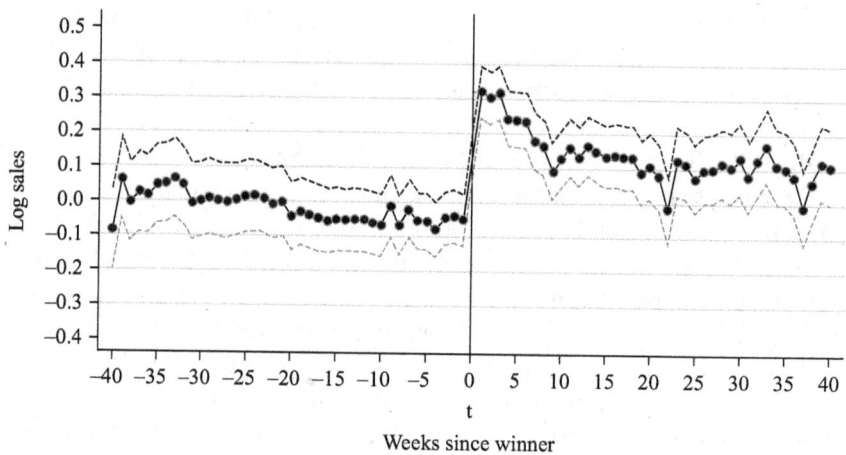

Figure 5.1
Retail level data for Lotto Texas wins.
Source: Guryan & Kearney (2008).

numbers: 10 or 65. *Subjects were asked to write down the number that the wheel stopped at. They were then asked the following two questions.*

1. *Comparative judgment question: Is the percentage of African nations among UN members larger or smaller than the number you just wrote?*
2. *Absolute judgment question: What is your best guess of the percentage of African nations among UN members?*

The answers to the second question were found to be anchored too closely on the irrelevant number that came up on the wheel of fortune: those who observed the number 10 answered 25 percent, and those who observed the number 65 answered 45 percent. This suggests anchoring on irrelevant information because the outcomes on the wheel of fortune are unrelated to the question asked.

In order to formalize anchoring in general, suppose that a problem, call it problem A, has a unique solution x^* (e.g., x^* is the actual percentage of African countries that are members of the UN in 1974). Consider the following two stages that are part of problem A.

Stage 1: The decision-maker is provided with some integer x_1 (call this an *anchor*), where $x_1 \neq x^*$. There is no presumption that x_1 has any relevance for the correct answer, x^*.

Stage 2: The decision-maker is asked two questions:

Q1 (Comparative judgment question): Is $x^* \gtreqless x_1$? This question serves to prime the individual and make the number x_1 more salient.

Q2 (Absolute judgment question): What is x^*?

Definition 5.5. *Consider the general problem A, and suppose that two different numbers/anchors x_1 and x_2 are given in stage 1 to two different individuals/groups, who are otherwise identical. The two different individuals/groups come up with respective answers, say, y_1 and y_2, to the absolute judgment question. Anchoring requires that $y_1 \neq x^*$, $y_2 \neq x^*$. An extreme form of anchoring exists if $y_1 = x_1$ and $y_2 = x_2$. A less extreme form of anchoring exists if $|y_i - x_i| < |y_i - x^*|$, $i = 1, 2$—that is, the answers are closer to the anchor than to the correct solution of problem A.*

Note that nothing in problem A requires the anchor to have any relevance for the optimal solution, x^*. The whole idea of anchoring is that completely irrelevant and uninformative anchors may influence the choices made by people.

Example 5.4. *The subjects in the experiments of Englich and Mussweiler (2001) were experienced trial judges with an average experience of 15 years. Subjects were asked to consider the case of a fictitious shoplifter accused of stealing from a supermarket for the 12th time. They were also supplied with detailed case material, including opinions from a psycho-legal expert and testimonies by the defendant and a witness. Opinions sought from other experienced and independent legal professionals indicated that the case material was complete and realistic; these professionals called for a mean sentence of 5.62 months with a standard deviation of 2.57.*

Subjects in the experiment were asked to determine an appropriate sentence. In two different treatments, the case material showed that the prosecutor had asked for a sentence of, respectively, 9 months (high anchor) and 3 months (low anchor). Subjects in the high anchor treatment chose a sentence of 8 months, and those in the low anchor treatment chose a sentence of 5 months. Experience did not mitigate the anchoring effect.

The anchoring phenomenon is remarkably robust across a wide range of domains, contexts, and frames. These include estimates of price, the probability of a nuclear war, the evaluation of lotteries and gambles, issues of legal judgment, and first offers in price negotiation. Anchoring also has the potential to explain a range of other phenomena. These include the hindsight bias, preference reversals, and nonlinear probability weighting.[3]

5.4 Hindsight Bias

Suppose that one wishes to make a *postdictive judgment*. This is a recall of a *predictive judgment* that one made in the past. The BRA assumes that postdictive judgments are perfect in the sense that the predictions made in the past are perfectly recalled (this follows from the assumption of *perfect recall*). However, the evidence suggests that people exhibit *hindsight bias*, relative to the perfect postdictive judgment. In common parlance, one appears "wiser in hindsight" (Fischhoff, 1975). Hindsight bias might appear to be an inexact phenomenon that lacks a definition—that is, simply a label in the sense alleged by the FFP. However, its use in behavioral economics is perfectly rigorous, as we see next.

Suppose that at time t an individual needs to compute the expected value of some random variable X that materializes at a future time period $t+j$, $j > 0$ (e.g., you are asked in December 2019 to guess the outcome of the September 2020 US presidential election). Let the information set I_t capture all possible information at time t that is required by the relevant economic theory for predicting the value of X. For instance, I_t might include past values of all possible relevant variables or even the construction of hypothetical scenarios that might influence X. Then, the BRA assumes that individuals can perfectly compute $E[X \mid I_t]$, where E is the mathematical expectation operator.

The conditional time t prediction, $E[X \mid I_t]$, gives the *predictive judgment*. The individual observes the time $t+j$ realization of X, denoted by x (e.g., the actual outcome of the September 2020 US presidential election), and is asked at the end of time $t+j$ to recall the time t prediction; this is the *postdictive judgment*. Statistically, this is given by $E[E[X \mid I_t] \mid I_{t+j}]$, where I_{t+j} is the date $t+j$ information set, and $I_t \subseteq I_{t+j}$ (because the information set can only get larger over time). In the BRA, the assumption of perfect recall guarantees equality of the predictive and the postdictive judgments,

$$E[X \mid I_t] = E\left[E[X \mid I_t] \mid I_{t+j}\right]. \tag{5.1}$$

However, evidence to the contrary is typically found. Consider the following definition and example of hindsight bias, which are perfectly rigorous.

Definition 5.6. *An individual is said to suffer from hindsight bias, or creeping determinism, if the following conditions hold:*

1. *The predictive and postdictive judgments differ—that is,*

$$E[X|I_t] \neq E\left[E[X|I_t]|I_{t+j}\right], and$$

2. *the postdictive judgment is biased in favor of the actual realization of the random variable X.*

Definition 5.6 can then be operationalized in a variety of ways, as shown next.

Example 5.5. *Motivated by a suggestion by Camerer et al. (1989) and Biais and Weber (2009), formalize the following simple rule.*

$$E\left[E[X|I_t]|I_{t+j}\right] = \alpha x + (1-\alpha)E[X|I_t]; \alpha \in [0,1] \qquad (5.2)$$

The individual has no hindsight bias if $\alpha = 0$ (this corresponds to the BRA, as in (5.1)). The most extreme form of hindsight bias arises if $\alpha = 1$, in which case one's postdictive judgment equals the actual outcome and may be unrelated to one's initial prediction. This is an extreme form of self-delusion in which the individual asserts, "I fully knew it all along."

Hindsight bias must be distinguished from learning. In learning, one learns to make better predictions of future events. However, under hindsight bias, the relevant issue is *remembered past predictions*—that is, postdictive judgments. There could be degrees of hindsight bias that are individual-specific, as captured by different values of α. Using individual-specific data, regression analysis, or other statistical techniques can help uncover the underlying preference parameter, α. Note that hindsight bias is not a heuristic. The relevant heuristic is given by (5.2), and the hindsight bias arises whenever $\alpha > 0$.

In an important result, Biais and Weber (2009) showed that financial market participants who were subject to hindsight bias would underestimate stock market volatility. We can demonstrate their idea through a simple example, although this result can be demonstrated more formally.

Suppose that risk averse investors are interested in investing in an asset, say, a stock. The underlying return on the asset has an unknown variance that is either high, σ_H^2, or low, σ_L^2. Obviously, the higher the variance, or the risk, the lower the amount that investors will wish to invest in the asset. They try to infer the unknown variance by using their observations of actual returns.

Suppose that an investor invests in the asset at time t and believes that the asset will give a return y when it matures at time $t+j$. The actual random variable that denotes the random return on the asset is X. At time $t+j$, the actual return is x, which is the realization of the random variable X. The prediction error in the investor's actual estimate of the return is $x - y$, which can be positive, negative, or zero. However, in order to calculate the term $x - y$ at time $t+j$, investors have to recall their initial estimate y that was made at time t. Denote the recalled estimate by $\hat{y}$. Thus, the perception of the investors about their prediction error is $x - \hat{y}$ (but the actual prediction error is $x - y$).

The more hindsight biased are the investors, the closer is their recalled estimate, $\hat{y}$, to the actual value x when they make their postdictive judgment. In the limiting case of perfect hindsight biasedness (corresponding to $\alpha = 1$ in example 5.5), investors believe that $\hat{y} = x$ and persuade themselves that they have made zero prediction error. But if they can predict returns correctly, then they infer that the asset return has very little variability. Thus, they err on the side of estimating the variance of stock returns to be low, σ_L^2. Whenever they invest again in this asset, they invest far too much relative to the predictions of the BRA because they underestimate the risk from holding the asset. Biais and Weber (2009) then estimate the hindsight bias of traders in a financial firm that has offices in London and Frankfurt. They find that more hindsight biased employees of this firm underestimate volatility of assets, choose to invest a higher amount in them, just as the theory predicts, and make lower profits.

Here is a final example on hindsight bias.

Example 5.6. *(Kamin & Rachlinski, 1995) A municipality may undertake flood precautions that cost $\$10^5$, but if the floods occur, they cause damages worth $\$10^7$. The efficacy of flood precautions is ex ante uncertain, but subjects were provided with meteorological and anecdotal data. One group of subjects, group A, was asked to predict the probability of a flood (this is the predictive judgment). Subjects in this group were told that if they found the probability of floods to be greater than 10 percent,* based on the meteorological and anecdotal data, then they should decide to take the precaution.

Another group of subjects, group B, was provided with the same meteorological and anecdotal data and asked to make a postdictive judgment. Group B was informed that the precautions had not been taken by the municipality and a flood had occurred. They were instructed that if their postdictive judgment was that the probability of a flood was greater than 10 percent, based on the same data provided to group A, then they should find the municipality guilty. In group A, 24 percent of the subjects thought that the precautions were merited, while 57 percent in group B found the municipality guilty. Clearly, group B exhibits hindsight bias relative to the predictions of group A.

5.5 The Availability Heuristic

Suppose that at time t, an individual needs to compute the expected value of some random variable X, the realization of which occurs at a future time period $t+j$, $j > 0$. The computation of $E[X \mid I_t]$ could be extremely cognitively challenging. For instance, individuals might not have immediate access to all possible relevant past information that is required to form the estimate. Their memory might be limited, selective, or strategic, and their recall might be subjective. Or, it might be the case that their attention is limited and some information in I_t may be relatively more salient or vivid (e.g., more vivid memories are more easily recalled). For all these reasons, in predicting X, individuals might use only a subset of the information $I'_t \subseteq I_t$ and potentially ignore the rest. By contrast, individuals in the BRA use all available information.

Definition 5.7. *Individuals are said to use the availability heuristic if they use the information set $I'_t \subseteq I_t$ in determining the expected value of X (where I'_t, I_t are defined above). In particular, the information included in I'_t is largely determined by an individual's personal experiences, the experiences of others in the individual's social network, the ease of recalling information, and the vividness/salience of information.*

Remark 5.1. *We often do not observe the information sets used by people, but we may use data on observables to infer whether the availability heuristic is being used. For instance, once we know the prediction of the relevant economic theory, $E[X \mid I_t]$, we can use the actual prediction $E[X \mid I'_t]$ and indirectly infer that the individual uses the* *availability heuristic. One method is to prime subjects by altering the vividness/salience of events/memories leading presumably to the use of different information sets, $I_t^1, I_t^2, I_t^3, \ldots$. One can then study observed predictions in each case, $E[X|I_t^1], E[X|I_t^2], \ldots$. If the responses are different, then the availability heuristic is likely to be in operation. In the BRA, varying vividness/salience does not make events more or less likely to be recalled, so the responses are predicted to be unchanged.*

Evidence for the availability heuristic comes from many sources. The typical experiments show that direct experience of a particular event increases the probability that one assigns to related events. Following on from the work of Lichtenstein et al. (1978), Pachur et al. (2012) show that there is a significant positive correlation between one's estimate of the annual mortality rate from various forms of cancer and the availability of information on cases of cancer from one's social network. Kuran and Sunstein (1999) introduce the idea of *availability cascades*, where the initial availability of some vivid/salient news leads to self-fulfilling bouts of emotional reaction followed by increased vividness/salience of the news and so on. Eventually, this may lead to the adoption of policies that might not initially have been justifiable in cost-benefit terms.

Example 5.7. *(Tversky & Kahneman, 1973) Subjects were asked to guess the probability that a randomly picked three-letter word from the dictionary either begins with the consonants r, k (event A) or ends with the consonants r, k (event B). Words beginning with the letters r or k are much easier to retrieve from one's memory, as compared to those that end with r or k. Hence, the vast majority of subjects reported that event A was more probable, but the correct answer is event B.*

Several studies show that events and stories highlighted in the media recently are more vivid and easier to recall from one's memory, with the result that subjects assign a greater probability to them (Lichtenstein et al., 1978; Eisenman, 1993). Kahneman (2011, p. 138) puts this in perspective: "The world in our heads is not a precise replica of reality."

5.6 The Conjunction Fallacy

The conjunction fallacy arises when people make mistakes about the set inclusion relation.

Definition 5.8. *(Conjunction fallacy) Given any two sets A, B, if $B \subseteq A$, then the conjunction fallacy arises if a decision-maker assigns a higher probability to the set B, $P(B) > P(A)$.*

The original experiments to demonstrate the conjunction fallacy were conducted by Tversky and Kahneman (1983) using the well-known *Linda problem*. Hertwig and Gigerenzer (1999) argued that the Linda problem is exhibited by only 15 percent of their subjects when the problem is presented in a *frequency format* as compared to a *probability format*. In a frequency format, one gives information of the form "3 out of 100 people have the condition C," while the same information in a probability format is that "3 percent of the people have condition C." More generally, a prominent criticism of the HBP has been that presenting information in a frequency format relative to a probability format makes decision-making more compliant with the prescriptions of classical statistics (see section 5.11.5 for a critical analysis).

For this reason, we present the Linda problem in its lesser-known frequency format version, due to Kahneman and Tversky (1996). They used a between-subjects design and gave the Linda problem to three groups of subjects (groups 1, 2, 3). Subjects in the experiments read the following description.

> Linda is in her early thirties. She is single, outspoken, and very bright. As a student she majored in philosophy and was deeply concerned with issues of discrimination and social justice. Suppose there are 1000 women who fit this description. How many of them are
>
> (a) high school teachers? [groups 1, 2, 3]
> (b) bank tellers? [groups 1, 2]
> (c) bank tellers and active feminists? [groups 1, 3]

After each choice we provide in square brackets which groups were given the corresponding choice. The set of people who are bank tellers and active feminists is smaller than the set of bank tellers alone (set inclusion principle). For group 1, the median response for choice (c) was statistically larger than the median response for choice (b), confirming the conjunction fallacy (see definition 5.8). There was a similar finding for the median choices of groups 1 and 3 when options (a) and (c) were compared.

In the more famous demonstration of the Linda problem, Tversky and Kahneman (1983) used Stanford students who were well trained in decision sciences and gave the following description.

Linda is 31 years old, single, outspoken, and very bright. She majored in philosophy. As a student, she was deeply concerned with issues of discrimination and social justice, and also participated in antinuclear demonstrations. Which of the following statements is most likely?

1. Linda is a bank teller (B).
2. Linda is active in the feminist movement (F).
3. Linda is a bank teller and is active in the feminist movement (BF).

Between 85 and 90 percent of the respondents rated the event BF as more likely relative to the separate events B and F. Thus, subjects exhibit the conjunction fallacy.

Subsequent evidence in Tentori et al. (2004) also supports the view that presenting information in natural frequencies does not eliminate the conjunction fallacy. Charness et al. (2010) find that incentives and group decision-making, as compared to individual decision-making, reduce the conjunction fallacy. However, Bonini et al. (2004) and Stolarz-Fantino et al. (2003) find that monetary incentives do not reduce the conjunction fallacy.

Let us consider the Bonini et al. (2004) study. In their experiments, subjects had to allocate €7 among the following three possible options. To facilitate comparison with the Linda problem, we use the same acronyms, B and F, for the two events.

1. Option B.
2. Option $B \wedge F$ (where $\wedge$ is the logical operator "and").
3. Option $B \wedge (\sim F)$, where $\sim F$ is the option "not F."

The third option controls for the objection that subjects may actually be interpreting option 1 as option 3—that is, the option B as $B \wedge (\sim F)$. It is a dominant action to bet on option B, because it is the largest of the following three sets: B, $B \wedge F$, and $B \wedge (\sim F)$. So, if subjects did not engage in the conjunction fallacy, we should observe that all subjects bet €7 on option B. Across all blocks of experiments, the average amount allocated to the three options was, respectively, €1.99, €3.15, and €1.86. The difference between the allocations to options 1 and 2 is statistically significant. The average percentage of subjects that engaged in the conjunction fallacy was 85.32, which is close to the figure of 85 percent reported in Tversky and Kahneman (1983).

5.7 Regression to the Mean

The *regression to the mean* phenomenon was first pointed out by Francis Galton (a half cousin of Charles Darwin) in 1886. He found that the height of adult children is closer to the average height, as compared to the average height of the parents. So taller-(resp. shorter)-than-average parents have children whose average height is smaller (resp. taller) than their average height.

Several fallacies arise from ignoring regression to the mean a phenomenon that is precisely defined in classical statistics. Most people ignore regression to the mean and hence make inferences that are statistically incorrect—that is, they exhibit a bias relative to the predictions of the BRA. One of our favorite examples of this bias is from Kahneman (2011, chapter 17). Israeli Air Force instructors found that praising pilots for executing complicated maneuvers reduced subsequent performance, but criticism for bad performance improved subsequent performance. They inferred that praise ought to be withheld but criticism was healthy (withhold the carrot but do not spare the stick). However, random luck played a huge part in the success of these complicated maneuvers, and regression to the mean implied that, on average, pilots who performed well (resp. not so well) this time were likely to do less well (resp. much better) next time. Praise or criticism probably plays little role in how the maneuvers are executed. The mistaken inference arose from ignoring regression to the mean.

In American professional sport, rookies who perform exceptionally well are typically not able to replicate their success in the following years. This is known as a *sophomore slump* and is consistent with the regression to the mean. In the Premier League in English football, a similar phrase, *second season syndrome*, highlights a slump in second-season performance after a football team has done well in the previous season. Conversely, teams that might not have done too well last season are often likely, on average, to do better this season. However, these phenomena need careful empirical testing to eliminate potentially confounding factors—for example, opposition coaches might study video of players who did well last season to counter them better this season through improved strategies.

Consider an investment firm where, unknown to its employees (i.e., the investors), the outcomes are governed, in addition to skill, by a fair bit of luck. Then, investors who are luckier in one time period will find that they are less successful, on average, in the next time period. Similarly, investors who are not so lucky now will be, on average, more successful in the future. In other words, there will be a weak, or no, temporal correlation in the returns earned by the investors. However, most investors are unlikely to accept this and ascribe their earnings to their skill; admitting otherwise would call into question the high-powered incentives within investment firms for doing well (Kahneman, 2011).

5.8 Necessary and Sufficient Conditions

An understanding of necessary and sufficient conditions is central to the BRA. After all, individuals who obey the BRA do not violate the laws of logic. However, people cannot always differentiate correctly between necessary and sufficient conditions. The classic experiment is due to Wason (1968). Let P and Q be two statements (e.g., think of the statement P as "It is a horse" and the statement Q as "It has a tail"). If $P \Rightarrow Q$ (i.e., if P implies Q), then a confusion between necessary and sufficient conditions arises if one concludes $Q \Rightarrow P$ or violates the negation $\sim Q \Rightarrow \sim P$ (where $\sim$ denotes the negation of a statement).

Indeed, professional economists, who are steeped in such logic, may also sometimes make similar errors. From the observation that most investors, including mutual and pension fund managers, find it very hard to beat the stock market (Malkiel, 1990), it is sometimes concluded that financial markets must be efficient (M. Rubinstein, 2001). However, Barberis and Thaler (2003) point out that this is a confusion between necessary and sufficient conditions. Market efficiency in finance (sometimes termed as the *efficient markets hypothesis*) implies that

prices equal fundamental values $\Rightarrow$ no arbitrage opportunities.

However, the absence of arbitrage opportunities is only a necessary, but not a sufficient, condition for stock prices to equal fundamental values. Hence,

no arbitrage opportunities $\not\Rightarrow$ prices equal fundamental values,

where the symbol $\not\Rightarrow$ is read as "does not imply." Thus, the difficulty in beating the stock market cannot be taken as evidence that prices equal fundamental values or that financial markets are efficient.

5.9 Confirmation Bias

A central feature in the BRA is a specification of how information is updated over time. The BRA requires individuals to use Bayes' law for this purpose. However, empirical evidence shows that people make systematic and significant departures from Bayes' law (see section 2.15.2). In particular, people, unless they intensely train to do otherwise, are subject to a *confirmation bias*—that is, their posterior beliefs are based on a biased interpretation of the existing evidence and are too close to their prior beliefs relative to the prediction of Bayesian updating. The philosopher and mathematician Bertrand Russell recognized this in a well-cited quotation from his 1918 book, *Proposed Roads to Freedom:* "If a man is offered a fact which goes against his instincts, he will scrutinize it closely, and unless the evidence is overwhelming, he will refuse to believe it. If, on the other hand, he is offered something which affords a reason for acting in accordance to his instincts, he will accept it even on the slightest evidence."

One of the most succinct descriptions of the confirmation bias has been given by Lord et al. (1979, p. 2099), which deserves to be read in full:

> Thus, there is considerable evidence that people tend to interpret subsequent evidence so as to maintain their initial beliefs. The biased assimilation processes underlying this effect may include a propensity to remember the strengths of confirming evidence but the weaknesses of disconfirming evidence, to judge confirming evidence as relevant and reliable but disconfirming evidence as irrelevant and unreliable, and to accept confirming evidence at face value while scrutinizing disconfirming evidence hypercritically. With confirming evidence, we suspect that both lay and professional scientists rapidly reduce the complexity of the information and remember only a few well-chosen supportive impressions. With disconfirming evidence, they continue to reflect upon any information that suggests less damaging "alternative interpretations." Indeed, they may even come to regard the ambiguities and conceptual flaws in the data opposing their hypotheses as somehow suggestive of the fundamental correctness of those hypotheses. Thus, completely inconsistent or even random data—when "processed" in a suitably biased fashion—can maintain or even reinforce one's preconceptions.

Confirmation bias is supported by the evidence (Dhami, 2020a, section 1.9.1). It has been formalized and defined in the model of Rabin and Schrag (1999). In this model, the decision-maker receives signals about the true state of the world. Signals are correctly perceived if they accord with one's prior beliefs. However, if they do not accord with the prior beliefs, then the individual misinterprets the signal with some probability; the degree of misrepresentation then captures the departure from standard Bayesian updating. This also clarifies the difference of this heuristic from simple hindsight bias. One of the results of this model is that it leads to overconfidence in one's predictive abilities because, ex post, the individual finds that the incorrectly computed posterior beliefs are closer to the prior beliefs, relative to Bayesian updating.

Indeed, if individuals update beliefs in this manner on a repeated basis and form overconfident predictions without any corrective mechanism, they may form long-lasting stereotypes and indulge in racial prejudices. Confirmation bias also explains why groups of people exposed to identical public information but holding incompatible beliefs feel vindicated by the same information. This occurs through various mechanisms that are highlighted in the quotation from Lord et al. For instance, in the 2020 US presidential election, given identical public information, some continued to maintain their initial beliefs that the election was rigged, but others stayed convinced that the election, was in fact, free and fair. For a similar reason, well-publicized shooting incidents are often used by people on both sides of the spectrum, those who support gun laws and those who oppose them, to stress the validity of their respective initial positions.

5.10 The Affect Heuristic

The BRA ignores the role of emotions in decision-making and assumes that humans make cold, calculated decisions, although as we argue in chapter 2, it is capable of being extended in this direction. There is now a burgeoning literature in behavioral economics that gives prominence to the salient role of emotions in many decisions (Dhami, 2019a, 2019d, 2020c). The *affect heuristic* highlights the fact that many events and experiences have emotional tags, positive or negative, associated with them, which also influence choices.

Zajonc (1980, p. 155) offers the following example that illustrates the affect heuristic: "We buy the cars we 'like,' choose the jobs and houses that we find 'attractive,' and then justify those choices by various reasons that might appear convincing to others who never fail to ask us, 'Why this car?' or 'Why this house?'... We need not convince ourselves. We know what we like." Thus, it is quite likely that we do not just see a car; we see a *sleek car*, a *cool car*, and an *ugly* car depending on the affect of the car on us. Slovic et al. (2002, p. 398) write: "We sometimes delude ourselves that we proceed in a rational manner and weight all the pros and cons of the various alternatives. But this is probably seldom the actual case. Quite often 'I decided in favor of X' is no more than 'I liked X.' ... We buy the cars we 'like,' choose the jobs and houses we find 'attractive,' and then justify these choices by various reasons." Kahneman (2011) notes that the affect heuristic substitutes the answer to a hard question (What do I think about it?) with the answer to an easier question (How do I feel about it?). This conserves cognitive resources, particularly in the case of complex and difficult problems that must be decided within a time constraint.

Unlike the other heuristics that we have discussed, the affect heuristic is not straightforward to formalize in a precise mathematical sense, although its implications are often clear in many circumstances. However, there has been a great deal of work in psychology and behavioral economics on empirical measures of emotions (Dhami, 2019a, 2020c). In particular, the emotion of guilt, surprise-seeking, inferring intentions of others, and reciprocal feelings all play a significant role in determining economic decisions. These emotions can be modeled formally using psychological game theory (Battigalli & Dufwenberg, 2020; Dhami, 2019a, sections 2.5, 3.6). We have already seen examples of the roles of guilt and shame in influencing choices in microfinance contracts in (section 3.2.2 in chapter 2).

In contrast, there has been less progress in building precise procedural models of heuristics that incorporate emotions, and this is likely to remain a challenging task.

5.11 Objections to the HBP

In this section, we consider the criticisms of the HBP, mainly leveled by the FFP. Many of these criticisms are discussed in a debate between Kahneman and Tversky (1996) and Gigerenzer (1996a). Although the original exchange remains worth reading, the literature has progressed significantly over the years. One of our aims is to offer an up-to-date evaluation of this debate, with the benefit of recent research findings.

5.11.1 Some Preliminaries
Gigerenzer and Brighton (2009) describe the HBP as follows.

> By the end of the 20th century, the use of heuristics became associated with shoddy mental software, generating three widespread misconceptions.
>
> S1 *Heuristics are always second-best.*
> S2 *We use heuristics only because of our cognitive limitations.*
> S3 *More information, more computation, and more time would always be better.*

To evaluate these statements, consider a simple optimization problem in the BRA. A decision-maker wishes to find the maximum value of an objective function $f(x, \theta)$, where x is some choice variable that is under the control of the decision-maker and θ is a parameter. The extension to many choice variables and to many parameters is straightforward, but we omit it. For instance, f could be a consumer's utility function, x could be a consumption choice, and θ could be a taste parameter; or f could be a firm's profit function, x could be an output/quality choice, and θ could be the corporate tax rate.

Suppose that the function f is strictly concave and x is chosen from the real valued interval of numbers $[0, \bar{x}]$. Readers unfamiliar with these terms can imagine that the function f is shaped like a hill with a single peak. In this case, we can use the theorem of maximum in mathematics to show that there is a unique maximum solution x^* (the top of the single peak on the hill) such that

$$f(x^*, \theta) > f(\hat{x}; \theta) \text{ for all } \hat{x} \in [0, \bar{x}] \text{ and } \hat{x} \neq x^*. \tag{5.3}$$

This sort of exercise is routine in the BRA.

For an individual who can use mathematical optimization and solve for the solution x^* (and people in the BRA can do so by assumption), then S1, S2, and S3 above are not misconceptions, as we show next.

1. From (5.3), heuristics are always second best because they can never result in a value of the objective function that is greater than $f(x^*, \theta)$. In terms of our analogy, we can get no higher than the peak of the hill. At best, if a heuristics-based solution also results in the choice x^*, then heuristics are as good as the optimization-based solution.

2. From (5.3), $f(x^*, \theta) > f(\hat{x}, \theta)$, for any $\hat{x} \neq x^*$. Hence, starting from $\hat{x}$ one can always improve on the value of objective function. In our analogy, starting from any point on the hill, which is not at the peak of the hill, we can increase our elevation by walking toward the peak. If an individual continues to choose $\hat{x}$, then cognitive, computational, or attentional limitations are possible contributing factors that prevent reaching the top of the hill.

3. Suppose that $\hat{x} \in [0, \bar{x}]$ and that $\hat{x} \neq x^*$ was chosen using a heuristics-based choice by an individual who does not have any cognitive, computational, or attentional limitations but has less information and time relative to an individual who uses an optimization-based approach. In this case, more information and time might produce an even better heuristics-based solution $\tilde{x}$ such that $f(\hat{x}, \theta) < f(\tilde{x}, \theta) < f(x^*, \theta)$. Thus, it is the case that more information and more time would always be better. In terms of our hill analogy, suppose that we were blindfolded, placed somewhere on the hill, not allowed to walk, and not told our location on the hill except that it is not the peak. In this case, by removing the blindfold (corresponding to being provided with additional information), we can improve our elevation by walking toward the peak.

Indeed, we appear here to be in the world of an *accuracy-effort trade-off* (Gigerenzer & Brighton, 2011). It is never the case that "less information/attention/computation/time is more." Gigerenzer and Brighton (2011, p. 5) write: "Even when information and computation are entirely free, there is typically a point where less is more." In the example described above, this is never the case.

Under what conditions might S1, S2, and S3 be applicable? They might be true, for example, if the underlying problem is misspecified—for example, incorrect objective function, f (or incorrect constraints in a more general problem). In the world described in the example, decision-makers know the correct objective function f; indeed, this is important in models of rational expectations that underpin all of modern macroeconomics. In richer situations than those depicted above, decision-makers may have several candidate objective functions, say, $f_1, f_2, f_3, \ldots$, in mind, but under the BRA decision-makers, they are assumed to converge toward the correct one through some underlying process of learning. However, empirical evidence shows that there is no guarantee that such a convergence will take place (Dhami, 2020b), and there are theoretical results that show the impossibility of learning the correct objective function on theoretical grounds (Dhami, 2020b, section 2.9).

S1, S2, and S3 are likely to be tremendously important, and the insights of Gigerenzer and Brighton (2011) very useful, when we have true uncertainty or the problem of unknown unknowns, which falls outside the remit of our example here, but we consider this problem in chapter 6. Indeed, it is in this domain that the FFP approach is of great interest and S1, S2, and S3 become important insights. By contrast, the HBP restricts itself mainly, but not exclusively, to variants of the example above, where S1, S2, and S3 do not apply. Thus, there is a fundamental misunderstanding in much of the literature as to the scope and the domain of applicability of the HBP and the FFP. This has led many people to erroneously pit one framework against the other, as if they addressed an identical problem; indeed the *great rationality debate* that we touch on later makes this error repeatedly.

5.11.2 Ecological Rationality

Why might some heuristics that use less information do better than more complex strategies? The FFP view is that the heuristics are better adapted to the environment as captured in the view that "the rationality of heuristics is ecological, not rational." Herbert Simon famously characterized bounded rationality as the two blades of a scissors. One of the blades is the mind, and the second is the environment. This implies that cognitive strategies cannot be looked at independently of their environment. The other possibility is that the environment really is one of true uncertainty.

In this case, the BRA has no bite and the HBP does not directly discuss this case, although we believe that the HBP approach identifies many heuristics that could also be enormously useful under true uncertainty.

How we do operationalize ecological rationality? After all, no precise definition is given. In behavioral economics, this problem is typically addressed by stressing that human decisions (including heuristics) are context, culture, history, time, and frame dependent (Dhami, 2016; Gintis, 2017). By way of analogy, social norms are often adapted to the social context in which they are situated. Insofar as they are fast and frugal, there is a sense in which their use by individuals is similar to heuristics.

An alternative formalization of this view, *the less is more effect*, is considered in section 6.6. Gigerenzer and Brighton (2009) also require heuristics to take account of the *less is more effect* or the *bias-variance dilemma* in satisfying the requirement of ecological rationality. We do not believe this to be an essential requirement for ecological rationality for the reasons that we explain in chapter 6. If we think of the environment as the context and the frame of a problem, then by ecological rationality, we refer to the context and frame dependence of preferences and beliefs. In the sense that we define ecological validity, we believe that the HBP satisfies it.

Another issue of ecological rationality that arises is the criticism that lab experiments might have low external validity (Levitt & List, 2007). This issue has already been thoroughly addressed in several recent publications that suggest that, to the contrary, a great deal of lab evidence has a high degree of external validity (Camerer, 2015; see section 3 of the introductory chapter in Dhami, 2016). Further support for the ecological rationality of heuristics in the HBP comes from the behavior of experts (see section 5.12).

5.11.3 One-Event Probabilities, Context, and Errors

Some of the arguments against the HBP can be dealt with relatively easily.

1. The frequentist approach in statistics requires a large number of repetitions. Hence, experimental evidence involving probabilities based on *singular events* may be suspect (Gigerenzer, 1991). For instance, in the famous Linda problem, whether Linda is a bank teller or a feminist is a singular event. In this case Gigerenzer (1991, 1993) argues that one can speak only about subjective probabilities in a Bayesian sense. Since it is possible to assign any subjective probabilities for a one-off event,

so the argument goes, the experimental results are uninformative about the violation of individual rationality. Kahneman and Tversky (1996) note that this view of probability is not universally held and that this issue applies to only 2 out of the 12 biases that they highlight. Furthermore, the responses show systematic biases, relative to the BRA, in one direction, which weakens the case for arbitrary subjective probabilities.

2. The HBP has been criticized for ignoring the context, content, and framing effects in their demonstration of biases (Gigerenzer et al., 1988; Gigerenzer, 1993). In other words, it is claimed that the HBP ignores ecological rationality. This claim is mistaken. Kahneman and Tversky (1996, p. 583) write: "The assumption that heuristics are independent of content, task and representation is alien to our position, as is the idea that different representations of a problem will be approached in the same way." Several examples can be given. The HBP showed that the conjunction fallacy is reduced in a frequency format (see section 5.6). The HBP also drew on the distinction between causal and noncausal base rates, which explains when the base rate is or is not ignored (Tversky & Kahneman, 1980).[4] The frame dependence of preferences is already a major finding in the HBP (Dhami, 2019a, 2020a).

3. The HBP has been criticized on the grounds that subjects may simply be making errors, could be inattentive, or may be suffering from temporary lapses of judgment; see Stanovich and West (2000) for a survey. Some of the more extreme suggestions that have been made to cast doubt on the HBP include the subjects' temporary insanity or difficult childhoods and entrapment by the experimenter (Kahneman, 1981, p. 340). The pattern of biases discovered by the HBP does not describe random mistakes but systematic mistakes; hence, these objections cannot be taken seriously. Furthermore, there is typically a great deal of heterogeneity among subjects who exhibit biases, which contradicts conformity with a single rational response.

5.11.4 "We Cannot Be That Dumb" Critique

Gilovich et al. (2002) outline the "we cannot be that dumb critique," which argues that stellar human achievements (e.g., discovering the structure of DNA and making space flights), are not consistent with the idea that people might be using simple judgment heuristics.

This appears to be a misunderstanding about the nature/process of scientific discoveries and the methodology of science. Scientists in all disciplines are likely to use simple heuristics to build initial intuitions about their problems. This, along with pure serendipity, is typical of the nature/process of scientific discoveries. For instance, James Watson reportedly gained insights on the double helix structure of DNA in a dream, and penicillin was discovered by Louis Pasteur while studying why silkworms were dying because of a bacterial infection. However, the methodology in science and the sociology of science are entirely different. Scientific methodology relies on refutability of theories, stringent empirical testing of theories, replication of the evidence, and transparency of the data. The sociology of science ensures, to a much greater degree as compared to economics and perhaps the other social sciences, that the editors and referees of the leading journals publish only peer-reviewed research that conforms to the scientific method. This has been a remarkably successful combination in producing great progress in science. Hence, there is no essential contradiction between scientific progress in science and the use of judgment heuristics by scientists to guide them on the way forward.

5.11.5 Frequency versus Probability Format and the HBP

Several critics of the HBP have argued that the biases created by heuristics in the HBP are eliminated, or substantially reduced, when data are presented in a frequency format rather than in a probability format (Gigerenzer et al., 1988, Gigerenzer, 1991, 1996, 2008). Our own reading of the evidence is as follows:

1. An entire class of heuristics in the HBP is unaffected by the distinction between the frequency and probability formats. This includes the representativeness heuristic (including gambler's fallacy, hot hand fallacy), anchoring, availability, hindsight bias, regression to the mean, confirmation bias, and the affect heuristic.

2. The frequency format might reduce biases, relative to the BRA, in the case of some heuristics, particularly in the case of the conjunction fallacy and in applications of Bayes' law. However, significant bias remains in applications of Bayes' law. After reviewing the relevant evidence, Kahneman and Tversky (1996, p. 585) cautiously noted: "Contrary to Gigerenzer's unqualified claim, the replacement of subjective probability judgments by estimates of relative frequency and the introduction of sequential random sampling do not provide a panacea against base-rate neglect."

Tversky and Kahneman (1983) themselves first highlighted the difference in results when information is presented in a frequency format relative to a probability format. They found that in a within-subjects design, the frequency format leads to fewer conjunction errors. However, the conjunction bias is found to be sufficiently high in a between-subjects treatment (Kahneman & Tversky, 1996); see the discussion in section 5.6. The anchoring heuristic was also found to be used when the information in example 5.3 was presented in a frequency format (Tversky & Kahneman, 1973, 1974).

The use of Bayes' law is critical to almost all areas of the BRA, and its acceptance in teaching and research in economics is an article of faith. Contrary evidence, which we review in section 2.15.2, is almost never discussed in university courses in economics. Our review of the evidence shows that the frequency format may increase compliance with Bayes' law, but violation of Bayes' law is still common in a frequency format.

3. It is possible that humans might have evolved to understand natural frequencies relatively better than percentages (Cosmides & Tooby, 1996; Pinker, 1997). However, most real world economic data is presented in percentage terms—for example, interest rates on mortgage borrowing; the forecasts of inflation and unemployment by central banks; various insurable risks; performance indicators on open days in universities; and the rates of return on portfolios. Thus, as a practical matter, one needs to understand human judgment and decision-making when information is presented in a probability format.

4. When conformity with Bayes' rule under a frequency format is claimed to be truly spectacular, it appears confounded, at least in some cases, by framing effects that not only provide the data in a frequency format but also facilitate conformity with the statistically correct solution. Consider, for instance, the problems given to 160 experienced gynecologists, reported in Gigerenzer (2008, pp. 16–18).

A. Probability format

Assume that you screen women in a particular region for breast cancer with mammography. You know the following about women in this region:

> *The probability that a woman has breast cancer is 1 percent (prevalence).*
>
> *If a woman has breast cancer, the probability is 90 percent that she will have a positive mammogram (sensitivity).*
>
> *If a woman does not have breast cancer, the probability is 9 percent that she will have a positive mammogram (false positive rate).*

A woman who tested positive asks if she really has breast cancer or what the probability is that she actually has breast cancer. What is the best answer?

1. "It is not certain that you have breast cancer, yet the probability is about 81 percent." [14]
2. "Out of 10 women who test positive as you did, about 9 have breast cancer." [47]
3. "Out of 10 women who test positive as you did, only 1 has breast cancer." [20]
4. The chance that you have breast cancer is about 1 percent." [19]

The numbers in the square brackets give the number of subjects out of 160 who chose that particular response. The option that is closest to the statistically correct answer is 4, but it is chosen by only 19 subjects (11.9 percent of the sample).

B. Frequency format

The italicized text in the probability format is changed as follows (the remaining information is identical):

Ten out of every 1000 women have breast cancer.
Of these 10 women, we expect that 9 will have a positive mammogram.
Of the remaining 990 women without breast cancer, some 89 will still have a positive mammogram.
Imagine a sample of women who have positive mammograms. How many of these women have cancer? ___ *out of* ___

In this case, 87 percent choose the correct answer.

There are two changes in this text relative to the one in the probability format. First, information is presented in a frequency format. Second, the problem is framed with a subtle difference that appears to aid statistical inference. Consider, for instance, the insertion of the explanations, "Of these 10 women" and "Of the remaining 990 women without breast cancer." This makes the set inclusion relation a lot clearer than the corresponding instructions in the probability format. The relative contribution of these two factors (frequency format and changed framing) is not clear. It does appear that with the altered framing, compliance with Bayes' rule may increase. This in itself is a valuable result, and there is now a growing literature that shows that the provision of information, particularly financial information that enhances financial literacy, ensures that people can make better choices (Bertrand & Morse, 2011).

We believe the following is the appropriate frame-equivalent analogue of the frequency format to the above problem when the information is presented in a probability format:

The probability that a woman has breast cancer is 1 percent (prevalence).

Of these 1 percent women who have breast cancer, we expect that 90 percent will have a positive mammogram (sensitivity).

Of the remaining 99 percent women without breast cancer, some 9 percent will have a positive mammogram (false positive rate).

A woman who tested positive asks if she really has breast cancer or what the probability is that she actually has breast cancer. What is the best answer?

To the best of our knowledge, this has never been tested.

5.11.6 Empirical Counterparts to the Heuristics

The FFP has criticized the availability heuristic for not specifying the exact empirical proxy for availability. As Gigerenzer and Brighton (2011, p. 18) put it: "The use of labels is still widespread ..., and it is therefore worth providing a second illustration of how researchers are misled by their seductive power. Consider the 'availability heuristic'... this label encompassed several meanings, such as the number of instances that come to mind ... the ease with which the first instance comes to mind ... the recency, salience, vividness, memorability, among others."

We now address this criticism. The availability heuristic is well defined in a mathematical sense and is eminently testable (see section 5.5). It arguably meets the standards of scientific rigor in economics. There are several examples in economics, where the exact empirical counterpart of a variable in an economic model is not fully specified. This arises because economic theories are necessarily a parsimonious description of complex reality. We give three examples from Nobel Prize–winning work in economics to illustrate this methodological point.

1. Friedman and Schwartz (1963) argue that an increase in the "money supply" increases inflation with "long and variable lags." Similar predictions also hold in New Keynesian models with frictions. However, there are at least four different empirical definitions of money supply (commonly known as M1, M2, M3, and M4), but theory does not specify which of these definitions is the most appropriate one, neither can "long and variable lags" be precisely defined. However, in this case, subsequent empirical research provided a useful guide to the appropriate definition of money supply and also helped to uncover the length of the lags.

2. Lucas (1988) shows that human capital is an important determinant of economic growth. But what is the precise measure of human capital (primary/secondary school education? university education? vocational

training?)? Similar predictions, without an exact empirical specification of the corresponding variable are offered in several modern growth theory models. It was left to the empirical literature to discover which measures of human capital were the most useful (Barro & Sala-i-Martin, 2003).
3. Kahneman and Tversky (1979) introduce the concept of *reference dependence* into economics. They do not specify the exact empirical proxy for reference points; however, they do propose the status quo and aspiration levels as candidates for a reference point. Other plausible candidates, identified in subsequent research, include a fair outcome, expected outcome, or entitlements based on norms (see Dhami, 2019b, section 2.4.4). It was again left to empirical work to discover the most suitable and appropriate reference point, depending on the application one uses.

For these reasons, we do not view the criticism of a lack of exact empirical proxy for the availability heuristic (and the other heuristics) to be a serious shortcoming of the HBP.

5.11.7 How Can Heuristics Explain Events A and Not A?

One can explain the gambler's fallacy and the hot hand fallacy in terms of the representativeness heuristic. This might sound paradoxical; see, for example, definitions 5.3 and 5.4. How can both negative and positive autocorrelation be explained by the same theory? Gigerenzer and Brighton (2011, p. 18) criticize the representativeness heuristic thusly: "No model of similarity can explain a phenomenon and its contrary; otherwise it would not exclude any behavior." They go on to write: "As it [representativeness heuristic] remains undefined, it can account even for A and non-A (Ayton and Fisher, 2004)."

We believe that this is likely to be a misunderstanding of how representativeness operates in these two different cases. Consider the empirical evidence from the same paper that Gigerenzer and Brighton (2011, p. 18) cite, Ayton and Fischer (2004). The key to providing a representativeness heuristic–based explanation for the gambler's and hot hand fallacies is to examine the domains in which these fallacies arise. Ayton and Fischer suggest that these domains are different. They propose that the hot hand fallacy is more likely to arise for *human performance* (e.g., the performance of basketball and tennis players), and the gambler's fallacy is more likely to arise for *inanimate processes* (such as throws of a die or tosses of a coin).

In Ayton and Fischer (2004), subjects were presented with various sequences of 21 binary outcomes—for example, each outcome is a success

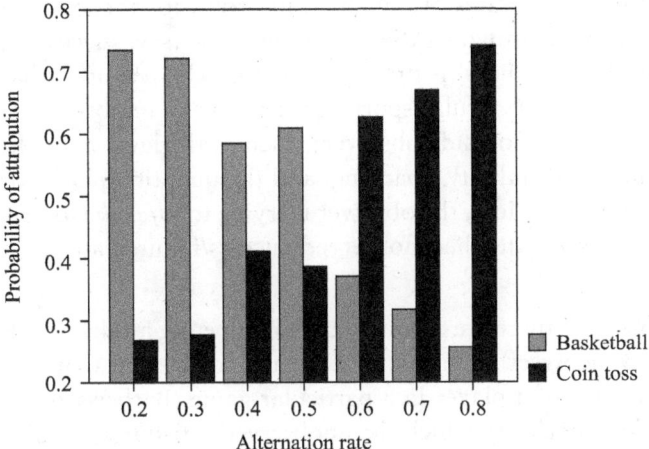

Figure 5.2
Does the given alternation rate arise from basketball shots or a coin toss?
Source: Ayton & Fischer (2004).

or a failure, as in the toss of a coin. The sequence of 21 outcomes had varying degrees of positive and negative autocorrelation. The *alternation rate* is the number of times a sequence changes direction, from success to failure or vice-versa, divided by 10. Subjects were then asked to guess the source of these sequences: *human skilled performance* (e.g., basketball shots or tennis serves), or an *inanimate process* (e.g., a coin toss or a binary-outcome roulette wheel).

The results for one of the comparisons is shown in figure 5.2. Sequences with low rates of alternation were rated by subjects to have more likely arisen from basketball shots rather than coin tosses. Conversely, sequences with high rates of alternation were rated as more likely to have come from a coin toss. These results highlight when the gambler's fallacy is more likely to arise (high alternation rates arising from an inanimate process) and when the hot hand fallacy is more likely to arise (low alternation rates and the involvement of human skills).

Why does this difference in results arise? We believe that subjects are solving quite different inference problems in each case.

1. In the case of inanimate processes, such as coin tosses, subjects are sure of the underlying probabilities of H and T if the coin is fair (50 percent each). Thus, subjects may switch too often in small samples to preserve the population proportions, as suggested by the representativeness heuristic. This leads to negative autocorrelation.

2. In predicting the success rates of outcomes in professional sport, the underlying distribution from which the binary outcome (say, success, S, or failure, F, in basketball shots) is drawn is unclear. The reason is that a streak of S, or of F, in a particular sporting event signals unobservable attributes about a player to outside observers, such as the level of confidence, fatigue, emotional stability, coaching, and the quantity/quality of training prior to the game. Here, the observer is trying to *infer the underlying model* that gives rise to the unobserved success/failure rates in a particular game.

Suppose, for instance, there are two subjective competing models (both possibly objectively incorrect) in the mind of an outside observer that give rise to the performance of a player in a particular game (Barberis et al., 1998): (a) a *trending model*, in which the unobserved attributes are particularly conducive to good performance, so that the player has a high success rate, and (b) a *mean reverting model*, in which success is intermingled with failure in such a way that the player achieves some mean level of success in the observed game. On observing a sequence of S, S, S, S, S (say, five consecutive successful shots by a player in a basketball game), an outside observer who uses the representativeness heuristics may infer that the observed sequence is representative of the trending model and not the mean reverting model. Thus, the observer may assign a high probability that the sixth shot will also be S. This leads to perceived positive autocorrelation.

By contrast, the true underlying model might well be a random model (which is neither trending nor mean-reverting), in which case, the correct statistical inference is a 50-50 chance of S on the sixth shot. In this case, if the outside observer is a sports market bettor, then the observed betting data on betting will immediately suggest a hot hand fallacy.

This reasoning potentially explains the evidence presented in figure 5.2. The key to the explanation lies in the different inference procedures for the cases of inanimate and animate processes. In particular, to our mind, there does not appear to be any inconsistency in using the representativeness heuristic to simultaneously explain the gambler's fallacy and the hot hand fallacy.

5.11.8 The Criticism of Appropriate Statistical Norms

Gigerenzer (1996) questions the appropriate "statistical norms" that apply to the experiments in the HBP, and in particular the experiments conducted by Kahneman and Tversky in the 1970s and 1980s. His argument is that the underlying model is not fully specified, which leaves unclear the appropriate statistical prediction. He writes (p. 592):

A convenient statistical principle, such as the conjunction rule or Bayes' rule, is chosen as normative, and some real-world content is filled in afterward, on the assumption that only structure matters. The content of the problem is not analyzed in building a normative model, nor are the specific assumptions people make about the situation.

This criticism potentially covers several points, which we address below.

1. *Normative standards of behavior*: The HBP did not advocate, invent, or defend a particular normative standard of behavior. It took the existing, and well-established, normative standard of behavior in economics, as encapsulated in the BRA. The objective in the foundational work done by Kahneman and Tversky in the 1970s and 1980s was to test whether people do actually conform to this normative standard. As noted earlier, in the BRA, the normative standard requires some of the following assumptions: people follow the law of large numbers; use all available information that the relevant economic model requires; follow Bayes' law to update their information sets; have perfect recall; are not influenced by irrelevant information; and have preferences that are context/frame independent.

In order to test the BRA, it is consistent with scientific methodology to test the individual assumptions in the BRA directly, or alternatively, to test a model that uses these assumptions plus other auxiliary assumptions. The HBP approach has often directly tested the assumptions behind the BRA framework, and one of the main findings is that the given normative standard in the BRA is violated.

This approach in the HBP also extends to the testing of theories in the BRA such as expected utility theory and exponential discounting. We have already shown that the axioms of rationality under risk give rise to expected utility theory and that the axioms of time discounting give rise to the exponential discounted utility model (see sections 2.5 and 2.6). One may then either test an economic model that uses these theories in conjunction with other auxiliary assumptions or directly test any of the axioms of rationality. It has proven simpler to directly test the individual axioms of rationality because they do not require the experimenter to have information on the utility function of a subject. For this reason, the testing of expected utility has largely employed tests of the independence axiom, while tests of exponential discounting have tested the stationarity axiom (see sections 2.12 and 2.13). In both cases, the relevant theories were rejected by the evidence. We see nothing objectionable in this approach, nor do tests of the relevant axioms imply that the researcher accepts the normative standard implied by expected utility theory or by exponential discounting.

An analogy from aerospace may help. The airframe of a proposed new airplane might be tested in a wind tunnel, without adding on all the other components in the airplane. This is not just an acceptable procedure in science and engineering; it is critical to the development of new findings and theories.

2. *Ecological rationality*: Implicit in the criticism of the HBP on the grounds of statistical norms is the view that it does not take account of ecological rationality. Interpreting ecological rationality as context and frame dependence of preferences, we have argued above that this criticism does not hold; Kahneman and Tversky (1996) have themselves addressed this criticism directly.

One may alter the environment within which a problem is embedded to analyze whether the appropriate decision changes. For instance, the FFP has done so by examining differences in behavior between a probability format and a frequency format to study the ecological rationality of behavior (section 5.11.5). This is interesting and useful, but of relevance to the HBP approach is that the BRA assumes human behavior to be identical in a frequency and a probability format. Hence, a demonstration of noncompliance with the predictions of the BRA in either a probability, or a frequency, format is sufficient to disprove this normative benchmark. However, if it were to turn out that people conformed with the BRA in a frequency format for most of the cases that the HBP considers (which they do not), then a newer version of the BRA may be proposed in a frequency format and retested. This is entirely consistent with how science progresses.

5.11.9 Systems 1 and 2

Both sides in the great rationality debate also differ about the appropriate models of the brain that may lead to a better understanding of the use of heuristics. This is not the focus of our book; the interested reader may consult Stanovich and West (2000) and Stanovich (2012). But we offer some brief remarks on this issue because it has a bearing on some of the criticism of the HBP.

Kahneman (2011) devotes the first third of his book to developing a two-system model of the brain, systems 1 and 2, that facilitates a deeper understanding of the biases relative to the BRA. To be sure, there is no universal agreement among psychologists about the appropriate models of the brain in this context (Stanovich & West, 2000). Kahneman fully recognizes that system 1 and system 2 are not meant to correspond with specific brain areas (p. 29) but are useful concepts that aid us in making greater sense of heuristics. In the natural sciences, atoms and genes were first hypothesized as useful concepts long before their material counterparts were discovered.

On a widespread view, the quick, reactive, and automatic system 1 is responsible for many errors relative to the BRA. System 2 has been likened to a *lazy controller* in Kahneman (2011); when it is called on to intervene in an unusual situation, the agenda (e.g., affective emotions, recalled memory, associations) is chosen by system 1. System 1 tries to make sense of a situation even when the events may have been generated purely randomly. Kahneman (2011, pp. 204–205) puts it as follows:

"The sense-making machinery of System 1 makes us see the world as more tidy, simple, predictable, and coherent than it really is. The illusion that one has understood the past feeds the further illusion that one can predict and control the future. These illusions are comforting. They reduce the anxiety that we would experience if we allowed ourselves to fully acknowledge the uncertainties of existence."

This systems distinction can be used to explain the law of small numbers, the gambler's and hot hand fallacies, and overconfidence in the ability to explain the future if one is subject to the hindsight bias. Indeed, this provides an altogether different view of the existence of heuristics that is not rooted in the bias-variance dilemma (see section 6.6).

5.12 Experts and the HBP Heuristics

Do experts use heuristics that are identified in the HBP? Do they exhibit biases relative to the BRA? If the answer is in the affirmative, then it lends further support to the ecological rationality of heuristics in the HBP.

There is now widespread evidence that many experts do exhibit biases relative to the BRA (Dhami, 2020a, section 1.18). The evidence comes from multiple domains. When making predictions about political events, experts were only slightly more accurate than chance. However, they were able to generate better ex post explanations for their predictions (Tetlock, 2002, 2006). Experts are typically more overconfident than laypeople who lack similar experience, and more experienced experts are more overconfident (Heath & Tversky, 1991; Glaser et al., 2007; Kirchler &

Maciejovsky, 2002). The realized returns on stocks are within the 80 percent confidence intervals of the returns predicted by senior finance professionals in only 36 percent of the cases (Ben-David et al., 2013).[5]

Mathematical psychologists exhibit the law of small numbers (Tversky & Kahneman, 1973). The perceived riskiness of various hazardous substances by toxicology experts is consistent with the affect heuristic (Slovic et al., 1999). Clinical psychologists underweight base rates relative to a Bayesian calculation (Meehl & Rosen, 1955). A meta study establishes that decision-makers who have the relevant expertise in the field suffer from the hindsight bias (Guilbault et al., 2004). Professional traders in a large investment bank were found to be hindsight biased (Biais & Weber, 2009).

Evidence supports the important role of anchoring on a given list price by estate agents (Northcraft & Neale, 1987). Evidence of anchoring is also found in legal judgment (Chapman & Bornstein, 1996; Englich & Mussweiler, 2001; Englich et al., 2006). Judges exhibit the false consensus effect (Solan et al. 2008). Finance professionals also exhibit a false consensus effect and they impute to others their own risk preferences (Roth & Voskort, 2014).

Experts, such as physicians and World Bank staff, exhibit framing effects, often of a similar magnitude to that observed with student populations (McNeil et al., 1982; Kahneman & Tversky, 1984; World Bank, 2015). Wholesale car market dealers exhibit limited attention (Lacetera et al., 2012). World Bank (2015) documents several kinds of biases among its professional staff. These include confirmation bias, susceptibility to sunk costs, and the influence of framing. World Bank (2015, p. 18) is candid in its assessment of expert bias: "This finding suggests that development professionals may assume that poor individuals may be less autonomous, less responsible, less hopeful, and less knowledgeable than they in fact are." World Bank also suggests potential solutions to the problem of expert bias; these include *dogfooding* (experts signing up and playing their own programs for real) and *red teaming* (having an adversarial outside team that tests the proposals).

Thus, the evidence suggests that many experts do use heuristics and exhibit biases relative to the BRA and that this is not necessarily eliminated, or even reduced, by market experience.

6

The Fast and Frugal Heuristics Research Program

6.1 Introduction

The work of Gerd Gigerenzer and others on the fast and frugal heuristics research program (which we abbreviate FFP) finds its motivation in the work of Herbert Simon (1955, 1978). The FFP's emphasis is on the *procedural rationality* of solutions. We have seen an application in section 4.5 to aspiration adaptation, based on Simon's work. The main domain of interest in the FFP is *large worlds*, or *true uncertainty* in our terminology in section 2.2. However, in some cases, notably in the use of the *priority heuristic*, FFP can also deal with *small worlds* (or *risk and subjective uncertainty* in our terminology).

We consider the foundational elements of the FFP in section 6.2, which begins with the plausible idea, also found in the HBP, that people may have an *adaptive toolbox of heuristics* from which they draw depending on the context and frame of the problem (*ecological rationality*). In principle, this is eminently plausible and consistent with the stated objective of procedural rationality. The FFP takes as given a *reference class of cues* and the *ecological validities of the cues* (their ability to differentiate between the given options in the reference class). In the simplest heuristic in the FFP, the *take-the-best heuristic*, the cues are ordered by their ecological validities, and the first cue that can discriminate between the choices (i.e., suggest that one choice is better than the other) is used to make the relevant choice. A simple cue could be to see whether one can recognize the objects in the given choice. The individual may then choose the first object that is recognized; this is the *recognition heuristic*. We also give a brief description of more complex heuristics. For instance, rather than choose the cue with the highest ecological validity, decision-makers may subjectively weight the cues in some manner and arrive at a decision. Cues can be ordered by means other than ecological validity, or require that cue discrimination must exceed a certain threshold value for it to be used to make a decisive choice.

We examine the criticisms of the HBP in chapter 5. However, the FFP has faced much less criticism, and there appears to be misunderstanding about several features of this research program. Economists have almost completely ignored the FFP.[1] Just as the HBP has benefited from a critical examination, we believe that the FFP may also benefit from constructive criticism. In particular, some of the most useful criticisms that can sharpen and improve results/predictions in a program often come from people who work outside that program. Section 6.3 gives a critical assessment of the FFP.

The analysis of the problem of decision-making under true uncertainty is arguably more challenging than under any of the other cases (certainty, risk, subjective uncertainty). We believe, based on the evidence, that the FFP has not yet given us a persuasive account of decision-making under true uncertainty. Economics has no optimization benchmark to offer in the case of true uncertainty, which makes it difficult to evaluate the performance of any candidate heuristic in the FFP (section 6.3.1). The FFP has compared the performance of its proposed heuristics against benchmarks claimed to be optimization benchmarks, typically logistic regression and weighted tallying. However, none of these benchmarks under true uncertainty is persuasive, and certainly none is recommended by any optimization theory in economics.

We consider two further issues in section 6.3. Section 6.3.2 discusses the difficulty of empirically validating the FFP based on experimenter-provided reference classes, cues, and ecological validities. Arguably the most interesting and relevant case for the FFP is to see how individuals uncover reference classes of cues and go about discovering their ecological validities. Or, under true uncertainty, do they even know if they should be searching for this information? Having the experimenter provide this information is far less enlightening. Recall from section 4.5 the infinite regress in search costs problem that partially motivated Herbert Simon's satisficing approach, leading ultimately to the incorporation of procedural rationality within the theory. Although the FFP invokes the work of Simon as the fountainhead for its approach, the experimenter-provided information in the FFP completely sidesteps the problem of how to resolve infinite regress in search costs. In any case, conformity with the heuristics in the FFP is not satisfactory in the cases of experimenter-provided information and of this assumption being slightly relaxed (subjects are given identical information to remember cues).

In section 6.3.3, we ask if it is a good option to train people in the use of statistics, particularly in a frequency format. Gigerenzer (2008) reports an improvement in the ability of doctors and children to use Bayes' law when trained in a frequency format. The problems used in these training programs typically involve simple conditional probability calculations, such as $P(A \mid B)$. However, in actual practice, doctors need to compute complex conditional probabilities such as $P(A \mid B, C, D, E, F \ldots)$, where $A, B, C, \ldots$ are events in some sample space. For instance, what is the probability that someone will die of a cardiac arrest (A), conditional on multiple contributing factors such as smoking (B), drinking alcohol (C), history of heart attacks in the family (D), cholesterol test scores (E), ethnic background (F), and so on? These complex calculations are virtually impossible to do whether one has been taught in a frequency format or a probability format. It is probably a more productive use of resources to allow doctors to use software to compute these complex conditional probabilities (as does the National Health Service in the UK). Of far greater importance is to decide on the relevant thresholds of these conditional probabilities, beyond which proactive medical treatment is needed. Finally, in section 6.3.4, we argue that the FFP is not yet able to predict which heuristic in the adaptive toolbox will be used in any particular situation, context, or frame. The inability to answer the central question in the FFP suggests that the program is at an early stage.

Section 6.4 considers the following twofold critique made by the FFP: (1) optimization-based and as-if models in economics are always dominated by heuristics-based models in prediction tasks, and (2) behavioral economics is a repair project for the BRA. Both arguments are incorrect. There is nothing inherently objectionable about optimization-based and as-if models on a priori grounds. Empirical evidence is the ultimate arbitrator among models. Optimization-based models may fail the empirical test (see several examples in chapters 2 and 3), although in some cases, this is on account of empirically rejected theories in the BRA such as expected utility theory. On the other hand, several examples of optimization-based and as-if models in this book organize well the empirical evidence, and there are cases where their predictions are indistinguishable from heuristics-based models (see sections 3.2.5, 3.2.6, 4.3, and 4.4). We argue in this book that prospect theory is a good as-if theory. The underlying psychological realism and richness of prospect theory enables it to make successful predictions, often in cases where, at the moment, it is not clear which heuristic would predict better. Furthermore, behavioral economics is not a repair project for expected utility or for the BRA. Models in behavioral economics are guided by the evidence and still face significant hostility from several quarters among the adherents of the BRA who would have more wholeheartedly welcomed it if it were a repair project.

Section 6.5 argues that the domains of choice in the HBP and the FFP programs are often nonoverlapping. The HBP largely considers situations of risk and uncertainty to which the BRA applies; the aim is to test the BRA. On the other hand, the FFP is typically interested in the *large worlds* situation (true uncertainty), where one cannot even list or imagine the possible outcomes and/or assign objective/subjective probabilities. Thus, a great deal of the debate that pits the two positions as adversarial is, in our view, unfortunate and misleading.[2] The main raison d'être of the FFP program is its attempt to answer the question of how people make decisions under true uncertainty. This is truly praiseworthy, but it is an objective that we do not believe has been accomplished yet. We highlight other potential avenues for the exploration of answers to the fundamental question of decision-making under true uncertainty, such as *social norms* and *mental models* (see chapter 3).

In section 6.6, we consider the *less is more effect*. When trying to uncover the unknown, but stochastic, relationship between two variables based on a sample of noisy observations, one faces the following trade-off. One could fit a function, say, using nonlinear regression, very close to the observed data points in the sample; in the extreme case one could connect all the data points in the sample. This is likely to generate an estimated function that has low bias in-sample, but that is because it fits too closely to the sample data that include the noise. However, if such a fitted function is then used to make predictions for a separate sample, also known as out-of-sample predictions, then the prediction errors from this function will have a high variance. This is because the realization of the noise terms in the new sample will, by definition, be different. This trade-off between bias and variance is known as the *bias-variance trade-off*. Roughly speaking, this trade-off is resolved by minimizing the sum of squares of errors for all possible out-of-sample data that one could obtain.

In section 6.6, we give a formal derivation of the bias-variance trade-off, with examples, and examine its implications for the choice of heuristics. Essentially, the FFP has criticized the HBP for focusing only on the bias term and ignoring the variance term in the bias-variance trade-off. We examine this criticism in three different subsections. Briefly, our arguments are as follows. First, it has not been demonstrated yet that human cognition and judgment use the bias-variance dilemma. The evidence from behavioral economics suggests that humans do not act as if they minimized the sum of squares of prediction errors, as in statistical problems of curve fitting, nor is there any reason why evolution would have chosen such a method for us. Second, the bias-variance dilemma does not apply to many of the heuristics in the HBP because these heuristics are not about prediction tasks; examples include the anchoring heuristic, conjunction fallacy, availability heuristic, confirmation bias, hindsight bias, and regression to the mean. Third, in tasks that involve predictions such as the gambler's fallacy and the hot hand fallacy (within the family of the representativeness heuristic), there may be no direct need to invoke the bias-variance dilemma.

6.2 The FFP

The FFP often differentiates itself from the HBP on the following grounds (Gigerenzer, 2008, 2014; Gigerenzer et al., 1999), which we paraphrase as follows:

1. The HBP suggests that people are fallible, hardwired with defective mental software, and prone to errors; that heuristics are bad; and that the appropriate normative norm of human behavior is the BRA (Gigerenzer, 1996, 2014; Gigerenzer et al., 1999).
2. In contrast, the FFP is designed to show that heuristics are good and do better than optimization methods once ecological rationality is taken into account.

The distinction between the two programs suggested above is not accurate. The HBP does not wish to prove that heuristics are good or bad. To the extent that researchers addressed that topic, it was to say that the heuristics they identified generally worked well but also led to severe and systematic errors relative to the BRA (which is demonstrably true). Their main goal was to test whether human behavior was consistent with the BRA, and they found it was not. But they went further by identifying various classes of heuristics that explain human behavior in different contexts and frames. The following two passages from Kahneman (2000, p. 682) show just how close the two sides in the debate really are on core issues and how misleading some of the debate on the relative positions of the two programs is:

> Contrary to a common perception, researchers working in the heuristics and biases (HB) mode are less interested in demonstrating human irrationality than in understanding the psychology of intuitive judgment and choice.

> All heuristics make us smart, more often than not.

Herbert Simon (1955) distinguished between *substantive rationality* (maximizing an objective function under constraints) and *procedural rationality* (the process/quality of decision-making). Simon's insight was that human beings may lack the information and the computational and cognitive ability to solve problems in the BRA (e.g., the problems in section 3.2.1). However, in actual practice, people do make decisions. Hence, he was interested in the cognitive processes that give rise to such decisions, which requires invoking procedural rationality rather than substantive rationality. Simon proposed the *satisficing heuristic* to operationalize procedural rationality, in which individuals set goals or targets, called aspiration levels (see section 4.5). The individual then searches for alternatives that give rise to different payoffs. Once an alternative attains the aspiration level, it is deemed as satisfactory, and further search is terminated. Empirical evidence is supportive of the theory (Caplin et al., 2011).

The FFP focuses on *procedural rationality*. It describes the process/method by which decisions are made and uses heuristics that are fast and frugal (economize on time and information). The HBP also focuses on fast and frugal heuristics, but its use of procedural rationality is different from the FFP. For instance, in the HBP, although procedural rationality is less well developed, it is reflected in some of the following ways: searching through the available information (availability heuristic); making undue use of prior information relative to the Bayesian benchmark (anchoring); using the law of small numbers in making decisions based on small samples (representativeness heuristic); being unduly influenced by one's own prior beliefs relative to the Bayesian benchmark (confirmation bias); using imperfect recall (hindsight bias).

In the FFP, procedural rationality is introduced by exploiting some of the following features: identifying a reference class, using cues to make decisions, ranking cues according to their ecological validity, deciding on the basis of the first discriminatory cue or tallying over cue values and using a weighted average of the cue values. In contrast to these methods, some of the most persuasive examples of fast and frugal heuristics come in the form of checklists, such as hospital checklists to reduce infections, and other simple algorithms that appear to work (Gigerenzer, 2014, especially chapter 3).

Example 6.1. *(Breiman et al., 1993) Hospitals use a simple decision tree to classify patients into those who face high and low risks. In principle, doctors may require a large battery of tests to determine the risk* classification of a patient. However, the decision tree uses only three variables. If the systolic blood pressure is below 91, the patient is immediately classified as high risk, and no further information is needed. If not, then patients older than 62.5 years and suffering from sinus tachycardia are classified as high risk. Otherwise, they are classified as low risk.

Example 6.2. *(McLeod & Dienes, 1996; McLeod et al., 2006) Consider the game of cricket (baseball will do as well), in which a batsman hits a ball from point A, in the air, and the ball takes a parabolic trajectory before landing at point B. Suppose that a fielder, who is stationed at point C, wishes to catch the ball before it lands on the ground at point B. Clearly, the fielder must start to run to catch the ball before it lands. The fielder must also form a prediction as to where the ball will land. In the BRA, the fielder is supposed to instantly use his knowledge of parabolic curves and incorporate the effects of wind speed and humidity in the air to predict that the ball will land at point B. The fielder is then predicted to run in a straight line from point C to point B (the shortest distance between two points is a straight line) and catch the ball.*

By contrast, most successful fielders run in a curved path from C to B and catch the ball. They do not appear to undertake any of the complex calculations prescribed by the BRA. Rather, they use a simple evolutionary heuristic, the gaze heuristic, that requires them to run in a curved path toward the ball. McLeod et al. (2006, p. 139) write: "The path of a fielder running to catch a ball is determined by the attempt to satisfy 2 independent constraints. The 1st is to keep the angle of elevation of gaze to the ball increasing at a decreasing rate. The 2nd is to control the rate of horizontal rotation necessary to maintain fixation on the ball."

This is an excellent example in which evolution has endowed us with a fast and frugal heuristic, possibly on account of our evolutionary history of hunting animals and escaping from predators. However, the heuristics in the FFP are not necessarily evolutionary at all. The heuristics that we use in investing in pension plans, choosing marriage partners, or deciding to introduce new products in the market are perhaps the result of culture, social norms, conscious deliberation, our prior experiences, and the experiences of our acquaintances.

The class of *one-good-reason heuristics* is based on checking a series of cue values that are arranged in decreasing order of *ecological validity* (these terms are described below). This class includes the *take-the-best* heuristic (Gigerenzer & Goldstein, 1996) and the *priority heuristic*

(Brandstätter et al., 2006). Often, these heuristics are used to answer quite simple questions that have binary answers. For instance, consider the following example: Which German city, in a sample of cities, has the highest population? Typically, the experimenter provides subjects with several cues and their ecological validities. For instance, some of the cues could be: Do you recognize the name of the city? Does the city have a football team? Does the city have an intercity train station? The cue can either differentiate between the cities or not.

Suppose that A and B are two cities in the sample and one poses the question: Is A more populous than B? A simple cue could be whether A and B are recognized (*recognition heuristic*). A cue value of 1 is given to the city that one recognizes, and 0 otherwise. Among two cities, the subject may (1) recognize at least one city or (2) not recognize both cities. Only in the first case is the recognition cue said to *discriminate* between the cities. Another cue could be to check whether the city has a football team. This cue is said to discriminate between pairs of cities if, say, one city has a football team and the other does not. If the decision-maker does not have information on whether a city has a football team, then this cue cannot discriminate between that pair of cities. The *ecological validity* of a cue in the FFP is its overall ability to discriminate in pairwise comparisons between the cities in the sample of cities under consideration.

The *take-the-best cue* then proceeds in the following manner.

1. *Search rule:* Examine the cues in decreasing order of ecological validity.
2. *Stopping rule:* Terminate search when the first cue that can discriminate between the cities is encountered.
3. *Decision rule:* Conclude that the city that the cue has discriminated in favor of is the larger of the two cities.

Gigerenzer and Goldstein (1996) used data on 83 German cities with nine ecological cues and compared the take-the-best heuristic with other methods such as tallying (giving equal values to all cues and adding them up), weighted tallying (adding weighted values of cues), and logistic regression (taking account of the probability, based on regression estimates, that a city is more populous, conditional on the cue values).

The authors show that, in some cases, the take-the-best heuristic outperforms the other methods in terms of the number of cities successfully identified as more populous. In other contexts, Borges et al. (1999) apply the recognition heuristic to stock market choices: for example, among two candidate stocks, pick the one that is recognized. The authors find that it outperformed several other methods of stock market investment such as mutual funds, market indices, and chance investment (or dartboard

Table 6.1
Determining which of two foods has more cholesterol

Cues / Ecological validity	Time 1	Time 3
Saturated fat (80%)	cake ? pie	cake > pie
Calories (70%)	cake > pie	cake > pie
Protein (60%)	cake > pie	cake > pie
Choice	cake	cake
Confidence	70%	80%

Source: Hoffrage et al., 2000.

portfolios). Czerlinski et al. (1999) also find support for the take-the-best heuristic against other alternatives, such as regression analysis, when the experimenter provides cues to the subjects and also their ecological validities. In this study, subjects had to guess high school dropout rates in 57 Chicago public high schools. The cues, many with high ecological validities, included percentage of low-income students and average SAT scores.

Example 6.3. *Consider the explanation of hindsight bias in Hoffrage et al. (2000). A hypothetical consumer, Patricia, has to decide, at time 1, which of two foods, a cake and a pie, has more cholesterol. She does not know the answer directly, so she uses cues to make an inference. She is provided by the experimenter with cues (saturated fat, calories, protein) and their ecological validities, stated as a percentage, just after the cue names; see table 6.1. The percentage of pairwise cases in which the cue can distinguish between the choices in the sample, called the ecological validity in the FFP, can only be defined with respect to a reference class of foods. Here, the reference class, selected by the experimenter, is a random sample of foods from a Chicago supermarket. If a cue favors choice A over B, we write A > B, and if the cue cannot discriminate between the two choices, we write A ? B. For the moment, consider only time 1. Saturated fat cannot determine whether a cake has more cholesterol relative to a pie (cake ? pie), but the cue with the next highest ecological validity, calories, can discriminate (cake > pie).*

Let us now use the steps described in the take-the-best heuristic at time 1. The cue with the highest ecological validity cannot discriminate (cake ? pie), so Patricia is predicted to evaluate the next cue, calories, which successfully discriminates in favor of cake (cake > pie). Hence, Patricia is predicted to choose cake. The confidence that Patricia has in her judgment equals the ecological validity of the first cue that is able to discriminate, in this case calories, so the confidence is 70 percent.

Having made her choice, Patricia is now asked to make the same choice at a future time, time 3. For whatever reason, she might have imperfect recall of her choice and the choice procedure at time 1. It is now assumed by the authors that "the cue values are not veridically remembered but show systematic shift towards feedback." We are not confident about the suitability of this inference and the reasoning preceding this inference; it assumes hindsight bias, the very phenomenon that it wishes to explain. The authors use this assumption to construct the information in column 3 of table 6.1. The inability of saturated fat to discriminate between cake and pie at time 1 turns into discriminatory evidence in favor of cake at time 3. Proceeding as above, cake is chosen with 80 percent confidence. This, the authors claim, explains hindsight bias.

While this is a useful illustrative example of how take-the-best works, we are not persuaded by its ability to explain hindsight bias; neither does this approach offer a persuasive method to update cues over time.

For future reference, we collect our critical observations in the following remark.

Remark 6.1. Example 6.3 highlights some of the important features of the FFP. The decision is made in a fast and frugal manner (limited number of cues), and the procedure for choice is clearly spelled out; hence, it satisfies procedural rationality. However, the assumptions that lie behind this method, which are often unstated, need closer examination.

1. If the cues and the reference class were not experimenter-provided, then, among different subjects, there is likely to be no agreement about the items in the reference class of foods that might be relevant for the required comparison. The number of items and the kinds of items included in the reference class determine the ecological validity of each cue (see example 6.3). There is also no obvious way of choosing a reference class. Hence, there would likely be no agreement between people about the precise ecological validities of the cues if this information were not provided by the experimenter to the subjects. Identical information on ecological validity is provided by the experimenter to the subjects to ensure uniformity of available information and common knowledge of beliefs about ecological validity. But this partly defeats the problem of finding out exactly how subjects make choices, particularly under true uncertainty.

2. In the far more interesting case, if subjects have to search for the relevant reference class and the cues, there is likely to be a separate prediction for each subject. This makes testing of the theory potentially very difficult. Furthermore, in an actual search problem for cues and their ecological validities, there is likely to be an infinite regress problem in search costs. It might well be that some heuristics, or some simple learning models, are employed to search for cues. This is consistent with the stated objectives of the FFP. However, limited progress in the FFP has been made in this direction. Some human actions simply involve motor skills that we might have acquired over the course of human evolution—for example, the use of the gaze heuristic to catch a ball (example 6.2).

3. The more interesting set of questions for social scientists is the choice of heuristics to solve cognitive, social, economic, and cultural problems. The FFP is evaluated on these issues in section 6.3.

4. Furthermore, in example 6.3, we only observe Patricia's choices but not the mental process that she engages in. Any number of theories / mental processes might have led to the choice of cake as the relevant answer to this binary question. Thus, this is a class of as-if theories despite the FFP's claim that the HBP provides only as-if theories.

5. As our final point, how do we accurately determine how much confidence Patricia has in her choices? Evaluating her confidence by the experimenter-provided cues and ecological validities does not sit easily with the empirical evidence on overconfidence, which does not relate to ecological validity at all (see section 2.11. How can we be sure that Patricia is not overconfident?

A range of other heuristics are considered in the FFP, such as LEX and LEXSEMI, which have been used to examine risky choices (Payne et al., 1993). Unlike the take-the-best heuristic, the LEX heuristic does not order cues by ecological validity but by some other measure of importance. The LEXSEMI heuristic imposes a slightly more stringent requirement for cues to discriminate between choices by requiring that the difference between the cue values exceeds a certain threshold (for instance, if one is comparing the outcomes in two lotteries, then the difference in outcomes must exceed a minimum threshold). The *elimination by aspects* (EBA) combines the LEX method with Herbert Simon's satisficing strategy.

Heuristics have also been used to make choices among objects with several attributes (Payne et al., 1993). Consider, for instance, the choice between cars that differ in attributes such as reliability, fuel consumption, price, safety, and horsepower. It is likely that the desirability of various attributes could be in conflict—for example, the car with the highest horsepower might also be the worst on the metric of fuel consumption. Edwards and Tversky (1967) suggest the weighted adding strategy (WADD), in which the attributes of each car, subjectively weighted, are added and the car with the highest such score is chosen. But the subjective weights also make WADD difficult to test. One may simply add all attributes (equal weighing strategy, EQW). In both cases, the choice of attributes matters; adding or deselecting the unobserved attributes used by people to make choices changes the rankings. The LEX heuristic would advocate choosing the car with the highest attribute value on the most important attribute, say, "Pick the most reliable car." The very fact that different people pick different cars suggests that the ranking of these attributes in terms of importance is also subjective. But the FFP does not have an underlying theory of how such a ranking might differ among individuals. Insofar as these attributes are subjective, and privately observed by the subjects, elicitation and predictions of such heuristics are vexed issues.

Simon's satisficing approach can be extended to multiple attributes as follows. Given a set of cues, one ranks the cues in some order of subjective importance and assigns each cue a satisficing level. Pick the first cue, and reject the alternatives whose cue value lies below the satisficing level. Then, move on to the next cue in order of importance and compare the surviving alternatives on their cue values relative to the aspiration level for this cue. Proceeding in this manner, if a unique alternative remains at some stage, it is chosen. If not, then some tie-breaking rule is used.

6.3 A Critique of the FFP

We organize the discussion in this section into several subsections in order to provide a clear separation between the distinct arguments.

6.3.1 What Is the Benchmark for Comparison?

Economic theories typically do not assume that people use regression analysis to make choices, although there is some use of regression analysis in economic theories of learning. In a leading book on economic theory (Mas-Colell et al., 1995) and in a recent analogue for behavioral economics (Dhami, 2016), the word *regression* does not even figure in the subject indices. Regression is a tool to test theories in economics, not a tool employed by economic theory to make predictions about how people behave.

The comparison between regression analysis and heuristics is often used in the FFP to demonstrate the superiority of heuristics over optimization for human decisions. Gigerenzer and Brighton (2011, p. 6) write: "Thus the scientific community would first have to rethink its routine use of multiple regression and similar techniques to facilitate accepting the idea that rational minds might not always weight but may simply tally cues." The word *weight* in this quotation refers to the beta coefficients in OLS regression.

The general statistical point made in the FFP is that regressions may overfit the data relative to tallying (unweighted addition of cue values) and relative to other heuristics such as take-the-best; hence, the performance of regressions in out-of-sample predictions may be inferior. This is well recognized in econometrics (see the *less is more effect* in section 6.6) and is not problematic for economists. However, regression analysis is not the optimization benchmark in any area of economics that we are aware of.

When the domain under consideration is true uncertainty (unknown unknowns), economics has no benchmark to offer, let alone regression analysis. Indeed, the use of regression analysis in such cases (which typically occurs in the FFP) is dubious because we cannot use variables in regression analysis that are unknown (see section 6.5).

6.3.2   Empirical Testing of Heuristics in the FFP

The FFP does not predict the choice of an appropriate heuristic from the adaptive toolbox (see section 6.3.4), the actual selection of cues by individuals, or the reference class in which ecological validity is to be determined. Furthermore, empirical tests have not been very successful in uncovering answers to these questions.

The take-the-best heuristic is one of the most tested heuristics in the FFP. There are two methods of introducing cues in tests of the take-the-best heuristic, both of which illustrate the enormous difficulties and pitfalls in testing the FFP.

1. *Inferences from givens*: Most empirical studies in the FFP use the inferences from givens approach. In this approach, the experimenter decides on the reference class, directly provides cues to subjects, and also reveals the ecological validities of the cues. As an experimental control, this is desirable because the experimenter can identify the information that is available to all subjects. However, it is unsatisfactory on two grounds.

(a) It may lead subjects to the very decisions that the experimenter wishes to predict by appropriate selection of cues and reference classes.
(b) It sidesteps the critical problem of how people search for reference classes and for the cues. Indeed, if such a subjective search for cues was employed by the subjects, there is likely to be substantial subjective variability in the reference class and the cues employed by people, giving rise to different predictions for each individual. This is potentially problematic for testing the FFP because any observed outcome can then be justified under the theory, unless there is a way to validate subject-specific data. Heterogeneity in subject responses is not problematic per se, but then one needs some underlying theory to take some account of the heterogeneity.

2. *Inferences from memory task*: This method corrects for the drawbacks of the first method (at least partially) and is closer in spirit to the suggestion of Gigerenzer et al. (1999)—namely, that cues should be drawn from memory; Gigerenzer and Goldstein (1996) suggested this even earlier. If implemented properly, then the only observables in this case are the actual decisions made by subjects in the lab. In this case, one needs a theory of how individuals choose a reference class, how they search for the relevant information, how they decide to give attention to various cues, and what heuristics they might use to order cues by ecological validity in the absence of full information. However, such a theory is missing from the FFP.

One potential solution, albeit a highly imperfect one, is to have two treatments, as in Bröder and Schiffer (2003).

(a) In treatment 1, all subjects observe the same information on a screen with all the relevant cues and their ecological validities. This is the case of experimenter-provided data on reference classes, cues, and their validities.

(b) In treatment 2, subjects are narrated the relevant information, pictorially or verbally, and then they have to retrieve the relevant information from their memory.

Two shortcomings of treatment 2 remain. First, although it solves the problem of cue recall from identical information, it does not solve the question of cue search in the real world. We still do not know if individuals would proceed to search for references classes, cue values, and their ecological validities in solving this class of problems if such information was not provided. Second, the experimenter only observes data on choices, so the problem of inferring that the subject actually used the take-the-best heuristic remains. We can never be sure what mental processes and solution methods were employed by the subjects. This places the FFP firmly in the domain of as-if theories. We stress these points because the FFP is predicated on procedural rationality and uses this to highlight its point of departure from HBP and indeed criticize the HBP for its as-if approach (particularly in its criticism of prospect theory).

Consider some illustrative examples of the potential problems that arise from inferring the use of heuristics in the FFP, based on observation of choice data. Suppose that the first cue in the take-the-best heuristic is the recognition cue (choose A over B, if A is recognized and B is not). It could be that the recognition cue is highly correlated with other sensible methods of determining the choice between A and B. For instance, Scheibehenne and Bröder (2007) show that mere name recognition of players for the 2005 Wimbledon matches correctly predicted 70 percent of the matches. However, more highly seeded players, who are also more likely to win, are also more likely to be recognized. So, choices between two players based on the official rankings of the players (which could well be consistent with the BRA or any other framework) may be indistinguishable from choices based on the recognition heuristic. A similar problem exists in choosing among stocks based on the recognition heuristic (Borges et al., 1999). More recognized stocks are also more likely to belong to larger, more established firms as compared to newer, transient firms that are more likely to run into problems. So, the choices made by someone who is simply more cautious and avoids newer, transient firms (also possibly consistent with the BRA) are also likely to be indistinguishable from someone who uses the recognition heuristic.

In both methods described above (inferences from givens and inferences from memory), and despite their shortcomings, conformity with the take-the-best heuristic is relatively low. The temporal evolution of some of these studies is clearly described in Bröder (2011). We summarize some of these results next; for the details and references, see Bröder (2011).

1. The prediction that all subjects use the take-the-best heuristic all the time is rejected; only 5 out of 130 participants used it all the time. This is admittedly a tough test for any theory in the social sciences.
2. When the percentage of subjects whose behavior best fitted with the take-the-best heuristic was used in a comparison with two other rules, Dawes' rule and Franklin's rule,[3] 28 percent of the subjects conformed to take-the-best.
3. When the cost of acquiring cues increased (costs were known and identical for all subjects), the conformity with the take-the-best increased.

Clearly, if cues are expensive to acquire, subjects are more likely to make their decisions based on the first cue they encounter. However, in the real world, unless all the cues have already been searched for first, the individual cannot compare their costs or even possibly know their costs or the costs of searching for the costs, and so on (infinite regress in search costs problem).

4. When the performance of the take-the-best with costly cue values is compared with compensatory strategies (e.g., Franklin's rule), more people use the latter.

5. When inferences from memory task are used, the predictions of 47 percent of the subjects are consistent with take-the-best in the verbal condition and 21 percent in the pictorial condition. However, as Bröder (2011), himself one of the authors of this study, notes (p. 375): "The results reported can also be accounted for by assuming people used a weighted additive strategy (e.g., Franklin's rule) that mimics take-the-best performance when the cue weights are noncompensatory." We have noted some of the other limitations of this study, above.

Clearly, if these results are taken as direct evidence for take-the-best, the evidence is weak.

Do subjects learn the ecological validity of cues if given a chance? Newell and Shanks (2003) gave cues to subjects and set the validity of these cues to 0.80, 0.75, 0.70, and 0.69. They then gave subjects a chance to learn to order the cues by their ecological validities. The authors set a learning trial period of 60 repetitions with feedback. They found that only 3 out of 16 subjects learned to order the cues in the correct order. Gigerenzer and Brighton (2011, p. 23) argue that the number of trials were too few and suggest that subjects would need at least 100 trials to learn to order all the cues correctly. This is an important limitation. In the real world, in many cases with significant consequences, opportunities to learn which cues to use might be limited. Consider, for instance, decisions such as marriage, divorce, number of children to have, choice of pension plan, choice of savings plans, choice of donating organs, and choice of consumer durables. For firms, infrequent choices include merger decisions and capital restructuring decisions. It might well be that, under such circumstances, alternatives to the heuristics proposed by FFP may be used; examples include social norms and public policy in the form of nudges.

Newell et al. (2002) report that a majority of their participants used some variant of frugal (in terms of the extent of information used) strategies. Using the criterion that subjects conform to all the features of the take-the-best (TTB) heuristic at least 90 percent of the time, they find that the behavior of only 33 percent of the subjects conform to the criterion. Gigerenzer et al. (2011) comment on these results (p. 381) in their book introduction (p. 381), objecting to the high figure of 90 percent. They also criticize the methodology of testing single theories, arguing (p. 381) in favor of running a horse race between models. However, when such competitive tests are run to show that TTB does better, the other candidates in the race are not necessarily persuasive.

For instance, Bergert and Nosofsky (2011) show that TTB does better than RAT (a weighted additive model). RAT works as follows: Suppose that a model has n features or cues. Then, assign weight w_i to the ith cue such that $w_i = \log\left(\frac{v_i}{1-v_i}\right)$, where v_i is the ecological validity of the ith cue. RAT requires choosing the model that maximizes $\sum_{i=1}^{n} w_i$. In order to get a unique prediction, this method requires a common set of cues across the subjects and common agreement about the ecological validity of cues. We are not aware of mechanisms that would satisfy such stringent conditions.

Many of the problems used in testing the take-the-best heuristic are relatively simple. For instance: Which city is more populous? Which of the players is likely to win a tennis match?[4] However, it is less clear which heuristics are used and how cues are generated to solve concrete economic problems that economists are interested in. These include problems such as the design of contracts, choice of savings and pension plans, choice of a mortgage, and the decision to donate organs. We do not have direct evidence of how individuals might search for cues in these cases, or how they might discover the ecological validities of these cues, or how they might even reach a common agreement about such things. In the absence of such an agreement, we are likely, in the best-case scenario, to have individual-specific predictions of take-the-best and other heuristics in the FFP that pose immense problems for testing these theories.

6.3.3 Training People in Using Statistics

Gigerenzer (2008, pp. 16–18) has advocated better training for people in statistical inference. Indeed, he has personally engaged in training medical doctors in the use of Bayes' rule in a frequency format. Building on this idea, some people, above all Ralph Hertwig (2017), have argued in favor of *boosts*, understood as efforts to enable people to exercise their own agency. Greater statistical literacy is a boost. We are certainly in favor of statistical literacy, and we agree that it is important to improve people's ability to exercise agency. We agree that, in principle, training in statistics is an excellent idea. In some cases, boosting people's capacities has proved, and might prove, a promising intervention, helping to reduce and perhaps eliminating biases. There is a great deal to learn about when boosting will work, and we are enthusiastic about trying to do that.

Still, a legitimate question remains: Which policy problems would it solve? Should a prime minister or a president focused, say, on clean air, highway safety, obesity, cigarette smoking, diabetes, savings, or poverty reduction emphasize statistical training as a top priority? As a high priority? Nudges have at least dented such problems and many other problems (Sunstein, 2013; Halpern, 2015; Benartzi et al., 2017). If, for example, the question is how to promote savings, automatic enrollment has a great deal of promise, while the track record of financial literacy is mixed (Willis, 2013). If the goal is to increase highway safety, to combat obesity, or to reduce greenhouse gas emissions, architectural solutions, including nudges, might well work better than efforts to teach people the difference between absolute and relative risk reduction. Nonetheless, we emphasize that boosting might prove helpful and perhaps more than that in areas that range from healthy food choices to decisions about whether to get mammograms and choices about financial planning. In these and other cases, boosting does deserve serious consideration.

These issues warrant sustained attention (Hertwig, 2017). For now, we focus on narrower questions. Gigerenzer (2008) reports that doctors and children make better statistical inferences when trained, and the learning effects of a frequency format are longer lasting than a probability format. This is a significant result. One would expect people to get better in statistical inference the more they are trained. Nonetheless, there remain several concerns.

1. Training people in statistics can be costly. Economists would ask for an assessment of the opportunity cost before justifying the policy on cost-benefit grounds. For instance, could the money be better spent by (a) providing public information and (b) using regulation to require more transparent selling of financial products? Patients using the National Health Service (NHS) in the UK are often provided direct information on the likely increase in life expectancy from taking various drugs, such as statins or blood thinners. Governments require financial firms to directly provide information to consumers on the annual percentage rate (APR), an all-inclusive figure for the cost of borrowing, to compare various financial products. Without comparing the costs and benefits of a program of statistical training of people against the alternatives, it is difficult to judge its efficacy. This is curious because the FFP criticizes other research programs for not pitting their theories against alternatives in a horse race.

2. Consider programs for imparting statistical training to doctors in order to teach them to compute conditional probabilities, such as $P(A|B)$, where A and B are events. For instance, A is the event that the patient has cancer and B is a positive result on a mammography test. By contrast, real world doctors are often interested in a range of conditioning factors that determine event A; hence, the appropriate medical diagnosis typically depends on more complex conditional probabilities of the form $P(A|B, C, D, E, \ldots)$. For instance, A is the event death from cardiac disease in the next 20 years; B is the overall level of cholesterol; C takes a value 1 if any of the grandparents die of a cardiac disease, and the value 0 otherwise; D is the ethnic background; E takes a value 1 if the patient drinks alcohol or smokes, and a value of 0 otherwise.

The actual computation of $P(A|B, C, D, E, \ldots)$ is a cognitively and computationally challenging problem, even in the frequency format. As a result, an alternative, which appears to be in place in the British NHS, enables doctors to compute $P(A|B, C, D, E, \ldots)$ directly on their computers using a predesigned software. Indeed, it is common for NHS patients tested for cholesterol (B) to be asked further questions ($C, D, E, \ldots$) by the doctor before the doctor presses a button on the computer to tell them the conditional probability that they might die in the next 10 years with and without the use of statins.

Arguably, of far greater importance is the issue of what doctors do with the number $P(A|B, C, D, E, \ldots)$ once they find it. If this turns out to be, say, 0.75, should they prescribe statins or not? Or, if the patient is suspected of cancer, should they recommend chemotherapy or not? In the UK, this problem is solved by setting a threshold, so that if $P(A|B, C, D, E, \ldots)$ exceeds the threshold, the doctors undertake the treatment. The cutoff is apparently determined using the best available medical statistics and medical know-how. Insofar as medical statistics are not good enough, this affects the quality of the medical decision irrespective of whether one has used a frequency format or a probability format to compute the relevant conditional probability. In both cases, one would benefit from an improvement in medical statistics.

6.3.4 Does the FFP Tell Us Which Heuristic to Use?

In the FFP, people draw on an adaptive toolbox of heuristics and pick a heuristic that is appropriate to the environment (Gigerenzer et al., 1999; Gigerenzer & Selten, 2001b). Which heuristic will be employed from the adaptive toolbox of heuristics for a given problem? Gigerenzer (2008, pp. 38, 39) and Gigerenzer and Brighton (2011) give identical answers.

Both refer to a single paper by Rieskamp and Otto (2006). However, this paper provides a limited and unsatisfactory framework to answer one of the most fundamental questions in the FFP. In our view, this remains an open and unresolved question.

Rieskamp and Otto (2006) use a model of reinforcement learning in which people learn to use only one of two models: a take-the-best model and a WADD model (see section 6.2). The set of cues and their ecological validities are provided to the subjects; we have already noted the criticisms of experimenter-provided cues and validities. Since the reinforcement learning model is an adaptive model, no other strategy than the ones initially considered can ever emerge from the model. The question that subjects have to answer is, which of two companies is more creditworthy? The cues include financial flexibility, efficiency, capital structure, and personal financial resources.

No underlying model is provided that explains how these factors translate into greater creditworthiness—certainly economics does not directly provide such a model. Thus, the particular sample of companies that is used (the given reference class) has its own particular ecological validities of cues, and one cannot rule out the role of other cues/factors in determining creditworthiness. Indeed, there is no evidence that the relevant actors in real life (e.g., shareholders who invest in these companies), judge their creditworthiness by using such cues and their ecological validities.

Within this setup, take-the-best proves to be superior to WADD and gets better as more feedback is provided. It is now well-known that the reinforcement learning model is dominated by a range of learning models and provides misleading results on the speed of learning (Dhami, 2020b). For instance, Chmura et al. (2012) show that the reinforcement learning model gives the worst performance among the set of learning models that they consider. Incidentally, Reinhard Selten, one of the authors of the idea that heuristics are drawn from the adaptive toolbox, is a coauthor on this study.

In a nutshell, we currently know very little about how heuristics are drawn from the adaptive toolbox.

One may also pose a similar question for heuristics in the HBP. What are the exact situations and contexts in which the individual heuristics in the HBP are used? We believe that progress can be made in answering this question. For instance, consider how we might distinguish between the following three prominent heuristics in the HBP program—availability, anchoring, and representativeness. We suggest using treatment effects to answer this question. Both availability and anchoring require giving subjects historical information that they can draw on (availability) or anchor on (anchoring). Yet they work through different mechanisms. Anchoring requires making comparative and absolute judgments (section 5.3), but availability does not. This can lead to different predictions depending on whether such judgments are required or not in different treatments. On representativeness, we propose starting with small samples and then varying the sample size to see the effects on behavior (availability and anchoring predict no effect). So, in principle, the treatment effects can provide a better understanding of when these heuristics are invoked and when they are not. Perhaps a similar strategy could be used for the FFP.

6.4 On Mathematical Optimization and As-If Theories

The FFP has criticized economic theories, particularly prospect theory (see the appendix to chapter 2), on the grounds that theories based on optimization are as-if theories (Gigerenzer, 2008). In other words, these theories do not explicitly model the mental processes that lie behind actual decision-making and assume that humans behave as if they followed these theories. We have argued that models in the FFP are also as-if models (see sections 6.2 and 6.3) because they do not model the underlying mental and cognitive processes.

The FFP position is summarized in the following from Gigerenzer (2016, p. 38):

> Although behavioral economists started out with the promise of greater psychological realism, most have surrendered to the as-if methodology. Cumulative prospect theory, inequity-aversion theory, hyperbolic discounting are all as-if theories. They retain the expected utility framework and merely add free parameters with psychological labels ... which is like adding more Ptolemaic epicycles in astronomy. The resulting theories are more unrealistic than the expected utility theories they are intended to improve on. Behavioral economics has largely become a repair program from expected utility maximization.

Optimization is simply a tool used both by the BRA and by behavioral economics. But behavioral economics and its approach, methodology, results, and conclusions are very different from the canonical approach taken in the BRA. Here is an extreme analogy. The classical Greeks recognized the smallest indivisible unit of matter that we now call atoms by the early fifth century BC, as does modern science. This should not be taken to mean that modern science and the classical Greek approaches to understanding the physical world have any fundamental similarity or that one is a repair program for the other. After all, the Greek approach was not an experimental science at all. It could not directly confirm or reject the existence of atoms, whereas experiments are central to modern science.

Optimization and as-if theories are not bad or undesirable per se, unless they are rejected after stringent empirical testing. This is a point that we have repeatedly emphasized; see sections 3.2.5, 3.2.6, 4.3, 4.4, and our earlier remarks on prospect theory being a good as-if theory. In physics, the sun and the earth are often modeled as points (e.g., in solving the two-body and the three-body problems), which is an as-if approach; however, the predictions are remarkably accurate. As-if optimization-based models are untenable if they conflict with the evidence. However, the success of behavioral theories such as prospect theory, inequity-aversion theory, and hyperbolic discounting is impressive; overall, in their respective domains, they arguably explain the evidence better than the alternatives. If better alternatives emerge in due course, they should be embraced; this is the methodological approach in behavioral economics.

Of course, it is appropriate to criticize as-if optimization-based models if their predictions are inconsistent with the relevant evidence. Indeed, such a criticism is the starting point of behavioral economics. It has shown, conclusively we believe, that several standard theories that are employed in conjunction with optimization-based models in economics, such as expected utility, exponential discounted utility, self-regarding preferences, and several refinements of Nash equilibrium are inconsistent with the evidence; see chapters 2, 3, and 4.

Behavioral economics is certainly not a rescue project for expected utility. A great deal of evidence-gathering effort has gone into behavioral economics to show that expected utility is untenable. Extensive evidence shows that although prospect theory is an as-if theory, overall, across the entire domain of applications, it outperforms other theories in situations of risk/uncertainty/ambiguity (Wakker, 2010; Dhami, 2019a). It is a leading example of a tenable as-if theory in behavioral economics. To be sure, there are other models, including models of heuristics, such as the priority heuristic, that can explain some of the puzzles that prospect theory explains (Brandstätter et al., 2006). However, the priority heuristic has been criticized on the grounds that its predictions do not hold outside the data set used in the paper and that its use of statistical techniques is questionable (Birnbaum, 2008).

As of now, the range of phenomena explained by prospect theory is too vast to be accounted for by any other theory. For instance, it is not immediately clear how any current heuristics-based model can account for the following behaviors that are explained under prospect theory (Dhami, 2019a): What explains the equity-premium puzzle? Why do drivers quit too early on a rainy day in New York? Why are incentive contracts low-powered? Why do firms exist? What accounts for the endowment effect? Why is human behavior so sensitive to goals? Why is skewness in returns to assets priced? What explains the Ellsberg paradox?

Recent theoretical work also suggests that there is a link between heuristics-based approaches in time discounting and optimization models (see sections 4.3, 4.4, and 4.6). The relevant heuristics in some of these cases are noncompensatory and lexicographic.[5] Yet, as shown in sections 4.3, 4.4, 4.6, choice behavior in the presence of these heuristics is equivalent to an optimization-based model. This suggests that the heuristics-based and optimization-based approaches might be closer than one imagines them to be, although these issues have been insufficiently explored. This also suggests that behavioral economics is not averse to the absence of optimization and does not necessarily ignore procedural rationality.

The FFP has also expressed strong reservation to optimization-based theories on the grounds that they have free parameters (see the quotation above from Gigerenzer, 2016). But there are statistical tests that enable us to determine whether these parameters add enough in the way of explanatory power that justifies their use or not (e.g., Akaike information criterion and the Bayesian information criterion). The FFP requires that the parameters so estimated in these models should be held fixed in every context and frame in order to make predictions. For instance, it is argued that the parameter of loss aversion should be held fixed in all cases. This is unnecessarily stringent and not supported by the evidence. We do know that human behavior is context dependent and frame dependent; examples and evidence abound in all areas of behavioral economics (Dhami, 2016). Behavior also depends on age, culture, gender, moods, and emotions. For instance, when disgust is induced, or when individuals have just experienced a loss, measured loss aversion increases. These are predictions that can be tested (and have been successfully tested) and allow one to take account of the richness of human behavior. We see nothing objectionable in this approach.

6.5 On Distinct Domains of Choices in the HBP and FFP

As noted earlier, the BRA makes no predictions under true uncertainty, but people do make decisions under true uncertainty. We remind readers that true uncertainty is not the same as ambiguity (see section 2.2). How do people make decisions under true uncertainty? This question lies at the frontiers of social science, and relatively little is firmly established. We have touched on these issues in chapters 2, 3, and 4. Below we offer further observations on this issue and also argue that the FFP and the HBP are best seen as operating in different domains.

1. *Overconfidence*: Even under true uncertainty (unknown unknowns), overconfident individuals (see section 2.11) may believe, incorrectly, that they can see through all possible future outcomes and can assign subjective probabilities to them. This effectively turns a situation of true uncertainty into a situation of subjective uncertainty, or even of ambiguity. One can then use any of the standard decision-making models, such as prospect theory (the special cases, expected utility and rank dependent utility, cannot deal with ambiguity), or even some heuristics-based model based on the insights of, say, the priority heuristic.

2. *Conservation of cognitive effort*: Individuals may not believe that they can see through all the possible outcomes and probabilities under true uncertainty. Exerting cognitive and search costs to explore possible unknowns and their probabilities may be too costly, or these factors may simply be unknowable. Individuals may then, in the spirit of the aspiration-adaptation framework, simply satisfice by assigning a zero probability to everything that is unknown or unimaginable and choose to focus on the known outcomes only. This also turns a situation of true uncertainty into one of subjective uncertainty. As in 1, they can now choose to employ any of the standard decision-making models, such as prospect theory. For an analogue of such thinking under risk, where people simply ignore events of very low probabilities and optimize over the rest, see section 4.14.

3. *Norms*: A tantalizing possibility is that individual behavior under true uncertainty might be determined by social or personal norms. Consider, for instance, marriage, arguably a problem in the domain of true uncertainty. One may decide to have a trial live-in relationship and make the marriage decision based on an evaluation of the live-in period. This is a norm in some societies but not others. Historically, in traditional Indian arranged marriages, several social norms appeared to be at work in making this decision. We discuss these issues in section 3.4. Indeed, narratives (section 4.11) and mental models (section 4.12) may also play a role similar to social norms in guiding decision-making under true uncertainty.

4. *Heuristics*: Individuals may realize that they just do not have enough data to make any optimization-based decisions under true uncertainty, so

they may resort to simple heuristics to make their choice. Such heuristics could be based on norms, conventions, personal experience, gut feeling, or simply the advice of a trusted person.

There is no presumption that our four speculative categories are nonintersecting. For instance, heuristics may themselves be determined by social norms, which might in turn have been optimized by society to conserve cognitive effort in order, partly, to prevent overconfident individuals from making choices that are suboptimal. When we speak of true uncertainty below, we only consider the very last potential explanation—that is, a heuristics-driven account of true uncertainty—as if it were a stand-alone explanation.

Our main claim in this section is that the domain of decisions in the HBP and the FFP accounts of heuristics is, in many cases, nonintersecting. However, in some cases, the domains intersect, as in the use of the priority heuristic to deal with risk and in the discussion on the efficacy of the frequency format relative to the probability format in reducing biases relative to the BRA. We have already dealt with these issues elsewhere in this book. For this reason, here we focus exclusively on the difference in domains between the two approaches.

The HBP demonstration of heuristics and biases mainly considers the domains of *risk and uncertainty alone.* In several of their most important demonstrations of biases in their pioneering work in the 1970s, Kahneman and Tversky explicitly provide data on outcomes and probabilities to subjects. Hence, these are situations of risk and uncertainty. This includes their demonstration of the law of small numbers (which includes the gambler's fallacy and hot hand fallacy); base rate neglect and violation of Bayes' law; conservatism or underweighting of the likelihood of a sample; hindsight bias; confirmation bias; regression to the mean; false consensus effect; conjunction fallacy; and confusion between necessary and sufficient conditions.

In other cases used in the HBP, the distinction between risk/uncertainty and true uncertainty is less clear; this includes the affect heuristic and the anchoring heuristic. To see this, consider the experiments reported in Kahneman (2011) to illustrate the anchoring heuristic (see section 5.3). Subjects were asked the following two questions:

1. *Comparative judgment question*: Is the height of the tallest redwood more or less than x_0 feet?
2. *Absolute judgment question*: What is your best guess about the height of the tallest redwood?

For many people who might only have experienced the height of the usual set of trees (e.g., eucalyptus and oaks are about 66 feet tall, and the silver birch is about 100 feet tall) and have no extra information on the height of redwood trees, it might be hard to imagine their heights (the tallest recorded was 377 feet tall). Two different anchor values of x_0 ($x_0^H = 1200ft$, $x_0^L = 180ft$) were used. Subjects in the high anchor condition (x_0^H) guessed the height to be substantially greater, thereby confirming the anchoring effect. One might wonder if in this case, subjects who did not know the answer faced true uncertainty—that is, it might not have been possible for them to imagine all the possible heights and the associated probabilities for redwood trees.

However, several other demonstrations of the anchoring heuristic (and the affect heuristic) clearly fall within the domain of risk/uncertainty, yet one still observes the relevant biases. Here are some examples. The affect heuristic was demonstrated with members of the British Toxicology Association who were aware of the relevant risks (Slovic et al., 1999). The anchoring heuristic was demonstrated with property experts who were given all relevant information to evaluate the relevant properties (Northcraft & Neale, 1987). Poetry reading sessions where self-evaluation was used exhibited anchoring (Ariely et al., 2006), and experienced trial judges exhibited anchoring in legal judgment (Englich & Mussweiler, 2001).

One can, therefore, safely conclude that the relevant domain that the HBP has used to demonstrate biases relative to the BRA was either *certainty, risk, or subjective uncertainty*, but not *true uncertainty*. We argue below that, by contrast, the domain of problems that the FFP deals with typically lie within the domain of *true uncertainty*, which it describes as *large worlds*. This observation on the FFP is important because we vitally need not only to understand human decision-making in such environments but also to highlight that many of the contributions of the FFP and the HBP lie in nonintersecting domains. In light of this, the characterization of the positions taken in the HBP and the FFP as adversarial, as has been the case in the *great rationality debate*, is inaccurate and muddies the waters.

The research agenda in the FFP speaks directly to problems of true uncertainty. It distinguishes between *small worlds* and *large worlds*, drawing on terminology originally introduced by Savage (1954). *Small worlds* corresponds to our use of the terms *risk* and *subjective uncertainty* and large worlds corresponds to our use of the term *true uncertainty*. In introducing their research agenda and summarizing their approach, Gigerenzer et al. (2011, p. xviii) write:

How should we make decisions in the large world—that is, when Bayesian theory or similar optimization methods are out of reach? ... In sum, the accuracy-effort trade-off indeed exists in a small world. In a large world, however, where there is no general accuracy-effort trade-off, heuristics can be more accurate than methods that use more information and computation, including optimization methods. Thus, one reason why people rely on heuristics is that these allow for decisions in both small and large worlds.

In this quotation, the greater accuracy of heuristics relative to other methods that rely on more computation/information is predicated on the *less is more effect*, which we explain in greater detail in section 6.6.

A good example of this approach for economists is in financial market investment. It would appear to us to be impossible to predict or even to imagine all possible outcomes and their associated probabilities in stock markets, so it is, arguably, a problem in true uncertainty. The standard assumption in financial economics is to treat this as a problem in risk and uncertainty, yet even in this case there may be no unique prediction (see example 6.5). Candidate optimization benchmarks that are typically used in the FFP to evaluate their heuristics against, such as logistic regression, require information that is simply not available under true uncertainty. But people do invest in the stock market. How do they do it? We draw on two examples that are frequently cited in the FFP as examples of successful heuristics (Gigerenzer et al., 2011).

Example 6.4. *Borges et al. (1999) study the performance of the recognition heuristic in choosing among stocks (which requires that among any two stocks, choose the one that can be recognized) against the performance of other mutual funds. In six out of eight tests, the performance of the recognition heuristic was better than the performance of selected mutual funds. Economists would need more data and tests to be persuaded by the results. The data was collected over a period of one year in the midst of a strong bull market that might have favored stocks that are more easily recognized. More tests would need to be done to disentangle the predictions of the recognition heuristic from competing explanations.*

Example 6.5. *Consider the following simple investment strategy. In a portfolio of N assets, invest a share $\frac{1}{N}$ in each asset. This is sometimes known as the $\frac{1}{N}$ heuristic. Treating the problem of financial investment as one of risk and uncertainty (but not true uncertainty), DeMiguel et al. (2009) compare the performance of the $\frac{1}{N}$ heuristic with 14 other optimal investment theories often recommended in finance.[6] They use calibrated* values and compare the performance of the alternative methods, based on Sharpe ratios, over a long simulated length of time. Optimization-based investment theories require the estimation of statistical moments of the underlying statistical distributions (e.g., the mean and the variance-covariance matrices), but these are assumed to be estimated with error. In contrast, there are no measurement errors involved with the use of the $\frac{1}{N}$ heuristic.

Thus, the trade-off is this: the $\frac{1}{N}$ heuristic is not sophisticated enough to take advantage of potentially greater profit opportunities that come from a more nuanced distribution of the portfolio, while the use of optimization-based methods involves measurement errors that are reflected in lower ex post profits. The authors then show that the $\frac{1}{N}$ heuristic outperforms all the optimal investment models; this also illustrates that more information and computation do not necessarily produce better results. However, the transmission mechanism based on measurements errors in the optimization-based methods, but not in the $\frac{1}{N}$ heuristic, is different from the one invoked in the less is more effect in section 6.6.

We offer three main comments on this work.

1. No evidence is given that people (as distinct from investment firms) do indeed use any of the optimal investment strategies described in the paper.
2. The $\frac{1}{N}$ heuristic does not belong to the class of heuristics used in the FFP (e.g., there are no reference classes, cues, or ecological validities involved in the $\frac{1}{N}$ heuristic).
3. The problem of investing in financial markets is arguably a problem of true uncertainty. For these reasons, DiMiguel et al. (2009) address a different class of issues: namely, that under true uncertainty that is characteristic of the real world, but not of the models that they employ, the $\frac{1}{N}$ heuristic may perform better than the optimization-based benchmarks that were developed under risk and subjective uncertainty.

As our final point in this section, it is a tantalizing possibility that people may employ heuristics in the HBP when dealing with true uncertainty, although these heuristics were not explicitly designed for such a purpose. Suppose one faces a problem in true uncertainty. Then, one may actually be influenced by an externally provided anchor or suggestion (anchoring heuristic); or by the availability of apparently similar information in the past (availability heuristic); or by the emotional tags associated with the given information (affect heuristic). It might also be the case that Herbert Simon's aspiration-adaptation theory may be used in such cases. We believe that it is worth exploring this possibility in future research.

This would provide a different account of decision-making under true uncertainty, as compared to the FFP.

6.6 The Less Is More Effect

Gigerenzer (2008) writes: "That simple heuristics can be more accurate than complex procedures is one of the major discoveries of the last decades." This is encapsulated in the *less is more effect*. In *prediction tasks*, there is a trade-off between unbiasedness and variance minimization, a well-known result in statistics (Gigerenzer, 2008, Gigerenzer & Brighton, 2011). To gain insights into the less is more effect, suppose that the true, but unknown, underlying data generation process that we would like to discover is given by

$$y = f(x) + \varepsilon, \tag{6.1}$$

where y is the dependent variable; x is a vector of independent variables; f denotes a function; and ε is a normally distributed noise term that has zero mean and variance σ^2. The observer has the data, given by n observations, on the independent and the dependent variables; this constitutes the sample $S = \{(x_i, y_i)\}_{i=1}^{n}$. Based on the given data, the observer would like to discover the true, but unobservable, underlying function f. However, the relation between x and y is stochastic because of the noise term, ε. Hence, the only option for the observer is to use the data S (known as the *training set* in models of machine learning) to generate an estimator $\hat{f}$ of f. In order to do so, the observer employs a standard statistical criterion: minimize a loss function, L, over a class F of possible candidate functions, conditional on the sample, S. More compactly, we can write this as

$$\hat{f} \in \arg\min_{f \in F} L(f \mid S), \tag{6.2}$$

where the dependence of the loss function on the sample, S, shows that the estimated function $\hat{f}$ depends on S. The class of all linear regression estimators, $F = F_{LR}$, is one possible domain of functions to focus on. For this case, we have $\hat{f}(x) = a + bx$, where a, b are regression coefficients that are estimated from the sample S by minimizing mean square errors. Different values of a and b, written compactly as the vector $\beta = (a, b)$, give rise to different members in the set F_{LR}. In this case, the loss function in (6.2) takes the specific form

$$L(\beta \mid S) = \sum_{i}^{n} (y_i - (a + bx_i))^2, \text{ where } \beta = (a, b). \tag{6.3}$$

If we are now given new data $S_1 = \{(x_i, y_i)\}_{i=1}^{m}$, not originally used to estimate $\hat{f}$, then this data contain the out-of-sample observations and are known as the holdout samples (or the *validation set*). Denote the expected mean square prediction error $E_{S_1}\left(y - \hat{f}(x)\right)^2$, created by our estimated function $\hat{f}$, where E_{S_1} is the expected value with respect to the new sample S_1. We can go further, and we might wish our estimator $\hat{f}$ to be robust to all possible holdout samples, not just the sample S_1. Suppose that the set of all possible holdout samples is given by the set, U. Then, we wish to find an estimator $\hat{f}$ that has the lowest expected mean square prediction error across all possible holdout samples, $E\left(y - \hat{f}(x)\right)^2$, where E is the expectation operator with respect to all possible holdout samples U.

We are now in a position to derive the formula for the bias-variance dilemma.

Proposition 6.1. *The expected mean square prediction error across all possible holdout samples U is given by*

$$E\left(y - \hat{f}(x)\right)^2 = E\left[\text{Bias}\left(\hat{f}(x)\right)^2\right] + E\left[V\left(\hat{f}(x)\right)\right] + \sigma^2, \tag{6.4}$$

where $\sigma^2 = E\left[(y - f(x))^2\right]$ *and*

$$E\left[\text{Bias}\left(\hat{f}(x)\right)^2\right] = E\left[\left(f(x) - E\left[\hat{f}(x)\right]\right)^2\right] \tag{6.5}$$

$$E\left[V\left(\hat{f}(x)\right)\right] = E\left[\left(E\left[\hat{f}(x)\right] - \hat{f}(x)\right)^2\right]. \tag{6.6}$$

Proof of Proposition 6.1. Using (6.1), we have

$$E\left(y - \hat{f}(x)\right)^2 = E\left[\left(f(x) + \varepsilon - \hat{f}(x)\right)^2\right].$$

Expanding the RHS and noting that $E\left[\varepsilon\left(f(x) - \hat{f}(x)\right)\right] = E\left(f(x) - \hat{f}(x)\right)E\varepsilon = 0$ and that $E\varepsilon^2 = \sigma^2$, we have

$$E\left[\left(f(x) + \varepsilon - \hat{f}(x)\right)^2\right] = E\left[\left(f(x) - \hat{f}(x)\right)^2\right] + \sigma^2.$$

Add and subtract $E\left[\hat{f}(x)\right]$ on the RHS to get

$$E\left(y-\hat{f}(x)\right)^2 = E\left[\left(\left(f(x)-E\left[\hat{f}(x)\right]\right)+\left(E\left[\hat{f}(x)\right]-\hat{f}(x)\right)\right)^2\right]+\sigma^2.$$

Expanding the first term on the RHS and noting that the expectation of the cross product is zero, we get

$$E\left(y-\hat{f}(x)\right)^2 = E\left[\left(f(x)-E\left[\hat{f}(x)\right]\right)^2\right]+E\left[\left(E\left[\hat{f}(x)\right]-\hat{f}(x)\right)^2\right]+\sigma^2$$

or

$$E\left(y-\hat{f}(x)\right)^2 = E\left[\text{Bias}\left(\hat{f}(x)\right)^2\right]+E\left[V\left(\hat{f}(x)\right)\right]+\sigma^2. \qquad \Box$$

Proposition 6.1 shows that if one is interested in minimizing expected mean square prediction errors, then one must pay joint attention to the bias and the variance of the estimator function across all possible holdout samples. The inherent noise in the system, σ^2, cannot be eliminated. However, in choosing the best estimator function, $\hat{f}$, one faces a trade-off between fitting the function too closely to the true function f (reducing bias) and the resulting increase in the variance of the function $\hat{f}$ in all possible holdout samples.

We illustrate the bias-variance trade-off through two examples shown in the two panels in figure 6.1.[7] In the upper panel, the true underlying, and unobserved, function, f, is nonlinear. Due to the noise term, the data points are shown scattered around this function. We estimate f by a linear function, $\hat{f}$, drawn from $F = F_{LR}$. We fit a different function $\hat{f}$ to several possible samples in the set U; several such fitted functions are shown as thick upward sloping straight lines in the upper panel. The average fitted function over all these samples is the function $E\left[\hat{f}(x)\right]$. The difference between the true function $f(x)$ and $E\left[\hat{f}(x)\right]$ gives the bias for each value of x. Since the bias can be positive or negative, we are interested in the mean sum of squares of these bias terms across values of the independent variable, x, given by $E\left[\text{Bias}\left(\hat{f}(x)\right)^2\right]$ (shown as the shaded area "Bias^2" in figure 6.1). The Bias^2 term is large because we are fitting a linear function to a true underlying function that is nonlinear. Thus, we are underfitting the data. However, since all the fitted linear functions appear relatively close to each other (three such functions are shown in the upper panel), they are close to the average function $E\left[\hat{f}(x)\right]$. Thus, the term $E\left[V\left(\hat{f}(x)\right)\right]$, shown as "Variance" in figure 6.1, is relatively small.

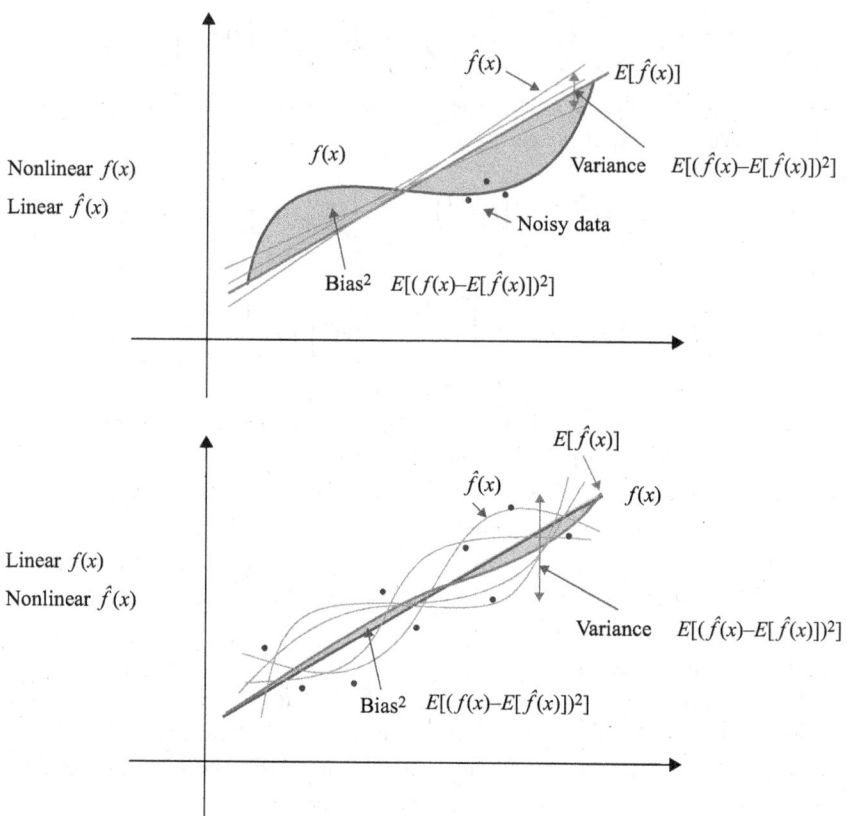

Figure 6.1
The bias-variance dilemma for two different cases.

Thus, fitting a linear function to a true nonlinear function produces low variance and high bias for the case shown in the upper panel.

The lower panel in figure 6.1 shows the case of a linear underlying true function, f, and fitted function, $\hat{f}$, that is highly nonlinear. Since the fitted function is a high degree polynomial, it fits very well the observed data points. The nonlinear fitted functions roughly average out to a straight line, shown as $E\left[\hat{f}(x)\right]$. The Bias^2 term (see shaded area) is relatively small. However, the variance of the fitted functions is high. In this case, we have overfitted the data because if we had instead fitted a more parsimonious function that had a poorer fit in-sample, it would have a better out-of-sample fit on average across all samples.

We seek a compromise between underfitting and overfitting the data by choosing the appropriate degree of the polynomial to fit (this is known as *regularization*). For lower order fitted polynomials, the bias is high but variance is low. For higher order fitted polynomials, bias is low but variance is high. Machine learning methods seek to optimize these trade-offs.

Proposition 6.1 lies at the heart of the *less is more* critique of the FFP. The bias-variance trade-off is statistically sound, but the relevant issue is whether it is useful to study human cognition. Gigerenzer and Brighton (2011, p. 12) write: "Our cognitive systems are confronted with the bias-variance dilemma whenever they attempt to make inferences about the world." However, we are not aware of any direct incontrovertible evidence in support of this assertion. Gigerenzer and Brighton cite Griffiths and Tenebaum (2006) and Oaksford and Chater (1998) as supporting evidence, but neither of these offers direct evidence that the human cognitive system considers the trade-off between bias and variance. In the absence of such an assertion, it is a leap of faith to assume that the human mind is so hardwired as to develop and use algorithms that consider the bias-variance trade-off. By implication, we also have no direct observations that the less is more effect is central to human cognition and decision-making. We do not deny the immense importance of proposition 6.1 in other areas such as machine learning, engineering, and public policy.

6.6.1 A Critique of the Bias-Variance Trade-off

We now examine other objections to the use of the bias-variance dilemma.

1. *Loss aversion and the objective function*: The objective function of minimizing the loss function in (6.3), which is used to prove proposition 6.1, gives equal weights to positive and negative forecast errors of the same magnitude. Loss aversion is now well established as an empirical phenomena, not just under certainty, risk, and uncertainty but also in the domain of temporal choices where losses are discounted less than gains (see sections 2.13 and 2.16.4). Thus, it is plausible to conjecture that, when engaged in prediction tasks, people will give different weights to negative and positive prediction errors; one would expect negative forecast errors to be more salient. If this were found to be true, then there is no presumption that proposition 6.1 will hold.

2. *Suitability of the error structure*: The error structure underlying the derivation of proposition 6.1 assumes that $E[\varepsilon] = 0$ and $V[\varepsilon] = \sigma^2$. By contrast, we now know from a great deal of evidence in behavioral economics, particularly in behavioral finance, that people make systematic prediction forecasting errors, not random ones. For an extended

period of time, such forecast errors can accumulate in the same direction, which leads to systematic divergence of stock market prices from the fundamental values (see our discussion of bubbles in financial markets in section 3.2.3). Insofar as real world data incorporate such systematic prediction errors, there is no guarantee that the assumptions on the error structure in proposition 6.1 are supported.

3. *Mental models*: In actual practice, there is likely to be a range of objectives other than the simple minimization of squares of prediction errors reflected in proposition 6.1. There is a growing literature on how people form *mental models* to understand complex reality in a manner that is unlikely to be the outcome of a bias-variance trade-off. We discuss mental models in section 4.12. In other cases, people might use social norms or narratives to make decisions in the face of true uncertainty (section 3.4). There is no presumption that social norms or narratives minimize the expected squares of prediction errors.

4. *Nonstationary environments and behavioral factors*: Unlike the assumption made in proposition 6.1 of a stationary (though stochastic) underlying environment, the real world environment typically is not stationary, as reflected in the models of complexity that we considered in section 4.9. In many cases, people do not know the true underlying model, but they try to form inferences about the correctness of competing models by examining the data. For instance, do stock market data come from an underlying model that is mean-reverting or trending? What if investors believe that the world switches between these two models depending on some underlying Markov transition process? Barberis et al. (1998) consider investor inference in such a scenario. This can explain stock market underreaction and overreaction relative to the rational benchmark. In other words, economic models require individuals to form beliefs on the relevant economic model and then update their beliefs by using observed data. It is possible that they never learn the true model and keep updating in the wrong direction (Dhami, 2020b, section 2.9). Furthermore, confirmation bias, hindsight bias, and overconfidence may furnish other powerful reasons why they cannot successfully learn the underlying models. However, all these critical considerations are missing from the purely statistical and mechanical exercise of minimizing prediction errors in (6.4).

5. *Decision tasks and prediction tasks*: Most of the tasks that economists are interested in are not *prediction tasks*; rather, these are *decision tasks* that require an appropriate decision theory, such as prospect theory, or

hyperbolic discounting. For instance, how much should a tax evader evade, given the probabilities of detection and fines? How much should one invest in a risky asset relative to a safe asset, given that the distribution of returns of the risky asset is known objectively/subjectively? As a taxi driver who chooses the hours of work, how many hours should the taxi driver work, conditional on a given wage? Should one buy a gym membership on a pay-as-you-go basis or on a fixed-fee basis? Should a firm preempt the introduction of a new product before its competitor firm does? For concrete and empirically supported answers to these questions from a behavioral economics perspective that is independent of the bias-variance dilemma, see Dhami (2016).

6.6.2 Implications of the Less Is More Effect for the HBP

An important criticism of the HBP by the FFP is that the HBP does not take account of the second term on the RHS of (6.4) (i.e., variance), so a demonstration of biased inference in the HBP gives an incomplete/misleading picture. However, there are several weaknesses with this argument.

The HBP was interested in potential biases that decision-makers may exhibit relative to the predictions of the BRA framework. It is important to realize that not all of these biases are statistical biases. For instance, an important element of the BRA is the assumption that people have complete and transitive preferences. A demonstration of nontransitivity, as in Lichtenstein and Slovic (1971), is a bias relative to the BRA, but not in a statistical sense.

Most heuristics in the HBP do not use the bias-variance trade-off as their justification, and as noted above, there is strong empirical support for these heuristics. In many cases, the relevant heuristics in the HBP may be used perhaps because they reduce the cognitive dissonance that would arise from an imperfect understanding of the world and from being shown up as incompetent in some domains (Kahneman, 2011). Confirmation bias and hindsight bias are not about predictive judgments but postdictive judgments, so they are backward looking, which has nothing to do with the bias-variance dilemma. Anchoring is about a previously given anchor; availability is about predicting on the basis of available information from memory; the representativeness heuristics is about inferring how likely a small population is to have come from some parent population (this includes the gambler's fallacy and the hot hand fallacy); not recognizing regression to the mean and the conjunction fallacy are also not about minimizing predictive error. Thus, the existence of an entire body of empirically successful, fast and frugal, ecologically rational heuristics that do not rely on the bias-variance dilemma suggests that its importance under risk and uncertainty, which is the domain used in the HBP, is overemphasized in the FFP. The bias-variance dilemma could be important under true uncertainty, but that is mainly the domain of the FFP, not the HBP.

7
Philosophical Foundations

7.1 Introduction

We now turn to some fundamental issues about bounded rationality, behavioral economics, and public policy. We offer two main claims. The first is that in light of behavioral findings, policymakers should adopt a working presumption in favor of respect for people's self-regarding choices, but only if those choices are adequately informed and sufficiently free from behavioral biases. These are important qualifications, calling for significant departures from standard economic approaches to welfare analysis.

The second is that the working presumption is itself rebuttable on welfare grounds. Even if people's self-regarding choices involve their *direct* judgments (as defined below), regulators should not *necessarily* respect them. The ends that people choose might make their lives go less well. For example, they might die prematurely or suffer from serious illness, and what they receive in return might not (on any plausible account of welfare) be nearly enough. The underlying reason might involve a lack of information or a behavioral bias, identifiable or not, in which case intervention can be made consistent with the working presumption. But the real problem might involve philosophical questions about the proper understanding of welfare and about what it means for people to have a good life. Still, regulators should proceed with great caution on the ground that reasonable people reasonably care about diverse goods and can make reasonable, and different, judgments about how much weight to give them. This point supports the working presumption and calls for humility in the face of self-regarding choices, certainly when choosers are sufficiently informed and sufficiently free from behavioral biases.

These points suggest that behavioral welfare economics, even as used in applied work and in government circles, must at least implicitly take a stand on the best understanding of welfare. We do not offer anything like a comprehensive account in this space, but in brief, we shall argue (1) that purely hedonic accounts, and even those that emphasize subjective well-being more broadly, ignore important aspects of what people legitimately care about; (2) that preference-based accounts pay too little attention to behavioral biases and to the ingredients of what is, for essentially all people, a good human life; and (3) that objective-good accounts may underplay human diversity and the heterogeneous goods that matter to reasonable people. The working presumption can be seen as a pragmatic way of accommodating points (1), (2), and (3). With respect to both theory and practice, it aspires to an "incompletely theorized agreement" (Sunstein, 2018b), a principle on which people can converge despite their disagreement or uncertainty about the most fundamental questions.

With an emphasis on human welfare, an illuminating and growing body of work explores whether and in what sense economists, lawyers, and others interested in behaviorally informed public policy can continue to insist on the sovereignty of individual preferences, while also acknowledging behavioral findings (for a highly selective account, see Allcott & Sunstein, 2015; Allcott & Kessler, 2019; Bernheim & Rangel, 2007, 2009; Bernheim, 2009; Thunström, 2019). For generations, economists have been committed to that form of sovereignty; as we have seen, behavioral findings have shaken that commitment. Our central aim here is to argue for a degree of humility, captured in the working presumption (see also Allcott & Sunstein, 2015).[1] As we shall see, this presumption can be disciplined by asking a series of subsidiary questions, and it should be accompanied by a distinction between *means paternalism* and *ends paternalism*, of special relevance to behaviorally informed law and policy. On welfarist grounds, we are more enthusiastic about means paternalism than about ends paternalism, though we are not prepared to rule the latter out of bounds.

To anchor the discussion, consider the following cases:

1. Sarah Masters recently bought a car. She considered a package with various safety features, including a camera designed to ensure rear visibility, but she rejected it; the package would have cost $75. Many consumers are making the same decision that Masters made.
2. Jerry Lancaster is significantly overweight (and, as a result, at heightened risk of getting diabetes and heart disease). He would like to diet, but he is not sure how. He goes to restaurants every day for lunch, and he tends to order high-calorie items. He is not aware of the caloric content of his orders. Many consumers act as Lancaster does.

3. Pamela Harston is eligible for the Earned Income Tax Credit, which is available to supplement the income of the working poor. She is aware of her eligibility. But she is not quite sure how to apply. She is also very busy. She thinks that she will apply next month. She has thought that for a long time. Many people are doing as Harston does: failing to apply for benefits for which they are eligible.

4. Edward Ullner is in his 30s; he is also healthy. In the midst of a pandemic, very much like the coronavirus pandemic of 2020, he is not especially worried. He does not believe that he will fall ill, and even if he does, he does not believe that he will suffer long-term harm. He does not wear a mask, and he does not stay at home.

In all of these cases, it is at least plausible to think that the relevant agent is making some kind of mistake, one that will produce serious harm. We could also believe, certainly in the case of Ullner, that harm to others is involved. But even if we bracket that possibility, the point remains: Ullner might be endangering his own life, perhaps because of an absence of information, perhaps because of unrealistic optimism, or perhaps because of both. On welfare grounds, regulators might want to respond in some way, perhaps with a nudge (Thaler & Sunstein, 2008), perhaps with an economic incentive, or perhaps with a ban or a mandate (Conly, 2013).

7.2 Choices and Welfare

Do people's choices promote their welfare? Exactly when? How, exactly, do behavioral findings bear on those questions? Some of the most careful and illuminating discussions of the underlying issues, at the intersection of economic theory and political philosophy, come from Bernheim (2016), who begins by noting that "standard welfare economics" associates welfare with choices. We can understand Bernheim's work as a particularly clear attempt to rescue the foundations of welfare economics while acknowledging behavioral findings. His work also bears directly on questions in policy and law, such as the legitimate domain of paternalism, and for that reason, it is worth careful attention here. He suggests that standard welfare economics invokes three general premises (Bernheim, 2016):

1. Each of us is the best judge of our own well-being.
2. Our judgments are governed by coherent, stable preferences.
3. Our preferences guide our choices: when we choose, we seek to benefit ourselves.

Something like these premises played a central role in the early decades of economic analysis of law, grounded in welfare economics (Posner, 1973), and similar premises to play a significant role in law and policy today. Bernheim (2016) recognizes that the resulting understanding "may fall short of a philosophical ideal" but urges that this "should not trouble us excessively" because it "captures important aspects of well-being and lends itself to useful implementation." That is an eminently reasonable claim, but it leaves open questions, and it remains to be specified; in some cases, it might also point in the wrong directions. Consider, for example, the question whether on welfare grounds a soda tax is a good idea (Allcott et al., 2019a, 2019b); whether energy efficiency regulations can be justified as a response to consumer mistakes (Allcott, 2016); whether heavy taxes on cigarettes might make smokers better off (Gruber & Mullainathan, 2005); whether motor vehicle safety regulation might provide people with "experience goods," such as rear visibility, and thus improve their lives by their own lights (Sunstein, 2019b); whether nudges or mandates might be a good idea in the context of a pandemic (to prevent harm to choosers, not to others). In these and other cases, falling short of a philosophical ideal might turn out to be a fatal flaw. (We will turn in due course to philosophical ideals.)

And what, exactly, is meant by the claim that the standard understanding "captures important aspects of well-being"? Perhaps the suggestion, empirical in nature, is that much of the time, satisfaction of people's preferences does, as a matter of fact, promote their well-being (properly understood), simply because they know what they like.[2] Bernheim (2016) makes something like this claim, invoking "the central Cartesian principle that subjective experience is inherently private and not directly observable." He adds: "We know how we feel; others can only make educated guesses. These considerations create a strong presumption in favor of deference to our judgments." (There are nice empirical questions here about whether subjective experience does, in fact, continue to be "inherently private" and whether people actually know what they like. Sometimes people might not know, in advance, what they will like, and sometimes people might not entirely know, at the time of experience, what they like.)

Bernheim (2016) also makes a separate argument, involving autonomy rather than welfare: "My views about my life are paramount because it is, after all, my life." This is a Kantian idea, suggesting the importance of respect for choosers, even if they err. People are ends, not means. Writing in this vein, Jeremy Waldron (2014) urges:

Deeper even than this is a prickly concern about dignity. What becomes of the self-respect we invest in our own willed actions, flawed and misguided though they often are, when so many of our choices are manipulated to promote what someone else sees (perhaps rightly) as our best interest? ... I mean dignity in the sense of self-respect, an individual's awareness of her own worth as a chooser.

An emphasis on the idea that people are making choices about their lives might reflect a commitment to respect for dignity and autonomy, not welfare at all.[3] That form of respect, rooted in a nonutilitarian framework that economists do not usually embrace, might stand as a decisive objection to paternalism in policy and law.[4]

Bernheim's emphasis on "the central Cartesian principle that subjective experience is inherently private and not directly observable" and on our unique knowledge of "how we feel" fits well with Mill's (2002/1863) epistemic argument for respecting freedom of choice and in particular his claim that the "ordinary man or woman has means of knowledge immeasurably surpassing those that can be possessed by anyone else." When people choose chocolate over vanilla, salmon over tuna, basketball over football, rest over recreation, or spending over saving, they do so because they know what they like. Outsiders are most unlikely to have that knowledge.[5]

For reasons we have explored, it is important to be cautious here. Let us return to behavioral findings and in particular to the cases of Masters, Lancaster, Harston, and Ullner. Even if people usually have unique knowledge of "how they feel," their knowledge on that count may not be perfect (T. Wilson, 2004). With respect to how people's choices will actually affect their welfare, external observers might know far better, especially if the area requires technical expertise (Bubb & Pildes, 2014). If I choose one kind of car over another, will my welfare be improved? What if I choose one kind of health care plan over another? Recall that choosers must solve a prediction problem; they must attempt to anticipate, at some point in advance of actual experience, the effects of one or another option on that experience (Kahneman et al., 1997).[6] To solve that problem, knowing how they feel is not enough. At a minimum, they must know how they will feel, and they might not know nearly enough to know that. In many circumstances, including those of a pandemic, the case for various mandates may well turn out to be plausible on welfare grounds; return to the case of Ullner. (Again, it is possible to defend mandates as a way of avoiding harms to third parties or as a way of solving collective action problems, but we are trying not to take the easy way out, conceptually speaking, and to focus on harms to choosers as such.) As a general rule, the claim for the epistemic advantages of choosers is more than plausible. Still, we have seen that it has taken a real battering from behavioral findings.[7]

7.3   Direct and Indirect Judgments

Many people are troubled by that apparent battering.[8] For current purposes, the most important challenge involves what Bernheim describes as premise 1. The behavioral findings we have explored seem to suggest that "people do not reliably exercise good judgment." More precisely, behavioral science shows that people sometimes make mistakes about what would promote their own well-being, and in some cases, they are not the best judges of what would do that.[9] If so, Mill's epistemic argument is severely undermined. For purposes of law and policy, the door would seem open to paternalism, not only in the form of nudges but also in the form of mandates and bans (Conly, 2013; Bubb & Pildes, 2014). At least this is so if welfare is our guide.

In what might plausibly be taken as an effort to reconstruct and even to rescue the essentials of standard welfare economics and Mill's basic account, Bernheim (2016) responds that the argument on behalf of paternalism "is faulty because it conflates what I will call direct and indirect judgments." In this way, Bernheim is attempting to lay the foundations for choice-oriented methods for conducting welfare analysis in the presence of behavioral biases. In his account, a direct judgment involves ultimate objectives or outcomes that people care about for their own sake. An indirect judgment, by contrast, involves alternatives that lead to those outcomes. We might understand direct judgments to involve intrinsic goods (such as enjoyment of a day or a month, or a sense of meaning in life) and indirect judgments to involve goods that are instrumental to their realization (such as a visit to a museum or a day off at a beach).

As an example of an indirect judgment, Bernheim points to a person, called Norma, who is choosing between two boxes, a red one containing a pear and a yellow one containing an apple. She prefers apples, but she chooses the red one, mistakenly ending up with a pear. This is a welfare-reducing indirect judgment, and Bernheim agrees that Norma has made a mistake. In his view, behavioral findings typically involve mistakes of that kind. More specifically: "Behavioral economics and psychology provide us with ample reason to question certain types of indirect judgments." In the face of a mistaken indirect judgment about money, safety, or health, a response might take the form of a mandatory disclosure, a warning, or some other kind of nudge, such as a default rule; in extreme cases, it might justify a ban (Conly, 2013). But, so long as we are speaking only of indirect judgments, we might insist that we have not departed radically from Mill's general anti-paternalistic framework, amending it only to say that for indirect judgments, his epistemic argument sometimes fails. The cases of Marston, Lancaster, Harston, and Ullner can be understood in precisely these terms.

We can link Bernheim's (2016) argument here with the suggestion that on welfare grounds, behavioral findings justify "means paternalism" but not necessarily "ends paternalism" (Sunstein, 2014b). The basic idea is that people are sometimes mistaken about how to get to their own preferred destination. On that view, behaviorally informed interventions increase navigability, writ very large. A GPS device is a form of means paternalism; it allows drivers to specify where they want to go (and helps them to get there). A calorie label can be seen as a form of means paternalism insofar as it improves people's ability to make their own choices about how to promote their ends. A default rule, automatically enrolling people in some program, can be seen as means paternalistic insofar as it is thought that (most) people prefer to be enrolled in that program (but do not enroll because they suffer from inertia) (Madrian & Shea, 2002).

Many efforts to increase navigability, embodying a form of means paternalism, retain freedom of choice and so can be seen as compatible with Mill's HARM PRINCIPLE (Sunstein, 2019a). But some do not. A ban on trans fats can be regarded as a form of means paternalism, at least if we are clear that the ban fits with, and does not undermine, people's ends (Conly, 2013). Occupational safety requirements (say, a ban on exposure to certain chemicals) can be seen in similar terms, even if they override the choices of unrealistically optimistic workers who would be willing to run the risks that those requirements eliminate (Akerlof and Dickens, 1982). When behavioral research finds that people are making a mistake, we have a behavioral market failure, in the sense that people's judgments lead to some kind of welfare loss, perhaps because of an identifiable behavioral bias (Bar-Gill, 2012; cf. Akerlof & Shiller, 2016). Much of behavioral law and economics is focused on that problem (Bar-Gill, 2012; Bubb & Pildes, 2014). As invoked for purposes of law and policy, behavioral market failures typically involve means paternalism rather than ends paternalism (Bar-Gill, 2012). To see the underlying issues, let us use Bernheim's terminology, distinguishing between direct and indirect judgments.

Does that distinction work? How helpful is it? Insofar as we are dealing with unambiguously indirect judgments, and thus respecting people's ends, the problem of unjustified paternalism seems to be reduced. But when, in ordinary practice, are those involved in law or policy dealing with direct judgments? An initial problem is that if Norma prefers apples to pears, it is natural to ask whether an indirect judgment is involved as well. Apples are good, but it would be hard to justify the conclusion that they are "ultimate objectives, or outcomes that people care about for their own sake." (Friendship might be an intrinsic good; not so much apples.) If Norma prefers apples to pears, it is probably because she thinks that they taste better or perhaps that they are healthier to eat. But perhaps she is wrong on either or both those counts. In other words, her preference for apples is itself an indirect judgment, and she might be badly mistaken, perhaps because of a behavioral bias.

The legal applications are numerous, including regulatory responses to unhealthy eating (Rabin, 2013b), insufficient savings (Bubb & Pildes, 2014), and "dark patterns" online (Luguri & Strahilevitz, 2019). Bernheim (2016) is alert to this point and adds:

> Now let us add a wrinkle: assume Norma's ultimate goal is to achieve certain mental states ("internal goods"). From that perspective, all consumption items ("external goods") are means to ends, and choices among them always involve indirect judgments. Moreover, just as Norma may misjudge the contents of a box, she may also misapprehend the relationships between consumption goods and mental states. *However, assuming she is sufficiently familiar with apples, pears, and bananas to understand the consequences of eating each, her indirect judgments among open boxes will be correctly informed, and hence will faithfully reflect her direct judgments.*

What is rightly added here is more than a wrinkle; it is fundamental to behaviorally informed law and policy and to behavioral welfare economics. Norma is probably not concerned only with internal mental states (she might well care about price, health, and morality), and this is a significant point, counting against purely hedonic accounts of welfare (sometimes favored by economists); but when it comes to food choices, her mental state is almost certainly something that she cares about. Consumption choices are typically means to ends, and in that sense, they typically involve indirect judgments.

Moreover, the assumption of sufficient familiarity might not turn out to hold. For many choices, people are not sufficiently familiar with the options "to understand the consequences" of each, and even if they are, they might suffer from some kind of behavioral bias, such as present bias.[10] In this light, we should add that for Norma's choice of apples to be a good measure of her welfare, she must not only be informed ("sufficiently familiar") but also free from any such bias. Modifying Mill, we might adopt this working presumption in favor of an amended version of premise 1, designed to orient behavioral welfare economics as applied to law and policy:

Working presumption *Each of us should be taken by outsiders to be the best judge of our own well-being, to the extent that we are adequately informed and sufficiently free of behavioral biases.*

The working presumption is an effort to build on choice-oriented methods for welfare analysis, as in Bernheim's approach, but for two reasons, it is more cautious. First, it is only a presumption. Second, it does not depend in any way on a distinction between direct and indirect judgments, or ends and means, though it is true that in application, it is usually likely to support interventions in the interest of means paternalism. Note also the words "should be taken by outsiders to be," as distinguished from the more dogmatic "are"; we return to the difference below.

Of course, there are questions about how to operationalize the working presumption, to which we will turn in chapter 9. If we care about welfare, it would make sense

1. to examine what choices people make when they are actually well informed;
2. to learn what consistent choosers, not affected by self-evidently irrelevant factors, end up choosing;
3. to see what choices people make when they do not suffer from limited attention and are in a position to evaluate all relevant facets of an option;
4. to use people's active choices rather than passive ones, which may be a product of inertia; and
5. to use otherwise unbiased choices, such as long-run choices based on a realistic understanding of facts, rather than biased ones, such as those that reflect present bias or optimistic bias (Allcott and Sunstein, 2015).

Ideas of this kind can be seen as an effort to draw on a broadly Millian understanding, respectful of consumer sovereignty and private choices, while also recognizing and giving weight to information deficits and behavioral biases.[11] They might provide a way to discipline behavioral welfare economics in areas that include savings behavior, decisions with respect to energy-efficient products, and choices of high-calorie or low-calorie food (Thunström, 2019).

By contrast, one of Bernheim's goals is to insist on respect for direct judgments. Instead of the working presumption above, he argues in favor of two premises (Bernheim & Taubinsky, 2018):

Premise A *With respect to matters involving either direct judgment or correctly informed indirect judgment, each of us is the best arbiter of our own well-being.*

Premise B *When we choose, we seek to benefit ourselves by selecting the alternative that, in our judgment, is most conducive to our well-being.*

In defense of premise A, Bernheim (2016) urges that existing economic research does not "provide evidence that people exercise poor direct judgment—for example, that they like certain goods or experiences 'too much' and others 'not enough.'" On the contrary, he maintains, "The occasional objection to a direct judgment entails nothing more than a difference of opinion between the analyst and the consumer as to what constitutes a good or fulfilling life." The conclusion might be right, but these are strong words—too strong, in our view, and for three separate reasons.

First, they disregard the possibility that people are genuinely making a mistake about what makes human lives, including their own, go well—not because of a mere difference of opinion between the analyst and the consumer but because that conclusion follows from any reasonable judgment about what it means for a human life to be good or fulfilling or to go well. (For example, longevity and health matter, even if they are not everything.) Second, they take a stand on some contentious philosophical issues about human welfare (a point taken up below). Third, they collapse the distinction between two very different questions: (1) Do people know what they will like before they have it? (2) Do people know what they like when they are having it? Even if we think the answer to the second question is usually yes, we have not answered the first question.

Repeating the basic claim elsewhere, Bernheim and Taubinsky (2018) add: "Thus there is no objective foundation for overturning the presumption in favor of a direct judgment and declaring the analyst's perspective superior." But the underlying issues are more complicated than that. It is true that if all we have is a difference of opinion between the analyst and the chooser, then we do not, by stipulation, have an "objective foundation" for favoring the views of the analyst. But what if the analyst has an actual data, suggesting that people's direct judgment produces large welfare losses (Levitt, 2016)? What if the analyst has information about what people are likely to like, and what if that information suggests that people's ex ante predictions are incorrect? What if the analyst has an account of what makes for a good or fulfilling life, and not simply an "opinion" (Feldman, 2010)?

7.4 Practice and Theory

We now offer three claims. The first is that for behavioral welfare economics and behaviorally informed law and policy, indirect judgments, or judgments about means, really are the coin of the realm. If we are speaking about inertia, present bias, unrealistic optimism, probability neglect (Sunstein, 2002), or limited attention, we are almost always dealing with judgments or decisions that might defeat people's own ends. And if we are speaking of default rules, disclosure, reminders, warnings, or uses of social norms, we are almost always dealing with efforts to encourage people to choose better means to achieve their own ends. Behavioral welfare economics typically deals with indirect judgments, and if it embraces paternalism, it is means paternalism (usually, at least).

The second is that with respect to direct judgments, behavioral welfare economics, like standard welfare economics, should proceed with humility. One reason is empirical; another is normative. To say that informed choosers are the best arbiters of their own welfare is to run afoul of a great deal of empirical evidence (and potentially to take a contested stand on how to think about the very idea of welfare). In the liberal tradition, time-honored ideas about autonomy and welfare do support a working presumption in favor of something like that proposition. But the presumption should be embraced with caution, and with an understanding of what kind of stand it is taking.

The third claim, and the most ambitious, involves the proper understanding of welfare. Put too simply, the claim is that each of the three prevailing theories in philosophical and economic circles—rooted in preferences, subjective well-being, and objective goods (Adler, 2011)—run into serious problems. Satisfaction of people's preferences, understood as their ex ante judgments about what to choose, will not always promote their welfare, simply because they might be inadequately informed or suffer from some kind of behavioral bias.

Impressed with this point, some social scientists now speak not in terms of preferences but in terms of subjective well-being, often measured hedonically: What is the quality of people's experience? Are they enjoying their moments? Their days? Their weeks? But the idea of subjective well-being can be vague and slippery, and we should not understand well-being or welfare in purely hedonic terms. People might choose to have a more meaningful life even if they end up sadder or more anxious. They might care about meaningfulness, not happiness or a lack of anxiety. People might choose a life that they consider to be better, even if they are more distressed as a result of choosing that life. Perhaps we can acknowledge these points, reject purely hedonic accounts, and nonetheless rely on subjective well-being, taking that concept to be broad enough to include everything that people (subjectively) care about, including a sense of meaning or purpose, or of doing good works, or of showing devotion to God. But suppose that people live under conditions of deprivation, injustice, and ignorance, such that their subjective well-being is relatively good even though their lives are short, unhealthy, and relatively brutal. If we care about welfare, ought we not to explore what kinds of lives people are actually able to live, and not rely entirely on subjective measures (Nussbaum, 2000)? To be sure, subjective experience matters; it is a large part of welfare. But it is not all that matters. These points might be taken to lead us to objective-good theories of well-being, asking questions about longevity, health, education, and more (Nussbaum, 2000). Across a certain domain, objective-good theories have considerable appeal. At the same time, what is good for John might not be good for Jane, and objective-good theories sometimes struggle (we think) to take account of heterogeneity.

The working presumption sketched above is not meant to take a stand on the deepest philosophical questions. But we shall try to bring the working presumption in contact with those questions and to show its appeal on pragmatic grounds. To simplify a complex story: The working presumption embodies an understanding that preference-based accounts of welfare must recognize that people might suffer from insufficient information and behavioral biases. It offers a highly qualified version of those accounts, and in important respects, it rejects them. The working presumption also recognizes that purely hedonic accounts of welfare, or even those that focus on subjective well-being, miss the fact that reasonable people reasonably care about things other than their moods, their subjective well-being, or even their lived experience. Recall that they might, for example, want to live meaningful lives. The working presumption need not be taken to embrace objective-good accounts of welfare, on the ground that reasonable people choose to live a great diversity of good lives, but it leaves open the possibility that some lives are objectively bad.

7.5 The Pervasiveness of Indirect Judgments

As applied to law and policy (Thaler & Sunstein, 2008; Conly, 2013; Mullainathan & Shafir, 2013), almost all of behavioral economics involves indirect judgments. The bulk of behavioral research involves such judgments as well (Kling et al., 2012). For example, the choice of one product over another—say, the Toyota RAV4 over the Toyota RAV4 Hybrid—will almost certainly be a result of a number of subsidiary indirect judgments: how the preferred vehicle looks, how it drives, how reliable it will be, how big it is, the storage space, the purchase price, the anticipated cost of operation, how often one will have to refuel. What is the direct judgment here?

We should agree that if a consumer named Susan makes some kind of clear mistake—she wants a smaller car and wrongly believes that the hybrid model is bigger—she is like Norma, selecting the wrong box. But suppose that Susan makes a subtler error: she is insufficiently responsive to fuel savings, in the sense that she would have saved a lot of money with the RAV4 Hybrid but, because of present bias, she decided against it (Gillingham et al., 2019). Unless we introduce other considerations (such as a liquidity constraint), Susan was mistaken. She was not, in this case, the best judge of her own well-being. Some kind of intervention would appear to be justified, perhaps in the form of clear disclosure of relevant information (if the disclosure works, as it might not, to overcome present bias).

Perhaps we should say that Susan was not "sufficiently familiar with" the two kinds of cars "to understand the consequences" of choosing one or the other, and so her indirect judgment between the two was not "correctly informed, and hence" did not "faithfully reflect her direct judgments." Fair enough. But if that is the case, it is tempting to ask: Exactly how much remains of the idea of deference to individual judgment in cases of genuine or realistic interest to law and public policy?[12] A great deal still, perhaps, but a lot less than suggested by standard economic theory. In many circumstances, people are undoubtedly good indirect choosers, likely better than anyone else, but when they lack information or suffer from a behavioral bias, their indirect choices will not be reliable. Whether particular choices fall in that category is an empirical question.

To broaden the viewscreen: Many laws and regulations involve externalities, and for that reason, much of the welfare analysis need not emphasize bounded rationality or draw on behavioral economics; it is conventional. For example, fuel economy regulations impose costs, which can be calculated and which are imposed largely on consumers in the form of higher sticker prices (Bento et al., 2019). Those regulations also reduce air pollution, including greenhouse gas emissions; monetization is more challenging here, but standard tools are available to do exactly that (Greenstone, 2013). To this extent, the welfare analysis should be familiar (Gayer & Viscusi, 2013). The distinctly behavioral dimension comes from possible errors on the part of consumers, who may not be giving sufficient weight to economic savings (from reduced gas usage) and time savings (from fewer visits to the gas station) (see the catalog in Gayer & Viscusi, 2013). For behavioral reasons, consumers may indeed make errors, which means that on welfare grounds, they might stand to gain a great deal from fuel economy mandates, even when those mandates override their choices (for a skeptical view, see Gayer & Viscusi, 2013; for a less skeptical view, see Allcott & Sunstein, 2015).

Consumers can, of course, choose fuel-efficient vehicles if they like. If they do not, perhaps it is because the less fuel-efficient vehicles are smaller or less powerful or inferior along some other dimension. The behavioral question is whether consumers neglect fuel economy because of (for example) present bias, myopic loss aversion, or limited attention or instead consider fuel economy but find it outweighed by other factors. The behavioral hunch is that present bias or limited attention do play a role, but a hunch is not evidence.[13] Behavioral welfare economics would carefully investigate the hunch and consider consumer savings to the extent that the evidence suggests that they are real.[14] In fact, that is a central, even defining, question in contemporary regulatory policy, bearing on energy-efficiency requirements as well as fuel-economy regulation (Allcott & Knittel, 2019; Allcott & Sunstein, 2015; Gayer & Viscusi, 2013).

7.6 Defining Direct Judgments

What about people's direct judgments? Do they deserve deference? When? To make progress on these questions, we have to know how to identify them, which means that we have to solve what might be called the *level of abstraction problem*. Return to the case of Norma. We could say that she prefers yellow box to red box, believing that yellow box contains apples; that is clearly an indirect judgment, because she wants an apple, not a pear. But we could also say that what she wants is a good snack rather than a less good snack (bracketing the question of what, exactly, makes a snack good) and that the choice of an apple is an indirect judgment. Or we could say that what she wants is a good afternoon, or day, or year, or life, and the choice of a good snack is instrumental to one of those things.

Suppose that direct judgments are described at the highest level of abstraction—say, having a good life (without specifying what that means, on the assumption that a good life, properly defined, is intrinsically good). If so, essentially all real world judgments are indirect judgments, in the sense that they are meant as ways of getting a good life. The problem is that if direct judgments are described at the highest levels of abstraction, and if the claim is that we must respect such judgments, outsiders (including regulators) are not much constrained even if they accept that claim. The reason is that outsiders (including regulators) are always, or almost always, dealing with indirect judgments, so long as direct judgments are taken at the highest levels of abstraction.

It would be possible to understand direct judgments at a lower level of abstraction. If so, there are plenty of direct judgments out there, operating at that lower level. Choosers make judgments about what kind of day they want to have or what kind of life they want to lead. They might prefer high-calorie, full-sugar soda to diet drinks, or pizza to salad, even if they gain weight. They might like basketball but not football. They might want to devote themselves to family. They might want to devote themselves to some cause. They might want to pursue art or sport. They might want to marry, or not. They might want to get drunk a fair bit, or not. They might want to live exciting, risk-filled lives, even at some cost to their health and longevity. Or they might want to live stable, risk-free lives, if that is the way of increasing the number of years they have on the planet. Which of the resulting judgments is direct, and which is indirect? More fundamentally: Does anything in behavioral economics demonstrate that people are mistaken with respect to these judgments?

That is not the easiest question to answer. It is one thing to insist that people choose inferior health care plans, given their situations (Gillingham et al., 2019); that they make some bad food choices (Rabin, 2013b), given their overall concerns; or that they do not purchase fuel-efficient motor vehicles when it would be in their economic interest to do so (Gillingham et al., 2019). It is quite another to insist that they choose the wrong sorts of days or lives. Do behavioral economists have anything to say on that question? If the answer is yes, it might be for empirical reasons. As we have seen, a body of research in behavioral science points to "hedonic forecasting errors," which occur when people make mistaken predictions about the effects of outcomes or options on their subjective well-being (Gilbert et al., 1998; Gilbert & Wilson, 2000).

Because the idea of "hedonic forecasting" is a bit narrow, we might ask whether people make "welfare forecasting errors"—that is, whether they make mistaken judgments about what will increase their welfare. They might think that their lives will be better if they marry, but they might be wrong. If so, we might be tempted to say that their judgment to marry was indirect, which would bring us back to the level of abstraction problem. And if they are making the wrong choices, it probably must, simply as a logical matter, be because of a lack of information or some behavioral bias, though we might not be able to identify it and it might not be part of the standard catalog of behavioral biases (see Kahneman et al., 2021, and the long catalog in Pohl, 2016).

7.7 Welfare

The largest question, of course, is how to define welfare. We have said that the philosophical literature distinguishes among three different theories: preference-based theories, subjective welfare theories, and objective-good theories (Adler, 2011). Economists are drawn to the first, but if welfare is what matters, and if respect for preferences leads to welfare losses, such theories have real problems. If those problems lead us to embrace hedonic theories, emphasizing subjective well-being, we can make real progress in understanding the idea of forecasting errors. People might think that they would be happier in California and therefore move there, but perhaps they would not be happier at all (Schkade & Kahneman, 1998).[15] People might think that they would be unhappier if they left their current personal situation (say, their job, their city, or their marriage), but they might be quite mistaken on that point (Levitt, 2016).[16]

Should we embrace subjective welfarism? Many people think so. But such theories have serious limitations. We have already signaled some of them, but to be more concrete, consider some cases:

1. John is deeply committed to public service; he wants to make the world better. He works long hours, and he does not especially enjoy it. His days are not a great deal of fun. But he does not want to do anything else.

2. Mary is a professional tennis player. She has been playing for most of her life. To her, tennis is not much fun. But she wants to pursue excellence. She aims to see how good she can get.

3. Frances is a lawyer. She is excellent at her job. She is an intense person. She likes winning; she finds it rewarding. But she also finds it stressful. She is not particularly happy.

These cases reflect what should be an obvious fact, which is that people care about things other than their hedonic state. To be sure, we could understand subjective welfare to include an array of values that go beyond hedonics; a sense of meaning, goodness, devotion, or excellence could be included in the catalog of what people care about. But if we do that, it is not clear that we are really speaking of the quality of people's experiences, which is often what is meant by subjective well-being. People care about things other than that quality. We have said that they might care about meaningfulness or excellence for their own sake, not because they affect the quality of their experiences. They might choose options that do not improve their experiences but make for a worthier or more meaningful life. (Of course it is true that a worthy life, or a meaningful life, might also have beneficial effects on people's experiences.)

It is for that reason that many people, including many economists, are drawn to preference-based theories, which can claim to take on board everything that people value, whether or not their experiences are improved. We have seen that choices can go badly wrong, in terms of what people care about, in the face of a lack of information or behavioral biases. But we can take that to be a friendly enough amendment to preference-based accounts. After all, it gives authority to (suitably purified) preferences. As we have seen, one problem is that preference-based accounts pay too little attention to behavioral biases; perhaps that problem can be handled with suitable purification of preferences. But there is another problem, which is the risk that such accounts might pay too little attention to the ingredients of what is, for essentially all people, a good human life (Nussbaum, 1993, 2013). If so, we might be drawn to objective-good accounts.

Such accounts take many forms. All of them would question the view that people's preferences deserve the kind of authority that many people, including many economists, would give them. Many philosophers embrace what they call "perfectionism," urging that some kinds of lives are simply better than others (Hurka, 1996).[17] Some liberals are perfectionists; they give pride of place to a distinctive understanding of freedom (Raz, 1985). Some perfectionists are Aristotelian, emphasizing Aristotle's notion of functioning and an understanding of what it means for a human being to be truly human (Foot, 2001).[18] Marx was a perfectionist (Elster, 1985). Some forms of perfectionism have religious foundations; consider Aquinas.

On grounds of either autonomy (invoking Kant) or welfare (invoking Mill), we might want to reject perfectionism (Conly, 2013). But to say the least, these are complicated normative questions, and nothing in standard economics, or behavioral economics, is equipped to solve them. It does seem reasonable and important to say that if preferences are an adaptation to injustice or acute deprivation, they do not deserve authority (Elster, 1983). (Suppose, for example, that women have grown up under conditions of widespread sex inequality and that their preferences have adapted to those conditions.) It also seems reasonable to say that if people's preferences lead them to have objectively terrible lives, something has gone wrong. Objectively terrible lives might be painful, brutal, or short. Perhaps we can say that in such cases objective-good accounts have force.

This is not the place to try to answer some of the deepest questions in political philosophy. Our main goal is to identify them. As John Rawls wrote in an unpublished manuscript, "We post a signpost. No deep thinking here; things are bad enough already." Notwithstanding the questions and doubts we have raised, it makes pragmatic sense to say that across a wide range of choices, people's informed and unbiased preferences generally deserve authority because they are the best available reflection of what people actually care about. An important qualification arises when people's preferences lead them in directions that make their lives go less well (by their own lights). If they care about their own welfare, and if their choices compromise their welfare, there is a problem. Another qualification arises when their preferences lead them in the direction of what is, by any reasonable account, an objectively bad life. Because the range of objectively good or not-bad lives is (in our view) very wide, we should much hesitate before bringing that qualification into play. All this is enough, we hope, to support an incompletely theorized agreement on the working presumption, in the form of a willingness to embrace it even if we are puzzled or disagree about the largest questions.

7.8 Paths Forward

In some cases, people lack information (Bar-Gill, 2012). In other cases, we can identify a behavioral market failure, in the sense that people fall prey to an identifiable behavioral bias, and their choices make their lives go worse by their own lights (Bubb & Pildes, 2014). When this is so, some kind of corrective response is likely to be a good idea, perhaps in the form of a nudge, perhaps in the form of a tax, perhaps in the form of a mandate. In a free society, and notwithstanding the philosophical concerns, it nonetheless makes pragmatic sense for those involved in law and policy to adopt a working presumption: *Each of us should be taken to be the best judge of what will promote our own well-being, to the extent that we are adequately informed and sufficiently free of behavioral biases.* In practice, that presumption can be disciplined by asking five subsidiary questions:

1. What do informed choosers choose?
2. What do active choosers choose?
3. In circumstances in which people are free of (say) present bias or unrealistic optimism, what do they choose?
4. What do people choose when their viewscreen is broad and they do not suffer from limited attention?
5. What do consistent choosers choose—that is, what do people choose when they are not affected by self-evidently irrelevant factors?

Some of these subsidiary questions can be answered empirically. Consider, for example, the question of whether and to what extent an absence of information leads consumers to fail to choose a fuel-efficient motor vehicle. Experiments might be designed to provide consumers with relevant information and see what they choose (Allcott & Knittel, 2019). The choices of informed consumers might be taken as the foundation for analysis. If most consumers make an active choice to enroll in overdraft protection programs under an opt-in regime, there is at least some reason to think that such programs are in their interests (Sarin, 2019).[19] (We are bracketing the potential benefits of targeted or personalized programs.) Experiments might also be designed to make the potential economic savings of (say) energy-efficient lightbulbs highly salient, at least potentially overcoming present bias and limited attention (Allcott & Taubinsky, 2015). If consumers choose or do not choose such lightbulbs in such circumstances, we will have learned something about what is likely to increase their welfare.

In principle, efforts to answer these subsidiary questions should help with cost-benefit analysis, where it is often challenging to know how to proceed when behavioral findings seem to cast doubt on standard uses of revealed preferences.[20] Answers to the subsidiary questions might also allow considerable room for regulatory interference with indirect judgments; such answers might well authorize means paternalism, often in the interest of increasing navigability.

With respect to people's ends, operating at a high level of abstraction, those who offer the working presumption insist on considerable deference to freedom of choice. But they recognize that the underlying justifications for the presumption, founded on ideas about autonomy and welfare, cannot avoid taking some kind of philosophical stand. They provide those justifications with conviction, but also with humility. Recognizing that large questions can be found in the background and sometimes the foreground, they hope to achieve an agreement on behalf of the presumption—an agreement among those who are uncertain about the most fundamental issues or who disagree intensely about how to resolve them.

8
Optimal Taxation and Regulation in Behavioral Economics

8.1 Introduction

In this chapter, we consider the use of traditional instruments, such as Pigouvian taxes and regulatory mandates and bans, to address policy problems. In doing so, we are particularly interested in public policy that takes the form of *hard paternalism*.

In chapter 9, by contrast, we focus on *libertarian paternalism*, such as information disclosure, warnings, and reminders, which are often characterized as a form of *soft paternalism*. The main distinction is that under hard paternalism, policies, such as taxes and regulatory mandates and bans, impose material costs on choosers. Under soft paternalism, by contrast, no such costs are imposed. Under soft paternalism, the behavior of any individual who satisfies the BRA is unlikely to be influenced. (Those who satisfy the BRA do not need reminders.) However, well-chosen policies are likely to improve the welfare of those who do not satisfy the BRA—for example, because they have present biased preferences that cause self-control problems, have limited attention, or are overconfident. Soft paternalism has evident appeal, and we shall devote considerable attention to explaining why. But in many cases, taxes, mandates, and bans might be well justified on welfare grounds.

In section 8.3, we outline a model of multiple selves that plays an important role in behavioral models of time discounting. The model can be used to explain many temporal choices that are puzzling in the BRA—for example, inadequate smoothing of consumption over the life cycle that leads to a sharp drop in consumption at retirement. A nasty shock awaits people who experience these sharp drops. Yet, under exponential discounted utility, EDU (see section 2.6), the main model in the BRA for decision-making over time, we should not observe such phenomena. In the BRA, we should also not observe people procrastinating, breaking new year resolutions, and checking themselves into drug or alcohol treatment centers. All these phenomena and others of this kind, where self-control issues and imperfect awareness of them play a role in decision-making, can be dealt with in a model of multiple selves.

In section 8.4, we introduce the concept of efficiency of taxes and then apply it to the case where consumers might pay limited attention to taxes. For instance, it is well-known that consumers pay less attention to taxes that are added at the check out counter than to taxes that are directly included in the sticker price (Chetty et al., 2009). We introduce *compensated demand curves*, which allows us to characterize efficiency of taxes in terms of their *deadweight loss*. We then show that consumers' increased inattention to a tax reduces inefficiency (or deadweight loss) on account of the tax. We briefly outline the implications for the choice of taxes by governments.

Firms often pass a part of the taxes levied on them as a price increase to consumers. Hence, the tax burden of a given increase in taxes is typically shared between the firm and the consumers. This is known as the problem of *tax incidence*. In section 8.5, we consider the problem of tax incidence under limited attention. We show that as consumer inattention to taxes worsens, firms can pass an increasingly large share of taxes onto consumers. Consumption taxes can sometimes be regressive with respect to income. In other words, the poorer individuals bear a disproportionate amount of these taxes. Hence, public policy has an important role to play in these cases. For instance, the government might refrain from increasing such taxes too much or engage in policy actions that reduce consumer inattention to such taxes.

In section 8.6, we consider public policy toward sugary drinks that takes the form of sugar taxes. In the BRA, individuals rationally choose to consume sugary drinks, taking full account of the present discounted value of marginal costs and benefits of such consumption. The view from behavioral economics is that individuals might underestimate the harm that consumption of sugary drinks causes to them in the future. Hence, they might overconsume because their present self does not fully internalize the costs to their future self. Taxes on sugary drinks in this case can be welfare improving. We provide a diagram to illustrate this principle.

In section 8.7, we consider a range of applications of present biased preferences and procrastination. In section 8.7.1, we fix basic ideas that link present biased preferences with procrastination when the actions taken by individuals have *current costs and future benefits*. These arguments can be reversed to show that for actions which have *current benefits and future costs*, the individual might preproperate (i.e., take the action too quickly). We then consider applications to job searching (section 8.7.2), meeting deadlines (section 8.7.3), and purchasing fertilizers (section 8.7.4).

In section 8.8, we consider some of the policy-relevant insights from *behavioral industrial organization* and how these insights impact the discussion on hard and soft paternalism. We use a simple Hotelling model of firm competition. A fraction of the consumers are inattentive in the sense that they do not pay attention to all components of the price that firms charge, particularly, to the prices of add-ons. For instance, inattentive consumers might not pay attention to bank overdraft charges while opening bank accounts or to expensive printer cartridges while buying printers, or they may overestimate their own future usage of a good (as in choosing a high annual fee for a gym membership that is independent of usage instead of choosing pay-as-you-go after paying a nominal fixed sign-up fee). The remaining fraction of consumers are fully attentive and pay attention to all components of the price, including all relevant surcharges.

We consider the implications of competition among firms when there is a mixture of attentive and inattentive consumers. We show that the presence of inattentive consumers can cross-subsidize attentive consumers, who end up paying a lower price for the product (because they see through the add-ons and do not buy them). Regulatory policies may serve to educate and inform inattentive consumers and may succeed in reducing inattention. Hence, firms cannot obfuscate as much by setting high unobserved add-on prices that inattentive consumers largely end up paying. If so, the welfare of attentive consumers may be reduced because they are required to pay a higher ticket price. Under a utilitarian social welfare function that takes account of the utilities of all consumers, including sophisticated consumers, the net welfare effects of policy might then be an empirical question. Furthermore, firms themselves might react to regulatory policy and try to create greater obfuscation in the form of cleverer add-ons. While these channels are plausible, we lack empirical support on their quantitative real world relevance. We also highlight several forms of regulatory policies that take account of some of these concerns.

8.2 An Introduction to Multiple Selves

The idea of multiple selves, well-known from psychology (and philosophy as well), may be explained by the following simple example, which illustrates several features of the failure of self-control together. It also highlights imperfect awareness of future self-control problems.

Example 8.1. *Suppose that an individual sets an alarm during the night (the night-self) to wake up in the morning (the morning-self). People often find it difficult to precommit to waking up on the alarm, because the night-self might not be able to predict accurately how the morning-self will react to the alarm. The morning-self may switch the alarm off, with possibly negative consequences for both selves. In this case, the night-self might benefit from a commitment technology that disciplines the morning-self. Manufacturers of alarm clocks seem aware of the problem, so they build a commitment device into the alarm clock through a snooze button that reactivates the alarm to set off after a short interval, thereby acting as a disciplining device on the morning-self.*

An even stronger precommitment from the night-self would be to place the alarm clock away from the bed, increasing the cost of the morning-self to reverse the night-self's decision. Perhaps the night-self does not often engage in this strong precommitment because it underestimates the degree of the self-control problem in its future selves.

This is, of course, a toy example. It can be extended to higher-stake situations—for instance, when gambling addicts take steps to prevent themselves from entering casinos; when cigarette addicts enter programs to quit; when alcohol addicts seek the help of Alcoholics Anonymous; and when people with weight problems enlist dieting strategies.

The simplest form of present biased preferences is the *quasi-hyperbolic form* that we stated in (2.23) in section 2.13. Consider time $t \in \Gamma = \{0, 1, 2, \ldots, T\}$ and real valued consumption c_t at time t. Let there be multiple selves of the same individual, one for each period. Each self who makes a decision in any time period $t \in \Gamma$, known as self-t, has *quasi-hyperbolic preferences* given by

$$U_t\left(c_t, c_{t+1}, \ldots, c_T\right) = u\left(c_t\right) + \beta \sum_{\tau=t+1}^{\tau=T} \delta^\tau u\left(c_\tau\right), \ 0 < \beta < 1. \tag{8.1}$$

As noted in section 2.13, the parameter $\beta \in (0, 1)$ in (8.1) shrinks the value of all future discounted utilities and creates a bias toward immediate gratification for each self, and $\delta > 0$ is the discount factor in the *exponential discounted utility* (EDU) model. Setting $\beta = 1$ in (8.1) gives rise to the EDU model, which is the main model of decision-making in the BRA (see appendix in chapter 2).

In making economic decisions, the self at time $t \in \Gamma$ must form beliefs about the behavior of all the future selves. Such beliefs reflect the *degree* of *self-awareness* of the current self at any time $t \in \Gamma$ (see example 8.1). Self-t has beliefs that the preferences of all the future *selves* at time $k > t$ are given by

$$U_k(c_k, \ldots, c_T) = u(c_k) + \hat{\beta} \sum_{\tau=k+1}^{\tau=T} \delta^\tau u(c_\tau), \, t < k \leq T-1, \tag{8.2}$$

where $\hat{\beta} \in (0, 1)$ is a subjective estimate of self-t about the actual β value of a future self at time k. In principle, one could have an entire series of estimates $\hat{\beta}_{k+1}, \hat{\beta}_{k+2}, \ldots, \hat{\beta}_{T-1}$ for all future selves. However, in (8.2) we have chosen a simpler case in which all these estimates are identical and given by $\hat{\beta}$. The relation between the actual impatience parameter of self-t, β, and the estimate, $\hat{\beta}$, for future selves is an important element in understanding many applications of libertarian paternalism. O'Donoghue and Rabin (2001) propose the following classification.

1. *Time consistents*: People with standard time consistent preferences behave as if they are using the EDU model, so

$$\beta = \hat{\beta} = 1. \tag{8.3}$$

These individuals imagine that they and none of their future selves ever have a present bias (over and above that caused by the presence of δ). This is the standard case in economics.

2. *Sophisticates*: Sophisticates know that they have a bias toward immediate gratification and believe that their future selves will also have an identical bias,

$$\beta = \hat{\beta} < 1. \tag{8.4}$$

3. *Partial naifs*: Partial naifs know that they have a bias toward immediate gratification but believe (mistakenly) that their future selves will have a smaller, but nonzero, bias,

$$\beta < \hat{\beta} < 1. \tag{8.5}$$

4. *Naifs*: Naifs know that their current selves are present biased but believe that their future selves will have no bias toward immediate gratification—that is, they believe that future selves are time consistent; hence,

$$\beta < \hat{\beta} = 1. \tag{8.6}$$

Evidence indicates that most people are partial naifs—that is, they fall within the two extremes of sophisticates and naifs.

In traditional economic analysis, individuals may impose *externalities* on other individuals. The role of public policy in this case is typically to use *Pigouvian taxes* that force the partial or full internalization of these externalities. In other words, externality-imposing individuals do not take full account of the marginal social costs (or benefits) of their actions. A Pigouvian tax, by directly taxing the externality-causing actions of individuals, forces them to take account of the appropriate social costs (or benefits).

In section 8.3, we consider public policy when there is consumption of *sin goods* in a framework with multiple selves. In this case, individuals impose externalities on their own future selves. Such externalities are known as *internalities*. We show in a formal model, where there is a mix of individuals with present biased and classical preferences, how optimal public policy might enable individuals to internalize the relevant internalities.

8.3 Multiple Selves, Internalities, and Public Policy

Consider the framework of multiple selves that was introduced above, in which an individual may be considered as a succession of multiple selves, and the self that makes decisions at time t is referred to as self-t. A *sin good* is any good that gives utility to the current self but disutility to the future selves of the same individual (e.g., smoking, alcohol consumption, texting while driving, procrastination). (Admittedly, the phrase *sin good* has awkward and perhaps unwelcome connotations; we use it because it has become conventional.)

Consider, for instance, smoking. The current self of an individual might be aware that future selves ought to smoke less and might also be aware of the long-term health risks associated with smoking, yet continue to smoke in the current period due, say, to present bias. Indeed, the decision by each self of the individual imposes costs, known as *internalities*, on the future selves (of the same individual). Recall that the term *externalities* in economics refers to the imposition of costs imposed by an individual on other individuals (negative externalities) or benefits conferred by an individual on other individuals (positive externalities), for which the externality-causing individual neither fully pays the costs nor receives full payments for the benefits given.

The decision to smoke in the future is made by the future selves of the (same) individual. It might also be the case that the current self lacks a commitment technology to bind the actions of the future selves. One possible commitment device takes the form of public policy. If the government is able to commit to levying *sin taxes* in the future, then it can partly, or fully, address the commitment problem faced by the current self. Empirically, the incidence and extent of smoking is negatively associated with income, and hence, cigarette taxes are regressive with respect to income. (It is also the case that a given unit of cost, imposed on poor smokers, might have a more serious negative impact on them than the same unit of cost imposed on wealthy smokers.) However, insofar as such taxes provide a commitment device to the current selves of individuals to control excessive consumption of an undesirable good, it might be welfare improving to levy such taxes (Gruber & Köszegi, 2001, 2004). To the extent that cigarette smoking imposes disproportionate costs on poor people (perhaps because they are disproportionate smokers), cigarette taxes might be progressive with the health, and on balance, they might be favored on distributional grounds. (Sugar taxes, taken up below, might be analyzed similarly; the cost might be borne particularly by people at the lower end of the income scale, or might be especially difficult for such people to bear, but they might also receive particular benefits in terms of health.)

If the current selves recognize the commitment role of such taxes, they might support such taxes. There is some evidence from Canadian smokers of a link between excise taxes on cigarettes and self-reported measures of happiness (Gruber & Mullainathan, 2005). Taxes are a form of hard paternalism. Taxes that reduce consumption of sin goods and reduce internalities for future selves are a variant of the standard Pigouvian taxes that are typically used to treat externalities in economic policy. We consider these issues below in a formal model where individuals choose privately their own consumption of the sin good and a policymaker chooses the appropriate welfare maximizing Pigouvian taxes.

Consider an individual whose multiple selves live over successive discrete time periods $t = 1, 2, 3, \ldots, T$. The individual consumes two kinds of goods every period: a sin good x_t and a composite good z_t (which aggregates all other goods consumed). Individuals maximize present discounted utility.

At any time t, the instantaneous, or time t utility of an individual is given by

$$u_t = (lnx_t - ax_{t-1}) + z_t; \, a \in (0,1). \qquad (8.7)$$

The time t utility of an individual is additively separable in the two goods, x_t, z_t, and quasilinear in the composite good z_t. In (8.7), the first term in the brackets, lnx_t, captures the current utility from the current consumption of the sin good, x_t. The second term in the brackets, $-ax_{t-1}$, captures the disutility arising from the immediately previous period's consumption of the sin good; hence, it captures the negative intertemporal consequences (internalities) of sin goods consumption. The parameter $a \in (0, 1)$ captures the weight given to the internality relative to current consumption of the sin good.

The disutility term, $-ax_{t-1}$, captures several potential effects that we have not formally modeled but that are potentially implicit in this reduced-form representation. It could capture habit formation effects so that a higher past consumption of the sin good requires a relatively greater current consumption of the sin good to achieve the same marginal utility from consumption of the sin good. For instance, drug users might need to take ever-increasing quantities of a drug in order to feel the same level of effect. Formalizing this effect would require stock-flow models in which the stock of habits evolves over time. Or the disutility term might capture health-related discomfort or extra health expenditures arising from past consumption of the sin good. Since the utility function is quasilinear in z_t, all income effects are absorbed by the composite good, and the changes in consumption of the sin good due to price changes reflect pure substitution effects only.

The individual has income equal to $I > 0$ in every time period. The unit price of the composite good is normalized to 1; hence, one may think of it as a *numeraire good*. For simplicity, we assume that the marginal cost of production of sin goods is identical to the marginal cost of production of the composite good (this is not restrictive for the conclusions we wish to draw below). Thus, under competitive market conditions, the unit price of the sin good is also 1.

Public policy has two elements. There is a *specific consumption tax* at the rate $\tau \in [0, 1]$ on the sin good only, and the resulting tax revenues are returned as lump-sum transfers to individuals. Each individual receives a lump-sum transfer α from the government.[1]

Thus, the budget constraint of an individual at time t, which equates total expenditure to total income at time t, is given by

$$(1 + \tau) x_t + z_t = I + \alpha. \tag{8.8}$$

The specific tax increases the effective price paid by the individual for each unit of the consumption of the sin good. In (8.8), the individual pays to the government taxes equal to τx_t. Substituting z_t from the budget constraint in (8.8) into the utility function in (8.7), we get

$$u_t(x_t, x_{t-1}) = (lnx_t - ax_{t-1}) + (I + \alpha - (1+\tau)x_t); a \in (0,1) \qquad (8.9)$$

Self-t does not have any means of binding the choices of future selves. In other words, private individuals lack a commitment device to influence the choices of future selves. Thus, self-t is only able to choose the time t consumption of the sin good, x_t, conditional on the history of choices, encapsulated in the time $t-1$ choice of the sin good, x_{t-1}. The optimal choice of the composite good at time t, z_t, is then found as a residual from (8.8).

We assume that there are two kinds of individuals—*classical* and *present biased*. There is a total population of N individuals of which N_1 individuals (or a fraction $\lambda = \frac{N_1}{N} \in [0,1]$) are *present biased*. They are assumed to have identical quasi-hyperbolic $(\beta, 1)$ preferences such that $\beta \in (0,1)$ (see section 2.13 for an explanation of these terms).[2] The remaining $N_2 = N - N_1$ individuals, or a fraction $1 - \lambda$, are *classical* individuals who do not discount the future at all and satisfy the requirements of the BRA (technically, they all use exponential discounted utility preferences with $\beta = \delta = 1$; see sections 2.6 and 2.13).

Consider first present biased individuals. The self-t of such an individual, $t = 0, 1, 2, \ldots, T$, has the following intertemporal preferences:

$$U_t(\beta, 1) = u_t + \beta \sum_{j=1}^{T-t} u_{t+j}; \beta \in (0,1) \qquad (8.10)$$

The preferences of the classical individuals are a special case of (8.10) when $\beta = 1$—that is, they are given by $U_t(1,1)$. As noted above, self-t can only make a choice of the time t consumption of the sin good, x_t, and the composite good at time t, z_t. Substitute (8.9) in (8.10) and collect terms corresponding to x_t,

$$U_t(\beta, 1) = [lnx_t - (1+\tau)x_t - a\beta x_t] + \phi, \qquad (8.11)$$

where

$$\phi = [\beta(lnx_{t+1} + I + \alpha - (1+\tau)x_{t+1}) + I + \alpha - ax_{t-1}] + \beta \sum_{j=2}^{T-t} u_{t+j}$$

is independent of x_t. Thus, in (8.11), only the first term in square brackets contains terms containing x_t. Hence, we can write the unconstrained maximization problem of a present biased individual as follows.

$$x_t^b(\beta) \in argmax\ U_t(\beta, 1) = [lnx_t - (1+\tau)x_t - a\beta x_t] + \phi;\ x_t \in \left[0, \frac{1+\alpha-z_t}{1+\tau}\right]$$
(8.12)

From (8.12), we get

$$\frac{dU_t(\beta, 1)}{dx_t} = \frac{1}{x_t} - (1+\tau) - a\beta.$$
(8.13)

From (8.13), it follows that $\frac{d^2 U_t}{dx_t^2} < 0$. Thus, the objective function $U_t(\beta, 1)$ is strictly concave and is defined over a compact set. Hence, a unique maximizer exists. Furthermore, $lim_{x_t \to 0} \frac{dU_t}{dx_t} = \infty$; hence, $x_t^b(\beta) > 0$, thus the present biased individual always consumes a positive amount of the sin good. Using (8.13), the unique solution can be written as

$$x_t^b = \frac{1}{(a\beta + 1 + \tau)}.$$
(8.14)

From (8.10), an increase in the value of β makes the individual more patient (lower present bias). From (8.14), x_t^b is decreasing (1) in β, so more patient, or less present biased, individuals consume smaller amount of the sin good, and (2) in τ, so higher consumption taxes deter consumption of the sin good.

Since classical consumers are just a special case with $\beta = 1$, we can directly use (8.14) to write the optimal consumption of the sin good for a classical individual as

$$x_t^c = \frac{1}{(a + 1 + \tau)}.$$
(8.15)

From (8.14) and (8.15) and using $\beta \in (0, 1)$, we have $x_t^c < x_t^b$—that is, present biased individuals consume a higher quantity of the sin good as compared to classical individuals.

In a world of unfettered free will, this is as far as the analysis can go. However, if we allow for a degree of paternalism on the part of the government, while staying within the ambit of traditional economic policy, then we can say more. In particular, for whatever reasons, it may be deemed that too much consumption of the sin good is harmful for individuals consuming it. In this case, the government may wish to use the policy instruments at its disposal to curtail consumption of the sin good. Let us now consider this possibility.

Two considerations must immediately be taken into account in any such analysis. First, any increase in sin taxes (increase in τ in our model) will deter the consumption of not only the present biased individuals but also the classical individuals (both x_t^b and x_t^c are decreasing in τ). This is an example of hard paternalism. In contrast to the position taken under libertarian paternalism, which does not influence the choices of classical individuals, hard paternalism is a more blunt instrument. Second, in order to implement such a policy, one needs some sort of ideal benchmark or yardstick that policy must implement; public policy then strives to move individual choices in the direction of this benchmark.

In the context of sin taxes, the natural benchmark to strive for in economics is the *first best allocation*. This arises when there are no distortionary taxes, $\tau = 0$ (although lump-sum taxes are available), and all individuals are classical individuals. We can recover this yardstick by setting $\tau = 0$ in (8.15). Denoting it by x^* we can write

$$x^* = \frac{1}{(a+1)}. \tag{8.16}$$

Next, we ask the following question. Is there a level of the distortionary tax, τ^*, such that present biased individuals, operating under this tax, will choose a level of sin good consumption that is identical to the first best allocation in (8.16)? To find this, we equate the RHS of (8.14) and (8.16) to get the required consumption tax

$$\tau^* = a(1-\beta). \tag{8.17}$$

The magnitude of the term $1-\beta$ may be interpreted as the degree of impatience of the present biased individual. Thus, the more impatient are present biased individuals (lower β or a higher $1-\beta$), the higher is the *corrective tax*, τ^*, that is required to push their consumption toward the first best allocation. The corrective tax is also increasing in the importance of the *negative internality*—that is, the size of the parameter a—which captures the harm caused to self-t from the consumption of sin goods by the previous self. Thus, the corrective tax also serves to internalize the externality that is caused by one self to the individual's other self. "Internalization of the externality" does not mean that the internality must be completely eliminated (a not uncommon misunderstanding). It means that, based on an appropriate yardstick, such as achieving a first best or a second best allocation, the marginal benefits and marginal costs of the reduction of the internality balance out, even if this does not eradicate the internality.

As we have said, such corrective taxes are also known as *Pigouvian taxes* in economics. Their role is typically to cause individuals to internalize the harm that they cause to other individuals. However, the same principle applies when the harm is caused by one self to the individual's other self. However, at the tax rate τ^*, given in (8.17), the consumption of classical individuals is not first best. This is a typical issue with such policies that impact all individuals in the same manner, yet the individuals are heterogenous. Hence, the optimality of a one-size-fits-all hard paternalistic policy needs to be judged by invoking other yardsticks, as we now examine.

From (8.14) and (8.15), the RHS is independent of time; hence we may drop the time subscripts. Substituting these optimal choices of sin good for the two types of individuals into the budget constraint in (8.8), we can recover their respective optimal choices of the composite good, z_t^b, z_t^c. These too are independent of time; hence, we may write them as follows.

$$z^b = I + \alpha - (1+\tau)x^b, \text{ where } x^b = \frac{1}{(a\beta + 1 + \tau)} \qquad (8.18)$$

$$z^c = I + \alpha - (1+\tau)x^c, \text{ where } x^c = \frac{1}{(a + 1 + \tau)} \qquad (8.19)$$

Substituting (8.18) and (8.19) into (8.9), we get the respective self-t indirect utilities of both types of individuals,

$$v_t^j(\alpha, \tau) = \left(\ln x^j - ax_{t-1}\right) + \left(I + \alpha - (1+\tau)x^j\right); j = b, c, \qquad (8.20)$$

where x^j, $j = b, c$, is given in (8.18) and (8.19).

Suppose that the objective function of the government (or the fiscal authority) is a utilitarian social welfare function. In each time period, $t = 1, 2, \ldots, T$, it wishes to choose its public policy optimally in order to maximize the sum of utilities of all individuals in society at time t. The sequence of moves in this case is as follows. At the beginning of every time period, t, the government announces the consumption tax rate, τ, and the lump-sum transfer, α, which is observed by individuals who then choose their optimal consumption of the sin good and the composite good. Looking forward, the government knows that the consumption choices of individuals are given by (8.18) and (8.19). In the parlance of game theory, the government behaves like a *Stackelberg leader*.

Following O'Donoghue and Rabin (2006), we assume that for any individual, the government at time t cares about the following measure of social utility for an individual of type $j = b, c$.

$$W_t^j(\alpha, \tau) = \left(\ln x^j - ax^j\right) + \left(I + \alpha - (1+\tau)x^j\right), j = b, c \qquad (8.21)$$

Comparing (8.12) and (8.21), the term $a\beta x_t$ is replaced by the term ax_t, and the time subscript has been removed. In other words, the social planner sets $\beta = 1$ in evaluating the social utility of the present biased individuals. By contrast, the classical individuals already have $\beta = 1$ as part of their preferences. Hence, the government has the following weighted utilitarian social welfare function in which the sum of social utilities of the two types of individuals, weighted by the proportions of the two types, is maximized:[3]

$$W(\alpha, \tau) = \lambda W_t^b(\alpha, \tau) + (1-\lambda) W_t^c(\alpha, \tau), \tag{8.22}$$

where W_t^j, $j = b, c$, is given in (8.21). The government is assumed to follow a balanced budget. Thus, total tax revenues from the collection of consumption taxes equal total tax expenditures on making lump-sum payments to the taxpayers: $N\alpha = N_1 \tau x^b + N_2 \tau x^c$. Dividing both sides by N and indicating the dependence of the optimal choices on the tax rate, τ, we can write the government budget constraint as

$$\alpha(\tau) = \lambda \tau x^b(\tau) + (1-\lambda) \tau x^c(\tau). \tag{8.23}$$

Substituting (8.23) in (8.22), the unconstrained maximization problem of the government is

$$\tau^* \in \text{argmax } W(\alpha(\tau), \tau) = \lambda W_t^b(\alpha(\tau), \tau) + (1-\lambda) W_t^c(\alpha(\tau), \tau), \tau \in [0, 1].$$

Using the envelope theorem (which requires using the condition (8.13) evaluated at zero), we get

$$\frac{dW}{d\tau} = \lambda \left[-a(1-\beta) \frac{dx^b}{d\tau} - x^b + \frac{d\alpha(\tau)}{d\tau} \right] + (1-\lambda) \left[-x^c + \frac{d\alpha(\tau)}{d\tau} \right]. \tag{8.24}$$

Denote the mean consumption of the sin good (across both types of individuals) by $\bar{x}(\tau) = \lambda x^b(\tau) + (1-\lambda) x^c(\tau)$. Then, using (8.23) we can rewrite (8.24) as

$$\frac{dW}{d\tau} = \lambda a(1-\beta) \left(-\frac{dx^b}{d\tau} \right) + \tau \frac{d\bar{x}(\tau)}{d\tau}. \tag{8.25}$$

The first term on the RHS in (8.25), which is positive because $\frac{dx^b}{d\tau} < 0$ (see (8.14)), is the *marginal social benefit* of increasing the consumption tax, τ, by a unit. It is the increase in marginal utility of the present biased individuals on account of the curtailment of sin good consumption below the privately optimal solution. Thus, each successive self suffers a lower level of internality from the sin good consumption of the immediately preceding self. The second term gives the *marginal social cost* of increasing τ in terms of a reduction in the tax revenues arising from taxing the reduced consumption of the sin good and, hence, a lower amount available for lump-sum redistribution. The optimal tax trades off the marginal benefit and the marginal costs. Suppose that the second-order condition is satisfied, $\frac{d^2 W}{d\tau^2} < 0$, when evaluated at τ^*.

Consider the special case where there are no present biased individuals ($\lambda \to 0$); then from (8.25), $\frac{dW}{d\tau} < 0$. Thus, the government sets a zero optimal consumption tax, $\tau^* = 0$. In other words, if all individuals were classical and rationally chose their consumption of the sin good (in the sense of maximizing exponential discounted utility), then there would be no role for sin taxes.

Since the first term on the RHS of (8.25) is positive, its magnitude drives how high the optimal sin tax will be. This term is higher, the higher is the degree of impatience or present biasedness, as captured in the term $1 - \beta$. The intuition is that the internalities are more severe (higher sin goods consumption) when present biasedness is higher. Hence, the marginal social benefit from curtailing the consumption of sin goods through taxes is higher in this case. A similar effect arises when the proportion of the present biased individuals increases, which corresponds to an increase in λ. In practice, this theoretical model imposes great informational requirements on the part of the government, as is the case in any such exercise. The craft of actual policymaking then would be to try to use the best empirical proxies available to enact actual policy.

8.4 Limited Attention and Deadweight Loss from Taxation

As noted earlier, in the BRA, individuals are assumed to possess unlimited attention, or to act *as if* they do. By contrast, extensive evidence (see section 2.10) shows that human behavior is inconsistent with unlimited attention. We have reviewed several implications of limited attention for public policy elsewhere. For instance, it might be valuable to send text message reminders for hospital appointments; to require firms to present information on the cost of borrowing in a simplified and standardized form (e.g., requiring banks to explicitly state the APR on loans); and to regulate price comparison websites. In this section, we are particularly interested in calculating the *efficiency costs of taxation* in the presence of limited attention.

Assume, as in section 8.3, that an individual who has income $I > 0$ consumes two goods, x and y, that are produced under competitive conditions. None of these is a sin good. The goods are produced under constant marginal costs of production. In particular, the marginal production cost of good x equals $c > 0$, and competitive firms have access to identical production technology. Suppose that the price of good y is normalized to 1 (the numeraire good) and the price of good x is p. Competitive markets ensure that $p = c$. There is a *specific consumption tax* on good x at the rate $\tau > 0$. The individual maximizes a utility function $u(x, y)$, which is increasing and concave in the two arguments. The budget constraint of the individual is given by

$$(p + \tau)x + y = I. \tag{8.26}$$

We may denote the total price paid by the individual for good x by the after-tax price $q = p + \tau$. Solving the individual's optimization problem gives the optimal consumption levels of the two goods as $x(q, I)$ and $y(q, I)$. These are sometimes known as *uncompensated* or Marshallian demand curves and show how the demand varies as the after-tax price, q, and income, I, vary. Substituting these demands in the utility function we get the indirect utility function

$$v \Leftrightarrow v(q, I) = u(x(q, I), y(q, I)). \tag{8.27}$$

We are particularly interested in the response of the optimal demand for good x to the after-tax price, q. The derivative $dx(q, I)/dq$ depends on the units in which the quantities and the prices are measured. Hence, it is preferable to consider instead the elasticity of demand for good x. This is defined as the percentage change in quantity demanded of good x resulting from a given percentage change in price and denoted by η, where $\eta = -\frac{dx(q,I)}{dq}\frac{q}{x}$. The multiplication by -1 ensures that price elasticity, η, is positive (if the demand curve for good x is downward sloping) and is independent of any units. Thus, we can use the size of η to infer the degree of responsiveness of quantity demanded of good x to changes in the after-tax price q.

The change in the price q can occur in one of two ways.

1. Suppose that the marginal cost, c, of each competitive firm increases by $\Delta > 0$. This will increase the price charged, p, and the after-tax price, q, by Δ each.
2. Suppose that the government increases the tax rate, τ, by $\Delta > 0$. This will directly increase the after-tax price, q, by Δ.

In the BRA, individuals have unlimited attention, so the source of the change in q is irrelevant to them. In particular, for the two cases above, which lead to an identical change in q equal to Δ, the resulting demand elasticities are identical. Thus, the following two elasticities, $\eta_{q,p} = -\frac{dx(q,I)}{dp}\frac{q}{x}$ and $\eta_{q,\tau} = -\frac{dx(q,I)}{d\tau}\frac{q}{x}$, which capture changes in q through changes in, respectively, p and τ, are identical: $\eta_{q,p} = \eta_{q,\tau}$.

By contrast, the evidence shows that individuals do not pay sufficient attention to taxes that are not displayed on price stickers but are added at the point of sale (Chetty et al., 2009). Thus, changes in q that work through changes in p (price on the stickers) are more salient than changes in q that arise through changes in less visible taxes, τ, added at the point of sale, even if the consumer is well aware of the magnitude of these taxes. This is a form of *limited attention to taxes*. Individuals simply do not pay sufficient attention to those components of price that are not directly visible; for a related framework based on *shrouded attributes*, see Gabaix and Laibson (2006). We capture limited attention, in our taxation context, by the following reduced-form assumption:

$$\eta_{q,\tau} = \theta \eta_{q,p}; \; \theta \in (0,1) \tag{8.28}$$

The assumption in (8.28) requires that less visible taxes are also less salient in the sense that they produce lower proportional changes in the quantity demanded relative to equivalent changes in q arising directly through change in the price, p.

We now wish to examine the effect of limited attention on the *deadweight loss of taxation*—a measure of the efficiency of taxes. In order to understand this concept, suppose that we lived in an ideal world where the government only levied *lump-sum taxes* (a fixed deduction from income, irrespective of individual characteristics and choices, such as a poll tax). Lump-sum taxes do not change relative prices of the two goods. By contrast, the tax τ in (8.26) is a *distortionary tax* because it alters the relative prices of the two goods.

Suppose that the lump-sum tax is denoted by T and that such a tax is available. In this ideal world, the budget constraint of the individual is given by

$$px + y = I - T. \tag{8.29}$$

As before, the individual chooses x, y to maximize utility $u(x, y)$ but is now subject to the new budget constraint in (8.29). Denote the optimal consumption bundles by $x(p, T, I)$ and $, y(p, T, I)$ and the indirect utility (obtained by substituting the optimal consumption bundles in the utility function $u(x,y)$) by

$$w \Leftrightarrow w(p,T,I) = u(x(p,T,I), y(p,T,I)).$$

Suppose our objective is now to determine the lump-sum tax, $T = T^*$, such that under this lump-sum tax, the individual derives the same level of utility as under the distortionary consumption tax, τ,

$$w(p, T^*, I) = v(q, I). \tag{8.30}$$

Under the restriction in (8.30), the total tax revenue raised from the individual under the distortionary consumption tax equals $\tau x(q, I)$ and the total tax revenue raised under the lump-sum, or nondistortionary, tax is T^*. The individual is indifferent under either of these two kinds of taxes because, from (8.30), they result in identical utility for the individual. Hence, a measure of the efficiency of the tax, or the deadweight loss arising from distortionary consumption taxes, denoted by DWL, is the difference in revenues under the two tax systems,

$$DWL = T^* - \tau x(q, I). \tag{8.31}$$

Suppose that the individual prefers variety in consumption of the two goods. This means that given two extreme consumption bundles of the two goods (say, 10 units of x and 0 units of y in one case; and 10 units of y and 0 units x in the other), the individual prefers the average consumption bundle (in this case, 5 units of x and 5 units of y) to either of the two extreme consumption bundles. Technically, we require that the indifference curves of the individual in the space of outcomes (x, y) are convex.[4] It can then be shown that $DWL > 0$—that is, the lump-sum taxes raise more tax revenue than distortionary taxes, keeping fixed the utility of the individual. In this sense, distortionary taxes are less efficient.

The intuition for this result is that the change in the relative prices of the two goods caused by the consumption tax does not allow the individual to indulge in as much variety in consumption as they would ideally want to. By contrast, lump-sum taxes do not constrain the preference for variety (although the lump-sum tax lowers the overall consumption of both goods if both goods are normal goods). Hence, distortionary taxes reduce the welfare of individuals relative to lump-sum taxes.[5] This assertion, of course, no longer needs to be true in a model of multiple selves with internalities, as we saw in section 8.3. In the presence of sin goods, distortionary taxes create a commitment device by reducing the internality-causing sin good, which can enhance welfare.

In order to explore the effects of limited attention on the deadweight losses arising through distortionary taxes, we need to relate DWL to the elasticity of demand. Recalling that the demand curve $x(q, I)$ is called the *uncompensated* or *Marshallian* demand curve, we are now interested in the *compensated*, or *Hicksian*, demand curve for good x. Such a demand curve arises from the exercise of ensuring that the individual derives identical levels of utilities under lump-sum taxes and distortionary taxes, as in (8.30).

The term *compensated demand curves* implies that we are carrying out compensations to the income of the individual, essentially by altering the income of the individual to $I - T^*$. Denote the compensated demand curve for good x by $x^c(q, w)$; this demand curve always slopes downward, while the Marshallian demand curve may not always slope downward. In other words, the demand curve $x^c(q, w)$ traces out the demand for good x by the individual for various levels of after-tax price, q, ensuring that the condition in (8.30) is satisfied.

As explained earlier, changes in q can arise either through p or through τ. In the former case, we denote this demand curve by $x^c_{p \to q}(q, w)$, and in the latter case by $x^c_{\tau \to q}(q, w)$. In the BRA, where we have unlimited attention, we have $x^c_{p \to q}(q, w) \Leftrightarrow x^c_{\tau \to q}(q, w)$. However, under limited attention, changes in q caused by changes in τ lead to relatively smaller changes in quantity demanded simply because the individual does not fully pay attention to such changes. This implies that the compensated demand curve $x^c_{\tau \to q}(q, w)$ is steeper—that is, there are more muted changes in demand arising from changes in τ as compared to the compensated demand curve $x^c_{p \to q}(q, w)$.

In figure 8.1, we measure the after-tax price on the vertical axis and the quantity on the horizontal axis, and we plot the two compensated demand curves, $x^c_{p \to q}(q, w)$ and $x^c_{\tau \to q}(q, w)$. The supply curve is horizontal at $p = c$. Before the imposition of the tax, the market equilibrium price is given by $p = c$, and the individual demands a quantity x_0.

Consider first the benchmark case of full attention, in which the demand curve is $x^c_{p \to q}(q, w)$, and the source of the after-tax price increase, via p or τ, has identical effects on demand. The total revenue and cost of profit maximizing competitive firms from supplying x_0 units is cx_0, and competitive firms make zero profits. The area under the demand curve captures the *individual's total willingness to pay for the good*. When the individual demands x_0 units, the total money paid by consumers to the firm is cx_0, and the remaining area under the demand curve, ADG, gives the *consumer surplus*.

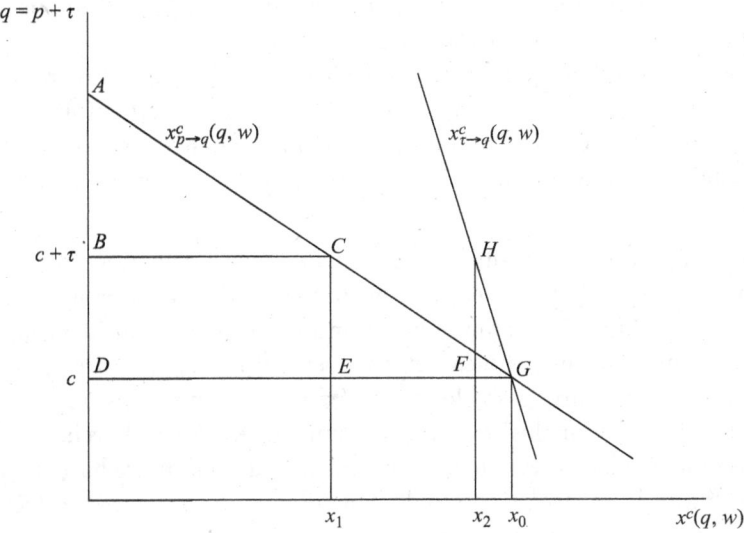

Figure 8.1
Deadweight loss of a consumption tax under limited attention.

Now consider the imposition of a consumption tax on good x given by $\tau > 0$. In competitive markets, the new after-tax price is $c + \tau$, and the consumer now demands a quantity x_1. The total revenue received by the firm in this new situation is cx_1, the total tax revenues collected by the government equal $BCED$, and the new consumer surplus is ABC. Of the original consumer surplus, ADG, we have, thus, accounted for the area $ABC + BCED$, but an amount CEG cannot be accounted for (either in terms of firm profits, government revenues, or consumer surplus).

It is as if this monetary amount is lost from the system. After all, if at the before-tax price, $p = c$, we had levied a lump-sum tax $T^* = BCED$, then there would have been an extra monetary amount CEG still available to the consumer as consumer surplus; it would not have been lost from the system. Using (8.31), this is the deadweight loss from the distortionary taxes.

Now introduce the possibility of limited attention, and consider the distinction between the two compensated demand curves, $x^c_{p \to q}(q, w)$ and $x^c_{\tau \to q}(q, w)$. There are two possibilities.

1. Suppose that, initially, $\tau = 0$. But the after-tax price increase takes place due to an increase in the marginal cost, c, of the inputs of the firm by an amount Δ. If Δ is identical to the value of τ in figure 8.1, then exactly

the same analysis as above with the demand curve $x^c_{p \to q}(q, w)$ applies, and we have deadweight loss equal to CEG.

2. Suppose instead that the after-tax price increases through an increase in the consumption tax. Given our assumption on limited attention, this increase in price is less salient for the individual; hence, the relevant demand curve is now $x^c_{\tau \to q}(q, w)$. The deadweight loss is now the smaller area HFG.

Therefore, the most important implication of limited attention for the efficiency of taxes is that the deadweight loss through distortionary taxation is reduced. Indeed, this might be an important policy consideration for governments. Given a choice between several taxes, they are likely to choose those that are less salient for individuals and firms and less likely to be noticed. For this reason, governments are typically reluctant to increase income taxes, which are very salient. Taxes that are harder to notice are more likely to be imposed, a phenomenon that is sometimes referred to as stealth taxes in the popular press.

Taubinsky and Rees-Jones (2018) provide evidence to show that taxes are less visible at low levels as compared to high levels. Hence, consumers might pay limited attention to changes in taxes when they are low. Thus, we expect small changes in taxes at low levels not to lead to appreciable changes in deadweight loss. A similar argument applies to increases in usage charges by firms that are often incremental and small, hence relatively unnoticed by consumers, leading to smaller efficiency losses. It is not uncommon for firms to increase prices in small but frequent increments on similar grounds.

8.5 Tax Incidence under Limited Attention

When governments levy taxes on firms, the firms might pass a part of the tax burden on to consumers as an increase in the price of the good. Thus, the burden of taxation is typically shared between firms and consumers. Determining the exact distribution of this burden is the problem of *tax incidence*. In this section, we briefly sketch the implications of limited attention for tax incidence.

In section 8.4, we derived the Marshallian demand curve for good x. Suppose that we index consumers by $i = 1, 2, \ldots, n$; then we can write consumer i's demand curve for good x by $x_i(q, I)$. If we aggregate this demand curve across all consumers in society, we get the aggregate demand curve, $D(q, I) = \Sigma^n_{i=1} x_i(q, I)$. Suppose that the supply curve for the good is given by $S(p)$, which, under competitive market conditions, is the firm's marginal cost curve. Thus, market clearing requires

$$D(q, I) = S(p). \tag{8.32}$$

Suppose that we have limited attention on the part of individuals, as in (8.28). Since aggregate demand is additive in the demands of individual consumers, we also get a similar form of limited attention at the aggregate level. Denote the two aggregate demand elasticities by $\epsilon_{q,p} = -\frac{dD(q,I)}{dp}\frac{q}{D}$ and $\epsilon_{q,\tau} = -\frac{dD(q,I)}{d\tau}\frac{q}{D}$, which capture the effect on D of changes in q that arise through, respectively, p and τ. It follows that the analogue of (8.28) for the aggregate demand curve is

$$\epsilon_{q,\tau} = \theta \epsilon_{q,p}; \ \theta \in (0,1). \tag{8.33}$$

Totally differentiate (8.32) to get

$$\left(\frac{\partial D}{\partial p} - \frac{\partial S}{\partial p}\right) dp + \frac{\partial D}{\partial \tau} d\tau = 0. \tag{8.34}$$

By definition, $q = p + \tau$. Hence, we have

$$\frac{dq}{d\tau} = 1 + \frac{dp}{d\tau}. \tag{8.35}$$

Define the price elasticity of supply by $\gamma = \frac{dS(p)}{dp}\frac{p}{S}$ (this captures the percentage change in quantity supplied arising from a given percentage change in price). Using (8.33)–(8.35) and using the formulas for $\epsilon_{q,p}$ and $\epsilon_{q,\tau}$, a few simple calculations allow us to derive the following formula.

$$\frac{dq}{d\tau} = \frac{\frac{q}{p}\gamma + (1-\theta)\epsilon_{q,p}}{\frac{q}{p}\gamma + \epsilon_{q,p}} \tag{8.36}$$

From (8.36), the RHS is decreasing in θ. Thus, the more inattentive are the consumers (i.e., lower θ), the higher is the LHS, or the higher is the increase in the after-tax price, q, following an increase in tax, τ. In other words, the less attentive are consumers to taxes, the greater is the tax burden that producers can shift on to consumers.

This opens up a potential role for public policy. Suppose that for good x, consumption taxation is regressive with respect to income—for instance, because it is consumed predominantly by the poor, who also end up paying more taxes. Since producers can pass on a greater share of taxes to inattentive consumers, this further increases the regressivity of the tax system. One policy response is to avoid levying such taxes or keep them at low levels. Another policy response is to increase public awareness of such taxes, say, through a program of greater financial and tax literacy.

8.6 Internalities and Tax Efficiency: An Application to Sugar Taxes

The empirical evidence is consistent with excessive sugar consumption for a significant share of the population in the West. Using US data, Alcott et al. (2019b) highlight excessive consumption of sugary drinks, which is 3–4 times higher than the world average. Furthermore, poorer households consume proportionally greater sugary drinks. Those with annual income below $25K consume 200 calories/day from sugary drinks while those with annual incomes above $75K consume 117 calories/day.

Why do some individuals consume excessive sugar despite the obvious health risks? The view in the BRA is that individuals choose rationally. They are assumed to be fully aware of the dangers of excessive sugar consumption, yet they make an informed consumption decision, taking into account the present discounted value of benefits and costs. In other words, the view from the BRA is that observed choices such as sugar-related obesity are rational choices of individuals that must be respected by the policymakers. Behavioral evidence about present bias raises the possibility that individuals might make choices based on present biased preferences. Recall that the rationality of decision-making over time is associated with exponential discounted utility (see section 2.6). The view from behavioral economics, based on evidence that contradicts exponential discounting and supports present biased preferences, is that sugar-related obesity is not a rational intertemporal decision. Indeed, the evidence shows that many people are frustrated with their self-control problems and choose to go on diets, and the dieting industry is itself a multibillion dollar industry.

If the behavioral arguments have merit, then a paternalistic policy response of levying taxes on sugar deserves serious consideration. Alcott et al. (2019b) list 39 countries that use or have tried to use such a tax. We now consider specifically a tax on producers.

Suppose that x is a sin good, such as a sugary drink. The government levies a specific tax $\tau > 0$ per unit on the sale of good x. This increases the marginal cost of firms, so that in competitive markets, their supply curve, which is given by their marginal cost curve, shifts upward by the amount of the tax. In figure 8.2, the original supply curve in the absence of taxes is shown as $S(\tau = 0)$. The imposition of the tax shifts the supply

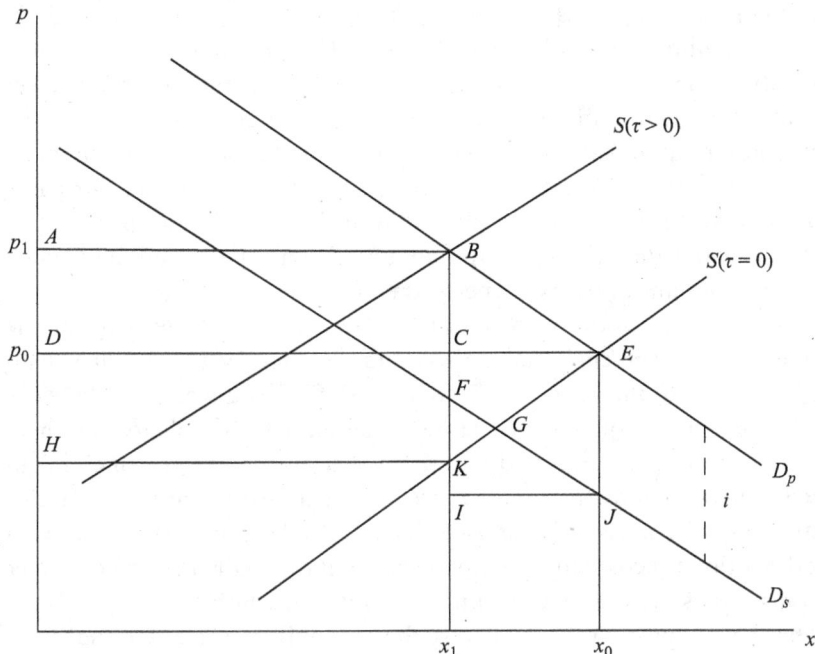

Figure 8.2
Efficiency of sugar taxes in the presence of internalities.

curve vertically upward by the amount of the tax, τ, and the new supply curve is shown as $S(\tau > 0)$.

Figure 8.2 also shows two demand curves. The (private) demand curve D_p shows the private marginal benefits to individuals from consuming good x. The area under D_p captures the total private benefits from consuming good x. However, the private benefits do not take account of the costs that are borne by the future selves of the same individual. In this sense, figure 8.2 gives a snapshot of the private benefits to the current self of an individual. We assume that the *internalities* caused to the future selves, which equal a monetary amount $i > 0$ per unit of consumption of good x, are not taken into account by the current self. If a benevolent social planner were to take account of these internalities, then the true marginal social benefit from the consumption of x is lower and shown by the (social) demand curve D_s.

Before the imposition of the tax, and based on the private demand curve D_p, the market equilibrium quantity of x is x_0, and the market equilibrium price is p_0; the market equilibrium is shown by the point E.

If, by contrast, one uses the social demand curve D_s, then the socially optimal equilibrium would be at the point G, corresponding to a lower quantity of the sin good x. After the imposition of the tax, the market equilibrium quantity of x is x_1 and the market equilibrium price is p_1; the new market equilibrium is shown by the point B. Notice that the price does not go up by the full amount of the tax because the tax burden is shared between firms and consumers. In figure 8.2, the tax per unit, τ, equals AH but the price goes up only by AD and the remaining burden of the tax per unit, DH, is borne by the producer.

After the imposition of the tax, the effective tax revenues paid by the firm to the government equal $DCKH$ and the effective tax revenues paid by consumers to the government equal $ABCD$. The government receives total tax revenues equal to $ABKH$. Let us suppose for simplicity that there are no income effects on good x so that the compensated and uncompensated demand curves for good x are identical (see section 8.4 for this distinction). As discussed in section 8.4, the deadweight loss arising from the distortionary consumption tax on account of a reduction in consumer surplus equals BCE. However, unlike section 8.4, where the marginal cost for firms was constant, here we have the case of increasing marginal costs and an upward sloping supply curve. Thus, the reduction in the quantity traded, which equals $x_0 - x_1$, also reduces the profits of firms by the area CEK; notice that over the interval $x_0 - x_1$, the price paid by consumers, p_0, exceeds the marginal cost of production for each unit of x; the area CEK is simply the addition (technically, the integral over $x_0 - x_1$) of all these differences. Thus, the total DWL is found by adding the deadweight loss from consumers (area BCE) and the fall in the profits of firms (area CEK). To summarize:

$$DWL = BCE + CEK$$

However, we also need to take account of internalities. The reduction in the consumption of x provides benefits to all future selves of individuals. The monetary benefit per unit on account of internalities is $i > 0$; hence, the total benefit caused by the reduction of $x_0 - x_1$ units equals the area $BEJF$. Thus, the net benefits, which could be positive or negative, from the imposition of the sugar tax are given by $BEJF - (BCE + CEK)$. Canceling common areas, the net benefit from the imposition of the sugar tax is given by

$$\text{Net Benefit} = GEJ - FGK.$$

The net benefit may be positive (indeed, for the curves shown in figure 8.2, this is the case) or negative. The precise answer depends on the relative elasticities of the demand and supply curves, the magnitude of the specific tax, and the size of the per unit internalities, $i > 0$, that are caused to the future selves. If positive, then there is an unassailable case for imposing such sin taxes. Clearly, this is a paternalistic intervention and a form of hard paternalism. However, there is no reason why hard paternalism cannot be used in conjunction with soft paternalism—for example, a combination of a policy of cigarette taxes plus mandatory warnings on cigarette packs of the health risks of smoking. Other intermediate forms of paternalism are possible. We will return to these issues in chapter 9. For a further discussion in the context of tobacco regulation, see DeCicca et al. (2020), and for public policy toward sugary drinks, see Alcott et al. (2019a, 2019b).

As noted above, there are relevant and perhaps important distributional issues. To speak broadly: Suppose that everyone who consumes a sugary drink consumes an identical quantity of the sugary drinks. A tax on such drinks could plausibly be understood to be regressive, in the sense that it would have a more severe impact on the poor than on the rich. (People often object to consumption taxes for that reason.) Or suppose that sugary drinks are consumed more by the poor than by the rich. If so, they could be understood as regressive for that very reason. For those who focus on distributional questions, is that a decisive objection? Not necessarily. Whether consumption of sugary drinks is uniform across the population or instead concentrated among the poor, poor people could be disproportionately benefited by the tax. On plausible assumptions, their welfare would be disproportionately increased (Allcott et al., 2019a, 2019b). Whether this would be true depends, of course, on the facts. The only point is that the apparent regressivity of an internalities-reducing tax (designed, say, to protect health) might be a mirage. The principal beneficiaries might be people who do not have a lot of money.

8.7 Present Biased Preferences and Procrastination: More Applications

Individuals who follow the exponential discounted utility model in the BRA are predicted to smooth consumption perfectly over their lifetimes. However, when individuals have present biased preferences, they place too much weight on instant gratification and may not adequately smooth consumption over their lifetimes. This may cause such individuals to overconsume in the present and save inadequately for retirement. Solutions to these problems, discussed elsewhere in this book, include the introduction of opt-out defaults that enroll individuals automatically in savings/pensions programs and novel savings vehicles (such as the SMarT savings program proposed in Thaler & Benartzi, 2004) that encourage savings through providing commitment devices to current selves. These interventions are a form of soft paternalism. In other problems of a similar nature, hard paternalism and regulation may be needed, as we show below.

Individuals typically receive staggered wage payments, with monthly payments being possibly the most common payment mode. This requires individuals to smooth consumption between successive paydays. Imagine a model of multiple selves in which each day of the month corresponds to a different self of the individual. Exponential discounters will smooth consumption perfectly. However, present biased individuals are likely to consume too much in the early part of the month, immediately after the payday, leaving insufficient income for the later part of the month.

People sometimes respond to insufficient income in the later part of the month by resorting to payday loans (which tide them over between successive paydays). Stark evidence of this phenomenon is found when income takes the form of wages, food stamp payments, or social security payments (Huffman & Barenstein, 2004; Shapiro, 2005; Stephens, 2003). It is likely to be welfare improving for an individual to be able to better smooth consumption between successive paydays. However, commitment devices that enable such smoothing are typically absent. Hence, governments often need to resort to hard paternalism by regulating payday loans. This can take the form of regulating the interest rate charged, which can be astronomical, the terms of the contract regarding penalties for late payments, and transparency about the costs of borrowing.

8.7.1 Procrastination: Fixing Ideas

An important insight from present biased preferences is that individuals might choose to *procrastinate*. To illustrate the main idea, think of an individual who lives for three time periods, $t = 1, 2, 3$. There is a single activity to be done that creates future benefit, $b_t > 0$, if done at time $t = 1, 2$, and a current cost, $c > 0$. Thus, the benefits depend on when the activity is done, but the cost is the same whenever the activity is done. The activity cannot be done at time $t = 3$. Time $t = 3$ might be thought of as the future date at which the benefits from the activity are enjoyed. This is an activity that has *current costs and future benefits*. Examples include cleaning one's room/car, organizing one's desk, preparing for an exam, doing a job search, mowing one's lawn, and giving up tempting but harmful activities.

The self of the individual at time $t=1$ (self-1) can do this activity or leave it to the self at time $t=2$ (self-2) to do it. Recall that self-3 never does the activity because it can only be done in the first two time periods. Each self decides independently whether to do the activity or not. The individual has quasi-hyperbolic preferences of the form $(\beta, 1)$ (see section 2.13). Denote the utility of self-t if the activity is undertaken at time $\tilde{t}$ by $u_t(\tilde{t})$.

Self-2 does the activity at time $\tilde{t}=2$ if

$$u_2(2) = \beta b_2 - c > 0 \Leftrightarrow \beta > \frac{c}{b_2}. \tag{8.37}$$

In (8.37), since the benefits accrue in the future, they are discounted by the present bias parameter β, but costs are incurred immediately; hence, they are not discounted. If self-1 does the activity at time $\tilde{t}=1$, then for this action to yield positive utility, we have

$$u_1(1) = \beta b_1 - c > 0 \Leftrightarrow \beta > \frac{c}{b_1}. \tag{8.38}$$

On the other hand, if self-1 does not engage in the activity, then self-1 derives utility from the activity of self-2. However, in this case, since the activity is either done, or not done, at time $t=2$, the benefits and costs both arise in the future so they are discounted. Hence, the utility of self-1, if self-2 engages in the activity, is

$$u_1(2) = \beta(b_2 - c), \tag{8.39}$$

and if self-2 does not engage in the activity and self-1 does not engage in it either, then there are neither costs nor benefits, so

$$u_1 = 0. \tag{8.40}$$

The β value of self-2 is not known to self-1, but self-1 forms an estimate $\hat{\beta}$ of the β value of self-2. The relation between β and $\hat{\beta}$ gives rise to the three possible cases described in section 8.2: time consistents ($\beta = \hat{\beta} = 1$), sophisticates ($\beta = \hat{\beta} < 1$), partial naifs ($\beta < \hat{\beta} < 1$), and naifs ($\beta < \hat{\beta} = 1$).

Using (8.37), self-1 believes that self-2 will engage in the activity if

$$\hat{\beta} > \frac{c}{b_2}. \tag{8.41}$$

Consider some possible equilibrium outcomes.

If $\beta < \frac{c}{b_1}$ and $\beta < \frac{c}{b_2}$, then from (8.37) and (8.38) both selves will not do the activity, so it never gets done. If $\beta > \frac{c}{b_2}$, then conditional on self-1 not doing the activity (say, because $\beta < \frac{c}{b_1}$), self-2 will definitely do it.

If $\hat{\beta} > \frac{c}{b_2}$ (i.e., (8.41) holds), then self-1 is confident that self-2 will do the activity. Suppose also that $\beta > \frac{c}{b_1}$ so that from (8.38), self-1 also derives positive utility from doing it. However, self-1 must now decide whether to do it or leave it for self-2 to do it. This requires comparing (8.38) and (8.39). If $u_1(2) > u_1(1)$ or $\beta(b_2 - c) > \beta b_1 - c$, then self-1 prefers to leave it for self-2 to do the activity. This can be simplified to

$$u_1(2) > u_1(1) \Leftrightarrow (b_1 - b_2) < c\left(\frac{1}{\beta} - 1\right). \tag{8.42}$$

The inequality in (8.42) is more likely to hold if b_1 and b_2 are close to each other (so doing the activity now rather than in the future does not buy significantly extra benefits for self-1), the cost of the activity, c, is high (it pays to defer costs for self-1 because they will be discounted), and β is low (future benefits are discounted by self-1).

Suppose that (8.42) holds so that self-1 prefers to defer the activity to self-2. Suppose also that $\beta < \frac{c}{b_2}$ (i.e., the actual β value of self-2 is low), and conditional on self-1 not having done the activity, self-2 also does not carry it out. In this case, self-1 has misplaced confidence (or overconfidence) that self-2 will do it, perhaps because self-1 is a partial naif or a naif. In that event, none of the selves will ever do the activity. This is a particularly bad outcome for the individual because if it were not for misplaced confidence in self-2, self-1 would actually find it profitable to undertake the activity (because $\beta > \frac{c}{b_1}$).

To fix ideas in a more concrete example, the individual might not clean their room today because they are fully confident that they will do it tomorrow. However, tomorrow, the taste for instant gratification prevents the individual from cleaning the room. The result is that the room never gets cleaned. How would a time consistent individual ($\beta = \hat{\beta} = 1$) behave in this situation? Suppose, for illustration, that benefits are identical in both periods, $b_1 = b_2 = b > 0$. Then, setting $\beta = 1$ in (8.42), we have $0 < 0$, which is not possible, so self-1 will not leave it for self-2 to do it. Using (8.38), if $\beta \equiv 1 > \frac{c}{b_1}$, then self-1 of a time consistent individual will do it immediately and there is no procrastination.

The main takeaway lesson from this simple exercise is that individuals with self-control problems may procrastinate, and current costs, even if they are not too large, may prevent them from taking timely actions.[6] One may also consider the implications when there are *current benefits but future costs* of actions (e.g., vacations, spending money with credit cards, watching a late night movie). In this case, the framework presented above can be extended to show that present biased individuals might preproperate (i.e., do the activity too quickly relative to a time consistent individual). The intuition is that because costs occur in the future, they are discounted too much, while benefits that occur immediately are undiscounted. We shall mainly be concerned about procrastination in the examples below.

8.7.2 Job Search and Hard Paternalism

Procrastination has several implications for policy. It also sometimes opens up avenues for hard paternalism. Consider, for instance, the problem of job search for the unemployed. There are two kinds of activities in searching for new jobs (Paserman, 2008; DellaVigna & Paserman, 2005): (1) getting information on new jobs, making CVs, filling out job applications, and attending interviews and (2) comparing the long-run costs and benefits of the alternative jobs and choosing among them. The first kind of activity is of the nature of *current costs and future benefits*, which we explored in section 8.7.1.

One prediction of the model is that individuals might procrastinate and be put off by the costs associated with the first activity, perpetuating their state of unemployment. Public policy can then be used to try to overcome these costs. For instance, in order to receive unemployment benefits, workers might need to register themselves at government job centers that guide them to construct CVs, provide online job search assistance, and highlight the importance of and provide preparation toward doing well in interviews. If attendance at job centers was voluntary and there were no implications for unemployment benefits from nonattendance, then this would be a form of soft paternalism. And if the process was easy and simple (and hence does not have "sludge"), people would be far more likely to choose to use it (Thaler & Sunstein, 2021).

In actual practice workers are typically required to register at the job centers; otherwise the unemployment benefits are withdrawn. Furthermore, those who register might be required to engage in periodic and mandatory face-to-face meetings with counselors who go through the relevant checklists and ask for data on the number of jobs applied for and follow-up actions taken. In other interventions, the length of time that workers can avail themselves of unemployment benefits is limited, which also encourages them to incur the relevant costs of the first activity (Fang & Silverman, 2009). Since this set of requirements is nonvoluntary for the unemployed (unless they wish to forgo the unemployment benefits), this is a form of hard paternalism, but one that is induced, at least in part, by the insights arising from behavioral models of time discounting. We do not mean necessarily to endorse this kind of intervention. But we do suggest that an understanding of such models, and of procrastination, makes them worth considering.

8.7.3 Deadlines; Buying Single Cigarette Packs

Consider students who need to complete an assignment, or consider any other activity that has some degree of flexibility on the completion date. Setting deadlines for university and college students is a form of hard paternalism. In many cases, these deadlines consist of a series of sub-deadlines that govern interaction between students and their supervisors (e.g., discuss the formal idea by date t_1, give a first draft to read by date t_2, and present a final draft by date t_3). Deadlines should not be needed if individuals are time consistent; they will plan optimally. However, in the presence of present bias and lack of full self-awareness of future self-control problems, individuals might procrastinate and keep putting off the completion of tasks until it is too late. This may compromise the quality of the task (e.g., a student leaving the assignment too late and then rushing to complete a work of low quality).

Ariely and Wertenbroch (2002) explore these ideas for executive education students who need to complete an assignment. In treatment 1, students could choose self-imposed deadlines and in treatment 2, they faced experimenter-provided, evenly spaced deadlines. In treatment 1, students did choose self-imposed deadlines when they could have chosen not to; as a result, there is a demand for deadlines. However, there was even less delay in completing the task in treatment 2, where the deadlines were exogenously imposed. The explanation of the results is threefold. First, the contrast between the two treatments suggests that students may have present biased preferences. Second, the imposition of self-imposed deadlines in treatment 1 shows that students have a degree of awareness of their self-control problems. Third, the fact that there is greater delay in treatment 1 relative to treatment 2 suggests that students have imperfect awareness of their self-control problems.

Smokers often buy single cigarette packs rather than several packs. This is puzzling because shopping trips are potentially costly and the per unit price of the cigarettes might be higher. One possible explanation might be found by applying our framework of multiple selves. Smoking creates current benefits but future costs, and hence there might be a tendency to buy too many cigarettes in order to minimize the fixed cost of going to a shop to buy them. However, if individuals have some degree of awareness of their self-control problems, then they might wish to limit the current purchase to a single pack. This may serve as a commitment device to smoke less, at least relative to the case where they buy multiple packs in a single trip (Wertenbroch, 1998).

8.7.4 Inducing Farmers to Buy Fertilizers

Duflo et al. (2011) consider an application of procrastination to the purchase of fertilizers in Kenya. To fix ideas, suppose that farmers grow two crops, crop 1 and crop 2, in two different seasons, so that there is a time interval between the harvesting of crop 1 and the planting of crop 2. When crop 1 is harvested, 97 percent of farmers say that they intend to buy fertilizers to use for crop 2. However, only 37 percent of the farmers actually buy fertilizers for crop 2. How might we explain this *intention-action divide*?

We can again appeal to our basic framework of present bias and limited awareness of self-control problems. After the harvesting of crop 1, there is a fixed cost to pay to buy fertilizers for the next crop (perhaps a trip to a nearby town and arranging for the transport to bring back the fertilizers). The benefits from this purchase accrue in the future. Hence, this a problem of current costs and future benefits. We know from our discussion in section 8.7.1 that this may lead to procrastination. The current selves of the farmers might always believe sincerely that in the future (and before fertilizers are required for crop 2) they will go out and buy the fertilizers. However, each self procrastinates and underestimates the self-control problems of the future selves. The result is that the harvest money from crop 1 might run out and by the time the fertilizers are actually required for crop 2, there is no money left to buy them.

One may think of two solutions to this problem. One could either subsidize the purchase of the fertilizer to make it more attractive—this is a form of hard paternalism. Alternatively, one could use a form of soft paternalism in which once farmers have the revenues in hand from the sale of crop 1, the fertilizer is delivered to their doorstep. This is a form of soft paternalism in the sense that there is no requirement for farmers to necessarily buy the fertilizer at the doorstep. The authors find that the second option is the more effective of the two. This experiment nicely contrasts the two forms of public policy response to a problem that has potentially serious welfare consequences for the poor. In this case, soft paternalism is relatively more effective.

8.8 Behavioral Industrial Organization, Bounded Rationality, and Policy

Economists distinguish between partial equilibrium and general equilibrium considerations. General equilibrium considerations take account of all possible spillovers of a policy on all economic actors and on all markets. Thus, partial equilibrium considerations that ignore such spillovers may not provide a complete account of the effects of a policy. This observation applies equally to classical taxation and regulation instruments in economics and to behavioral policy instruments.

There is a growing literature on *behavioral industrial organization*, surveyed in Heidhues and Köszegi (2018), that considers the general equilibrium effects of behavioral policy. To describe some of the central insights from this literature, we first introduce a simple model of *Hotelling competition* among two firms; consumers in this model have behavioral biases. Once we draw the relevant implications from the model, we offer a critical evaluation of the insights from this literature.

We should point out that there is an older literature on bounded rationality within firms whose insights are as relevant today as they were then, but this has not been the focus in modern behavioral industrial organization. This literature tried to address the question of decision-making within diverse subunits within the firm who might have conflicting goals/aspirations. Other features of these models include separation of ownership and control, search costs of gathering information, and incomplete contracts (Simon, 1955; Cyert & March, 1963; Radner, 1992, 1996). We believe that in future research, it would be fruitful to follow up on the insights from this literature too.

The main, but not the only, behavioral bias introduced in the modern behavioral industrial organization literature is that firms offer prices for a product that consist of two components: a directly observed price component, q, and a less directly visible price component, a (short for *add-on*, which the reader might think of as a surcharge). Thus, the total price, p, for the product is given by $p = q + a$. Let us assume that $a \in [0, \bar{a}]$, where $\bar{a}$ is some maximum possible add-on. *Sophisticated consumers* observe both price components, q and a. *Naive consumers* observe q but do not observe (or do not pay attention to) the add-on component a. Neglect of the component *a* takes several forms in the behavioral industrial economics literature. We consider some of these forms below.

1. Naive consumers may simply ignore the component *a*. For instance, consumers have been found to ignore sales taxes that are added at the cash register (Chetty et al., 2009) or to ignore bank overdraft charges when opening a bank account (Armstrong & Vickers, 2012).

2. Naive consumers might have present biased preferences, as in our hyperbolic discounting model (see section 2.13), so they might form an incorrect estimate of the future use of the product. For instance, an overestimate of the future use of a gym membership that is exploited by firms through a pay-as-you-go contract that requires paying a high upfront fee (DellaVigna & Malmendier, 2004, 2006). *Projection bias* on the part of consumers, in which they estimate their future usage of a product based too closely on their current usage/preferences, is likely to lead to similar results (Loewenstein et al., 2003). Ausubel (1991) showed that the most likely explanation for why consumers borrow at high rates on credit cards is that they underestimate the amount they will need to borrow in the future (perhaps because of overconfidence, projection bias, present biased preferences, or a combination of these factors).

3. In other settings, consumers may incorrectly estimate some underlying statistical moments of the usage of their product. For instance, Grubb (2009) shows that if mobile phone consumers underestimate the variance of their phone usage, then they can be exploited by firms who offer a convex pricing scheme for their call usage (i.e., each successive unit of usage increases unit price at an increasing rate). Risk averse consumers who correctly estimate the variance of their mobile phone usage may prefer instead concave pricing schemes. Another example comes from Spiegler (2006), who shows why people who use the *law of small numbers* (see section 5.2) might value the services of quacks. A quack only has to be proved right once, or a small number of times, for a subscriber to the law of small numbers to start believing in the efficacy of the quack's treatment. Such an individual uses the small sample of observed successes of the quack to infer the properties of the population distribution of successes of the quack, which might, in actual practice, be no better than tossing a coin and choosing heads.

Let us be agnostic for the moment about the exact reason why inattentive consumers do not pay attention to the add-on component, *a*, in prices.

Hotelling price competition between firms is a stylized representation of competition between two firms, A and B, for consumers who are uniformly located in the interval [0, 1]. One may imagine a linear city of length 1 mile and the two firms are located at the two ends of the city; firm A is located at 0 and firm B at 1. Let us denote a generic location in this city by $x \in [0, 1]$. Firm $i = A, B$ charges a price $p_i = q_i + a_i$. The two firms compete by offering directly observed prices, q_i, and add-ons, a_i. Both firms have an identical marginal cost of supplying one unit of the good, equal to $c > 0$.

Each consumer demands one unit of the good and assigns a value v to the single unit. If the consumer does not buy the good then they receive a utility of 0. A consumer who travels a distance $x \in [0, 1]$ to buy the 1 unit incurs a transportation cost of tx^2, where $t > 0$.

Let us start with the special case where all consumers pay equal and full attention to the two components q_i and a_i; such consumers are *fully attentive*. Hence, there is no reason why firms should choose any add-ons. It follows that each firm optimally sets $a_i = 0$, A, B. Thus, we can directly consider competition between the two firms in the overall prices, p_A and p_B.

The utility of a consumer who is located at $x \in [0, 1]$ is found by deducting the total cost of the purchase, the price and the transportation cost, from the value, v, of the good.

$$U = \begin{cases} v - p_A - tx^2 & \text{if buying from A} \\ v - p_B - t(1-x)^2 & \text{if buying from B} \end{cases} \quad (8.43)$$

The method of solution is fairly straightforward and standard in economics, but we provide the details for the benefits of interdisciplinary readers. We can find a location $x_c \in [0, 1]$ such that a consumer who is located at x_c is indifferent to buying from A or B. In other words, such a consumer derives identical utility from buying from either firm. Using (8.43), we have $v - p_A - tx_c^2 = v - p_B - t(1 - x_c)^2$, so solving out for x_c, we have

$$x_c = \frac{p_B - p_A + t}{2t}. \quad (8.44)$$

To the left of the location x_c, all consumers prefer to buy from A because they are even closer to A and incur lower transaction costs. Similarly, to the right of location x_c, all consumers prefer to buy from B because they are even closer to B and incur lower transportation costs. Let us assume that the consumer located at x_c always prefers to buy the good,

$$v - p_A - tx_c^2 \geq 0. \tag{8.45}$$

If (8.45) holds, then all consumers, on either side of x_c, also prefer to buy the good. This is because to the left (resp. right) of x_c, everyone incurs a lower transport cost by buying from firm A (resp. firm B), hence deriving even higher utility than the consumer at location x_c.

We can now determine the demand curves facing each of the two firms. Recall that consumers are distributed uniformly over the interval [0, 1]. Everyone to the left of x_c buys from A, so the demand facing firm A is

$$D_A = \int_0^{x_c} dz = x_c = \frac{p_B - p_A + t}{2t}, \tag{8.46}$$

while everyone to the right of x_c buys from B, so the demand facing firm B is

$$D_B = \int_{x_c}^1 dz = 1 - x_c = 1 - \frac{p_B - p_A + t}{2t}. \tag{8.47}$$

Given the demands, each firm $i = A, B$ maximizes its profits, given by $\pi_i = D_i(p_i - c)$, where $D_i p_i$ is the total revenue and $D_i c$ is the total costs, so the difference gives total profits. For instance, for firm A, we have

$$\pi_A = \frac{p_B - p_A + t}{2t}(p_A - c). \tag{8.48}$$

Differentiating (8.48),

$$\frac{d\pi_A}{dp_A} = \frac{p_B - p_A + t}{2t} - \frac{1}{2t}(p_A - c). \tag{8.49}$$

The second-order condition is satisfied because $\frac{d^2\pi_A}{dp_A^2} = \frac{-1}{t} < 0$. At an interior solution, we can solve $\frac{d\pi_A}{dp_A} = 0$ using (8.49) for p_A to get

$$p_A = \frac{1}{2}(p_B + t + c). \tag{8.50}$$

The expression in (8.50) is also known as the *reaction function* of firm A. It shows the best response of A, in terms of a choice of price p_A, to any price p_B set by B. We can derive a similar reaction function for B and solve the two reaction functions together. Since the reaction function of firm B is symmetric and the marginal costs are identical, we can restrict our choices to a symmetric Nash equilibrium in prices $p_A^* = p_B^* = p^*$. Thus, in equilibrium, if any one firm chooses the price p^*, then the best response of the other firm is also to choose the price p^*. Setting $p_A = p_B = p^*$ in (8.50), we get

$$p^* = t + c. \tag{8.51}$$

Thus, in a symmetric Nash equilibrium, facing fully attentive consumers, each firm sets the price given in (8.51). We leave it to the reader to check that in equilibrium, each firm gets half the market share ($D_A = D_B = \frac{1}{2}$), and the profit of each firm is

$$\pi_A = \pi_B = \frac{t}{2}. \tag{8.52}$$

The unit transport cost t may be taken as an index of how competitive the market is. Obviously, if $t = 0$, then consumers incur no transport costs (it is as if the firms from whom they buy are located at their doorsteps). In this case, using (8.51), each firm optimally sets its price equal to the marginal cost, $p^* = c$, and makes no profits (this can be checked by setting $t = 0$ in (8.52)). Technically, this outcome is the same as under Bertrand competition, a popular form of price competition used in economics. When $t = 0$, consumers get the lowest price possible and the consumer surplus is at its maximum. On the other hand, as t increases, the market becomes more imperfect, and the gap between the optimal price and the marginal cost increases, so firms' profits increase and consumer surplus falls.

Now consider the opposite extreme where all consumers are *inattentive* in the sense that they completely ignore the add-on component of price, a. From (8.46) and (8.47), the demand facing each firm is decreasing in the price set by the firm—that is, D_i is decreasing in p_i, $i = A, B$. Since $p_i = q_i + a_i$, but inattentive consumers only observe q_i (but not a_i), each firm can expand its demand by setting the add-on price as high as possible (i.e., $a_i = \bar{a}$) and the directly observed price as low as possible. Denote by q_i^* the component of the optimal price that is observed by consumers. Hence, using (8.51), the definition $p_i = q_i + a_i$, and $a_i = \bar{a}$, we have

$$p^* = q_i^* + \bar{a} = t + c. \tag{8.53}$$

Comparing (8.51) and (8.53), inattentive consumers are not disadvantaged. In both cases, they pay an identical price of p^* (although they believe that they are paying a price q_i^*). Thus, market competition protects boundedly rational consumers in this case (Grubb, 2015). From (8.53), we have

$$q_i^* = t + c - \bar{a}. \tag{8.54}$$

If $\bar{a}$ is high enough, then q_i^* might be quite low. In some cases, there could be price floors, so that a very low price, q_i^*, might be infeasible, hence disallowing inattentive consumers to be protected by market competition. For instance, consider the market for printers, where consumers ignore the price of printer cartridges. In order to increase profits, firms can make their printers incompatible with printer cartridges of other firms and set high prices for them. But inattentive consumers ignore these add-ons and still buy the printers (Miao, 2010). In this case, setting the price of printers too low (low q_i^*) might simply induce consumers to buy a new printer rather than a new cartridge. Similar considerations apply to the sale prices of consumer durables where the add-on is the price of the warranty (C. Michel, 2017). There could also be a legal requirement in some countries that prevents the retail price of a good to fall below the wholesale price.

Having considered separately the polar cases of fully attentive and inattentive consumers, suppose now that each firm knows that a fraction μ of the consumers is inattentive and the remaining fraction $1 - \mu$ is fully attentive. If firms maximize expected profits, then the analogue of (8.53) is

$$p^* = q_i^* + \mu\bar{a} = t + c.$$

Thus, the analogue of (8.54) is

$$q_i^* = t + c - \mu\bar{a}. \tag{8.55}$$

Since fully attentive consumers anticipate the add-ons, they can protect themselves from being exploited by the high prices of these add-ons. For instance, suppose that hotels levy steep charges for room telephone calls. Then, fully attentive consumers might be able to protect themselves by either their mobile phone or using a public telephone booth (Gabaix & Laibson, 2006). Similarly, a fully attentive consumer might choose not to buy a printer if it is not compatible with cheaper printer cartridge brands.

Remark 8.1. *(Cross-subsidy from inattentive to fully attentive consumers) Let us assume that fully attentive consumers can costlessly protect themselves against the add-ons and will not buy the add-ons (such as extended warranties, costly calling charges in hotels, or printers that are incompatible with print cartridges of cheaper brands). Thus, inattentive consumers ignore add-ons and fully attentive consumers only pay the price q_i^*. Then, an important lesson can be drawn from (8.55). The presence of inattentive consumers reduces the price, q_i^*, by an amount*

$\mu\bar{a}$ that depends on the fraction of inattentive consumers. This is a form of cross-subsidization of the fully attentive consumers at the expense of the inattentive consumers (Gabaix & Laibson, 2006). In many cases, inattentive consumers might be less literate and poorer; hence, such cross-subsidization is regressive with respect to incomes. Thus, for instance, bank accounts may be offered free of cost, but the costs are recouped through high interest rate charges on consumers whose bank accounts are overdrawn; typically, these are poorer consumers who are faced with unanticipated expenses (Armstrong & Vickers, 2012).

We make four further observations:

1. Consider the case of perfect competition (i.e., $t \to 0$) and only inattentive consumers; so from (8.54), $q_i^* = c - \bar{a}$. If we have the case $c - \bar{a} < v < c$, then consumers will buy the good (because $v > q_i^*$), yet it is socially undesirable to produce the good because $v < c$. Thus, naivete creates economic inefficiencies and distortions in production.

2. The demand facing each firm is decreasing in its price. Hence, in the presence of inattentive consumers, each firm will wish to innovate to produce new technologies of obfuscation that allow for an increase in maximum possible add-ons, $\bar{a}$ (Heidhues et al., 2016). If $\bar{a}$ can be increased, then the observed component of price, q_i^*, can be decreased (see (8.54)), leading to an expansion of demand for each firm under imperfect competition (especially under the assumptions made in remark 8.1). Thus, another implication of naivete is that it might lead firms to pursue more devious strategies for obfuscation.

3. In the BRA, competition is almost always good and forms the basis of classical antitrust policies and theory of regulation. In particular, greater competition is supposed to reduce the prices that consumers pay and lead to greater efficiency. However, under bounded rationality, this basic axiom of regulation economics may not be valid. Suppose, for instance, that we have only inattentive consumers and a price floor, given by $\underline{q} \leq c - \bar{a}$. Then, an increase in competition, as captured by a reduction in t in our model above, is not able to reduce the price, q_i^* in (8.54). When such price floors do not exist, then competition will reduce prices, even under bounded rationality; however, competition might not necessarily produce more efficiency in terms of higher quality and lower obfuscation (Spiegler 2006; Carlin, 2009; Gamp & Krähmer, 2019; Heidhues et al., 2016).

4. Suppose that inattentive consumers were to realize that they are inattentive and hire an expert or use an intermediary to give them advice on

their purchase decisions. Would this not solve the problem? Not necessarily. Suppose, for instance, that inattentive consumers use price comparison websites as the relevant intermediary. Then, firms could respond by quoting low headline prices on the price comparison website but use high surcharges (Ellison & Ellison, 2009; Armstrong & Zhou, 2011). If firms are confident that intermediaries will be reasonably successful in ensuring high take-up of their (possibly inferior) products, they may increase prices, further cutting down on consumer surplus. A second problem in some areas (for instance, in financial advice) is that intermediaries might actually push the sale of inferior financial products because they receive a greater commission from selling these products (Murooka, 2015).

Heidhues and Köszegi (2018) make several observations on the implementation and unexpected effects of soft paternalism. We now consider some of these observations in light of the discussion above. Consider, for instance, a utilitarian welfare function, or any social welfare function that places weight on the utilities of the inattentive and the fully attentive consumers. Now consider any libertarian paternalistic policy, such as a nudge to inattentive consumers (e.g., financial literacy, clearer labeling/descriptions of products), that reduces the fraction, μ, of inattentive consumers in society. From remark 8.1, we know that this reduces the cross-subsidy received by fully attentive consumers who are worse off, while some of the inattentive consumers are better off. Since welfare measures take account of the utilities of both inattentive and fully attentive consumers, on net, we cannot say if any policies that help inattentive consumers are overall welfare improving.

Consider another example. Suppose that some regulatory intervention, perhaps a form of soft paternalism, increases the likelihood that consumers will attend to late fees associated with credit card payments. Inattentive consumers will be less likely to pay late fees, because they are not aware of them. Fully attentive consumers will not change their behavior, but companies might respond to the intervention by (for example) imposing or increasing annual fees. On balance, there might be no welfare gain.

That is certainly possible, but we offer two cautionary notes. First, assuming interpersonal comparisons of utility (Adler, 2011), the gainers might gain more in terms of welfare than the losers lose, especially if the gainers are at the lower end of the economic ladder (see also remark 8.1). Second, the consequence of effective nudges, in cases of this kind, might not in fact be a loss of a cross-subsidy. Some evidence suggests that behaviorally informed interventions, including nudges, can help the inattentive without harming the fully attentive (see Agarwal et al., 2013; Sarin, 2019). To be sure, this evidence remains to be fully explained.

A second observation, already incorporated in our example on credit card payments, is related to the well-known *Lucas critique* in economics. In response to regulatory intervention, such as mandatory disclosure or contract simplification, firms could respond and choose new and perhaps more devious methods to increase profits (Piccione & Spiegler, 2012; Murooka & Schwarz, 2018). To evaluate this concern, consider a few possibilities from US regulatory policy:

1. The Department of Transportation requires airlines to include taxes and other fees in posted prices.
2. The Federal Trade Commission forbids hotels and resorts from adding hotel fees at checkout time.
3. The Consumer Financial Protection Bureau forbids online companies from automatically enrolling people into certain programs (such as costly insurance packages).
4. The Department of Labor mandates fee and performance disclosures for investment options in certain plans.
5. The Department of Energy requires various appliances, such as refrigerators and microwave ovens, to come with energy-efficiency disclosures.

For all of these policies, it is easily imaginable that firms will respond in some way—perhaps by making disclosure more complex and confusing (Persson, 2018), perhaps by inducing information overload, perhaps by seeking to divert consumers' attention in some way, perhaps by altering some other contract term or product attribute. If so, the intervention might turn out to be futile, producing no net welfare gain. Or, it might even be counterproductive, making consumers or investors worse off on net.

This possibility cannot be ruled out, whether we are speaking of soft or hard paternalism. But it is only a possibility. It might turn out to be net beneficial to regulate, simply because of the costs, to firms, of attempting a response (Sarin, 2019). There is evidence, for example, that something like 4 has helped investors (Kronlund et al., 2020), that something like 3 has helped consumers (Sarin, 2019), and that something like 1 has helped travelers (Bradley & Feldman, 2020). One analysis suggests that something like 2 would help consumers (Sullivan, 2017). None of this demonstrates that the concern is baseless. But how companies will respond to soft paternalism, and whether the response will eliminate a potential welfare gain, is an empirical question and cannot be answered in the abstract.

There are cases, however, where potentially harmful reactions by firms in response to regulatory policies can be ignored. For instance, when the supplier itself is a state monopoly, with an explicit aim of consumer welfare, it is unlikely to engage in devious practices post regulation. In other cases, there is no private market. For instance, nudges that induce greater organ donations in a situation where demand for organs is independent of supply are unlikely to be subject to the criticism of devious firm responses.

The insights arising from the behavioral industrial organization literature are plausible and thought-provoking. However, we have little empirical evidence of the effectiveness or the importance of the transmission channels that are invoked in the theoretical models. The models themselves are extremely simplified toy version stories of real world markets, and it is not clear how useful their predictions are for the actual functioning of markets. The concerns here are similar to those that are invoked by the literature on complexity and agent-based models in thinking about macroeconomics relative to the mainstream macroeconomic models (see sections 3.7 and 4.9). This is not to underestimate the potential usefulness of the insights coming out of behavioral industrial organization but rather to await stringent empirical testing of the predictions before we are confident enough to design policy based on these predictions. Furthermore, the game theoretic equilibrium concepts used in this literature, such as mixed strategy Nash equilibrium, do not find adequate empirical support, at least in the lab evidence, nor is it easy to provide an economic interpretation of such mixed strategies. Whether such tools are more useful to model strategic interaction outside the lab is an open question.

9
Libertarian Paternalism in Theory

9.1 Introduction

This chapter turns to more specific issues in public policy. In the BRA, observed choices reflect the underlying preferences of individuals. Suppose, for example, that John Smith chooses chocolate ice cream over vanilla ice cream; that Mary Jones chooses to live in New York rather than London; that Frank Williams chooses to spend money this year rather than save money for the future. In all of these cases, and many others, we might want to insist that outsiders, especially those who work for the government, should let Smith, Jones, and Williams do as they wish. As we have emphasized, however, behavioral evidence demonstrates that Smith, Jones, and Williams, and countless others like them, sometimes do not make choices that are in their best interests (Thaler & Sunstein, 2021; Dhami, 2016).

We have referred to the canonical text on these questions, *On Liberty*, where J. S. Mill (2002/1863) insisted:

> The only purpose for which power can be rightfully exercised over any member of a civilized community, against his will, is to prevent harm to others. His own good, either physical or moral, is not a sufficient warrant. He cannot rightfully be compelled to do or forbear because it will be better for him to do so, because it will make him happier, because, in the opinion of others, to do so would be wise, or even right.

Mill offered a number of separate justifications for his famous HARM PRINCIPLE, but as we have noted, his most emphatic, and the most relevant here, is epistemic: choosers are in the best position to know what is good for them. In Mill's view, the problem with outsiders, including government officials, is that they lack the necessary information. Mill (2002/1863) insists that the individual "is the person most interested in his own well-being," and the "ordinary man or woman has means of knowledge immeasurably surpassing those that can be possessed by any one else." When society seeks to overrule the individual's judgment, it does so on the basis of "general presumptions," and these "may be altogether wrong, and even if right, are as likely as not to be misapplied to individual cases." If the goal is to ensure that people's lives go well, Mill concludes that the best solution is to allow people to find their own path. That conclusion is echoed in Hayek's (2013, p. 384) suggestion that "the awareness of our irremediable ignorance of most of what is known to somebody [who is a chooser] is the chief basis of the argument for liberty." For Hayek, the key contrast is between the chooser, who knows a great deal, and the outsiders, who show "irremediable ignorance," especially if they are social planners. These ideas play a defining role in much of discussion on public policy in the BRA.

We have also seen that, in the BRA, individuals are often believed to be self-regarding, although other-regarding preferences are not inconsistent with the BRA. Self-regarding individuals are generally focused on their own welfare, not on the welfare of those whom they affect, which, as noted, gives rise to an important role for public policy to internalize the externalities that they cause. Examples of relevant policy interventions include Pigouvian taxes to regulate the emission of pollution by firms, subsidies to consumers to buy electric cars, and tax-exempt charitable contributions. Regulation (such as fuel economy limits for motor vehicles and emissions limits for power plants) might also be used to reduce externalities, though it is cruder and less efficient than Pigouvian taxes.[1]

In section 9.2, we consider a range of choices where it is not clear that people are acting in their own interests, taking their life as a whole. For instance, can people always or necessarily be said to be acting in their interests, including their long-term interests, if they refuse to get vaccinated? If they choose unhealthy diets? If they smoke cigarettes? If they text while driving? If they procrastinate in choosing their pension plans? If they make hasty decisions with respect to marriage or divorce? If they do not save for retirement? It is true that rational choosers care about things other than health and wealth and that they discount the future. But even so, we provide evidence to show that in many cases, self-control and other problems induce people to make suboptimal choices that are hard to justify as in their own interests, taking account of the long term.

We have referred to libertarian paternalism (LP), but in section 9.3, we outline the basic idea in more detail. LP is an umbrella term for policy interventions, often called *nudges*, that are designed to preserve freedom of choice (the L in LP) while also steering people in directions that will promote their welfare. LP leaves unchanged the choices of those who satisfy the assumptions in the BRA. At the same time, LP also nudges those who might violate these assumptions (e.g., have self-control problems) into choices and outcomes that are best for them, as judged by themselves. A GPS device is an example of LP; it increases navigability while also allowing people to choose their own destination (and if they like, their own route).

In some cases, LP favors disclosure of information; in some cases, LP favors warnings and reminders; in some cases, LP favors automatic enrollment (opt out as opposed to opt in); in some cases, LP favors active choosing. Consider, for instance, the introduction of various default options, such as automatic enrollment in savings programs. LP can be used, and is being used, in multiple domains to help choosers by increasing their welfare. Both private and public institutions can enlist LP to promote desirable goals. Of course, we have also seen that behavioral findings might justify more aggressive interventions, and we take up that idea again in the following chapter.

Finally, we offer a critical discussion of a contractarian approach to these problems, originally due to the 1986 Nobel laureate in economics, James M. Buchanan, and explored and defended in detail by Robert Sugden.

In section 9.4, we consider the possibility that governments themselves might make errors, suffer from behavioral biases, or fail to act as benevolent social planners. These are important concerns, and they help to explain why libertarian paternalism is libertarian. Importantly, they apply whether we think of policy in the framework of libertarian paternalism or within the BRA. We also respond to some critical evaluations of LP and nudges.

Section 9.5 considers several examples of nudges to illustrate how they may be used to improve human agency and to improve individual welfare.

9.2 Mistakes and Welfare

An understanding of the role of heuristics, and of bounded rationality, raises some pointed questions: Was Mill right? Do individuals really know what is in their best (including their long-term) interests at all times? To build on the discussion in chapter 7 and to concretize these questions, consider the following empirically documented examples, E1–E6, of human behavior; the examples are just that; they do not by any means exhaust the scope of behavioral findings.

E1. Individuals may overconsume some goods (sugar, saturated fat, alcohol, tobacco) and suffer ill health, a shorter life span, and a lower quality of life.

E2. Individuals may procrastinate too much, fail to complete their projects on time, fail to consolidate their finances in a timely manner that might be more conducive to their long-term interests, not enroll in suitable pension plans, and take up annual gym memberships when a pay-as-you-go membership could have saved them money.

E3. Individuals might under save for their retirement (the data indicate a sharp drop in consumption at retirement; Bernheim et al., 1997) or retire too soon.

E4. Individuals might make marriage and divorce decisions too hastily. They might also make purchase decisions on impulse, in a hot state, and regret it afterward.

E5. Individuals might be misled by manipulative or deceptive, but not untruthful, advertising by firms that cleverly frame the options so as to encourage certain choices (Akerlof & Shiller, 2016). Such advertising might exploit people's lack of information, reliance on heuristics, or behavioral biases; as a result, people might lose a great deal of money or make choices that adversely affect their health and well-being.

E6. Individuals might not purchase fuel-efficient vehicles or energy-efficient refrigerators. Focusing on the short term, they save money in the present but lose money over a period of years, and with any reasonable discount rate, they are likely to be making an unjustifiable choice.

Under normative preferences, we should not observe these phenomena. The BRA would argue, for instance, that individuals rationally choose to consume unhealthy foods (perhaps because they are delicious to eat); never procrastinate (but instead optimally delay); perfectly smooth consumption over their lifetime; choose to marry, divorce, and make their purchases rationally; and make frame-invariant choices, provided the frames are informationally equivalent. It should not be controversial to suggest that individuals might be insufficiently informed and make poor choices for that reason. The behavioral claim is that these and other examples cannot be adequately explained by reference to lack of information. Distinctly behavioral explanations are necessary. For example, they might point to self-control problems, present bias, and unrealistic optimism.

We do not mean to deny that, in cases that appear to show mistakes relative to the BRA benchmark (as in E1–E6), it is possible that some people, or most people, are doing exactly what they should do. This is largely an empirical question. Many people might consume less than healthy foods not because they are present biased but because they greatly enjoy them and have made a fully rational judgment that trades off present discounted values of costs and benefits. With Mill, we agree that third parties, including public officials, should be humble about their potential ignorance and should hesitate before concluding that people have erred. But against Mill, we urge that in many cases, people's decisions are not in their interests; they do not, in fact, promote their welfare.

9.3 Libertarian Paternalism

In actual practice, a combination of private responses, public policy, and self-imposed control mechanisms might be used to remedy the problems described in E1–E6. Such remedies may involve the following:

1. Recall from chapter 8 that corrective taxes, such as sugar taxes and cigarette taxes, both of which can be understood as responding not only to externalities but also to internalities, arise when people impose costs on their own future selves without taking these costs fully into account in the same manner that a benevolent social planner would. In such cases, corrective taxes might be justified on welfare grounds.
2. Automatic enrollment in free school lunch and breakfast plans for poor children might be designed to respond to the possibility that parents will fail to sign up their children.
3. Many companies have adopted SMarT (short for *Save More Tomorrow*) savings plans, by which individuals agree to save a fraction of future increases in their incomes (Benartzi & Thaler, 2004); individuals might be automatically enrolled in such plans or asked whether they want to be.
4. Some governments have adopted cooling-off periods for divorce and 21-day return policies for impulse purchases.
5. Regulations might require financial firms to state the annual percentage interest rates (APR) on their financial products, perhaps with updates and reforms to APR to ensure simplicity and intelligibility.
6. Regulations might require clear, color-coded declarations of the key nutritional facts of food products, such as calories, saturated fats, and salt content.
7. Clear, simple labels so that people can see, and appreciate, the potential economic and social benefits of fuel-efficient automobiles and energy-efficient appliances.

As we have noted, E1–E6 are easily explained within a behavioral economics framework. These and countless other problems, some costing money and lives, can arise from a range of judgment heuristics and biases (Thaler & Sunstein, 2021; Dhami, 2019c, 2020a). Many individuals exhibit self-control problems as a result of present biased preferences; this typically leads to temporally suboptimal outcomes such as inadequate savings for retirement, obesity, procrastination, and drug use (Dhami, 2019c). Many people report that they would prefer to save more or prefer the median portfolio to their own. While self-reports should be taken with many grains of salt, they are at least suggestive.

We have said that some behaviorally informed approaches are discussed under a more general term: soft paternalism. This term includes (1) libertarian paternalism, which preserves freedom of choice, to which we have referred (Thaler & Sunstein, 2003, 2021; Sunstein & Thaler, 2003); (2) asymmetric paternalism (Camerer et al., 2003), which does not affect people who are fully rational but tries to help people who are not; and (3) light paternalism (Loewenstein & Haisley, 2008), which tries to enhance freedom of choice without restricting it. Despite their diversity, such approaches share two important features:

1. They allow people to go their own way—that is, to reject the direction suggested by the paternalist.
2. They reflect a form of means paternalism rather than ends paternalism, in the sense that they are respectful of the chooser's desires with respect to the ultimate destination (see chapter 7). It is for this reason that a GPS device is a defining example of libertarian paternalism. People who do not like the route suggested by a GPS device can simply select their own. In addition, users of a GPS device exercise agency in choosing their ultimate location.

In the relevant cases, the policy is introduced by a planner or a choice architect (who may work in the private or public sector). The objective is to enlist policies that do not affect, or affect minimally, the choices of fully rational individuals, but at the same time nudge others in a direction that is in their considered best interests, again as judged by themselves. By considered best interests, we mean the decisions that would be made by individuals if they had complete information and were free from behavioral biases (relative to the BRA). It is in that sense that individuals are enabled to make choices that make them better off, again as judged by themselves (Thaler & Sunstein, 2021). In some cases, it can be challenging to know whether this criterion is met; if so, it may be best to insist on a particular form of choice architecture: active choosing (Sunstein, 2018a).

Instead of nudging people to select a particular health care plan, for example, a choice architect might simply ask people: Which would you like to choose? That approach directly engages individual agency, and it might seem to have a kind of neutrality. Note, however, that it may be difficult or perhaps impossible to avoid some kind of steering of individual choices. Any website has to have some kind of layout. Any form that elicits information has to choose the order in which the questions are asked. When individuals are given choices and information, they are necessarily framed in a particular manner and already embed a certain choice architecture. Many examples can be given (Thaler & Sunstein, 2021), from doctors who advise patients on a choice of treatment to architects who advise clients about house designs, to interior decorators who advise people on alternative interior designs.

Consider the arrangement of food items in a cafeteria. On plausible assumptions, boundedly rational consumers, who pay special attention to items placed at eye level, could benefit from the placement of healthy options at eye level, relative to unhealthy snacks; this is an example of a nudge (Thaler & Sunstein, 2021). Consumers with normative preferences are not influenced by the arrangement of items, so little cost is imposed on them. Because the intervention of the choice architect is designed to steer choosers in a particular direction, a form of paternalism is involved. But, ultimately, it is the consumer who exercises choice; in this sense, the proposal respects consumer sovereignty.

There are many other examples of libertarian paternalism. To protect people with allergies, food might come with labels alerting people that it contains peanuts, eggs, milk, or shellfish. Doctors might send text messages to patients, reminding them of an appointment (or to take their medicines). Nozzles for dispensing different types of fuel (e.g., diesel and regular gasoline) are often different sizes or colors to prevent incorrect use. Many cars produce a beeping sound if the driver is not wearing a seat belt or if they are about to hit something while reversing. Automatic electric switches in cars and offices are often used to conserve energy or prevent batteries from running out. Default options in savings and pension plans are meant to enable people to save more or invest better; employees might have certain choices filled in by default, on the ground that those choices are in the interest of most employees. Government warnings on cigarette packs tell consumers of the risks of smoking. Many cash machines dispense cash only after the bank card has been taken out first so that it doesn't get left behind. A social media company might label certain posts as false or disputed, or refer users to sites where they can obtain more information.

We have emphasized that some instances of bounded rationality reflect self-control problems. These problems are often a product of present biased preferences in conjunction with a model of multiple selves; this can be shown rigorously (Dhami, 2019c, 2020c). This appears to be a common source of misunderstanding of the rationale for nudges. We outline some of the basic machinery of multiple self models in chapter 8.

Remark 9.1. *(Dhami, 2019c, chapter 3) People who have the present biased preferences in (8.2) will exhibit the behaviors outlined in E1–E4 in section 9.2 even if they satisfy all other features of the BRA. The degree to which they exhibit such behavior, and whether the behavior is to procrastinate or preoperate, will depend on their degree of self-awareness, as captured by the three cases in (8.4), (8.5), and (8.6).*

The interaction of default savings options, seen as nudges, and employee matching contributions is studied in Blumenstock et al. (2018) within the framework of present biased preferences, as in (7.2). For a rigorous theoretical model that shows the importance of the role of default options in the presence of present biased preferences and different degrees of self-awareness of future self-control problems, see section 5.8 in Dhami (2020c). This theoretical model uses the concept of a perception perfect equilibrium in O'Donoghue and Rabin (1999a, 1999b) to derive predictions that are supported by the empirical results in Blumenstock et al. Those results show that default options have a significant effect on private savings behavior, and while these particular data come from Afghanistan, the numerical estimates are comparable to those from numerous Western studies. This suggests that the model captures important and general features of human behavior.

Critics have objected to several features of libertarian paternalism. Sugden (2008, 2013) has used the *contractarian approach*, in which appeals are directly made to individuals, stressing the personal advantage to each individual from taking a particular action. Sugden places a particular emphasis on opportunity and increasing it; he is skeptical of the idea that nudges, or other interventions, can increase people's welfare, which (in his view) is difficult to assess or observe. The interested reader can get acquainted with some of the features of alternative proposals in Dhami (2020c, chapters 3, 5).

Building on the work of James Buchanan, Sugden invokes contractarianism both to justify the basic institutions of society and to establish the foundations of an account of what regulators legitimately do (Buchanan,

1986; Sugden, 2019). We doubt that contractarianism can do this kind of work; it is one thing to offer a contractarian account of some kind, as a defense of basic institutions, and quite another to use the same account to constrain regulators considering how and whether to interfere with voluntary arrangements.

Put that issue to one side and consider: For Buchanan and Sugden, what kind of contract is involved? What do we know about the parties? What do they know about themselves? What kind of information do they have? Do they suffer from behavioral biases? And what is the role of welfare? In our view, the answer to the last question is central; to know what regulators should and should not do, it is critical to know about the effects of their options on people's lives (which is to say, their welfare). In an arresting passage, Buchanan (1964) writes:

> The "market" or market organization is not a means toward the accomplishment of anything. It is, instead, the institutional embodiment of the voluntary exchange processes that are entered into by individuals in their several capacities. That is all there is to it. Individuals are observed to cooperate with one another, to reach agreements, to trade.

Is that really all there is to it? Maybe so. But then, why should anyone approve of the market? Embodying processes of voluntary exchange cannot be self-justifying; if the consequence is to make both sides worse off, the outcome should not be celebrated, and if the consequence is to harm people at the bottom of the economic ladder, the same conclusion should hold. Recall that for Mill, the central point was that people's voluntary choices are likely to promote their welfare, and that outsiders would be at an epistemic disadvantage. We think that Mill was doing battle on the right ground, at least; whether or not welfare is everything, it is something, and without resort to it, it is hard to evaluate intervention or non-intervention with voluntary choices. Avoiding Mill's welfarist claim, grounded in his form of utilitarianism, Sugden (2019) defends a kind of contractarianism in the following way:

> Social arrangements are not assessed from the standpoint of a benevolent social planner. Instead they are assessed from the several viewpoints of individual members of society, considered as potential parties to an agreement or "social contract." In evaluating a social institution, a contractarian theorist does not ask whether aggregate welfare is maximized. Instead, he asks whether it is in the interest of each individual to accept the rules of that institution, on the condition that everyone else does the same.

This understanding of contractarianism raises many questions and doubts. We should be willing to agree that arrangements should be assessed from the standpoint of members of society. (From what other standpoint would they be assessed?) It is also true that if accepting an institution is in the interest of everyone, it should be accepted. But that is a very demanding criterion. The institution of marriage is not good for everyone; it is good if and because it makes human life better. The same can be said for the corporate form. And what counts as a social institution? What does it mean to say that it is "in the interest of each individual to accept the rules of" an "institution, on the condition that everyone else does the same"? What must the individual know to conclude that accepting the rules of an institution are in their interest?

Putting that question to one side, does this mean that each individual's welfare must be improved, at least by his or her own lights? (Evidently not, on Sugden's account; at least, that is a possible implication of the claim that the "contractarian theorist does not ask whether aggregate welfare is maximized"). Is the judgment of each individual authoritative, even in the absence of information or in the presence of a behavioral bias? (Evidently so, on Sugden's account, though this is not clear.) And when an institution is being evaluated by each individual, to what is it being compared? What is the baseline?

Of course, we should approve of the rules of an institution if those rules are really in the interest of each individual. By stipulation, it would appear that those rules improve everyone's welfare. But offhand, it is hard to identify any social institution that it is in the interest of each individual to accept. Free labor markets are generally a good idea (we think), but they are certainly not in the interest of *each* individual, compared to imaginable alternatives. Free markets in transportation are certainly not in the interest of *each* individual, compared to imaginable alternatives. The point here should be familiar; any social institution creates losers. But if no institution is in the interest of *each* individual, then we need other criteria to evaluate social institutions. Human welfare is one candidate. Of course the idea of welfare needs to be specified if we accept it, and of course distributional considerations greatly matter; we want to know who is helped and who is hurt, and what is happening to the most disadvantaged members of society.

Offering a modern restatement of the contractarian tradition, Buchanan (1986) writes:

> If politics is to be interpreted in any justificatory or legitimating sense without the introduction of supra-individual value norms, it must be modelled as a process within which individuals, with separate and potentially different interests and values, interact for the purpose of securing individually valued benefits of cooperation. If this presupposition about the nature of politics is accepted, the ultimate model of politics is contractarian.

We are not sure what Buchanan means by "supra-individual value norms"; let us simply stipulate that we are not introducing them. But what does he mean by saying that if we do not introduce them, we "must" model politics as a process by which individuals interact in order to secure the benefits of cooperation? Why must we do that? Buchanan (1986, p. 65) explicitly states that in his view, the contractarian approach is "a generalization of the market." Endorsing this view, Sugden (2019, p. 84) adds what he calls the Individual Opportunity Criterion, which holds "that it is in each individual's interest to have more opportunity rather than less." But is it, really? By definition? Why is that in each individual's interest if it does not make their life go better?

We agree that more opportunity is much better than less, but in some cases, giving people more opportunity introduces frustration, confusion, and error. Many sellers know that; they create more options with the goal of promoting their own economic interest, at the expense of choosers. Respect for voluntary agreements has to be justified by reference to something that matters. On Millian grounds, the most natural candidate is welfare, though we might want instead to speak in deontological terms, emphasizing the importance of respect for persons. Our central point is that voluntary arrangements should not be embraced because they are voluntary arrangements. They have to be good for the people who enter into them.

In an influential discussion, Loewenstein and Chater (2017) offer a very different set of claims, calling for interventions that go well beyond nudges. They argue that there should be no presumption that all biases relative to the BRA could be corrected with nudges. For instance, climate change is a complex problem that requires traditional regulation, including mandates and bans (perhaps along with a set of nudges). They add that the real problem could be structural, justifying large-scale interventions, not merely nudges. Because that is the real problem, it might be much better to address the power and the self-interested decisions of large institutions (oil and gas companies, food producers, tobacco companies)—and inadequate, or altogether wrong, to focus on mistaken choices by uninformed or behaviorally biased choosers. Here too climate change is an example. Obesity could also be caused by structural factors (e.g., relative prices of food) that might not be directly related to present biased preferences. Nudges alone might not eliminate the problem. They might do far too little.

We do not disagree with these claims; they might well be right. Many problems, including climate change, cannot be handled with nudges.

When externalities are involved (as in the case of pollution), corrective taxes are a standard prescription, not nudges. We might respond to behavioral market failures (such as present bias and unrealistic optimism) with behaviorally informed interventions that are more coercive (see also Conly, 2013). The ban on trans fats is one example; others include compulsory seat belt laws, cigarette taxes, sugar taxes, and bans on menthol-flavored cigarettes. Those who embrace libertarian paternalism need not reject this view. They view nudges not as a cure-all but as useful additions to the existing stock of public policy instruments. We have defended a working presumption in favor of respect for freedom of choice (see chapter 7) under specified conditions and assuming that there is no harm to others; but nothing in that presumption rules out bans and mandates to deal with climate change, and it should not be taken as a rejection of structural changes.

There is also a growing literature on the unexpected effects of nudges; see Dhami (2020c, section 5.6). Some nudges might be *ineffective*; if people really want candy, they might find it, even if it is not at the checkout counter. Some nudges might be *counterproductive*; if people are automatically enrolled as organ donors, they might rebel and opt out. An emerging literature explores "nudges that fail" and attempts to specify their boundary conditions (Sunstein, 2018b). When people have strong antecedent preferences, they might not be much influenced by a nudge; they might ignore a warning or choose to opt out. And if people are prone to show reactance—to rebel against an influence *because* it is an *influence*—they might reject a nudge.

As any first year undergraduate student in economics knows, there are partial equilibrium effects of policy, and there are general equilibrium effects of policy. The latter give due consideration to the effects of proposed policies on all possible economic actors in society and on all possible markets. These effects are necessarily complex, and this is as true for behavioral public policy as it is for traditional economic policy. The standard approach to take account of potential general equilibrium effects is to run pilots and test for all possible effects that can be unearthed before implementing the policy. Advocates of libertarian paternalism subscribe to similar stringent testing of their proposals before they are implemented. They should be, and usually are, alert to the risk that nudges will fail and even prove counterproductive.

9.4 Government Error

Many people have raised the possibility that nudging might be carried out by choice architects who are neither benevolent nor competent. We agree that choice architects might be ill-motivated. They might act on the basis of their own self-interest or be affected by powerful private interests. We would emphasize that they may not have important or necessary information—what followers of Friedrich Hayek call "the knowledge problem." A choice architect might believe that people are suffering from a behavioral bias when, in fact, they simply care about something that the architect does not see, does not appreciate, or does not value. We can go further. Choice architects are emphatically human (bracketing the role of algorithms and artificial intelligence), and they might themselves suffer from behavioral biases, including present bias, unrealistic optimism, and availability bias. If elected policymakers are responsive to what their constituents want, they might replicate widespread biases. Their own decisions, including their nudges, might have unintended effects. Nor is the bureaucracy immune from biases; there is a pervasive problem of behavioral bureaucrats. That is one reason why nations might need a kind of choice architecture for choice architects; constitutional orders can be understood in exactly that way. A requirement of cost-benefit analysis, imposed for any expensive regulation (nudges, mandates, bans) is also a form of choice architecture for choice architects.

Concerns of this kind apply to any government action, nudge or not. For example, regulatory capture, say, by lobbyists, is a pervasive possibility. Economists have long been aware of the political economy of regulation; it is an established field in economics (Laffont & Tirole, 1993). But if we are concerned about nonbenevolent motives, a lack of information, or behavioral biases on the part of public officials, we should be especially troubled by mandates and bans rather than nudges, which preserve freedom of choice. A central point of libertarian paternalism is to ensure that individuals can exercise their freedom of choice. A central reason for preserving that freedom is a fear of government ignorance or malevolence.

With respect to nudges, many people have pointed to the risk of government error. To illustrate that risk, Gigerenzer (2015) offers the following example. Letters sent out to women for mammography screening (a form of nudge) state that early detection reduces breast cancer mortality by 20 percent. However, in absolute terms, it reduces mortality from 5 to 4 for every 1000 women after 10 years. Gigerenzer (2015, p. 363) views the information in a percentage form as a misleading nudge to benefit the mammography industry (political economy considerations) and prefers education to nudging so that people can make a more informed decision. On page 364, he writes: "Democratic governments should invest less in nudging and more in educating people to become risk savvy."

With respect to this particular example, Gigerenzer is convincing. But, in thinking about appropriate tools, we do not do well to contrast a misleading nudge with a perfect, and evidently hypothetical, educational approach (perfect by stipulation). No one should favor misleading nudging. (Nudges can certainly be used for bad purposes, as when people are defaulted into some option that is not in their interests.) Nor is there any contradiction between nudging people and educating them to be more risk savvy. We can and should do both. Such efforts can easily go in parallel, which might be even more efficacious. In addition, the same safeguards that would need to be applied to prevent potentially misleading education may also be used to prevent potentially misleading nudges. Choice architecture is inevitable in both cases (Thaler & Sunstein, 2021). Gigerenzer (2015) appears to believe that the rationale for nudges lies in arguments for what he calls "latent irrationality" (p. 361). In his view, those who believe in LP think that human beings are "hardly educable" (p. 361). They "prefer nudging to educating people." He adopts an idiosyncratic definition of nudging, which he calls "its original meaning," though it has been used only by its critics: "a set of interventions aimed at overcoming people's stable cognitive biases by exploiting them" (p. 363). Continuing this theme, he writes: "As I will argue in some detail, the dismal picture of human nature painted by behavioral economists and libertarian paternalists is not justified by psychological research." In his view, "nudging people without educating them means infantilizing the public." He adds, "the interest in nudging as opposed to education should be understood against the specific political background in which it emerged. In the US, the public education system is largely considered a failure, and the government tries hard to find ways to steer large sections of the public who can barely read and write. Yet this situation does not apply everywhere." We have several comments. The unifying theme is consistent with one of our general themes throughout: those who emphasize behavioral biases and bounded rationality do not believe that people are stupid or irrational. They believe that life is complex and, for many people, hard.

1. A GPS device is useful for human beings, even if we do not have a dismal picture of human nature. It helps people to get where they want

to go. As we have seen, many nudges have that characteristic; consider reminders, disclosures, and warnings (Sunstein, 2013).

2. Though people can define terms however they wish, the stated definition of nudges in Gigerenzer (2015) has not been embraced by the vast majority of behavioral economists or by any public official who has engaged in nudging, and it is inconsistent with its standard meaning. Many nudges, such as information, reminders, and warnings, are explicitly educative (Sunstein, 2016), so it is difficult to understand the claim that those who embrace nudging "prefer nudging to educating people." (Is a double-sided setting for office printers a way of "infantilizing the public"?)

3. If we consider nudges that have actually been adopted by governments or been under serious consideration (see chapter 10), we will find that they rarely depend on controversial psychological research. Whatever their force, the objections to the HBP in the FFP are irrelevant to most nudges. Think back to reminders, disclosures, and warnings. Default rules are a prominent kind of nudge, and they are usually (but not always) powerful. That claim does not depend on a "dismal picture of human nature."

4. One of us (Sunstein) has worked in the US government for extended periods of time, and in that capacity, he did not try hard, or at all, "to steer large sections of the public who can barely read and write." On the contrary, many of the nudges in which he has been involved are explicitly educative; they involve disclosure of information, which requires a capacity to read (Sunstein, 2013). Some of those nudges involved default rules, as in the case of automatically enrolling poor children in free school meal programs (to which they were legally entitled). We are not aware of any US official who has tried "to steer large sections of the public who can barely read and write" (for a catalog of nudges in the UK, see Halpern, 2015).

5. Nations all over the world—including the UK, Canada, Ireland, Japan, Australia, the US, New Zealand, Qatar, India, and the Netherlands—have created behavioral insight teams, or nudge units, to help solve policy problems (Halpern, 2015). The resulting initiatives have rarely, if ever, depended on controversial psychological research. Many of them have produced significant social benefits.

6. People do use fast and frugal heuristics, and they often work well. However, even when we account for ecological rationality (i.e., there is a clear context and frame in which the decision is situated), heuristics create biases relative to the BRA benchmark. We have covered this point in detail. Corrections of those biases through educative nudging (or efforts

to teach statistical literacy) may sometimes be a good idea, particularly when biases lead to a reduction in welfare. Such corrections need not and general do not "exploit" behavioral biases.

7. Recall our discussion of overconfidence in sections 3.2.4 and 2.11. Overconfidence creates departures of behavior from the BRA benchmark (Kahneman & Tversky, 1996; Dhami, 2016). In his criticism of nudges, Gigerenzer (2015, p. 371) gives a prominent role to overconfidence, discounting most of the existing evidence that seems to find it. Although there are difficulties in measuring overconfidence, behavioral economics has documented impressive evidence on it using novel methods not cited in Gigerenzer; see, for instance, the surveys in Malmendier and Taylor (2015) and Malmendier and Tate (2015). This evidence indicates that overconfidence may harm people's self-interest. In contrast, Gigerenzer (2015, p. 371) takes the view that when overconfidence exists, it may promote people's self-interest: "If you earn your money by forecasting exchange rates or the stock market, you had better be overconfident." By contrast, the evidence from behavioral economics indicates that more overconfident people may churn their portfolios more and lose money (Dhami, 2020a) and that more overconfident managers of firms may engage in greater merger activity, which is characterized by a high rate of eventual failure.

Gigerenzer (1993) has argued that if the relevant questions/events are sampled randomly, then overconfidence disappears. For instance, if subjects are asked an IQ question and the question is randomly drawn from the set of all possible IQ questions, then the claim is that overconfidence disappears (i.e., the subjects' assessment of the accuracy of their answers is close to the actual number of correct answers). Kahneman and Tversky (1996) address this issue in their twofold reply. First, not all individuals are overconfident in all possible situations. Second, even when the questions are randomly sampled, empirical evidence shows that overconfidence remains, provided the questions are not too easy. There is also the nontrivial problem of defining the "set of all possible IQ questions" from which random sampling is to be undertaken.

8. Some of the problems that nudges have successfully tackled in actual practice come from self-control problems due to present-biased preferences. Such preferences, say, in the form of hyperbolic discounting, are found not just in humans but also in close primate relatives, suggesting that these were inherited from a common evolutionary ancestor; see section 2.13 and Dhami (2019c).

9.5 Remedies

Once we uncover departures from perfect rationality, as encapsulated in the BRA, what should we do? We have seen that nudges are one possibility and that they hardly exhaust the alternatives, and a fuller answer will depend on identification of the *we*. The private sector cannot enact law, but it can do a great deal. For example, hospitals, doctors, and nurses might be alert to behavioral biases, including present bias and overconfidence, and they might deal with patients in a way that does not exploit, and that helps counteract, those biases. They might use nudges, such as reminders and warnings, and reference to ordinary practice. In fact, many hospitals, doctors, and nurses, informed by behavioral findings, are now doing exactly that.

Dealing with public health problems, officials at the World Health Organization (WHO) are enlisting behavioral economics to encourage people to make healthier choices. In 2020 and 2021, the WHO relied on a team of behavioral scientists, supported by a technical advisory group and charged with responding to an assortment of health problems. In 2020, the WHO released a report on vaccination updates and acceptance in connection with the Covid-19 pandemic, with an assortment of recommendations rooted directly in behavioral science (WHO, 2020). Nations that are concerned with road safety might explore ways to nudge drivers to reduce the risk of accidents; Sweden's Vision Zero has done so, with considerable success. Many nations, including Germany and Switzerland, have relied on behavioral economics to address climate change; a prominent approach in both nations is to automatically enroll households and businesses in green energy, with the belief (vindicated by evidence) that enrollment rates will be far higher with opt-out than with opt-in. The result has been significant reductions in greenhouse gas emissions. All over the world, public officials have used reminders, information disclosure, and default rules to address policy priorities, including obesity, diabetes, heart disease, Covid-19, poverty, and sex discrimination.

We have said that while a great deal of behavioral economics has explored the potential of libertarian paternalism, there is also a keen interest in other tools, including taxes, subsidies, mandates, and bans (Sunstein, 2020). Social security mandates, including forced savings, might be a response to present bias, and as we have seen, soda taxes might be a way to reduce internalities. Many nations require people to wear seat belts while driving cars and helmets while driving motorcycles. Some food safety and occupational health regulations might also have a behavioral justification (Conly, 2013). Some nations have considered prohibitions on menthol-flavored cigarettes. The issues here are quite complex and beyond the scope of the present discussion. Our only suggestion is that if the goal is to improve human welfare, all of the relevant tools should be explored with reference to behavioral findings.

Challenging libertarian paternalism in particular, Gigerenzer (2015, p. 367) writes:

> There are multiple other reasons for harmful behavior, including the fast food and tobacco industry's multi-billion-dollar advertisement campaigns to seduce people into unhealthy lifestyles and the failure of educational systems worldwide to teach children statistical thinking. Libertarian paternalists, like the behavioral economists they draw upon, make a case against the human mind and thereby turn a blind eye to flaws in human institutions.

Nothing could be further from the truth. Some libertarian paternalists have spent most of their working lives on flaws in human institutions. The goal of libertarian paternalism is to provide an additional tool for public policy that imposes no restrictions on individual liberty. As we have said, it does not deny the potential role of other regulations that might achieve a similar purpose. It adds to the menu of policy choices for policymakers. In order to reduce smoking, the government can use prohibitions (as noted, forbid menthol-flavored cigarettes or cigarettes with addictive levels of nicotine), impose high cigarette taxes, use a nudge (print an appropriate warning on cigarette packages), or do all of the above. More choices may sometimes be worse than fewer, but libertarian paternalism can hardly be blamed for adding to the menu of choices.

We have mentioned that some people argue for "boosts" such as an increase in statistical literacy, on the theory that they improve people's capacity for agency (Hertwig, 2017). On one view, boosts are an alternative to nudges, and in some ways better. We agree that boosts can be an excellent idea. In thinking about their relationship with nudges, it is important to consider five points.

First, some nudges are meant to improve people's capacity for agency and belong in the same family as boosts. Consider information (e.g., about caloric content); warnings (e.g., about the consequences of paying late); and reminders (e.g., that a doctor's appointment is coming up).

Second, many nudges make life simpler and so allow people to put their focus and attention where they wish. Consider a GPS device or a default rule. In that sense, they do not undermine people's agency; on the contrary, they promote it.

Third, nudges have an established track record (Halpern, 2015) with impressive cost-effectiveness (Benartzi et al., 2017). The empirical evidence for boosts is less robust, certainly for the most important public policy issues.

Fourth, it is not so easy to identify boosts that could provide significant help in addressing the principal problems faced by the world's governments (though we agree that statistical literacy would be a step forward). If one is advising the prime minister of the UK, the chancellor of Germany, or the president of the US, what boosts would one recommend to successfully address (for example) highway safety, opioid addiction, obesity, greenhouse gas emissions, or immigration? We do not mean to suggest that this is an impossible question to answer. But the answer is not exactly obvious.

Fifth, boosts and nudges can be complements, not alternatives. With respect to savings policy and poverty reduction, for example, it might well be a good idea to have both. If the goal is to reduce deaths on the highway, boosting drivers' capacities is important; nudges, in the form of improved technologies designed to increase safety, can save a lot of lives (not least because they overcome limited attention).

10

Libertarian Paternalism in Practice

In this chapter, we consider a number of specific policies that have been motivated by the findings from behavioral economics, many falling under the rubric of libertarian paternalism. We focus mainly on policy choices in the US, though close analogues can be found in nations all over the world.

In section 10.1, we provide a general overview of the worldwide increase in the use of behavioral economics in public policy. In section 10.2, we propose a simple framework for thinking about behavioral public policy that is based on the acronym FEAST (fun, easy, attractive, social, and timely). Section 10.3 discusses two possible institutional structures to implement behavioral public policy: integrated within existing institutions or set up within new units (e.g., a nudge unit). In section 10.4, we consider a number of behaviorally informed public policies in the US, their implementation, and their impact. Examples include default rules, savings policies, school meals, finance, health care, and payroll statements.

Section 10.5 considers the effects of mandatory disclosure requirements for nutrition, finance, health care, and fuel economy. We also explore the effect of disclosure on competition. Section 10.6 considers the effects of structuring choices, both in terms of the number and the complexity of choices. Section 10.7 turns to the effect of salience on choices.

10.1 Behavioral Public Policy around the World

We have emphasized that, all over the world, bounded rationality and behavioral economics have been attracting high-level attention from policymakers (Thaler & Sunstein, 2021; Halpern, 2015; Organisation for Economic Cooperation and Development, 2010). Both the developed and the developing world are increasingly recognizing the opportunities. With respect to new policy initiatives, developments and applications have been proceeding at an exceptionally rapid pace, so much so that any account will rapidly become out of date.

In North America, Europe, Japan, Australia, New Zealand, and the Middle East, important initiatives enlist tools such as disclosure, warnings, and default rules, and they can be found in multiple areas, including fuel economy, finance, energy efficiency, environmental protection, highway safety, smoking, health care, and obesity (with behavioral findings playing an unmistakable role in efforts to combat obesity). As a result, behavioral findings and nudges have become important reference points for regulatory and other policymaking in multiple nations.

Some of the most prominent efforts can be found in the UK. Those efforts began in 2010 under former prime minister David Cameron, who created a Behavioural Insights Team, sometimes described as "the Nudge Unit," with the specific goal of incorporating an understanding of human behavior into policy initiatives. In its early years, the official website stated that its "work draws on insights from the growing body of academic research in the fields of behavioral economics and psychology which show how often subtle changes to the way in which decisions are framed can have big impacts on how people respond to them" (Cabinet Office, n.d.).

Now partly private, the Behavioural Insights Team has become far more ambitious. It is working in over thirty nations. It has used behavioral insights to promote initiatives in numerous domains, involving smoking cessation, energy efficiency, organ donation, consumer protection, employment, crime, sex equality, Covid-19, and compliance strategies in general. Other nations have expressed keen interest in the work of the team, and its operations are continuing to expand. In 2012, the US created its own behavioral insights team, now called the Office of Evaluation Sciences, and many other nations have done so, including Australia, Singapore, the Netherlands, Germany, Canada, Qatar, Lebanon, Saudi Arabia, India, and Japan.

It is important to note that most of the world's behavioral work is undertaken by people in departments and ministries who have a large repertoire of responsibilities and are not dedicated behavioral teams. Under former president Barack Obama, the White House relied heavily on behavioral findings, working with the Department of Transportation, the Environmental Protection Agency (EPA), the Social Security Administration, the Department of the Treasury, the Department of Health and Human Services (HHS), and many more. President Joe Biden is continuing this work, often with impressive results. Something similar can be said of many other nations, including Germany, Denmark, Sweden, and Canada.

Behavioral economics has drawn considerable attention in Europe. The Organisation for Economic Development and Cooperation (2010) published a *Consumer Policy Toolkit* that recommends a number of initiatives rooted in behavioral findings. In the European Union, the Directorate-General for Health and Consumers (2010) showed the influence of behavioral economics. A report from the European Commission, called *Green Behavior*, enlists behavioral economics to outline policy initiatives to protect the environment (European Commission, 2012; iNudgeYou, n.d.). Private organizations, including social media companies, are also using behavioral insights to promote a variety of environmental, health-related, and other goals. Important work has been undertaken at the United Nations, the World Bank, and the World Health Organization; as noted, the last of these created its own behavioral insights project in 2020, supported by a technical advisory group, consisting of specialists in behavioral economics and behavioral insights.

In the US, regulatory efforts have been directly informed by behavioral findings, and behavioral economics has played an unmistakable role in numerous domains, including the Credit Card Accountability Responsibility and Disclosure Act (Credit CARD Act), the Affordable Care Act, and the Dodd-Frank Wall Street Reform Act (Sunstein, 2013). Indeed, something very close to the idea of nudging is built directly into a prevailing executive order on regulation, which amounts to a kind of mini-constitution for the regulatory state: "Each agency shall identify and consider regulatory approaches that reduce burdens and maintain flexibility and freedom of choice for the public. These approaches include warnings, appropriate default rules, and disclosure requirements as well as provision of information to the public in a form that is clear and intelligible" (Exec. Order No. 13,563, 2011). Executive Order No. 13,707 (2015) is even more explicit, calling out "behavioral science insights" in plain terms and directing agencies to consider those insights.

It is clear that behavioral findings are having a large impact on regulation, law, and public policy all over the world. That impact is likely to grow over the next decades. Notably, the use of behavioral findings cuts across conventional political divisions and tends to appeal to people with diverse views in diverse nations. Because behavioral findings suggest the possibility of low-cost, high-impact interventions (Benartzi et al., 2017), they often attract considerable attention in economically challenging times.

10.2 FEAST

Behavioral findings proved especially relevant to efforts to combat the Covid-19 pandemic of 2020–2021. Behavioral economics and nudging were especially attractive and came into widespread use—not only by governments but also by private institutions, including hospitals, universities, and ordinary businesses, large and small. Those social distancing markers, indicating where people should stand in line? They are nudges.

To organize these and other efforts involving public health and safety (operating in normal times as well as during a pandemic), a simple framework can be captured in an acronym: FEAST. The idea builds on the EAST framework from the Behavioural Insights Team (2014). EAST refers to four ideas: easy, attractive, social, and timely.

The first idea, explicitly informed by behavioral economics, is that if you want people to do something, make it *easy* for them. They have to know what to do and how to do it, and it should not be too burdensome, painful, or costly. Automatic enrollment significantly increases participation rates simply because people do not have to exert effort to enroll. Whenever the goal is to change behavior, the best question is often overlooked: Why aren't people doing it already? After obtaining the answer, public officials, employers, schools, and others can take steps to remove the barrier. If we focus on E, we might think that the preferred approach is straightfoward: make it automatic. And if that is not possible, the second best is also simple: make it easy. A striking example of the effect of automaticity is the default setting on printers: if the setting is to print double-sided, people will use a lot less paper (Egebark & Ekstrom, 2016).

It matters whether an option or message is *attractive*. A simple and vivid communication has more impact than a dull and complicated one. With respect to Covid-19, officials in Ireland made excellent use of this insight with striking informational signs. The same is true of New Zealand. (Of course, it is also true that sometimes warnings should not exactly be attractive; they should be vivid. Graphic health warnings are an example.)

As we have emphasized, people also tend to be affected by what most other people do; hence the S for *social* in EAST. Notifying people of the actions of the majority can be a powerful nudge. If people learn that they are conserving less energy than other people, they start to conserve more energy (Allcott, 2011). Publicizing a current norm can greatly alter behavior. There is also evidence that even if a norm is not yet current but is emerging, publicizing that fact can be effective (Sparkman & Walton, 2017). It is worth underlining that finding: when people learn that other people are increasingly engaging in certain behavior, they are more likely to do it too, even if it has not yet attracted majority support. This might be true in the domain of exercising, healthy eating, or environmentally friendly behavior.

Timing is important. People's attention is limited, and they sometimes forget to do things. Often it is best to provide them with information (including warnings) right before they make a decision, not the night before or when their minds are focused elsewhere. In the context of Covid-19: when nations started to relax stay-at-home orders and business shutdowns, they probably did best if they arranged health-related messages so that people saw them immediately before they made health-related choices. For example, such messages might be provided in grocery stores, including social distancing signals that give people general reminders and also guidance about where to stand in line.

For policymakers all over the world, EAST has proven useful. But it is missing something essential: *fun*. Hence our modest, behaviorally informed amendment, adding the F for FEAST.

What is the best way to encourage people to eat more vegetables? A Stanford University study tried two different methods (Turnwald et al., 2019). The first involved labels that emphasized health benefits. The second used labels that emphasized enjoyment and taste. Both worked, but enjoyment proved to be the more powerful motivator. The health-focused labels increased vegetable consumption by 14 percent, which is a large improvement. The enjoyment-focused labels increased vegetable consumption by 29 percent, which is an even more impressive improvement.

Behaviorally informed marketers are keenly aware of the importance of enjoyment and fun. For example, Amazon sells certain products with what it calls frustration-free packaging. That means that there isn't much plastic, wiring, or cardboard to deal with. Better still, frustration-free packaging also turns out to be green packaging; it contains less solid waste, and the materials are recyclable. The company is making a smart behavioral bet, which is that the idea of frustration-free packaging will make customers smile—and attract many more of them than would be motivated by the abstract idea of sustainability.

No one thinks that a pandemic is fun. But if they are alert to behavioral findings, leaders can produce a sense of optimism, unity, hope, and more than a few smiles instead of despair, anger, division, and fear.

Prime Minister Jacinda Ardern of New Zealand even managed to have some fun with the lockdown, describing the Tooth Fairy and the Easter Bunny as essential workers, legally authorized to carry on their work. In general, New Zealand has succeeded in meeting the pandemic not only with firmness, calm, and determination but also with wit, a call to unity (emphasizing that the nation is a team of five million), and a consistent sense of good cheer. Its mantra has been, "Be kind."

For Covid-19, the most important parts of the FEAST framework were the E for easy and the S for social. Complexity and confusion are mortal enemies of public health; good norms are its best friends. But here is a plea to leaders at all levels, even in dark times: do not neglect the F. Human beings need it.

10.3 Institutionalizing Behavioral Insights: Two Approaches

What is the best method for implementing behavioral insights? It is certainly possible to rely entirely on existing institutions. We could imagine a system in which an understanding of behavioral economics is used by current officials and institutions, including leaders at the highest levels. For example, the relevant research could be enlisted by those involved in promoting competitiveness, environmental protection, public safety, consumer protection, and economic growth—or in reducing private and public corruption and combating poverty, infectious diseases, and obesity. Focusing on concrete problems rather than abstract theories, officials with well-established positions might be expected to use that research, at least on occasion. (Leaders of private institutions could do, and are doing, the same thing.)

If the relevant officials have both knowledge and genuine authority, they might be able to produce significant reforms simply because they are not akin to a mere research arm or a think tank. Even a single person, if given the appropriate authority and mission, could have a large impact. On one model, the relevant officials would not engage in new research, or at least not in a great deal of it. They would build on what is already known (and perhaps have formal or informal partnerships with those in the private sector who work on these issues). In an important sense, this approach is the simplest because it does not require new offices or significant additional funding but only attention to the relevant issues and a focus on the right appointments. In Canada, Sweden, Denmark, Germany, and the US, this kind of approach has proved highly successful, with the adoption of many behaviorally informed reforms.

A quite different approach would be to create a new institution such as a behavioral insights team or a "nudge unit" of some sort (as in the UK, the US, Australia, Germany, the Netherlands, Qatar, India, and an increasing number of nations). Such an institution could be organized in different ways, and it could have many different forms and sizes. On a minimalist model, it would have a small group of knowledgeable people (say, 5) bringing relevant findings to bear and perhaps engaging in, or spurring, research on their own. On a more ambitious model, the team could be larger (say, 30 or more), engaging in a wide range of relevant research. A behavioral insights team could be created as a formal part of government (the preferred model, to ensure real impact) or could have a purely advisory role.

Whatever its precise form, the advantage of such an approach is that it would involve a dedicated and specialized team, highly informed and specifically devoted to the relevant work, with expertise in the design of experiments. If the team could work with others to conduct its own research, including randomized controlled trials, it might be able to produce important findings (as has been done in the UK, Australia, and the US, and similar efforts are occurring elsewhere). The risk is that such a team would be akin to an academic adjunct, a kind of outsider, without the power or ability to initiate real reform. Authority greatly matters. The UK has had the most experience with this kind of approach, and it has succeeded in part because it has enjoyed high-level support and access. In this domain, one size does not fit all, but it is noteworthy that a growing number of nations have concluded that it is worthwhile to have a dedicated team. Of course, the two approaches might prove complementary.

10.4 Examples of Behavioral Public Policies

We now turn to a series of examples, with an emphasis on behaviorally informed policies playing a role in public policy, particularly in the US. We refer to efforts in that country because of our own familiarity with them; similar efforts can be found in other nations.

10.4.1 Default Rules

If there were an Olympic competition for behaviorally informed tools, default rules would win the gold medal. They often have very large effects, transforming outcomes in ways that combat poverty, improve the environment, increase savings, and protect consumers (Jachimowicz et al., 2019). It is important to see that default rules can be used for good or for ill. If people are automatically enrolled in programs that do not help them, they might end up paying money for nothing at all (Luguri & Strahilevitz, 2019). *Dark patterns*, understood as online forms of manipulation that attempt to take people's money, often use default rules, in which people do not explicitly consent to make certain payments and might not even know that they are doing that. It is, therefore, important to ensure that default rules are transparent and that they are actually working to increase people's welfare.

A great deal of research has attempted to explore exactly why default rules have such a large effect on outcomes (Jachimowicz et al., 2019; Gale et al., 2009; Dinner et al. 2011; Carroll et al. 2009). There are three major explanations (E. Johnson & Goldstein, 2013). The first involves inertia and procrastination. To alter the effect of the default rule, people must make an active choice to reject the default. In view of the power of inertia and the tendency to procrastinate, people may simply continue with the status quo. The second factor involves what might be taken to be an implicit endorsement of the default rule. Many people appear to conclude that the default was chosen for a reason; they believe that they should not depart from it unless they have particular information to justify a change. Third, the default rule might establish the reference point for people's decisions; the established reference point has significant effects because people dislike losses from that reference point (the behavioral finding of loss aversion). If, for example, the default rule favors energy-efficient lightbulbs, then the loss (in terms of reduced efficiency) may loom large and there will be a tendency to continue with energy-efficient lightbulbs. But if the default rule favors less efficient (and initially less expensive) lightbulbs, then the loss in terms of up-front costs may loom large, and there will be a tendency to favor less efficient lightbulbs.

Consider the endowment effect, which means that people place greater value on goods that they physically own compared to the same goods when they are in the hands of others (Thaler, 2015). If, for example, you are given a coffee mug, a lottery ticket, or an exemption from a risk, you will likely demand more money to give it up than you would give to get it in the first place. The reasons for the endowment effect, and its boundary conditions, remain to be clearly established, but it appears to be produced in part by loss aversion: people are reluctant to give up what they have.

It is important to note that even if the effects of default rules are large, and they often are (Jachimowicz et al., 2019), they might not always be positive (Weimer, 2020). People might be defaulted into a pension plan, and many of them might benefit (and not opt out). But some people might be defaulted into such a plan and lose because they could use the money for something now (and even so, they might not opt out). If people are defaulted into a green energy plan, and if it is more expensive than a dirtier energy source, they might lose (and might not opt out). Because of the power of inertia, there is always a risk that a default rule will help some while hurting others. This point in favor of personalized defaults, a topic taken up below, strongly suggests a general point, which is that nudges should be subject to the same kind of welfare analysis as any other policy tool. On net, are people being helped or hurt? Cost-benefit analysis is a standard way to answer that question, though it is far from perfect (Sunstein, 2020).

10.4.2 Policies on Savings

In many nations, employers have long asked workers whether they want to enroll in pension plans. Even when enrollment is easy, and the benefits of enrolling seem high, the number of employees who enroll, or opt in, has often been relatively low (Madrian & Shea 2002; Gale et al. 2009). An increasing number of employers have responded by changing the default to automatic enrollment, by which employees are enrolled unless they opt out. The results are clear: significantly more employees end up enrolled with an opt-out design than with opt-in (Gale et al. 2009). This is so even when opting out is easy. Importantly, automatic enrollment has significant benefits for all groups, with increased anticipated savings in particular for Hispanics, African Americans, and women (Orszag & Rodriguez 2009; Papke et al., 2009; Chiteji & Walker 2009).

In Denmark, the large effects of automatic enrollment have been demonstrated with great rigor; indeed, the impact of automatic enrollment significantly exceeds the impact of tax incentives (Chetty et al., 2014). The expensive option of tax incentives is far less effective than the cheap alternative of automatic enrollment. There is a general lesson here; sometimes nudges are far more effective than expected and indeed far more cost-effective than more familiar tools (Benartzi et al., 2017).

In the US, the Pension Protection Act of 2006 (PPA) draws directly on behavioral findings by encouraging employers to adopt automatic enrollment plans. The PPA provides nondiscrimination safe harbors for elective deferrals and for matching contributions under plans that include an automatic enrollment feature, as well as by providing protections from state payroll-withholding laws to allow for automatic enrollment. Building on these efforts, the Obama administration, with personal involvement from President Obama, undertook significant initiatives to encourage employers to adopt such plans, in part by making it easier for them to do so (Obama 2009; Internal Revenue Service 2009). An important part of automatic enrollment plans is automatic escalation, which can ensure that default contribution settings do not produce unduly low savings levels (Benartzi & Thaler, 2013).

Continuing work, both theoretical and empirical, is exploring the use of automatic enrollment to promote savings and the circumstances in which one or another approach is optimal. Of course, many nations have social security programs, in which savings are mandatory; such programs might be understood as a (coercive) response to inertia, present bias, limited attention, and unrealistic optimism. Perhaps automatic enrollment programs should supplement social security programs. Some people believe, however, that the best approach is to increase the amount of money that people must contribute to social security programs, which means that the area involves vigorous debates between advocates of coercive paternalism and advocates of libertarian paternalism.

10.4.3 School Meals

The National School Lunch Act (Healthy Hunger-Free Kids Act of 2012) takes steps to allow "direct certification" of eligibility, thus reducing complexity and introducing a form of automatic enrollment. Under the program, children who are eligible for benefits under certain programs will be "directly eligible" for free lunches and free breakfasts and hence will not have to fill out additional applications (Healthy Hunger-Free Kids Act of 2012). To promote direct certification, the US Department of Agriculture (USDA, 2011) issued an interim final rule that is expected to provide up to 270,000 children with school meals. The aggregate effects of direct certification are much larger, allowing participation by millions of additional children. According to recent counts, the number has been in the vicinity of 15 million. It is worth pausing over that number.

10.4.4 Finance

Nudges, including default rules, are an important part of credit markets, and sensible nudging is doing a great deal to help consumers (Agarwal et al., 2013). One example is the Federal Reserve Board's switch in 2020 of the default rule, undertaken as part of its effort to protect consumers from high bank overdraft fees (12 C.F.R. § 205.17). To provide that protection, the board issued a regulation in 2009 banning banks from automatically enrolling people in overdraft "protection" programs. Now (in 2020), customers have to sign up (12 C.F.R. § 205.17(b)). In justifying the regulation, the board drew directly and extensively on the behavioral literature, with specific reference to the retirement issue (Willis, 2013; Sarin, 2019).

Interestingly, the available evidence, cataloged in an important article (Willis, 2013), suggests that the effect has not been as large as might be expected. The reason is that banks have used behaviorally informed strategies, including loss aversion, to encourage people to opt in to the program in significant numbers. Nonetheless, large numbers of people are no longer enrolled in the programs (Sarin, 2019). The overall level of opt-in seems to be around 15 percent (Willis, 2013); to that extent, the opt-in default has been sticky. Moreover, the largest proportion of people who opt in are those who actually exceed their checking limits (Zywicki, 2013). For such people, it is not implausible to think that opting in is a good idea.

More generally, the bulk of the gains for the Credit CARD Act have come from behaviorally informed mandates and bans, targeting shrouded attributes such as late fees and overuse fees. It appears that these provisions are saving consumers over $10 billion annually, and the savings are concentrated among people with low credit ratings (Agarwal et al., 2013). There is a large lesson here as well. Under certain circumstances, bans on product attributes, if they are shrouded, can protect consumers (and also employees and investors) (Sarin, 2019).

10.4.5 Health Care

Many provisions of the Affordable Care Act (ACA) show the influence of behavioral economics and an appreciation of bounded rationality. A provision of the ACA required that by a specific date, employers with over 200 employees must automatically enroll employees in health care plans, while also allowing employees to opt out (Affordable Care Act, 2010). Another provision, the Community Living Assistance Services and Supports Act (CLASS Act, 2010), created a national voluntary long-term insurance program. The ACA provided for an automatic enrollment system, whereby employers enroll employees in that program unless they opt out. In addition, the ACA contains an automatic payroll deduction system for the payment of premiums.

On February 4, 2010, the Centers for Medicare & Medicaid Services (CMS) provided guidance to states via a State Health Official letter (Centers for Medicare & Medicaid Services, 2010). In cases where states are able to obtain all the information necessary to determine eligibility, states are permitted to automatically enroll and renew eligible children in Medicaid or the Children's Health Insurance Program (CHIP). This allows states to initiate and determine eligibility without a signed program application as long as the family or child consents to be enrolled in Medicaid or CHIP.

After enactment, these various provisions of the ACA were put under serious pressure, in part on political grounds; some of them were repealed. But their original enactment attests to the power of behavioral insights in national legislatures.

10.4.6 Payroll Statements

In 2010, the Department of Homeland Security changed the default setting for payroll statements from paper to electronic, thus reducing costs (Orszag 2010). Many government agencies have done something similar. Changes of this kind will not exactly balance a nation's budget, but they can save significant sums of money for both private and public sectors.

10.5 Disclosure

Disclosure can take many forms, from the short and sweet to the long and sour. It can operate like a GPS device, telling people how to get where they want to go, or like a nightmare, leaving people badly confused. A great deal of work needs to be done to learn when disclosure is effective and exactly why (Loewenstein et al., 2014; Sunstein, 2020). But there is no question that disclosure is proving to be an appealing nudge and that much of what has been done is behaviorally informed.

When mandatory disclosure requirements are imposed, it is often because less-informed consumers are interacting with better-informed sellers and the incentives of the consumers and sellers are at least arguably misaligned. Consider, for example, interactions between an automobile seller and a potential customer. The seller has better information about the safety of the cars it sells; the customer may have a greater interest in driving a safe car. Or consider interactions between a chain restaurant and its patrons. The restaurant has better information about the nutritional properties of the food it sells; the customer may have a greater interest in eating nutritious food.

There are also situations in which disclosure serves the purpose of helping to protect consumers against themselves. Some of these cases involve *behavioral market failures*. We have seen that behavioral economics enlarges the potential scope of justifiable regulation by introducing the concept of internalities, mentioned above—costs that individuals impose on themselves but fail to internalize at the time of decision. For example, smokers may enjoy smoking, but not so much lung cancer. Those who eat a lot of food, and gain weight, may love their meals, but not the health problems that come from them. Those who spend a lot of money today may not be so happy to find that they have nothing to spend tomorrow. We have already seen that nudges can respond to the problem, and if they are behaviorally informed, they might stipulate format, framing, and other requirements that take account of cognitive and other factors in such a way as to make the relevant disclosure more effective.

10.5.1 Nutrition
In the domain of nutrition, a number of disclosure requirements are in place. For example, in 2020, the USDA issued a final rule requiring provision of nutritional information to consumers with respect to meat and poultry products. Nutrition facts panels must be provided on the labels of such products; the panels must contain information with respect to calories and both total and saturated fats (9 C.F.R. § 317.309). The rule is behaviorally informed; it clearly recognizes the potential importance of framing. If a product lists a percentage statement such as "80% lean," it must also list its fat percentage. This requirement helps to avoid the confusion that can result from selective framing; a statement that a product is 80 percent lean, standing by itself, makes leanness salient and may therefore be misleading.

In a related vein, the USDA abandoned the food pyramid used for decades as the central icon to promote healthy eating. The pyramid was long criticized as insufficiently informative; it did not offer people any kind of clear path with respect to healthy diet and did not connect to people's actual experience with food (Heath & Heath, 2010). In response, the USDA replaced the pyramid with a new, simpler icon, consisting of a plate with clear markings for fruit, vegetables, grains, and protein. The plate is accompanied by straightforward guidance, including "Make half your plate fruits and vegetables," "Drink water instead of sugary drinks," and "Switch to fat-free or low-fat (1%) milk." This approach has the key advantage of informing people what to do if they seek to have a healthier diet.

In 2014, the Food and Drug Administration (FDA) proposed to improve and clarify the nutrition facts panel on most foods. The proposal is an unambiguous nudge, and it is behaviorally informed. Hence the FDA's (2014) explanation states:

Changes in labeling may also assist consumers by making the long-term health consequences of consumer food choices more salient and by providing contextual cues of food consumption. We note that the behavioral economics literature suggests that distortions internal to consumers (or internalities) due to time-inconsistent preferences, myopia or present-biased preferences, visceral factors (e.g., hunger), or lack of self-control, can also create the potential for policy intervention to improve consumer welfare.... Consistent with predictions based on models of bounded rationality, consumers can systematically make suboptimal dietary choices because they discount future health consequences relative to immediate benefits more than they would if they chose according to their underlying or true preferences, leading them to regret their decisions at a later date. To the extent that some form of intrapersonal market failure characterizes diet-related decisions, changes in labeling may assist consumers by making the long-term health consequences of consumer food choices more salient and by providing contextual cues of food consumption.

The final version of the rule embeds these insights; there is no question that it is strongly influenced by behavioral findings.

10.5.2 Finance

In the context of financial products, disclosure played a key role in the Credit CARD Act (2009). One of its provisions is a small nudge: every month, companies must disclose the interest savings from paying off the full balance within 36 months instead of making only minimum payments every month. It is easy to be skeptical about disclosure requirements of this kind, but the consequence has been to reduce interest payments by $74 million a year—not a huge amount, but far from trivial (Agarwal et al., 2013).

The Credit CARD Act contains other, seemingly modest provisions designed to limit credit card fees. For example, companies are forbidden to impose fees on cardholders who go over their credit limit unless cardholders agree to opt in to authorize that practice. In addition, banks must give cardholders a 45-day advance notice of rate increases, and they must inform cardholders of their right to cancel the account before such increases go into effect. Cardholders must also be provided with statements that inform them exactly how long it would take to pay the outstanding balance if they made only the minimum monthly payments.

These provisions have contributed to substantial decreases in both over-limit fees and late fees—with the overall package saving US credit card users billions of dollars annually. Cardholders with low credit scores appear to be the biggest beneficiaries. To be sure, and importantly, the package includes mandates and bans (behaviorally informed) as well as nudges, but there is no question that nudges have played a beneficial role.

10.5.3 Health Care
The ACA includes a large number of nudges designed to promote accountability and informed choice with respect to health care. Indeed, ACA is, in significant part, a series of disclosure requirements, many of which are meant to inform consumers in a way that is alert to behavioral findings. Under the ACA, a restaurant that is part of a chain with 20 or more locations doing business under the same name is required to disclose calories on the menu board. Such restaurants are also required to provide in a written form (available to customers on request) additional nutrition information pertaining to total calories and calories from fat, as well as amounts of fat, saturated fat, cholesterol, sodium, total carbohydrates, and more (Affordable Care Act, 2010). There continues, of course, to be a dispute about the actual effects of disclosure requirements of this kind, and further evidence is indispensable (Sunstein, 2020; for a finding of positive results, in the sense of decreased caloric intake, see Bollinger et al. (2010); for less positive results, see Finkelstein et al. (2020) and Downs et al. (2009)).

In a similar vein, § 1103 of the ACA calls for "immediate information that allows consumers to identify affordable coverage options." It requires the establishment of an internet portal for beneficiaries to easily access affordable and comprehensive coverage options, including information about eligibility, availability, premium rates, cost sharing, and the percentage of total premium revenues spent on health care rather than administrative expenses.

Implementing a provision of the ACA, the HHS finalized a rule to require insurance companies to provide clear, plain-language summaries of relevant information to prospective customers. The rule includes basic information, including the annual premium, the annual deductible, a statement of services that are not covered, and a statement of costs for going to an out-of-network provider. These are simply a few examples; the Affordable Care Act contains many others (Sunstein, 2011).

10.5.4 Fuel Economy
Automobile manufacturers have long been required to disclose the fuel economy of new vehicles as measured by miles per gallon (MPG). This disclosure is a nudge that helps to promote informed choice. As both behavioral scientists and the EPA (2009) have emphasized, however, MPG

is a nonlinear measure of fuel consumption. For a fixed travel distance, a change from 20 to 25 MPG produces a larger reduction in fuel costs than does a change from 30 to 35 MPG or even from 30 to 38 MPG.

Evidence suggests that many consumers do not understand this point and tend to interpret MPG as linear with fuel costs. When it occurs, this error is likely to produce inadequately informed purchasing decisions when people are making comparative judgments about fuel costs. Consumers tend to underestimate the cost differences between low-MPG vehicles and tend to overestimate the cost differences between high-MPG vehicles (Allcott 2011). By contrast, an alternative fuel economy metric, such as gallons per mile, could be far less confusing. Recognizing the imperfections and potentially misleading nature of the MPG measure, the Department of Transportation and EPA mandated a radically revised and behaviorally informed label including a clear statement about anticipated fuel savings (or costs) over a five-year period (Sunstein, 2013).

10.5.5 Disclosure and Competition

If disclosure requirements are straightforward and simple, they should facilitate comparison-shopping and hence market competition. Drawing directly on behavioral research, the Department of Treasury's (2009) account of financial regulation emphasizes the value of requiring that "communications with the consumer are reasonable, not merely technically compliant and non-deceptive. Reasonableness includes balance in the presentation of risks and benefits, as well as clarity and conspicuousness in the description of significant product costs and risks." The department's analysis goes on to say that one goal should be to

> harness technology to make disclosures more dynamic and adaptable to the needs of the individual consumer .... Disclosures should show consumers the consequences of their financial decisions .... [The regulator] should [ ] mandate or encourage calculator disclosures for mortgages to assist with comparison shopping. For example, a calculator that shows the costs of a mortgage based on the consumer's expectations for how long she will stay in the home may reveal a more significant difference between two products than appears on standard paper disclosures.

In keeping with this theme, the Consumer Financial Protection Bureau is authorized to ensure that "consumers are provided with timely and understandable information to make responsible decisions about financial transactions" (Dodd-Frank Act, 2010). The bureau is also authorized to issue rules that ensure that information is "fully, accurately, and effectively disclosed to consumers in a manner that permits consumers to understand the costs, benefits, and risks associated with the product or service, in light of the facts and circumstances" (Dodd-Frank Act, 2010).

To accomplish this task, the bureau is authorized to issue model forms with "a clear and conspicuous disclosure that, at a minimum—(A) uses plain language comprehensible to consumers; (B) contains a clear format and design, such as an easily readable type font; and (C) succinctly explains the information that must be communicated to the consumer" (Dodd-Frank Act, 2010; Riis & Ratner, 2015). In addition, the director of the bureau is required to "establish a unit whose functions shall include researching, analyzing, and reporting on ... consumer awareness, understanding, and use of disclosures and communications regarding consumer financial products or services" and "consumer behavior with respect to consumer financial products or services, including performance on mortgage loans." Note that new technologies make it possible to inform consumers of their own choices and usages, an approach that may be especially important when firms have better information than consumers do about such choices and usages (Kamenica et al., 2011).

To the same end, in 2020, the Department of Labor issued a final rule requiring disclosure to workers of relevant information in pension plans. The rule is designed to require clear, simple disclosure of information about fees and expenses and to allow meaningful comparisons, in part through the use of standard methodologies in the calculation and disclosure of expense and return information (29 C.F.R. §2550.404a-5). Evidence suggests that the rule, which was clearly informed by behavioral economics, has produced substantial savings for investors (Kronlund et al., 2020). In a similar action, the Department of Transportation required US air carriers and online travel agents to alter their web interfaces to incorporate all ticket taxes in up-front, advertised fares. Evidence suggests that this behaviorally informed intervention, designed to overcome shrouded prices, has been highly effective and saved consumers a lot of money (Bradley & Feldman, 2020).

Yet another example is a final rule of the Department of Education (2010a) that promotes transparency and consumer choice with respect to for-profit education by requiring institutions to provide clear disclosure of costs, debt levels, and graduation and placement rates. These disclosures must be included "in promotional materials [the institution] makes available to prospective students" and be "prominently provide[d] ... in a simple and meaningful manner on the home page of its program Web site" (34 C.F.R. § 668.6); Department of Education, 2010b).

10.6 Structuring Choices

Complexity can also create problems through a phenomenon known as choice over-load. In the traditional view, having more choices helps, and never harms, consumers or program participants. This view is based on the reasonable judgment that, if an additional option is not better than existing options, people will simply not choose it. In general, more choices are indeed desirable, but an increasing body of research offers certain potential qualifications, especially in unusually complex situations (Sethi-Iyengar et al., 2004). For example, there is some evidence that enrollment may decline (Sethi-Iyengar et al., 2004) and asset allocations may worsen (Iyengar and Kamenica, 2010) as the menu of investment options in a 401(k) plan expands.

Responding to this general problem in the context of prescription drug plans (specifically discussed in Thaler & Sunstein, 2008), CMS took steps to maintain freedom of choice while also reducing unhelpful and unnecessary complexity (Abaluck & Gruber, 2011). The Medicare Part D rules require sponsors to ensure that when they provide multiple plan offerings, those offerings have meaningful differences. The rules also eliminate plans with persistently low enrollments, on the ground that those plans increase the complexity of choices without adding value (see also Korobkin 2013).

10.7 Salience

It is often possible to promote social goals by making certain features of a product or a situation more salient to consumers. Increasing salience can be an effective nudge (Kronland et al., 2020; Sarin, 2019). Consider the response to Covid-19, which consists in large part of making certain safeguards highly salient (staying home, washing one's hands, social distancing, wearing masks). Or consider alcohol taxes. There is evidence that when such taxes are specifically identified in the posted price, increases in such taxes have a larger negative effect on alcohol consumption than when they are applied at the register (Chetty et al., 2009; Finkelstein, 2009).

In the context of fiscal policy, there is a question whether to provide stimulus payments in the form of a one-time check or in the form of reduced withholding. Would one or another approach lead to increased spending? A one-time stimulus payment has been found to have significantly greater effects in increasing spending than does an economically equivalent reduction in withholding (Sahm et al., 2011). A potential explanation, with support in the evidence, involves the importance of salience or visibility. Indeed, a majority of households did not notice the withholding changes in the relevant study, and households who found "a small but repeated boost to their paychecks" appear to be less likely to use the money for significant purchases.

There are large issues here about how to design optimal taxes in the light of bounded rationality. Suppose that people have limited attention, and that attention is heterogeneous across a population. As Farhi and Gabaix (2020) show, a corrective (Pigouvian) tax might be set too low if it is equivalent to the monetary value of the corrected externality; the reason is that people might not pay attention to it. In the face of limited attention, the optimal tax should be higher; it should be equal to the monetary value of the externality, divided by the attention that people give to the tax. (If attention is at 50%, the externality will not be corrected unless the tax is doubled.) Things get more complicated in the face of heterogeneity in attention, where uniform taxes can generate inefficiencies. In principle, a blunt instrument, such as a regulation (say, an emissions limit), could turn out to be better than corrective taxes (Farhi & Gabaix, 2020).

In the face of internalities—perhaps produced by present bias, overconfidence, or inertia—it is natural to consider a nudge. For many consumers, the potential savings of energy-efficient products may not be salient at the time of purchase, even if those savings are significant. The *Energy Paradox* refers to the fact that some consumers do not purchase energy-efficient products even when it is clearly in their economic interest to do so. Empirical work suggests that nonprice interventions—for example, making the effects of energy use more salient—can alter decisions and significantly reduce electricity use. There is evidence that such interventions can lead to private as well as public savings (Howarth et al., 2000).

At the same time, there is a risk that some or many people will not pay attention to them, even if policymakers try to ensure that they do so. In that case, a corrective tax might be the right way to reduce internalities (Farhi & Gabaix, 2020). We might conclude, then, that Pigouvian taxes, responding to the externalities, might be accompanied by behaviorally informed taxes, responding to the harms that people do to their future selves. But here again, the problem of limited attention might rematerialize if some or many people pay too little attention to the taxes—again giving rise to a possible argument in favor of a blunt instrument, such as a fuel-economy rule or an energy-efficiency rule.

As we have noted, some people are concerned that corrective taxes or regulation might have unwelcome distributional consequences insofar as they impose disproportionate harm on poor people. An increase in the price of energy might have modest negative effects on the welfare of wealthy people but serious adverse effects on the welfare of poor people. On that count, nudges have real advantages insofar as they target internalities in particular (Farhi & Gabaix, 2020). A real question, of course, is whether they will succeed in doing that, though there is some reason to think that poor people will be especially attentive to possible economic savings (see Mullainathan & Shafir, 2013).

A possible response to consumer or investor mistakes is to identify and reconsider the frame through which people interpret information. There is evidence that some consumers may not seriously consider annuities in retirement to insure against longevity risk—the risk that they will outlive their assets—because they do not fully appreciate the potential advantages of annuities (Brown, 2007). One hypothesis is that some people evaluate annuities in an investment frame that focuses narrowly on risk and return (Brown et al., 2008). Looking through such a frame, consumers focus on the risk that they could die soon after the annuity purchase and lose all of their money. Some evidence suggests that efforts to shift consumers into a consumption frame, which focuses on the end result of what they can consume over time, help consumers appreciate the potential benefits of annuities (Brown et al., 2008). The goal here is not to suggest a view on any particular approach to retirement; it is merely to emphasize that the choice of the relevant frame will often matter.

11
Epilogue

Human beings are boundedly rational in the sense that they depart in systematic ways from the BRA. In the last decades, we have learned a great deal about those departures and hence obtained novel understandings of human judgment and decision-making. Our aim here has been to describe those understandings, with reference to existing evidence and models, and thus to identify appropriate foundations for both social science and public policy.

The heuristics and biases approach, inaugurated by Daniel Kahneman and Amos Tversky, is one of the most important research programs in social science and certainly one of its stellar achievements. It showed that the empirical evidence is fatally inconsistent with the BRA. Since the 1970s, there has been increased formalization of the heuristics and biases program, and continuing empirical research has clarified and deepened its foundations. Since the 1970s, the program has also been intensely scrutinized and criticized, to its great benefit.

We have presented a formalized version of the various heuristics in one place, evaluated the criticisms of the approach, and described how these criticisms can be answered, and existing understandings improved, by a fuller consideration of the evidence and the emerging models. We have tried to offer a state of the art treatment of bounded rationality, with reference to that evidence and those models.

We have also considered the foundations of behavioral welfare economics, with reference to the limit of Mill's HARM PRINCIPLE, the proper domain of freedom of choice, and the uses of libertarian paternalism or nudging. We show that libertarian paternalism has been adopted in many contexts, often to good effect. Most of the time, it does not depend on controversial psychological claims.

The BRA approach deals with situations of certainty, risk, subjective uncertainty, and ambiguity. In contrast to these situations, many interesting and important real-life problems belong to the domain of *true uncertainty*, where it is not possible to even imagine the set of all possible future states. Furthermore, many real world problems are *NP-complete*—that is, the time required to solve them grows too fast as the problem becomes more complicated. In fact, problems like this, such as the traveling salesman problem, cannot be solved in polynomial time. How do people solve such problems? As we have seen, decision-making under true uncertainty is a vexed problem.

The relative neglect of true uncertainty in economics is astonishing. The other social sciences do not provide a coherent framework in this regard either. More research is needed on how people make decisions in this case. We also need to have a basic agreement on what constitutes a benchmark in these situations against which proposed alternatives can be evaluated. Should this benchmark take an ex ante perspective (prior to the resolution of true uncertainty) or an ex post perspective (after the resolution of true uncertainty)? Heuristics that were designed for evaluating the BRA may, in our view, also be potentially interesting candidates to think about decision-making under true uncertainty. Or it could be that mental models and social norms might have evolved to deal with such cases. It is staggering that the black box of true uncertainty remains so impenetrably black.

On the most fundamental questions, a great deal remains to be learned. At the same time, this book should be seen as a celebration. Over recent decades, we have learned a great deal about bounded rationality, and about what it specifically entails. That understanding has helped not only to improve predictions about what people will do but also to develop practices and policies that are improving human lives, not least by lengthening them.

Notes

Acknowledgments

1. https://journals.sagepub.com/home/mic

Chapter 1

1. Namely, that the long-run relation between unemployment and inflation is vertical and the expectations response to a change in inflationary policy (e.g., money supply or interest rate changes) is gradual, as people slowly adjust their expectations. During this expectations adjustment period, economic policy may exploit the trade-off between inflation and unemployment by reducing unemployment at the cost of higher inflation. By contrast, under rational expectations, such expectations change instantaneously to a change in inflationary policy, so economic policy is not effective, even in the short run.

2. For discussions and surveys of bounded rationality, see also Hogarth and Reder (1986), Selten (1990, 1998), Conlisk (1996), Munier et al. (1999), Spiegler (2011), and Dhami (2016, 2020a).

3. Our use of the term *methodological individualism* throughout refers to its standard usage in economic theory. We do not mean to object to methodological individualism as defended by Jon Elster in many places; see, e.g., Elster (1982).

Chapter 2

1. For a more formal and satisfactory definition of Savage acts and probabilistic sophistication, see Dhami (2019a, section 1.3).

2. The Ellsberg paradox is named after Daniel Ellsberg, a former US military analyst who caused a national political controversy in 1971 when he released the Pentagon Papers, which contained a top-secret Pentagon study of the US government's decisions in the Vietnam War, to the leading national newspapers.

3. We have drawn all these quotations from an article by Robert J. Szczerba in *Forbes*, Jan. 5, 2015, titled "15 Worst Tech Predictions of All Time." See also a nice list of such situations in Gigerenzer (2014, pp. 41–42).

4. The interested reader can consult Dhami (2020a) for a more detailed discussion, including emerging attempts to provide the relevant underlying behavioral

theory. For an attempt to formalize limited attention, see Gabaix (2014, 2019, 2020) and Farhi and Gabaix (2020).

5. For a contrary view that contests the idea that individuals are overconfident, see Gigerenzer (2018, section 2.4).

6. Incidentally, Paul Samuelson and many others who knew the work of Allais opined that the Nobel Prize was given too late. That Allais's earlier work was in French and not widely read might have been a contributory factor.

7. Here we are assuming that when considering choices between lotteries, the decision-maker does not integrate existing wealth with the choices in the lotteries—a form of mental accounting that is supported by the evidence (Anderson et al., 2012; Fafchamps et al., 2014).

8. Here are the details. The indifference between \$250 received now and \$350 received in a year's time implies $250 = 350e^{-\theta}$, so $\theta = \ln\left(\frac{7}{5}\right) = 0.336$. Finally, indifference between \$3,000 received now and \$4,000 in a year's time implies $3000 = 4000e^{-\theta}$, so $\theta = \ln(4/3) \cong 0.29$.

9. Here are the relevant calculations. (1) $15 = 20e^{-\frac{\theta}{12}}$, so $\theta = 12\ln\left(\frac{4}{3}\right) = 3.452$. (2) $15 = 50e^{-\theta}$, so $\theta = \ln\left(\frac{50}{15}\right) = 1.204$. (3) $15 = 100e^{-\theta 10}$, so $\theta = \frac{1}{10}\ln\left(\frac{100}{15}\right) = 0.190$.

10. For a formal exposition that subadditivity can explain the common difference effect and, more importantly, that the evidence supports subadditivity, see Dhami (2019c).

11. We do not survey the early literature on the topic, but it is well covered in Benjamin (2018).

12. For attempts to correct for subadditivity to get at the true underlying subjective distribution, see Clemen and Ulu (2008), Prava et al. (2016), and Benjamin et al. (2018).

13. For an early study that documents neglect of base rates by clinical psychologists, see Meehl and Rosen (1955).

14. For more evidence on the neglect of base rates, see Grether (1980), who found that likelihoods were more salient than base rates, although the latter were not altogether ignored. See also Grether (1992) for an extension of his earlier work.

15. For an account of the competing theories, see Barbey and Sloman (2007).

16. For the axiomatic foundations of this utility function, see al-Nowaihi et al. (2008).

17. Abdellaoui (2000) and Abdellaoui et al. (2005) find that there is no significant difference in the curvature of the weighting function for gains and losses. For the Prelec function (see definition 2.11), we know that the parameter α controls the curvature. However, the elevation (which in the Prelec function is controlled by the parameter β) can be different in the domains of gains and losses.

Chapter 3

1. Psychological game theory is a part of the tool kit of behavioral game theory (Geanakoplos et al., 1989; Dhami, 2019d; Battigalli & Dufwenberg, 2020). Its main distinguishing feature, relative to classical game theory, is that beliefs of the players directly enter into their utility function, which allows us to model emotions in a formal manner. Such beliefs may be determined endogenously.

2. Constant returns to scale is an assumption on the technology that firms use to produce output, and it guarantees that an increase in inputs by a given percentage amount, say, 10%, leads to the same percentage increase in output, in this case by 10%.

3. One can invoke asymmetric information to argue that JL contracts perform a screening role, but it is unclear if this alone can account for the existence of such contracts. Peer pressure and social identity have also been invoked to explain the success of JL contracts. However, the empirical counterparts of these constructs are not specified, and these typically tend to be catch-all terms that try to capture the social connnections between borrowers. For a critical discussion of the literature and the references, see Dhami et al. (2020) and Dhami (2019d, section 3.6).

4. Readers interested in pursuing a formal introduction to psychological game theory may consult Dhami (2019d, sections 2.5, 3.6) and Battigalli and Dufwenberg (2020).

5. In their experimental design, Dhami et al. (2020) use the induced beliefs design of Ellingsen et al. (2010) to implement mutual knowledge of positive expectations. They improve the induced beliefs design by asking permission from the subject before conveying their private signal to the other players in order to address deception concerns raised in the literature.

6. For surveys, see Andreoni et al. (1998), Slemrod and Yitzhaki (2002), Slemrod (2018), and Alm (2019).

7. See, in particular, Yaniv (1999) and Bernasconi and Zanardi (2004), who were also the first to suggest a prospect theory analysis to tax evasion.

8. One of us was invited by HMRC to give a talk on tax evasion in their London office circa 2013. Among the questions asked at the end of the talk was how the work of Dhami and al-Nowaihi (2007) could enable HMRC to reduce evasion. The reply was that loss aversion plays a key role in reducing evasion; hence, any measures by HMRC to increase the visibility of tax offenders might act to increase the loss aversion of taxpayers by identifying evasion as a particularly socially undesirable activity. The naming and shaming of taxpayers, as an offical HMRC policy, began a few months later. The authors have no evidence, however, that the talk may have contributed toward such a policy.

9. Dhami and al-Nowaihi (2007) show that moral costs of tax evasion, in the form of stigma costs, alone cannot explain the observed extent of tax evasion.

10. *Strategies* in classical game theory refers to 'complete contingent plans of actions. However, in static games of full information such as the prisoner's dilemma game, we may use the terms *strategies* and *actions* interchangeably.

11. See, for instance, Fehr and Gächter (2000), Fehr et al. (2002), Fehr and Fischbacher (2004), Elster (2011), Dhami (2016), and Gintis (2017).

12. For an approach to behavioral economics that is based on Popper (1959/ 1934, 1963) and takes account of the extensions in the form of the Duhem-Quine thesis and the work of Lakatos (1970), see the introductory chapter in Dhami (2016).

13. We are grateful to Ali al-Nowaihi for this example.

14. The trust game is a two-player game in which a trustor and a trustee are initially given a sum of money by the experimenter. The trustor then decides to make a monetary investment i in the trustee; this is a measure of trust. The experimenter multiplies this investment by a multiplier $m > 1$ so that the trustee receives a monetary amount mi. In the final stage, the trustee decides to return an amount r to the trustor; this is a measure of trustworthiness. The BRA predicts, under self-regarding preferences, that $i = r = 0$. Yet, significant levels of trust and trustworthiness are found in experiments; for a survey, see Dhami (2019b).

15. In public goods games, a group of subjects makes simultaneous voluntary contributions toward a public good whose benefits are shared equally by everyone in the group, irrespective of the contributions. Under the BRA, which assumes self-regarding preferences, and using relatively weak technical conditions, the prediction is that everyone will free-ride and voluntarily contribute nothing. Yet, we find that voluntary contributions are high, particularly when a punishment option is present in which contributors can punish noncontributors. For a survey of the results from public goods games and the different patterns of punishments among Western and non-Western subject pools, see Dhami (2019b).

16. The dictator game is a two-player game in which a dictator who is given an endowment by the experimenter must decide to share a part of the endowment, including the option to not share at all, with a passive receiver. The prediction of the BRA, under self-regarding preferences, is that the dictator should not share any endowment. However, the average endowment shared in experiments ranges between 15 percent and 20 percent. For a survey and extensions of these experiments, see Dhami (2019, Vol. II).

Chapter 4

1. In an insightful paper that was perhaps ahead of its time, Akerlof and Yellen (1985) show that even small amounts of irrationality (relative to the benchmark levels of rationality in macroeconomics) can produce large economic fluctuations. However, these insights were either ignored within mainstream macroeconomics or taken as as curiosities with respect to the standard framework.

2. There is also a set of attribute-based models under risk and uncertainty in which the two attributes are outcomes and probabilities. For an introduction to these models, see Dhami (2019a).

3. An equivalence relation on a set is a binary relation that satisfies reflexivity, symmetry, and transitivity. For instance, consider the set of students in a large university and define the equivalence relation "having the same year of birth as."

4. The explanation of the gain-loss asymmetry requires an explicit consideration of the case $z_L < z_S < 0$, which we have omitted; the interested reader can see the relevant proofs in Dhami (2019c).

5. This framework can be extended to incomplete information and to other classes of games.

6. For an extension of this discussion to problems of public goods provision and exploitation of common resources, see Roemer (2018).

7. See, for instance, Samuelson and Bazerman (1985), Ball et al. (1991), and Tor and Bazerman (2003).

8. As explained in the introduction, rational expectations requires that the subjective expectations of people are essentially the same as the mathematical expectations taken for the correct, possibly stochastic, underlying model that describes the economic phenomenon under study.

9. For surveys of complexity theory and agent-based models that are written for economists, see Epstein and Axtell (1996), Tesfatsion (2002), Arthur (2006), Beinhocker (2006), Beinhocker et al. (2019), Hommes (2013), Kirman (2010), Haldane (2016), and Dhami (2020b). For a more technical treatment, see Hommes and LeBaron (2018). For a beautifully simple introduction to complexity, see Mitchell (2009).

10. These include prejudice/hatred; legal decree (as in South Africa's apartheid regime); and purely economic reasons in which the richer people locate into neighborhoods with more expensive housing, better schools / public services, and lower crime. When segregation is created by purely economic reasons, it might, in turn, lead to prejudice and a lack of mutual understanding, hence creating yet another reason for segregation. Thus, the different explanations for segregation cannot often be neatly separated from each other.

11. For more examples and a rich discussion of these issues, see Scheffer (2009).

12. For $\lambda \leq 1$ starting from any initial value of $x_0 \in (0, 1]$, the population will collapse to zero, and this is a stable steady state. For any value $\lambda \in (1, 2)$, the system steadily approaches the stable steady state $x^* > 0$, which is found by setting $x_t = x_{t+1} = x^*$ in (4.24) and solving out for x^*. A similar analysis holds for the interval $\lambda \in (2, 3]$. Beyond $\lambda > 3$, the system exhibits interesting oscillations. When $\lambda \in (3, 3.44949]$, starting from any initial value x_0, the system permanently oscillates between two values found by solving the fixed points of $x = f(f(x)) = f^2(x)$. When $\lambda \in (3.44949, 3.54409]$, another bifurcation occurs, and the system exhibits a limit cycle of period 4. As λ increases between the values $3.54409 < \lambda < 3.56995$, successive bifurcations occur more and more quickly and one gets limit cycles of period $8, 16, 32, \ldots$.

13. For an application of chaotic dynamics to the Cobweb model with nonlinear supply curves, see Hommes (2018).

14. In more general models, each genotype may induce a probability distribution over the possible phenotypes. For instance, genes determine that humans have fingerprints. However, the exact fingerprint is unique to each human. We abstract from these considerations.

15. For other adjustment processes, see Hofbauer and Sigmund (1998) and Samuelson (1997).

16. For the expected utility functional in (2.37), the coefficient of relative risk aversion is given by the calculation of the unit-free number $\frac{-xu''(x)}{u'(x)}$, where u is the utility function for outcomes, u' is the first derivative of the utility function, and u'' is the second derivative.

17. Al-Nowaihi and Dhami (2011) formalize the precise mathematical sense in which this function is steep—that is, close to $p = 0$ and $p = 1$. They show that, for the Prelec function, $\lim_{p \to 0} \frac{w(p)}{p} = \infty$ (i.e., the ratio of the probability weight to the probability tends to infinity as p tends to zero), and also $\lim_{p \to 1} \frac{1-w(p)}{1-p} = \infty$.

18. See also Radelet and Ackers (1996) and Polinsky and Shavell (2007).

19. More formally, the CPF zero-underweights infinitesimal probabilities, i.e., $\lim_{p \to 0} \frac{w(p)}{p} = 0$, and zero-overweights near-one probabilities, i.e., $\lim_{p \to 1} \frac{1-w(p)}{1-p} = 0$.

Chapter 5

1. Kahneman and Tversky (1996, p. 584) themselves offered a blunt assessment of the criticisms of their position: "The position described by Gigerenzer is indeed easy to refute but it bears little resemblance to ours. It is useful to remember that the refutation of a caricature can be no more than a caricature of a refutation."

2. The weak law of large numbers can be strengthened to the *strong law of large numbers,* which guarantees almost sure convergence of the sample mean to the population mean. However, its scope of application is smaller than that of the weak law.

3. The interested reader can pursue the details and the relevant references for all the claims in this paragraph in Dhami (2020a, section 1.6.3).

4. In the Linda problem, it is plausible that she is a member of the feminist movement (causal base rates). However, if this is substituted by a noncausal description (e.g., Linda drinks black tea in the morning), then the conjunction fallacy is unlikely to arise (see section 19.3.3 in Dhami, 2016).

5. See also chapter 5 in Gigerenzer (2014) for more discussion on simple rules of thumb followed by experts in the financial markets that prevent good stock market predictions.

Chapter 6

1. None of the core texts in any area of economics, with the exception of Dhami (2016, Part 7; 2020a), give an adequate treatment of either the HBP or the FFP approaches. This is clearly unsatisfactory.

2. We fully realize that some heuristics in the FFP apply to the domain of risk and subjective uncertainty (e.g., the priority heuristic).

3. Dawes' rule or tallying prescribes the following. In choosing between options A and B, consider the entire set of cues and tally the cue values in favor of each

of the options. Then pick the option that has a higher number of cues in its favor. Franklin's rule prescribes a weighted combination of the cues to choose between the options.

4. See section 6.5 for a more complex problem: Which stocks to invest in? But we show that the problem cited there falls outside the ambit of the FFP.

5. Compensatory heuristics are those that give equal weight to the cues. Noncompensatory heuristics allow for unequal weights.

6. This work is reprinted as chapter 34 in Gigerenzer et al. (2011).

7. We are grateful to Raúl Rojas, professor of artificial intelligence, Freie Universität Berlin, for giving us permission to print figure 6.1 from his lecture notes.

Chapter 7

1. The presumption could be fortified with reference to the potentially self-interested or malevolent incentives of those who seek to interfere with people's judgments. We are bracketing that important point here; we will return to it in chapter 9.

2. For a series of objections, see Conly (2013).

3. Some questions about this idea are raised in Sunstein (2014a).

4. For a defense of coercive paternalism, see Bubb and Pildes (2014). By design, Bubb and Pildes do not engage this kind of normative objection: "We thus put aside various external critiques that could be, and have been, mounted. Autonomy or liberty-based political theories argue, for example, that these values should have priority over welfare maximization." The only point is that if a Kantian idea, of the sort invoked by Bernheim (2016) and Waldron (2014), is in play, it would serve as a check on imaginable claims in behaviorally informed law and policy.

5. A rejoinder can be found in Conly (2013): "We don't regard it as insulting to assume that the man on the street can't do quantum mechanics, because he can't (unless you're on a very special street). The paternalist believes that it is the facts that suggest a change in the status we accord people, a change from what we might have thought about ourselves to a more realistic acceptance of our inabilities. The suggestion here is simply that we should treat people in accordance with their real abilities and their real limitations."

6. Sunstein (2019b) finds what seems to be a significant mistake on the part of consumers with respect to a technology designed to make driving safer.

7. Ambitious accounts are Conly (2013) and Bubb and Pildes (2014).

8. For different perspectives, see Allcott and Sunstein (2015), Bernheim and Taubinsky (2018), and Goldin (2017).

9. For some vivid examples, see Abaluck and Gruber (2011, 2013), Afendulis et al. (2015), and Bhargava et al. (2015, 2017).

10. Cigarette smoking is an example (Masiero et al., 2015).

11. Akerlof and Shiller (2016) is in the same vein, though it emphasizes the active efforts by sellers to exploit those deficits and biases, or to phish for them.

12. Recall Bernheim's acknowledgment of the possibility that "all consumption items ('external goods') are means to ends, and choices among them always involve indirect judgments." It is true that some governments impose coercive controls on intimate aspects of people's lives—as, for example, by criminalizing same-sex relations—and these controls might, at some point, be defended on behavioral grounds. But in the institutions that are now using behavioral economics, indirect judgments are the lay of the land, and the same is true of academic research that finds mistakes or recommends a behaviorally informed intervention.

13. The hunch is questioned in Gayer and Viscusi (2013) and in Allcott and Knittel (2019); it is supported in Gillingham et al. (2019).

14. The issue remains debated and, in our view, unresolved (Allcott & Knittel, 2019; Gayer & Viscusi, 2013; Gillingham et al., 2019).

15. Bernheim and Taubinsky (2018) raise a number of objections to reliance on subjective well-being. As noted, it is right to insist that subjective well-being is not the only thing that people care about; for example, choosers might sacrifice their subjective well-being for the sake of others, for the sake of living meaningful lives, or for the sake of moral goals. But the case for relying on choices, rather than subjective well-being, is not made by that point. In some contexts, choices really are an effort to promote subjective well-being, and they go wrong.

16. In general, Levitt (2016) finds excessive caution in making life-changing decisions.

17. For a defense of liberal perfectionism, see Raz (1985); for critiques of perfectionism, see Rawls (1991) and Conly (2013). For a general account, see Zalta (2017).

18. Nussbaum (2000) can be placed in the same extended family. For an especially clear treatment, see Nussbaum (1993).

19. It is important to be careful here; active choices might be uninformed or behaviorally biased.

20. One example is the continuing dispute over the benefits to consumers of fuel-economy and energy-efficiency requirements (Allcott & Taubinsky, 2015). Another example is the dispute, also continuing, about how to value reductions in smoking; to what extent do they improve the welfare of former smokers? (Levy et al., 2018). The framework introduced in Levy et al. is highly compatible with the analysis here.

Chapter 8

1. Economists distinguish between two kinds of consumption taxes. Ad valorem taxes are imposed as a percentage of the price of a good. Specific taxes are imposed per unit of consumption of a good.

2. In a richer model, we may assume a distribution of β values across the individuals who have $(\beta, 1)$ preferences. However, the minimal assumptions that we have made are sufficient for deriving most of the critical insights.

3. Technically, we have $W(\alpha, \tau) = N_1 W_t^b(\alpha, \tau) + N_2 W_t^c(\alpha, \tau)$. Maximizing W is equivalent to maximizing the function W/N. Using the definition of $\lambda = N_1/N$ gives rise to (8.22).

4. An indifference curve shows all combinations of the two goods, x and y, that provide an identical level of utility to the individual.

5. The reader can find formal treatments of the concept of DWL in most microeconomics or public economics books.

6. For numerical examples that distinguish between the behavior of selves with various degrees of awareness of future self-control problems, see O'Donoghue and Rabin (1999a,b).

Chapter 9

1. For the classic analysis in economics of the relative efficacy of regulation versus Pigouvian taxes in the face of uncertainty about the marginal benefits and the marginal costs of of externality reduction, see Weitzman (1974).

References

Abaluck, J., & Gruber, J. (2011). Choice inconsistencies among the elderly: Evidence from plan choice in the Medicare Part D Program. *American Economic Review, 101*(4), 1180–1210.

Abaluck, J., & Gruber, J. (2013). *Evolving choice inconsistencies in choice of prescription drug insurance* [NBER Working Paper No. 19163]. https://www.nber.org/papers/w19163

Abdellaoui, M. A. (2000). Parameter-free elicitation of utility and probability weighting functions. *Management Science, 46*(11), 1497–1512.

Abdellaoui, M. A., Vossmann, F., & Weber, M. (2005). Choice-based elicitation and decomposition of decision weights for gains and losses under uncertainty. *Management Science, 51*(9), 1384–1399.

Abreu, D., & Brunnermeier, M. K. (2003). Bubbles and crashes. *Econometrica, 71*(1), 173–204.

Acemoglu, D., & Jackson, M. O. (2012). Social norms and the enforcement of laws. *Journal of the European Economic Association, 15*(2), 245–295.

Acemoglu, D., Reed, T., & Robinson, J. A. (2013). Chiefs: Economic development and elite control of civil society in Sierra Leone. *Journal of Political Economy, 122*(2), 319–368.

Adler, Matthew. (2011). *Well-being and fair distribution: Beyond costbenefit analysis*. Oxford University Press.

Afendulis, Christopher, Sinaiko, Anna D., & Frank, Richard G. (2015). Dominated choices and Medicare Advantage enrollment. *Journal of Economic Behavior and Organization, 119*(C), 72–83.

Affordable Care Act (The Patient Protection and Affordable Care Act of 2010), Pub. L. No. 111-148, 124 Stat. 119 (2010).

Agarwal, S., Chomsisengphet, S., Mahoney, N., & Stroebel, J. (2013). *Regulating consumer financial products: Evidence from credit cards* [NBER Working Paper No. 19484].

Ahmed, A. S., & Duellman, S. (2013). Managerial overconfidence and accounting conservatism. *Journal of Accounting Research, 51*(1), 1–30.

Ainslie, G. W. (1975). Specious reward: A behavioral theory of impulsiveness and impulse control. *Psychological Bulletin, 82*(4), 463–496.

Ainslie, G. W. (1992). *Picoeconomics.* Cambridge University Press.

Ainslie, G. (2015). The cardinal anomalies that led to behavioral economics: Cognitive or motivational? *Managerial and Decision Economics, 37*(4–5), 261–273.

Ajzen, I. (1977). Intuitive theories of events and the effects of base-rate information on prediction. *Journal of Personality and Social Psychology, 35,* 303–314.

Akerlof, George, & Dickens, William. (1982). The economic consequences of cognitive dissonance. *American Economic Review, 72*(3), 307–319.

Akerlof, G. A., & Shiller, R. J. (2009). *Animal spirits: How human psychology drives the economy and why it matters for global capitalism.* Princeton University Press.

Akerlof, George, & Shiller, Robert. (2016). *Phishing for phools: The economics of manipulation and deception.* Oxford University Press.

Akerlof, G. A., & Yellen, J. L. (1985). Can small deviations from rationality make significant differences to economic equilibria? *The American Economic Review, 75*(4), 708–720.

Aktas, N., de Bodt, E., Bollaert, H., & Roll, R. (2016). CEO narcissism and the takeover process: From private initiation to deal completion. *Journal of Financial and Quantitative Analysis, 51*(1), 113–137.

Alesina, A., & Fuchs-Schündeln, N. (2007). Goodbye Lenin (or not?): The effect of communism on people. *American Economic Review, 97*(4), 1507–1528.

Alesina, Alberto, & Giuliano, Paola. (2014). Family ties. In Philippe Aghion & Steven N. Durlauf (Eds.), *Handbook of economic growth* (Vol. 2A, pp. 177–216). Elsevier.

Alesina A., & Giuliano, P. (2015). Culture and institutions. *Journal of Economic Literature, 53*(4), 898–944.

Alesina, A., Giuliano, P., & Nunn, N. (2013). On the origins of gender roles: Women and the plough. *Quarterly Journal of Economics, 128*(2), 469–530.

Alesina, A., & Glaeser, E. L. (2004). *Fighting poverty in the US and Europe: A world of difference.* Oxford University Press.

Allais, M. (1953). Le comportement de l'homme rationnel devant le risque, critique des postulats et axiomes de l'ecole Américaine. *Econometrica, 21,* 503–546.

Allcott, H. (2011). Social norms and energy conservation. *Journal of Public Economics, 95*(9–10), 1082–1095.

Allcott, Hunt. (2016). Paternalism and energy efficiency: An overview. *Annual Review of Economics, 8*(1), 145–176.

Allcott, Hunt, & Kessler, Judd. (2019). The welfare effects of nudges: A case study of energy use social comparisons. *American Economic Journal: Applied Economics, 11*(1), 236–276.

Allcott, Hunt, & Knittel, Christopher. (2019). Are consumers poorly informed about fuel economy? Evidence from two experiments. *American Economic Journal: Economic Policy, 11*(1), 1–37.

Allcott, H., Lockwood, B. B., & Taubinsky, D. (2019a). Regressive sin taxes, with an application to the optimal soda tax. *Quarterly Journal of Economics, 134*(3), 1557–1626.

Allcott, H., Lockwood, B. B., & Taubinsky, D. (2019b). Should we tax soda? An overview of theory and evidence. *Journal of Economic Perspectives, 33*(3), 202–227.

Allcott, H., & Mullainathan, S. (2010). Behavior and energy policy. *Science, 327*(5970), 1204–1205.

Allcott, H., & Rogers, T. (2014). The short-run and long-run effects of behavioral interventions: Experimental evidence from energy conservation. *American Economic Review, 104*(10), 3003–3037.

Allcott, Hunt, & Sunstein, Cass R. (2015). Regulating internalities. *Journal of Policy Analysis and Management, 34*(3), 698–705.

Allcott, Hunt, & Taubinsky, Dmitry. (2015). Evaluating behaviorally motivated policy: Experimental evidence from the lightbulb market. *American Economic Review, 105*(8), 2501–2538.

Allen, F., Morris, S., & Postlewaite, A. (1993). Finite bubbles with short sale constraints and asymmetric information. *Journal of Economic Theory, 61*(2), 206–229.

Allingham, M. G., & Sandmo, A. (1972). Income tax evasion: A theoretical analysis. *Journal of Public Economics, 1*(3–4), 323–338.

Alm, J. (2019). What motivates tax compliance? *Journal of Economic Surveys, 33*(2), 353–388.

al-Nowaihi, A., Bradley, I., & Dhami, S. (2008). A note on the utility function under prospect theory. *Economics Letters, 99*(2), 337–339.

al-Nowaihi, A., & Dhami, S. (2006a). A note on the Loewenstein-Prelec theory of intertemporal choice. *Mathematical Social Sciences, 52*(1), 99–108.

al-Nowaihi, A., & Dhami, S. (2006b). A simple derivation of Prelec's probability weighting function. *Journal of Mathematical Psychology, 50*(6), 521–524.

al-Nowaihi, A., & Dhami, S. (2008). *A general theory of time discounting: The reference-time theory of intertemporal choice*. [Working Paper 08/22] University of Leicester, Department of Economics.

al-Nowaihi, A., & Dhami, S. (2009). A value function that explains the magnitude and sign effects. *Economics Letters, 105*(3), 224–229.

al-Nowaihi, A., & Dhami, S. (2010). *Composite prospect theory: A proposal to combine prospect theory and cumulative prospect theory* [University of Leicester. Discussion Paper 10/11].

al-Nowaihi, A., & Dhami, S. (2011). Probability weighting functions. In *Wiley encyclopedia of operations research and management science*. Wiley.

al-Nowaihi, A., & Dhami, S. (2015). Evidential equilibria: Heuristics and biases in static games of complete information. *Games, 6*(4), 637–677.

al-Nowaihi, A., & Dhami, S. (2018). *Foundations for intertemporal choice* [CESifo Working Paper Series No. 6913]. SSRN: https://ssrn.com/abstract=3167146

Anderson, C., Brion, S., Moore, D. A., & Kennedy, J. A. (2012). A status enhancement account of overconfidence. *Journal of Personality and Social Psychology, 103*(4), 718–735.

Andreoni, J., Erard, B., & Feinstein, J. (1998). Tax compliance. *Journal of Economic Literature, 36*(2), 818–860.

Andreoni, J., & Miller, J. H. (1993). Rational cooperation in the finitely repeated prisoner's dilemma: Experimental evidence. *Economic Journal, 103*(418), 570–585.

Arad, A., & Rubinstein, A. (2012). The 11-20 money request game: A level-k reasoning study. *American Economic Review, 102*(7), 3561–3573.

Ariely, D., Loewenstein, G., & Prelec, D. (2006). Tom Sawyer and the construction of value. *Journal of Economic Behavior and Organization, 60*, 1–10.

Ariely, D., & Wertenbroch, K. (2002). Procrastination, deadlines, and performance: Self-control by precommitment. *Psychological Science, 13*(3), 219–224.

Arifovic, J., Boitnott, J. F., & Duffy, J. (2019). Learning correlated equilibrium: An evolutionary approach. *Journal of Economic Behavior and Organization, 157*(C), 171–190.

Armstrong, Mark, & Vickers, John. (2012). Consumer protection and contingent charges. *Journal of Economic Literature, 50*(2), 477–493.

Armstrong, Mark, & Zhou, J. (2011). Paying for prominence. *Economic Journal, 121*(556), F368–F395.

Arthur, W. B. (1994). Inductive reasoning and bounded rationality. *American Economic Association Papers and Proceedings, 84*, 406–411.

Arthur, W. B. (2006). Agent-based modeling and out-of-equilibrium economics. In K. Judd & L. Tesfatsion (Eds.), *Handbook of computational economics: Vol. 2. Agent-Based Computational Economics* (pp. 1551–1564). Elsevier B.V.

Arthur, W. B. (2015). *Complexity and the economy*. Oxford University Press.

Aumann, R. J., & Brandenburger, A. (1995). Epistemic conditions for Nash equilibrium. *Econometrica, 63*, 1161–80.

Ausubel, Lawrence M. (1991). The failure of competition in the credit card market. *American Economic Review, 81*(1), 50–81.

Ayton, P., & Fischer, I. (2004). The hot hand fallacy and the gambler's fallacy: Two faces of subjective randomness? *Memory and Cognition, 32*, 1369–1378.

Bacharach, M. (1999). Interactive team reasoning: A contribution to the theory of cooperation. *Research in Economics, 53*(2), 117–147.

Bacharach, M. (2006). *Beyond individual choice: Teams and frames in game theory* (N. Gold & R. Sugden, Eds.). Princeton University Press.

Ball, S. B., Bazerman, M. H., & Carroll, J. S. (1991). An evaluation of learning in the bilateral winner's curse. *Organizational Behavior and Human Decision Processes, 48*(1), 1–22.

Banerjee, A., & Duflo, E. (2011). *Poor economics: A radical rethinking of the way to fight global poverty*. Public Affairs.

Banerjee, A., & Mullainathan, S. (2008). Limited attention and income distribution. *American Economic Review, 98*(2), 489–493.

Banerjee, S., Humphery-Jenner, M., & Nanda, V. (2015). Restraining overconfident CEOs through improved governance: Evidence from the Sarbanes-Oxley Act. *Review of Financial Studies, 28*(10), 2812–2858.

Baptista R., Farmer, D. J., Hinterschweiger, M., Low, K., Tang, D., & Uluc, A. (2016). *Macroprudential policy in an agent-based model of the UK housing market* [Bank of England Staff Working Paper No 619].

Bar-Gill, Oren. (2012). *Seduction by contract: Law, economics, and psychology in consumer markets*. Oxford University Press.

Bar-Hillel, M. (1980). The base rate fallacy in probability judgements. *Acta Psychologica, 44*, 211–233.

Bar-Hillel, M., & Wagenaar, W. A. (1991). The perception of randomness. *Advances in Applied Mathematics, 12*, 428–454.

Bar-Ilan, A. (2000). *The response to large and small penalties in a natural experiment* [Working Paper]. University of Haifa, Department of Economics.

Bar-Ilan, A., & Sacerdote, B. (2001). *The response to fines and probability of detection in a series of experiments* [National Bureau of Economic Research Working Paper 8638].

Bar-Ilan, A., & Sacerdote, B. (2004). The response of criminals and noncriminals to fines. *Journal of Law and Economics, 47*(1), 1–17.

Barberis, N., & Huang, M. (2008). Stocks as lotteries: The implications of probability weighting for security prices. *American Economic Review, 98*(5), 2066–2100.

Barberis, N., Shleifer, A., & Vishny, R. (1998). A model of investor sentiment. *Journal of Financial Economics, 49*, 307–343.

Barberis, N., & Thaler, R. H. (2003). A survey of behavioral finance. In G. Constantinides, M. Harris, & R. Stultz (Eds.), *Handbook of the economics of finance* (pp. 1051–1119). North-Holland.

Barbey, A. K., & Sloman, S. A. (2007). Base-rate respect: From ecological rationality to dual processes. *Behavioral and Brain Sciences, 30*(3), 241–254.

Bardsley, N., Cubitt, R., Loomes, G., Moffatt, P., Starmer, C., & Sugden, R. (2010). *Experimental economics: Rethinking the rules*. Princeton University Press.

Barro, R. J., & Sala-i-Martin, X. I. (2003). *Economic growth* (2nd ed.) MIT Press.

Battigalli, P., & Dufwenberg, M. (2007). Guilt in games. *American Economic Review, 97*(2), 170–176.

Battigalli, P., & Dufwenberg, M. (2020). *Belief-dependent motivations and psychological game theory* [CESifo Working Paper No. 8285]. SSRN: https://ssrn.com/abstract=3598771

Bauckhage, C. (2021). Insights into internet memes. *Proceedings of the International AAAI Conference on Web and Social Media, 5*(1), 42–49.

Bazerman, M. H., & Samuelson, W. F. (1983). I won the auction but don't want the prize. *Journal of Conflict Resolution, 27*(4), 618–634.

Bebchuk, L. A., Fried, J. M., & Walker, D. I. (2002). Managerial power and rent extraction in the design of executive compensation. *University of Chicago Law Review, 69*(3), 751–846.

Becker, G. S. (1968). Crime and punishment: An economic approach. *Journal of Political Economy, 76*(2), 169–217.

Behavioural Insights Team. (2014, April 11). *EAST: Four simple ways to apply behavioural insights*. https://www.bi.team/publications/east-four-simple-ways-to-apply-behavioural-insights/

Beinhocker, E. D. (2006). *The origin of wealth: Evolution, complexity, and the radical remaking of economics*. Harvard Business School Press.

Beinhocker, E. D., Arthur, W. B., Axtell, R., Bednar, Bouchaud, J-P., Colander, D., Crockett, M., Farmer, J. D., Hausmann, R., Hommes, C., Kirman, A., Page, S., & Wilson, D. S. (2019, March 19). Economics after neoliberalism: Complexity economics is inclusive economics. *Boston Review*.

Bellman, R. (1952). On the theory of dynamic programming. *Proceedings of the National Academy of Sciences USA, 38*(8), 716–719.

Bénabou, R. (2015). The economics of motivated beliefs. Jean-Jacques Laffont lecture. *Revue d'economie politique, 125*(5), 665–685.

Bénabou, R., Falk, A., & Tirole, J. (2018). *Narratives, imperatives, and moral reasoning*. Princeton University Press. https://scholar.princeton.edu/sites/default/files/rbenabou/files/morals_april_2_2020_snd.pdf

Bénabou, R., & Tirole, J. (2002). Self-confidence and personal motivation. *Quarterly Journal of Economics, 117*(3), 871–915.

Bénabou, R., & Tirole, J. (2016). Mindful economics: The production, consumption, and value of beliefs. *Journal of Economic Perspectives, 30*(3), 141–164.

Benartzi, S., Beshears, J., Milkman, K. L., Sunstein, C. R., Thaler, R. H., Shankar, M., Tucker, W., Congdon, W. J., & Galing, S. (2017). Should governments invest more in nudges? *Psychological Science, 28*, 1041–1055

Benartzi, S., & Thaler, R. H. (1995). Myopic loss aversion and the equity premium puzzle. *Quarterly Journal of Economics, 110*(1), 73–92.

Benartzi, S., & Thaler. R. H. (2004). Save more tomorrow: Using behavioral economics to increase employee savings. *Journal of Political Economy, 112*, S164–S187.

Benartzi, S., & Thaler, R. H. (2013). Behavioral economics and the retirement savings crisis. *Science, 339*(6124), 1152–1153.

Ben-David, I., Graham, J., & Harvey, C. (2013). Managerial miscalibration. *Quarterly Journal of Economics, 128*(4), 1547–1584.

Benjamin, D. J. (2018). *Errors in probabilistic reasoning and judgment biases* [USC Dornsife Institute for New Economic Thinking Working Paper No. 18-21].

Benjamin, D., Moore, D., & Rabin, M. (2017). *Biased beliefs about random samples: Evidence from two integrated experiments* [NBER Working Paper 23927].

Benjamin, D., Moore, D., & Rabin, M. (2018). *Biased beliefs about random samples: Evidence from two integrated experiments* [Global Research Unit Working Paper No. 2018-014].

Bentham, J. (1789). *An introduction to the principle of morals and legislations*. Reprinted, Blackwell, 1948.

Bento, Antonio, Jacobsen, Mark R., Knittel, Christopher R., & van Benthem, Arthur A. (2019). *Estimating the costs and benefits of fuel economy standards* [NBER Working Paper No. 26309]. https://www.nber.org/papers/w26309

Bergert, F. B., & Nosofsky, R. M. (2007). A response-time approach to comparing generalized rational and take-the-best models of decision making. *Journal of Experimental Psychology: Learning Memory and Cognition, 331*, 107–129.

Bernard, T., & Taffesse, A. S. (2014). Aspirations: An approach to measurement with validation using Ethiopian data. *Journal of African Economies, 23*(2), 189–224.

Bernasconi, M., & Zanardi, A. (2004). Tax evasion, tax rates and reference dependence. *FinanzArchiv, 60*(3), 422–445.

Bernheim, B. D. (2009). Behavioral welfare economics. *Journal of the European Economic Association, 7*(2–3), 267–319.

Bernheim, B. D. (2016). The good, the bad, and the ugly: A unified approach to behavioral welfare economic. *Journal of Benefit-Cost Analysis, 7*(1), 12–68.

Bernheim, B. D., & Rangel, A. (2007). Toward choice-theoretic foundations for behavioral welfare economics. *American Economic Review, 97*(2), 464–470.

Bernheim, B. D., & Rangel, A. (2009). Beyond revealed preference: Choice-theoretic foundations for behavioral welfare economics. *Quarterly Journal of Economics, 124*(1), 51–104.

Bernheim, B., Skinner, D., Skinner, J., & Weinberg, S. (1997). *What accounts for the variation in retirement wealth among U.S. households?* [NBER Working Paper 6227].

Bernheim, B. D., & Taubinsky, D. (2018). Behavioral public economics. In B. Douglas Bernheim, Stefano DellaVigna, & David Laibson (Eds.), *Handbook of behavioral economics: Vol. 1. Foundations and applications* (pp. 381–516). Elsevier.

Bertrand, M., Karlan, D., Mullainathan, S., Shafir, E., & Zinman, J. (2010). What's advertising content worth? Evidence from a consumer credit marketing field experiment. *Quarterly Journal of Economics, 125*(1), 263–305.

Bertrand, M., & Morse, A. (2011). Information disclosure, cognitive biases, and payday borrowing. *Journal of Finance, 66*(6), 1865–1893.

Bertrand, M., & Mullainathan, S. (2001). Are CEOs rewarded for luck? The ones without principals are. *Quarterly Journal of Economics, 116*(3), 901–932.

Bertrand, M., & Schoar, A. (2006). The role of family in family firms. *Journal of Economic Perspectives, 20*(2), 73–96.

Bettman, J. R., & Weitz B. A. (1983). Attributions in the board room: Causal reasoning in corporate annual reports. *Administrative Science Quarterly, 28*(2), 165–183.

Bhargava, Saurabh, Loewenstein, George, & Sydnor, Justin. (2015). *Do individuals make sensible health insurance decisions? Evidence from a menu with dominated options* [NBER Working Paper No. 21160]. https://nber.org/papers/w21160

Bhargava, Saurabh, Loewenstein, George, & Sydnor, Justin. (2017). Choose to lose: Health plan choices from a menu with dominated option. *Quarterly Journal of Economics, 132*(3), 1319–1372.

Biais, B., & Weber, M. (2009). Hindsight bias, risk perception and investment performance. *Management Science, 55*(6), 1018–1029.

Bicchieri, C. (2006). *The grammar of society: The nature and dynamics of social norms*. Cambridge University Press.

Binmore, K. (1998). *Game theory and the social contract: Just playing*. MIT Press.

Birnbaum., M. H. (2008). Evaluation of the priority heuristic as a descriptive model of risky decision making: Comment on Brandstätter, Gigerenzer, and Hertwig (2006). *Psychological Review, 115*, 253–262.

Black, F. (1986). Noise. *Journal of Finance, 41*(3), 529–543.

Blanchard, O. J., & Fischer, S. (1989). *Lectures in macroeconomics*. MIT Press.

Blumenstock, J., Callen, M., & Ghani, T. (2018). Why do defaults affect behavior? experimental evidence from Afghanistan. *American Economic Review, 108*(10), 2868–2901.

Bocskocsky, A., Ezekowitz, J., & Stein, C. (2014). *The hot hand: A new approach to an old fallacy* [Paper presentation]. MIT Sloan Sports Analytics Conference.

Bollinger, B., Leslie, P., & Sorenson, A. (2010). *Calorie labeling in chain restaurants* [NBER Working Paper No. 15648]. www.nber.org/papers/w15648

Bombardini, M., & Trebbi, F. (2012). Risk aversion and expected utility theory: An experiment with large and small stakes. *Journal of the European Economic Association, 10*(6), 1348–1399.

Bonini, N., Tentori, K., & Osherson, D. (2004). A different conjunction fallacy. *Mind & Language, 19*, 199–210.

Bonner, B. L., & Bolinger, A. R. (2013). Separating the confident from the correct: Leveraging member knowledge in groups to improve decision making and performance. *Organizational Behavior and Human Decision Processes, 122*(2), 214–221.

Booker, C. (2004). *The seven basic plots: Why we tell stories*. Bloomsbury.

Bookstaber, R., & Kirman, A. (2018). Modelling a heterogeneous world. In C. Hommes & B. LeBaron, (Eds.), *Handbook of computational economics* (Vol. 4, pp. 769–795). Elsevier.

Bordalo, P., Coffman, K., Gennaioli, N., & Shleifer, A. (2016). Stereotypes. *Quarterly Journal of Economics, 131*(4), 1753–1794.

Börgers, T., & Sarin, R. (2000). Naïve reinforcement learning with endogenous aspirations. *International Economic Review, 41*, 921–950.

Borges, B., Goldstein, D. G., Ortmann, A., & Gigerenzer, G. (1999). Can ignorance beat the stock market? In G. Gigerenzer, P. M. Todd, & the ABC Research Group (Eds.), *Simple heuristics that make us smart*, pp. 5972. Oxford University Press.

Bowles, S. (1998). Endogenous preferences: The cultural consequences of markets and other economic institutions. *Journal of Economic Literature, 36*(1), 75–111.

Bowles, S., & Gintis, H. (2011). *A cooperative species: Human reciprocity and its evolution*. Princeton University Press.

Bradley, S., & Feldman, N. (2020). Hidden baggage: Behavioral responses to changes in airline ticket tax disclosure. *American Economic Journal: Economic Policy, 12*(4), 58–87.

Brandstätter, E., Gigerenzer, G., & Hertwig, R. (2006). The priority heuristic: Choices without tradeoffs. *Psychological Review, 113*, 409–432.

Brase, G. L. (2002a). Which statistical formats facilitate what decisions? The perception and influence of different statistical information formats. *Journal of Behavioral Decision Making, 15*, 381–401.

Brase, G. L. (2002b). Ecological and evolutionary validity: Comments on Johnson-Laird, Legrenzi, Girotto, Legrenzi, and Caverni's (1999) mental-model theory of extensional reasoning. *Psychological Review, 109*, 722–728.

Brase, G. L., Fiddick, L., & Harries, C. (2006). Participant recruitment methods and statistical reasoning performance. *Quarterly Journal of Experimental Psychology, 59*, 965–976.

Braun-Munzinger, K., Liu, Z., & Turrell, A. (2016). An agent-based model of dynamics in corporate bond trading [Bank of England Staff Working Paper No 592].

Breiman, L., Friedman, J. H., Olshen, R. A., & Stone, C. J. (1993). *Classification and regression trees*. Chapman and Hall.

Brennan, G., & Buchanan, J. (1980). *The power to tax: Analytical foundations of a fiscal constitution*. Cambridge University Press.

Bröder, A. (2011). The quest for take-the-best: Insights and outlooks for experimental research. In G. Gigerenzer, R. Hertwig, & T. Pachur (Eds.), *Heuristics: The foundations of adaptive behavior*, 363–380. Oxford University Press.

Bröder, A., & Schiffer, S. (2003). Take the best versus simultaneous feature matching: Probabilistic inferences from memory and effects of representation format. *Journal of Experimental Psychology: General, 132*, 277–293.

Brown, J. R. (2007). *Rational and behavioral perspectives on the role of annuities in retirement planning* [NBER Working Paper No. 13537]. http://www.nber.org/papers/w13537

Brown, J. R., Kling, J. R., Mullainathan, S., & Wrobel, M. V. (2008). Why don't people insure late-life consumption? A framing explanation of the under-annuitization puzzle. *American Economic Review, 98*, 304–309.

Brunner, C., Camerer, C. F., & Goeree, J. K. (2011). Stationary concepts for experimental 2 x 2 games: Comment. *American Economic Review, 101*(2), 1029–1040.

Brunnermeier, M., & Parker, J. (2005). Optimal expectations. *American Economic Review, 95*(4), 1092–1118.

Bubb, R., & Pildes, R. (2014). How behavioral economics trims its sails and why. *Harvard Law Review, 127*(6), 1593–1678.

Buchanan, J. M. (1964). What should economists do? *Southern Economic Journal, 30*, 213–219.

Buchanan, J. (1967). *Public finance in democratic process: Fiscal institutions and the individual choice*. University of North Carolina Press.

Buchanan, J. M. (1986). *Liberty, market and state: Political economy in the 1980s*. New York University Press.

Buehler, R., Messervey, D., & Griffin, D. W. (2005). Collaborative planning and prediction: Does group discussion affect optimistic biases in time estimation? *Organizational Behavior and Human Decision Processes, 97*(1), 47–63.

Burson, K. A., Larrick, R. P., & Klayman, J. (2006). Skilled or unskilled, but still unaware of it: How perceptions of difficulty drive miscalibration in relative comparisons. *Journal of Personality and Social Psychology, 90*(1), 60–77.

Busse, M. R., Lacetera, N., Pope, D. G., Silva-Risso, J., & Sydnor, J. R. (2013). Estimating the effect of salience in wholesale and retail car markets. *American Economic Review, 103*(3), 575–579.

Cabinet Office. (n.d.). Behavioural Insights Team. www.cabinetoffice.gov.uk/behavioural-insights-team

Camerer, C. F. (1987). Do biases in probability judgment matter in markets experimental evidence? *American Economic Review, 77*, 981–997.

Camerer, C. F. (1989). Does the basketball market believe in the 'Hot Hand'? *American Economic Review, 79*, 1257–1261.

Camerer, C. F. (1990). Do markets correct biases in probability judgment? Evidence from market experiments In J. Kagel & L. Green (Eds.), *Advances in behavioral economics* (Vol. 2, pp. 125–172). Ablex Publishers.

Camerer, C. (1995). Individual decision making. In J. Kagel & A. E. Roth (Eds.), *Handbook of experimental economics*. Princeton University Press.

Camerer, C. F. (2003). *Behavioral game theory: Experiments in strategic interaction*. Princeton University Press.

Camerer, C. F. (2015). *The promise and success of lab-field generalizability in experimental economics: A critical reply to Levitt and List.* https://papers.ssrn.com/sol3/papers.cfm?abstract_id=1977749

Camerer, C. F., Babcock, L., Loewenstein, G., & Thaler, R. H. (1997). Labor supply of New York City cabdrivers: One day at a time. *Quarterly Journal of Economics, 112*(2), 407–441.

Camerer, C., Issacharoff, S., Loewenstein, G., O'Donoghue, T., & Rabin, M. (2003). Regulation for conservatives: Behavioral economics and the case for asymmetric paternalism. *University of Pennsylvania Law Review, 151,* 1211–1254.

Camerer, C. F., Loewenstein, G., & Weber, M. (1989). The curse of knowledge in economic settings: An experimental analysis. *Journal of Political Economy, 97,* 1232–1254.

Camerer, C. F., & Lovallo, D. (1999). Overconfidence and excess entry: An experimental approach. *American Economic Review, 89,* 306–318.

Capen, E. C., Clapp, R. V., & Campbell, W. M. (1971). Competitive bidding in high-risk situations. *Journal of Petroleum Technology, 23*(6), 641–653.

Caplin, A., Dean, M., & Martin, D. (2011). Search and satisficing. *American Economic Review, 101*(7), 2899–2922.

Caplin, A., & Leahy, J. (2001). Psychological expected utility and anticipatory feelings. *Quarterly Journal of Economics, 116,* 55–79.

Carlin, Bruce I. (2009). Strategic price complexity in retail financial markets. *Journal of Financial Economics, 91*(3), 278–287.

Carpenter, J. P., & Seki, E. (2011). Do social preferences increase productivity? Field experimental evidence from fishermen in Toyama Bay. *Economic Inquiry, 49*(2), 612–630.

Carroll, G. D., Choi, J. J., Laibson, D., Madrian, B. C., & Metrick, A. (2009). Optimal defaults and active decisions. *Quarterly Journal of Economics, 124,* 1639–1674.

Casscells, W., Schoenberger, A., & Graboys, T. B. (1978). Interpretation by physicians of clinical laboratory results. *New England Journal of Medicine, 299,* 999–1000.

Centers for Medicare & Medicaid Services (2010, February 4). *Express lane eligibility option* [SHO # 10-003]. https://www.medicaid.gov/federal-policy-guidance/downloads/sho10003.pdf

Chapman, G. B., & Bornstein, B. H. (1996). The more you ask for, the more you get: Anchoring in personal injury verdicts. *Applied Cognitive Psychology, 10,* 519–540.

Charness, G., & Gneezy, U. (2012). Strong evidence for gender differences in risk taking. *Journal of economic behavior and organization, 83*(1), 50–58.

Charness, G., Karni, E., & Levin, D. (2010). On the Conjunction Fallacy in Probability Judgment: New Experimental. *Games and Economic Behavior, 68,* 551–556.

Charness, G., & Levin, D. (2009). The origin of the winner's curse: A laboratory study. *American Economic Journal: Microeconomics, 1*(1), 207–236.

Chen, G., Crossland, C., & Luo, S. (2015). Making the same mistake all over again: CEO overconfidence and corporate resistance to corrective feedback. *Strategic Management Journal, 36*(10), 1513–1535.

Chetty, R., Friedman, J. N., Leth-Petersen, S., Nielsen, T. H., & Olsen, T. (2014). Active v. passive decisions and crowd-out in retirement savings accounts: Evidence from Denmark. *Quarterly Journal of Economics, 129*(3), 1141–1219.

Chetty, R., Looney, A., & Kroft, K. (2009). Salience and taxation: Theory and evidence. *American Economic Review, 99*(4), 1145–1177.

Chiteji, N., & Walker, L. (2009). Strategies to increase the retirement savings of african american households. In W. G. Gale, et al. (Eds.), *Automatic*, (pp. 231–260). R. R. Donnelley.

Chmura, T., Goerg, S. J., & Selten, R. (2012). Learning in experimental 2x2 games. *Games and Economic Behavior, 76*(1), 44–73.

Cho, I. K., & Matsui, A. (2005). Learning aspiration in repeated games. *Journal of Economic Theory, 124*(2), 171–201.

Chung, S. H., & Herrnstein, R. J. (1967). Choice and delay of reinforcement. *Journal of the Experimental Analysis of Behavior, 10*(1), 67–74.

Cialdini, R., Kallgren, C., & Reno, R. (1990). A focus theory of normative conduct: A theoretical refinement and reevaluation of the role of norms in human behavior. *Advances in Experimental Social Psychology, 24*, 201–234.

CLASS Act, 42 U.S.C. §300 (2018).

Clemen, R. T., & Ulu, C. (2008). Interior additivity and subjective probability assessment of continuous variables. *Management Science, 54*(4), 835–851.

Clotfelter, C. T., & P. J. Cook. (1993). The gambler's fallacy in lottery play. *Management Science, 39*, 1521–1525.

Colander, D., & Kupers, R. (2014). *Complexity and the art of public policy: Solving society's problems from the bottom up.* Princeton University Press.

Colman, A. M., Pulford, B. D., Omtzigt, D., & al-Nowaihi, A. (2010). Learning to cooperate without awareness in multiplayer minimal social situations. *Cognitive Psychology, 61*, 201–227.

Conlisk, J. (1996). Why bounded rationality? *Journal of Economic Literature, 34*(2), 669–700.

Conly, Sarah. (2013). *Against autonomy: Justifying coercive paternalism.* Cambridge University Press.

Cooper, A. C., Woo, C. Y., & Dunkelberg, W. C. (1988). Entrepreneurs' perceived chances for success. *Journal of Business Venturing, 3*, 97–108.

Cosmides, L., & Tooby, J. (1996) Are humans good intuitive statisticians after all? Rethinking some conclusions from the literature on judgment under uncertainty. *Cognition, 58*, 1–73.

Crawford, V. P. (2013). Boundedly rational versus optimization-based models of strategic thinking and learning in games. *Journal of Economic Literature, 51*(2), 512–527.

Crawford, V. P. (2021). Efficient mechanisms for level-k bilateral trading. *Games and Economic Behavior, Elsevier, 127*(C), 80–101.

Credit Card Accountability Responsibility and Disclosure Act of 2009, Pub. L. No. 111–24, 123 Stat. 1734.

Croson, R., & Sundali, J. (2005). The gambler's fallacy and the hot hand: Empirical data from casinos. *Journal of Risk and Uncertainty, 30*, 195–209.

Cyert, R. M., & March, J. G. (1963). *A behavioural theory of the firm*. Prentice-Hall.

Czerlinski, J., Goldstein, D. G., & Gigerenzer, G. (1999). How good are simple heuristics? In G. Gigerenzer, P. M. Todd, & the ABC Research Group. *Simple heuristics that make us smart*. Oxford University Press.

Daley, D. J., & Kendall, D. G. (1964). Epidemics and rumors. *Nature, 204*, 1118.

Daley, D. J., & Kendall, D. G. (1965). Stochastic rumors. *IMA Journal of Applied Mathematics, 1*, 42–55.

Dalton, P., Ghosal, S., & Mani, A. (2016). Poverty and aspirations failure. *Economic Journal, 126*, 165–188.

Darai, D., & Grätz, S. (2010). *Golden balls: A prisoner's dilemma experiment* [Working Paper 1006]. University of Zurich.

Datta, S., & Mullainathan, S. (2014). Behavioral design: A new approach to development policy. *Review of Income and Wealth, 60*(1), 7–35.

DeCicca, P., Kenkel, D. S., & Lovenheim, M. F. (2020). *The economics of tobacco regulation: A comprehensive review* [NBER Working Paper No. 26923].

Dekel, E., & Lipman, B. L. (2010). How (not) to do decision theory. *Annual Review of Economics, 2*, 257–282.

DellaVigna, S., & Malmendier, U. (2004). Contract design and self-control: Theory and evidence. *Quarterly Journal of Economics, 119*(2), 353–402.

DellaVigna, S., & Malmendier, U. (2006). Paying not to go to the gym. *American Economic Review, 96*(3), 694–719.

DellaVigna, S., & Paserman, M. D. (2005). Job search and impatience. *Journal of Labor Economics, 23*(3), 437–466.

Delli Gatti, D., Di Guilmi, C., Gaffeo, E., Giulioni, G., Gallegati, M., & Palestrini, A. (2005). A new approach to business fluctuations: Heterogeneous interacting agents, scaling laws and financial fragility. *Journal of Economic Behavior and Organization, 56*(4), 489–512.

De Long, J. B., Shleifer, A., Summers, L., & Waldmann, R. (1990). Noise trader risk in financial markets. *Journal of Political Economy, 98*, 703–738.

DeMiguel, V., Garlappi, L., & Uppal, R. (2009). Optimal versus naive diversification: How inefficient is the 1/N portfolio strategy? *Review of Financial Studies, 22*, 1915–1953.

Denzau, A. T., & North, D. C. (1994). Shared mental models: Ideologies and institutions. *Kyklos, 47*(1), 3–31.

Department of Agriculture. (2011). Direct Certification and Certification of Homeless, Migrant and Runaway Children for Free School Meals. 76 C.F.R. §§22,785, 22,793.

Department of Education. (2010a). Program Integrity Issues. 75 C.F.R. §§66,832.

Department of Education. (2010b). Department of Education Establishes New Student Aid Rules to Protect Borrowers and Taxpayers. https://www.legistorm.com/stormfeed/view_rss/68409/organization/69539/title/department-of-education-establishes-new-student-aid-rules-to-protect-borrowers-and-taxpayers.html

Department of Treasury. (2009, December 4). FinancialStability.gov TARP Transactions Data: Asset Guarantee Program. www.data.gov/raw/1260

Directorate-General Health and Consumer Protection (SANCO). (2010). *Consumer affairs.* http://ec.europa.eu/consumers/docs/1dg-sanco-brochure-consumer-behaviour-final.pdf

Dhami, S. (2016). *The foundations of behavioral economic analysis.* Oxford University Press.

Dhami, S. (2017). *Human ethics and virtues: Rethinking the omo-economicus model* [CESifo Working Paper No. 6836].

Dhami, S. (2019a). *The foundations of behavioral economic analysis: Vol. 1. Behavioral decision theory.* Oxford University Press.

Dhami, S. (2019b). *The foundations of behavioral economic analysis: Vol. 2. Other-regarding preferences.* Oxford University Press.

Dhami, S. (2019c). *The foundations of behavioral economic analysis: Vol. 3. Behavioral time discounting.* Oxford University Press.

Dhami, S. (2019d). *The foundations of behavioral economic analysis: Vol. 4. Behavioral game theory.* Oxford University Press.

Dhami, S. (2020a). *The foundations of behavioral economic analysis: Vol. 5. Bounded rationality.* Oxford University Press.

Dhami, S. (2020b). *The foundations of behavioral economic analysis: Vol. 6. Behavioral models of learning.* Oxford University Press.

Dhami, S. (2020c). *The foundations of behavioral economic analysis: Vol. 7. Further topics in behavioral economics.* Oxford University Press.

Dhami, S., & al-Nowaihi, A. (2007). Why do people pay taxes? Expected utility versus prospect theory. *Journal of Economic Behaviour and Organization, 64*, 171–192.

Dhami, S., & al-Nowaihi, A. (2010a). Optimal income taxation in the presence of tax evasion: Expected utility versus prospect theory. *Journal of Economic Behavior and Organization, 75*, 313–337.

Dhami, S., & al-Nowaihi, A. (2010b). *A proposal to combine "prospect theory" and "cumulative prospect theory"* [University of Leicester Discussion Papers in Economics 10/11].

Dhami, S., & al-Nowaihi, A. (2013). An extension of the Becker proposition to non-expected utility theory. *Mathematical Social Sciences, 65*(1), 10–20.

Dhami, S., & al-Nowahi, A. (2021). Behavioral economics and rationality. In Markus Knauff & Wolfgang Spohn (Eds.), *Handbook of rationality*. MIT Press https://mitpress.mit.edu/books/handbook-rationality

Dhami, S., al-Nowaihi, A., & Sunstein, C. (2018a). Heuristics and public policy: Decision making under bounded rationality [Special issue]. *Studies in Microeconomics, 7*(1), 7–58.

Dhami, S., Arshad, J., & al-Nowaihi, A. (2020d, June). *Psychological and social motivations in microfinance contracts: Theory and evidence* [CESifo Working Paper No. 7773]. SSRN: https://ssrn.com/abstract=3432821

Dhami, S., & Beinhocker, E. (2019). *The behavioral foundations of new economic thinking*. SSRN: https://ssrn.com/abstract=3454822 or http://dx.doi.org/10.2139/ssrn.3454822

Dhami, S., & Hajimoladarvish, N. (2020). *Mental accounting, loss aversion, and tax evasion: Theory and evidence* [CESifo Working Paper No. 8606]. SSRN: https://ssrn.com/abstract=3710348

Dhami, S., Wei, M., & al-Nowaihi, A. (2019). Public goods games and psychological utility: Theory and evidence. Special issue on Psychological Game Theory in *Journal of Economic Behavior and Organization, 167*(C), 361–390.

Dimmock, S. G., Kouwenberg, R., Mitchell, O. S., & Peijnenburg, K. (2016). Ambiguity aversion and household portfolio choice puzzles: Empirical evidence. *Journal of Financial Economics, 119*, 559–577.

Dimmock, S. G., Kouwenberg, R., & Wakker, P. P. (2016). Ambiguity attitudes in a large representative sample. *Management Science, 62*, 1363–1380.

Dinner, I., Johnson, E. J., Goldstein, D. G., & Liu, K. (2011). Partitioning default effects: Why people choose not to choose. *Journal of Experimental Psychology: Applied, 17*(4), 332.

Dodd-Frank Act, 12 U.S.C. §5511 (2010).

Dohmen, T., Falk, A., Huffman, D., & Sunde, U. (2006). *Seemingly irrelevant events affect economic perceptions and expectations: The FIFA world cup 2006 as a natural experiment* [IZA Discussion Paper No. 2275]. SSRN: https://ssrn.com/abstract=928830

Dosi, G., Fagiolo, G., Napoletano, M., Roventini, A., & Treibich, T. (2015). Fiscal and monetary policies in complex evolving economies. *Journal of Economic Dynamics and Control, 52*, 166–189.

Downs, J. S., Loewenstein, G., & Wisdom, J. (2009). Strategies for promoting healthier food choices. *American Economic Review, 99*(2), 159–164.

Drexler, A., Fischer, G., & Schoar, A. (2014). Keeping it simple: Financial literacy and rules of thumb. *American Economic Journal: Applied Economics, 6*(2), 1–31.

Duesenberry, J. S. (1949). *Income, saving and the theory of consumption behavior*. Harvard University Press.

Duflo, E., Kremer, M., & Robinson, J. (2011). Nudging farmers to use fertilizer: Theory and experimental evidence from Kenya. *American Economic Review*, 101(6), 2350–2390.

Dunning, D., Johnson, K., Ehrlinger, J., & Kruger, J. (2003). Why people fail to recognize their own competence. *Current Directions in Psychological Science*, 12(3), 83–87.

Dyer, D., Kagel, J. H., & Levin, D. (1989). A comparison of naive and experienced bidders in common value offer auctions: A laboratory analysis. *Economic Journal*, 99(394), 108–115.

Eddy, D. M. (1982). *Probabilistic reasoning in clinical medicine: Problems and opportunities*. In D. Kahneman, P. Slovic, & A. Tversky (Eds.), Judgment Under Uncertainty: Heuristics and Biases, pp. 249–267. Cambridge University Press.

Edwards, W. (1954). The theory of decision making. *Psychological Bulletin*, 51(4), 380–417.

Edwards, W. (1962). Subjective probabilities inferred from decisions. *Psychological Review*, 69(2), 109–135.

Edwards, W. (1968). Conservatism in human information processing. In B. Kleinmutz (Ed.), *Formal representation of human judgment*, 359–369. Wiley.

Edwards, W., & Tversky, A. (1967). *Decision making: Selected readings*. Penguin.

Egebark, J., & Ekstrom, M. (2016). Can indifference make the world greener? *Journal of Environmental Economics and Management*, 76, 1–13.

Ehrlinger, J., Johnson, K., Banner, M., Dunning, D., & Kruger, J. (2008). Why the unskilled are unaware: Further explorations of (absent) self-insight among the incompetent. *Organizational Behavior and Human Decision Processes*, 105(1), 98–121.

Eisenman, R. (1993). Belief that drug usage in the United States is increasing when it is really decreasing: An example of the availability heuristic. *Bulletin of the Psychonomic Society*, 31, 249–252.

Ellingsen, T., Johannesson, M., Tjøtta, S., & Torsvik, G. (2010). Testing guilt aversion. *Games and Economic Behavior*, 68(1), 95–107.

Ellison, G. (1993). Learning, local interaction and coordination. *Econometrica*, 61, 1047–1071.

Ellison, G., & Ellison, S. F. (2009). Search, obfuscation, and price elasticities on the internet. *Econometrica*, 77(2), 427–452.

Elster, J. (1982). The case for methodological individualism. *Theory and Society*, 11(4), 453–482.

Elster, Jon. (1983). *Sour grapes: Studies in the subversion of rationality*. Cambridge University Press.

Elster, J. (1989). Social norms and economic theory. *Journal of Economic Perspectives*, 3(4), 99–117.

Elster, J. (1999). *Alchemies of the mind: Rationality and the emotions*. Cambridge University Press.

Elster, J. (2011). Norms. In P. Bearman & P. Hedström (Eds.), *The oxford handbook of analytical sociology* (pp. 195–217). Oxford University Press.

Engelmann, D., & Fischbacher, U. (2009). Indirect reciprocity and strategic reputation building in an experimental helping game. *Games and Economic Behavior*, 67(2), 399–407.

Englich, B., & Mussweiler, T. (2001). Sentencing under uncertainty: Anchoring effects in the courtroom. *Journal of Applied Social Psychology*, 31, 1535–1551.

Englich, B., Mussweiler, T., & Strack, F. (2006). Playing dice with criminal sentences: The influence of irrelevant anchors on experts' judicial decision making. *Personality and Social Psychology Bulletin*, 32(2), 188–200.

Engström, P., Nordblom, K., Ohlsson, H., & Persson, A. (2015). Tax compliance and loss aversion. *American Economic Journal: Economic Policy*, 7(4), 132–164.

Environmental Protection Agency. (2009). Fuel Economy Labeling of Motor Vehicles: Revisions to Improve Calculation of Fuel Economy Estimates. 74 C.F.R. §§61,537, 61,542, 61,550–53.

Epstein, J. M., & Axtell, R. (1996). Growing artificial societies: Social science from the bottom up. Brookings Institution Press and MIT Press.

Ericson, K. M. M., White, J. M., Laibson, D., & Cohen, J. D. (2015). Money earlier or later? Simple heuristics explain intertemporal choices better than delay discounting does. *Psychological Science*, 26(6), 826–833.

Ertan, A., Page, T., & Putterman, L. (2009). Who to punish? Individual decisions and majority rule in mitigating the free rider problem. *European Economic Review*, 53(5), 495–511.

European Commission. (2012). *Science for Environment Policy: Future Brief: Green Behaviour*. https://ec.europa.eu/environment/integration/research/newsalert/pdf/FB4_en.pdf

Evans, J., Handley, S. J., Perham, N. Over, D. E., & Thompson, V. A. (2000). Frequency versus probability formats in statistical word problems. *Cognition*, 77, 197–213.

Exec. Order No. 13,563 (*Improving regulation and regulatory review*), 76 C.F.R. §14 (2011).

Exec. Order Np. 13,707 (*Using behavioral science insights to better serve the american people*), 80 C.F.R. §181 (2015).

Eyster, E., & Rabin, M. (2005). Cursed equilibrium. *Econometrica*, 73(5), 1623–1672.

Fafchamps, M., Kebede, B., & Zizzo, D. J. (2014). *Keep up with the winners: Experimental evidence on risk taking, asset integration, and peer effects* [Discussion Paper 14-03]. University of East Anglia, CBESS.

Fang, H. M., & Silverman, D. (2009). Time-inconsistency and welfare program participation: Evidence from the NLSY. *International Economic Review*, 50(4), 104377.

Farhi, E., & Gabaix, X. (2020). Optimal taxation with behavioral agents. *American Economic Review*, 110(1), 298–336.

Farmer, J. D., Mealy, P., & Beinhocker, E. D. (2019). *A new generation of models for public policy* [mimeo INET Oxford].

Fehr, E., & Fischbacher, U. (2004). Third-party punishment and social norms. *Evolution and Human Behavior, 25*(2), 63–87.

Fehr, E., Fischbacher, U., & Gächter, S. (2002). Strong reciprocity, human cooperation, and the enforcement of social norms. *Human Nature, 13*(1), 1–25.

Fehr, E., & Gächter, S. (2000). Cooperation and punishment in public goods experiments. *American Economic Review, 90*(4), 980–994.

Fehr, E., & Gächter, S. (2002). Altruistic punishment in humans. *Nature, 415*, 137–140.

Fehr, E., & Leibbrandt, A. (2011). A field study on cooperativeness and impatience in the tragedy of the commons. *Journal of Public Economics, 95*(9–10), 1144–1155.

Fehr, E., & Schmidt, K. M. (1999). A theory of fairness, competition and cooperation. *Quarterly Journal of Economics, 114*(3), 817–868.

Fehr, E., & Schmidt, K. (2006). The economics of fairness, reciprocity and altruism: Experimental evidence and new theories. In S. C. Kolm & J. M. Ythier, (Eds.), *Handbook of the economics of giving, altruism and reciprocity* pp. 615–691 Elsevier.

Fehr, E., & Schurtenberger, I. (2018a). Normative foundations of human cooperation. *Nature Human Behavior, 2*, 458–468.

Fehr, E., & Schurtenberger, I. (2018b). *The dynamics of norm formation and norm decay* [Working Paper Department of Economics]. University of Zurich.

Feldman, Fred. 2010. *What is this thing called happiness?* Oxford University Press.

Ferraro, P. J., & Price, M. K. (2013). Using nonpecuniary strategies to influence behavior: Evidence from a large-scale field experiment. *Review of Economics and Statistics, 95*(1), 64–73.

Fershtman, C., & Gneezy, U. (2001). Discrimination in a segmented society: An experimental approach. *Quarterly Journal of Economics, 116*(1), 351–377.

Feynman, R. (1965). *The character of physical law.* MIT Press.

Figlewski, S. (1979). Subjective information and market efficiency in a betting model. *Journal of Political Economy, 87*, 75–88.

Finkelstein, A. (2009). E-Z tax: Tax salience and tax rates. *Quarterly Journal of Economics, 124*(3), 969–1010.

Finkelstein, E. A., Ang, F. J. L., & Doble, B. (2020). Randomized trial evaluating the effectiveness of within versus across-category front-of-package lower-calorie labelling on food demand. *BMC Public Health, 20*(1), 1–10.

Fischer, David Hackett. (1989). *Albion's Seed: Four British Folkways in America.* Oxford University Press.

Fischhoff, B. (1975). Hindsight biased foresight: The effect of outcome knowledge on judgment under uncertainty. *Journal of Experimental Psychology: Human Perception and Performance, 1*, 288–299.

Fishburn, P. C. (1978). On Handa's "New theory of cardinal utility" and the maximization of expected return. *Journal of Political Economy, 86*(2), 321–324.

Fishburn, P. C., & Rubinstein, A. (1982). Time preference. *International Economic Review, 23*(3), 677–694.

Food and Drug Administration. (2014). *Regulatory impact analysis for final rules on "food labeling: Revision of the nutrition and supplement facts labels."* https://www.fda.gov/media/98712/download

Foot, Philippa. (2001). *Natural goodness.* Clarendon Press.

Forsythe, R., Nelson, F., Neumann, G. R., & Wright, J. (1992). Anatomy of an experimental political stock market. *American Economic Review, 82*(5), 1142–1161.

Frederick, S., Loewenstein, G., & O'Donoghue, T. (2002). Time discounting and time preferences: A critical review. *Journal of Economic Literature, 40*(2), 351–401.

Friedman, M. (1953). *The methodology of positive economics.* University of Chicago Press.

Friedman, M. (1968). The role of monetary policy: Presidential address delivered at the 80th Annual Meeting of the American Economic Association. *American Economic Review, 58*(1), 1–15.

Friedman, M., & Schwartz, A. J. (1963). *A monetary history of the united states, 1867–1960.* Princeton University Press.

Fudenberg, D., & Tirole J. (1991). *Game theory.* MIT Press. Gabaix, X. (2014). A sparsity-based model of bounded rationality. *Quarterly Journal of Economics, 129*(4), 1661–1710.

Gabaix, X. (2019). *Behavioral inattention* [NBER Working Paper No. 24096].

Gabaix, X. (2020). A behavioral new Keynesian model. *American Economic Review, 110*(8), 2271–2327.

Gabaix, X., & Laibson, D. (2006). Shrouded attributes, consumer myopia, and information suppression in competitive markets. *Quarterly Journal of Economics, 121*(2), 505–540.

Gächter, S., & Falk, A. (2002). Reputation and reciprocity: Consequences for the labour relation. *Scandinavian Journal of Economics, 104*(1), 1–26.

Gächter, S., & Thöni, C. (2005). Social learning and voluntary cooperation among like-minded people. *Journal of the European Economic Association, 3*(2–3), 303–314.

Galasso, A., & Simcoe, T. S. (2011). CEO overconfidence and innovation. *Management Science, 57*(8), 1469–1484.

Gale, W., Iwry, J., & Walters, S. (2009). Retirement savings for middle and lower-income households: The pension protection act of 2006 and the unfinished agenda. In W. G. Gale et al. (Eds.), *Automatic* (pp. 11–27) R. R. Donnelley.

Gamp, T., & Krähmer, D. (2019). *Deception and competition in search markets* [Mimeo]. Humboldt-Universität zu Berlin.

Gayer, T., & Viscusi, W. Kip. (2013). Overriding consumer preferences with energy regulations. *Journal of Regulatory Economics, 43*(3), 248–264.

Geanakoplos, J., Pearce, D., & Stacchetti, E. (1989). Psychological games and sequential rationality. *Games and Economic Behavior, 1*(1), 60–79.

Genicot, G., & Ray, D. (2017). Aspirations and inequity. *Econometrica, 85*(2), 489–519.

Gennaioli, N., & Shleifer, A. (2010). What comes to mind. *Quarterly Journal of Economics, 125*(4), 1399–1433.

Gigerenzer, G. (1991). How to make cognitive illusions disappear: Beyond "heuristics and biases." In W. Stroebe & M. Hewstone (Eds.), *European review of social psychology*, (Vol. 2, pp. 83–115). Wiley.

Gigerenzer, G. (1993). The bounded rationality of probabilistic mental models. In K. I. Manktelow & D. E. Over (Eds.), *Rationality: Psychological and philosophical perspectives* (pp. 284–313). Routledge.

Gigerenzer, G. (1996a). On narrow norms and vague heuristics: A reply to Kahneman and Tversky. *Psychological Review, 103*, 592–596.

Gigerenzer, G. (1996b). The psychology of good judgment: Frequency formats and simple algorithms. *Medical Decision Making, 16*, 273–280.

Gigerenzer, G. (2008). *Rationality for mortals: How people cope with uncertainty*. Oxford University Press.

Gigerenzer, G. (2014). *Risk savvy: How to make good decisions*. Viking.

Gigerenzer, G. (2015). On the supposed evidence for libertarian paternalism. *Review of Philosophy and Psychology, 6*, 361–383.

Gigerenzer, G. (2016). Towards a rational theory of heuristics. In R. Frantz & L. Marsh (Eds.), *Minds, models, and milieux: Commemorating the centennial of the birth of Herbert Simon* (pp. 34–59). Palgrave Macmillan.

Gigerenzer, G. (2018). The bias bias in behavioral economics. *Review of Behavioral Economics, 5*, 303–336.

Gigerenzer, G., & Brighton, H. (2009). Homo heuristicus: Why biased minds make better inferences. *Topics in Cognitive Science, 1*, 107–143.

Gigerenzer, G., & Brighton, H. (2011). Homo heuristicus: Why biased minds make better inferences. In G. Gigerenzer, R. Hertwig, & T. Pachur (Eds.), *Heuristics: The foundations of adaptive behavior* (pp. 2–27). Oxford University Press. (Reprinted from "Homo heuristicus: Why biased minds make better inferences," 2009, *Topics in Cognitive Science*, 1, 107–143.)

Gigerenzer, G., & Gaissmaier, W. (2011). Heuristic decision making. *Annual Review of Psychology, 62*, 451–482.

Gigerenzer, G., & Goldstein, D. G. (1996). Reasoning the fast and frugal way: Models of bounded rationality. *Psychological Review, 103*, 650–669.

Gigerenzer, G., & Hoffrage, U. (1995). How to improve Bayesian reasoning without instruction: Frequency formats. *Psychological Review, 102*, 684–704.

Gigerenzer, G., Hell, W., & Blank, H. (1988). Presentation and content: The use of base rates as a continuous variable. *Journal of Experimental Psychology: Human Perception and Performance, 14*, 513–525.

Gigerenzer, G., Hertwig, R., & Pachur, T. (Eds.) (2011). *Heuristics: The foundations of adaptive behavior*. Oxford University Press.

Gigerenzer, G., & Selten, R. (Eds.). (2001a). *Bounded rationality: The adaptive toolbox*. MIT Press.

Gigerenzer, G., & Selten, R. (2001b). Rethinking rationality. In G. Gigerenzer & R. Selten (Eds.), *Bounded rationality: The adaptive toolbox,* pp. 1–12. MIT Press.

Gigerenzer, G., Todd, P. M., & the ABC Group (Eds.) (1999). *Simple heuristics that make us smart*. Oxford University Press.

Gilbert, Daniel, & Wilson, Timothy. (2000). Miswanting: Some problems in the forecasting of future affective states. In Joseph P. Forgas (Ed.), *Feeling and thinking: The role of affect in social cognition*. Cambridge University Press.

Gilbert, Daniel, Wilson, Timothy D., Pinel, Elizabeth C., & Blumberg, Stephen J. (1998). Immune neglect: A source of durability bias in affective forecasting. *Journal of Personality and Social Psychology, 75*(3), 617–638.

Gilboa, I., Postlewaite, A., Samuelson, L., & Schmeidler, D. (2014). Economic models as analogies. *Economic Journal, 124*, F513–F533.

Gillingham, Kenneth, Houde, Sebastien, & van Benthem, Arthur A. (2019). *Consumer myopia in vehicle purchases* [NBER Working Paper No. 25845]. https://www.nber.org/papers/w25845

Gilovich, T., Griffin, D., & Kahneman, D. (2002). *Heuristics and biases: The psychology of intuitive judgement*. Cambridge University Press.

Gilovich, T., Vallone, R., & Tversky, A. (1985). The hot hand in basketball: On the misperception of random sequences. *Cognitive Psychology, 17*, 295–314.

Giné, X., Cuellar, C. M., & Mazer, R. K. (2014). Financial dis-information: Evidence from an audit study in Mexico [Policy Research Working Paper 6902]. World Bank.

Gintis, H. (2009). *The bounds of reason: Game theory and the unification of the behavioral sciences*. Princeton University Press.

Gintis, H. (2017). *Individuality and entanglement: The moral and material bases of social life*. Princeton University Press.

Girotto, V., & Gonzalez, M. (2001). Solving probabilistic and statistical problems: A matter of information structure and question form. *Cognition, 78*, 247–276.

Glaser, M., Langer, T., & Weber, M. (2007). On the trend recognition and forecasting ability of professional traders. *Decision Analysis, 4*, 176–193.

Glaser, M., Nöth, M., & Weber, M. (2004). Behavioral finance. In D. J. Koehler & N. Harvey (Eds.), *Blackwell handbook of judgment and decision making* (pp. 527–546). Blackwell.

Glaser, M., & Weber, M. (2007). Overconfidence and trading volume. *Geneva Risk and Insurance Revue, 32*, 1–36.

Gneezy, U., & Potters, J. (1997). An experiment on risk taking and evaluation periods. *Quarterly Journal of Economics, 112*(2), 631–645.

Goel, A. M., & Thakor, A. V. (2008). Overconfidence leadership selection and corporate governance. *Journal of Finance, 63*, 2737–2784.

Goetzmann, William N., Kim, Dasol, & Shiller, Robert J. (2016, March 19). Crash beliefs from investor surveys. SSRN: https://ssrn.com/abstract=2750638 or http://dx.doi.org/10.2139/ssrn.2750638

Goldin, Jacob. (2015). Which way to nudge? Uncovering preferences in the behavioral age. *Yale Law Journal, 125*(1), 226–270.

Goldin, Jacob. (2017). Libertarian quasi-paternalism. *Missouri Law Review, 82*, 669–682.

Goldin, J., & Homonoff, T. (2013). Smoke gets in your eyes: Cigarette tax salience and regressivity. *American Economic Journal: Economic Policy, 5*(1), 302–336.

Gollaher, D. L. (2000). *Circumcision: A history of the world's most controversial surgery.* Basic Books.

Gorodnichenko, Y., & Roland, G. (2021). Culture, institutions and democratization. *Public Choice, 187*, 165–195.

Green, B. S., & Zwiebel, J. (2013). *The hot hand fallacy: Cognitive mistakes or equilibrium adjustments? Evidence from baseball* [mimeo]. Stanford University.

Greenstone, Michael. (2013). Developing a social cost of carbon for US regulatory analysis. *Review of Environmental Economics and Policy, 7*(1), 23–46.

Greif, A. (1994). Cultural beliefs and the organization of society: A historical and theoretical reflection on collectivist and individualist societies. *Journal of Political Economy, 102*(5), 912–950.

Greif, A., & Tabellini, G. (2012). *The clan and the city: Sustaining cooperation in china and europe* [Innocenzo Gasparini Institute for Economic Research Working Paper 445].

Grether, D. M. (1980). Bayes' rule as a descriptive model: The representativeness heuristic. *Quarterly Journal of Economics, 95*(3), 537–557.

Grether, D. M. (1992). Testing Bayes' rule and the representativeness heuristic: Some experimental evidence. *Journal of Economic Behavior and Organization 17*, 31–57.

Grether, D. M., & Plott, C. (1979). Economic theory of choice and the preference reversal phenomenon. *American Economic Review, 69*(4), 623–638.

Griffin, D., & Tversky, A. (1992). The weighing of evidence and the determinants of confidence. *Cognitive Psychology, 24*(3), 411–435.

Griffiths, T. L., & Tenenbaum, J. B. (2006). Optimal predictions in everyday cognition. *Psychological Science, 17*(9), 767–773.

Grubb, Michael D. (2009). Selling to overconfident consumers. *American Economic Review, 99*(5), 1770–1805.

Grubb, Michael D. (2015). Consumer inattention and bill-shock regulation. *Review of Economic Studies, 82*(1), 219–257.

Gruber, J., & Hungerman, D. M. (2008). The church versus the mall: What happens when religion faces increased secular competition? *Quarterly Journal of Economics, 123*(2), 831–862.

Gruber, J. H., & Köszegi, B. (2001). Is addiction rational? Theory and evidence. *Quarterly Journal of Economics, 116*(4), 1261–1303.

Gruber, J. H., & Köszegi, B. (2004). Tax incidence when individuals are time-inconsistent: The case of cigarette excise taxes. *Journal of Public Economics, 88*(9–10), 1959–1987.

Gruber, J. H., & Mullainathan, S. (2005). Do cigarette taxes make smokers happier? *B. E. Journals: Advances in Economic Analysis and Policy, 5*(1), 145.

Guilbault, R. L., Bryant, F. B., Brockway, J. H., & Posavac, E. J. (2004). A meta-analysis of research on hindsight bias. *Basic and Applied Social Psychology, 26*, 103–117.

Guiso, L., Sapienza, P., & Zingales, L. (2004). The role of social capital in financial development. *American Economic Review, 94*(3), 526–556.

Guiso, L., Sapienza, P., & Zingales, L. (2008a). Social capital as good culture. *Journal of the European Economic Association, 6*(2–3), 295–320.

Guiso, L., Sapienza, P., & Zingales, L. (2008b). Trusting the stock market. *Journal of Finance, 63*(6), 2557–2600.

Guryan, J., & Kearney, M. S. (2008). Gambling at lucky stores: Empirical evidence from state lottery sales. *American Economic Review, 98*(1), 458–473.

Guyon, N., & Huillery, E. (2014). *The aspiration-poverty trap: Why do students from low social background limit their ambition? Evidence from France* [mimeo].

Haigh, M. S., & List, J. A. (2005). Do professional traders exhibit myopic loss aversion? An experimental analysis. *Journal of Finance, 60*(1), 523–534.

Haldane, A. G. (2016). The dappled world [mimeo] Bank of England. https://www.bis.org/review/r161115a.pdf

Hall, B. J., & Murphy, K. J. (2000). Optimal exercise prices for executive stock options. *American Economic Review, 90*, 209–214.

Hall, B. J., & Murphy, K. J. (2002). Stock options for undiversified executives. *Journal of Accounting and Economics, 33*, 3–42.

Halpern, D. (2015). *Inside the nudge unit: How small changes can make a big difference.* W. H. Allen.

Hammerstein, P., & Selten, R. (1994). Game theory and evolutionary biology. In R. Aumann, & S. Hart (Eds.), *Handbook of game theory* (Vol. 2, pp. 929–993). North-Holland.

Handa, J. (1977). Risk, probability, and a new theory of cardinal utility. *Journal of Political Economy, 85*(1), 97–122.

Hansson, P., Rönnlund, M., Juslin, P., & Nilsson, L. G. (2008). Adult age differences in the realism of confidence judgments: Overconfidence, format dependence, and cognitive predictors. *Psychology and Aging, 23*, 531–544.

Härdle, W., & Kirman, A. (1995). Nonclassical demand: A model-free examination of price quantity relations in the Marseille fish market. *Journal of Econometrics, 67*(1), 227–257.

Harrison, G. W., & List, J. A. (2008). Naturally occurring markets and exogenous laboratory experiments: A case study of the winner's curse. *Economic Journal, 118*, 822–843.

Harstad, R. M., & Selten, R. (2013). Bounded-rationality models: Tasks to become intellectually competitive. *Journal of Economic Literature, 51*(2), 496–511.

Haushofer, J., & Fehr, E. (2014). On the psychology of poverty. *Science, 344*(6186), 862–867.

Hayek, Friedrich. (2013). The market and other orders. In Bruce Caldwell (Ed.), *The collected works of F. A. hayek*. University of Chicago Press.

Healthy, Hunger-Free Kids Act of 2012, Pub. L. No. 111–296, 124 Stat. 3183.

Heath, C., & Heath, D. (2010). *Switch: How to change things when change is hard*. Broadway.

Heath, C., & Tversky, A. (1991). Preference and belief: Ambiguity and competence in choice under uncertainty. *Journal of Risk and Uncertainty, 4*, 5–28.

Heidhues, P., & Köszegi, B. (2017). Naivete-based discrimination. *Quarterly Journal of Economics, 132*(2), 1019–1054.

Heidhues, P., & Köszegi, B. (2018). Behavioral industrial organization. In D. Bernheim, S. DellaVigna, & D. Laibson (Eds.), *Handbook of behavioral economics* (Vol. 1 pp. 517–612). Elsevier.

Heidhues, P., Köszegi, B., & Murooka, T. (2016). Exploitative innovation. *American Economic Journal: Microeconomics, 8*(1), 1–23.

Helson, H. (1964). *Adaptation level theory: An experimental and systematic approach to behavior*. Harper and Row.

Henrich, J. (2017). *The secret of our success: How culture is driving human evolution, domesticating our species, and making us smarter*. Princeton University Press.

Henrich, J., Boyd, R., Bowles, S., Camerer, C., Fehr, E., Gintis, H., & McElreath, R. (2001). Cooperation, reciprocity and punishment in fifteen small-scale societies. *American Economic Review, 91*, 73–78.

Herrmann, B., Thöni, C., & Gächter, S. (2008). Antisocial punishment across societies. *Science, 319*(5868) 1362–1367.

Hertwig, R. (2017). When to consider boosting: Some rules for policy-makers. *1*, 143–161.

Hertwig, R., & Gigerenzer, G. (1999). The conjunction fallacy revisited: How intelligent inferences look like reasoning errors. *Journal of Behavioral Decision Making, 12*, 275–305.

Hirshleifer, D., Low, A., & Teoh, S. H. (2012). Are overconfident CEOs better innovators? *Journal of Finance, 67*(4), 1457–1498.

Hofbauer, J., & Sigmund, K. (1998). *Evolutionary games and population dynamics*. Cambridge University Press.

Hoffrage, U., Hertwig, R., & Gigerenzer, G. (2000). Hindsight-bias: A byproduct of knowledge updating? *Journal of Experimental Psychology: Learning Memory and Cognition, 26*, 566–581.

Hogarth, R. M., & Reder, M .W. eds. (1986). The behavioral foundations of economic theory: Proceedings of a conference october 13–15, 1985. *Journal of Business, 59*(4), S181–S505.

Hogg, R. V., McKean, J. W., & Craig, A. T. (2005). *Introduction to mathematical statistics* (6th ed.). Prentice Hall.

Hommes, C. H. (2013). *Behavioral rationality and heterogeneous expectations in complex economic systems*. Cambridge University Press.

Hommes, C. H. (2018). Carl's nonlinear cobweb. *Journal of Economic Dynamics and Control, 91*, 7–20.

Hommes, C., & LeBaron, B. (2018). *Handbook of computational economics: Vol. 4, heterogeneous agent modelling*. North-Holland.

Hong, H., & Kubik, J. D. (2003). Analyzing the analysts: Career concerns and biased earnings forecasts. *Journal of Finance, 58*, 313–352.

Hong, H., & Stein, J. (1999). A unified theory of underreaction, momentum trading, and overreaction in asset markets. *Journal of Finance, 54*, 2143–2184.

Hong, H., & Stein, J. (2007). Disagreement and the stock market. *Journal of Economic Perspectives, 21*, 109–128.

Hotz, V. J., & Scholz, J. K. (2003). The earned income tax credit. In R. Moffitt (Ed.), *Means-tested transfer programs in the United States*, (pp. 141–198). University of Chicago Press.

Howarth, R. B., Haddad, B. M., & Paton, B. (2000). The economics of energy efficiency: Insights from voluntary participation programs. *Energy Policy, 28*, 477–486.

Hribar, P., & Yang, H. (2015). CEO overconfidence and management forecasting. *Contemporary Accounting Research, 33*(1), 204–227.

Huck, S., Szech, N., & Wenner, L. M. (2018). *More effort with less pay: On information avoidance, belief design and performance* [mimeo]. University College London.

Huffman, D., & Barenstein, M. (2004). *A monthly struggle for self-control? Hyperbolic discounting, mental accounting, and the fall in expenditure between paydays* [IZA Discussion Paper 1430].

Hurka, Thomas. (1996). *Perfectionism*. Oxford University Press.

Internal Revenue Service. (2009, September). *Retirement and savings initiatives: Helping Americans save for the future*. Retrieved from http://www.irs.gov/pub/irs-tege/rne_se0909.pdf

iNudgeYou. (n.d.). *Resources*. https://www.inudgeyou.com/en/resources

Iyengar, S., & Kamenica, E. (2010). Choice proliferation, simplicity seeking, and asset allocation. *Journal of Public Economics, 94*, 530–539.

Iyengar, S. S., & Lepper, M. R. (2000). When choice is demotivating: Can one desire too much of a good thing? *Journal of Personality and Social Psychology, 79*(6), 995–1006.

Jachimowicz, Jon, Duncan, Shannon, Weber, Elke U., & Johnson, Eric J. (2019). Why and when defaults influence decisions: A meta-analysis of default effects. *Behavioral Public Policy, 3*(2), 159–186.

Jehiel, P. (2005). Analogy-based expectation equilibrium. *Journal of Economic Theory, 123*(2), 81–104.

Jensen, R. (2012). Do labor market opportunities affect young women's work and family decisions? Experimental evidence from India. *Quarterly Journal of Economics, 127*(2), 753–792.

Jensen, R., & Oster, E. (2009). The power of TV: Cable television and women's status in India. *Quarterly Journal of Economics, 124*(3), 1057–1094.

Jevons, W. (1905). *Essays on economics*. Macmillan.

Johnson, D. D. P., McDermott, R., Barrett, E. S., Cowden, J., et al. (2006). Overconfidence in wargames: Experimental evidence on expectations, aggression, gender and testosterone. *Proceedings of the Royal Society B, 273*, 2513–2520.

Johnson, E., & Goldstein, D. (2013). Decisions by default. In E. Shafir (Ed.), *The behavioral foundations of public policy* (pp. 417–427). Princeton University Press.

Kagel, J. H. (2015). Laboratory experiments: The lab in relationship to field experiments, field data, and economic theory. In G. R. Fréchette & A. Schotter (Eds.), *Handbook of experimental economic methodology* (pp. 339–359). Oxford University Press.

Kagel, J. H., & Levin, D. (1986). The winner's curse and public information in common value auctions. *American Economic Review, 76*(5), 894–920.

Kagel, J. H., & Levin, D. (2001). Behavior in multi-unit demand auctions: Experiments with uniform price and dynamic Vickery auctions. *Econometrica, 69*(2), 413–454.

Kagel, J. H., Levin, D., & Harstad, R. M. (1995). Comparative static effects of number of bidders and public information in second-price common value auctions. *International Journal of Game Theory, 24*(3), 293–319.

Kagel, J. H., & Richard, J-F. (2001). Super-experienced bidders in first-price common value auctions: Rules of thumb, Nash equilibrium bidding and the winner's curse. *Review of Economics and Statistics, 83*(3), 408–419.

Kahan, D. M. (2013). Ideology, motivated reasoning, and cognitive reflection. *Judgment and Decision Making, 8*(4), 407–424.

Kahan, D. M., Peters, E., Dawson, E. C., & Slovic, P. (2017). Motivated numeracy and enlightened self-government. *Behavioral Public Policy, 1*(1), 54–86.

Kahneman, D. (1981). Who shall be the arbiter of our intuitions? *Behavioral and Brain Sciences, 4*, 339–340.

Kahneman, D. (2000). A psychological point of view: Violations of rational rules as a diagnostic of mental processes (commentary on Stanovich and West). *Behavioral and Brain Sciences, 23*, 681–683.

Kahneman, D. (2003). Maps of bounded rationality: Psychology of behavioral economics. *American Economic Review, 93*, 1449–1475.

Kahneman, D. (2011). *Thinking fast and slow*. Farrar, Strauss, Giroux.

Kahneman, D., Sibony, O., & Sunstein, C. R. (2021). *Noise: A flaw in human judgment*. Harper Collins Publishers.

Kahneman, D., Slovic, P., & Tversky, A. (Eds.). (1982). *Judgment under uncertainty: Heuristics and biases*. Cambridge University Press.

Kahneman, D., & Tversky, A. (1972a). On prediction and judgment. *Oregon Research Institute Bulletin, 12*(4).

Kahneman, D., & Tversky, A. (1972b). Subjective probability: A judgment of representativeness. *Cognitive Psychology, 3*(3), 430–454.

Kahneman, D., & Tversky, A. (1979). Prospect theory: An analysis of decision under risk. *Econometrica, 47*(2), 263–291.

Kahneman, D., & Tversky, A. (Eds.) (1982). *Judgement under uncertainty: Heuristics and biases*. Cambridge University Press.

Kahneman, D., & Tversky, A. (1984). Choices, values, and frames. *American Psychologist 39*(4), 341–350.

Kahneman, D., & Tversky, A. (1996). On the reality of cognitive illusions: A reply to Gigerenzer's critique. *Psychological Review, 103*, 582–591.

Kahneman, D., & Tversky, A. (2000). *Choices, values and frames*. Cambridge University Press.

Kahneman, D., Wakker, P. P., & Sarin, R. (1997). Back to Bentham? Explorations of experienced utility. *Quarterly Journal of Economics, 112*(2), 375–405.

Kamenica, E., Mullainathan, S., & Thaler, R. (2011). Helping consumers know themselves. *American Economic Review, 101*(3), 417–422.

Kamin, K. A., & Rachlinski, J. J. (1995). Ex post-ex ante: Determining liability in hindsight. *Law and Human Behavior, 19*, 89–104.

Kandori, M., Mailath, G. J., & Rob, R. (1993). Learning, mutation, and long-run equilibria in games. *Econometrica, 61*, 29–56.

Karandikar, R., Mookherjee, D., Ray, D., & Vega-Redondo, F, (1998). Evolving aspirations and cooperation. *Journal of Economic Theory, 80*(2), 292–331.

Karlan, D., Morten, M., & Zinman, J. (2012). *A personal touch: Text messaging for loan repayment* [Working Paper 17952]. National Bureau of Economic Research.

Kay, J., & King, M. (2020). *Radical uncertainty: Decision-making for an unknowable future*. The Bridge Street Press.

Keren, Gideon, (Ed.). (2011). *Perspectives on framing*. Psychology Press.

Kermack W. O., & McKendrick, A. G. (1927). A contribution to the mathematical theory of epidemics. *Proceedings of the Royal Society, 115*(772), 701–721.

Keynes, J. M. (1921). *A treatise on probability*. Macmillan.

Keynes, J. M. (1936). *The general theory of employment, interest and money*. Macmillan.

Khadjavi, M., & Lange, A. (2013). Prisoners and their dilemma. *Journal of Economic Behavior and Organization, 92*, 163–175.

Kirchler, E., & Maciejovsky, B. (2002). Simultaneous over and underconfidence: Evidence from experimental asset markets. *Journal of Risk and Uncertainty, 25*, 65–85.

Kirman, A. P. (1992). Whom or what does the representative individual represent? *Journal of Economic Perspectives, 6*(2), 117–136.

Kirman, A. (2010). *Complex economics: Individual and collective rationality*. Routledge.

Kirman, A., & Vriend, N. (2001). Evolving market structure: A model of price dispersion and loyalty. *Journal of Economic Dynamics and Control, 25*(3–4), 459–502.

Kling, Jeffrey, Mullainathan, Sendhil, Shafir, Eldar, Vermeulen, Lee, & Wrobel, Marian V. (2012). Comparison friction: Experimental evidence from medicare drug plans. *Quarterly Journal of Economics, 127*(1), 199–235.

Knight, F. H. (1921). Risk, uncertainty and profit: University of illinois at urbana-champaign's academy for entrepreneurial leadership historical research reference in entrepreneurship. SSRN: https://ssrn.com/abstract=1496192

Kolm, S.-C. (1973). A note on optimum tax evasion. *Journal of Public Economics, 2*(3), 265–270.

Kolmogorov, A. N. (1950). *Foundations of the theory of probability*. Chelsea Publishing Co. (Original German work published in 1933).

Korobkin, R. B. (2013). Relative value health insurance: The behavioral law and economics solution to the health care cost crisis. *Journal of Scholarly Perspectives, 10*(1), 51–68.

Korvost, M., & Damian, M. F. (2008). The differential influence of decades and units on multidigit number comparison. *Quarterly Journal of Experimental Psychology, 61*(8), 1250–1264.

Köszegi, B., & Rabin, M. (2006). A model of reference-dependent preferences. *Quarterly Journal of Economics, 121*(4), 1133–1165.

Kreps, D. M. (1990). *A course in microeconomic theory*. Harvester Wheatsheaf.

Kronlund, M., Pool, V., Sialm, C., & Stefanesco, I. (2020). *Out of sight no more? The effect of fee disclosures on 401K investment allocations* [NBER Working Paper No. 27573]. www.nber.org/papers/w27573

Krueger, J. I. (2007). From social projection to social behaviour. *European Review of Social Psychology, 18*(1), 1–35.

Krueger, J., & Mueller, R. A. (2002). Unskilled, unaware, or both? The contribution of social-perceptual skills and statistical regression to self-enhancement biases. *Journal of Personality and Social Psychology, 82*(2), 180–188.

Kruger, J., & Dunning, D. (1999). Unskilled and unaware of it: How difficulties in recognizing one's own incompetence lead to inflated self-assessments. *Journal of Personality and Social Psychology, 77*(6), 1121–1134.

Kuhn, T. (1962). *The structure of scientific revolutions*. University of Chicago Press.

Kunreuther, H., Ginsberg, R., Miller, L., et al. (1978). *Disaster insurance protection: Public policy lessons*. Wiley.

Kunreuther, H., & Pauly, M. (2004). Neglecting disaster: Why don't people insure against large losses? *Journal of Risk and Uncertainty, 28*(1), 5–21.

Kunreuther, H., & Pauly, M. (2005). Insurance decision making and market behaviour. *Foundations and Trends in Microeconomics, 1*(2), 63–127.

Kuran, T., & Sunstein, C. (1999). Availability cascades and risk regulation. *Stanford Law Review, 51*(4), 683–768.

Kyle, A. S. (1985). Continuous auctions and insider trading. *Econometrica, 53*, 1315–1336.

Lacetera, N., Pope, D. G., & Sydnor, H. (2012). Heuristic thinking and limited attention in the car market. *American Economic Review, 102*(5), 2206–2236.

Laffont, J-J., & Tirole, J. (1993). *A theory of incentives in procurement and regulation*. MIT Press.

La Ferrara, E., Chong, A., & Duryea, S. (2012). Soap operas and fertility: Evidence from Brazil. *American Economic Journal: Applied Economics, 4*(4), 1–31.

Laibson, D. (1997). Golden eggs and hyperbolic discounting. *Quarterly Journal of Economics, 112*(2), 443–478.

Laibson, David. (2018, May). Private paternalism, the commitment puzzle, and model-free equilibrium. *American Economic Review, 108*, 1–21.

Lakatos, I. (1970). Falsification and the methodology of scientific research programmes. In I. Lakatos & A. Musgrave (Eds.), *Criticism and the growth of knowledge*. Cambridge University Press.

Lamberson, P. J. (2016). Diffusion in networks. In Yann Bramoullé, Andrea Galeotti, & Brian Rogers (Eds.), *The oxford handbook of the economics of networks*, pp. 479–503. Oxford University Press.

Landier, A., & Thesmar, D. (2009). Financial contracting with optimistic entrepreneurs. *Review of Financial Studies, 22*, 117–150.

Larrick, R. P., Burson, K. A., & Soll, J. B. (2007). Social comparison and confidence: When thinking you're better than average predicts overconfidence (and when it does not). *Organizational Behavior and Human Decision Processes, 102*(1), 76–94.

Lazear, E. P. (2004). Balanced skills and enterpreneurship. *American Economic Review, 94*(2), 208–211.

Ledyard, J. (1995). Public goods: A survey of experimental research. In J. H. Kagel & A. E. Roth (Eds.), *The handbook of experimental economics*, pp. 111–194. Princeton University Press.

Lee, C. M. C., Shleifer, A., & Thaler, R. H. (1991). Investor sentiment and the closed-end fund puzzle. *Journal of Finance, 46*, 76–110.

Lei, V., Noussair, C. N., & Plott, C. R. (2001). Nonspeculative bubbles in experimental asset markets: Lack of common knowledge of rationality vs. actual irrationality. *Econometrica, 69*(4), 831–859.

Leijonhufvud, A. (1973). Life among the econ. *Economic Inquiry, 11*(3), 327–337.

Levitt, S. D. (2004). Understanding why crime fell in the 1990s: Four factors that explain the decline and six that do not. *Journal of Economic Perspectives, 18*(1), 163–190.

Levitt, S. (2016). *Heads or tails: The impact of a coin toss on major life decisions and subsequent happiness* [NBER Working Paper No. 22487]. www.nber.org/papers/w22487

Levitt, S. D., & List, J. A. (2007). What do laboratory experiments measuring social preferences reveal about the real world? *Journal of Economic Perspectives, 21*(2), 153–174.

Levy, Helen G., Norton, Edward C., & Smith, Jeffrey A. (2018). Tobacco regulation and consumer surplus: How should we value foregone consumer surplus? *American Journal of Health Economics, 4*(1), 1–25.

Lewis, D. K. (1979). Prisoners' dilemma is a Newcomb problem. *Philosophy and Public Affairs, 8*(3), 235–240.

Lichtenstein, S., & Slovic, P. (1971). Reversals of preferences between bids and choices in gambling decisions. *Journal of Experimental Psychology, 89*, 46–55.

Lichtenstein, S., & Slovic, P. (Eds.). (2006). *The construction of preference*. Cambridge University Press.

Lichtenstein, S., Slovic, P., Fischhoff, B., Layman, M., & Combs, B. (1978). Judged frequency of lethal events. *Journal of Experimental Psychology: Human Learning and Memory, 4*, 551–578.

Liebenstein, H. (1950). Bandwagon, snob, and veblen effects in the theory of consumers' demand. *Quarterly Journal of Economics, 64*(2), 183–207.

Lin, S. W., & Bier, V. M. (2008). A study of expert overconfidence. *Reliability Engineering and System Safety, 93*(5), 711–721.

Lind, B., & Plott, C. R. (1991). The winner's curse: Experiments with buyers and with sellers. *American Economic Review, 81*(1), 335–346.

Loewenstein, G. (1987). Anticipation and the valuation of delayed consumption. *Economic Journal, 97*, 666–684.

Loewenstein, G. (2008). *Exotic preferences: Behavioural economics and human motivation*. Oxford University Press.

Loewenstein, G., & Chater, N. (2017). Putting nudges in perspective. *Behavioural Public Policy, 1*(1), 26.

Loewenstein, G., & Haisley, E. (2008). The economist as therapist: Methodological ramifications of "light" paternalism. In A. Caplin & A. Schotter (Eds.), *The foundations of positive and normative economics: A handbook* (pp. 210–247). Oxford University Press.

Loewenstein, G. F., & Prelec, D. (1992). Anomalies in intertemporal choice: Evidence and an interpretation. *Quarterly Journal of Economics, 107*(2), 573–597.

Loewenstein, G., O'Donoghue, T., & Rabin, M. (2003). Projection bias in predicting future utility. *Quarterly Journal of Economics, 118*, 1209–1248.

Loewenstein, G., Sunstein, C. R., & Golman, R. (2014). Disclosure, psychology changes everything. *Annual Review of Economics, 6*(1), 391–419.

Loewenstein, G. F., Weber, E. U., Hsee, C. K., & Welch, E. S. (2001). Risk as feelings. *Psychological Bulletin, 127*, 267–286.

Logue, A. W. (1988). Research on self-control: An integrating framework. *Behavioral and Brain Sciences, 11*(4), 665–679.

Loomes, G., Starmer, C., & Sugden, R. (1991). Observing violations of transitivity by experimental methods. *Econometrica, 59*(2), 425–439.

Loomes, G., & Sugden, R. (1982). Regret theory: An alternative theory of rational choice under uncertainty. *Economic Journal, 92*(368), 805–824.

Lord, C. G., Ross, L., & Lepper, M. R. (1979). Biased assimilation and attitude polarization: The effects of prior theories on subsequently considered evidence. *Journal of Personality and Social Psychology, 37*(11), 2098–2109.

Lucas, R. E. (1988). On the mechanics of economic development. *Journal of Monetary Economics, 22*, 3–42.

Luce, R. D., & Raiffa, H. (1957). *Games and decisions*. Wiley.

Luguri, James, & Strahilevitz, Lior. (2019). *Shining a light on dark patterns* [University of Chicago, Public Law Working Paper No. 719]. https://papers.ssrn.com/sol3/papers.cfm?abstract id=3431205

Luttmer, E. F. P., & Singhal, M. (2011). Culture, context, and the taste for redistribution. *American Economic Journal: Economic Policy, 3*(1), 157–179.

Mabe, P. A., & West, S. G. (1982). Validity of self-evaluation of ability: A review and meta-analysis. *Journal of Applied Psychology, 67*(3), 280–296.

Macchi, L. (2000). Partitive formulation of information in probabilistic problems: Beyond heuristics and frequency format explanations. *Organizational Behavior and Human Decision Processes, 82*, 217–236.

Mackie, G. (1996). Ending footbinding and infibulation: A convention account. *American Sociological Review, 61*(6), 999–1017.

Madrian, Brigitte, & Shea, Dennis. (2002). The power of suggestion: Inertia in 401(k) participation and savings behavior. *Quarterly Journal of Economics, 116*(4), 1149–1187.

Malkiel, B. (1990). *A random walk down Wall Street*. Norton.

Malmendier, U., & Tate, G. (2005). CEO overconfidence and corporate investment. *Journal of Finance, 60,* 2661–2700.

Malmendier, U., & Tate, G. (2008). Who makes acquisitions? CEO overconfidence and the market's reaction. *Journal of Financial Economics, 89,* 20–43.

Malmendier, U., & Tate, G. (2015). Behavioral CEOs: On the role of managerial overconfidence. *Journal of Economic Perspectives, 29*(4), 37–60.

Malmendier, U., Tate, G., & Yan, J. (2011). Overconfidence and early-life experiences: The effect of managerial traits on corporate financial policies. *Journal of Finance, 66,* 1687–1733.

Malmendier, U., & Taylor, T. (2015). On the verges of overconfidence. *Journal of Economic Perspectives, 29*(4), 3–8.

Mani, A., Mullainathan, S., Shafir, E., & Zhao, J. (2013). Poverty impedes cognitive function. *Science, 341*(6149), 976–980.

Mankiw, N. G., & Zeldes, S. P. (1991). The consumption of stockholders and nonstockholders. *Journal of Financial Economics, 29*(1), 97–112.

Manzini, P., & Mariotti, M. (2006). A vague theory of choice over time. *Advances in Theoretical Economics 6*(1), Article 6.

March, J. G., & Shapira, Z. (1987). Managerial perspectives on risk and risk taking. *Management Science, 33,* 1404–1418.

Mas-Colell, A., Whinston, M., & Green, J. R. (1995). *Microeconomic theory*. Oxford University Press.

Masiero, Marianna, Lucchiari, Claudio, & Pravettoni, Gabriella. (2015). Personal fable: Optimistic bias in cigarette smokers. *International Journal of High Risk Behaviors and Addiction, 4*(1), e20939.

Mattauch, Linus, & Hepburn, Cameron. (2016). Climate policy when preferences are endogenous—and sometimes they are. *Midwest Studies in Philosophy, 40*(1), 76–95.

Maynard Smith, J., & Price, G. R. (1973). The logic of animal conflict. *Nature, 246,* 15–18.

McConnell, Brent. (2006). *Endogenous preferences and welfare evaluations* [Minnesota Legal Studies Research Paper, DP06–50].

McLeod, P., & Dienes, Z. (1996). Do fielders know where to go to catch the ball, or only how to get there? *Journal of Experimental Psychology: Human Perception and Performance, 22,* 531–543.

McLeod, P., Read, N., & Dienes, Z., (2006). The generalized optic acceleration cancellation theory of catching. *Journal of Experimental Psychology, 32*(1), 139–148.

McNeil, B. J., Pauker, S. G., Sox, H. C., Jr., & Tversky, A. (1982). On the elicitation of preferences for alternative therapies. *New England Journal of Medicine, 306,* 1259–1262.

Mead, W. J., Moseidjord, A., & Sorensen, P. E. (1983). The rate of return earned by leases under cash bonus bidding in OCS oil and gas leases. *Energy Journal, 4*(4), 37–52.

Meehl, P. E., & Rosen, A. (1955). Antecedent probability and the efficiency of psychometric signs, patterns or cutting scores. *Psychological Bulletin, 52,* 194–216.

Mehra, R., & Prescott, E. C. (1985). The equity premium: A puzzle. *Journal of Monetary Economics, 15*(2), 145–161.

Meikle, N. L., Tenney, E. R., & Moore, D. A. (2016). Overconfidence at work: Does overconfidence survive the checks and balances of organizational life? *Research in Organizational Behavior, 36,* 121–134.

Menkhoff, L., Schmeling, M., & Schmidt, U. (2013). Overconfidence, experience, and professionalism: An experimental study. *Journal of Economic Behavior and Organization, 86,* 92–101.

Metzger, M. (1984). Biases in betting: An application of laboratory findings. *Psychological Reports, 56,* 883–888.

Meulbroek, L. K. (2001). The efficiency of equity-linked compensation: Understanding the full cost of awarding executive stock options. *Financial Management, 30*(2), 5–30.

Miao, Chun-Hui. (2010). Consumer myopia, standardization and aftermarket monopolization. *European Economic Review, 54*(7), 931–946.

Michel, C. (2017). Market regulation of voluntary add-on contracts. *International Journal of Industrial Organization, 54,* 239–268.

Michel, J. B., et al. (2011). Quantitative analysis of culture using millions of digitized books. *Science, 331*(6014), 176–182.

Mill, J. S. (2002). *On liberty*. In Dale E. Miller, (Ed.), *The basic writings of John Stuart Mill: On liberty, the subjection of women, and utilitarianism, 3,* 11–12. Random House (Original work published 1863).

Miller, J. B., & Sanjurjo, A. (2018). Surprised by the gambler's and hot hand fallacies? A truth in the law of small numbers. *Econometrica, 86*(6), 2019–2047.

Mitchell, M. (2009). *Complexity: A guided tour*. Oxford University Press.

Mombardini, M., & Trebbi, F. (2012). Risk aversion and expected utility theory: An experiment with large and small stakes. *Journal of the European Economic Association, 10*(6), 1348–1399.

Moore, D. A., & Healy, P. J. (2008). The trouble with overconfidence. *Psychological Review, 115*(2), 502–517.

Mullainathan, S. (2002). A memory-based model of bounded rationality. *Quarterly Journal of Economics, 117*(3), 735–774.

Mullainathan, S., Schwartzstein, J., & Shleifer, A. (2008). Coarse thinking and persuasion. *Quarterly Journal of Economics, 123*(2), 577–619.

Mullainathan, S., & Shafir, E. (2013). *Scarcity: Why having too little means so much*. Times Books.

Munier, B., Selten, R. Bouyssou, D., Bourgine, P., Day, R., Harvey, N., Hilton, D., Machina, M. J., Parker, P., Sterman, H., Sterman, J., Weber, E., Wernerfelt, B., & Wensley, R. (1999). Bounded rationality modeling. *Marketing Letters, 10*(3), 233–248.

Murooka, T. (2015). *Deception under competitive intermediation* [Working paper].

Murooka, Takeshi, & Schwarz, Marco A. (2018). The timing of choice-enhancing policies. *Journal of Public Economics, 157*, 27–40.

Nash, J. F. (1950). Equilibrium points in n-person games. *Proceedings of the National Academy of Sciences of the United States of America, 36*(1), 48–49.

Navarro, A. D., & Fantino, E. (2009). The sunk time effect: An exploration. *Journal of Behavioral Decision Making 22*, 252–270.

Nelson, R. R., & Winter, S. G. (1982). *An evolutionary theory of economic change*. Harvard University Press.

Nelson, R. R., & Winter, S. G. (2002). Evolutionary theorizing in economics. *Journal of Economic Perspectives, 16*(2), 23–46.

Newell, A., & Simon, H. A. (1972). *Human problem solving*. Prentice-Hall.

Newell B. R., & Shanks, D. R. (2003). Take the best or look at the rest? Factors influencing "one-reason" decision making. *Journal of Experimental Psychology: Learning Memory and Cognition, 29*, 53–65.

Newell B. R., Weston N. J., & Shanks D. R. (2002). Empirical tests of the fast- and frugal heuristic: Not everyone "takes-the-best." *Organization Behavior and Human Decision Processes, 91*, 82–96.

North, Douglass C. (1990). *Institutions, institutional change and economic performance*. Cambridge University Press.

Northcraft, G. B., & Neale, M. A. (1987). Experts, amateurs, and real estate: An anchoring-and-adjustment perspective on property pricing decisions. *Organizational Behaviour and Human Decision Processes, 39*, 84–97.

Novemsky, N., & Kahneman, D. (2005). The boundaries of loss aversion. *Journal of Marketing Research, 42*(2), 119–128.

Nunn, N. (2008). The long-term effects of Africa's slave trades. *Quarterly Journal of Economics, 123*(1), 139–176.

Nunn, N., & Wantchekon, L. (2011). The slave trade and the origins of mistrust in Africa. *American Economic Review, 101*(7), 3221–3252.

Nussbaum, Martha C. (1993). Non-relative virtues: An Aristotelian approach. In Martha C. Nussbaum & Amartya Sen (Eds.), *The quality of life*. Clarendon Press.

Nussbaum, Martha C. (2000). *Women and human development: The capabilities approach*. Cambridge University Press.

Nussbaum, M. C. (2013). *Creating capabilities: The human development approach*. Belknap Press.

Oaksford, M., & Chater, N. (1998). *Rational models of cognition.* Oxford University Press.

Obama, B. (2009, September 5). *Weekly address.*

Ockenfels, A., & Selten, R. (2005). Impulse balance equilibrium and feedback in first price auctions. *Games and Economic Behavior, 51*(1), 155–170.

O'Donoghue, T., & Rabin, M. (1999a). Incentives for procrastinators. *Quarterly Journal of Economics, 114*(3), 769–816.

O'Donoghue, T., & Rabin, M. (1999b). Doing it now or later. *American Economic Review, 89*(1), 103–124.

O'Donoghue, T., & Rabin, M. (2001). Choice and procrastination. *Quarterly Journal of Economics, 116*(1), 121–160.

O'Donoghue, T., & Rabin, M. (2006). Optimal sin taxes. *Journal of Public Economics, 90*(1011), 1825–1849.

O'Donoghue, T., & Rabin, M. (2015). Present bias: Lessons learned and to be learned. *American Economic Review, 105*(5), 273–279.

Okada, E. M., & Hoch, S. J. (2004). Spending time versus spending money. *Journal of Consumer Research, 31*, 313–323.

Organisation for Economic Cooperation and Development. (2010). *Consumer policy toolkit.* https://www.oecd.org/digital/consumer/consumer-policy-toolkit-9789264079663-en.htm

Orszag, P. R. (2010, March 29). White House Office of Management and Budget, Director, SAVEings. Retrieved from www.whitehouse.gov/omb/blog/10/03/29/SAVEings/

Orszag, P. R., & Rodriguez, E. (2009). Retirement security for latinos: Bolstering coverage, savings, and adequacy. In W. G. Gale et al. (Eds.), *Automatic: Changing the way America saves* (pp. 173–198). R. R. Donnelley.

Ostrom, Elenor (2000). Collective action and the evolution of social norms. *Journal of Economic Perspectives, 14*, 137–158.

Pachur, T., Hertwig, R., & Steinmann, F. (2012). How do people judge risks: Availability heuristic, affect heuristic, or both? *Journal of Experimental Psychology: Applied, 18*, 314–330.

Papke, L. E., Walker, L., & Dworsky, M. (2009). Retirement savings for women: Progress to date and policies for tomorrow. In W. G. Gale et al. (Eds.), *Automatic: Changing the way America saves* (pp. 199–230). R. R. Donnelley.

Paserman, M. D. (2008). Job search and hyperbolic discounting: Structural estimation and policy evaluation. *Economic Journal, 118*(531), 1418–1452.

Payne, J. W., Bettman, J. R., & Johnson, E. J. (1993). *The adaptive decision maker.* Cambridge University Press.

Pension Protection Act of 2006, Pub. L. No. 109-280, 120 Stat. 780.

Persson, P. (2018). Attention manipulation and information overload. *Behavioural Public Policy, 2*(1), 78–106.

Pettigrew, Richard. (2020). *Choosing for changing selves*. Oxford University Press.

Phelps, E., & Pollack, R. A. (1968). On second best national savings and game equilibrium growth. *Review of Economic Studies, 35*(2), 185–199.

Piccione, Michele, & Spiegler, Ran. (2012). Price competition under limited comparability. *Quarterly Journal of Economics, 127*(1), 135–197.

Pinker, S. (1997). *How the mind works*. Norton.

Pohl, Rudiger F. (Ed.). (2016). *Cognitive illusions*. Routledge.

Polak, B. (1999). Epistemic conditions for Nash equilibrium, and common knowledge of rationality. *Econometrica, 67*, 673–676.

Polinsky, A. M., & Shavell, S. (2007). The theory of public enforcement of law. In Polinsky, A. M., & Shavell, S. (Eds.), *Handbook of law and economics* (Vol. 1, Chapter 6, pp. 405–454). Elsevier.

Popper, K. (1959). *The logic of scientific discovery*. Hutchinson. (Original work, *Logik der Forschung*, published 1934).

Popper, K. (1963). *Conjectures and refutations: The growth of scientific knowledge*. Routledge and Kegan Paul.

Posner, Richard. (1973). *Economic analysis of law*. Kluwer.

Pöystia, L., Rajalina, S., & Summala, H. (2005). Factors influencing the use of cellular (mobile) phone during driving and hazards while using it. *Accident Analysis and Prevention, 37*(1), 47–51.

Prava, V., Clemen, R., Hobbs, B., & Kenny, M. (2016). Partition dependence and carryover biases in subjective probability assessment surveys for continuous variables: Model-based estimation and correction. *Decision Analysis, 13*(1), 51–67.

Prelec, D. (1998). The probability weighting function. *Econometrica, 66*(3), 497–528.

Prelec, D., & Loewenstein, G. (1998). *The red and black: Mental accounting of savings and debt. Marketing Science, 17*(1), 4–28.

Puri, M., & Robinson, D. (2007). Optimism and economic choice. *Journal of Financial Economics, 86*(1), 71–99.

Quattrone, G. A., & Tversky, A. (1984). Causal versus diagnostic contingencies: On self deception and the voter's illusion. *Journal of Personality and Social Psychology, 46*(2), 237–248.

Quiggin, J. (1982). A theory of anticipated utility. *Journal of Economic Behavior and Organization, 3*, 323–343.

Quiggin, J. (1993). *Generalized expected utility theory*. Kluwer.

Rabin, M. (2002). Inference by believers in the law of small numbers. *Quarterly Journal of Economics, 117*(3), 775–816.

Rabin, M. (2013a). Behavioral optimization models versus bounded-rationality models in decisions. *Journal of Economic Literature, 51*(2), 528–543.

Rabin, M. (2013b). Healthy habits: Some thoughts on the role of public policy in healthful eating and exercise under limited rationality. In A. Oliver, (Ed.), *Behavioral public policy*, pp. 115–147. Cambridge University Press.

Rabin, M., & Dimitri, V. (2010). The gambler's and hot-hand fallacies: Theory and applications. *Review of Economic Studies, 77*(2), 730–778.

Rabin M., & Schrag, J. (1999). First impressions matter: A model of confirmatory bias. *Quarterly Journal of Economics, 114*(1), 37–82.

Rabin, M., & Vayanos, D. (2010). The gambler's and hot-hand fallacies: Theory and applications. *Review of Economic Studies, 77*, 730–778.

Radelet, M. L. & Ackers, R. L. (1996). Deterrence and the death penalty: The views of the experts. *Journal of Criminal Law and Criminology, 87*(1), 1–16.

Radner, Roy, (1992). Hierarchy: The economics of managing. *Journal of Economic Literature, 30*, 1381–1415.

Radner, R. (1996) Bounded rationality, indeterminacy, and the theory of the firm. *Economic Journal, 106*(438), 1360–1373.

Rajagopal, P., & Rha, J.-Y. (2009). The mental accounting of time. *Journal of Economic Psychology, 30*, 772–781.

Rapoport, A. (1988). Experiments with N-person social traps I: Prisoners' dilemma, weak prisoners' dilemma, volunteers' dilemma, and largest number. *Journal of Conflict Resolution, 32*(3), 457–472.

Rapoport, A., & Budescu, D. V. (1992) Generation of random binary series in strictly competitive games. *Journal of Experimental Psychology, 121*, 352–364.

Rapoport, A., & Budescu, D. V. (1997). Randomization in individual choice behavior. *Psychological Review, 104*, 603–617.

Rawls, John. (1991). *Political liberalism.* In Jacob T. Levy (Ed.), *Oxford handbook of classics in contemporary political theory*. Oxford University Press.

Ray, D. (2006). Aspirations, poverty and economic change. In A. Banerjee, R. Bénabou, & D. Mookerjee (Eds.), *Understanding poverty*, pp. 409–421. Oxford University Press.

Raz, Joseph. (1985). *The morality of freedom*. Oxford University Press.

Read, D., Frederick, S., & Scholten, M. (2013). DRIFT: An analysis of outcome framing in intertemporal choice. *Journal of Experimental Psychology Learning Memory and Cognition, 39*(2), 573–588.

Read, D., Loewenstein, G., & Rabin, M. (1999). Choice bracketing. *Journal of Risk and Uncertainty, 19*(1–3), 171–197.

Rees-Jones, A. (2018). Quantifying loss-averse tax manipulation. *Review of Economic Studies, 85*(2), 1251–1278.

Rieskamp, J., & Otto, P. (2006). SSL: A theory of how people learn to select strategies. *Journal of Experimental Psychology: General, 135*, 207–236.

Riis, J., & Ratner, R. (2015). Simplified nutrition guidelines to fight obesity. In R. Batra, P. A. Keller & V. J. Strecher (Eds.), *Leveraging consumer psychology for effective health communications: The obesity challenge*. M. E. Sharpe.

Robbins, J. M., & Krueger, J. I. (2005). Social projection to ingroups and outgroups: A review and meta-analysis. *Personality and Social Psychology Review*, 9(1), 32–47.

Roemer, J. (2015). Kantian optimization: A microfoundation for cooperation. *Journal of Public Economics*, 127, 45–57.

Roemer, J. (2018). *A theory of cooperation in games with an application to market socialism* [mimeo].

Romer, P. (2016). The trouble with macroeconomics. *The American Economist*, 20, 1–20.

Ross, L., Greene D., & House, P. (1977). The false consensus effect: An egocentric bias in social perception and attribution processes. *Journal of Experimental Social Psychology*, 13, 279–301.

Roth, B., & Voskort, A. (2014). Stereotypes and false consensus: How financial professionals predict risk preferences. *Journal of Economic Behavior and Organization*, 107, 553–565.

Royal Society for the Prevention of Accidents. (2005). *The risk of using a mobile phone while driving*. https://www.rospa.com/rospaweb/docs/advice-services/road-safety/drivers/mobile-phone-report.pdf

Rubinstein, A. (2003). Economics and psychology? The case of hyperbolic discounting. *International Economic Review*, 44(4), 1207–1216.

Rubinstein, A. (2006). Dilemmas of an economic theorist. *Econometrica*, 74(4), 865–883.

Rubinstein, M. (2001, May–June). Rational markets: Yes or no? The affirmative case, *Financial Analysts Journal*, 57(3), 15–29.

Sahm, C. R., Shapiro, M. D., & Slemrod, J. (2011). *Check in the mail or more in the paycheck: Does the effectiveness of fiscal stimulus depend on how it is delivered?* [Finance and Economics Discussion Series No. 2010-40]. http://www.federalreserve.gov/pubs/feds/2010/201040/201040pap.pdf

Samuelson, L. (1997). *Evolutionary games and equilibrium selection*. MIT Press.

Samuelson, P. A. (1937). A note on measurement of utility. *Review of Economic Studies*, 4(2), 155–161.

Samuelson, P. (1963). Risk and uncertainty: A fallacy of large numbers. *Scientia*, 98, 108–113.

Samuelson, W. F., & Bazerman, M. H. (1985). The winner's curse in bilateral negotiations. In V. L. Smith (Ed.), *Research in experimental economics* (Vol. 3), pp. 105–137. JAI Press.

Sarin, Natasha. (2019). Making consumer finance work. *Columbia Law Review*, 119(6), 1519–1596.

Savage, L. J. (1954). *The foundations of statistics.* Wiley. Rev. ed., 1972, Dover Publications, 1972.

Scarpetta, S., Hemmings, P., Tressel, T., & Jaejoon, W. (2002). *The role of policy and institutions for productivity and firm dynamics: Evidence from micro and industry data* [OECD Working Paper No. 329].

Schank, R. C., & Abelson, R. P. (1977). *Scripts, plans, goals and understanding: An inquiry into human knowledge.* Erlbaum.

Scheffer, M. (2009). *Critical transitions in nature and society.* Princeton University Press.

Scheibehenne, B., & Bröder, A. (2007). Predicting Wimbledon 2005 tennis results by mere player name recognition. *International Journal of Forecasting, 23,* 415–426.

Schelling, T. C. (1971). Dynamic models of segregation. *Journal of Mathematical Sociology, 1*(2), 143–186.

Schkade, David, & Kahneman, Daniel. (1998). Does living in California make people happy? A focusing illusion in judgments of life satisfaction. *Psychological Science, 9*(5), 340–346.

Scholten, M., & Read, D., (2006). *Beyond discounting: The trade-off model of intertemporal choice* [Working Paper LSE-OR 06.88]. London School of Economics and Political Science.

Scholten, M., & Read, D. (2010). The psychology of intertemporal trade-offs. *Psychological Review, 117*(3), 925–944.

Scholten, Marc, Read, Daniel, & Stewart, Neil. (2019, December). The framing of nothing and the psychology of choice. *Journal of Risk and Uncertainty, 59,* 125–149.

Schram, A., & Charness, G. (2015). Inducing social norms in laboratory allocation choices. *Management Science, 61*(7), 1531–1546.

Schwarz, N., Strack, F., Hilton, D., & Naderer, G. (1991). Base rates, representativeness, and the logic of conversation: The contextual relevance of irrelevant information. *Social Cognition, 9,* 67–84.

Seinen, I., & Schram, A. (2006). Social status and group norms: Indirect reciprocity in a repeated helping experiment. *European Economic Review, 50*(3), 581–602.

Selten R. (1998). Aspiration adaptation theory. *Journal of Mathematical Psychology, 42*(2), 191–214.

Selten, R. (1990). Bounded rationality. *Journal of Institutional and Theoretical Economics (JITE) / Zeitschrift für die gesamte Staatswissenschaft, 146*(4), 649–658.

Selten, R. (2001). What is bounded rationality? In G. Gigerenzer, & R. Selten (Eds.), *Bounded rationality: The adaptive toolbox.* (pp. 1–12). MIT Press.

Selten, R., & Chmura, T. (2008). Stationary concepts for experimental 2×2 games. *American Economic Review, 98*(3), 938–966.

Selten, R., Chmura, T., & Goerg, S. J. (2011). Stationary concepts for experimental 2 × 2 games: Reply. *American Economic Review, 101*(2), 1041–1044.

Selten, R., Pittnauer, S., & Hohnisch, M. (2012). Dealing with dynamic decision problems when knowledge of the environment is limited: An approach based on goal systems. *Journal of Behavioral Decision Making, 25*, 443–457.

Sen, A. (2002). *Rationality and freedom*. Belknap Press.

Sethi-Iyengar, S., Huberman, G., & Jiang, W. (2004). How much choice is too much? Contributions to 401(k) retirement plans. In O. S. Mitchell, & S. P. Utkus, (Eds.), *Pension design and structure: New lessons from behavioral finance*. Oxford University Press.

Shafir, E., & Thaler, R. H. (2006). Invest now, drink later, spend never: The mental accounting of delayed consumption. *Journal of Economic Psychology, 27*, 694–712.

Shah, A. K., Mullainathan, S., & Shafir, E. (2012). Some consequences of having too little. *Science, 338*, 682–685.

Shapiro, J. M. (2005). Is there a daily discount rate? Evidence from the food stamp nutrition cycle. *Journal of Public Economics, 89*(23), 303–325.

Shiller, R. (1981). Do stock prices move too much to be justified by subsequent changes in dividends? *American Economic Review, 71*, 421–436.

Shiller, R. (2015). *Irrational exuberance* (3rd ed.). Princeton University Press.

Shiller, Robert J. (2017). Narrative economics [Cowles Foundation Discussion Paper Number 2069]. *American Economic Review, 107*(4), 967–1004.

Shiller, Robert J. (2019). *Narrative economics: How stories go viral and drive major economic events*. Princeton University Press.

Shleifer, A. (2000). *Inefficient markets: An introduction to behavioral finance*. Oxford University Press.

Simon, H. A. (1955). A behavioral model of rational choice. *Quarterly Journal of Economics, 69*(1), 99–118.

Simon, H. A. (1957). *Models of man*. Wiley.

Simon, H. A. (1978, December 8). *Rational decision-making in business organizations* [Nobel Memorial Lecture].

Simon, H. A. (1982). *Models of bounded rationality*. MIT Press.

Simon, H. A. (1986). Rationality in psychology and economics. *The Journal of Business, 59*(4), S209–S224.

Simon, H. A. (2000). Bounded rationality in social science: Today and tomorrow. *Mind and Society, 1*(1), 25–39.

Skinner, J., & Slemrod, J. (1985). An economic perspective on tax evasion. *National Tax Journal, 38*, 345–353.

Slemrod, J. (2018). *Tax compliance and enforcement* [National Bureau of Economic Research Working Paper No. 24799].

Slemrod, J., & Yitzhaki, S. (2002). Tax avoidance, evasion and administration. In A. J. Auerbach, & M. Feldstein (Eds.), *Handbook of public economics* (Vol. 3, pp. 1423–1470). Elsevier Science.

Sloman, S. A., Over, D., Slovak, L., & Stibel, J. M. (2003). Frequency illusions and other fallacies. *Organizational Behavior and Human Decision Processes, 91,* 296–309.

Slovic, P., Finucane, M., Peters, E., & MacGregor, D. G. (2002). The affect heuristic. In T. Gilovich, D. Griffin, & D. Kahneman (Eds.), *Heuristics and biases: The psychology of intuitive judgment* (pp. 397–420). Cambridge University Press.

Slovic, P., MacGregor, D. G., Malmfors, T., & Purchase, I. F. H. (1999). *Influence of affective processes on toxicologists' judgments of risk* (Report No. 99–2). Decision Research.

Smith, V. L., Suchanek, G. L., & Williams, A. W. (1988). Bubbles, crashes, and endogenous expectations in experimental spot asset markets. *Econometrica, 56*(5), 1119–1151.

Solan, L., Rosenblatt T., & Osherson D. (2008). False consensus bias in contract interpretation. *Columbia Law Review, 108,* 1272–1300.

Soman, D. (2001). The mental accounting of sunk time costs: Why time is not like money. *Journal of Behavioral Decision Making, 14,* 169–185.

Sparkman, G., & Walton, G. M. (2017). Dynamic norms promote sustainable behavior, even if it is counternormative. *Psychological Science, 28*(11), 1663–1674.

Spiegler, R. (2006). The market for quacks. *Review of Economic Studies, 73*(4), 1113–1131.

Spiegler, R. (2011). *Bounded rationality and industrial organization.* Oxford University Press.

Staats, B. R., Milkman, K. L., & Fox, C. R. (2012). The team scaling fallacy: Underestimating the declining efficiency of larger teams. *Organizational Behavior and Human Decision Processes, 118*(2), 132–142.

Stango, V., & Zinman, J. (2014). Limited and varying consumer attention: Evidence from shocks to the salience of bank overdraft fees. *Review of Financial Studies, 27*(4), 990–1030.

Stanovich, K. E. (2012). On the distinction between rationality and intelligence: Implications for understanding individual differences in reasoning. In K. Holyoak, & R. Morrison (Eds.), *The Oxford handbook of thinking and reasoning* (pp. 343–365). Oxford University Press.

Stanovich, K. E., & West, R. F. (2000). Individual differences in reasoning: Implications for the rationality debate [Target article and commentaries]. *Behavioral and Brain Sciences, 23,* 645–726.

Starmer, C. (2000). Developments in non-expected utility theory: The hunt for a descriptive theory of choice under risk. *Journal of Economic Literature, 38,* 332–382.

Stephens, M., Jr. (2003). 3rd of the month: Do social security recipients smooth consumption between checks? *American Economic Review*, 93(1), 406–422.

Stiglitz, J. E. (2018). Where modern macroeconomics went wrong. *Oxford Review of Economic Policy*, 34(1–2), 70–106.

Stokey, N., Lucas, R. E., & Prescott, E. (1989). *Recursive Methods in Economic Dynamics*. Harvard University Press.

Stolarz-Fantino, S., Fantino, E., Zizzo, D. J., & Wen, J. (2003). The conjunction fallacy: New evidence for robustness. *American Journal of Psychology*, 116, 15–34.

Strotz, R. H. (1955). Myopia and inconsistency in dynamic utility maximization. *Review of Economic Studies*, 23(3), 165–180.

Sugden, R. (1989). Spontaneous order. *The Journal of Economic Perspectives*, 3(4), 85–97.

Sugden, R. (1998). Normative expectations: The simultaneous evolution of institutions and norms. In A. Ben-Ner & L. Putterman (Eds.), *Economics, value, and organization* (pp. 73–100). Cambridge University Press.

Sugden, R. (2004). *The economics of rights, cooperation and welfare* (2nd ed.). Macmillan.

Sugden, R. (2008). Why incoherent preferences do not justify paternalism. *Constitutional Political Economy*, 19, 226–248.

Sugden, R. (2013). The behavioural economist and the social planner: To whom should behavioural welfare economics be addressed? *Inquiry: An Interdisciplinary Journal of Philosophy*, 56(5), 519–538.

Sugden, R. (2019). *The community of advantage: A behavioural economist's defence of the market*. Oxford University Press.

Sullivan, M. W. (2017). *Economic issues: Economic analysis of hotel resort fees*. Bureau of Economics Federal Trade Commission.

Sunstein, C. R. (1996). Social norms and social roles. *Columbia Law Review*, 96(4), 903–968.

Sunstein, Cass R. (2002). Probability neglect. *Yale Law Journal*, 112(1), 61–107.

Sunstein, C. R. (2011). Empirically informed regulation. *University of Chicago Law Review*, 78, 1349–1429.

Sunstein, C. R. (2013). *Simpler*. Simon and Schuster.

Sunstein, Cass R. (2014a, January). Is deontology a heuristic? *Iyyun: The Jerusalem Philosophical Quarterly*, 63, 83–101.

Sunstein, Cass R. (2014b). *Why nudge? The politics of libertarian paternalism*. Yale University Press.

Sunstein, C. R. (2016). The council of psychological advisers. *Annual Review of Psychology*, 67(1), 713–737.

Sunstein, C. R. (2017). Default rules are better than active choosing (often). *Trends in Cognitive Sciences*, 21, 600–606.

Sunstein, C. R. (2018a). "Better off, as judged by themselves": A comment on evaluating nudges. *International Review of Economics, 65*(1), 1–8.

Sunstein, Cass R. (2018b). *Legal reasoning and political conflict.* Oxford University Press.

Sunstein, Cass R. (2019a). *On freedom.* Princeton University Press.

Sunstein, Cass R. (2019b). Rear visibility and some unresolved problems for economic analysis. *Journal of Benefit-Cost Analysis, 10*(3), 317–350.

Sunstein, C. R. (2020). *Behavioral science and public policy (elements in public economics).* Cambridge University Press.

Sunstein, C. R., & R. H. Thaler. (2003) Libertarian paternalism is not an oxymoron. *University of Chicago Law Review, 70,* 1159–1202.

Sutter, M. (2007). Are teams prone to myopic loss aversion? An experimental study on individual versus team investment behavior. *Economics Letters, 97*(2), 128–132.

Sutter, M., Haigner, S., & Kocher, M. G. (2010). Choosing the carrot or the stick? Endogenous institutional choice in social dilemma situations. *Review of Economic Studies, 77*(4), 1540–1566.

Tabellini, Guido. (2008). The scope of cooperation: Values and incentives. *Quarterly Journal of Economics, 123*(3), 905–950.

Taubinsky, D., & Rees-Jones, A. (2018). Attention variation and welfare: Theory and evidence from a tax salience experiment. *Review of Economic Studies, 85*(4), 2462–2496.

Taylor, P., & Jonker, L. (1978). Evolutionary stable strategies and game dynamics. *Mathematical Biosciences, 40,* 145–156.

Tenney, E. R., Logg, J. M., & Moore, D. A. (2015). (Too) optimistic about optimism: The belief that optimism improves performance. *Journal of Personality and Social Psychology, 108*(3), 377–399.

Tentori, K., Bonini, N., & Osherson, D. (2004). The conjunction fallacy: A misunderstanding about conjunction? *Cognitive Science, 28,* 467–477.

Terrell, Dek. (1998). Biases in assessments of probabilities: New evidence from greyhound races. *Journal of Risk and Uncertainty, 17,* 151–166.

Terrell, Dek, & Farmer, A. (1996). Optimal betting and efficiency in parimutuel betting markets with information costs. *Economic Journal, 106,* 846–868.

Tesfatsion, L. (2002). Agent-based computational economics: Growing economies from the bottom up. *Artificial Life, 8*(1), 55–82.

Tetlock, P. E. (2002). Cognitive biases in path-dependent systems: Theory driven reasoning about plausible pasts and probable futures in world politics. In T. Gilovich, D. W. Griffin, & D. Kahneman (Eds.), *Inferences, heuristics and biases: New directions in judgment under uncertainty.* Cambridge University Press.

Tetlock, P. E. (2006). *Expert political judgment: How good is it? How can we know?* Princeton University Press.

Thaler, R. H. (1980). Toward a positive theory of consumer choice. *Journal of Economic Behavior and Organization, 1*, 39–60.

Thaler, R. H. (1981). Some empirical evidence on dynamic consistency. *Economics Letters, 8*, 201–207.

Thaler, R. (1985). Mental accounting and consumer choice. *Marketing science, 4*, 199–214. (Reprinted as "Mental accounting and consumer choice," 2008, *Marketing Science, 27*[1], 15–25.)

Thaler, R. H. (1988). Anomalies: The winner's curse. *Journal of Economic Perspectives, 2*(1), 191–202.

Thaler, R. H. (1999). Mental accounting matters. *Journal of Behavioral Decision Making, 12*(3), 183–206.

Thaler, R. H. (2015). *Misbehaving: The making of behavioral economics* (reprint ed.). Norton.

Thaler, R., & Benartzi, S. (2004). Save More Tomorrow: Using behavioral economics to increase employee saving. *Journal of Political Economy, 112*(S1), S164–S187.

Thaler, R. H. & Sunstein, C. R. (2003). Libertarian paternalism. *American Economic Review: Papers and Proceedings, 93*, 175–179.

Thaler, R. H., & Sunstein, C. R. (2008). *Nudge: Improving decisions about health, wealth, and happiness*. Penguin Books.

Thaler, R. H., & Sunstein, C. R. (2021). *Nudge: Improving decisions about health, wealth, and happiness* (2nd ed.). Penguin Books.

Thunström, Linda. (2019). Welfare effects of nudges: The emotional tax of calorie menu labeling. *Judgment and Decision Making, 14*(1), 11–25.

Thurner, S., Farmer, J. D., & Geanakoplos, J. (2012). Leverage causes fat tails and clustered volatility. *Quantitative Finance, 12*(5), 695–707.

Tobias, R. B. (1999). *Twenty master plots and how to build them*. Piatkus.

Tomasello, M. (2014). *A natural history of human thinking*. Harvard University Press.

Tor, A., & Bazerman, M. H. (2003). Focusing failures in competitive environments: Explaining decision errors in the Monty Hall game, the acquiring a company game, and multiparty ultimatums. *Journal of Behavioral Decision Making, 16*(5), 353–374.

Touron, D. R., & Hertzog, C. (2004). Distinguishing age differences in knowledge, strategy use, and confidence during strategic skill acquisition. *Psychology and Aging, 19*, 452–466.

Turnwald, B. P., et al. (2019). Increasing vegetable intake by emphasizing tasty and enjoyable attributes: A randomized controlled multisite intervention for taste-focused labeling. *Psychological Science, 30*(11), 1603–1615.

Tversky, A., & Gilovich, T. (1989a). The cold facts about the 'hot hand' in basketball, *Chance, 2*, 16–21.

Tversky, A., & Gilovich, T. (1989b). The hot hand: Statistical reality or cognitive illusion? *Chance, 2*, 31–34.

Tversky, A., & Kahneman, D. (1971). Belief in the law of small numbers. *Psychological Bulletin, 76,* 105–110.

Tversky, A., & Kahneman, D. (1973). Availability: A heuristic for judging frequency and probability. *Cognitive Psychology, 5*(2), 207–232.

Tversky, A., & Kahneman, D. (1974). Judgment under uncertainty: Heuristics and biases. *Science, 185,* 1124–1130.

Tversky, A., & Kahneman, D. (1980). Causal schemas in judgments under uncertainty. In M. Fishbein (Ed.), *Progress in social psychology* (pp. 49–72). Erlbaum.

Tversky, A., & Kahneman, D. (1981). The framing of decisions and the psychology of choice. *Science, 211*(4481), 453–458.

Tversky, A., & Kahneman, D. (1983). Extensional vs. intuitive reasoning: The conjunction fallacy in probability judgment. *Psychological Review, 90,* 293–315.

Tversky, A., & Kahneman, D. (1992). Advances in prospect theory: Cumulative representation of uncertainty. *Journal of Risk and Uncertainty, 5*(4), 297–323.

Tversky, A., & Koehler, D. J. (1994). Support theory: A nonextensional representation of subjective probability. *Psychological Review, 101*(4), 547–567.

Tyran, J-R., & Feld, L. P. (2006). Achieving compliance when legal sanctions are non-deterrent. *Scandinavian Journal of Economics, 108*(1), 135–156.

Ullmann-Margalit, Edna. (2006). Big decisions: Opting, converting, and drifting. *Royal Institute of Philosophy Supplement, 58,* 157–172.

Van Boven, L., & Loewenstein, G. (2005). Cross-situational projection. In M. Alicke, J. Krueger, & D. Dunning (Eds.), *The self in social judgment* (pp. 43–64). Psychology Press.

Von Neumann, J., & Morgenstern, O. (1944). *Theory of games and economic behavior.* Princeton University Press.

Voors, Maarten J., Nillesen, Eleonora E. M., Verwimp, Philip, Bulte, Erwin H., Lensink, Robert, & Van Soest, Daan P. (2012). Violent conflict and behavior: A field experiment in burundi. *American Economic Review, 102*(2), 941–964.

Wakker, P. P. (2010). *Prospect theory for risk and ambiguity.* Cambridge University Press.

Waldron, Jeremy. (2014). It's all for your own good. [Review of the book *Why nudge?*, by Cass Sunstein]. *The New York Review.* https://www.nybooks.com/articles/2014/10/09/cass-sunstein-its-all-your-own-good/

Wallace, C., & Young, P. H. (2015). Stochastic evolutionary game dynamics. In H. P. Young & S. Zamir (Eds.), *The handbook of game theory* (Vol. 4, pp. 327–380). Elsevier.

Wason, P. C. (1968). Reasoning about a rule. *Quarterly Journal of Experimental Psychology, 20,* 273–281.

Weimer, D. L. (2020). When are nudges desirable? Benefit validity when preferences are not consistently revealed. *Public Administration Review, 80*(1), 118–126.

Weinstein, N. D. (1980). Unrealistic optimism about future life events. *Journal of Personality and Social Psychology, 39*(5), 806–820.

Weisbuch, G., Kirman, A., & Herreiner, D. (2000). Market organisation and trading relationships. *Economic Journal, 110*(463), 411–436.

Weitzman, M. L. (1974). Prices vs. quantities. *Review of Economic Studies, 41*(4), 477–491.

Wertenbroch, K. (1998). Consumption self-control by rationing purchase quantities of virtue and vice. *Marketing Science, 17*(4), 317–337.

Whitt, S., & Wilson, R. K. (2007). The dictator game, fairness and ethnicity in postwar Bosnia. *American Journal of Political Science, 51*(3), 655–668.

Williams, A. F., & Lund, A. K. (1986). Seat belt use laws and occupant crash protection in the United States. *American Journal of Public Health, 76*(12), 1438–1442.

Willis, L. E. (2013). When nudges fail: Slippery defaults. *The University of Chicago Law Review, 80*(3), 1155–1229.

Wilson, E. O. (2012). *The social conquest of earth*. Liveright Publishing Corporation.

Wilson, Timothy. (2004). *Strangers to ourselves: Discovering the adaptive unconscious*. Belknap Press.

Windschitl, P. D., Kruger, J., & Simms, E. (2003). The influence of egocentrism and focalism on people's optimism in competitions: When what affects us equally affects me more. *Journal of Personality and Social Psychology, 85*, 389–408.

World Bank. (2015). *World development report: Mind, society, and behaviour*.

World Health Organization. (2020). Behavioural considerations for acceptance and uptake of COVID-19 vaccines. *WHO Technical Advisory Group on Behavioural Insights and Sciences for Health*. https://www.who.int/publications/i/item/9789240016927

Wright, J. D., & Ginsburg, D. H. (2015). Behavioral law and economics: Its origins, fatal flaws, and implications for liberty. *Northwestern University Law Review, 106*(3), 1033–1090.

Yaari, Menahem E. (1978). Endogenous changes in tastes: A philosophical discussion. In H. W. Gottinger & W. Leinfellner (Eds.), *Decision theory and social ethics* (pp. 59–98). Springer.

Yaniv, G. (1999). Tax compliance and advance tax payments: A prospect theory analysis. *National Tax Journal, 52*(4), 753–764.

Yitzhaki, S. (1974). A note on income tax evasion: A theoretical analysis. *Journal of Public Economics, 3*(2), 201–202.

Young, H. P. (1993). The evolution of conventions. *Econometrica, 61*(1), 57–84.

Young, P. H. (1998). *Individual strategy and social structure: An evolutionary theory of institutions*. Princeton University Press.

Zajonc, R. B. (1980). Feeling and thinking: Preferences need no inferences. *American Psychologist, 35*(2), 151–175.

Zalta, Edward N. (Ed.). (2017). Perfectionism in moral and political philosophy. *Stanford encyclopedia of philosophy*. https://plato.stanford.edu/entries/perfectionism-moral/

Zhao, C. (2018). *Representativeness and similarity* [mimeo]. University of Hong Kong.

Zhao, L., Cui, H., Qiu, X., Wang, X., & Wang, J. (2013). SIR rumor spreading model in the new media age. *Physica A: Statistical Mechanics and its Applications, 392*(4), 995–1013.

Zhong, C-B., Loewenstein, J., & Murnighan, J. K. (2007). Speaking the same language: The cooperative effects of labeling in the prisoner's dilemma. *Journal of Conflict Resolution, 51*(3), 431–456.

Zywicki, T. J. (2013). *The economics and regulation of bank overdraft protection* [George Mason University Law and Economics Research Paper No. 11–43]. https://papers.ssrn.com/sol3/papers.cfm?abstract_id=1946387

Index

Page numbers in italic indicate a figure and page numbers in bold indicate a table on the corresponding page.

Abdellaoui, M. A., 446n17
Abreu-Matsushima mechanisms, 77
Abstraction, level of, 354–356
Accuracy-effort trade-off, 290–291
Acquire a company game, 172, 209–211
Acquisition utility, 261–262
Active choosing, 405, 408–409
Adaptive expectations, 3–4, 192–193
Adaptive rules, 15, 166, 213, 215–216
Adaptive toolbox of heuristics, 305, 323
Add-ons, 392
  fully attentive consumers and, 397–398
  inattentive consumers and, 363, 394
Ad valorem taxes, 452n1
Affect heuristic, 16
  definition of, 236, 269, 288–289
  examples of, 329–330, 332
  narratives and, 174, 241–242
Affordable Care Act (ACA), 425, 433–434, 437
Age, overconfidence and, 63
Agent-based models (ABMs)
  applications of, 212, 225–226
  definition of, 172–173
  features of, 114, 166–167
  Lucas critique, 224, 225
  strengths and weaknesses of, 223–225
  UK housing sector example of, 221–223
Agents, 37
Aggregation of risk, 175–176, 249–250
Agriculture, Department of (USDA)
  automatic enrollment plans, 432
  disclosure requirements, 435–436
Akaike information criterion, 327
Akerlof, G. A.,, 213, 448n1
Alesina, A., 162, 164
Allais, Maurice, 38, 66, 446n6
Allais paradox, 28, 65–68, 99
Allingham, M. G., 134–138
Allingham-Sandmo-Yitzhaki (AYS) framework, 134–136
al-Nowaihi, A., 72, 97, 136–137, 185, 201, 256
Alternating-offers bargaining games, 78
Alternation rate, 299, *299*
Amazon frustration-free packaging, 427
Ambiguity. *See also* Decision theory
  definition of, 32–33
  true uncertainty versus, 34
American Economic Association, Friedman's address to, 3
Analogy-based equilibrium, 77, 246

Anchoring heuristic, 16
  definition of, 267, 277
  examples of, 275–278, 276, 329–330
  expert bias and, 304
  irrelevance of bias-variance dilemma to, 19, 339
  under true uncertainty, 332
  when to use, 324–325
Animal spirits, 128
Annual percentage rate (APR), mandated disclosure of, 322, 407
Annuities, consumer evaluation of, 442
Anticipal utility, 177–178, 189
Anticipatory utility, 177
Anxiety, decision-making and, 55–56, 179, 303, 352. *See also* Affect heuristic; Emotional states
Applied economics, 9
Aquinas, Thomas, 358
Arbitrageurs, 129
Ardern, Jacinda, 428
Ariely, D., 390
Aristotle, 357
Arrow, Kenneth, 255
Arthur, W. B., 214, 215
Ashenfelter, Orley, 262
As-if theories, 93
  in economic methodology, 157–159
  fast and frugal heuristics research program on, 307–308, 325–327
Aspiration-adaptation theory, 14–15
  conservation of cognitive effort and, 328
  cooperation problem, 192–195, **192**
  coordination problem, 195–197
  definition of, 171, 190–191
  infinite regress problem in search, 171, 191
  under true uncertainty, 332
Asymmetric paternalism, 408
Asymptotically stable steady states, 15, 173, 230, 232–233
Attention, assumptions of Bayesian rationality approach, 24, 52, 56–57, 59–60. *See also* Limited attention

Attribute-based models of time discounting, 14–16, 93
  definition of, 169–170, 180
  under risk and uncertainty, 448n2
  similarity relation in time preferences, 170, 183
  trade-off model of attribute choice, 170, 184–185
  vague time preferences model, 170, 181–182
Attribute choice, trade-off model of, 14, 184–185
Attribution bias, 62, 130, 224
Auctions, common value. *See* Common value (CV) auctions, bidding behavior in
Aumann, R. J., 53
Australia, libertarian paternalism in, 424, 429
Ausubel, Lawrence M., 393
Autocorrelation, positive/negative, 267
Automatic enrollment plans, 407, 431–432
  default rules, 429–431
  health care, 433–434
  payroll statements, 434
  savings plans, 431–432
  school meals, 432–433
Automatic escalation, 432
Autonomy, choice and, 344–345
Availability cascades, 282
Availability heuristic, 16, 19
  definition of, 267–268
  examples of, 281–282
  irrelevance of bias-variance dilemma to, 339
  mental models and, 244
  narratives and, 174
  under true uncertainty, 332
  when to use, 325
Axioms of rationality for time discounting, 25
  definition of, 48–52
  discounted utility model, 70, 72
  evidence on, 69–76

exponential discounted utility model, 69–70, 142, 178, 186, 361
  violations of, 70–76
Axioms of rationality under risk, 25, 44–47
Ayton, P., 298–300

Bans. *See also* Mandates; Regulations
  Bayesian rationality approach to, 6
  libertarian paternalism and, 6–7, 20–21
Baptista R., 222
Barberis, N., 338
Bardsley, N., 58
Bargaining impasse, 78
Bar-Hillel, M., 84
Bar-Ilan, A., 257
Base rates
  base rate neglect, 10, 29, 90–92, 329, 446n14
  base rate overuse, 90
  causal, 85
  incidental, 85
Battigalli, P., 56
Bayesian information criterion, 327
Bayesian rationality approach (BRA), 1–7. *See also* Bayes' law; Dynamic programming; Mathematical optimization
  assumptions in, 2–3, 10, 12, 24, 37, 52, 79–80
  attention in, 24, 52, 56–57, 59–60
  behavioral economics compared to, 156–157
  computational ability in, 24, 52, 56–57
  consistent preferences in, 24–25, 27–28, 40–41, 56–58
  continued adherence to, 12–14, 37–38, 157–158
  decision-makers in, 37
  decreasing absolute risk aversion in, 135
  definition of rationality in, 23
  emotional states in, 26–27, 55–56

empirical rejection of, 4–7, 11–13, 37–38, 443
  harm principle, 6, 19, 347, 403–404, 443
  intellectual history of, 1–3
  limitations of, 3–4
  rational expectations in, 3–4, 24, 445n1
  rationality in choices made over time, 47–52, 361–362
  rationality in strategic interaction, 52–54
  rationality under certainty, 38–43
  rationality under risk and uncertainty, 43–47
  self-regarding preferences in, 26–28, 54–55, 403–404
  utility function in, 41–43
Bayes' law
  alternatives to, 92
  in Bayesian rationality approach, 13, 37, 52, 142, 161, 273, 286, 293–295, 301
  departure of human behavior from, 29, 84–88, 87, 128, 149, 329
  equation for, 84, 87
  frequency versus probability format and, 294–297, 307, 321
  modification of, 89–92
Bazerman, M. H., 208–210
Becker, Gary, 256–257
Becker paradox, 256–257
Becker proposition, 256–257
Behavioral decision theory. *See* Decision theory
Behavioral economics, 19–21. *See also* Libertarian paternalism (LP)
  Bayesian rationality approach compared to, 156–157
  Bernheim's premises for, 350–351
  big-push program, 5–6, 11
  choices and welfare in, 343–346
  concept of welfare in, 356–358
  direct judgements in, 341, 346–351, 354–356
  emotional states in, 55–56

Behavioral economics (cont.)
  fast and frugal heuristics research
    program on, 307–308
  freedom of choice in, 20–21, 345,
    347, 360, 404, 408, 414–415,
    425, 440, 443
  harm principle, 6, 19, 347,
    403–404, 443
  increasing acceptance of, 2, 4–7, 11
  incremental program, 5–6, 12
  indirect judgements in, 346–351,
    353–354
  lack of information or behavioral
    bias in, 341–343
  means paternalism, 342, 347
  perfectionism in, 357–358, 452n17
  practice and theory in, 351–353
  procedural rationality, 5, 11–12,
    139, 170, 265, 305, 310–311
  sample cases for, 342–343
  sovereignty of individual
    preferences and, 341–343
  subsidiary questions for, 359–360
  working presumption for, 349,
    358–360
Behavioral frictions to learning, 224
Behavioral game theory, 77, 141,
  146–147
Behavioral industrial organization, 20
  Hotelling competition, 363,
    392–394
  unexpected effects of soft
    paternalism in, 399–401
Behavioral market failures,
  434–435
Behavioral models of game theory, 77,
  141
Behavioral models of heuristics-based
  choice, 14–16
  aspiration-adaptation theory, 171,
    188–197
  attribute-based models of time
    discounting, 14–16, 93, 169–170,
    180–185
  choice bracketing, 175–176,
    245–251
  evidential reasoning, 162, 198–202

evolutionary game theory, 8, 15,
  146–147, 173, 226–233, 227,
  230, 449n14
fundamental misunderstandings
  about, 289–291
heuristics-based models of
  intertemporal choice, 170,
  185–188
introduction to, 169–177
Kantian rationality, 171, 203–207
low probability events, attitudes
  toward, 176–177, 251–259
macroeconomic implications of
  bounded rationality, 172–173,
  211–226
mental accounting and prospect
  theory, 170–171, 188–190
mental models, 175, 242–245
narrative economics, 174–175,
  234–242
opportunity costs, 177, 259–263
original prospect theory, 176,
  253–255
risk as feelings theory, 169,
  177–180, *178*
stochastic social dynamics,
  173–174, 231–234
sunk costs, 177, 259–263
winner's curse in financial markets,
  172, 207–211
Behavioural Insights Team (UK), 424,
  426
Beinhocker, E. D., 159
Beliefs
  common knowledge of, 127
  optimal belief management, 63–64
  updating with Bayes' law. *See* Bayes'
    law
Bellman, Richard E., 109, 116
Bellman equation, 116
Bénabou, R., 235
Benartzi, S., 247, 248
Benchmarks
  for fast and frugal heuristics
    research program, 18–19
  for heuristics and biases research
    program, 18–19

Benefits, marginal, 259
Benjamin, D., 90, 91, 92
Bergert, F. B., 321
Bernard, T., 197
Bernheim, B. D., 343–344, 346, 347, 350, 451n4, 452n12, 452n15
Bertrand competition, 395–396
Best and worst axiom, 45
Better than average effect, 61
Better than median effect, 61
Betting behavior. *See* Gambler's fallacy
Biais, B., 279–280
Biases. *See also* Heuristics and biases research program (HBP); Overconfidence
　attribution, 62, 130
　confirmation, 16, 19, 88–89, 244, 269, 286–288, 339
　definition of, 265
　expert, 270, 303–305, 450n5
　hindsight, 16, 19, 267, 278–281, 303–304, 313–314, 329, 339
　left-digit, 60
　present bias for current consumption, 75–76, 385–392
　projection, 56, 393
　sampling, 80–83, 82
　self-serving, 78, 130
　systematic, 129, 293
Bias-variance dilemma, 8, 19, 292
　critique of, 308–309, 337–339
　definition of, 331
　examples of, 333–337, *336*
　formula for, 334–335
　implications for heuristics and biases research program, 339–340
Bicchieri, C., 150
Biden, Joe, 424
Big-bang approach, 112
Big-push program, 5–6, 11
Binary preference relation, 39
Blumenstock, J., 410
Boltzmann equilibrium, 213
Bonini, N., 284
Bookstaber, R., 214
Boosts, 321–322, 420–421

Borges, B., 331
Bounded rationality, case for, 109–110. *See also* Mathematical optimization
　introduction to, 109–114
　macroeconomic implications of bounded rationality, 172–173, 211–226
　macroeconomy as complex, adaptive system, 113–114, 165–167
　methodology in economics, 112–113, 156–161
　preferences and beliefs, 113, 161–165
　social norms, 12, 54, 56, 112, 149–156, 308, 327–329
　strategic interaction, 10, 52–54, 76–79, 112, 143–149
Bracketing, choice. *See* Choice bracketing
Brain
　mind as a Swiss army knife view, 86
　natural frequency algorithm of, 86
　two-system model of, 302–303
Brandenburger, A., 53
Breast cancer examinations, behavior toward, 176, 258
Brighton, H., 289–303, 317, 320, 323, 337
British Toxicology Association, 330
Broad bracketing, 15
　definition of, 175, 246
　risk aggregation, 249–250
Bröder, A., 318, 319, 320
Bubb, R., 451n4
Bubbles in financial markets, 111, 126–127
Buchanan, James M., 405, 410, 412
Budget constraints of individual, 116, 368–369, 372, 375, 376
Buy to let investors (BTL), 222

Cab driver behavior, choice bracketing in, 69, 246–247, 251
Cab problem, 84–88
Camerer, C. F., 63, 89, 273, 279

Cameron, David, 424
Cancellation heuristic, 254
Capen, E. C., 208
Capital punishments, Becker paradox for, 176, 256–257
Carpenter, J. P., 163
Case-based decision theory, 36
Categorical thinking, 92
Causal base rates, 85
Centers for Medicare & Medicaid Services (CMS), 433
CEO overconfidence, 63, 130–131
Certainty, rationality under, 10, 38–43
  assumption of, 40–41
  binary preference relation in, 39
  certainty equivalents, 57, 94–95, 107, 248
  consistent preferences in, 24–25, 27–28, 40–41, 56–58
  continuity in, 42–43
  definition of, 31, 40–41
  example of, 39–40
  utility function in, 41–43
Certainty effect, 66
Certainty equivalents, 57, 94–95, 107, 248
Chaotic dynamics, 14, 114, 172–173, 219–221, 220, 449n13
Charness, G., 150, 284
Chater, N., 337, 413
Chen, Steve, 35
Chetty, R., 60
Children's Health Insurance Program (CHIP), automatic enrollment in, 434
Choice bracketing, 245–251
  broad, 15, 175, 246, 249
  definition of, 245–246
  equity-premium puzzle, 175, 247–249
  examples of, 246–247
  introduction to, 175–176
  myopic loss aversion in, 246
  narrow, 21, 175–176, 245–246, 251
  risk aggregation in, 175–176, 249–250

Choices. *See also* Choice bracketing
  choice over-load, 440
  structuring of, 440
  welfare and, 343–346
Cho-Kreps intuitive criterion, 78
Cigarette taxes, 21, 344, 367, 407, 414
Cigarette use
  bans on menthol-flavored cigarettes, 21, 414, 420
  choice bracketing in, 175, 246
  purchase of single cigarette packs, 390–391
  vividness of risky outcomes in, 179
Classical game theory (CGT)
  assumptions in, 143
  common knowledge in, 53
  epistemic foundations of, 52–53
  equilibrium concepts in, 3–4, 10, 26, 52–54, 78–79, 143
  evidential reasoning and, 147, 162, 198–202, **200**
  infinite regress problem in, 26, 53
  methodological individualism in, 10, 12, 15, 37, 78–79, 143–144, 445n3
  rationality assumptions under, 52–54, 76–79
  strategic interaction in, 52–54, 76–79, 112, 143–149, 447n10
Classical individuals, 369–373
Classical neoclassical economics, 2
Clemen, R. T., 83
Climate change
  behavioral economics and, 413–414, 419
  models of, 224
Coalescing heuristic, 254
Coarse thinkers, 245
Cobweb model, 449n13
Coefficient of loss aversion, 103
Coefficient of relative risk aversion, 248
Coercive paternalism, 451n4
Cognitive ability, limited, 232
Cognitive effort, conservation of, 87, 201, 328–329

Cognitive tax, 59–60
Combination heuristic, 254
Common consequence violation of expected utility, 67–68
Common difference effect, 25, 28, 71–76
Common knowledge, 10, 26, 53, 127, 143
Common-pool resource problems, Kantian rationality in, 204–207
Common priors, 10, 26, 53, 143–144
Common ratio violation of expected utility, 67
Common value (CV) auctions, bidding behavior in, 171–172
  acquire a company game, 172, 209–211
  winner's curse, 172, 207–211
Community Living Assistance Services and Supports Act (CLASS Act), 433
Compensated demand curve, 362, 378
Compensatory heuristics, 451n5
Competition, Bertrand model of, 395–396
Competition, Hotelling model of, 363, 392–394
  cross-subsidy from inattentive to fully attentive consumers, 397–399
  fully attentive consumers, 394–396
  inattentive consumers, 396–399
  naive consumers, 392–393
  reaction function in, 395–396
  sophisticated consumers, 392–393
Completeness axiom, 44–45
Complex, adaptive system, macroeconomy as, 113–114, 165–167
Complexity theory, 8, 15, 172, 212–215. *See also* Macroeconomic implications
Composite Prelec probability weighting function (CPF), 258–259, 259, 450n19
Composite prospect theory, 16, 177, 258–259
Compound lotteries, 45–46

Computational ability, assumptions of Bayesian rationality approach, 2, 24, 52, 56
Conditional cooperation, 194–195
Conditional reciprocity, 147, 202
Confirmation bias, 16, 19
  definition of, 269, 286–288
  irrelevance of bias-variance dilemma to, 339
  mental models and, 244
  risk and uncertainty in, 329
Conjunction fallacy, 19
  definition of, 268, 282–283
  irrelevance of bias-variance dilemma to, 339–340
  Linda problem, 268, 283–284, 450n4
  risk and uncertainty in, 329
Conly, Sarah, 451n4
Consequentialist reasoning, 169, 177
Conservation of cognitive effort, 328
Conservatism, 10, 29, 61, 66, 88–92, 257, 329
Consistent preferences
  criterion of internal consistency, 27–28
  definition of, 24–25, 40–41
  evidence on, 56–58
Constant returns to scale, 447n2
Consumer Financial Protection Bureau, 400, 438–439
Consumer Policy Toolkit, 425
Consumer surplus, 261, 378–379, 384, 396, 399
Consumption taxes. *See* Pigouvian (corrective) taxes; Taxation
Contagion, spread of narratives through, 15, 174–175, 234–242
  affect heuristic and, 236
  characteristics of narratives in, 235–236
  epidemiological models of, 237–242, 240
  network theory of, 237
  phishing equilibrium in, 236
Contagion rate, 238–242

Contented households, in neighborhood segregation problem, 217–218
Continuity axiom, 42–43
  rationality in choices made over time, 48, 69–76
  rationality under risk, 45
Contractarianism, 405, 410–413
Contracts, microfinance. *See* Microfinance contracts, optimization in
Control, illusion of, 130
Conventions, 153–154
Cooling-off periods, 407
Cooperation, 112, 143
  aspiration-adaptation theory and, 192–195
  in prisoner's dilemma game, 146–149, 192–195, 201
Coordination, 112, 143, 226–231, 227, 230
Corporate bond trading, agent-based models of, 225
Corrective taxes. *See* Pigouvian (corrective) taxes
Correlated equilibrium, 127, 149, 225
Costs
  current, 362, 386–390
  future, 362, 389
  marginal, 177, 259
  marginal social, 374
  opportunity, 16, 177, 259–263
  sunk, 16, 77, 177, 259–263, 304
Covid-19 pandemic, libertarian paternalism in, 344, 419, 424, 426–428, 440
Craven, T.A. M., 35
Crawford, V. P., 127, 138–141, 190
Credit Card Accountability Responsibility and Disclosure Act (Credit CARD Act), 425, 433, 436
Cross-subsidy from inattentive to fully attentive consumers, 397–399
Cues, 17, 305
Culture, 113
  definition of, 161–162
  effect of institutions on, 163–165
  effect on institutions, 162–163
  transmission of, 162
Cumulative prospect theory. *See* Prospect theory, cumulative
Current benefits and future costs, 389
Current costs and future benefits
  example of, 386–389
  fertilizer purchases, 391–392
  job searches, 389–390
Cursed equilibrium, 77, 211, 246
Czerlinski, J., 313

Darai, D., 202
Dark patterns, 430
Darwin, Charles, 173, 226, 284
Datta, S., 60, 243, 245
Dawes' rule, 450n3
Deadlines, 390–391
Deadweight loss, 362, 376–380, *379*
Decision-makers, 37
Decision tasks, 338–339
Decision theory, 8, 10–11, 36, 92–93. *See also* Attribute-based models of time discounting; Expected utility theory (EU); Lotteries; Probability weighting function; Prospect theory, cumulative
  ambiguity in, 32–33
  certainty in, 31
  decision weighted utility, 99
  rank dependent utility theory, 11, 29, 36, 96, 99–101
  risk in, 31
  subjective uncertainty in, 31–32
  taxonomy of situations in, 29–36
  true uncertainty in, 33–36
Decision weighted utility (DWU), 99
Decision weights
  definition of, 99–100
  under prospect theory (PT), 105–106
Decreasing absolute risk aversion, 135
Default options, 7, 21, 405, 409–410
Default rules, 429–431
Defection, in prisoner's dilemma game, 192–195, 201

Delay-discounting models, heuristics for, 170, 185–188
Demand curve
 compensated (Hicksian), 362, 378
 indifference, 453n4
 uncompensated (Marshallian), 375, 378, 380
De Niro, Robert, 64
Denmark, automatic enrollment plans in, 431
Denzau, A. T., 242
Description invariance assumption, 68–69
Descriptive norms, 151
Diagnostic significance, 98
Dictator game, 164, 447n16
Dimmock, S. G., 33
Direct judgements
 definition of, 346, 354–356
 examples of, 346–351
 lack of information or behavioral bias in, 341–343
 legal applications of, 348
 level of abstraction problem and, 354–356
Disappointment aversion, 36
Disclosure requirements, 434–439
 competition and, 438–439
 financial products, 436–437
 fuel economy, 437–438
 goals, 434–435
 health care, 437
 nutrition, 435–436
Discontented households, in neighborhood segregation problem, 217–218
Discounted utility (DU) model, 50–51, 70, 72
Discount function, 50–51
Discount rate, 51–52, 69–70, 74, 364
Disposition effect, 274
Distortionary consumption taxes, 377–378, 384, 453n5
Distortionary taxes, 376
Dodd-Frank Wall Street Reform Act, 425, 438–439
Dogfooding, 304

Domains of choice, 307–308, 327–333
Dominance heuristic, 254–255
Dotted S-shaped curve, 98
Drexler, A., 59
DRIFT (difference, ratio, interest, and finance) model, 170, 187–188
Duflo, E., 391
Dufwenberg, M., 56
Duhem-Quine thesis, 448n12
Dunning, D., 62
Dunning-Kruger effect, 61–62
Dyer, D., 209
Dynamic general stochastic equilibrium (DGSE) models, 214–215
Dynamic optimization problem, 109–110, 115–119
Dynamic programming, 4, 8, 109–110, 115–119
Dynamics
 chaotic, 14, 114, 172–173, 219–221, *220*, 449n13
 evolutionary, 173
 replicator, 173, 229, 233
 stochastic social dynamics, 8, 15, 156, 173–174, 231–234, *234*
Dynamic stochastic general equilibrium (DSGE), 14

Earned income tax credit (EITC), 60, 343
Ecological rationality of heuristics, 265, 269–270, 291–292, 302, 305
Ecological validity of cues, 17, 305, 311, 312, 320–321
Economic actors, 37
Economic methodology, 112–113, 156–161
Edison, Thomas, 35
Education, Department of, 439
Edwards, W., 89, 316
Efficiency costs of taxation, 374–380
Efficient markets hypothesis (EMH), 62, 126, 128, 286
Ehrlinger, J., 62
Einstein, Albert, 156

El-Farol problem, 215–216
Elimination by aspects (EBA), 315
Ellingsen, T., 447n5
Ellison, G., 232
Ellsberg, Daniel, 445n2
Ellsberg paradox, 32–34, 327, 445n2
Elster, Jon, 150, 445n3
Emergent phenomena, 14
  definition of, 172, 212–213
  emergent properties, 114
  example of, 215–216
  neighborhood segregation as, 216–218, 218, 449n10
Emotional states, 26–27. *See also* Affect heuristic
  in classical game theory, 79
  in decision-making, 55–56
  loss aversion and, 327
  in microfinance contracts, 110
  projection bias, 56
  risk as feelings theory, 169, 177–180, 178
  spread of narratives and, 241–242
Empirical counterparts to heuristics, 17, 269–270, 297–298
Empirical expectations, 26, 151
Empirical testing of heuristics, 317–321
Endgame effect, 126, 199
Endowment effect, 36, 69, 430
Ends paternalism, 342, 347, 408
Energy, Department of, 400
Energy-efficient products, decisions about, 344, 350, 369, 407, 430, 441, 452n20
Energy Paradox, 441
Englich, B., 277
Enrollment, automatic, 407, 431–432
  default rules, 429–431
  health care, 433–434
  payroll statements, 434
  savings plans, 431–432
  school meals, 432–433
Entrepreneurs
  heuristics improving financial literacy of, 59
  overconfidence of, 63

Environmental Protection Agency (EPA), 424, 438
Environments, simple taxonomy of, 29–36
  ambiguity, 32–33
  certainty, 31
  lotteries, 29–30
  risk, 31
  subjective uncertainty, 31–32
  true uncertainty, 33–36
Epidemiological models, application to narrative economics, 237–242, 240
Equality heuristic (1/N heuristic), 331–332
Equal weighing strategy (EQW), 316
Equilibrium, 3, 4, 10, 26. *See also* Nash equilibrium
  analogy-based, 246
  Boltzmann, 213
  in classical game theory, 52–54, 143
  correlated, 127, 149, 225
  cursed, 211, 246
  dynamic general stochastic, 214–215
  evidential, 127, 201–202
  general equilibrium considerations, 392
  history dependent equilibria, 78
  in Hotelling competition model, 395–396
  impulse balance, 190
  Kantian, 127, 171, 204
  monomorphic, 173, 227
  partial equilibrium considerations, 392
  phishing, 236
  polymorphic, 173, 227
  punctuated, 174, 233
  quantal response, 78
  sequential, 211
  statistical, 213
Equity-premium puzzle, 15, 56, 69, 175, 247–249
Equivalence relation, 181, 448n3

Ergodic states, 233
Error structure, suitability of, 337–338
Ethicality, 162
Euler equations, 214–215, 221
European Union, libertarian paternalism in, 424, 425
  institutionalization of behavioral insights, 428–429
  policies on savings, 431
Events, heuristic explanations of, 298–300
Evidential equilibrium, 127, 147, 201–202
Evidential games, 201–202
Evidential reasoning (ER), 147, 162, 198–202, **200**
Evolutionary game theory, 8, 15, 146–147, 226–231
  asymptotically stable steady state, 173, 230, 232–233
  coordination game, 227–231, **227**, **230**
  evolutionary stable strategies in, 173, 227–231
  monomorphic versus polymorphic equilibrium in, 173, 227
  phenotypes in, 226–228, 449n14
  replicator dynamics in, 173, 229, 233
Evolutionary stable strategy (ESS), 15, 173, 227–231
Expectations
  adaptive, 3
  rational, 3–4
Expected mean square prediction error, 334
Expected outcome, 102, 298
Expected return per dollar of evaded tax, 136
Expected utility functional, 25, 96, 450
Expected utility theory (EU), 3, 10, 11, 29, 35–36, 46–47, 93–96
  additional violations of, 69
  anomalies under, 135–138
  attitudes to risk in, 95
  axioms of rationality under risk in, 44–47
  in Bayesian rationality approach, 142
  certainty equivalents in, 57, 94–95, 107, 248
  common consequence violation, 67–68
  common ratio violation, 67
  definition of, 44, 93
  examples of, 94–96
  refutations of, 52, 64–69, 96
  St. Petersburg paradox, 93–94
  tax evasion problem and, 134–138
Expected wealth, 102
Experienced net utility, 261–262
Expert bias, 270, 303–305, 450n5
Exponential discounted utility (EDU), 3, 10, 25, 49–52
  anticipal utility in, 178
  discount factor in, 50–52, 69–70, 74, 364
  equation for, 116
  outcome-time pairs in, 169, 186
  refutations of, 28, 142, 361
Extended warranties, 169, 180
Externalities
  definition of, 366
  internalization of, 366, 371
Extrinsic motivation, 58

Fair outcome, 102, 298
Fallacies
  conjunction, 19, 88–89, 268, 282–284, 339
  gambler's, 16, 19, 267, 273–274, 298–300, **299**, 329, 339
  hot hand, 16, 19, 267, 274–275, 276, 298–300, **299**, 329, 339
  planning, 8
False consensus effect, 147, 198, 304, 329. *See also* Evidential reasoning (ER)
Farhi, E., 441

Fast and frugal heuristics research
    program (FFP), 16–19, 265,
    305–309, 313–314, 315, 331
  bias-variance dilemma, 8, 19, 292,
    308–309, 331–340, *336*
  choice of heuristics in, 307,
    323–325
  critique of, 18, 316–325
  domains of choice in, 307–308,
    327–333
  ecological validity of cues in, 17,
    305, 311, 312, 320–321
  elimination by aspects, 315
  empirical testing of heuristics in,
    306, 317–321
  equal weighing strategy, 316
  examples of, 310–314
  foundational elements of, 305–306
  heuristics and biases research
    program versus, 265, 269–270,
    289–303, 308–309, 450n1
  lack of benchmark for, 18–19, 306,
    316–317
  LEX heuristic, 315–316
  motivation for, 305
  on optimization-based and as-if
    models, 307–308, 325–327
  priority heuristic, 312
  procedural rationality, 5, 11–12,
    139, 170, 265, 305, 310–311
  recognition heuristic, 18, 305, 312
  reference class of cues in, 305
  risk and subjective uncertainty in,
    305
  statistical training in, 307, 321–323
  take-the-best heuristic, 17–18, 305,
    311–315, **313**
  true uncertainty in, 305–306, 308,
    327–333
  weighted adding strategy, 316, 324
FEAST (fun, easy, attractive, social,
    and timely) framework, 21–22, 423,
    426–428
Federal Reserve Board, 432
Federal Trade Commission, 400
Feelings, risk as, 14, 36, 93, 169,
    177–180, *178*

Fehr, E., 13, 55, 138–139, 152
Fehr-Schmidt model, 138–139
Felicity, 50
Fershtman, C., 163
Fertilizer purchases, hard paternalism
    and, 391–392
Feynman, R., 157
Field studies, 5, 158
Financial fragility, 226
Financial market investment. *See also*
    Choice bracketing
  applications of the gambler's fallacy
    to, 274
  behavioral market failures,
    434–435
  bubbles in, 111, 126–127
  corporate bond trading,
    agent-based models of, 225
  disclosure requirements in, 436–437
  disposition effect, 274
  efficient markets hypothesis, 62,
    126, 128, 286
  equity-premium puzzle, 15, 56, 69,
    175, 247–249
  expert bias in, 279–280, 450n5
  heuristics for, 331–332
  investor sentiment, 128–129, 213
  investor sentiment in, 128
  noise traders, 11, 129
  non-optimizing individuals and
    firms, 111, 127–131
  regression to the mean and, 285
  winner's curse in, 172, 207–211
Firm competition, Hotelling model of,
    363, 392–394
  cross-subsidy from inattentive to
    fully attentive consumers,
    397–399
  fully attentive consumers, 394–396
  inattentive consumers, 396–399
  naive consumers, 392–393
  reaction function in, 395–396
  sophisticated consumers, 392–393
First best allocation, 371
Fischer, I., 298–300
Fishburn, P. C., 49
Fittest, survival of, 173, 226–227

Food and Drug Administration (FDA), 435–436
Food pyramid, 435
Ford, Betty, 258
Fourfold classification of risk, 68, 102–103, 105–107, **106**
Framing, 68–69, 442
Franklin's rule, 320, 450n3
Frederick, S., 70
Freedom of choice
   preservation of, 20–21, 360, 404, 408, 414–415, 425, 440, 443
   respect for, 345, 347
Frequency format, 17, 86–88, 87, 270, 283–284, 294–297
Friedman, Milton, 3, 13, 16, 38, 112, 157, 297
Fuchs-Schündeln, N., 164
Fuel economy, disclosure of, 354, 407, 437–438, 452n20
Fully attentive consumers, 394–399

Gabaix, X., 376, 441
Gächter, S., 152, 199
Gain-loss asymmetry, 10, 28, 70–72
Galton, Francis, 284
Gambler's fallacy, 16, 19, 339
   definition of, 267, 273–275
   representativeness heuristic-based explanation for, 298–300, 299
   risk and uncertainty in, 329
Gambles, definition of, 29–30
Games against nature, 29–30
Game theory. *See also* Classical game theory (CGT)
   behavioral, 77, 141, 146–147
   common knowledge in, 53
   epistemic foundations of, 52–53
   evolutionary, 8, 15, 146–147, 173, 226–233, **227**, 230, 449n14
   psychological, 56, 78–79, 110, 447n1
Gender inequity, mental models of, 244
General equilibrium considerations, 392
Genotypes, 226, 449n14

Gigerenzer, Gerd, 5, 16, 265, 305, 312. *See also* Fast and frugal heuristics research program (FFP)
   advocacy for statistical training, 321–322
   on ecological validity of cues, 318, 320
   on frequency versus probability format, 307
   on less is more effect, 333, 337
   libertarian paternalism, 415–418, 420
   on Linda problem, 283
   objections to heuristics and biases research program, 266, 289–303, 450n1
   on small versus large worlds, 330
   on superiority of heuristics, 317
Gilovich, T., 266, 293
Giné, X., 59
Gintis, Herbert, 41, 58, 143, 159, 203
Givens, inferences from, 317–318
Glaser, M., 63
Glazer-Perry mechanisms, 77
Gneezy, U., 163
Goals
   evaluation of outcomes relative to, 96
   goal-setting behavior, 69, 149, 251, 310
   goal systems, 197
   moral, 452n15
   multiple or conflicting, 197, 392
   promotion of. *See* paternalism; salience
   sensitivity to, 327
   shared, 203
Goldstein, D. G., 312, 318–319
Government error, libertarian paternalism and, 415–418
GPS devices, 347, 405, 408, 416–417, 420
Grameen Bank, 120
Grätz, S., 202
Great Depression, narratives about, 242
Great rationality debate, 17, 291, 330

Great Recession, narratives about, 242
Green Behavior (European
　Commission), 425
Greif, A., 163
Grether, D. M., 57, 90, 446n14
Griffin, D., 90
Griffiths, T. L., 337
Grubb, Michael D., 393
Guilt, 56
　guilt aversion, 79, 110, 121–126,
　　131–134, 138, 153
　moral norms and, 153
　social norms and, 152
Guryan, J., 275

Hansson, P., 63
Hard-easy effect, 61
Hard paternalism, 20. *See also*
　Procrastination; Taxation
　bans, 6–7, 20–21
　definition of, 361
　insights from behavioral industrial
　　organization, 20, 363, 392–394,
　　399–401
　mandates, 6–7, 20–21, 344
　multiple selves, 153–154, 361–374
　policy-relevant insights from
　　behavioral industrial
　　organization, 363
Hardwiring, evolutionary, 226
Harm principle, 6, 19, 347, 403–404,
　443
Harrison, G.W., 209
Harsanyi's purification agenda, 148
Harstad, R. M., 8, 126, 127,
　138–141
Hayek, Friedrich, 415
Health and Human Services (HHS),
　Department of, 424
Health care policies, 433–434, 437
Healthy Hunger-Free Kids Act, 432
Heckman, James, 225
Hedonic criteria, 20, 63, 342, 348,
　352, 357
Hedonic forecasting errors, 356
Heidhues, P., 392
Henrich, J., 155, 162

Herrmann, B., 164
Hertwig, Ralph, 283, 321
Hertzog, C., 63
Heuristics. *See* Fast and frugal
　heuristics research program (FFP);
　Heuristics and biases research
　program (HBP); *Individual
　heuristics*
Heuristics and biases research
　program (HBP), 16–17, 265–270.
　See also Biases; Representativeness
　heuristic
　affect heuristic, 16, 174, 236,
　　241–242, 269, 288–289,
　　329–330, 332
　anchoring heuristic, 19, 267,
　　275–278, 276, 304, 325,
　　329–330, 332, 339
　availability heuristic, 19, 244,
　　267–268, 281–282, 325, 332,
　　339
　benchmarks for, 18–19
　choice of heuristics in, 323–324
　confirmation bias, 16, 19, 244, 269,
　　286–288, 329, 339
　conjunction fallacy, 268, 282–284,
　　339
　criticism of appropriate statistical
　　norms, 270, 300–302
　domains of choice in, 307–308,
　　327–333
　ecological rationality of heuristics
　　in, 269–270, 291–292, 302
　empirical counterparts to heuristics
　　in, 270, 297–298
　expert bias, 270, 303–305, 450n5
　explanations of event and its
　　negation, 270, 298–300
　fast and frugal heuristics research
　　program versus, 265, 308–309
　frequency versus probability format
　　in, 270, 283–284, 294–297
　gambler's fallacy, 16, 19, 267,
　　273–274, 298–300, 299, 329,
　　339
　hindsight bias, 16, 19, 88–89, 267,
　　278–281, 313–314, 339

hot hand fallacy, 16, 19, 267,
  274–275, 276, 298–300, 299,
  329, 339
 necessary and sufficient conditions,
  268, 286
 objections to, 269–270, 289–303,
  450n1
 one-event probabilities in, 269–270,
  292–293
 regression to the mean, 16, 62,
  88–89, 268, 284–285, 339
 significance of, 38, 265, 443
 two-system model of brain in,
  302–303
 "we cannot be that dumb" critique,
  17, 269–270, 293–294
Heuristics-based choice, behavioral
 models of. See Behavioral models of
 heuristics-based choice
Hicksian demand curve, 362, 378
Hindsight bias, 16, 19, 329
 definition of, 267, 278–279
 examples of, 279–281
 expert bias, 303–304
 irrelevance of bias-variance
  dilemma to, 339
 remembered past predictions in,
  279–281
 take-the-best heuristic and,
  313–314
History, role of, 113, 161–165
History dependent equilibria, 78
Hoffrage, U., 313
Homeland Security, Department of,
 434
Hong, H., 127
Hotelling competition, 363, 392–394
 cross-subsidy from inattentive to
  fully attentive consumers,
  397–399
 fully attentive consumers, 394–396
 inattentive consumers, 396–399
 naive consumers, 392–393
 reaction function in, 395–396
 sophisticated consumers, 392–393
Hot hand fallacy, 16, 19
 definition of, 267, 274–275

example of, 275, 276
 irrelevance of bias-variance
  dilemma to, 339
 representativeness heuristic-based
  explanation for, 298–300, 299
 risk and uncertainty in, 329
Hotz, V. J., 60
Housing sector, agent-based model of,
 221–223
Human performance, hot hand fallacy
 applied to, 298–300, 299
Hyperbolic discounting, 10, 70,
 73–76, 142, 169

Illusion of control, 130
Immediate gratification, 72, 75–76
Immigrant households, neighborhood
 segregation of, 216–218, **218**
Impatience, 48, 50, 72
Impulse balance equilibrium, 190
Impulse purchases, return policies for,
 407
Inanimate processes, gambler's fallacy
 applied to, 298–299, 299
Inattentive consumers, 396–399
Incidental base rates, 85
Income tax evasion, 134–138
Incremental program, 5–6, 12, 112
Independence axiom, 25, 45
Indifference curve, 453n4
Indirect judgements
 examples of, 346–351
 pervasiveness of, 353–354
Individualism, methodological. See
 Methodological individualism
Individual liability microfinance
 contracts. See Microfinance
 contracts, optimization in
Individual Opportunity Criterion,
 413
Induced beliefs design, 447n5
Inductive reasoning, 214–216
Inertia, 351. See also Automatic
 enrollment plans; Nudges;
 Procrastination
 aspiration-adaptation theory and,
  193–195

Inertia (cont.)
  automatic enrollment plans and, 347, 349, 430–432
  mental models and, 243–245
Inferences
  from givens, 317–318
  from memory task, 318–320
  potential problems of, 319–320
  of underlying model, 298–300
Infinite regress problem, 26, 53, 171, 191
Inflation
  money supply and, 297
  unemployment and, 295, 445n1
Information, limited, 232
Information criterion, 327
Injunctive norms, 151
Instantaneous utility function, 50
Instant gratification, 385–386, 388. *See also* Procrastination
Institutions, 113, 161–162
  definition of, 161
  effect of preferences on, 162–163
  effect on preferences, 163–165
  institutionalization of behavioral insights, 423, 428–429
Instrumental rationality, 79
Insufficient reason, principle of, 33
Insurance, reluctance to purchase, 255–256
Integration/segregation heuristics, 188–190
Intention-action divide, 60, 391
Intentionality, joint, 15, 79, 147, 171, 203
Internal consistency, 27
Internalities, 20
  definition of, 366
  multiple selves, 153–154, 361–374
  negative, 371
  tax efficiency and, 382–385, *383*
Intertemporal optimization problem under uncertainty, 109–110, 115–119
Intrinsic motivation, 58
Intuitive criterion, 78
Inverse S-shaped curve, 98

Investment. *See* Financial market investment
Investor sentiment, 128–129, 213
ITCH (intertemporal choice heuristic) model, 170, 187–188
Iyengar, S. S., 56

Japan, libertarian paternalism in, 424
Job searches, hard paternalism and, 389–390
Joint intentionality, 15, 79, 147, 171, 203
Joint liability microfinance contracts. *See* Microfinance contracts, optimization in
Jonker, L., 229
Journal of Economic Literature, 138
Judgement
  direct, 341, 346–351, 354–356
  indirect, 346–351, 353–354
  lack of information or behavioral bias in, 341–343

Kagel, J. H., 209
Kahneman, Daniel, 5, 16, 265, 443, 450n1. *See also* Heuristics and biases research program (HBP); Original prospect theory (OPT); Prospect theory, cumulative
  on affect heuristic, 288
  on biases in producing full sampling distribution, 81
  cab problem, 84–88
  on conjunction fallacy, 283–284
  on frequency versus probability format, 294–295
  on judgment heuristics, 112
  on one-event probabilities, 292–293
  on overconfidence, 418
  on predictions of economic models, 13
  refutations of expected utility, 38, 58, 68–69
  on risk/uncertainty, 329
  two-system model of brain, 302–303
Kandori, M., 232

Kantian equilibrium, 127, 171, 204–207
Kantian protocol, 171
Kantian rationality, 15, 79, 147, 171, 203–207
Kearney, M. S., 275
Keeping up with the Joneses, 55
Kermack-McKendrick model, 15, 174, 237–242, 240
Kirman, A., 214
Knight, Frank, 33
Knightian uncertainty. See True uncertainty
Knowledge problem, 414
Kolm, S.-C., 256
Köszegi, B., 392
Kouwenberg, R., 33
Krueger, J. I., 198, 201
Kruger, J., 62
Kuhn, T., 157
Kunreuther, H., 253, 255–256
Kuran, T., 282

Labor, Department of
 disclosure requirements, 439
 Lucas critique and, 400
Lacetera, N., 60
Lack of a benevolent policymaker criticism, 21
Laffer curve, 240, 242
Laffont, J-J., 21
Laibson, D., 376
Lakatos, I., 448n12
Lamberson, P. J., 238
Large numbers, law of, 271, 450n2
Larger-later (LL) rewards, 74–75, 184–188
Large worlds. See True uncertainty
Law of large numbers, 271, 450n2
Law of small numbers, 267, 271–272, 303–304, 329, 393
Lazy controller, System 1 as, 303
Leadership overconfidence, 63, 130–131
Left-digit bias, 60
Legal entitlements, 102

Legislation
 Affordable Care Act, 425, 433–434, 437
 Community Living Assistance Services and Supports Act, 433
 Credit Card Accountability Responsibility and Disclosure Act, 425, 433, 436–437
 Dodd-Frank Wall Street Reform Act, 425, 438–439
 Healthy Hunger-Free Kids Act, 432
 Pension Protection Act, 431
 Sarbanes-Oxley Act, 63
Lei, V., 126
Lepper, M. R., 56
Less is more effect. See Bias-variance dilemma
Level-k models, 77, 146, 211
Level of abstraction problem, 354–356
Levin, D., 209
Levitt, S. D., 257
Levy, Helen G., 452n20
Lewyt, Alex, 35
LEX heuristic, 315–316
LEXSEMI heuristic, 315
Libertarian paternalism (LP), 7, 21, 443. See also Behavioral economics; Nudges; Public policy, behaviorally informed
 boosts in, 321–322, 420–421
 choice over-load, 440
 contractarian approach to, 405, 410–413
 criticism of, 410–414, 420
 default options, 7, 21, 405, 409–410
 definition of, 20–21, 404–405
 disclosure requirements, 434–439
 examples of, 409–410
 FEAST (fun, easy, attractive, social, and timely) framework for, 21–22, 423, 426–428
 goals of, 420
 government error and, 415–418
 institutionalization of behavioral insights, 22, 423, 428–429
 introduction to, 403–405

Libertarian paternalism (LP) (cont.)
  mistakes and welfare in, 405–407
  objections to, 21
  remedies under, 407, 419–421
  salience in, 440–442
  structuring of choices, 440
  theory of, 407–414
  worldwide use of, 423–425
Lichtenstein, S., 57–58, 282, 339
Light paternalism, 408
Likelihood of sample, underweighting of, 29, 88–92, 329
Like-mindedness, evidential reasoning and, 198–202
Limited attention, 10, 20–21, 28, 56
  efficiency costs of taxation and, 362, 374–380
  evidence on, 59–60
  tax incidence under, 362, 380–382
Limited information, 232
Limited memory/recall, 92
Lind, B., 209
Linda problem, 268, 283–284, 450n4
Linear probability weighting, 64, 96
List, J. A., 209
Loan to income (LTI) ratio, 222
Loan to value (LTV) ratio, 222
Loewenstein, G., 36, 70, 178, 199, 413
Logistic map, 219–221, 220
Lord, C. G., 287
Loss aversion
  bias-variance dilemma and, 337
  coefficient of, 103
  definition of, 102
  emotional states and, 327
  libertarian paternalism and, 430, 433
  myopic, 246
  tax evasion problem and, 137, 447n8
Lotteries, 25, 99. *See also* Situations, taxonomy of
  anticipatory emotions in, 180
  compound, 45–46
  definition of, 29–30, 92–93
  equation for, 29

low probability events, attitudes toward, 176–177, 251–259
  simple, 43
  single-outcome, 31
  split, 254
Lovallo, D., 63
Low bandwidth, problem of, 59–60
Low hanging policy fruit, 60
Low probability events, attitudes toward, 16, 176–177, 251–259
  behavioral evidence for, 176, 255–258
  composite prospect theory, 16, 177, 258–259
  original prospect theory, 176, 253–255
  probability weighting function and, 251–253, 252, 254, 450n17
Lucas, R. E., 297
Lucas critique, 224, 225, 399–401
Luce, R. D., 158
Lump-sum taxes, 376
Luttmer, E. F. P., 162

Machine learning, bias-variance dilemma in, 8, 19
Macroeconomic implications, 211–226
  adaptive rules, 215–216
  agent-based models, 172–173, 212, 221–226
  chaotic dynamics, 172–173, 219–221, 220, 449n13
  complexity theory, 172, 212–215
  emergent phenomena, 14, 114, 172, 212–213, 215–218, **218**, 449n10
  inductive reasoning, 214, 215–216
  macroeconomy as complex, adaptive system, 113–114, 165–167
  neighborhood segregation problem, 216–218, **218**
  persistent randomness, 172, 213–214, 226, 231–232
  rational expectations in, 211–212
  self-organizing systems, 213

statistical equilibrium, 213
stochastic social dynamics, 8, 15, 156, 173–174, 231–234, *234*
Magnitude effect, 10, 28, 70, 71
Malmendier, U., 131, 418
Managerial overconfidence, 63, 130–131
Mandates, 344. *See also* Hard paternalism
 Bayesian rationality approach to, 6
 libertarian paternalism and, 6–7, 20–21
Mandatory disclosure requirements, 22
Manzini, P., 181
Marginal benefits, 259
Marginal costs, 177, 259
Marginal social benefits, 373–374, 383
Marginal social costs, 374
Mariotti, M., 181
Market competition
 disclosure and, 438–439
 inattentive consumers and, 396–397
 non-optimizing individuals and firms, 111, 127–131
Marshallian demand curve, 375, 378, 380
Marx, Karl, 358
Mas-Colell, A., 47
Mathematical optimization, 109–112, 114–115
 bubbles in financial markets, 111, 126–127
 dynamic programming, 4, 8, 109–110, 115–119
 fast and frugal heuristics research program on, 307–308, 325–327
 heuristics for temporal choices and delay-discounting models, 185–188
 mental accounting and prospect theory, 188–190
 in microfinance contracts, 110, 111, 119–126, 131–134, 447n3
 non-optimizing individuals and firms, 111

tax evasion problem, 111, 134–138, 447nn7–10
 three-way leaders debate on, 111–112, 138–142
Mathematical statistics, departure of human behavior from, 28–29, 79
 assumptions of Bayesian rationality approach, 79–80
 Bayes' law, 29, 84–88, *87*, 128, 149, 329
 conservatism, 10, 29, 61, 66, 88–92, 257, 329
 probability distribution, 80–83, *82*
Mead, W. J., 208
Mean, regression to, 16, 62, 268, 284–285, 329, 339
Mean reverting models, 300
Means paternalism, 20, 342, 347, 408
Medicare & Medicaid Services, automatic enrollment in, 433–434, 440
Mehra, R., 248
Meikle, N. L., 62
Memory tasks, inferences from, 318–320
Mental accounting and prospect theory, 170–171, 188–190
Mental models, 15, 175, 242–245, 308
 bias-variance dilemma and, 338
 definition of, 175, 242–243
 examples of, 243–244
 inertia in abandoning, 243–245
Menthol-flavored cigarettes, ban on, 21, 414, 420
Methodological individualism, 10, 12, 15, 37, 78–79, 143–144, 445n3
Methodology in economics, 112–113, 156–161
Microfinance contracts, optimization in, 119–126, 447n3
 effort choices in, 122–126, *123*, *125*
 examples of, 131–134
 financing model, 119–120
 guilt and shame aversion, 121–126, 131–134

Microfinance contracts, optimization in (cont.)
  introduction to, 56, 110–111
  public repayment of loans in, 120–121
Microfounded macroeconomic models, 165–166
Middle East, libertarian paternalism in, 417, 424
Miles per gallon (MPG), 437–438
Mill, John Stuart, 6
  anti-paternalistic framework, 345, 347, 411
  harm principle, 19, 347, 403–404, 443
Mind as a Swiss army knife view, 86
Mistakes, welfare and, 405–407
Mitchell, M., 213
Mixed net gains/losses, integration of, 188–190
Mixed strategy Nash equilibrium, 52, 78, 160, 275, 401
Models, mental, 175, 242–245
Modern neoclassical economics. *See* Bayesian rationality approach (BRA)
Monetary and fiscal policies, agent-based models of, 225
Monetary sunk costs, 259–263
Monomorphic equilibrium, 173, 227
Monotone increasing/decreasing games, Kantian rationality in, 204–207
Monotonicity axiom, 48
Moral norms, 56, 151, 153
Morgenstern, O., 46–47
Motivated cognition, 63–64
Motivation, intrinsic versus extrinsic, 58
Motor vehicle safety regulation, 344
Mouselab software, 78
Mullainathan, S., 60, 245
Multiple selves, 361–374
  awareness of self-control problems and, 453n6
  degree of self-awareness in, 364–365
  example of, 363–366

  internalities and, 366–374
  naifs, 365
  partial naifs, 365
  public policy and, 366–374
  social norms and, 153–154
  sophisticates, 365
  time consistents, 365
Mussweiler, T., 277
Mutations, 226–227
Myopic best replies, 232
Myopic investor behavior, 248
Myopic loss aversion, 246

Naive consumers
  definition of, 365
  in Hotelling competition model, 392–393
Narrative economics, 15, 234–242
  affect heuristic, 236
  characteristics of narratives in, 235–236
  definition of, 174–175
  epidemiological models of, 237–242, 240
  network theory of, 237
  phishing equilibrium in, 236
Narrow bracketing, 15
  definition of, 175–176, 245–246
  equity-premium puzzle and, 15, 56, 69, 175, 247–249
  example of, 246
  explanations for, 251
  risk aggregation in, 249–250
Nash, J. F., 52
Nash bargaining, 202
Nash equilibrium, 127
  in Bayesian rationality approach, 37, 142
  in classical game theory, 24, 52–54, 78–79
  emotional states and, 79
  in Hotelling competition model, 395–396
  mixed strategy, 52, 78, 160, 275, 401
  perfect, 24, 53, 142
  in prisoner's dilemma game, 145, 196, 205–207

National Health Service (UK), 307, 322
National School Lunch Act, 432
Native households, neighborhood segregation of, 216–218, **218**
Natural frequency algorithm, 86
Natural selection, 226–227
Necessary and sufficient conditions, 16, 268, 286, 329
Negative autocorrelation, 267
Negative framing, 68–69
Negative internality, 371
Neighborhood segregation problem, 216–218, **218**, 449n10
Neoclassical economics. *See* Bayesian rationality approach (BRA)
Network theory, 237
Newell B. R., 320
New York cab driver behavior, choice bracketing in, 69, 246–247, 251
New Zealand, libertarian paternalism in, 424, 428
Noise traders, 11, 129
Noncompensatory heuristics, 451n5
Nonconsequentialist reasoning, 169
Nonlinear probability weighting, 10, 64–68
    Allais paradox, 65–68
    Russian roulette example, 64–65
Non-optimizing individuals, 111
Nonstationary environments, bias-variance dilemma and, 338
Nontransitivity, 339
Normative standards of behavior, 151–153, 301–302
    personal norms, 151, 327–329
    social norms, 12, 54, 56, 112, 149–156, 308, 327–329
North, D. C., 242
Nosofsky, R. M., 321
NP-complete, 115, 444
Nudges, 20–21, 344, 404–405. *See also* Automatic enrollment plans; Disclosure requirements
    boosts versus, 420–421
    default savings options, 410
    disclosure, 434–439
    effectiveness of, 413–414
    examples of, 409–410
    finance, 436–437
    fuel economy, 437–438
    government error in, 415–418
    health care, 437
    increased salience as, 440–441
    nutrition, 435–436
Numeraire good, 368
Nutritional facts, mandatory disclosure of, 407, 435–436

Oaksford, M., 337
Obama, Barack, 424, 431
Objections to heuristics and biases research program, 269–270
    criticism of appropriate statistical norms, 270, 300–302
    ecological rationality of heuristics, 291–292
    empirical counterparts to heuristics, 270, 297–298
    explanations of event and its negation, 270, 298–300
    frequency versus probability format, 270, 294–297
    fundamental misunderstandings, 289–291
    one-event probabilities, 269–270, 292–293
    two-system model of brain, 302–303
    "we cannot be that dumb" critique, 17, 269–270, 293–294
Objective-good theories, 356–358
O'Donoghue, T., 365, 372, 410
Office of Evaluation Sciences (US), 424
Oil lease auctions. *See* Common value (CV) auctions, bidding behavior in
Oligopoly theory, 202
One-event probabilities, 17, 269–270, 292–293
One-good-reason heuristics, 311
1/N heuristic, 331–332
On Liberty (Mill), 403
Opportunity costs, 16, 177, 259–263
Optimal belief management, 63–64
Optimal taxation. *See* Taxation

Optimism
  calculation of, 100–101
  leadership impact on, 427
  narrative impact on, 242
  preservation of, 63
  unrealistic, 21, 343, 351, 359, 406, 414–415, 432
  winner's curse and, 207–211
Optimization, mathematical. *See* Mathematical optimization
Order axiom, 44, 48
Organisation for Economic Development and Cooperation, 425
Original prospect theory (OPT), 176, 253–255. *See also* Prospect theory, cumulative
Ostrom, Elenor, 152
Other-regarding preferences, 10, 13, 26–27, 55
Otto, P., 324
Outcome-time pairs. *See* Temporal decisions, rationality in
Outward similarity, 272–273
Overconfidence, 10, 28, 328
  Dunning-Kruger effect, 61–62
  evidence on, 61–64
  expert bias, 303–304
  managerial, 63, 130–131
  nudges and, 418
  overestimation, 28, 61–62
  overplacement, 28, 61
  overprecision, 28, 61–62
Overdraft protection programs, 359
Overestimation, 28, 61–62
Overplacement, 28, 61
Overprecision, 28, 61–62
Owner-occupiers, 222

Pachur, T., 282
Pareto optimality, 153, 207
Partial equilibrium considerations, 392
Partial naifs, 365
Pasteur, Louis, 293
Paternalism. *See also* Hard paternalism; Libertarian paternalism (LP); Soft paternalism
  asymmetric, 408
  coercive, 451n4
  ends, 342, 347, 408
  light, 408
  means, 20, 342, 347, 408
Pauly, M., 255
Payoff dominance, 78, 155
Payroll statement policies, 434
Pension Protection Act of 2006 (PPA), 431
Pentagon Papers, 445n2
Perfect Bayesian Nash equilibrium, 24, 53, 142
Perfectionism, 357–358, 452n17
Perfect recall, assumption of, 278
Persistent errors, 129
Persistent randomness, 172, 213–214, 226, 231–232
Personal commitment, overconfidence and, 130
Personal norms, 151, 327–329
Pessimism, 100–101
Phenotypes, 226–228, 449n14
Philosophical foundations. *See also* Welfare
  Bernheim's premises for, 350–351
  choices and welfare, 343–346
  direct judgements, 341, 346–351, 354–356
  indirect judgements, 346–351, 353–354
  lack of information or behavioral bias, 341–343
  means paternalism, 20, 342, 347, 408
  perfectionism, 357–358, 452n17
  philosophical ideals, 344
  practice and theory, 351–353
  respect for self-regarding choices, 341–343
  subsidiary questions, 359–360
  working presumption, 349, 358–360
Philosophical ideals, 344
Phishing equilibrium, 236

Pigouvian (corrective) taxes, 20, 21, 368–369, 403–404, 452n1
  cigarette taxes, 21, 344, 367, 407, 414
  definition of, 371
  efficacy of, 441–442, 453n1
  justification of, 407, 414
  marginal social benefit of, 373
  marginal social cost of, 374
  multiple selves and, 153–154, 361–374
  pollution taxes, 6
  role of, 366, 371–372
  soda taxes, 21, 344
  sugar taxes, 362, 382–385, 383, 407, 414
Pildes, R., 451n4
Planning fallacy, 8
Players, 37
Plott, C., 57, 209
Polak, B., 53
Pollution taxes, 6
Polymorphic equilibrium, 173, 227
Popper, K., 157, 448n12
Positive autocorrelation, 267
Positive framing, 68–69
Postdictive judgments, 267, 278
Poverty
  aspirations and, 197
  intergenerational transmission of, 243
  limited attention and, 59–60
Prediction tasks. *See* Bias-variance dilemma
Predictive judgments, 267, 278
Preference-based theories, 357–358
Preference reversals, 10, 28, 57–58
  hyperbolic discounting, 10, 70, 73–76, 142, 169
  quasi-hyperbolic discounting function, 75–76, 364
Preferences
  binary preference relation, 39
  consistent, 24–25, 27–28, 40–41, 56–58
  continuity property of, 42–43
  emotional states and, 26–27, 55–56
  expected utility theory of, 44–47
  institutions and, 161–165
  malleability of, 113
  other-regarding, 10, 13, 26–27, 55
  self-regarding, 10, 13, 26–28, 54–55
  sovereignty of, 341–343
Prelec, D., 97
Prelec function, 97–98, 251–252, 252, 446n17, 450n17
Preplay communication, 78
Prescott, E. C., 248
Prescription drug plans, 440
Present biased individuals, 369–374, 386, 389
Present biased preferences and procrastination, 75–76, 362–363, 385–392
  current benefits and future costs, 389
  current costs and future benefits, 386–389
  deadlines, 390–391
  example of, 386–389
  fertilizer purchases, 391–392
  intention-action divide, 391
  job searches, 389–390
  purchase of single cigarette packs, 390–391
Presidential elections, evidential reasoning about, 200, **200**
Price competition, Bertrand model of, 395–396
Price competition, Hotelling model of, 363, 392–394
  fully attentive consumers, 394–396
  inattentive consumers, 396–399
  naive consumers, 392–393
  reaction function in, 395–396
  sophisticated consumers, 392–393
Primitives, preferences as
  decision-making over time, 25
  rationality under certainty, 39
  rationality under risk and uncertainty, 44
Principle of insufficient reason, 33
Priority heuristic, 305, 312, 450n2

Prisoner's dilemma game, 52, 112, 144–149
  aspiration adaptation in, 14–15
  aspiration-adaptation theory and, 192–195, **192**
  cooperation in, 12, 146–149, 192–195, 201
  defection in, 192–195, 201
  equilibrium concepts in, 54, 145
  Kantian equilibrium in, 204–207
  mixed strategy in, 193
  Nash equilibrium in, 205–207
  normal form game, 144–145, **144**
  social rationality in, 79, 147
Private rationality, 4, 10, 15, 112, 171
Probabilities, 10, 29, 292–293. *See also* Probability weighting function
  decision weighted utility, 99
  low probability events, attitudes toward, 176–177, 251–259
  nonlinear probability weighting, 64–68
  one-event, 292–293
  probability distributions, biases in producing, 80–83, *82*
  source-dependent, 33
  subadditivity in, 75, 82–83, 446n10, 446n12
  subjective, 31–36, 44, 47, 89, 154, *178*, *179*, 292–293, 308, 328
Probability format, 17, 86–88, *87*, 270, 283–284, 294–297
Probability weighting function, 96–99, *98*, 179
  composite Prelec, 258–259, *259*, 450n19
  linear, 64
  for low probability events, 251–253, *252*, *254*, 450n17
  nonlinear, 64–68
Procedural aspects of decision-making, 183
Procedural rationality, 5, 11–12, 14, 138–140, 170–171, 190, 265, 305, 310

Procrastination, 362–363, 385–392
  current benefits and future costs, 389
  current costs and future benefits, 386–389
  deadlines, 390–391
  example of, 386–389
  fertilizer purchases, 391–392
  intention-action divide, 391
  job searches, 389–390
  purchase of single cigarette packs, 390–391
Profit maximization, 114
Projection bias, 56, 393
Proposed Roads to Freedom (Russell), 287
Prosociality, 162
Prospect theory, composite, 16, 177, 258–259
Prospect theory, cumulative, 11, 18, 29, 36, 96, 101–107
  decision weights under, 105–106
  definition of, 176
  fourfold classification of risk in, 68, 102–103, 105–107, **106**
  low probability events in, 253
  mental accounting and, 170–171, 188–190
  performance of, 326–327
  prospect theory utility, 104–105
  reference dependence in, 68–69
  reference points in, 102
  tax evasion problem and, 136–137
  utility function under, 103–104, *104*
Prospect theory, original (OPT), 101, 176, 253–255
Psychological game theory, 56, 78–79, 110, 447n1
Public economics, behavioral, 20
Public goods games, 163–164, 447n15
  evidential reasoning in, 198–199
  Kantian rationality in, 204–207
Public policy, behaviorally informed. *See also* Behavioral economics; Paternalism; Welfare
  behavioral industrial organization, 20, 363, 392–401

Bernheim's premises for, 350–351
choices and welfare, 343–346, 440
default rules, 429–431
direct judgements in, 341–343, 346–351, 354–356
disclosure requirements, 434–439
FEAST (fun, easy, attractive, social, and timely) framework, 423, 426–428
health care, 433–434
indirect judgements, 346–351, 353–354
institutionalization of behavioral insights, 423, 428–429
introduction to, 341–343
lack of information or behavioral bias in, 341–343
multiple selves and, 153–154, 361–374
payroll statements, 434
perfectionism in, 357–358, 452n17
philosophical ideals and, 344
practice and theory in, 351–353
salience, 440–442
savings plans, 431–432
school meals, 432–433
structuring of choices, 440
subsidiary questions for, 359–360
working presumption for, 349, 358–360
worldwide use of, 423–425
Punctuated equilibria, 174, 233
Puzzles
equity-premium, 15, 56, 69, 175, 247–249
Yitzhaki, 135, 136

Quantal response equilibria, 77, 78, 147
Quasi-hyperbolic discounting function, 75–76, 364
Quasi-hyperbolic preferences, 364
Quattrone, G. A., 200
Query theory of value, 36
Quiggin, J., 99, 255

Rabin, M., 138–141, 273, 274, 287, 365, 372, 410
Raiffa, H., 158
Randomized control trials (RCTs), 5, 429
Randomness, persistent, 172, 213–214, 226, 231–232
Rank dependent utility theory (RDU), 11, 29, 36, 96, 99–101
RAT, 321
Rational actor model, 1, 37
Rational expectations
in Bayesian rationality approach, 3–4, 24, 445n1
bubbles in financial markets, 126–127, 222
macroeconomic implications, 172, 211–212, 291
requirements of, 449n8
self-fulfilling prophesy, 167
Rationality
Bayesian. See Bayesian rationality approach (BRA)
under certainty. See certainty, rationality under
in choices made over time. See temporal decisions, rationality in
concept of, 23, 54–56
private, 4, 10, 15, 112, 171
procedural, 5, 11–12, 14, 138–140, 170–171, 190, 265, 305, 310
under risk and uncertainty, 10, 25, 43–47, 64–69
social. See social rationality
in strategic interaction, 10, 52–54, 76–79, 112, 143–149
substantive, 11, 310
Rationalizability, 149, 155
Rawls, John, 358
Reaction function, 395–396
Read, D., 184
Recognition heuristic, 18, 305, 312, 331
Red teaming, 304
Red traffic light running, 176, 257
Reduction axiom, 45–46
Rees-Jones, A., 380

Reference class of cues, 305
Reference dependence, 10, 68–69, 298
Reference points, 96, 102
Regression analysis, 316–317
Regression to the mean, 16, 62, 88–89, 268, 284–285, 339
Regret aversion, 36
Regularization, 337
Regulations, 6, 19–20, 425. *See also* Hard paternalism; Libertarian paternalism (LP); Public policy, behaviorally informed
  bans, 6–7, 20–21
  disclosure requirements, 434–439
  efficacy of, 453n1
  energy-efficiency, 344, 350, 369, 407, 430, 441, 452n20
  fuel economy, 354, 407, 437–438, 452n20
  government error in, 415–418
  insights from behavioral industrial organization, 20, 363, 392–394, 399–401
  mandates, 6–7, 20–21, 344
  motor vehicle safety, 344
  self-regarding preferences and, 403–404
Relativity, theory of, 156
Remembered past predictions, hindsight bias from, 279
Reminders, 20–21
Renters, 222
Replicator dynamics, 173, 229, 233
Representative agent framework, 14, 165
Representativeness heuristic, 16, 270–275
  definition of, 266–267
  definition of representativeness in, 272–273
  event and its negation explained by, 270
  example of, 273
  gambler's fallacy, 16, 19, 267, 273–274, 329, 339
  hot hand fallacy, 16, 19, 267, 274–275, 276, 329, 339
  law of small numbers, 267, 271–272, 329, 393
  role in evolution of narratives, 174
  theorem for, 270–271
Reproductive success, evolutionary, 226–227
Research programs
  big-push, 5–6, 11
  incremental, 5–6, 12
Resident phenotypes, 226–228
Rieskamp, J., 324
Risk, 9. *See also* Uncertainty
  aggregation of, 175–176, 249–250
  attitudes to, 95
  definition of, 23, 31
  fourfold classification of, 68, 102–103, 105–107, **106**
  in heuristics and biases research program, 329–330
  rationality under, 10, 25, 43–47, 64–69, 448n2
  risk as feelings theory, 14, 36, 93, 169, 177–180, *178*
Risk aversion, 95, 224–225, 248
Risk dominance, 78
Risk-loving decision-makers, 69, 95, 107
Risk-neutral decision-makers, 95, 256
Robbins, J. M., 198
Rockefeller, Happy, 258
Romer, Paul, 14
Rubinstein, A., 49, 78
Russell, Bertrand, 287
Russian roulette, 64–65

Sacerdote, B., 257
Sales tax, limited attention and, 60
Salience, 36, 440–442
Sampling distribution, biases in producing, 80–83, 82
Samuelson, Paul, 66, 70–76, 175, 249–250, 446n6
Samuelson, W. F., 208–210
Sanctions
  mental models and, 175, 243
  social norms and, 26, 132–133, 151–154, 243

Sandmo, A., 134–138
Sarbanes-Oxley Act, 63
Satisficing, 190–191
Satisficing heuristic, 14–15, 310
Saurmann, Heinz, 191
Savage, Leonard, 66, 330
Savage acts, 32, 44
Savings plans, 407, 410, 431–432
Schelling, T. C., 216
Schiffer, S., 318
Schmidt, K. M., 13, 55, 138–139
Scholten, M., 184
Scholz, J. K., 60
School meals, automatic enrollment in, 407, 432–433
Schrag, J., 287
Schram, A., 150
Schurtenberger, I., 152
Schwartz, A. J., 297
Scientific methodology, misconceptions about, 293–294
Scripts, narratives as, 235–236
Seat belt usage, 176, 258, 414
Second season syndrome, 284
Segregation, neighborhood, 216–218, 218, 449n10
Segregation/integration heuristics, 188–190
Seki, E., 163
Self-control problems, 20, 76, 410. See also Libertarian paternalism (LP)
  degree of self-awareness of, 364–365
  multiple selves, 153–154
  multiple selves model and, 361–374
Self-fulfilling prophesy, 126
Self-interested motivations, 12
Self-organizing systems, 213
Self-regarding preferences, 10, 13
  direct judgements in, 341
  rationality and, 26–28, 54–55
  relevant policy interventions for, 403–404
  sovereignty of individual preferences and, 341–343
Self-serving bias, 78, 130

Selten, Reinhard, 8, 115, 126, 127, 138–141, 191, 324
Sen, A., 27
Sequential equilibrium, 53, 211
Set inclusion principle, 86, 87, 268, 283. See also Conjunction fallacy
Shafir, E., 262
Shame aversion, 56, 110, 121–126, 131–134, 152
Shared understandings, social norms as, 152
Sharpe ratios, 332
Shiller, R., 174, 213, 235, 236, 242
Shleifer, A., 128
Shrouded attributes, 5, 376, 433
Silver lining principle, 189–190
Similarity relation in time preferences, 14, 170, 183
Simon, Herbert, 5, 7, 14, 38, 113, 170, 265–266, 291, 305–306, 310, 332
Simple increasing elasticity (SIE), 72
Simple lotteries, 43
Singhal, M., 162
Single-outcome lotteries, 31
Sin goods, 366, 369–370
Singular events, 292–293
Sin taxes. See Pigouvian (corrective) taxes
SIR model. See Kermack-McKendrick model
Situations, taxonomy of, 29–36
  ambiguity, 32–33
  certainty, 31
  lotteries, 29–30
  risk, 31
  subjective uncertainty, 31–32
  true uncertainty, 33–36
Slovic, P., 57–58
Smaller-sooner (SS) rewards, 74–75
  in delay-discounting models, 185–188
  in trade-off model of attribute choice, 184–185
Small numbers, law of, 267, 271–272, 303–304, 329, 393
Small worlds. See Risk

SMarT (Save More Tomorrow) savings plans, 407
Smith, Adam, 2
Smith, Maynard, 228
Smith, V. L., 126
Smoking
  bans on menthol-flavored cigarettes, 21, 414, 420
  choice bracketing in, 175, 246
  cigarette taxes, 21, 344, 367, 407, 414
  purchase of single cigarette packs, 390–391
  vividness of risky outcomes in, 179
Snob consumption, 55
Social norms, 12, 308, 327–329
  conformity with, 152–156
  conventions versus, 154
  descriptive versus injunctive, 151
  emotional states and, 56
  empirical expectations, 151
  equilibrium concepts in, 54
  examples of, 149–150
  normative expectations, 151
  role of, 112, 149–156
  sanctions in, 152–153
Social projection. See Evidential reasoning (ER)
Social rationality, 4, 79, 112, 156
  classical game theory and, 79, 147
  joint intentionality, 15, 79, 147, 171, 203
  Kantian rationality, 15, 171, 203–207
  team reasoning, 15, 171
Social Security Administration, 424
Soda taxes, 21, 344
Soft paternalism, 346, 408. See also Libertarian paternalism (LP)
  definition of, 361
  insights from behavioral industrial organization, 399–401
Sophisticated consumers, 365, 392–393
Sophomore slump, 284
Source-dependent probabilities, 33
Spiegler, R., 8, 393
Split lottery, 254
Stable steady state, 449n12
Stackelberg leader, 372
Standard welfare economics, 343–344
Stanovich, K. E., 266, 293, 302
Starmer, C., 69
Static game of complete information, 52–53
Stationarity axiom, 25, 49, 52, 73
Statistical equilibrium, 213
Statistical norms, criticism of, 17, 270, 300–302
Statistical theory. See Mathematical statistics, departure of human behavior from
Statistical training, value of, 307, 321–323
Status quo, as reference point, 18, 40, 102, 140, 160, 298
Stein, J., 127
Stochastically dominated lotteries, 99
Stochastically stable steady state, 15, 232, 233
Stochastic social dynamics (SSD), 8, 15, 156, 173–174, 231–234, *234*
Stokey, N., 116
Stolarz-Fantino, S., 284
St. Petersburg paradox, 93–94
Strategic interaction, rationality in, 10, 52–54, 76–79, 112, 143–149
Strategies, definition of, 447n10
Strong law of large numbers, 450n2
Structuring of choices, 440
Subadditivity, 75, 82–83, 446n10, 446n12
Subgame perfection, 115
Subject deception, 58
Subjective expected utility (SEU), 44
Subjective experience, 344–345
Subjectively known outcomes, 31
Subjective probabilities, 31–36, 44, 47, 89, 154, *178*, 179, 292–293, 308, 328
Subjective uncertainty, 31–32, 330, 450n2
Subjective welfare, 356–357, 452n15
Substantive rationality, 11, 310

Sufficient conditions, 16, 88–89, 268, 286
Sugar taxes, 362, 382–385, *383*, 407, 414
Sugden, Robert, 405, 410, 412
Sunk costs, 16, 77, 177, 259–263, 304
Superficial similarity, 266–267, 272–273
Survival of the fittest, 173, 226–227
Sweden, libertarian paternalism in, 419, 425, 428
Systematic biases, 129, 293
Systems 1 and 2, 302–303

Tabellini, G., 164
Taffesse, A. S., 197
Take-the-best heuristic
 definition of, 17–18, 305
 empirical testing of, 319–321
 performance of, 311–315, *313*, 324
Tallying, 450n3
Targets, evaluation of outcomes relative to, 96
Tate, G., 131, 418
Taubinsky, D., 380, 452n15
Taxation. *See also* Pigouvian (corrective) taxes
 ad valorem taxes, 452n1
 deadweight loss from, 362, 376–380, *379*
 distortionary taxes, 376–378, 384, 453n5
 earned income tax credit, 60, 343
 internalities and tax efficiency, 382–385, *383*
 Laffer curve, 240, 242
 limited attention and, 60, 362, 374–380
 lump-sum taxes, 376
 sales tax, 60
 tax incidence, 362, 380–382
Tax efficiency, internalities and, 382–385, *383*
Tax evasion problem, 69, 111, 134–138, 447nn7–10
Taxonomy of situations, 29–36
 ambiguity, 32–33
 certainty, 31
 lotteries, 29–30
 risk, 31
 subjective uncertainty, 31–32
 true uncertainty, 33–36
Taylor, P., 229
Taylor, T., 418
Team reasoning, 15, 77, 79, 147, 171
Temporal decisions, rationality in, 10, 47–52. *See also* Attribute-based models of time discounting; Exponential discounted utility (EDU)
 attribute-based models of time discounting, 14–16, 93, 169–170, 180–185, 448n2
 axioms of rationality for time discounting, 25, 47–52, 69–76
 discounted utility model, 50–51, 70, 72
 evidence on, 69–76
 heuristics-based models of intertemporal choice, 170, 185–188
 hyperbolic discounting, 10, 70, 73–76, 142, 169
 multiple selves, 153–154, 361–374, 453n6
 outcome-time pairs, 25, 48
 outcome-time pairs in, 25, 48
 time inconsistency, 70, 76
Tenenbaum, J. B., 337
Tentori, K., 284
Tetlock, P. E., 62
Thaler, Richard, 7, 58, 70, 72–76, 156, 208, 247–248, 261–262
Theory of relativity, 156
Thöni, C., 199
Time consistent choices, 70
Time consistents, 365, 387
Time discounting, attribute-based models of, 169–170, 180–185
Time discounting, axioms of rationality in, 25, 48–52, 69–76. *See also* Exponential discounted utility (EDU)
Time inconsistent choices, 70, 76

Tirole, J., 21
Tobias, R. B., 236
Tomasello, M., 79, 203
Touron, D. R., 63
Trade-off model of attribute choice, 14, 170, 184–185
Training sets, 333
Transaction utility, 261–262
Trans fats ban, 21
Transitivity axiom, 44–45, 57–58
Transportation, Department of, 424
  disclosure requirements, 438
  Lucas critique and, 400
Travelling salesman problem, 444
Treasury, Department of, 424, 438
Trending models, 300
True uncertainty, 9, 305, 306, 308
  avenues for future research, 444
  decision-making under, 112, 327–329
  definition of, 23, 33–34
  examples of, 34–36
  fast and frugal heuristics research program and, 327–333
  overconfidence and, 328
  prevalence of, 23–24, 444
Trust game, 162–163, 447n14
Tversky, Amos, 5, 7, 16, 90, 112, 265, 316, 443. *See also* Heuristics and biases research program (HBP)
  analysis of presidential elections, 200
  cab problem proposed by, 84–88
  on conjunction fallacy, 283–284
  on frequency versus probability format, 294–295
  objections to heuristics and biases research program, 450n1
  on one-event probabilities, 292–293
  on predictions of economic models, 13
  refutations of expected utility, 38, 58, 68–69
  on risk/uncertainty, 329
  on sampling biases, 81
  on source-dependent probabilities, 33

Two-colors example, 32–33
Two-system model of brain, 302–303

Ulu, C., 83
Uncertainty, 9. *See also* True uncertainty
  attribute-based models under, 448n2
  confusion resulting from varied meanings of, 23
  in heuristics and biases research program, 329–330
  intertemporal optimization problem under, 109–110, 115–119
  rationality under, 43–47, 64–69
  subjective, 31–32, 135, 305, 330, 450n2
  true, 33–36, 305, 306, 308
Uncompensated demand curve, 375, 378, 380
Underinference, 90–92
Underlying models, inference procedures for, 298–300
Underweighting (conservatism), 10, 29, 61, 66, 88–92, 257, 329
Unemployment
  inflation and, 295, 445n1
  job search, 389–390
United Kingdom
  housing sector, agent-based model of, 221–223
  libertarian paternalism in, 424, 429
  National Health Service, 307, 322
  tax gap in, 134
Unknown unknowns, 23
Unreasonable attitudes toward risk, 69
Unsophisticated investors, 129
Utility. *See also* Expected utility theory (EU); Exponential discounted utility (EDU)
  acquisition, 261–262
  anticipal, 177–178, 189
  anticipatory, 177
  decision weighted, 99
  decision weighted utility, 99
  discounted, 50–51, 70, 72

expected utility functional, 96, 450
experienced net, 261–262
instantaneous, 50
rank dependent, 11, 29, 36, 96, 99–101
rank dependent utility theory, 11
subjective expected, 44

Vague time preferences model, 170, 181–182
Validation sets, 334
Van Boven, L., 199
Vayanos, D., 274
Verhulst, Pierre, 219
Violation of completeness of preferences, 10
Vividness of risky outcomes, decision-making and, 179
Von Neumann, J., 46–47

Wakker, P. P., 33, 47, 100, 106
Waldron, Jeremy, 344, 451n4
Wallace, C., 233
War
  leader overconfidence and, 63
  narratives during, 242
  preferences impacted by, 164
Warnings, 20–21
Warranties, extended, 169, 180
Wason, P. C., 286
Watson, James, 293
Watson, Thomas, 34–35
Weber, M., 162, 279–280
"We cannot be that dumb" critique, 17, 269–270, 293–294
Weighted adding strategy (WADD), 316, 324
Welfare, 6, 356–357
  choices and, 343–346
  forecasting errors for, 356
  hedonic criteria, 20, 63, 342, 348, 352, 357
  mistakes and, 405–407
  objective-good theories of, 356–358
  preference-based theories of, 356–358

sovereignty of individual preferences and, 341–343
subjective, 356–357, 452n15
Wertenbroch, K., 390
West, R. F., 266, 293, 302
Whitt, S., 164
Wiener process, 233
Wilson, R. K., 164
Winner's curse, 15, 172, 207–211
World Bank, 59, 304, 425
World Health Organization (WHO), 419, 425
World Values Survey (WVS), 162

Yitzhaki, S., 134–138
Yitzhaki puzzle, 135, 136
Young, H. P., 232
Young, P. H., 232, 233, 234
Yunus, Muhammad, 120

Zajonc, R. B., 288
Zanuck, Darryl, 35
Zhao, C., 92
Zipf's law, 226